BROKEN VOWS

by the same author

BLIND EYE TO MURDER

KLAUS BARBIE

THE PAPERCLIP CONSPIRACY

RED WEB

MAXWELL: THE OUTSIDER

TINY ROWLAND

THE PERFECT ENGLISH SPY

HEROES OF WORLD WAR II

MAXWELL: THE FINAL VERDICT

NAZI GOLD

BLOOD MONEY

FAYED

BRANSON

THE PAYMASTER

BROKEN DREAMS: VANITY, GREED AND THE SOURING OF BRITISH FOOTBALL

CONRAD AND LADY BLACK: DANCING ON THE EDGE

THE SQUEEZE

NO ANGEL: THE SECRET LIFE OF BERNIE ECCLESTONE

SWEET REVENGE: THE INTIMATE LIFE OF SIMON COWELL

BRANSON: BEHIND THE MASK

BROKEN VOWS

Tony Blair:
The Tragedy of Power

TOM BOWER

FABER & FABER

First published in 2016
by Faber & Faber Ltd
Bloomsbury House
74–77 Great Russell Street
London WC1B 3DA

Typeset by Faber & Faber Ltd
Printed in the UK by CPI Group (UK) Ltd, Croydon, CR0 4YY

A CIP record for this book
is available from the British Library

ISBN 978-0-571-31420-1

FSC
www.fsc.org
MIX
Paper from
responsible sources
FSC® C101712

2 4 6 8 10 9 7 5 3 1

To Veronica

Contents

CONTENTS

Contents

Photographs

The winning team in 1997: Peter Mandelson, Alastair Campbell, Blair and Gordon Brown (Tom Stoddart/Getty Images)

The Blairs move into Downing Street, 2 May 1997 (Rebecca Naden/ PA Archive/PA Images)

Blair's first Cabinet (Rex Shutterstock)

Blair and Bill Clinton, with Cherie Blair and Hillary Clinton, February 1998 (Jamal A. Wilson/AFP/Getty Images)

Blair with General Sir Charles Guthrie and General Sir Mike Jackson in Macedonia, May 1999, during the Kosovo war (Rex Shutterstock)

Celebrating the millennium at the Dome on New Year's Eve 1999 (Rex Shutterstock)

Three Cabinet secretaries: Robin Butler, Richard Wilson and Andrew Turnbull (Martin Keene/PA Archive/PA Images; Stefan Rousseau/PA Archive/PA Images; Tom Pilston/*Independent*/Rex Shutterstock)

George Bush and Blair at Camp David, 2001 (Mario Tama/AFP/ Getty Images)

Chief of staff Jonathan Powell, director of communications Alastair Campbell and director of government relations Sally Morgan (Alisdair Macdonald/Rex Shutterstock)

Chiefs of the defence staff: Admiral Mike Boyce, General Mike Walker and Air Marshal Jock Stirrup (Ian Waldie/Getty Images; Toby Melville WPA/Getty Images)

Blair and Brown during the 2005 election campaign (Peter Nicholls/
PA Archive/PA Images)

Blair at the Sedgefield election count with Reg Keys (John Giles/PA
Archive/PA Images)

Blair with Sheikh Mohammed bin Zayed al-Nahyan, the crown
prince of Abu Dhabi; Paul Kagame, the president of Rwanda;
Nursultan Nazarbayev, the president of Kazakhstan; and Libyan
leader Muammar Gaddafi (Richard Lewis/PA Archive/PA Images;
Adrian Dennis/Getty Images; Alastair Grant/Getty Images; Peter
Macdiarmid/Getty Images)

27 June 2007: the Blairs leave Downing Street after ten years (Matt
Dunham/AP/Press Association Images)

Blair, Rupert Murdoch and Wendi Deng (photograph © Hannah
Thomson)

Blair with President Goodluck Jonathan of Nigeria and Jamie Dimon,
J. P. Morgan's chief executive, November 2010 (Citizen Report/
Abayomi Adeshida)

Blair at Ariel Sharon's funeral in Jerusalem, January 2014 (Amos Ben
Gershom/GPO via Getty Images)

Every effort has been made to trace or contact all copyright holders.
The publishers would be pleased to rectify any omissions or errors
brought to their notice at the earliest opportunity.

Introduction

October 2007. Cherie Blair had just telephoned to cancel that evening's dinner engagement 'due to an emergency'. She and the African president were due to discuss the creation of a justice ministry in his impoverished country. 'I understand –' he began, but was interrupted.

'I can't come,' said Cherie, 'but Tony says he'd happily join you.'

'Excellent,' said Paul Kagame, the ruler of Rwanda, a land-locked nation famous for its gorillas and thousand rolling hills, where 11 million people earn an average daily wage of $2.

Celebrated as the poster boy for British aid to Africa, the president was sitting in the penthouse apartment of a luxury hotel near Chelsea football ground that cost £2,100 per day. He had flown to London in his private jet after addressing the United Nations in New York. His four-day visit matched his celebrity. He would deliver a lecture to Britain's power brokers at the London School of Economics, then address the Conservative Party conference in Blackpool as David Cameron's guest, and finally meet Gordon Brown, the new prime minister, in Downing Street. Taking their lead from Tony Blair, all of Kagame's hosts ignored the fact that their guest was widely accused of being a mass murderer.

Ever since Britain had learned of the horrendous genocide during the early 1990s of 800,000 Rwandan Tutsis by the dominant Hutu tribe, its government had turned a blind eye to the reprisals orchestrated by Kagame, a Tutsi. And now, to the president's delight, his hero was coming for dinner. Blair arrived, warmly embraced his host and shook hands with David Himbara, a fifty-two-year-old Rwandan economist personally recruited by the president to rebuild their country's economy with financial aid from Britain and America.

'You're a hero,' Kagame had told Blair when the first millions of pounds were donated in 1999. 'You're the man I've been looking for. You're giving us beautiful pounds to spend as we wish.'

Eight years on, in the penthouse suite, Himbara watched as the president and the world-famous former prime minister bonded in mutual admiration. 'They charmed each other,' he would recall. 'They both said to each other how great the other was.' Blair felt pride that Kagame's pledge to transform his country into the 'Singapore of Africa' was, thanks to his inspiration, coming true.

The former prime minister, a youthful fifty-four, slim and tanned, set out his stall. 'I've always been interested in you. You are a man with a vision, a leader I've always admired. Now you need advisers to show you how to run a government, and I'm your man.'

Blair continued his pitch: 'I learned by bitter experience during ten years as prime minister the problems of getting the government machine to deliver what I wanted. I created a Delivery Unit, and that was a great success. It transformed everything. I want to bring that success to Africa.'

'Yes,' said Kagame repeatedly. He agreed to welcome Blair's team.

The following day, Himbara arrived at Blair's new headquarters in Grosvenor Square, which Blair had rented for £550,000 a year following his resignation three months earlier. On the walls of the corridor leading to his office were photographs showing him with world leaders. The overwhelming impression was of entering the presence of a global celebrity. For two hours, Blair explained to Himbara how twelve experts, employed by his new Africa Governance Initiative (AGI), would work inside the president's office and Rwanda's economic ministry to improve the government's effectiveness. Himbara, formerly a professor of economics in South Africa, was relieved that Blair's experts would be more skilled than the 'DFID types' – untalented British civil servants sent after 1999 by Clare Short's Department for International

Development. But, unlike Blair, Himbara doubted that Kagame would take advice. 'That evening,' he recalled a couple of years later, 'they lied to each other.'

Blair was thrilled by Kagame's enthusiasm. AGI, his banner programme, had been launched effortlessly. After the frustrations of Downing Street, he intended to modernise Africa and, through his Faith Foundation, heal religious intolerance across the world. Both charities would be financed by his personal income and bequests from the philanthropic billionaires who congregated at the annual World Economic Forum in Davos. Soon after, he solicited annual donations of about £1 million for AGI in Rwanda from David Sainsbury, the former science minister, and Bill Gates.

Within a year of AGI's launch, Jonathan Reynaga, a former Downing Street aide, arrived in Kigali, the Rwandan capital, to embed himself and his team. By then, Blair had introduced Kagame to the international circuit of leaders' conferences across America and in Davos. He was presenting the president as Africa's 'Mr Clean'; no one mentioned the continuing massacre of Hutus in the neighbouring Congo by militia dispatched by Kagame. Nor did Blair's audience refer to the systematic theft by Kagame's armed forces of diamonds, gold and other precious minerals from Congo to finance their lifestyle. After all, the president's virtues were also hailed by Bill Clinton, Blair's ally.

The following year, 2008, Blair was welcomed by Himbara at Kigali airport, having stepped off a commercial flight from Nairobi. Like all visitors, he was impressed by Kigali's clean streets, new skyscrapers, Internet network and stock exchange. Soon he was telling his host how British and American aid was transforming the country into the continent's showcase. But Himbara knew the truth: the Internet rarely worked because the country lacked electricity, and the stock exchange listed exactly seven corporations – three of which were foreign-owned, with another belonging to the president. The legacy of Belgium's colonial occupation was a nation of illiterate subsistence farmers lacking the means to build a modern infrastructure. Despite all the millions in aid, the life of Rwandans outside the capital remained dire. 'Twelve AGI staff cannot turn around a dysfunctional state,' Himbara reflected. 'How do you start in a country where most people can't spell?'

Blair was more optimistic. As soon as he was ensconced in the presidential palace, his conversation with Kagame centred on him as an experienced leader willing to offer his advice at any time. At the end, Kagame summoned Himbara. 'Please arrange for Mr Blair to fly back to London on my private jet,' he ordered. Shortly after, Blair and his staff climbed aboard the $30 million Bombardier BD-700 'Global Express' to fly non-stop to Stansted. The cost of the round-trip flight – about $400,000 – was billed to the Rwandan government.

A year later, Blair returned to Kigali, again on the president's jet. Conditions were not as impressive as they had been on his last visit. Kagame feared the outcome of the upcoming elections but, since Blair paraded him as a model of African democracy, they could not be cancelled. Although there was no meaningful opposition party and Kagame was guaranteed over 90 per cent of the vote, his paranoia was causing fatal repercussions. Any journalist or businessman who was critical of the government was beaten up; his personal doctor had been murdered. A UN investigation into Kagame's attacks against the Hutus in the Congo during the 1990s was due to report that the president was guilty of genocide.

Suspicious of any independent-minded Rwandan, Kagame forbade Himbara to spend time alone with Blair during his visit. Himbara carefully obeyed the orders until he bid Blair farewell outside the president's palace. 'Jump in and come with me,' Blair ordered, pulling Himbara into the limousine. 'I'm a dead man,' thought Himbara, as Blair asked him to recite his fears. By the end of their journey to the airport, Blair had heard that 'It's getting nasty here. People are disappearing.' He did not comment. Once again, he boarded the president's jet and flew towards Europe.

At Christmas, Himbara joined his family in Johannesburg. Fearing for his life, he did not return to his country. Even in South Africa he wasn't safe. Another Rwandan exile, a personal friend living near by, was murdered by a hit squad. Although Kagame duly won the 2010 election with 93 per cent of the vote, the leaders of the small opposition party were being hunted down. Their beheaded corpses, hacked by machetes, were strewn about the countryside.

Blair ignored those events. Instead, he hailed his protégé's success. 'The popular mandate received by President Kagame in the recent presidential election is a testament to the huge strides made under his formidable leadership,' he said. In Britain, police in London announced that a plot hatched in Kigali to murder two Rwandan exiles had been foiled.

In 2012, Himbara heard that Tony Blair would be addressing an 'Executive Leadership Conference' in Johannesburg. He paid $450 for a ticket and sat in the front row. At question time, he raised his hand. 'How is your Rwandan project going?' he asked Blair. 'I had to run for my life. But, for you, it's business as usual. Why?'

'Oh, David,' replied Blair, 'Good to see you, man. Next question.'

At the end of the session, Blair walked out, avoiding Himbara's gaze. Five years after leaving Downing Street, he was accountable to no one. He had bidden good riddance to Parliament, civil servants and the Labour Party. Democracy, he had decided, hindered effective government. Casualties like David Himbara were not his concern.

Two years later, in 2014, after several more trips to Kigali and meetings with Kagame at Davos and elsewhere, Blair was sent a report by the US Department of State describing the murderous oppression in Rwanda. Again, he said nothing. The following year, he was equally silent after Congressional hearings in Washington denounced the murders of Kagame's opponents.

Three months on, in June 2015, one of Kagame's associates, General Karenzi Karake, the head of Rwanda's intelligence service, arrived at Heathrow on an official visit. To his surprise, he was arrested on an international warrant for 'war crimes against civilians' issued in Spain. He was immediately imprisoned. To resist his extradition to Spain, he hired Cherie Blair. In defence of her client, she told the magistrate that the general was 'a hero in Rwanda and they very much want him home as soon as possible'. Karake was released on bail of £1 million. Two months later, he was freed on a legal technicality before the charges were heard, and flew back home. Kagame's opponents were shocked. Cherie, like her husband, was hailed by Kagame as a hero.

Since his resignation in June 2007, Tony Blair's relations with dictators have been, and continue to be, bewildering. The defining events of his ten years as prime minister were the humiliation of Slobodan Milošević, the Serbian dictator, and the toppling of Iraqi president Saddam Hussein. In the cause of democracy, Blair defiantly risked his office to remove leaders he repeatedly described as evil. Set free from government, a different Tony Blair emerged from the politician who had spoken on behalf of New Labour. Eleven years after risking his reputation to topple Saddam, he publicly justified strong, authoritarian government. 'You also need efficacy,' he wrote in the *New York Times*. 'You need effective government taking effective decisions.' He recalled that in 2001 the British army and not Whitehall's civil servants had solved the foot-and-mouth epidemic that ravaged the nation's cattle. Soldiers and corporate chief executives rather than democratically elected representatives are, he argued, the best managers.

Since he left Downing Street, the accusations against Blair have grown. The image of a career carefully balanced between global charity and his commercial consultancies has become frayed. Despite his efforts to remain invisible, regular reports have described a global traveller jetting between Asia, the Middle East, Africa, Europe and America to earn millions of pounds by offering advice to sheikhs, presidents and dictators.

His new pitch, refined since his first meeting with Kagame, was perfectly delivered on 13 May 2015 to President Buhari of Nigeria. After his arrival at Abuja airport on a jet chartered by Evgeny Lebedev, the son of the former KGB colonel who owned the London *Evening Standard*, Blair was whisked to the Hilton Hotel. Besides Lebedev, his entourage included Nick Thompson, the head of the AGI, his police protection officer and a personal assistant. The following morning, he called on Andrew Pocock, the British High Commissioner. The routine was familiar. In every country he visits, Blair expects the British embassy to provide a comprehensive security briefing. In Nigeria, he was especially interested in the threat posed by Boko Haram, the Islamic terror group murdering hundreds of civilians in the north of the country. Armed with classified information, he then sped in a motor cavalcade to the office of Muhammadu Buhari, recently elected as president and committed to ridding his country of endemic corruption. Getting access to the new president even before his inauguration was a notable achievement. Blair's reputation overcame many hurdles.

In their first meeting, Blair introduced himself as 'Britain's most successful prime minister'. With the benefit of age, experience and hindsight, he explained to Buhari, he had learned how to focus on important matters and work the system. 'I pioneered the skills to make government work effectively,' he told the president. 'The Delivery Unit is the leader's weapon to make his government effective across the civil service and country.' He offered Buhari the benefit of that expertise. AGI would establish a delivery unit within his government, with paid staff.

Buhari, a former army general who had orchestrated a successful coup in 1983, looked bored. The wizened politician, famous for imprisoning his opponents without trial until he was deposed in a counter-coup and jailed for three years, stared intently at Lebedev. The Russian seemed equally uninterested in Blair's sermon. Buhari's assistant had earlier asked why Lebedev was included in the meeting. 'It's his plane,' replied a member of Blair's staff, 'and he's interested in Blair's work against Ebola in Sierra Leone.'

'Could you all leave us alone now?' Blair announced. 'I have a personal message for the president from David Cameron.' Twenty minutes later, the two men emerged. Buhari was noticeably disgruntled. Blair, he told an aide, had used his access to tout for business on behalf of Tony Blair Associates, his commercial calling card. He had offered the sale of Israeli drones and other military equipment to help defeat the Islamic uprising. 'Blair is just after business,' muttered Buhari.

During the drive back to the airport, Lai Yahaya, the local AGI organiser, asked Blair whether he was mixing charity and business. 'We don't do business in Africa,' the statesman replied. 'Don't worry. Only AGI and charitable work. We only do business in the Middle East and Asia.' Yahaya was unconvinced. He had heard about Blair working the system in other African countries where AGI operated.

Two weeks later, Yahaya called Buhari's office to ask whether the president would accept AGI's experts. 'Don't push the AGI stuff,' he was told. 'The president was not happy with Blair pushing the Israeli business.' (Buhari subsequently ignored Blair's calls on behalf of the Saudi crown prince.)

Six weeks later, in London, Blair met Bukola Saraki, the president of the Nigerian senate, ranked by the constitution as the third most powerful person in the country. Just before the meeting, Blair was briefed by Yahaya that Buhari was vigorously campaigning to rid Nigeria of its endemic corruption and did not welcome Blair seeking a business deal. 'They're concerned that you're pretending to be something else, using AGI to get access.'

'That's the problem with being the most successful prime minister,' came the reply. 'Britain is a country which doesn't like success.'

Blair ignored Yahaya's warning. During his conversation with Saraki, he discussed opportunities to introduce investors from the Middle East to Nigeria. 'We'd like that,' said Saraki, aware that Blair represented a wealth fund based in Abu Dhabi.

Yahaya was unaware of more glaring conflicts of interest. Two months earlier, Blair had posed with Ehud Barak, the former Israeli prime minister, at a college fund-raiser near Tel Aviv. Like Blair, since leaving office Barak had become a wealthy businessman. In Israel, he and Blair had become known as 'the twins'. Blair presented a perplexing conflict of interests: he was simultaneously the envoy of the international Quartet, the contact group established in 2002 by the US, Russia, the UN and the EU to negotiate peace between Israel and the Palestinians; he was also conducting business in Israel and the Arab countries; and, finally, he relied on the expertise and money of the British government to execute both undertakings. Was it a coincidence that, just two weeks later, Blair resigned as the Quartet's envoy?

For Yahaya, his surprise at the conversation with Blair was tempered by the Delivery Unit's global fame. A new book, *How to Run a Government* by Michael Barber, the founder of Blair's unit in Downing Street, had become a 'must read' across the developing world. However, unknown to those African politicians lectured by Blair about his government's unqualified success in improving Britain's health, education, housing and society, the unit was dismantled in 2005, four years after its creation. Since then, most independent observers have come to regard the unit as unsatisfactory. That fact has not deterred Blair's salesmanship. His genius since becoming prime minister in 1997 has been to pursue his causes regardless of any discomfiting misfortunes. With charisma and guile, he won three successive elections and, in the Blairite gospel, those unprecedented victories meant that he was successful. But, for others, there is a difference between success at the polls against weak opponents and success in government.

Fully understanding Blair's record has not been possible until recently, partly because the politicians, officials and military officers involved are only now giving candid explanations about their role in the New Labour era, and also because Blair's career after 2007 has cast a new light on his legacy.

Since his resignation, some Britons have remained admirers, while for others disappointment has grown. For the former, the extensive construction of new hospitals and schools and the dismantling of social barriers during his decade as prime minister remain a glorious achievement. Others, recalling the high expectations of May 1997, list the lost opportunities as a tragic waste. The principal complaint by the disenchanted is that the man who proclaimed his intention to be 'purer than pure, whiter than white' above all things broke that vow and revealed himself to be untruthful.

The invasion of Iraq, the critics say, was approved by Parliament because of his deception. Their anger has intensified during the years since his premiership, not least because while selling his services on the strength of the connections he made while in power, he continues to use the trappings of state to earn tens of millions of pounds. Even his close friends are puzzled about his quest for wealth, and their bewilderment is compounded by ignorance. None of them knows about his activities in Rwanda and Nigeria, or about the source of his lucrative business across the Middle East, Asia and America. So, has he undergone a metamorphosis since 2007, or is the man now consorting with a mass murderer and several vile dictators showing his true character?

At the outset of my research, in 2013, answering such a question was not my primary aim. Indeed, I knew little about Blair's commercial career. Rather, my original focus was on what had happened during his days in government. The genesis of the book was a friendly but impassioned argument I had over dinner with a close friend of Blair. She insisted that, thanks to his time in government, only 20 per cent of eleven-year-olds entered secondary school illiterate, whereas in 1997 it was 30 per cent. I believed that there had been no genuine improvement in literacy and numeracy during the Blair years. The argument continued over the following days, and by the end I realised that no one really knew what had happened during that hectic decade – not only in education but in energy, immigration, health, social welfare, defence and, of course, the events that led Britain and America into two disastrous wars.

There are many books describing aspects of those subjects. Most are partial memoirs or gossipy accounts of life among Blair's inner circle (the best being Andrew Rawnsley's two volumes). In addition, Alastair Campbell's diaries provide a useful timetable and a remarkable testament to the prejudices of Blair's supreme adviser, while Jonathan Powell's slim record provides a crude study in self-deception. No book adequately delves beyond the spin masters' smoke and mirrors to reveal what the government actually achieved. The thirty-six books I read all perpetuate myths and, occasionally, falsehoods about the central events of the period from 1997 to 2007. All ignore the eyewitness accounts by anonymous civil servants who saw so much but have generally kept their counsel. Even those books, articles or TV documentaries that reveal unknown facts about, for example, education or the build-up to the Iraq war present a mosaic rather than a full narrative.

Like, I suspect, the majority of my readers, I lived through the Blair era. I wrote two books covering that period: one exposing the dishonesty of Geoffrey Robinson in 2001, and a critical biography of Gordon Brown in 2004. In both, my focus was on a flawed politician; Blair was a subsidiary figure, albeit an important one. I later came across him while writing biographies of Bernie Ecclestone and Richard Branson; in neither case was his reputation enhanced. With all four mavericks, Blair's conduct often seemed inexplicable to me. Yet, in hindsight, with the exception of Brown, there was a link between him and the other three: money, and the power of money. That did not appear to be relevant until I researched this book.

In 2013, despite the familiarity from the previous books, and despite absorbing huge amounts of information about the period, I realised that my understanding of Blair's government was limited. Beyond the headlines, sensational resignations or accusations of deception was a mystery. That contentious dinner party bequeathed a riddle: what actually happened during those years? Like most people, I viewed the charismatic, charming communicator as something of an enigma, but suspected that the full story would never be known. His band of loyalists, I knew, would not reveal his flaws. The best way to discover the truth about an unknown, Karl Marx famously proposed, is to write a book. I have taken his advice.

My study focuses on five areas: health, education, immigration, energy and the wars. Health and education represented, according to Blair, huge successes for Labour, while the inside story of immigration has never been told. Regarding energy, I failed to understand why not a single power station was built throughout Blair's decade in power, exposing Britain to potential blackouts. The wars speak for themselves. Regarding Iraq, all the key military officers and many of the civil servants and politicians have broken their silence; I also had the benefit of the televised testimony of about 190 witnesses to the Chilcot inquiry. The road to war in Afghanistan has not been previously explored. It is a shocking story, but understandable in the context of Blair's approach in other areas of his premiership. In other words, the same characteristics that persuaded Blair to dispatch troops to fight in Iraq and Afghanistan decided the fate of Britain's education, our health service and the nature of our society. Iraq was not an aberration; it was consistent with his administration of government throughout his decade in office. The story of his tenure reveals the nature of the man today.

To discover what happened after 1997, I sought out all the retired senior civil servants who had worked in those five areas during Blair's decade. I interviewed dozens of junior and senior officials, permanent secretaries and all the Cabinet secretaries. Next, I spoke with successive junior ministers and Cabinet ministers. For the wars, I interviewed most of the principal senior military officers, chiefs of staff and all four chiefs of the defence staff. In total, over two hundred people were interviewed, some of them several times. A handful refused to speak to me but, in the light of what others told me, I know that their contribution would have been mostly irrelevant. Those who agreed to speak were credible eyewitnesses. The result is the fullest narrative yet available about the workings of the Blair government.

To those readers who suspect my motives, let me declare the following. I voted for Blair in 1997 and excitedly watched his drive from Islington to Downing Street. Like the majority of Britons, I did believe that this was a new dawn. Before the election, I had met socially many of those close to Blair, including Peter Mandelson and Alastair Campbell, and had no reason to distrust them. I have met Blair once – at a Hampstead dinner party in 1996 to celebrate Mandelson's birthday – and was bemused to discover that Labour's leader knew nothing about Harold Wilson (with whom I had spent two memorable weeks as a BBC TV producer during the October 1974 election) or any of his predecessors. Besides that, I did not doubt that he was sincere.

In 2003, I supported the invasion of Iraq. I believed the prime minister's warning that Iraq possessed weapons of mass destruction and even, to the bemusement of friends, followed the government's advice to stock up on tinned goods and spare batteries. Thirteen years later, I am neither disenchanted nor angry about Blair or his party. I am not a Labour supporter, but I remain mightily influenced by the student radicalism I absorbed during the 1960s at the then uniquely blessed London School of Economics. So please accept that what follows – my twenty-first book – while fuelled by curiosity is not motivated by prejudice. Rather, I was compelled to research this book because, like most Britons, I could not understand how the 'whiter than white' prime minister of 1997 evolved into a derided carpetbagger. Were we all fooled at the outset by a brilliant actor, or did an honest man fall victim to the temptations of power? Did he embark on government in bad faith or, infected by vanity and unmoored values, did he slowly lose his way amid situations he did not understand? Will his still loyal friends, after reading this book, retreat from their high ground? Or are Blair's critics, as he asserts, guilty of mean-spirited ingratitude? Will history, as he believes, hail his greatness?

Shimon Peres, the veteran Israeli statesman, told Blair during one of their early meetings that every successful political leader needs to be a narcissist and paranoiac to survive. 'Not one or the other,' said Peres, 'but both at the same time.' Blair acknowledged that wisdom. His unshakeable self-belief is an essential prop that keeps him afloat during his involuntary exile from Britain.

Many believe redemption is impossible for a man so tarnished. For the moment, the best way to judge the man is to uncover the previously unknown story of his government. Discovering the truth was a surprise to me, and perhaps will be for you too.

PART 1

NEW LABOUR TAKES CHARGE

MAY 1997–MAY 2001

ONE

The Beginning

One week before the 1997 general election, Tony Blair was facing Robin Butler, the fifty-nine-year-old Cabinet secretary. On the eve of his landslide victory, Blair had invited Britain's most important civil servant to his home in Islington for a meeting. Uppermost in Butler's mind as he drove from Downing Street to north London was the fate of Jonathan Powell, Blair's chief of staff.

Ever since Blair had first met Powell in Washington in 1993, the Foreign Office diplomat had fed Blair's suspicion that most civil servants were unimaginative conservatives opposed to modernising Britain. Two years after that meeting, Powell had resigned from his job and joined Blair's private office, and over the following years Blair came to accept Powell's belief that Whitehall's inertia would sabotage New Labour's mission. Anticipating his party's victory, Blair expected Powell to move into Downing Street and issue orders to his former colleagues.

'When I arrive next week,' Blair told Butler as the two men faced each other, 'I want Jonathan to be my principal private secretary.'

'I advise very strongly against that,' replied Butler. 'You'll need someone experienced to operate the levers of power. You'll have Alex Allan for the first three months. After that, see how it goes.' Allan was an experienced civil servant trusted by Butler.

'I see,' replied Blair.

'There are some things that a PPS has to do that should not be done by a political adviser,' explained Butler. 'Like relations with the Palace, civil-service appointments and intelligence matters.' He mentioned another factor. Powell's elder brother Charles, also a former Foreign Office official, had been a close adviser to Margaret Thatcher, and Butler believed that Thatcher had been brought down in 1990 partly because her reliance on Powell had isolated her from others.

Not mentioned was Jonathan Powell's reputation. Many in Whitehall considered him to be politically naive and even trivial. His belief in himself extinguished any self-doubt. Butler, a former head boy at Harrow school and now an accomplished patrician on the eve of retirement, was seeking to protect the young future prime minister from an early mistake.

'Right,' said Blair reluctantly, 'let's keep Allan for the first three months and see how it goes.'

Butler was relieved. Sharp words, he thought, had been exchanged in the stand-off. 'I'll make the legal arrangements using an order-in-council to give him and Alastair Campbell the necessary powers,' he told Blair. Powell would remain Blair's chief of staff and would be given executive authority to issue orders to civil servants.

Blair smiled. In their confrontation he had acted with the self-confidence of an insider, although he had been bored after an hour. 'Amiable but out of date,' he told himself as he bid his visitor farewell. His natural politeness had concealed his judgement that Butler's protests were the death rattle of the old mandarin class. Under his regime, Whitehall would be occupied by a network of friends ruled by himself as self-styled chief executive. By giving both Powell and Campbell, his spokesman, executive powers, he had cleared his first obstacle. Henceforth the civil servant's tainted advice would be ignored. Blair had modernised the Labour Party. Now he would modernise Britain.

'He's scared of me,' Butler concluded during the drive back to Whitehall. 'He didn't even ask me how to make the government machine work.' He was puzzled by Blair. Since they had first met in 1993, his attempts to explain Whitehall had been ignored. First, he had sent the young MP the transcript of a lecture describing the problems of governing Britain.

Blair did not respond. Then, several weeks before the 1997 election, they had met in Westminster. Butler had been beguiled by Blair's charm but only in hindsight did he realise that the future prime minister had not asked how Whitehall intended to implement Labour's election manifesto. Only later did he understand his mistake. Blair had not asked how prime ministers operated because he was focused on winning power. Despite his lifelong experience, Butler had missed the signs of a politician's fearless conceit. 'He didn't really get what was going on inside Blair's head,' noted Campbell in his diaries.

Over the following days, the headlines were dominated by predictions of a Labour landslide. Blair's cautionary words – 'I take nothing for granted' – were greeted amid unusual bitterness by Prime Minister John Major's accusations that Blair was telling 'bare-faced lies' by predicting that a new Tory government would abolish the state pension and levy VAT on food. Beyond the cynical abuse, *The Times* columnist Matthew Parris speculated whether Labour's appeal to Britain's middle class spelt the end of the Conservative Party and the abandonment of the working class. Simon Jenkins, another shrewd commentator, was awed by New Labour's 'discipline of vacuity' so that 'an entire political generation has been chloroformed to utter waffle by a leader who is not politically bold'. Nevertheless, everyone agreed that on Friday 2 May the removal van would arrive in Downing Street and eighteen years of British history would be derided.

A week after their confrontation in Islington, Butler and Blair met again in the Cabinet room in Downing Street. Millions of television viewers were watching reruns showing the smiling victor greeting Labour supporters at an all-night party in the Royal Festival Hall and, later, as the century's youngest prime minister, walking in the sunshine along Downing Street to witness the beginning of his eulogy that 'a new dawn has broken'. 'This is a dream come true,' the playwright Colin Welland was saying on TV. 'I'm going to be able to pick up my four-year-old grandson and tell him he has got a future.'

Exhausted by the campaign, Blair had been re-energised by the excitement he had witnessed on the pavements as he had been driven from Islington towards Westminster. The clapping crowds, he would accurately say, were 'liberated, yearning for change in their country'. His message was addressed to those in the middle ground, voicing their hopes and fears and giving reassurance about taxes and the economy. Yet none of the jubilant supporters spraying the media with guffaws about 'a new era' and 'history is changing' could have imagined the strained atmosphere inside 10 Downing Street.

After welcoming Blair, Butler told him, 'We have studied your manifesto and are ready to help you implement it.' Blair smiled, concealing his disbelief. Thirteen years later, he would write that he found those words strangely disturbing. In his punctilious manner, Butler went through the routine housekeeping list: the senior appointments that Blair would make that day; the seniority of ministers and the seating plan in Cabinet meetings; and the allocation of government houses for ministers. The final item covered the process by which Britain's nuclear weapons were activated.

Blair was then presented with a bundle of files. In the traditional manner, the civil service had prepared a detailed schedule for implementing Labour's manifesto. Butler was proud of the achievement, but the reaction unsettled him. Glowering at Butler from the side, Powell interpreted the files as an attempt to overawe Blair. Butler, he thought, was 'an old-school Cabinet Secretary who was anxious to assert control over a new and inexperienced prime minister'.

'Butleshanks', as the Blairites demeaningly called the Cabinet secretary, was puzzled by Powell's hostility. 'I never saw it as putting the frighteners on him at all,' Butler would say, mystified. The first sign of his reduced status was his exclusion from Blair's Monday-morning discussion with his confidants about the upcoming week's agenda. Powell's attitude, Butler lamented privately, was 'quite ridiculous and ludicrous'.

Butler's humiliation was repeated over the following hours across Whitehall. Freshly appointed ministers arrived in their departments expecting their civil servants to be untrustworthy Tories. During their brief moments with Blair to receive their appointments, any suspicions they may have built up over eighteen years of opposition had not been discouraged. For many, the only surprise was their new responsibility. With some exceptions, Blair had jettisoned his pre-election plans.

George Robertson, a jocular fifty-one-year-old career politician, arrived in Downing Street believing that he would emerge with the Scottish portfolio. The man who Blair feared talked too much was unprepared for his appointment as defence secretary, a brief he had never considered. Chris Smith, a former charity worker, had spent two years developing Labour's health policy but at the last moment Gordon Brown had taken offence at Smith's ideas, so, bowing to his chancellor's objections, Blair made Smith culture secretary. Health he entrusted to Frank Dobson, a mainstay of old Labour. The NHS had never aroused Blair's interest. '24 hours to save the NHS' had been one of several key election pledges made up on the spur of the moment by a Labour speechwriter. 'Tony didn't discuss health when we met in Downing Street,' recalled Dobson. 'He only mentioned my daughter Sally, who was part of his election team.'

While Blair decided on the remaining 191 appointments, Dobson made his way across Whitehall to the health department's headquarters and stepped into a government departmental building for the first time. 'He looked aghast to have been appointed,' recalled the senior civil servant who welcomed him. On Dobson's desk was a thick folder prepared over the previous months. In simple terms, Graham Hart, the permanent secretary, and his officials outlined the problems and alternative policies for the national health service. 'I won't need that,' said Dobson, pushing the file to one side. 'I'll read the manifesto and we'll do that.' He gazed suspiciously at the perplexed officials. 'Everything's OK,' he said as he leaned back in his upholstered chair. 'Labour will save the NHS.' His audience suppressed their unanimous opinion that their new boss knew nothing about the health service.

Two hundred yards away, Margaret Beckett, a former deputy leader of the party and, in 1994, one of Blair's rivals for the leadership alongside John Prescott, had just entered the Department of Trade and Industry. To her surprise, she was greeted by hundreds of clapping civil servants. Without a word, she walked unsmiling into the waiting lift. 'I never expected such a welcome,' she told Michael Scholar, her permanent secretary. Scholar, a principled public servant, had organised the reception to win Beckett's trust. Her hostility suggested that he would fail.

As in other parts of the civil service, the department had compiled a five-hundred-page plan based on Labour's manifesto, speeches and policy documents. 'This is to achieve your objectives,' said Scholar, offering Beckett a timetable for briefings. 'Nice to be here,' she replied, pushing the thick brief aside. Either hostile or lazy, she would never open the file and refused to meet civil servants for briefings.

Below her in the same building John Battle, a former councillor, would enter his office as the new energy minister. During a two-minute telephone conversation with Blair, Battle was told: 'Stick to the party's election manifesto and look after the coal mines.' In fact, Labour had no energy plan other than to follow the Tories' policies. On his first day, Battle denounced his officials to their faces. 'He was', noted a hurt Scholar, 'strangely blinkered and distrustful.'

Officials in other buildings were not as downhearted. General Charles Guthrie, the chief of the defence staff, had been delighted by George Robertson's appointment. Some weeks before the election, over breakfast with Blair in a private room at Claridge's hotel, Guthrie had stacked the odds in Robertson's favour. 'David Clark', said the general, referring to Labour's shadow defence spokesman, 'is not the right man for the department.' Blair accepted the advice with a trace of gratitude. Compared to the lawyers, academics and dissolute parliamentarians vying to be ministers in the new government, the general's openness was disarming. On 2 May, Robertson crossed Whitehall and received a rousing welcome in the ministry's main building, not least from Guthrie.

Gordon Brown had been similarly cheered as he entered the Treasury. 'Thank you,' he said, before walking up a staircase lined with portraits of his predecessors. His smile disappeared once he sat behind his desk in the large chancellor's office. Speaking without warmth, he issued instructions regarding where to seat his closest advisers – Ed Balls, Geoffrey Robinson and Charlie Whelan – and gave orders that would revolutionise the Bank of England by enshrining its independence. Terry Burns, the permanent secretary, suggested slight modifications, in so doing confirming Brown's suspicions that Burns was untrustworthy. He resolved to neutralise him at once.

By contrast, Jack Straw had appreciated the applause of hundreds of civil servants as he arrived at the Home Office in Queen Anne's Gate. Like most government officials, they had become weary of John Major's fractious administration, and were drained by the previous home secretary Michael Howard's abrasive complaints about their obstruction of his demands. In his brief speech of thanks, Straw praised his audience, promised to listen to their advice and expressed his intention to work 'within the system'. His list of priorities included human rights and crime, the territory that the new prime minister had memorably captured from the Tories during the election with the slogan 'Tough on crime, tough on the causes of crime'.

Shortly afterwards, Straw was closeted in a conference room with Richard Wilson, his permanent secretary, and other senior officials. 'Implement our manifesto,' said Straw. 'That will take us through the next two years, and then we'll look to you for ideas.'

The officials smiled. 'This is refreshing,' thought one. 'He's got emotional intelligence. He's more open than Michael Howard. We can work for him.' Everyone suppressed their surprise as Straw then revealed that he had not discussed Labour's policies for the Home Office with Blair. 'I'm not interested in immigration,' Straw told Tim Walker, head of the Immigration and Nationality Department (IND).

'Howard had played up immigration,' thought Walker, 'Straw wants to play it down.' Straw believed immigration had become toxic under Howard, a situation that he intended to defuse.

Many of the new ministers, Robin Butler assumed, would want to discuss their responsibilities at the first Cabinet meeting. To restore good relations with Blair, he diligently offered a draft agenda. The reply was jolting. 'I've decided to make the Bank of England independent,' Blair revealed.

'The Cabinet will want to discuss and decide that,' replied Butler.

'Oh, they won't mind,' said Blair. 'We'll ring round and they'll agree.'

'It was my idea,' he would later write. 'I kept control of the economy but was pleased to let Brown take the credit.'

Butler was surprised that a tradition established three hundred years earlier was being jettisoned so casually. Since Robert Walpole became Britain's first prime minister in 1721, his successors had abided by the custom that the Cabinet would be consulted on major decisions. In Blair's vision, all traditions needed to be re-justified in order to survive. Collective government, ranking the prime minister as first among equals, reflected weakness. With presidential powers, he would govern with a handful of like-minded friends who, united by ambition and a desire for secrecy, would meet in his small office. 'My core staff', wrote Blair, 'were knitted together like a regiment, imbued with a common purpose and with a camaraderie that had a spirit of steel running through it.' Members of the Cabinet were not included. In addition to Powell and Campbell, there was Anji Hunter, his confidante since his teens, who acted as gatekeeper, his pollster Philip Gould and Peter Mandelson, the political genius who invented New Labour and fashioned Blair's image. During those early days, few outsiders could accurately measure Blair's disdain for the Labour Party members, especially those appointed as ministers. Their appointment was secured on condition that his orders were unquestioningly obeyed.

Although before the weekly meetings Cabinet ministers would receive the traditional agenda covering parliamentary, foreign and home affairs, Blair continued to ignore Butler's drafts. Powell took over that task, thus denying any dissidents an opportunity to launch complaints. The discipline Blair had imposed since becoming party leader would continue in government. He was a man in a hurry, and Cabinet meetings would be limited to forty minutes, during which he would address his government, expecting complete loyalty. That, he mistakenly assumed, had been Margaret Thatcher's method.

The change in approach surprised other leading civil servants besides Butler – Brian Bender, for instance, the senior Cabinet Office official responsible for Europe. In a conversation with Robin Cook after the new foreign secretary's meeting with Blair three days after the election, Bender listened to an unusual complaint.

'I'm chairing the committee about joining the euro but no one has given me the key documents,' said Cook.

'Well, I'll see what I can do in the future,' replied Bender.

Bender approached Jonathan Powell and asked, 'Will the single currency be discussed in the first Cabinet?'

'Don't worry about that,' replied Powell with noticeable impatience. 'We'll tell them what the line is.'

Perplexed, Bender asked Peter Mandelson how the new prime minister would operate before making major decisions. 'You'll find', replied the minister without portfolio, 'that he will helicopter in and then focus.'

Still uncertain, Bender addressed Blair directly. 'I assume you will want to implement the manifesto pledges?'

'Don't feel spellbound by every word we used,' came the reply, implying that the manifesto should be ignored.

'Blair doesn't trust anyone,' Bender silently concluded.

On 8 May, as twenty-one ministers arrived in Downing Street for their first Cabinet meeting, Blair asked Butler, 'What do people call each other in the Cabinet?'

'The Conservatives were formal,' replied Butler, 'but Labour governments have used first names.'

'Call me Tony,' Blair told his ministers, with a flash of the familiar smile. His audience was rapt. Thanks to his emotional appeal, their leader had delivered an unimaginable 179-seat majority in the Commons. Even his critics in the room acknowledged their leader's talent as a communicator who gave the impression of enjoying every-one's company.

Blair started as he intended to continue: the chief executive imposing his will on former lawyers, TV producers, councillors and teachers with no experience of managing large organisations. 'The Bank of England will be made independent,' he announced. There were no comments. Everyone knew the form from their years in opposition: decisions were presented and voicing an opinion would not be looked on kindly. Next, Blair spoke about 'the line to take', focusing on how policies should be presented.

During the election campaign, simple phrases had spread Blair's promise to Britain: 'the future not the past'; 'the many and not the few'; 'duty to others'; and 'Britain deserves better'. He described his country as a community working together in 'a fair society'. His vision for Britain promised 'progressive' politics to 'modernise the nation'. The campaign song, 'Things Can Only Get Better', played over captions promising renewal, recovery and change, had energised voters to believe Blair's vision to 'end the crisis of faith' because, under New Labour, 'we will be a beacon to the world if people unite behind our mission to modernise our country'. And, finally, 'The future then, not the past.'

His ministers embraced every word. Even the left-wing Clare Short, responsible for international development, believed his declaration that 'The Britain of the elite is over. The new Britain is a meritocracy.' In the very first Cabinet meeting, she offered to give up her official car. 'You can keep it, Clare,' Blair said soothingly.

Sitting against the wall, Alastair Campbell epitomised the enigma of Tony Blair. The trusted propagandist had been employed as a political writer on Robert Maxwell's *Daily Mirror*. Without complaint, he had ignored journalism's duty towards objectivity and loyally served the infamous fraudster until Maxwell's sudden death. In serving Blair, simi-lar nuances had been embraced to establish New Labour as the natural party of government. Blurring the distinction between left and right had been one reason for the party's landslide victory. In a pre-election film, Blair had offered a 'different type of politics rooted in values and convictions but not quite left or right', adding with sincerity, 'I will not promise anything I can't deliver.'

Much of that message had been crafted by Campbell and was endorsed by Blair's belief that 'communication is fifty per cent of the battle in the information age'. Ensuring that Labour supporters in the media repeated the message had paved the way to victory. The most important ally had been John Birt, the BBC's director general, who had contributed money to Blair's campaign to become party leader while still employed by the corporation.

Like Jonathan Powell, Campbell had been given special powers by an order-in-council and had taken control of the government's media officials. Immediately, he dominated the Cabinet room. The weak feared his wrath, while the strong basked in his admiration. Campbell's skulduggery complemented Blair's apparent purity. Quite simply, he was indispensable to Blair's success.

His one rival as the dominant force in the new administration (besides Blair himself) was Peter Mandelson. Ever since Blair had become the party's leader, together the three men had focused on winning the upcoming election. During the three years after 1994, Blair was to rewrite Labour's constitution and utter slogans in verbless tirades aimed at crushing the Tories: 'New Labour. New Britain. The party renewed. The country reborn.' The language, the spectacle and the tactics had awakened the imagination of the electorate, but beyond the words there had been limited preparation in terms of realising Blair's ambitions. Now it was time for the hard work to begin.

One obstacle, the cabal knew, would be John Prescott, the obdurate representative of traditional Labour, a man burdened by a chip on his shoulder. To keep him onside, Blair had acceded to his demand to be both deputy prime minister and the supremo of a massive department embracing the environment, the regions and transport. The former waiter, Blair anticipated, would not interfere in running the government.

Blair ended his homily in the Cabinet room with a smile. Shortly after, he summoned Butler and furiously denounced the two ministers who had raised questions. 'From now on', he ordered, 'I want to know in advance about anything they want to bring up.'

The second Cabinet meeting lasted just thirty-five minutes.

TWO

Uninvited Citizens

After eighteen years in opposition, there was a long list of revisions that did not require Downing Street's approval. The most controversial would become immigration.

The last Commons clash on this issue had been fought over Michael Howard's bill in 1996. Alarmed by the increase in the number of foreigners claiming asylum in Britain, the Tories had proposed a list of restrictions that Jack Straw had vigorously opposed.

Britain had been a historic safe haven for those escaping persecution. Until the fall of the Berlin Wall in 1989, many fleeing the Soviet Union and other East European dictatorships had been welcomed. Among the 4,000 refugees arriving every year were politicians and artists from Africa and South America. Their applications automatically involved MI5, and were governed by the Geneva international convention signed in 1951. Asylum would be awarded only to those able to prove persecution by their government, and there was no legal guarantee such requests would be granted.

By 1995, that approach had changed. Third World economic migrants were entering Britain as tourists and then, after their six-month visas expired, claiming asylum. That year, applications rose to 43,000. Pertinently, the number of asylum-seekers in the rest of Europe had fallen dramatically because borders were being tightened. 'Britain was no longer a haven but a honey pot,' declared Howard. Unlike in other European countries, successful applicants were given generous cash benefits, subsidised housing and free health care. Home Office officials estimated that in 1995 over £200 million was paid out in benefits and only 5 per cent of those claiming asylum were genuine refugees. In Howard's opinion, the Home Office was losing control. Dilatory judges were allowing skilful lawyers to exploit a crumbling system. If the law were not changed, another 75,000 foreigners would claim asylum within the year.

To stop the racket, Howard's bill made it illegal to employ unrecognised asylum-seekers, withdrew benefits from those who failed to apply properly and stipulated procedures to remove bogus applicants as swiftly as possible. He also created a 'white list' naming those countries recognised as tyrannies whose nationals could genuinely be seeking asylum, and a 'safe' list whose nationals should have no reason to fear for their lives. Applications for asylum by nationals from the 'safe' countries would be automatically denied. Following the announcement of the bill, the number arriving in Britain dropped from 43,000 to 29,000 during 1996. Immigration from the Indian subcontinent also fell.

At first, Blair said nothing about the bill. He believed that immigration was good for the economy. Beyond that, he was oblivious to potential political problems arising from immigration or bogus asylum-seekers. As he would subsequently write, 'We had come to power with a fairly traditional but complacent view of immigration and asylum.' But Straw was genuinely angry. Free to oppose Howard in the Commons, he described the home secretary's focus on the number of immigrants as 'racist'. He was supported by Gerald Kaufman, an acerbic Labour MP, who characterised the legislation as 'vicious'. Blair was eventually forced into making a public comment, damning Howard for playing the immigration card as a sop to his party and the electorate.

A succession of human-interest stories now strengthened the Labour case, in particular one concerning a group of failed Algerian asylum-seekers on hunger strike in Rochester prison in protest at their deportation orders. Tim Walker and other Home Office officials believed that Howard was prepared to let them die. His nonchalance was widely criticised.

A second victim of the bill who received considerable publicity was Viraj Mendis, a Sri Lankan who was pulled out of a church and deported. A third was a family of Nigerians destined for deportation who were seeking sanctuary in a church in Stoke Newington.

'We are seen as a soft touch,' said Howard defensively. 'My bill will prevent the abuse of the law.'

'Wicked,' retorted Straw. Not granting asylum to the Nigerians, he went on, was racist because Nigerians needed visas to enter Britain while Americans didn't. According to Straw, all asylum-seekers arriving in Britain were genuinely fleeing from oppression and torture. Bogus claimants were products of Tory racism. He pledged to repeal Howard's 'arbitrary and unfair' law. Labour's manifesto, he predicted, would also include legislation to promote racial equality among those employed in the public sector.

Straw's damnation of Howard's bill resonated among those directly affected. In the dying months of a discredited Conservative government, the immigrant communities assumed that Straw would be the next home secretary and pinpointed one particular pledge in the Labour manifesto. At Straw's behest, the party promised to remove the 'primary purpose rule' – a regulation enshrined by the Home Office to prevent bogus marriages being used to enter Britain. The targets were naturalised immigrants from India and Pakistan living in Britain who sought to marry citizens living in the subcontinent and bring them back to Britain. That was forbidden unless they could prove that the primary purpose was genuinely to marry and not a ruse to enable a non-resident to live in the UK. For years, the law had kept out many suspect fiancés and members of the immigrants' extended families.

Straw had a special interest in the rule. Many of his constituents in Blackburn originated from the subcontinent, and they were pleading for the right to be united with their wives and family – real or acquired – in Britain. Straw wrote a pamphlet called 'Firmer, Faster, Fairer' that praised tolerance and reflected his belief in the benefits of immigration, and he promised to repeal the 1996 Immigration Act and abolish the primary purpose rule. Blair agreed with Straw that 'the rule is a mistake and should be removed'.

'Because I represent Blackburn', Straw told Tim Walker, 'and have been the shadow Home Office minister for many years, I know a great deal about immigration and asylum.' The primary purpose rule, he ordered, was to be abandoned immediately. 'There will be about 10,000 immigrants a year coming from India and Pakistan,' he predicted with certainty. 'I don't like letting illiterates from the subcontinent into Britain,' he added, 'but people have the right to choose their wives.' In passing, he also mentioned that 'Tony's not interested in immigration. He wants the manifesto commitment quickly implemented.'

Mike O'Brien, the junior minister responsible for immigration, silently noted that 'Straw's also not interested in asylum.'

One official sought to persuade the home secretary that he misunderstood marriage in the subcontinent. 'Marriage in India', she told him, 'is an important part of the economy. Families are prepared to pay large sums to arrange for their daughters to enter Britain, not least so they can follow.' She added that in Somalia the word 'brother' had a different definition to that in Britain. Straw was dismissive and, although he would never approve of any proposed legal definition of a dependant or a family, he waved her advice aside. Immigration, he told officials, was not a problem and was certainly not a priority.

Taking his lead from Straw, Richard Wilson had no interest in immigration. His attitude was reinforced by the absence of any policy directive from Robin Butler. 'Blair', observed Butler, 'never discussed immigration. I doubt if he ever thought about it.' It was clear that Straw's proposals had barely been discussed with his leader. Accordingly, the primary purpose rule was abolished and more immigrants from the subcontinent were made eligible to enter Britain. While Labour would formally retain Britain's border controls with Europe, their enforcement was relaxed.

In that halcyon year, the consequences did not materialise: Straw had inherited the legacy of Howard's restrictions. The number of asylum-seekers arriving in Britain began to fall in 1997 from 32,500 towards 20,000 in 1999; immigrants from non-EU countries remained static at about 150,000. After deducting the number of Britons emigrating, 'net' migration was under 100,000. Straw also inherited an unmentioned difficulty: the 52,000 applications for asylum that were piled up, unprocessed, at the IND's headquarters in Croydon.

Within the Home Office, the immigration department was an unloved backwater where some 5,000 civil servants were charged with scrutinising bulging files, highlighting discrepancies. In a forbidding atmosphere, newly appointed officials duly noted that most applications were riddled with lies. Their work rarely led to solutions but invariably to appeals. 'Our task is often hopeless,' Walker told Straw during his first visit to the centre. 'Their efforts to get in are always greater than our efforts to keep them out.' Straw was told that the IND's task could be relieved only if the number of applicants fell or the conditions of entry were modified.

He agreed. Officials were told to rewrite Howard's restrictive index of approved nations. 'Increase the countries on the list,' Straw ordered. Asylum was to be granted to beleaguered Afghans, Nigerians and others. The unusually legalistic home secretary also asked officials to redefine 'persecution'. Among those to be granted asylum were gays fleeing maltreatment in Africa and Roma suffering in Europe.

By the end of May, human-rights activists recognised that the 1996 Act had been swept aside. One lawyer even challenged the state's right to withhold benefits from asylum-seekers who had, as required by the Act, failed to register their claim immediately, citing a clause in the 1948 Assistance Act that guaranteed the state's duty of care towards the poor. Judge Andrew Collins, sympathetic towards Labour's intentions, agreed that the 1948 act neutralised Howard's prohibitions. Normally, the Home Office would have appealed the judge's decision, but officials assumed that Blair wanted all immigrants, including suspect asylum-seekers, to be treated generously. Accordingly, even failed applicants became entitled to welfare benefits.

In 2011, Blair would write, 'Law and order – and to an extent immigration – were to me utterly mainstream and vital points of what the government was about.' In reality, Downing Street's directive to ministers was not to mention immigration. Blair was just not interested in the subject.

Any doubts about that message were removed by the government's announcement soon after the election that it would introduce a human-rights bill, under which suspect asylum-seekers would be guaranteed the right to have their cases heard by a judge in Britain rather than a European judge in Strasbourg. The change was interpreted across the world as the beginning of a new tolerance, described by Blair as 'placatory signals'. In reality, his nonchalant dismissal of the topic would come back to haunt him.

THREE

Restoring a Vision

Four days after the election, Frank Dobson was summoned to Downing Street.

'How's it going, Frank?' Blair asked.

'I'm implementing the manifesto,' Dobson replied proudly.

Blair smiled. He had barely thought about New Labour's health policy. On the Saturday morning after the election, in a telephone conversation with Alan Milburn, a former Trotskyite from a coal-mining village in County Durham, Blair had confessed his ignorance about the NHS. 'You'll be the junior health minister,' he said. Milburn seemed a natural choice. He had made his reputation as a backbencher who asked awkward questions about the health service based on sensitive information leaked to him by a senior NHS manager.

'What should I do?' asked Milburn.

'We need a health policy.'

The service, Blair believed, was in crisis. However, he was uncertain about the solution.

Dobson did not share those qualms, and had already ordered Graham Hart, the department's permanent secretary, to restore the NHS to the purity of its founders' vision in 1948. The Tories' system of targets and league tables, along with the Patient's Charter introduced in 1994, were rescinded. Simultaneously, Dobson abolished the Tories' schemes to improve the quality of NHS care by empowering patients to choose their treatment and creating competition between hospitals.

'I've ended the internal market and GP fund-holders,' Dobson told Blair. 'Now it's co-operation, not competition and arguments.'

The NHS at that point employed a million people and absorbed about a tenth of Britain's GDP. In the manifesto, Blair had promised that £100 million would be saved by terminating the internal market's red tape. That money, he had written, would be used to reduce the waiting lists for admission to hospital, which were at their highest level since 1948. One hundred thousand people would immediately be helped, even though 1.1 million would remain on the lists.

That inheritance, Blair believed, was symbolic of the Tories' disdain for the NHS. In comparison with other countries, Britons had a lower life expectancy and less chance of surviving cancer. With inadequate government funding, many hospital buildings were derelict, there were insufficient doctors and the use of new technology was limited. A plan introduced in 1988 to make the training of nurses more academic was producing 'too posh to wash' recruits who were reluctant to perform the traditional chores. The £100 million, predicted Dobson, would begin to solve these problems. 'We hoped that all it would need was just a bit more money,' recalled John Hutton, a junior health minister. Beyond that, on his own initiative Dobson had ignored the plans devised by Chris Smith over the previous year to refine the Tories' introduction of market economics into the NHS. Any proposal to change Aneurin Bevan's blessed legacy was heresy.

Back in 1991, Ken Clarke, the then health minister, had concluded that the NHS was weakened by the Luddite practices of the NHS's own employees. To undermine their damaging self-interest, Clarke had created an internal market. His purpose was to provide faster and cheaper treatment for the public; to allow NHS hospitals to become more independent from Whitehall as so-called 'trusts'; to give financial power to GPs as 'fund-holders' to select and 'pay' for the treatment and hospital care of their patients; and to use private hospitals to reduce NHS waiting times. Robin Cook, Labour's spokesman at the time, had opposed all these ideas.

In 1996, in an unusual innovation, Chris Smith had been encouraged by Stephen Dorrell, the Conservative health minister, to speak to his departmental officials so that he might understand the incentives and competition that had been crafted to cure the NHS's chronic inefficiency.

'We need to rethink how to provide what did not exist in 1948,' Dorrell told those civil servants in the department who still worshipped Nye Bevan's 'covenant of past ideas'. The famous quip, 'The British have only one religion, the NHS, and Tories are seen as non-believers,' still resonated. Dorrell's White Paper, 'A Service with Ambitions', summarised the cures developed by trial and error to reduce management costs and end the paternalism of the staff running the NHS to suit their own rather than their patients' interests. Over the previous six years, the NHS had gradually placed GPs rather than administrators in the central role as leaders of the service, responsible for directing the expenditure of money to improve primary care. By using incentives and competition, GPs were encouraged to focus on the quality of treatment rather than on the number of people passing through hospitals. The innovation had been rewarded by a continuous rise in productivity. Taxpayers were getting more for their money and a record number of people were being treated. The downside was that the increasing demand for treatment by a growing and ageing population was not being met by sufficient expansion of the service.

In crafting Labour's health policy, Smith appeared to accept that Clarke's innovations were improving productivity, but he intended to add refinements. At the same time, he could not resist mocking Dorrell and the Tories' NHS as 'a shambles'. Among the solutions he expected – by 10.30 a.m. on his first day in office – was the dismissal of Alan Langlands, the forceful and intelligent chief executive of the service.

Echoing that policy, Blair had told a meeting of the heads of the royal colleges and the BMA before the election that he intended to clear out all the top NHS officials, including Langlands. Unanimously, his audience had protested that the NHS's chief was sound, not least because he opposed both the introduction of market forces into the service and the use of private hospitals. Blair retreated, but he lost his trust in Smith. For the moment he did not grasp the consequences of the fundamentally conservative medical trade unions' objections to any shift from the gospel that the NHS should be free of state controls. For them, introducing competitive pricing through the internal market offended Bevan's idealistic purity. Blair accepted their protests, which in turn were endorsed by Dobson.

During his first substantial meeting in Downing Street about the NHS, at which Alan Langlands was present, Blair's new health minister summed up his department's officials as 'dumbos appointed on a sleepy afternoon. They're second-rate, basically incompetent.'

Dobson's opinion was shared by Robert Hill, Blair's special adviser on the NHS, who was also at the meeting. The civil servants, believed Hill, 'had not got a clue as to how to get a grip on the service, which had been left completely fragmented by the internal-market reforms.' Hill did not recognise that civil servants in Whitehall set policy; they didn't manage services.

Neither Blair nor Dobson appeared to be embarrassed by the presence of Langlands. On the contrary, Blair shared Dobson's dismay that Labour had inherited a public sector that, in their opinion, and despite the evidence, was largely unreformed. 'The state was still as it had been in 1945,' Blair later wrote, although he was unsure what to do about it. Nevertheless, the reforms introduced since 1991 were to be dumped.

Faced with Dobson's caustic appraisal, Langlands trod carefully. Although sympathetic to Labour, he knew that Robert Hill, whom he marked down as 'well-meaning but an ideologue who would not listen', shared Dobson's disdain. Yet voicing any disagreement, he understood, would be unhelpful. The prime minister, he suspected, was uncertain about Dobson. Hours before he was appointed health minister, Downing Street had alerted officials in the department to expect Peter Mandelson as their new boss. To switch from Smith to Mandelson and end up with Dobson suggested Blair had no clear vision for the NHS.

'It's clear from the manifesto', Langlands now told Blair, 'that your policy is to abolish GP fund-holders.'

'Should we be getting rid of them?' asked Blair uncertainly.

He had forgotten his approval of Smith's plan for an amended GP fund-holding scheme. Although he instinctively accepted Thatcher's idea that monopolies should be broken up, New Labour's ideology provided no obvious alternative to central control of the NHS. 'Save the NHS' was only a slogan, behind which lay no new ideology, values or policy.

Any doubts were silenced by Dobson. 'I'm taking control,' said the new minister. Although the manifesto had pledged not to return to the top-down management of the 1970s, Blair did not object as Dobson went on to explain how the NHS would revert to the command-and-control system first developed in 1948. Over the following weeks, Dobson's officials did not dare ask how one man in Whitehall could supervise 520 executives running the NHS's 100 health authorities and 420 hospital trusts. With their jobs at stake, silence was advisable.

'We're not going to close St Bart's, are we?' Blair asked Langlands next. Closing the famous London hospital was part of Tory 'rationalisation' to improve community care. Concentrating medical expertise and new technology across a larger area provided better treatment than relying on an unplanned network of hospitals developed over the past century.

'That's in the plan,' replied Langlands.

'I don't understand community care,' said Blair. 'I don't want St Bart's to close.'

Langlands made no comment. After a brief pause, Blair mentioned the huge discrepancies in treatment across the country. 'How can they get it right in Newcastle and not Newquay?' he asked.

'There are some good ones and some tail-enders,' Langlands replied, 'just like in your Cabinet.'

Blair appeared to agree. 'Good,' he said, bringing the meeting to a close despite the unanswered questions.

Dobson returned to his department. Under the orders of his deputy Alan Milburn, everything inherited from the Tories would be reversed, echoing his wishes. 'I'll come down like a ton of bricks', Milburn threatened a group of NHS managers, 'if anyone uses the private sector.' He further told Langlands, 'We'll abolish the NHS trusts.'

'That's the one thing that is working,' replied Langlands.

'Right, we'll keep them,' said Milburn, 'but GP fund-holding, the internal market and the idea of independent hospitals must go.' In his understanding, Labour had settled on a policy of ending any independence of hospitals from Whitehall's total control and restoring what he called his ministry's 'care and maintenance' of the NHS.

Dobson and Milburn's demand for a complete reversal of previous government policy exposed their misunderstanding of the internal market. Among the NHS's weaknesses was its inability to price good-quality treatment. Since the 1980s, the Tories had accused the medical profession of obstructing improvements to the NHS. Doctors were interested in more cash – when it became their income – but caring for money that was to help the taxpayer caused discord. Like all NHS staff, GPs and consultants were unwilling to be constrained by budgets. 'My job', the doctors incanted to ministers, 'is to treat my patients. Your job is to provide the money.' The Tory answer was to set up an internal market between providers – the hospitals – and purchasers – the GPs. Being empowered to choose between different services provided by different hospitals would force NHS staff to consider costs and pricing, a normal procedure in the private market. By introducing a tariff, the NHS would get value for money and at the same time challenge vested interests.

The plan's introduction in 1991, forcing GPs to make choices when treating their patients, had caused grief for the NHS's ideological purists. The only solution, agreed Labour's supporters, was more money. Blair joined the chorus trumpeting that the internal market was a curse and should be abolished.

Graham Hart, the permanent secretary in the health department, was dismayed. Over half Britain's GPs had signed up to the fund-holders scheme. Research showed that the patients of those GPs incentivised by payments and preferential access were being treated faster and better in hospitals. And that was precisely Dobson's complaint: patients served by GPs opposed to fund-holding were noticeably worse off. Dobson and Milburn were adamant: 'We're not having a two-tier service.' The alternative scenario seems not to have occurred to them: namely, if all patients were served by GP fund-holders, all would benefit. Hart resisted explaining that to Dobson, reasoning, 'He would suspect that I was a Tory.'

Persuaded by the medical professionals that competition under-mined the public-service ethos, Dobson and Milburn believed that Britain should rely upon the altruism of the NHS staff, who, to their mind, were wholly motivated by their social conscience to help patients. Blair agreed. Choice, he believed, entrenched inequality because only the middle class possessed the ability to make effective use of it. 'Cream-skimming' was unacceptable because choice led to unequal life expec-tancy and, owing to duplication, waste. With his blessing, the system of fund-holders was abolished, but Dobson agreed to keep a watered-down scheme that still incorporated the internal market's 'providers and purchasers'. No one was quite sure whether Dobson understood the resulting confusion, and Blair was not told about the muddle in the NHS, nor did he seem aware of it in government policy.

At 10 a.m. on the Wednesday after the election, Blair bounced into the regular weekly meeting of Whitehall's permanent secretaries. Radiating idealism and energy, and dressed in his shirtsleeves, he conveyed mis-sionary zeal. 'My motives', he said, 'are the same as yours. Public service. You all have a huge wealth of experience, and we will rely on you.' Some officials would depart enthused, but Graham Hart was disappointed by the answers he received to particular questions. Labour's plan, Blair had said, was to 'reintegrate the NHS without reorganisation'. Hart was ready to implement the new government's policies by abolishing trust hospitals and GP fund-holders, but Blair's refusal to set up a Cabinet committee for the NHS was puzzling. He appeared unaware of the fiendish complications of running the world's second-largest business. 'He doesn't have the faintest idea about the NHS,' Hart concluded.

Blair left the meeting with misgivings of his own. The top civil servants, he complained on his return to his office, were not as impressive as generally assumed by politicians. They were only good for supplying raw data, and their advice was best ignored. He would rely on his confidants to change Britain.

Dobson was not a member of the inner clique but he stood in the vanguard. Embraced by Blair as a signal of reassurance to the trade unions and to the NHS staff that they had Labour's support, Dobson could silence fractious nurses. 'I'm the heart and soul of the NHS,' he told one of their conferences, 'so trust me. The NHS is the envy of the world.' He never reflected that no other country had adopted the British model, not least because it made no sense to manage the health of nearly 60 million people from Whitehall. 'The NHS is a secret garden,' Dobson told his officials. 'It moves like a giant ocean tanker. It only becomes political when it goes wrong.'

The first tremors of trouble, from either garden or tanker, were felt one week after the election. 'The NHS is running on empty,' Hart told Dobson. Treasury officials had not replied to any of Hart's previous warnings. In the months before the election, Gordon Brown had expressly forbidden any additional spending on the NHS because the economy he was inheriting, he said, was in crisis. He spoke about 'sticking to Tory spending plans' but intended to spend 0.6 per cent less on the NHS than the Tories, while increasing taxes. In truth, as Hart knew, the economy was growing, with a low debt of 37.6 per cent of GDP.

'There will be a winter crisis,' Langlands told Dobson. Waiting times would grow unless more staff were hired.

'No, there won't,' replied Dobson. 'We're in charge now and it won't happen.'

'It will unless we get more money.'

Dobson was obdurate, so Langlands passed his warning on to Blair, who in turn protested to Brown. 'It's all very difficult,' replied his chancellor in what would become a familiar routine. 'We're not going to solve this today.'

Blair persisted. More money and improving morale thanks to Labour, he said, would solve all the problems.

In early July, Dobson was telephoned by a Treasury official. 'The chancellor would like to see you, but come alone,' he was told. One hour later, Dobson returned and summoned Hart. 'Gordon wants to give us a lot of money,' he announced.

'How much?'

'One billion quid.'

'How did he arrive at that?'

'It wasn't explained.'

'It can't be a final settlement,' said Hart. 'We need discussions and a plan. When can we talk about it?'

'He said there could be no discussion. Take it or leave it by 10 p.m.'

Dobson was clearly in awe of Brown and the insiders around Blair. Hart said nothing. Brown was reverting to the old ways of throwing money at a problem rather than attempting to understand it. In particular, he had not understood that the publication of waiting lists had been invented by the Tories to shame bad NHS managers, but then the hospitals with the longest lists received government money. Paying hospitals to reduce such lists had been condemned for rewarding the worst. Brown ignored that discovery. Dobson said nothing further, took the money and distributed it to hospitals around the country.

Two months later, newspapers reported an increase in premature deaths, cancelled operations and what they called 'Third World hospital wards'. The NHS was still short of money. Blair was angry. Brown agreed to a further infusion of cash but insisted that he should broadcast the announcement to demonstrate his control over the economy. If Blair refused, he said, no more money would be released. Blair protested again, saying the NHS was being sabotaged, but he didn't dare overrule his chancellor. Their argument raged for two months, while the size of the waiting lists rose until they were 14 per cent higher than in 1996. It was impossible for Brown to sit on his hands any longer.

'Go and see Gordon,' Dobson told Langlands in early December. 'I've been told that I'm not required.' Brown's attitude towards his colleagues, many were discovering, was peculiar.

Langlands made his way to the chancellor's office. After reminiscing that Brown's father, the minister of Kirkcaldy's largest church, had married Langlands's parents, the two engaged in a bitter argument. 'Give me the answers to these nine questions tomorrow,' snapped Brown, ending their dispute by handing over a list drawn up by his department.

The following day, Langlands returned with the required sheet of responses. 'I can't give these to the chancellor,' a Treasury civil servant told him. 'It's too hard-hitting. You cannot talk to the chancellor like this.' The stand-off was resolved by Brown agreeing to pledge more money, but without a public announcement.

Blair did not ask Dobson how waiting lists would be reduced, he just willed him to do so. By then, Dobson had discovered that the number of available hospital beds had, as part of a deliberate policy, declined since 1948 from 480,000 to 190,000. He rejected the advice that modern medicine did not require them. To prove that the NHS was once again safe under Labour, he ordered an immediate increase to 246,000. Blair did not ask how such an increase matched New Labour's agenda. Millions were spent on extra beds, money that could have gone towards patient care. Jonathan Powell would be candid about the folly of unrealisable ambitions: 'We had prepared a hundred-day plan on coming into government but not an overall strategy for what we were trying to achieve.'

This early episode involving the NHS suggested that Blair was ambivalent about the requirements for governing. A telltale sign was the fate of the red box left outside Blair's flat in Downing Street every night. The case contained important memoranda from across Whitehall that Blair needed to read and annotate to guide civil servants and ministers. Officials recalled that by 7 a.m. Margaret Thatcher had written comments on every paper in her box. Blair rarely completed even half the work.

Those problems had been anticipated by Robin Butler, who had persuaded Blair to use Alex Allan as his private secretary for three months. To his surprise, Blair discovered Allan's value, telling Butler at the end of the period, 'He's very good. I want to keep him.'

'Too late,' replied Butler. 'He's going to Australia.' To his surprise, Blair appeared to have no recollection of their earlier discussion. The official resisted offering a solution. 'He's left with Jonathan Powell and the problem,' he decided.

On the eve of Butler's retirement, one final task for the loyal civil servant was to guide Blair in the selection of his successor. At Blair's request, he hosted a dinner at his home for the prime minister, Peter Mandelson and the Lord Chancellor Derry Irvine, who had admitted the young Blair to his chambers to practise at the bar and ever since had been a trusted adviser. Aware of his own inexperience, Blair relied on Mandelson's and Irvine's judgements to make the critical appointment. Butler was asked by Blair to debate with Irvine whether the combined post of Cabinet secretary and head of the civil service should be split. In the end, Blair was convinced by Butler's argument that they should remain together.

A few days later, Blair asked his closest confidants to select what Mandelson would call 'a reforming Cabinet secretary'. Their choice was Richard Wilson, the permanent secretary at the Home Office. With little thought, Blair directed that the Old Radleian be presented to the press as a moderniser. Powell scoffed. Wilson, he said, was a classic Establishment appointment. 'Very odd-looking,' agreed Campbell disparagingly. 'With huge great ears and a face that didn't quite map together. He didn't seem naturally on our wavelength.'

The selection of Wilson revealed Blair's indifference to the machinery of government. Whoever had been appointed would be excluded from his den, especially by Powell. In Butler's words, the Cabinet had been quickly reduced to 'a weekly meeting of political friends'.

Musing later with an official, Blair offered his understanding about the future: 'Our job is to have the vision. Your job is to carry it out.'

'It's not as simple as that,' replied the official. 'There's the money too.'

'That's Gordon's job. I don't get on with him. We're like an unhappy marriage. But he's the details man, and I'm the front man.'

The conversation trailed off.

Blair's candour revealed both his strengths and his weaknesses. 'You could take Jonathan away from me,' he added, 'but not Alastair.'

Blair acknowledged that he relied on his scriptwriter more than on anyone else. Politicians, it is said, should be judged by their choice of their closest associates.

FOUR

The Gospel

Unlike Frank Dobson, David Blunkett arrived at his department with a detailed plan. Over the previous two years, the new secretary of state for education had spent many hours with Blair discussing the fate of working-class children. Just after the first Cabinet meeting, Blair invited Blunkett to Downing Street. He arrived with Michael Bichard, the permanent secretary of what Blunkett dismissed as a dysfunctional department focused on administration rather than education.

Blunkett had already clashed with Robin Butler about his senior aides. 'If you rock the boat too much,' Blair warned Blunkett, 'they'll get you.'

Until Bichard's appointment in 1995, only one of Blunkett's officials had taught in a school. 'Education was the Tories' biggest failure,' Blair told Bichard, 'and education is Labour's number-one priority.' To emphasise his commitment, days after the election he stood on the ground floor of the department's eighth-floor atrium, looking up at hundreds of officials crammed onto balconies. 'Building a modern society depends on education,' he exhorted his audience with passion. 'My job depends on what you're doing.' The wild applause was encouraging.

Blunkett was never quite sure what Blair's 'modernisation' meant. He assumed that it involved ridding Britain of the old politics, empowering people to embrace 'citizenship' and join the knowledge economy. The fuzziness was intentional. Blairites had banned the word 'ideology'. In its place, Blunkett acknowledged, 'Tony didn't have one set of values to drive across the board.' Unlike the old socialists, Blair offered a concoction of intentions rather than a set of principles. Within the first weeks, the absence of a firm ideological base was causing confusion for John Prescott at transport and Harriet Harman at welfare. Both politicians, limited by their intellect and lack of new policies to inspire their departments to produce realistic improvements, were struggling. Jack Cunningham at agriculture was also adrift. He disliked his civil servants, and the sentiment was returned towards a wayward minister ostentatiously enjoying the perks of his office. Education was the exception. Blunkett arrived with a clear route map agreed with Blair and based on a fundamental change from old Labour.

The transformation had begun in the early 1990s, during dinner parties among Blair's friends in Hackney and Islington. As with so many young parents across Britain, their conversation would return to a familiar topic: the disappointing standard of local state schools. The Blairs knew that using private education could be a fatal handicap for an ambitious Labour politician. Nevertheless, they refused to entrust their children to failing schools. They heaped the blame for their dilemma on Thatcher's indifference to state resources. John Major had been little better. Since 1995, the education budget had been cut to its lowest level since the mid-1950s and the department was relegated to middle-ranking ministers. The Conservatives, Blair believed, were deliberately undermining state schools in order to champion private education. While only 7 per cent of Britain's children were privately educated, 20 per cent of university entrants came from private schools, and half of all Oxbridge students were from public schools.

Blair was a beneficiary of that privilege. Fettes, his Scottish private school, and St John's College in Oxford had provided enviable advantages. By improving state schools, he wanted to remove the social inequalities suffered by children from poor backgrounds. Such children, he argued, deserved the same opportunities as those born to the wealthiest. Realising his ambition, he believed, depended on confronting an educational establishment filled not with Tories but with left-wing academics – Marxist schoolteachers and ideological trade unionists.

The Left's anger had been particularly roused in 1994 by Chris Woodhead, the head of Ofsted, the regulator established by the Tories to inspect schools and report on their performance. On the basis of his staff's reports, Woodhead, a leading evangelist for the depoliticisation of education, had denounced 30 per cent of teachers as unsatisfactory. In a headline-capturing declaration, he demanded that no fewer than '15,000 incompetent teachers' should be instantly dismissed, especially the champions of 'progressive education'. Blair sympathised with the sentiment, although he did not appreciate the history behind the headlines.

After the publication of a report in 1967 by Bridget Plowden, an amateur educationalist, describing primary schooling, Britain's education system had become an ideological battleground. Masked by a scattering of platitudes about improving schools, Plowden recommended the destruction of traditional education. Children, she wrote, should no longer sit in rows of desks but instead gather in groups around tables to encourage self-learning. She also recommended that the eleven-plus examination, a three-part test (English, maths and intelligence) taken in one day that irrevocably determined a child's educational fate – either to blossom in a grammar school or be consigned to failure in a secondary modern school – should be abandoned. Grammar schools should be replaced by non-selective comprehensives that mixed children of all standards. With cross-party support, successive Labour and Conservative governments implemented her recommendations.

Within ten years, educationalists had become divided over the consequences of Plowden's changes. For left-wing academics, schools were ideal locations for engineering the removal of class distinctions. In the Left's ideology, all children start as equals, regardless of genetics or social background. If parental choice, testing and selection were prevented, middle-class children would beneficially influence those in the classroom whose home life was blighted by crime, drug addiction and deprivation. The Left had also welcomed Harold Wilson's decision to centralise teacher training in universities. Like-minded academics

could persuade their student teachers to use education for social engineering. Self-learning became the mantra; teachers would no longer be
required to guide the learning process. 'Phonics' was abolished as a
way to teach reading, and traditional basic textbooks were discarded.
Instead, children discovered how to read by themselves using books
sanitised of unwelcome stereotypes.

By the 1990s, Blair understood the consequences. Amid a notable
decline in educational standards, the closure of grammar schools and
indiscipline in classrooms, over 30 per cent of children were leaving
school illiterate or innumerate. Yet, while aspiring parents became disillusioned with comprehensives, Labour's support for non-selective
schools remained solid.

The dilemma for Blair was whether poor education was the fault
of schools and their teachers or whether those on the left of his party
were correct to blame poverty and a child's social background. The
ideological battle between the left-wing educational establishment and
the Tories centred on whether poverty could be overcome by a school's
culture. Did elitism, excellence and discipline – based on choice and
selection in state schools – give deprived children the chance of a good
education? Or, as argued by the Left, did choice and selection prevent
the majority of disadvantaged children receiving a good education so
that a few could benefit at grammar schools?

In 1994, Blair had hesitated about engaging in that battle. Labour's
educational establishment, he knew, denied outright that any schools
were failing. 'There's no such thing as a bad teacher,' they proclaimed
in unison. They opposed selection at any stage in the educational process and wanted to limit parent power because in both cases the middle
class would be favoured. They wanted the middle class to use the ailing
schools that the Blairs were resisting for their own children in Islington.
Such prejudice excused the Left from questioning why literacy and
numeracy were successfully taught in private schools. Blair spoke publicly about the importance of discipline in the classroom but rarely
mentioned the curriculum. Amid Tory ridicule that Labour lacked any

education policy, he needed to resolve his dilemma between what he wanted and what he believed, and in particular whether he would challenge Labour's opposition to Thatcher's 1988 Education Reform Act.

The Tories had become alarmed by the capture of education since the 1960s by the 'progressives', especially in the Institute for Education in London and in the Department for Education in Westminster. The Left's pursuit of equality, in their opinion, was harming children. The abandonment of traditional teaching methods had effectively consigned the 30 per cent of teenagers who were innumerate or illiterate to lifelong failure. In Thatcher's opinion, as the demand for manual labour declined, those children would become permanently unemployed.

The 1988 Act imposed on schools a national curriculum with a 'basic syllabus' of the 'Three Rs' plus testing. The important innovation was the publication of schools' results in league tables. Their performance would be monitored by Ofsted, a new regulator. With that information, parents were empowered to choose the best schools. Those with poor academic results that failed to attract children would be forced to improve or close.

Six years later, improvement was patchy, with the Tories blaming the educational establishment for sabotaging their policies. To overcome that obstruction, in 1996 they introduced compulsory literacy and numeracy hours for all primary schools. Blair's predicament was that Labour's educationalists condemned the innovation, and much more besides. Rather than join the Tories in pulling aside the lack of disclosure that protected inadequate teachers and struggling schools, Labour was committed to denying parents any information about a school's performance, abolishing Ofsted and ending all choice. 'Ghettoisation', as the Left described parental selection, would be replaced by an entirely comprehensive system.

Blair disagreed with that ideology, and after his election as party leader he signalled his sympathy towards the aspiring middle classes by removing Ann Taylor as shadow education minister for being too favourable to teachers. Taylor's replacement by Blunkett would be hailed as a milestone.

Blair next declared war on the educational establishment. 'We should build on what's good from the Tories,' he declared. Britain's children, he said in a dramatic speech in 1995, were being betrayed by the system. Labour, he added, would keep the Tories' tests, league tables and streaming, and even enhance Ofsted's powers. Oxbridge's prejudice in favour of excellence would not be challenged.

Blunkett was encouraged by Blair to intensify the assault at the annual conference of the National Union of Teachers in 1995. 'There is a culture of complacency and lack of ambition in some schools,' the new shadow minister told the outraged delegates. Comprehensive schools were failing the majority of children. Many teachers, he believed, were lazy, poorly trained and had low expectations. 'We have a crap teaching profession,' he would later say, referring to the anarchy in some schools.

There were, however, important aspects of the 1988 Act that Blair opposed. To escape the control of the local education authorities (LEAs), the Tories had given some of the money from their budgets directly to schools. This could then be used by the 1,198 grant-maintained schools to fund extra classes – for example, in music – or to amend their curriculum.

Five years later, Tony and Cherie Blair enrolled their eldest children at the Oratory, a grant-maintained Catholic school in Fulham. There was uproar. Both Left and Right accused Blair of hypocrisy, with the former infuriated by their leader's endorsement of the divisions created by the Conservatives. To persuade the Left that Labour was ideologically different to the Conservatives, Blair promised to end the privileges of the grant-maintained schools and to terminate the assisted-places scheme that paid for 38,000 poor children to attend private schools. That decision revealed his confusion. He refused to close the last 164 grammar schools and protected the new city technology colleges (CTCs), despite their dependence on selection and private finance. He also adopted the Tories' plan for 200 specialist schools that selected 10 per cent of their intake.

Compounding the confusion, Blunkett solemnly promised his party conference: 'Read my lips. No selection by examination or interview.' To further pacify the Left, he agreed that disruptive pupils would not be expelled. Inclusivity would rule and 'special needs' schools would be closed.

By cherry-picking and promising the Left half of a golden age, Blair hoped to create a coalition to reform education. 'Some things the Conservatives got right,' he inserted into Labour's 1997 manifesto. 'We will not change them.' The manifesto partly focused on class sizes and laptops, and to assuage the Left's passion for uniformity it omitted mentioning the standard of teaching in classrooms. Blair himself said nothing about Harriet Harman, the shadow minister for welfare, sending her children to private schools.

Blair's ideological confusion was disguised by adopting ideas suggested by Michael Barber, a key ally of Blunkett. Barber, a former official in the National Union of Teachers, somersaulted in 1995 and attacked what he called 'the dark side of the moon' among his former allies. Teachers, he said, echoing Blair, should cease tolerating failure in poor communities. They should abandon their conviction that only money could change education, and they should be accountable. But there was an awkward outcome to his conversion.

Unlike the Tories, Barber believed that all children share the same abilities and, regardless of their social background, can, with the right education, be successful. In the policies that he and Blunkett presented to Blair, they stressed that every child would benefit from an 'accessible and personalised' education. By default, they denigrated special technical colleges that trained plumbers, carpenters and electricians.

Barber tempted Blair with an additional hymn. Education, he said, should be driven by measurement. Targets would change the culture of schools. As an instinctive dogmatist, Blair was persuaded that improvement could be achieved by setting what they variously called strategies, standards, benchmarks, performance indicators and measurements by examinations. He also echoed another of Barber's gospels: 'It's standards, not structures.' By that, Blair and Barber meant that Labour would focus on what happened in the classroom. To their critics, that was tokenism. To avoid a conflict within the party, they both refused to challenge the local education authorities. The LEAs' officials controlled the teachers in the classroom. Nothing could change without removing their doctrinaire influence.

Blair now directed his speeches at his left-wing critics. 'To those who say where is Labour's passion for social justice,' he proclaimed, 'I say education is social justice. Education is liberty. Education is opportunity.' As so often, he also urged 'modernisation'. On one theme he remained consistent: the changes in schools would be imposed from Whitehall. Control over education was to be centralised. London would micro-manage all the LEAs. To effect that change, he empowered Blunkett, Bichard and Barber to execute a radical plan across the Department for Education. Presentation was Blair's driver of change. To convince the electorate of action, he expected regular announcements of Green Papers, White Papers, legislation and the creation of new schools.

Blunkett was his ideal ally, spreading New Labour's message immediately after election day. In a frenzy of diktats, he announced a succession of White Papers, including 'Excellence in Schools', 'Excellence in the Cities', 'Pupil Learning Credits' and 'Education Action Zones' (EAZs). He also proclaimed the creation of more specialist schools (1,000 to be opened by 2002), more faith schools, a Leadership Incentive Grant and a programme of Leading Edge Partnerships. With every publication, the most important task was to guarantee coverage by the media. Then, forgetting what Blair had said before the election, he promised to devolve power to local people and give schools more freedom from the LEAs and the national curriculum, as well as the right to receive extra money from business.

Ever since the original criticism of teachers and comprehensive schools, Blair and Blunkett had hardened their dislike of the Left's ideology that all children are born with the same ability, while excellence is merely destructive elitism. To neutralise the Left, Blair engaged in a battle of slogans about equality. He spoke about children benefiting from 'equality of outcome' and 'equality of opportunity'. His weapons were targets and tests.

On 13 May 1997, English teachers were told by Blunkett to achieve 'a dramatic improvement' by raising standards for eleven-year-olds. By 2002, they were ordered, 80 per cent of this age group should be able to reach level four or the average mark of the Standard Assessment Test (SAT) examinations. Under the Tories in 1996, only 57 per cent of children had reached that level. Secondary schools were told that children at sixteen would be expected to achieve five 'good' A*–C passes at GCSE, well above what was achieved during the Tory era. To enforce the changes, Barber established a standards and effectiveness unit to name and shame failing schools. Blunkett said he would resign if the targets were not met. Tory pragmatism had been replaced by Stalinist five-year plans.

Blair approved the ruthlessness. Schools that failed the Ofsted test were given two years to improve or would be closed. Eighteen were 'named and shamed' during the first flood of announcements, initiatives and laws. They were to be reopened under the 'Fresh Start' programme, another initiative to transform run-down schools with new staff, refurbished buildings and a revised curriculum to match the children's needs. In parallel, Blunkett announced the construction of new schools and the recruitment of 35,000 teachers. Pertinently, there was no mention of retraining or dismissing any of the existing 400,000 teachers, or of reforming the curriculum. For both Blair and Blunkett, confronting the teachers amounted to no more than boycotting their annual conference and giving head teachers the power to reward performance with special payments. Nearly every teacher in England, it later emerged, was rewarded with a payment.

Blair still worried about his pet concern. 'Why are the schools in my constituency so awful?' he asked Chris Woodhead during their first meeting soon after the election, with Blunkett in attendance. The director of Ofsted was the media star whom Blair could neither ignore nor dismiss.

'Give me 2,000 inspectors and I can solve a lot,' Woodhead replied. 'Schools need to be held to account.' Inspection, he continued, would reveal faults in a school, but his task force was not permitted to tell teachers how to improve. Something more prescriptive was required. 'Ofsted should be used in a constructive way, but the improvements must be forced upon schools by the department.'

'Yes,' said Blair, appearing to agree.

'Teacher training', explained Woodhead, 'is the heart of the problem. We must change it.'

'Yes, yes, yes,' said Blair. 'Let's do that.'

'Bad teachers and inadequate head teachers unable to control anarchy in classrooms are to blame. Bad discipline leads to academic decline.'

Blair nodded. 'What's the cure?' he asked.

'It's bottom up,' explained Woodhead. 'Dismiss every bad teacher and head teacher. We've got to tackle the problem in each school, root out the enemy in every classroom. And then we'll get rid of the malign influence of the LEAs. The LEAs are failing schools.'

'You can't inspect your way to success,' interrupted Blunkett.

The exchange revealed an irreconcilable disagreement between Woodhead and Barber, Blunkett and Bichard. Woodhead, like the Tories, focused on the quality of every teacher and advocated that schools should be set free from the dead-hand control of local authority officials. Blair's team disagreed.

Woodhead was puzzled. Did Blair not understand that his proposed improvements required a drastic change to the organisation and management of the educational system? 'They want change and think they know how to do it,' he thought, 'but they have no real understanding how change happens.' He did not conceal his irritation. Blair, he considered, was 'being taken in by Blunkett's and Barber's whacky initiatives'.

At the meeting, Blair simply applauded Blunkett's fanfare. In his desire for faster change, the details evoked little interest. In the days that followed, he never summoned experts to consider the quality of Labour's literacy and numeracy strategy. Many applauded his 'quick grasp of detail'; they did not realise that his gift for headlines ignored the problem.

That autumn, Blunkett ordered primary schools to devote one hour every day to English and another to maths. The hours were hailed as New Labour triumphs. In reality, they had been first announced in 1995. However, the Tory programme was different from Michael Barber's. The Tories had told teachers what to teach; Blair ordered schools *how*. The detailed maths curriculum instructed teachers on how to use every minute in an 'interactive style' for 'whole class teaching'. The best and the worst pupils would be taught together.

Blair personally endorsed that directive despite two evident flaws: 'whole class teaching' forced the best pupils to progress at the rate of the worst; and, as Professor Margaret Brown of King's College, London, one of Britain's foremost experts on maths education, noted, 'interactive teaching' disregarded how children understood maths. Student teachers, warned Brown, were not learning how to teach maths.

In the rush of those early months, all these contradictions were easily overlooked. However, because education was so important, Blair appointed a special education adviser in Downing Street. His choice was Andrew Adonis, an Oxford graduate whose political activism first as a Liberal Democrat and then as a Labour councillor convinced him of the credibility of the Conservatives' education policies. 'If you want to reform education,' Adonis told Blair, 'you should make me the minister, not keep me in No. 10.'

A civil servant who overheard this conversation cautioned Blair, 'Like so many bright things in No. 10, Adonis is full of ideas but without experience.' Blair nodded. Whether he understood the criticism about a frenetic realist was hard to discern.

New Labour values continued to be wrapped in impenetrable jargon. Typically, Anthony Giddens, the architect of the Third Way, said, 'The crisis of democracy comes from it not being democratic enough.'

Giddens's way with language would be dissected by a group of permanent secretaries gathered at a seminar held by him at the British Academy
on Pall Mall, during a fierce debate about the validity of the Third Way.
At the end, the civil servants were divided about Giddens but still uniformly loyal to the government's ambitions, symbolised by Blair's vow
to be 'whiter than white'. After witnessing Tory sleaze, Blair's pledge
counted among Whitehall's senior mandarins. The smokescreen of slogans served New Labour well, until unexpected revelations eclipsed his
triumphalism.

FIVE

Broken Vows, Part 1

Long before the election, Tony Blair had come to rely on Geoffrey Robinson. The former Jaguar executive, who lived in a suite at Grosvenor House on Park Lane, was an unashamed millionaire who since his election as an MP in 1976 had attached himself to Gordon Brown as an adviser on finance and industry. Both Brown and Blair had accepted hospitality in Robinson's five homes around Europe and were grateful for his financial help in maintaining their parliamentary offices while in opposition. Neither suspected the murky source of his fortune nor knew that he had deposited millions of pounds in a secret offshore account.

To reward his help, Blair had agreed to Brown's demand that Robinson be appointed paymaster general, a sinecure to be used as the chancellor required. Presented by Brown as a key member of the Treasury team, Robinson assumed he had the authority to roam across Whitehall as a problem-solver. His methods were unconventional. In telephone conversations he demanded loyalty and reminded officials, 'We're here for a long time, so why don't you get on with me and do it our way.' One Treasury official muttered, 'It's a sad day. We've never previously allowed spivs to set foot inside this building.'

Like others in Brown's entourage (known as the 'Hotel Group' for enjoying the hospitality at Grosvenor House), Blair seized on Robinson's invitation to spend part of his 1997 summer holiday at the millionaire's neoclassical villa in Tuscany. He and his wife Cherie would then move on to a French chateau owned by a High Court judge. They did not conceal from their friends a fondness for life as guests of the super-rich. The only requirement for a prime minister was to be certain that his host was honest. If Blair had made any enquiries, he would have discovered that Robinson failed his own test set in 1994 about those people who 'just by hiding money in the right places can avoid paying tax altogether'. There were other skeletons in Robinson's career that were about to rattle Blair's 'pure' image.

Blair returned to London at the end of August 1997 in some despair. His holiday at Robinson's Italian estate had been interrupted by an ugly spat caused by him leaving Peter Mandelson in charge of the government. Mandelson's lofty self-portrayal as acting prime minister attracted newspaper headlines such as 'Who's in Charge?' and accusations that the minister was hysterically rude. John Prescott had aggravated the problem on camera by holding a jar containing a crab next to his smirking face and addressing it as 'Peter'. 'Peter has let his ego run out of control,' noted Alastair Campbell somewhat gleefully about a 'disastrous' summer, and temporarily stopped talking to Mandelson.

Blair walked into 10 Downing Street fretting that after his first hundred days he was at a loss what to do. The mood has changed, he told Brian Bender. The quality of his ministers, he complained, was dire. The bad ones, his officials had already noticed, were ignored. The only ones Blair could unhesitatingly rely upon were Brown and Mandelson. They at least understood how to sell New Labour. 'No. 10's bright new young things have brought huge enthusiasm,' thought Bender.

Three days later, Princess Diana's midnight death in Paris provided Blair with an unexpected opportunity to cure his frustration. Those hearing the news as they awoke in Britain and across much of the world on 31 August were deeply shocked by the senseless death of a beautiful icon. Many were traumatised by the pictures of the crashed car, the vigil outside the Paris hospital where Diana's death was confirmed and the anticipated reaction after her two young boys were told the news.

During the morning, the nation's emotions intensified. Britons needed a leader who could express the country's grief. Neither the

46

Queen nor Prince Charles was prepared to speak. Blair was the natural alternative. After consulting Campbell, he composed his eulogy on a piece of paper and stood in front of the church in Trimdon, in his Sedgefield constituency. 'She was the people's princess and that's how she will stay, how she will remain in our hearts and in our memories for ever.' An outstanding performer delivering the perfect words with the appropriate gestures, Blair proved his genius as a communicator to mourners across the globe.

The Queen, by contrast, was criticised for failing to respond to the country's mood by remaining in Balmoral to console the two boys rather than returning to London to lead the nation's mourning. The symbol of her alleged insensitivity was the refusal to break protocol and raise Buckingham Palace's flag to half-mast. Amid open and growing criticism of the monarch, Blair would claim the credit for persuading the Queen to return to London five days later, inspect the vast floral tribute outside Kensington Palace and address the nation on TV. The public's anger dissipated, but the reason for it was not forgotten.

For Blair, the public criticism of the Queen validated his agenda to modernise the country. As he claimed credit for rescuing the monarchy from embarrassment, the rousing phrases tripped off his tongue: Britain as 'the beacon to the world'; 'Britain as the best': 'The glory of the British people'; and 'We must be able to build from this a more compassionate Britain.' His words offered no answers to the problems his country faced, but they did sprinkle stardust on their speaker. The media was briefed about the 'deep involvement' of Blair and Campbell in the funeral arrangements. The prime minister himself would deliver the reading on faith, hope and love from 1 Corinthians in Westminster Abbey. Blair was in his element and, according to Campbell, was praised by the Spencer family. 'Tony Blair has this week taken on the mantle of Disraeli and Baldwin', wrote Peter Riddell glowingly in *The Times*, 'as a bridge between the people and the Palace.'

The royal family was less grateful. Its relations with Blair had been 'frosty' from the outset and did not improve after he emerged from the prime minister's traditional annual September weekend at Balmoral to explain that the monarchy intended to 'change and modernise'. The Queen was entitled to expect sound advice from her prime minister, but Blair failed to accept that it should remain secret and not be read by the royal family in the media, as briefed by Campbell.

'Modernisation' was the theme of his speeches during that month, both in attacking the trade unions and in enthusing the party at its annual conference. 'Our destiny', he said, was to modernise Britain and Europe. The conference was ecstatic, while the polls showed he enjoyed a 93 per cent approval rating.

Three months after this unexpected success, the frisson of joy within Downing Street had evaporated. Rivalries, jealousies and personal insecurities were plaguing Blair's household. At the centre of the bickering was Cherie. Insecure about her unphotogenic appearance, she was sensitive to media criticism about her clothes and later about a pendant she wore to ward off evil spirits. Contrary to newspaper profiles, she was not the outstanding lawyer they proclaimed and was not pursuing a glittering career at the Bar; on the other hand, she was instinctively political and keen to participate in her husband's government. But, if her ambitions were realised, she knew the consequences would be fatal, so she festered with mounting resentment over her exclusion by Blair's entourage from the discussions about the affairs of state constantly echoing around her own home.

There were other problems. Money was a serious concern. Having agreed with Gordon Brown that the Blairs would use the larger flat in 11 Downing Street while the chancellor occupied the flat at No. 10, she had complained to Robin Butler about the shabby state of the accommodation. The carpet was worn, the kitchen old, her daughter's mattress needed replacing and the stale smell of Ken Clarke's cigars stuck to every fabric. 'I won't sleep in Ken Clarke's bed,' her husband told everyone, and spent his first night as prime minister in the brass bed brought from his home in Islington, which was soon after replaced by a new bed costing £3,500 that had been bought by Cherie's close friend and lifestyle adviser Carole Caplin. 'And his lavatory is cracked!' Cherie complained to Robin Butler, adding that she needed a new dustbin. In any other country, a leader's request for household replacements would have been granted automatically, but Cherie's haughty tone insulted Butler. Tact towards Downing Street officials, he noted, was alien to her. Unlike most of her predecessors, her prickly attitude towards the staff began the moment she entered Downing Street and dumped her bags at the entrance door, expecting someone to carry them upstairs. Her imperious manner sparked wry reminiscences about her raid on the No. 10 flat in the hours just before Brown arrived in Downing Street, ordering a sofa and a TV set to be pushed across the corridor into No. 11.

The Blairs had already irritated officials over the time and money wasted even in advance of their arrival. Just before the election, Robin Butler had spent hours with them poring over the floor plans of the Downing Street accommodation. Dissatisfied, the Blairs decided to remain in Islington. The police and the security agencies built guard huts around the house and ordered bombproof glass for their home, only for Cherie, with little grace, to change her mind. The pattern would become familiar.

Unflattering stories appeared in newspapers about her accompanying Blair to a summit abroad with a hairdresser and beautician. Irritated by the betrayal, Cherie fumed when the civil service asked for repayment of the costs. She also discovered the disadvantage of publicity. Each newspaper account describing her fixation with money would also mention her drunken, adulterous father, Tony Booth, a well-known, prickly actor who had abandoned his family when she was a child. Instead of remaining in the shadows like her predecessors, Cherie offered herself as a target. To avoid further embarrassment, Blair vetoed the new kitchen and offered to pay for the whole refurbishment.

Arguments about money were compounded by the simultaneous dispute between Cherie and Blair about Anji Hunter, Blair's girlfriend during his teenage years, who had been an intimate assistant since 1994.

Cherie strenuously opposed Blair bringing Hunter into Downing Street. She had discovered an old collection of affectionate notes between him and his former flame in a cardboard box, and this sparked an irrational jealousy against the good-looking, well-turned-out blonde who, unlike herself, possessed 'more than one dress'.

In a succession of attacks, including one ferocious outburst in front of Hunter, at the end of which the prime minister's wife stormed out of Blair's office, Cherie demanded that the assistant be fired. Blair pleaded that a prime minister was entitled to employ people he trusted. His misery was aggravated by Fiona Millar, Campbell's partner, who worked as Cherie's personal assistant. Millar had promised to 'keep Cherie biography-free' by rejecting media requests to interview the prime minister's wife. In the current dispute, she was angry that Campbell supported Blair.

After a succession of exhausting arguments, Blair persuaded Cherie that Hunter be allowed to stay. Michael Levy, the party's fund-raiser, was asked to broker a suitable job description for her with the civil service. (The irony lost on Blair was that Levy was worried about his own position: he hoped he would receive a peerage, but Mandelson was agitating against it.) Levy duly delivered the title 'special assistant for presentation and planning'.

To assuage her humiliation, Cherie sent Hunter a note outlining the restrictive terms of her employment: 'In so far as your job brings you into contact with me, that will be kept to a minimum . . . I trust this is clear.' In the aftermath of Blair's premiership, Cherie admitted to Levy that she had let her husband down.

Other personalities were causing aggravation. The failing marriage of Robin Cook had become spectacularly public when a newspaper exposed his adulterous relationship with his assistant; at welfare, Harriet Harman was proving to be a persistent irritant who 'fussed and fretted', in Blair's words, while failing to deliver a scheme for welfare reform; and Charlie Whelan, Brown's aggressive publicist, was ceaselessly machinating against Blair on his master's behalf. Mandelson had attracted endless criticism, not least for his manipulation of the media after leaking that Chris Patten was the subject of a security investigation thanks to his book of reminiscences describing his governorship of Hong Kong, a ruse aimed at diverting attention away from Cook's problems. The spin rebounded. 'Peter Mandelson seems to be suffering from midsummer madness verging on megalomania,' sniped Francis Maude, the Tory frontbencher. The Camelot-like atmosphere of the first few weeks in power had truly evaporated.

In the aftermath of Princess Diana's funeral, Gordon Brown, jealous about his colleague's easy return to the spotlight, told Blair that he rejected the suggestion that the government should announce its intention to be admitted to the European Monetary Union (EMU). Brown knew how to poke a sensitive spot. Those who had discussed membership of the euro with Blair were surprised by his poor grasp of the technical consequences. In his desire to lead Europe, he had pledged to join the currency union, subject to a referendum. Briefed by Campbell, the *Financial Times* had for weeks reported that Britain was 'moving towards' becoming part of the EU's inner group. Then, in mid-October, Blair gave Philip Webster of *The Times* an interview expressing his intention to join the euro in the near future. He expected Brown to continue his pre-election support, although both were uncertain whether the government could win the referendum. In the interview, Blair accepted that Britain would not join in the first phase in 1999, but thereafter the options were open. Webster, a reliable journalist, then spoke to Charlie Whelan. On Brown's behalf, and without consulting the Cabinet, Whelan gave a contradictory briefing, with the result that *The Times* led with the headline 'Brown Rules Out Single Currency for the Lifetime of This Parliament'.

'I cannot believe what Gordon has done,' exclaimed Blair in disbelief. 'He has damaged our credibility in a way that could take ages to restore. And all over something where there is in fact no division.' For the first time, he sensed the depth of Brown's fury that he was not prime minister. But the chancellor was impregnable: there was no question of getting rid of him.

Ever since Blair decided in 1994 that he would ignore his informal understanding made during the 1980s that the older man could have the first run for the leadership, Brown had promoted his own supposed superior intellect to expose Blair's vulnerabilities, especially his inferior understanding of politics. Every effort by Blair to placate his chancellor and lead the government as equal partners was misinterpreted by Brown as an attempt to deny him his rightful elevation. Somehow he believed that he could have won the 1994 leadership election, whereas his support was limited to just 9 per cent of Labour MPs. Brown's fury at Blair's 'betrayal' was well concealed by Blair's entourage until after the election. They had laughed off the chancellor's petulant reaction to Blair's plan for a high-profile party for pop stars, actors and London's 'luvvies' in 10 Downing Street, when the Treasury had rapidly arranged a rival party for other celebrities to be held next door the day before. But the rivalry over the euro was of a different order, a major issue on which prime minister and chancellor should be seen to be thinking as one. Blair, said Peter Riddell, quoting an insider, is 'well aware what a disaster it's been . . . They have exposed damaging flaws in the way that the government is run.' 'Theirs is not a relationship,' said Andrew Turnbull, the Treasury permanent secretary, 'it's a pathology.'

To clear the air, Blair asked Brown to see him in his office. Unless we stay as a team, he warned, 'we're dead. You'll ruin the government.' Brown was undaunted. If he had been prime minister, he too would have favoured membership. For two weeks, Blair struggled to understand Brown's obstruction, until he had no alternative but to acknowledge defeat and issue a statement: 'We do not propose to enter a single currency this parliament.' The public, still wholly supportive of the government and unaware of Brown's animosity, was bemused. The ruffled atmosphere settled until, on 8 November, a bombshell exploded.

David Hill, a Labour loyalist and one of Blair's spokesmen, was asked by a journalist if Bernie Ecclestone, the chief executive of Formula One, had made a large donation to the party. 'Good God, I've no idea,' replied Hill. A few hours later, Hill emphatically denied the suggestion. The following day, the *Sunday Telegraph* reported that Ecclestone's unquantified donation had persuaded the Labour government to exempt Formula One from a European directive that banned tobacco companies from sponsoring the sport. The paper described the donation as a crude bribe because Formula One's lucrative sponsorship deals with these companies – especially Philip Morris, the producer of Marlboro cigarettes – were threatened by Labour's manifesto commitment to end financial relations between all sports and tobacco companies.

Inside Downing Street there was panic. For a prime minister who had deliberately used the vocabulary of trust to highlight Tory sleaze during the election and who had promised that he would be 'whiter than white', the allegation of corruption was shattering. Labour's 'moral crusade', Blair had said, embraced compassion, integrity, community and honesty. Now, television news programmes illustrated their reports of 'corruption' by broadcasting pictures of Ecclestone walking up Downing Street. Viewers would assume it was the historic moment when Formula One had paid cash for access, but the images had been recorded earlier in the week at a charity event. How Blair now regretted the 'sleaze' soundbite. 'The consequences were disastrous,' he admitted. 'I couldn't see us doing some of the things the Tories had done.'

Unknown to the public, Ecclestone had indeed donated £1 million to the Labour Party, and was discussing a further contribution of £3 million. Although he was a Tory voter and contributor to the Conservative Party, he and his representatives had met Blair and paid the sweetener. On the Monday morning after the exposure, Brown appeared on BBC Radio 4's *Today* programme. Asked about the donation, he lied, denying any knowledge of Ecclestone's gift.

Events were moving beyond the government's control. 'This was the kind of issue', Campbell noted in his diary, 'that [Blair] hated most of all, though in truth there was nothing wrong about the way the decision was reached.' Blair, he continued, had 'nothing to hide' because 'the policy on banning was made after the donation was received, which blows the idea [Ecclestone] bought a change.' The £1 million, wrote

Campbell mistakenly, had been brought in by Michael Levy, Blair's friend and successful fund-raiser.

A false version of events was being swiftly embedded. In reality, the financial relationship had been initiated by Jonathan Powell, who himself would disingenuously write, 'Our sin in this case was one of naivety.' Combined with those inaccuracies was Blair's own, written thirteen years later: 'To be fair to [Ecclestone], he made no link whatsoever between the gift and the policy . . . not even implicitly.' That was also untrue. Blair had been explicitly told by an emissary of the businessman that £1 million would be donated on condition that Formula One was exempted from the ban. The agreement was made because Blair and Ecclestone had forged a good relationship by then.

The two men had first met at the British Grand Prix in Silverstone in 1996. Blair's visit had been organised by Powell after Ecclestone had featured in the *Sunday Times* Rich List as Britain's highest-paid businessman. Powell telephoned David Ward, a former Labour Party official employed in Formula One. 'Do you know how we can contact Ecclestone?' he asked, and wondered whether Ecclestone might become a Labour donor. 'Blair has already been invited to visit Silverstone in July,' replied Ward, 'and we can arrange for him to meet Bernie.'

On the day, Ecclestone welcomed Blair into his motorhome. The two leaders bonded instantly. The following day, Powell telephoned Ward. Would Ecclestone consider donating to the Labour Party? 'Nowadays', continued Powell, 'we don't consider anything less than £1 million.'

'Are you serious?' asked Ward incredulously.

Both knew New Labour had set a tariff for peerages and access – a sliding scale depending on wealth and importance to the party – but this amount for a simple donation was unprecedented. Ecclestone nevertheless agreed to consider the proposition. A meeting was arranged with Blair in the House of Commons. After a twenty-minute conversation, Ecclestone was taken by Michael Levy to another office.

'We would be grateful', said Levy, 'if you could make a significant contribution, something around £1 million.'

Ecclestone listened, said nothing and after five minutes took his leave. 'He's amateurish,' he told Ward.

In early January 1997, Levy telephoned Max Mosley, Ecclestone's trusted partner in the transformation of Formula One from a sport for enthusiasts into a global business, to ask again for £1 million. By then Philip Morris was agitating against the European ban on tobacco companies sponsoring sport. '£1 million', Mosley told Ecclestone, 'will give us access and help us on tobacco.' His words fell on fertile ground.

Ecclestone was furious that, despite big donations to his party, John Major had failed to secure him the promised knighthood. In revenge for that snub and to please the tobacco companies, Ecclestone agreed to pay £1 million to Labour. Ward passed the news on to Powell with a caveat: 'I will support Bernie Ecclestone's contribution so long as I can talk to Tony and outline the sensitive issues around Formula One.' Powell agreed.

Soon after, Ward was seated opposite the prime minister in Blair's living room in Islington. Powell and Peter Mandelson, who had welcomed Ward into the house, remained outside. 'You're getting £1 million from Ecclestone,' Ward told Blair, 'but you must understand that the issue of tobacco sponsorship will arise in a European directive, and we believe that a better way to achieve the same outcome is by a voluntary global agreement. We just want a transition period.' The problem, Ward added, was the officials in Brussels, who were stubbornly resisting such a period. 'There is no need for controversy, but we will want your help,' he concluded. At the end of twenty minutes, Blair said, 'I understand.' Back in Ecclestone's Knightsbridge office, Ward was given a personal cheque by the billionaire, although both knew that Labour remained committed to banning tobacco sponsorship of all sports.

On 15 May, Frank Dobson announced in the House of Commons that the government intended to implement the ban. Tessa Jowell, his junior minister, repeated the same pledge in Brussels. Soon after, Levy invited Ward to his home in north London and set about reassuring him that the government was sticking to their agreement to change the law. Sitting in the garden, he asked, 'Is Bernie thinking of giving more money to Labour? We wondered if he would commit himself to giving Labour £1 million every year for the life of the current parliament.'

'There are problems,' Ward replied.

'We must arrange another meeting with Tony,' Levy soothed.

Soon after, Levy spoke to Powell. 'The prime minister needs to meet Bernie.'

'OK,' replied Powell.

The arrangements were made soon after. Blair's agreement to meet Ecclestone in Downing Street, Ward reassured Mosley, was directly linked to their conversation in his Islington home before the election: another donation would protect the tobacco companies' sponsorship of Formula One.

Seated in a circle in a small ground-floor room in Downing Street with Blair, Powell, Ward and Ecclestone, Mosley addressed the prime minister, as he would later say, 'lawyer to lawyer'. Eloquent and precise, Mosley said, 'We don't oppose the end of tobacco advertising but we just want a gradual elimination so that alternative sponsors can be found.'

Blair nodded. If phased reduction was denied, Mosley explained, 50,000 British jobs as well as F1 Digital TV could easily be relocated outside the EU. Blair looked over at Ecclestone. The businessman wanted Blair to know that there was no contest between Dobson and himself. With a snap of his fingers Britain could lose its Grand Prix and the lucrative motor-sport industry. Those who ignored his warnings, Ecclestone implied, were always surprised that he did what he said.

'Let's keep in touch about this,' said Blair after thirty-five minutes. The three visitors departed convinced that an understanding had been reached.

Shortly after, Mosley bumped into Mandelson at a reception in Lancaster House. 'How's it going?' he asked.

'The whole of Whitehall is reverberating to the sound of grinding gears,' said Mandelson, implying that Formula One's request was being granted.

The following Monday, Ward heard that Blair had given an order to 'sort out the Formula One problem'. Powell explained that the government was seeking an exemption in Brussels from the directive. Shortly after, Tessa Jowell called Mosley. Blair, she said, had ordered that Formula One should be given special exemption until October 2006. Ecclestone's money had forced Dobson to reverse the ban on tobacco sponsorship.

Although Levy would mischievously write, 'To my knowledge [Blair] never altered any of his policies because of any of the big-money donations I brought in,' he did criticise Blair for what followed.

Ecclestone's success was leaked to a journalist and, the day after the Sunday newspaper's report, Ward rushed to Downing Street to confront Powell and Campbell. He discovered 'total chaos'. 'They didn't want to listen to me,' he told Mosley, adding that Powell and Campbell, anxious to protect the prime minister, would cast Ecclestone as the villain and encourage Blair, if necessary, to lie. At Mosley's suggestion, Ward telephoned Powell and urged that the government stay silent about the donation. The suggestion of a conspiracy to suppress the truth hardly appealed to Blair or his entourage. On the contrary, ignoring Ecclestone's interests, Blair had already asked Derry Irvine, the Lord Chancellor, to limit the damage.

By then, Blair's confidence in his former pupil master had been shaken by Irvine's arrogance and misunderstanding of the media. The extravagant manner of Britain's most senior lawyer would later be compared to Cardinal Wolsey's behaviour, and in that vein Irvine blamed Blair for the disaster. 'He could not believe how badly we had fucked it up,' noted Campbell. Irvine advised that any confession of the truth was 'utterly absurd', and suggested that the government should create a smokescreen.

Acting on Irvine's advice, Blair and Gordon Brown concocted a ruse. They ordered Tom Sawyer, the party's general secretary, to write a letter to Patrick Neill, the commissioner for standards in public life, based on a lie. The letter referred to a new code of conduct for party funding. Sawyer mentioned that the Labour Party had accepted a donation from

Ecclestone while in opposition, and that 'Mr Ecclestone has since the election offered a further donation'. So far, wrote Sawyer inaccurately, the second offer had been refused out of fear of a potential conflict of interest because of the tobacco exemption. He asked Neill whether the party's concern was justified. The letter was sent on 7 November. On the same day, David Hill, as he would later admit, continued using evasions and menaces to deflect journalists' questions.

Wracked by fear, Blair was not sleeping. His fate depended upon the ability of his clique – especially Alastair Campbell – to manage the media. After the election, the PR man had introduced himself to government information officers as 'a believer in strategic communications'. Few officials immediately understood that in the daily battle for favourable headlines they were to serve Blair's interests and not the media's. 'We must not let the press think they can push us around,' Campbell said. While working for Robert Maxwell, he and other *Mirror* journalists were routinely ordered to distort the news, a practice that Campbell imported into Downing Street. Frightening people was his strategy. His misfortune was that Hill's denials about Ecclestone were denying him his accustomed influence over the media. Blair, he realised, 'was taking a real hit. We had made a big mistake in not going upfront. We were looking shifty and shabby.'

Patrick Neill only contributed to Blair's plight. Regardless of the truth, he replied to Sawyer the same day, the appearance of taking Ecclestone's money had raised questions of honesty and offended the rules. Therefore, he recommended, not only should the second donation be refused, but Ecclestone's first should be returned. In Downing Street, the panic intensified. No one had anticipated that interpretation. Campbell suggested limiting the damage by admitting some truth. Accordingly, Hill told journalists that Ecclestone had given the party 'over £5,000'. At the same time, another Downing Street spokesman said that, during their meeting in No. 10, Ecclestone made 'no request regarding policy'. That lie was quickly contradicted by Campbell. Ecclestone's donation, he admitted, was made to change Labour's policy.

'Tony Blair has started talking,' Ecclestone cursed. 'It's third-rate behaviour.' Besieged by journalists, he was told that Blair had finally admitted receiving the donation. 'Well, if Mr Blair said that, he wouldn't lie, would he?' Ecclestone replied.

'How much did you give?' he was asked.

'£1 million,' said Ecclestone.

His admission was explosive. Off message, Jack Straw publicly admitted that Blair had 'been aware of the second offer from Mr Ecclestone when they met at Downing Street'. After implying that the additional £3 million had persuaded Blair to accommodate Ecclestone's wishes, Straw then promptly headed for the bunker.

The ammunition against Blair was so strong that no one even referred to the manifesto's pledge to 'clean up public life'. To close down the horror, Campbell arranged Blair's first post-election television interview. The prime minister's words were carefully rehearsed. He resisted Irvine's advice of total disclosure, refused to apologise and instead blamed Ecclestone. Even 'before any journalist had been in touch' with Downing Street, Blair told his audience, the Labour Party had notified Ecclestone that, despite his 'firm commitment' of paying another £1 million, 'we couldn't accept further donations'. Only then, said Blair, had the government asked Neill about the probity of the first donation, and as a result it would of course be repaid. To tilt the balance further in his favour, Blair added: 'I think that most people who have dealt with me think I'm a pretty straight sort of guy – and I am.'

Despite his damnation in the Commons by William Hague for a 'shabby tale of evasion', the lies saved Blair but left Ecclestone's reputation damaged. 'I've been hung out to dry,' he complained.

Blair was shaken by the crisis. In an unusual post-mortem, he privately admitted his dishonesty. To avoid chaos in the future, Cherie advised, he needed to organise 'proper decision-making structures' to resolve 'the lack of clarity in his office'. The truth, she implied, was that Powell, Levy and Campbell had failed to protect her husband.

Derry Irvine was harsher. Blair's mistake, said the lawyer, was to believe his own propaganda and trust that Campbell could spin an escape from anything. In his grandiose manner, Irvine had lectured his employer, whom he would call 'the boy', that solving the malpractice required legal, not journalistic, minds. That reprimand evoked from Campbell a rare confession: 'I have been evasive too often ... The problem had been a lack of precision and a lack of candour.'

In concluding the inquest, Brian Bender mentioned that Blair must hope that his team 'would return to [the] rigour of [the] Wilson and Callaghan years'. Blair agreed, without realising that Wilson's premiership had been damned for serial dishonesty, while Callaghan had developed a corrupt relationship with a banker who loaned the prime minister sufficient money to buy a farm in Sussex in exchange for a knighthood.

The self-flagellation included Mandelson giving a lecture entitled 'Effective Communication in the Public Sector' to civil servants in Whitehall. Referring to the Ecclestone scandal, Mandelson told his audience, without blushing, 'Honesty is the first principle of good communications ... and the purpose of communications is not to stall or to hide but to put in context and to explain.' The cynics in the audience chortled. Mandelson had never previously spoken about Labour's moral mission or 'the right thing to do'. His writ had always been 'This is how we win', and he intended to continue in the same vein.

The tumult disrupted relations among Blair's closest advisers, especially between Mandelson and Brown. Ever since he withdrew his bid to be party leader in 1994, Brown's venom had been directed at Mandelson in particular. 'Mendelsohn', he said, emphasising the Germanic lineage, was 'a menace'. Previously, the two had been close allies, but Mandelson's support for Blair's leadership bid had devastated Brown. The depressive Scot was incapable of maintaining civilised relations with anyone other than subservient ultra-loyalists. By October 1997, he was brazenly ignoring the most senior officials in Blair's office. Even Powell was ignored for thirteen years.

Unflattering stories about Brown spread, especially after the EMU row, and the chancellor was convinced that Mandelson was the source. 'Call the dogs off,' he snapped at Blair. In response, Mandelson was reported to have cried during an emotional interview with a psychiatrist. Campbell, he complained, had become too grand, and in addition was undermining him, keeping him off television. Mandelson suspected that he himself was even disliked by Fiona Millar. He next remonstrated in Blair's Downing Street den that he was fed up with being 'treated like dirt'.

'The attention-seeking was becoming absurd,' sighed an insider who lamented Mandelson's exaggeration of his status. Increasingly, Blair was buffeted by arguments among his team. There was even a dispute about who could claim the credit for the election victory.

Amid all the bitter emotions, Blair relied on each of those loyalists. Mandelson was his political genius, Brown his financial expert, Campbell his protector and Hunter his confidante. At the end of May, before departing for the 'People's Banquet', a lunch he hosted with the Queen for 350 'ordinary people' in Banqueting House, Blair told the four of them, 'I could not survive without you.' Yet each, in their different way, was making his survival more difficult.

SIX

The Battle Plan

'I know we have an army, navy and air force but I don't know any more,' Blair told a senior RAF officer soon after he stepped into Downing Street. He opted to rely on General Charles Guthrie, the chief of the defence staff, to educate him.

'Call me Tony,' said Blair as they sat on the sunlit terrace of Downing Street's garden.

'I shall call you Prime Minister,' replied Guthrie.

Blair, who had avoided serving in the cadet force at school, was receptive to the blood-and-guts aura the general had acquired over his years of service, which included a tour as the SAS commander during a guerrilla war in Yemen. For his part, Guthrie understood the politician's ambition to change the world. The Tories' hesitation over intervening in the conflict in Bosnia, which had ended two years earlier after 200,000 deaths, or in Rwanda in 1994, where at least half a million were murdered, had aroused Blair's anger. Under New Labour, explained the forty-four-year-old, Britain's military power would be deployed to save mankind.

The men soon bonded over a mutual enjoyment of tennis and agreement about a newspaper article describing the Blair doctrine. 'If good men do nothing,' Blair had written, adapting Edmund Burke, 'evil prospers.' Neither Blair nor Guthrie anticipated how those seven words would transform British politics.

Guthrie had raced to London on 2 May to greet George Robertson, his new boss. Labour's manifesto had pledged an exhaustive review of Britain's military forces. Ever since the end of the cold war in 1989, successive Tory defence ministers had orchestrated incoherent policies, and the defence budget had been savagely cut, leaving the underfunded military floundering amid a 'what-should-we-do?' syndrome. Guthrie, like all the military chiefs, welcomed Labour's commissioning of the first serious strategic review since 1990 to decide the purpose of Britain's annual £21 billion military budget.

Unlike in previous reviews, Labour invited hundreds of experts to participate in an unprecedented roadshow aimed at conceiving the new 'defence diplomacy'. Emphasising idealism rather than money, Blair abandoned Britain's tradition of fighting wars only to protect the national interest. Instead of pursuing its policy of promoting peace, the country would in future wage war to improve the conditions of foreign people, even if there was no direct benefit to Britain.

At the outset of the review, the MoD was tasked with examining thirty scenarios that might redefine Britain's global role. 'Can you give me some guidance on the nature and scope of future military operations?' Rear Admiral Nigel Essenhigh, a chief in the defence staff, asked Robertson.

'That's above my pay grade,' replied the politician.

'They haven't thought about the political circumstances of committing Britain to war,' realised Essenhigh.

Soon after this conversation, Blair's resolve was tested. On 10 July, while he and Guthrie were discussing the review in Downing Street, a message was brought to the general on a silver platter.

'What does it say?' asked Blair.

'Apparently the SAS have just killed a Serbian warlord,' said Guthrie, describing an unplanned shoot-out while three fugitives were fishing. After aborting dozens of similar missions, Guthrie was pleased by the success, but Blair became agitated. Worried about the possibility of the deaths being declared unlawful, he 'showed real fear'. The tension was relieved by Alastair Campbell. 'We can turn this to our advantage. We can say, "Evil Srebrenica warlords killed."' Blair looked relieved. And so it came to pass. Disaster was averted, and reports duly described the Serbs as murderers who had opened fire first.

'We must do this more often,' Clare Short told Guthrie, pinning the general to the wall at the next Cabinet meeting.

'Clare's sound on killing people,' Guthrie observed.

A day or two later, Blair asked Guthrie about the SAS entering Zimbabwe to deal with Robert Mugabe, who had threatened to seize all white-owned land without compensation and persecute the farmers. Guthrie demurred: 'Without support in a land-locked country our men will all get eaten up.' Logistics, explained the general, was the key to successful operations.

Blair nodded. 'How about Angola?' he asked. 'We should stop the atrocities there.'

'We could dispatch a few troops to help logistics at the port for a few weeks,' suggested Guthrie.

Undeterred, Blair mentioned reports of another war: 'I'm very worried about the massacres around the great lakes in the Congo.'

'We've got nothing left except the Black Watch,' Guthrie replied. 'They're seven hundred very fine men, but they can't stop a war in an area the size of Europe.'

Agitated by Africa's plight, which he would call 'a moral scar on the conscience of the world', Blair's reliance on Guthrie did not stop his pushing for a ban on the use of anti-personnel mines, despite the army's protests. But, in consolation, he sided with the military against the Foreign Office on another hotly debated issue.

'We've been stitched up by Cook,' protested Guthrie, after Robin Cook had agreed that British soldiers should be subject to the International Criminal Court rather than British justice. 'I'm a simple soldier,' he continued. 'I just tell people the truth.'

Blair halted his 'pompous' foreign secretary's scheme, and further vetoed Cook's 'ethical' decision to ban arms sales to Indonesia and Saudi Arabia.

His other critic had also declared herself. 'You don't understand central Africa, Tony,' said Clare Short from the end of the Cabinet table.

'Well, thank you, Clare,' replied Blair with a smile.

Those early exchanges provided little help to the officials grappling for a new purpose for the military. In previous generations, Whitehall officials brandishing PhDs would have rigorously scrutinised Blair's ideas. But ever since the Tories had virtually eliminated that breed of expert from the Ministry of Defence, none of the chiefs was served by staff officers with the intellect to question the shift from fighting defensively in Germany against the Russians to a global commitment to impose liberal values. Whitehall's defence specialists had heard about von Moltke and von Clausewitz, Germany's famed military strategists, but, unlike the legions of academics employed by the Pentagon in Washington, few had actually studied the subject or read more than the basic military manuals. They were unable to examine the wisdom of Blair's directive that the military would no longer sit in Dover waiting for the enemy but instead should be equipped to fight across the world in support of moral causes.

Not surprisingly, the ministry's first draft was rejected as 'wholly inadequate' by Kevin Tebbit, a senior official in the Foreign Office who was about to become the director of GCHQ, the intelligence agency responsible for intercepting signals and cyber-traffic. 'It's been written by people who don't know what's needed,' Tebbit told his colleagues. 'I'll write the foreign-policy framework myself.'

The problem was that for over sixty years the bulk of Britain's military – its tanks and infantry – had been deployed with the aim of resisting a Soviet advance across West Germany. The British plan was to retreat towards the Atlantic until, at the last moment, nuclear weapons would be fired at Russia from submarines, and the world would be changed for ever. After the collapse of Soviet communism, that scenario was barely imaginable, but the mindset and education of Britain's senior military officers had not evolved.

Blair envisaged Britain executing Cook's ethical foreign policy from the Baltic to the Balkans and across the Middle East to the Indian subcontinent. Alternatively, to win universal praise he would seize the chance to repeat an operation similar to Thatcher's Falklands victory. 'Blair's ideas', noted Essenhigh, 'filtered down by osmosis' for Tebbit to turn into what Essenhigh would call 'an elegant and commendably brief document'. Under the headline 'Expeditionary Warfare', Tebbit provided the blueprint for Blair's foreign and defence policy. In ringing Blairite phrases, he described Britain's armed services being speedily transported across the globe to engage in a 'just war' or to provide humanitarian relief as 'a force for good'.

No one from Guthrie down questioned whether 'a force for good' was an intellectually coherent military strategy that matched Britain's resources or merely a bumper-sticker slogan, while no one in the Foreign Office or MoD asked whether Britain had sufficient money to pay for Blair's ambitions. Rather, there was uniform relief that he was seeking to give the military a new purpose. With some joy, Guthrie began brokering between the three services, defence officials and the politicians to produce a shopping list of the equipment needed to realise Blair's philosophy.

'Expeditionary warfare', Guthrie recorded, required new helicopters and vehicles for the army, new aircraft for the RAF and two new aircraft carriers for the navy. Despite being in supreme command, Guthrie decided not to oppose the navy's demand for the carriers to land troops supported by aircraft. He suspected that the carriers' estimated cost of £3.7 billion by the time of their anticipated launch in 2012 was deeply unrealistic. He also presumed that the protection of the carriers at sea would be beyond Britain's capability, but accepted that the politics behind their creation was overwhelming. George Robertson was keen because the ships would be built in Scotland, while Blair never questioned whether spending an increasing amount on the navy at the army's expense made sense. Experts predicted that the true cost for the carriers throughout their service would rise to over £50 billion, and in addition the navy would need to buy new aircraft. In those heady days, not everything made sense, but for the new prime minister Guthrie's presence was reassuring.

That November, Blair wanted to publicise his commitment to rescuing the oppressed in Europe. Accompanied by Guthrie and Campbell, he flew with a group of journalists on a day trip to meet British troops in Bosnia. During his brief visit, he was enthused by the military's support and discipline. They would provide the backbone to his ambition to lead Europe. On the return flight to London, fired by his foreign fame, Blair began briefing the journalists.

'He doesn't have a clue what he's saying,' an aide warned Campbell, as Blair stood near by.

'Fuck off, Tony,' snapped Campbell, pushing Blair aside. 'Let Charles do this.'

Blair returned meekly to his seat. 'Is that OK, Alastair?' he asked, as Campbell thrust Guthrie forward to 'exaggerate the military's capabilities and disguise the problems on the ground'.

'Now there's a real politician,' Cherie would say about Guthrie, unaware that, despite the general's loyalty, he had voted Conservative in 1997.

The whirlwind of summit conferences soon after the election had encouraged Blair's vainglory. Never before had he stood in the midst of such famous fans, with even Campbell looking on awestruck from the sidelines. Blair flew 25,000 miles in the first seven weeks, enjoying the congratulations of the elite club of fellow world leaders in Brussels, Amsterdam, Denver, Hong Kong and Madrid – topped by Bill Clinton telling him that Helmut Kohl had crowned him his natural heir as Europe's leader.

Any doubts about his place in world affairs had been swept aside during the Amsterdam summit, as hundreds of cameras followed him as he coolly cycled past, waving to the German chancellor. Well prepared for the meeting, Blair had basked in his rivals' tolerance of their differences and the media's praise. The Europeans' applause was loudest for his decision that Britain would sign the social chapter, a list of regulations to protect and enhance the rights of employees that the Tories had resisted. Despite the extra costs imposed on British businesses, Blair denied any contradiction between this and his constant enthusiasm for a more flexible labour market. His ambition, he confided to his aides, was to metamorphose from national politician to charismatic global statesman. 'Believes that he was the big player who could take over the whole show,' noted Campbell in his diary. 'He loved this stuff.'

Over a three-hour private dinner at the Pont de la Tour restaurant by the Tower of London – chosen to headline the two Blairs bonding with the two Clintons – Blair swallowed his 'older brother's' sermon about leading the new world. Tarnished in America by allegations of his harassment of women, Clinton spoke of Blair as his natural successor who would shape their new 'progressive' agenda across the world. Casting aside old alliances and ideologies, Blair's 'soulmate and political ally' declared that the new prime minister should follow the trail he himself had blazed. Boosted by images and slogans of hope, their new politics would lead the world to 'modernisation' – that word again. Pertinently, in comparing Cherie Blair to Hillary Clinton, 'the most reviled presidential spouse in the history of the United States', Tim Hames in *The Times* wrote sympathetically that Cherie 'is unlikely to endure such a fate . . . Try as her husband's political opponents might, the mantle of dragon lady will not fit his wife. The public reaction here is more likely to be sympathy bordering on affection.' During the honeymoon period, the infighting within Downing Street between Cherie and her husband's closest confidants remained unknown to the public.

Shortly after, Blair flew by Concorde to Denver for a summit of the G8 heads, the elite of the elite. Warmly greeted by the leaders of China and Japan, and loudly cheered in a rodeo stadium, Blair mentioned to Jonathan Powell that the public adulation reinforced his wish of 'wanting to make Britain count for something again'. He was the idealist who could 'no longer ignore what happens in other countries, but would intervene to end human rights abuses'. In Moscow, Boris Yeltsin's toast was 'To a young energetic leader who is so popular in his country'.

'The world needs our leadership,' Blair convinced himself. The opinion polls showed Labour's support up from 44 per cent at the election to 58 per cent, with no fewer than 72 per cent of those asked expressing their satisfaction with Blair. The balloon was momentarily deflated on 1 July during an uncomfortable ceremony marking the end of British rule in Hong Kong that had Blair standing in a monsoon downpour near the snivelling governor, Chris Patten, mourning the end of British rule, and Cherie, who was complaining about her sodden clothes. On top of that, the discussions with China's leaders were disappointing.

Another dampener came at a summit in Luxembourg. Since Britain, according to its chancellor, was not joining the euro, Blair was excluded from discussions about the currency among Europe's other leaders. Inevitably, Campbell would brief newspapers that Britain's prime minister had scored a victory, leading to headlines such as 'Blair Wins', accompanied by Campbell's concoction that Blair and Brown were a dream team. Brown was not pleased. 'I have to tell you bluntly', he told Campbell, 'that this will be very bad if it's seen as Tony succeeding where I have failed.'

Brown's bigger problem erupted on 29 November. Chris Blackhurst, a respected journalist, reported in the *Independent* that the fortune of paymaster general Geoffrey Robinson was linked to a multimillion-pound secret offshore trust in Guernsey. Brown had repeatedly pledged sanctions against Britons who evaded tax by burying their millions in tax havens. In their conversations together, Robinson had been unapologetic about his undisclosed trust. He had reason to feel confident.

Just four weeks after the Ecclestone affair had subsided, Blair had bowed to Brown's advice that neither of them could demand unvarnished honesty from their benefactor. Both hoped that Terry Burns, the permanent secretary at the Treasury, would lie to protect the paymaster. To their disappointment, Burns refused. While Robinson obfuscated, Blair nevertheless defended his man. 'Geoffrey Robinson', he told the Commons, 'is an exceptionally able minister.' Without asking for an investigation of Robinson's finances, he added that it was not 'remotely clear' that his benefactor had avoided taxes. 'He has probably paid more UK tax than either you or me,' he taunted the Tories.

By Christmas, the row seemed to be over. Newspapers retreated under Robinson's threats to sue for defamation. Polly Toynbee described him in the *Guardian* as 'an honest man'; Campbell declared, 'He is staying'; while Blair said, 'I do not want a war with Gordon.'

Since the election, there had been no respite. After Christmas at Chequers and the anguish of seeing his father becoming speechless as a consequence of a stroke, an exhausted Blair flew with his family to the Seychelles for a week's holiday in a rented plantation lodge. On one evening beneath the palm trees, he was Richard Branson's guest for a dinner prepared by the chef of the former Shah of Persia. From the beach, he issued a New Year's message that Labour would 'tackle the problems of poverty'. He returned on 5 January, saying, 'We need a strategy for the party.' He might have added, 'And for its senior members.' Three days later, while he was flying to Japan and writing a long memorandum to himself about education and welfare reform, Westminster was convulsed by the publication of a sympathetic biography of Brown by Paul Routledge.

The book's sensational disclosure was that 'Gordon Brown is convinced he could have beaten Tony Blair in a contest for Labour's leadership and that the prime minister broke a secret pact between them.' Routledge alleged that Blair had agreed before 1994 that Brown would be prime minister first, and only afterwards would it be Blair's turn. Brown's accusation of betrayal dominated the news. Blair called him from Tokyo. The chancellor repeated the denial he had already made in public: that he had not co-operated with Routledge. Unfortunately for him, his handwritten corrections were scattered across the copy of Routledge's manuscript held by the publisher. 'He's a sad, sad man,' Blair told Campbell. 'He will never, ever get over it.' He did not, however, publicly deny the story that day, although he would subsequently dismiss Brown's version.

While Blair sat out the storm, news came that Margaret Cook had simultaneously published a book damning her adulterous husband Robin. 'Do you realise', Blair said to Campbell, 'we are carrying the whole show, you, me, one or two others?' Referring to Cook, he added, 'I'm surrounded by these weak vessels who can bring the rest of us down.' Amid the media furore, trivialising what journalist Simon Jenkins called 'an intriguing guide to the chancellor's dudgeons and grudge', no one highlighted that Blair's government was being sabotaged from within. To rectify that situation, Campbell summoned Andrew Rawnsley of the *Observer*. Referring to 'someone who has an extremely good claim to know the mind of the prime minister', Rawnsley was soon reporting that 'It is time, in the words of the same person, for Mr Brown to get a grip on his psychological flaws.' Naturally, when Campbell was asked about a split, he would deny 'silly and counterproductive' claims of a rift. A ponderous leader in *The Times* describing 'a chastened chancellor' made it clear that even the media was underestimating the battle. But the primed grenade had been thrown into the room. Now Blair and Campbell waited to see whether Brown would be silenced.

Blair sat at the next Cabinet meeting with a rictus smile. One of his strengths was his ability to conceal his anger. His even temperament betrayed no stress. Along the table was Harriet Harman, who 'complained interminably' and was 'impossible'. Then there was the preening Cook, failing to apply himself to the grind of governmental work, and near to him was Brown, furiously scribbling and refusing to participate. Behind him sat Richard Wilson. The Cabinet secretary had advised Blair to strengthen his position by forging alliances with other ministers in committees. Blair had ignored the suggestion. He was untroubled by his tendency to divide rather than unite his Cabinet, or indeed his party. Besides eight Cabinet ministers and his loyal Downing Street staff, he had little interest in those regarded as his obedient flock. He would drive all his reforms from his office. 'Tony was not a natural chairman', wrote Powell. 'He didn't as a rule feel bound to follow an agenda or sum up the discussion.' Modernising depended on destruction. He was bored by process. He feared descending into the world of delegates at the UN reading out prepared briefs. He would not allow tedium to prevent change. No minister would dare challenge him, except Brown, and he was even refusing to discuss his Budget. To show his contempt, the chancellor let Blair discover his thoughts by reading the *Guardian*, and rather than mend fences, displayed his resentment by authorising Charlie Whelan to express his intention to 'put the boot into the bastards to prevent them getting away with murder'.

Those sentiments reflected Brown's predetermined reaction to Robertson and Guthrie as they enthusiastically unveiled a draft of the defence review in late February 1998. Their script recounted the military's 'strategic mobility' to provide 'power projection' across the globe. The two new aircraft carriers were described as indispensable because, 'in almost all operations, maritime forces will be essential to help deliver ground forces to the theatre'. Britain's military would be equipped to fight simultaneously a major battle and a small engagement of limited duration, or fight two medium-sized conflicts concurrently.

All this appealed to Blair. Unlike Margaret Thatcher and John Major, he had not required his staff to provide a comprehensive briefing to explain Britain's military capabilities. Since his election, he had sat only once with the chiefs for a ninety-minute discussion and, as they themselves later noted, he had not asked the kind of technical questions posed by his predecessors. Blair appeared uninterested in scrutinising the consequences of fundamental changes.

Thirty years earlier, Britain had withdrawn its military from any engagement east of Suez. Now, Blair ordered a return, without asking about the additional cost of protecting his aircraft carriers from an attack by a land-based missile. His principal adviser remained Guthrie, whom he had grown to trust over drinks. 'Charles,' a voice from Downing Street would say, 'would you come over? The prime minister wants a word.' During their conversation about the strategic defence review, the two men never discussed the carriers. The undiscussed dilemma, Guthrie must have known, was finding the additional billions of pounds to organise an unprecedented naval task force.

The next step caused some trepidation. George Robertson was required to present the defence review to the Cabinet for their approval. As Blair feared, it was John Prescott's question that exposed his minister's weakness.

'Why do we need the bugger?' he asked, referring to the nuclear deterrent. 'How many targets can we even hit?'

'Four,' replied Robertson, muddling up warheads, missiles and targets and ignoring his briefing paper, which showed that Britain's missiles could hit about 150 targets. Nevertheless, the new policy was approved. After the meeting, Blair told Robertson, 'It's best if you don't brief the Cabinet again.'

Robertson was due to present the final draft of the review to the Overseas Policy and Defence Committee (OPX) chaired by Blair on 27 March. Although Brown had already made a habit of not attending OPX meetings, refusing to discuss budgets except on his terms, this one was too important to ignore. In anticipation of the chancellor's disapproval, Admiral Essenhigh had been asked at the last moment to make the twenty-minute presentation rather than Robertson. His staff, 'helped by a bottle of sherry', had prepared the PowerPoint slides about the expeditionary forces. At the end, Brown burst from his sulk and snapped, 'I thought we're here to discuss the budget, not this stuff.'

'Brown sent me looks which could kill,' Essenhigh would recall. 'Filthy and grumpy.'

'Any money spent on defence', volunteered Clare Short, 'is wasted.'

Blair looked helpless. He had not read his brief nor discussed the restructuring of Britain's defence and foreign policy with the chancellor. 'Before they get to the money,' he said, 'they need guidance on core principles.'

'We need to save money,' said Brown.

The meeting was heading towards the buffers. 'Prime Minister,' interrupted Essenhigh, 'could we just look at this slide again to remind the committee? It is the heart of the argument.'

'Yes,' said Blair, 'and leave it up.'

He at last began following Essenhigh's briefing note, which high-lighted the questions he should ask, and also the script for his conclud-ing remarks. Both the review and the budget were approved. Brown appeared to have been defeated. 'You saved the day,' Robertson, who had floundered against Brown's unanticipated attack, told Essenhigh as they walked across Whitehall after the two-hour meeting. The military officers were unimpressed. Neither the prime minister nor his ministers seemed able to run or lead.

The following day, Brown insisted on saving a further £200 million a year from the defence budget. Robertson appealed to Blair. 'Sort it out with Gordon,' came the answer. Robertson was unprepared to chal-lenge Brown as his officials lacked the Treasury's computer models to analyse their own budgets. To try to help his beleaguered minister, Blair called Brown early one morning but was rebuffed. The defence review was paralysed.

'It's an absolute disgrace,' Guthrie told Blair in Downing Street, three months after the OPX meeting. 'We did what was required.'

'Oh, it's not as bad as that,' interrupted Jeremy Heywood, Brown's principal private secretary.

'You're not important,' said Guthrie sharply. 'You're the Treasury erk [*sic*].'

'Yes, we must do something,' said Blair. 'This is putting me in an extremely difficult position. Please go to Gordon and fix it.'

'It's your job to get Brown to deliver what he agreed,' countered the general.

'Politics doesn't work like that,' concluded Blair. He had decided to limit the number of arguments about money with Brown to ten per year.

'Brown's against it', thought Guthrie, 'because Blair's for it.'

Guthrie confronted Brown. After a bitter exchange, he left No. 11 with the promise of a nine-figure increase to the defence budget. 'The £100 million soon disappeared,' Essenhigh would later say.

'Enough is enough,' declared Robertson, knowing that Blair had refused to become further involved. Essenhigh was asked to produce a final budget. After all the grandiose promises about a new era, the review was reduced to horse-trading between the three services. Over a weekend in July 1998, Essenhigh made what he would call 'heroic assumptions' to bridge the funding gap. Instead of a £200 million shortfall every year, he calculated the annual gap was over £2 billion. He squared the circle by making cuts based upon untested efficiencies and aspirations of 'smart procurement'. The sorry result was endorsed by Blair.

Those invited by Robertson to celebrate the publication of the strategic defence review booklet at a party in Whitehall spoke about a new era. 'A change of flavour,' said one admiral, thrilled that the British fleet would once again be sailing east of Suez. A government spin doctor conjured the hymn for the new dawn: 'Go first, go fast and go home.' No one questioned the revival of imperial expeditions or mentioned the obvious weakness: the military had not been ordered to devise plans for any stated objective. An army sent to war without a goal was doomed to fall off the cliff. But the abundant mention of 'strategy' satisfied Blair that the nation's defence was in safe hands.

SEVEN

Old King Coal

By June 1998, Blair had realised the error of many of his ministerial appointments, not least at the DTI. That month, he accepted an invitation from Michael Scholar, the permanent secretary at Trade and Industry, to visit the demoralised department for half a day. The principal problem, he soon realised, was Margaret Beckett, a tribal politician whose hallowed status within the Labour family fed his fear that she would join with others to revive old Labour.

Blair had arrived in Downing Street with little thought about an energy policy. Having served briefly as the shadow minister, he believed the subject was uncontroversial. Oil prices were low in 1997 – about $18 a barrel – and most experts assumed that the world would continue to enjoy an oil glut for many years. To please the party's left wing, he could afford to appoint John Battle, a former councillor in Bradford, as the relevant minister serving under Beckett.

During his first telephone conversation with Blair, Battle was told to stick to the party's election manifesto. The formula was bland. 'We want secure, diverse and sustainable energy at competitive prices,' Battle would say. Although the party was committed to reducing carbon dioxide emissions by 20 per cent by 2010 – a tougher target than would be agreed at Kyoto – the high costs had deterred Blair from giving government support to renewable energy from wind and solar panels. For the same reason, he approved the moratorium on the building of new nuclear power stations, as announced by the Tories in 1989. Accordingly, other than platitudes about conservation and greener power stations,

Blair's only instruction to Battle was to protect the coal mines' supply to the stations for as long as possible. That, he knew, would be a problem because, compared to other fuels, British coal was expensive and un-green.

Battle's first days at the DTI's headquarters had ruffled feathers. The new minister had instantly denounced his officials, although there were few to criticise as the energy section had been run down by the Tories. Those few experts who remained found Battle immune to the complexities of the electricity market and the generation of power. 'He was', noted Michael Scholar, 'strangely blinkered and distrustful of civil servants.'

Scholar's initial unease had been placated six days after the election by Blair's introduction to all the permanent secretaries at the Wednesday-morning meeting. Like most of his colleagues, Scholar had walked back into Whitehall afterwards feeling inspired. In calculating his own priorities, he assumed that Blair intended to continue the policies designed in 1982 by Nigel Lawson.

Lawson had believed in allowing competition to dictate Britain's supply. The welfare of consumers, he said, was better served by the market than by a government. After the miners' strike was defeated in 1985, the Tories, supported by Labour, privatised the gas and electricity industries. Both were subject to regulators who encouraged the new companies to earn high profits in the hope that the 'market for energy' would attract investors and spark competition. Those expectations did not materialise.

The new owners had inherited an excess of power stations – nuclear, coal- and gas-fired plants. They invested very little and pocketed huge profits. Then electricity prices plummeted. Convinced that the halcyon days of gas supplies from the North Sea were permanent, in 1992 the Tories abolished the Department for Energy and inserted the remnants into the DTI. Everyone was satisfied. Britain's economic growth was based on cheap electricity, and its suppliers continued to earn good returns. Both Blair and Gordon Brown endorsed Britain's market as the most open in the world. Their one act of retribution on the 'benign neglect' of the Tory years was to impose a £5.2 billion windfall tax on all the privatised utilities, including the power-generating companies, in order to recover some of their excess profits and to finance three of Brown's passions: the introduction of winter fuel payments for the elderly; the New Deal, a welfare-to-work programme for the long-term unemployed; and the financing of a University for Industry, which developed into an expensive flop. The only outcry was Battle's tribal criticism of the free market for causing 'havoc' to the coal industry.

British coal's fate was threatened by the construction of new gas generators. The Tories 'dash for gas' meant 41 per cent of the nation's electricity was now generated from coal, down from 74 per cent. Britain's coal mines faced bankruptcy. 'Irresponsible', was Battle's judgement to the Commons. 'I have stopped it,' said the new minister.

Coal's fate was first considered after the election by a Cabinet committee chaired by Brown. The single meeting (it did not meet again) ended without a decision. Disdainful of the Cabinet machine, Blair summoned another gathering in March 1998 to hear Anna Walker, the DTI's director of energy, describe her plans for a review. Blair, the chief executive of Britain plc, sat in shirtsleeves holding a latte; his ministers, he expected, could settle the dispute with quick decisions.

By then, any confidence he had in Battle had evaporated. The junior minister, he was told, lost official briefing papers in his chaotic office and struggled to distinguish between the important and the trivial. Beckett seemed unwilling to compromise. She asked few questions, proposed no original policies and denounced her civil servants for any mistakes. Her officials replied that ministers were always presented with options. In the DTI, however, the traditional practice had been interrupted ever since Beckett had written insulting comments to one official for advancing an argument supporting the free market for gas. She suspected he was a Tory and, despite Blair's support of markets, displayed her disagreement through earthy comments. The result was a stand-off that encouraged Beckett to sidestep her department. Senior

civil servants discovered that she and John Prescott were meeting without their knowledge to discuss the fate of the nuclear industry.

'This is absolutely, deeply shocking,' Scholar told Beckett.

'Well, that's the way I'm doing it,' she replied.

'It's going to be a disaster if you carry on like this without information.'

'Where would I get information from?'

'From the experts in this department.'

'I don't trust them. They're in the pockets of the nuclear industry.'

Scholar knew that was untrue but, to prove his mettle to Beckett, he
threatened his experts, 'I'll fire the lot of you if you're in the pockets of
the industry.'

Nothing transpired except further distrust. A review of Labour's policies delivered by Beckett's staff in May 1998 persuaded Blair that the
department was dysfunctional. He was angry that Battle, with Prescott's
support, believed that the use of gas to generate electricity was part of
a Tory plot to destroy the coal industry. Battle and Prescott advocated
rigging the market in favour of coal. The review recommended that the
construction of gas-powered generators should be halted, and that the
government should subsidise new coal-fired power plants. 'They just
don't get it,' Blair raged. Old Labour and the trade unions, he cursed,
wanted to reverse privatisation and undermine New Labour's support
for markets. He was prepared to give coal a chance, but not with more
taxpayers' money. William Rickett, an energy expert working in the
Cabinet Office, was asked to assist Mandelson in orchestrating old
Labour's retreat. The bid failed.

The natural solution would have been to reprimand Beckett and
Battle. Instead, Blair summoned Brown, Geoffrey Robinson, Beckett,
Battle and Geoff Norris, Downing Street's energy adviser, to decide
whether Britain should subsidise its coal mines. In his role as chief
executive, he expected his precise focus to resolve the disagreement.

'Is the market rigged against British coal?' he asked Anna Walker.

'No,' replied Walker, who explained that British coal was plagued by disadvantages, not least that the mines were so deep. Britain could import much cheaper coal.

Blair waited for his ministers to join the discussion. None spoke. Fearful of angering Labour's backbenchers, Brown and Beckett resisted putting their heads above the parapet.

Robinson broke the silence. 'I'll sort it out,' he offered.

'Right,' said Blair.

Over the next days, Robinson telephoned and frightened DTI officials in what Michael Scholar would describe as 'the most monstrous way' to urge the department to provide financial support for Britain's mines.

'I don't like this,' Walker told Robinson after consulting a government lawyer. 'You haven't got the legal powers to do what you want.'

To avoid potential illegalities and a judicial review, Blair ordered Robinson to let up. He summoned Walker back to Downing Street. As they went through the options, Blair refused to approve any pit closures. Coal should be given a chance, he told her, by stopping the 'dash for gas'. Then he was told that Brown was unexpectedly waiting outside his office. 'Call him in,' he told his private secretary. 'We need his brains on this.'

The official returned, saying, 'Sorry, Prime Minister, the chancellor says that he would prefer not to be involved.' Blair's face fell, but he made no comment.

To delay any pit closures, he decided that coal should be protected for another five years. Simultaneously, to make coal appear more attractive, no more gas plants would be built and the subsidy for nuclear power (which produced 25 per cent of Britain's electricity) would be reduced. The meeting ended. 'It's a fudge,' concluded Rickett.

Blair had ignored the contradiction created by subsidising coal at the expense of championing the environment and providing cheap electricity. Party politics overrode his better instincts. The government was now committed to sending more miners down the pits to produce expensive coal, in so doing irrevocably damaging their health. At the same time, the trade unions were complaining that the DTI was not distributing the £6 billion of compensation the government had allocated to sick miners with sufficient speed.

Taking up their complaint, Battle and Beckett castigated their civil servants for applying statutory safeguards too rigorously. 'It's undignified for the claimants,' said Beckett. The tests were modified and payments accelerated. Within months, unscrupulous lawyers were accused of pocketing taxpayers' money. Blair voiced no concern. He did not mention that appointing Battle was a mistake or ask for new thoughts about producing energy, but he did succumb to Mandelson's criticism of Beckett for failing to promote British business. In early July 1998, he agreed that she would be replaced – by Mandelson. Blair would have preferred to keep his political genius in Downing Street, but Mandelson's demands to prove his abilities beyond political intrigue had become irresistible.

The new minister's arrival at the DTI delighted the civil servants. Working with a serious player close to the prime minister was stimulating. The first day's preliminaries were routine. 'You need to disclose to me', Scholar told Mandelson, 'any material interests you have which could influence your position as chief regulator in the land.'

'I have nothing except a few savings,' answered Mandelson. Scholar wrote the reply down.

Mandelson proceeded to show a minimum of interest in energy. No one was surprised. Other than urging the advantages of an even more competitive market to lower prices, he made little comment in October about the publication of his department's White Paper, 'The Review of Energy Sources for Power Generation'. The policy was mentioned in Cabinet but there was no discussion. Few took the government's commitment to decarbonise Britain's energy supply seriously because Blair refused to raise the necessary taxes to finance the expensive restructuring required. Ministers realised that the important decisions had already been taken. Like so many White Papers, it disappeared into oblivion.

Mandelson was more interested in commissioning a White Paper about competition to show how high-tech businesses could be revital-ised with government subsidies and looser planning and immigration rules. This was the heart of New Labour. Although its authors in the DTI condemned their own work as 'a worthless confection, a complete waste of time', Alastair Campbell gave the publication show-biz promo-tion. 'The prime minister', he told journalists, 'is thrilled.'

However, the publication was overshadowed by Mandelson's riposte to an American journalist about Labour's traditional prejudice against the wealthy. 'We are intensely relaxed', he said, 'about people becom-ing filthy rich, so long as they pay their taxes.' Those who questioned how rules and subsidies would improve the economy were told, 'Don't worry. We'll have a bill on this.' In New Labour's lexicon, legislation was the equivalent of governing.

With Blair's blessing, Mandelson was already anticipating how British industry could be reshaped, unaware that Gordon Brown was intent on exacting revenge for Mandelson switching his support to Blair in 1994.

EIGHT

The Wall Crumbles

In mid-June 1998, home secretary Jack Straw was told about a rise in the number of asylum-seekers arriving in Britain. Labour's mood music, said Tim Walker, the head of the Immigration and Nationality Department (IND), had removed the deterrent legislation erected by Straw's predecessor Michael Howard. The guarantee of welfare benefits was encouraging the increase. Most asylum-seekers were under threat from either criminals or warlords rather than governments, or else were economic migrants lying about their persecution and nationality. Despite that dishonesty, the government's liberal policy was persuading more judges to rule against deportation, impervious to the consequences of their decisions. Asylum and immigration, Walker continued, would become important issues.

Straw raised the issue with Blair. 'Isn't immigration the sort of issue which can blow up in our face?' he asked.

'Immigration won't be an issue,' replied Blair. 'Immigration is good for Britain.' The *Daily Mail* and *Daily Express*, he continued, were 'not concerned', so it was not an issue.

'Tony's not interested,' Straw told Walker.

In fact, Straw himself agreed with Blair, and was untroubled by increasing immigration. In 1997, he had told his officials that only 10,000 foreigners would take advantage of the abolition of the primary purpose rule. Instead, over 150,000 immigrants would arrive during 1998. Straw's mistake was compounded by the unpredicted steep increase in applications for asylum.

Tim Flesher, a senior member of the IND, explored Straw's intentions in his first conversation with the minister. 'We need to send a message about our attitudes,' suggested Flesher. 'Should we welcome legal immigrants and encourage them with the promise of British citizenship? And should we be tough on the rest? There are no rules to distinguish between a good and a bad Kosovan.'

In a separate conversation, Walker told Straw, 'Under the rules, we can exclude only the extreme cases at the margins.'

'Well, do your best,' Straw replied to both.

'It's defeatist but also realistic,' thought Walker, who offered another condition to keep the numbers down. 'Why don't we stipulate that immigrants must speak English before we grant them British nationality? To make British nationality a prize?'

'No,' replied Straw.

The minister's response was confusing. In private, he showed no alarm about the statistics, yet in public he wanted to show that he was not an easy touch. He told the Commons he favoured strong controls, especially at the borders. Then he added, 'We mustn't be soft but we must be fairer.' Neither side was satisfied with his confusing answer. Indeed, some Labour supporters criticised his intention to deter bogus asylum-seekers as authoritarian.

His true position depended on the new law planned for 1999. Straw summoned Michael Eland, a Home Office official responsible for policy, telling him, 'I want to make the application process for asylum faster.' Eland was told to prepare laws to establish the National Asylum Support Service, which would help migrants live in Britain. That measure did not strike Eland as tough towards immigrants. Straw's proposals, he judged, would actually help bogus applicants. IND officials returned to Straw and asked for guidance.

'We must not let immigration get out of control,' Straw told Tim Flesher. 'But we don't want to stop immigration, just control the flow.'

'That is no solution to the problems of immigration,' replied Flesher. Straw was deaf to such warnings. Immigration, he countered, would no longer be a problem. He was more interested in crime, and delegated immigration to Mike O'Brien, a junior minister and lawyer.

Since arriving at the Home Office in May 1997, O'Brien had become 'appalled'. During his first visit to Croydon, the headquarters of the IND, he discovered that the staff were demoralised, negative and overwhelmed by a two-year backlog of applications for asylum. One official greeted Labour's victory as 'the relief of Mafeking . . . The Home Office mandarins were not competent,' O'Brien decided. Yet the new rules introduced by Straw had increased the number of legal challenges available to asylum-seekers over the decisions made by IND officials.

The gloom had been compounded by the dismissal of a thousand officials, with another thousand due to join them. The departures had been planned four years earlier, after the Home Office and Treasury had approved the computerisation of immigration procedures. Siemens had been contracted by the Home Office to replace the IND's archaic paper files with a seamless electronic process. The cost, according to the Treasury, would be paid for by sharply reducing the number of civil servants. The computers were due to come into operation in late 1998 and, as the redundancies began, the remaining personnel began moving to a new building.

In the hiatus, Straw was under pressure from IND officials to clarify the government's policy. Britain's asylum laws, he was told, were constantly being broken by thousands of Albanians and Iraqis who were entering Britain by posing as Kosovan refugees, the latter being exposed because none could speak any language or dialect used in Kosovo. They were economic migrants, not asylum-seekers. The IND needed new guidelines.

The answer was the new immigration Act due in 1999. As an introduction, O'Brien wrote a White Paper called 'Fairer, Faster, Firmer'. The government pledged to treat genuine asylum-seekers efficiently and fairly, and to keep the doors firmly closed to bogus applicants. Curiously, the White Paper's arguments cited the 1997 immigration statistics rather than the higher figures of 1998. O'Brien also stated that the largest number of migrants were white Britons returning from abroad. The uninformed reader would not know that immigration from the subcontinent was soaring, but the paper did propose a sting. To discourage bogus applicants, Straw and Walker had concocted a scheme during a train journey to Brussels: cash benefits would be replaced by vouchers that could be exchanged only for food, and not for cigarettes or alcohol. Their plan was opposed by some within the Home Office as too complicated, but Straw was insistent. 'Gordon has agreed to pay, and Tony supports the idea,' he told O'Brien.

Officials at the IND remained confused. Although Straw rejected the request by some Labour supporters to open the doors to migrants by removing all restrictions on entry, he was not closing them firmly. Fearing what Blair called 'a hysterical reaction' from Labour's heartlands, Straw also refused to acknowledge in public that most asylum-seekers were just seeking a better standard of living. His mixed signals encouraged officials in Croydon to approve suspect applications rather than engage in what was becoming an endless appeals process involving a new breed of lawyer appearing before judges whose interpretation of human rights favoured bogus applicants.

'We've got the worst of all worlds,' said Flesher. 'O'Brien is not a leader of deterrence.' The Labour government spoke about more deportations but, since the Treasury refused to provide additional money, there were insufficient staff for the time-consuming operation. And at that moment, June 1999, the IND collapsed. The department was paralysed. Siemens revealed that its computer system was defective, but failed to cure its mistakes or offer an alternative.

'All hell's broken loose,' lamented a hapless official. 'We've jumped off the cliff and there is nowhere to land.'

'It's going pear-shaped,' admitted another. 'We've lost control.'

At a meeting with Straw, IND officials admitted the certain prospect of chaos. The overloaded old system had been dismantled and the best staff had long gone. After a further visit to Croydon, O'Brien reported that the 'pile of files is vast' and, even worse, many folders could no longer be found.

Straw's and O'Brien's anger was diverted by their civil servants onto the Treasury. Home Office officials were paralysed by the Treasury's original decision to place the financial risk and control of the system with Siemens. By surrendering control to an outside company, immigration into Britain was at the mercy of unhelpful Germans. While IND officials argued about blame and Croydon careered towards meltdown, deportations declined, delays in the application process increased the backlog and, as the news about the chaos spread, hundreds of thousands more migrants were attracted to Britain. Disappearing after arrival, they knew, would be easy. The solution, Straw was told, was to hire 5,000 new staff, a proposal that was rejected by Brown. 'What more do you want to plug the loopholes?' Straw asked Stephen Boys-Smith, the new head of the IND. Boys-Smith, a conscientious official, looked puzzled.

Days later, Richard Wilson moved to Downing Street as Cabinet secretary and was replaced by David Omand, a former director of GCHQ. Omand was soon declaring that immigration had become 'a failure of policy. It's a shifting landscape and we have an administration problem.' The calamity, his fellow officials agreed, reflected an absence of 'joined-up government'.

The statistics confirmed that the problem was accelerating. After the abolition of the primary purpose rule, immigration from non-EU countries had risen by 50,000 to 200,000. Applications for asylum had increased to 46,000. The Labour government, Tim Walker concluded, watching from his new job in Whitehall, was indeed seen as 'a soft touch'. Blair's lack of interest risked turning a bad situation into a crisis. The only amusing diversion was Alastair Campbell's call to the head of the IND in the midst of the emergency. 'Are there are any good-news stories', he asked, 'that we can use for the Sundays?'

After Christmas, the media turned against Labour. Reports described Kent council as being inundated by thousands of unexpected asylum-seekers landing in Dover. As the arrivals were dispersed to abandoned housing estates across the country, the local communities in those areas protested that blocks of flats and even streets had become foreign territory.

Blair continued to show no interest in the problem. Instead, he announced the government's relaxation of the conditions for those applying to enter Britain as students. More foreign students in Britain, he said, would boost the country's income. In the speech being drafted for the party conference he did not disguise his sympathies. He would attack 'the old prejudices where foreign means bad; where multiculturalism is not something to celebrate but a left-wing conspiracy to destroy their way of life'. He signalled that not only were more migrants welcome, but anyone who encouraged integration into the British way of life, with its implication of superiority, was a borderline racist. Those who warned about the danger of allowing political Islam to be nurtured in Britain's mosques and schools were also labelled racist. For those who supported a multicultural Britain, patriotism was a form of racism. They interpreted any emotional connection to the British way of life as discrimination against those who did not share that sentiment.

Blair's encouragement of foreign students surprised IND officials. If these proposals were implemented, Straw was told, bogus students would 'attend' sham language schools and remain in Britain after their visas had expired. In reply Straw faced both ways. Labour, he said, would open the door to students, immigrants and genuine asylum-seekers. At the same time, the 1999 Act showed his determination to stop illegal entry. Bogus marriages had been outlawed, lorry drivers smuggling migrants into Britain would be fined £2,000 per person and benefits for asylum-seekers would be reduced. His officials remained unconvinced. Without publicly admitting the fact, the government had strengthened the rights of asylum-seekers.

Previously, under the Tories a passport officer could deny entry to a suspected applicant and immediately order his or her departure from the country. Under the 1999 Act, Straw allowed applicants to appeal and stay in Britain until their case was finally decided. Dedicated law-yers patrolling Heathrow promised their clients lengthy delays, while sympathetic judges, in the opinion of IND officials, increasingly inter-preted the 'facts' to favour the asylum-seekers.

The courts rapidly became clogged, while bogus applicants were freed from overcrowded detention centres with the promise of wel-fare benefits and public housing. Iraqis, Iranians and Kosovans already resident in Britain encouraged their 'families' to join them. The news about the country's new tolerance spread around the world, encour-aging Kurds, Tamils, Sri Lankans and Cypriots to enter as tourists before applying for asylum. Migrants from the Balkans, Afghanistan and Somalia headed for Calais to jump on a lorry and be smuggled in. The police resisted any involvement, and Straw did not demand that Brown finance new detention facilities and more staff. Everyone looked the other way.

In early 1999, Home Office officials reported that people smug-glers and lawyers were schooling applicants on what to tell immigra-tion officers, and marriage rackets were flourishing. Over the course of the year, IND received tens of thousands of new applications from migrants who had destroyed their identity documents, making it impossible to know which country they could be deported to. By June 1999, the backlog of applications for asylum rose to 125,000, compared to 52,000 in 1997. The number of immigrants legally entering Britain rose to 360,000, although the government minimised the number by speaking only about a 'net migration of 219,000'.

That autumn, the new Act was tested. Straw's somersault from criticising Michael Howard's bill in 1996 to enacting his own controls encouraged a media outcry. In reaction, No. 10 finally asked the Home Office for information, and Straw paid them a visit. 'If Downing Street was irritated by the Home Office's failure to produce the results Blair wanted,' Omand noted, 'a chain would be yanked, and the media reports from Campbell's briefing signalled that Straw's stock in Downing Street had fallen.'

Straw returned to his office from Downing Street visibly annoyed by Blair's irritation over the fact that the number of asylum-seekers had not been sharply reduced. To his officials, he appeared surprised that the courts were embracing the sentiment of Labour's new legislation. 'What more do you want to stop this?' he asked Boys-Smith. 'Shall we rewrite the UN Charter?' His forlorn question was mixed with anger at Downing Street. The machinery of government, he complained, was being frustrated by the innumerable specialist 'units' randomly established by Blair to implement his ideas, and by Blair's arguments with Brown.

Straw was particularly stung by Brown saying that he refused to 'waste more money' on building new prisons. Brown disparaged Michael Howard's policy of longer sentences in order to teach prisoners to work. Without new prisons, overcrowding developed and convicts had to be released earlier. David Ramsbotham, the chief inspector of prisons, protested that Straw was 'totally ineffectual' at reforming the sordid institutions. Straw blamed Blair's unending dispute with Brown for undermining Blair's own homily that 'what mattered to me was crime and immigration'.

Brown's refusal to release money to hire more officials and lawyers for the Home Office 'fed back into the system,' in Omand's experience, 'and then nothing happened. We just had to plug away to get more money, but Downing Street and the Treasury were not joined up.' Blair was paralysed by not understanding how to make his government work. 'Well, you must do what's necessary,' he routinely concluded discussions.

'We were unprepared for the explosion in asylum claims through 1998 and 1999,' he would write in 2010, claiming to be unaware that IND officials had been warning Straw about the effect of Labour's policies. 'We were quickly dubbed the asylum capital of Europe,' Blair admitted.

His self-portrayal as the victim of unpredictable events is undermined by the telephone call made by Liz Lloyd, a close aide in Downing Street, to Michael Eland in late autumn 1999. 'What can be done?' she enquired. Worried about the media headlines, Lloyd emphasised that the government disliked appearing soft. 'Is the Home Office on top of this?' she asked, concerned about the looming possibility that the Tories might use the growing numbers in their next election campaign. Since Eland could not give a satisfactory reply, Straw and Boys-Smith were summoned to Downing Street. For thirty minutes, Blair expressed his anger about judges who found loopholes to help the asylum-seekers, and then blamed the Home Office for failing to stop them coming. The improving economy, he said, and the lack of ID cards were the reasons for the upsurge. The government's policies were not at fault.

The prime minister was soon contradicted. Labour's new laws, said Boys-Smith, had created 'a gravy train for lawyers' who were 'corrupting the system'. That had been exposed by a test composed by the IND staff. A group of Kosovan applicants were asked to identify well-known landmarks – cafés, schools and streets – in Priština, the capital of Kosovo. On the first day, all the Albanians posing as Kosovans were exposed as liars. On the second day, another group of Albanian suspects passed the test. The lawyers had briefed their clients.

'You must work on this, Jack,' Blair told his home secretary, 'and find ways to stop it.' He did not, however, ask Omand any questions about the chaos in the IND, nor about the administration of immigration. The prime minister, senior Home Office officials were discovering, did not understand the problems. 'He just went mad about how long it takes to get things done,' said Omand. Neither Blair nor Straw mentioned the rising number of lawful immigrants from India and Pakistan, nor did they consider how to provide housing, schools and health care for an additional 300,000 people a year. Nor did they question whether the immigrants would influence the lives of the British working class. Immigration, they both still believed, was a Tory issue.

The final item on the agenda that day was whether Britain would sign the EU's new asylum law. Straw had arrived at the meeting hoping to discuss the proposed change, which ordered migrants to apply for asylum in the first EU country they reached. Every member state was then compelled to respect that country's decision. Boys-Smith expected Blair to say, 'Jack, what are we going to do?' Instead, the prime minister ignored the issue. 'I was shocked by Blair's lack of focus,' recalled Boys-Smith. 'He was totally uninterested in a question of principle, which was a loss of sovereignty. He didn't realise the importance.' Britain signed the law.

Towards the end of 1999, the Treasury finally agreed to finance the employment of more immigration officers. But the politicians no longer believed that manpower was the problem. Mike O'Brien blamed his officials for providing the wrong information, a criticism that was echoed by Blair. The civil service, the prime minister would write, 'wasn't greatly inclined to the radical action the system needed'. They were not closet Tories sabotaging a Labour government, he wrote, but they suffered 'inertia . . . They tended to surrender, whether to vested interests, to the status quo or to the safest way to manage things – which all meant: to do nothing.'

NINE

A Government Adrift

Blaming civil servants for the government's failures had become popular among Blair's inner circle. Officials, Blair complained, were slow, begrudging and not so brilliant. The civil service was incapable of reproducing men of the quality of Burke Trend, the legendary Cabinet secretary of the 1960s. Too many current civil servants, he was convinced, disliked politicians and felt that the country would be better managed without their interference.

Echoing Blair's thoughts, Jonathan Powell blamed civil servants for not offering solutions but instead frustrating his master's 'ambition for action'. Radical change, Powell would write, had proved to be 'extremely difficult' because civil servants imposed 'the most effective brakes'. Negativism, cynicism and 'a culture where the word "brave" is a warning rather than praise', he believed, was irresistibly piling regulations upon Blair, who 'found himself banging his head against a brick wall of difficulties'.

To the service itself, Blair appeared the author of his own misfortune. In *The Times* he had written an article entitled 'Why Britain Needs a New Welfare State', in which he outlined 'the boldest benefits shake-up since Beveridge', but which raised questions without offering any answers. In his desire for reform, he had entrusted Harriet Harman to work with Frank Field, the former director of Shelter, the charity for the homeless, whose robust experience with those living on welfare would influence his ideas for reforms. Blair's misgivings about Harman had surfaced soon after her appointment. During a

93

two-hour discussion before the election he had advised her not to oppose her Tory predecessor Peter Lilley's plan to reorganise state pensions, but the suggestion had been ignored. 'It's too good to throw away as an election issue,' Harman had urged. After his first weeks as prime minister, Blair knew that the chance of sensible reform had been irrevocably lost, effectively stymied by Harman's raving diatribes against Field.

The task was complicated by further disagreements between Blair and Brown. Blair advocated new ideas to save the 'vast sums' being wasted by promoting welfare-to-work. Opposing him, Brown emphasised that the money was not going to the impoverished. Nor could they agree about sickness and disability benefits, and especially payments to single parents, an issue that had already provoked a rebellion by Labour MPs.

Field, a mild character, was drowned out by the hysteria. 'Blunkett Declares War on Brown' was one newspaper headline, highlighting the ripple effect of the arguments, as Brown demanded that the Treasury control all welfare policy. Civil servants could only observe that if the politicians disagreed, how could any reforms be implemented? The problem was aggravated, as Richard Wilson discovered, by Blair's appointments. Field, in Blair's view, had promised to deliver the 'unthinkable' but had supplied the 'unfathomable', while Harman was simply 'no good'. Exasperated by her incompetence, Blair had once got so tired of her 'interminable complaints' during a telephone call that he simply handed the receiver to Mandelson. She continued talking, unaware that the prime minister had left the building.

In the end, Blair fired both ministers. Welfare reform, a priority in May 1997, was derailed. He established a Cabinet committee to resolve the problem, but then Brown set up his own committee to assert his supremacy over the domestic agenda. Eventually, Brown and his adviser Ed Balls reluctantly attended Blair's committee. Balls spent the whole time whispering in Brown's ear, 'driving Tony absolutely crazy', as Powell records. Exasperated by the bickering, Blair agreed that Brown could introduce a complex system of means-tested tax credits to help the poor. He did not understand the seismic implications of importing a welfare scheme developed in America. The Inland Revenue would abandon its historic and sole job of tax collection to become a welfare agency distributing money. Blair did not ask if Brown understood his own revolution; nor did any official across Whitehall. Such was the consequence of Blair's rejection of traditional Cabinet government. To avoid leaks, he resorted to informal conversations without civil servants, a class he now regarded as pawns.

Instead of blaming himself, he expressed his disappointment to Richard Wilson. 'I feel like I'm sitting in a Rolls-Royce and I can't find the key,' he told the Cabinet secretary.

'Well, what you shouldn't try to do is to get out and push it yourself,' Wilson countered, resenting Blair's hostility. 'You need a chauffeur. We're plagued by the problem, what is government good at?' he confessed. The Tories had reduced the number of civil servants and started to 'drain government of its role'. That left Whitehall's 'soggy middle', with too many unenterprising civil servants and poor financial controls. But, complained Wilson, nothing would be achieved by Blair constantly urging civil servants to modernise, or by Jeremy Heywood haranguing everyone that nothing was changing fast enough. Incoherence could not be implemented. Wilson's request for Blair to explain his message received at best idealistic verbiage – and his reward was exclusion from the policy unit.

'The problem with the traditional civil servants', Blair repeated, 'is not obstruction but inertia.' To allay Blair's fears, Wilson began drafting a plan to strengthen the prime minister's office, unaware that Blair had asked John Birt, the BBC's former director general, now employed as an unpaid adviser, to do the same.

To reinsert himself into the decision-making process, Wilson would routinely creep into Blair's office to scrutinise his diary and discover what he was doing hour by hour, day by day, and then offer his help. When Blair refused to involve him, Wilson threatened to resign. Civil servants, he told Blair, performed well for effective ministers. Good government required good politicians. And with that exchange the fault line became unmistakable. Could one man govern Britain without understandable policies, or without caring about his supporters? One Blairite minister complained that 'Blair no longer appreciates the ambitions of others. Having risen to the top so rapidly, he has become insensitive to the careers of others.' The direction of the NHS, said Wilson, showed that its latest problems were created by Blair and his ministers rather than by civil servants.

In December 1997, junior health minister Alan Milburn and his special assistant Simon Stevens had published a ninety-two-page White Paper called 'The NHS: Modern and Dependable'. Blair wrote in the foreword, 'This White Paper begins a process of modernisation . . . In my contract with the people of Britain, I promised that we would rebuild the NHS.' The government rejected the Conservatives' open market in favour of 'integrated care based on partnership and driven by performance'. Abolishing competition and choice, he predicted, would save £1 billion from 'wasted resources' and the money would flow from 'red tape to patient care' since 'we'll put doctors and nurses in the driving seat'.

In conversations with his health ministers, Blair revealed little understanding about the counter-revolution he had approved. Nor did the minister for health, Frank Dobson, understand. Both men had relied on Milburn and Stevens to produce the government's health policy – a policy that the party had failed to compose while in opposition. In the preparatory discussions, Blair had never offered any ideas other than memorably suggesting, 'Hospitals are too much like unemployment benefit offices. They need to be modernised.' It was modernisation without meaning.

Blair had launched the White Paper with the promise of an extra £1.5 billion for the NHS. Not to be outdone, Brown rushed to the Commons to announce that he was giving the service an extra £21 billion, a 50 per cent increase over three years. Both men believed that extra money would automatically produce improvements. For once, the chancellor's headlines outshone the prime minister's, but Blair was not worried. 'That £21 billion is real money,' he told the Commons. But, within a week, NHS chief Alan Langlands heard that Brown's announcement was a ruse. By triple counting the same sum over three years, the chancellor had inflated the true amount – just £8.6 billion. The public exposure of this trickery by a think tank aroused cynicism about the government's refined spin machine. Blair remained unconcerned. 'That £21 billion is real money,' he repeated in Parliament. Not to be outdone, he also announced an extra £30 million would be spent on A&E. Later, on three separate occasions, he announced that an extra £30 million was being spent on other NHS services, without clarifying that he was always committing the same money.

By then, Brown had seized on a much bigger tool to promote himself as defender of the NHS. The Tories had developed the Private Finance Initiative (PFI), a scheme for building hospitals in partnership with the private sector. Under the plan, a private company financed, built and maintained a hospital. While retaining ownership, it rented the premises to the state for about thirty years, after which the building reverted to the financier. Under Tory health minister Stephen Dorrell's scheme, the private sector assumed the financial risk. Dorrell had negotiated loans for about ten new hospitals and GP surgeries, but the contracts remained unsigned because the financiers were uncertain about Labour's attitude.

Brown seized on the idea and allowed Geoffrey Robinson to negotiate more generous deals than the Tories had envisaged. To get their quick support, the financiers were allowed to transfer all the risk onto the state. By deft accounting, Brown excluded the costs from the national debt and presented himself as the godfather of seventy new hospitals.

Among the first to be built was the Princess Royal University Hospital in Bromley. Over the thirty years, the private consortium expected to earn a gross profit of 70.6 per cent. Blair confessed he was unconcerned by complaints of profiteering or accusations that he was mortgaging the future to win popularity. 'It doesn't matter how hospitals are funded,' he told his party, 'so long as they get built.' His attitude towards money was as hazy as his attitude towards undesirable ministers.

In the summer of 1998, Blair acknowledged that Dobson was 'unimpressive'. In the jargon he used, he was 'not communicating a sense of progress and direction'. Yet he did not consider dismissing him. Elsewhere, greedy hangers-on were generating turbulence. Derek Draper, a friend of Peter Mandelson's, had offered an undercover journalist access to the 'seventeen most important people' in the government for cash; then David Heathcoat-Amory, a Conservative MP, challenged Robinson about a £200,000 payment recorded in the late Robert Maxwell's accounts. 'I never asked for the money and wasn't paid,' Robinson replied.

In July 1998, Blair appeared to endorse Robinson's lie when Alastair Campbell's rebuttal unit was ordered to jump on the story. 'We can state categorically', said Campbell, 'that Geoffrey Robinson did not receive £200,000 [from Maxwell].' At Blair's direction, Labour MPs on the parliamentary standards committee rallied to Robinson's defence, and after a soft reprimand he was embraced once again by his charmed circle.

'Every time the Conservatives have made an allegation it has been proved to be worthless,' said Blair. The premature retirement of Terry Burns, who had steadfastly rejected Brown's bullying to lie on Robinson's behalf, had annoyed the Tories, but still Robinson stayed. At the same time, Blair inaccurately denied intervening on Rupert Murdoch's behalf with Romano Prodi, the Italian prime minister, for favoured treatment in a TV deal.

On reflection, Blair realised that using subterfuge to protect his relationships with the rich would lead him towards a cesspit. Murdoch was worth protecting, but not Robinson. As a result, Richard Wilson was dispatched to negotiate the paymaster's resignation. First, he visited Brown, only to leave swiftly after the chancellor refused to agree to

Robinson's departure. Next, he called on Robinson personally. 'Rough old game, politics,' Wilson told the paymaster. However, supported by Brown, Robinson rejected 'a dignified exit', and the Cabinet secretary retreated. Blair then agreed to meet Robinson, and after an hour's conversation withdrew the dismissal. He refused to gamble on Brown's reaction if he sacked the paymaster.

Blair left for his summer holiday. Since Robinson was tarnished, he accepted an invitation from Prince Girolamo Strozzi, a new friend and the owner of a fifty-room villa in Tuscany. One unresolved problem was Jonathan Powell. Despite his title and powers, Powell's gauche judgement was confusing things rather than helping to solve problems. In July 1998, he faced the sack but was then reprieved with a part-time role in Northern Ireland. Blair was left without a suitable co-ordinator, which undermined his ambition to modernise the NHS.

Too much of the new NHS funding was being spent on structures – buildings and organisations – rather than on patient treatment. The government's policies were failing to make the NHS either more efficient or more responsive. Alan Langlands blamed Frank Dobson, who in turn, despite lacking any previous managerial experience, cursed his advisers as 'pointy-heads' for being 'too clever' and trying to outsmart him. In his disdain, he marginalised Christopher Kelly, the new permanent secretary, from any involvement. As a result, Kelly was not invited to a stock-take in late 1998 in the Cabinet room. Dobson's slide-show presentation to Blair listed a blitz of innovations devised by Robert Hill, Blair's health adviser, and Alan Milburn.

Milburn believed that tough regulators were the answer. To monitor the NHS's standards, his department had launched the Commission for Health Improvement, which would later have its name changed to the National Care Standards Commission, which in turn would be replaced by the Care Quality Commission, signalling the repeated failure of executives. In what he would later call 'the architecture for change', Milburn also promoted the National Institute for Health and Clinical Excellence (NICE) to control the cost and effectiveness of new treatments, and NHS Direct, a scheme designed during the Tory era to provide the public with easy access to medical advice.

To Dobson's surprise, 'Blair didn't want to go anywhere near the launch of NHS Direct with a bargepole,' as he put it. Instead, to score a quick public-relations hit, Blair launched Health Action Zones (HAZs) in twenty-six deprived areas. These were intended to remove health inequalities and raise the life expectancy of Britons to the highest levels in western Europe. The annual cost of the initiative was estimated at over £100 million. Yet in the rush to satisfy Blair's demand for delivery, Dobson refused to commission pilot schemes to test the plan.

Blair never challenged his health minister, not least because, other than replacing competition by co-operation, his 'master plan' was to rely on doctors to make decisions based on needs rather than finance. So he nodded through Milburn's changes.

'They're well meaning,' he later told Mandelson about Dobson and Milburn, 'but they're scratching the surface.'

'Why did you appoint Frank?' Mandelson asked.

'I didn't exactly have a choice,' Blair replied unconvincingly.

Mandelson would blame 'naivety and nervousness of government' for Blair's vacillation. Equally baffled by Dobson's appointment, Charles Clarke, Neil Kinnock's former chief of staff and a junior education minister since 1998, mentioned an organic weakness: 'Blair's real delinquency was that he wasn't interested in finding the right people to do the job – civil servants or ministers. He was a bad judge of people.' The result, Langlands concluded, was that 'Dobson spent a lot of time patrolling the borders instead of crossing them.'

The 'implosion' of the NHS, in Milburn's expression, hit just before Christmas 1998. Blair had shared Dobson's expectation that the government could trust the hospitals to use the extra millions of pounds to reduce waiting lists. Instead, the lists grew for the second year in succession by another 100,000 people to 1.3 million. In public Dobson blamed the Conservatives, but in private he complained that the manifesto pledge had been a 'crazy' confection by Peter Hyman, Blair's speechwriter. The reality was a shortage of beds and nurses, and the sick abandoned on trolleys in corridors. Then Britain was struck by a flu epidemic. One hundred thousand people were going down with the bug every week. 'Chaos in the NHS', blazed the headlines. Labour had boasted that the NHS was the envy of the world, yet in France, where about 300,000 people were falling sick weekly, GPs coped without a hitch.

Blair was baffled. France's success could be explained by the country spending more on health, so that one doctor was employed for 344 people compared to 625 people per doctor in Britain. But that did not explain why 30,000 Britons died prematurely every year because of negligence by hospitals, or why annually 100,000 patients became seriously ill from infections caught in British hospitals, of whom an estimated 5,000 died.

Blair had hit an ideological wall. Only the state could be trusted to manage the NHS, he believed, but he did not know why the state was failing. Like Gordon Brown, he trusted NHS employees to dedicate themselves to serving those in need but, beyond spending yet more money, both men ruled out any dilution of the NHS's monopoly. So, Blair concluded, the fault must be Dobson's after all.

He was urged by his Downing Street advisers to tell Dobson that his department was failing. An appointment was arranged. As usual, Blair looked at himself in the mirror before seeing Dobson. His habits rarely altered, and the meeting followed a familiar pattern: the minister came, Blair circled around the topic, and then he bid him farewell.

'You failed to challenge him,' Powell exclaimed.

'Yes, I did,' replied Blair. 'The guy knows that I want change.'

Those around the PM could conclude only that their boss was in an odd state of mind, or even caught up in a fantasy. In his own briefing notes before the meeting, Dobson had been told by officials at No. 10 that 'The prime minister is particularly interested in the private sector.' He now returned to his department to report, 'Well, he didn't raise it with me and I didn't raise it with him.'

The persistent media criticism persuaded Blair to consider the ideas of Julian Le Grand, a leftish professor of social policy at the London School of Economics who, unusually, advocated 'market socialism'. Since 1994, Le Grand had occasionally talked with Blair about the use of competition to achieve social ends. 'You can't expect hospitals to reform on their own,' he had told him. 'The NHS staff serve their own interests ahead of their patients'. Change comes with pressure. Carrots and sticks are needed.' In the contest between pragmatists and purists, Le Grand believed, patients should be encouraged to choose their doctors, using taxpayers' money to buy treatment either from the NHS or from private hospitals. 'Choice', he had emphasised, 'will encourage the NHS to deliver what the users want, or they will go elsewhere. Even the helpless want choice and quality.' Inferior hospitals with less money would be shamed into improving.

Blair was unconvinced. He remained certain of the selflessness of NHS staff. More importantly, choice was a Tory concept. He could not foresee that a series of academic studies would demonstrate how choice and competition between hospitals raised standards.

The trouble was, his core beliefs were not borne out by the facts. 'Blair didn't know what he wanted,' Wilson realised. Since there was no Cabinet committee focused on the NHS and the full Cabinet was not allowed to discuss the subject, Blair protected himself not only from criticism, but also from any constructive discussion.

'No one complained,' recalled culture minister Chris Smith, 'because no one knew anything different.'

During thirty-minute Cabinet meetings, Dobson said nothing. Bullying his minister was inconceivable for Blair. 'Tony didn't complain about anything,' Dobson would report to his department.

In theory, there was an arrangement in place to deal with the situation. Before the election, David Simon, the chairman of BP, had been asked to become a trade minister. Simon also had an unannounced role in which he was to advise on how to manage a government – the art of building a team, creating a culture that sought to set objectives, conduct meetings and review results. He encouraged Blair to hold all-day summits at Chequers to discuss 'goals' with civil servants, ministers and outside consultants. An away-day at Chequers in early September 1998 matched that prescription. Blair stressed modernisation with fairness, while Brown emphasised productivity, skills, education, tax credits and the global economy.

Shortly after, Simon realised that Blair was not listening to him. The prime minister's apathy over organisation and management was incurable. He relied almost solely on instinct and his ultra-loyalist team. None of those brothers-in-arms was tempted to advise that what worked in opposition was too crude for government. Blair, they realised, knew no other way of working. Discussions amid the formality of a Cabinet were uncongenial to a communicator who enjoyed coming to a decision after several conversations and a night's sleep, after which he would emerge with not only a policy, but also the required sales pitch.

The consequences of Blair's disorderliness erupted just before Christmas. His approval of Geoffrey Robinson's continued presence in the government not only challenged his own reputation, but also annoyed the Brownites who enjoyed Robinson's hospitality. Perversely, they had become outraged that, while their paymaster was tainted, Blair had allowed Mandelson to rise ever higher in the government's pecking order. Fuelled by Brown's antagonism towards Blair and their own hatred of Mandelson, Paul Routledge, a *Daily Mirror* journalist sympathetic to Brown, and Charlie Whelan set about poisoning the minister's reputation. They possessed a signed agreement from 1996 recording a £373,000 loan from Robinson to Mandelson for the purchase of a house in Notting Hill Gate. Mandelson had not declared that loan to Michael Scholar at the DTI, although he knew that Scholar's department was investigating Robinson's offshore trust. He had concealed a conflict of interest. Routledge planned to reveal the loan, without realising that Robinson was at that moment facing his own crisis: he had failed to declare in the Commons register of interests his receipt of £200,000 from Robert Maxwell.

Blair already knew some of the story. After the summer break, Michael Wills, a newly elected MP, had told Charlie Falconer, a lawyer and close friend of Blair's, about Robinson's loan. Falconer had a duty to tell the prime minister. Blair also knew that the DTI had commissioned a new investigation into Robinson's relationship with Maxwell. Still Mandelson held off telling Scholar. In November, Blair again ignored demands for Robinson's resignation and once more defended the paymaster in the Commons. Simultaneously, Mandelson resisted David Heathcoat-Amory's demand for a robust investigation of thirteen examples of Robinson's 'wilful disregard' of the law. Blair's fate depended upon Brown's caprice. To deflect pressure from Robinson, he could order Mandelson's destruction, or he could tiptoe away and hope the temple would remain standing.

The imbroglio intensified after Blair was told that Ron Davies, the Welsh secretary, had been robbed by a male prostitute on Clapham Common. His instant resignation was praised in the media as 'the coming of age of the Blair government' – without their realising that Blair had concealed from the outset that Davies had been lying to the police about the circumstances of the incident. In the ensuing discussion about gays in politics, journalist Matthew Parris declared on BBC TV that Mandelson was gay. Days later, Nick Brown, the new minister of agriculture, was accused by the *News of the World* of paying £100 to rent boys in order to be kicked around a room, and admitted his sexuality. A 'gay mafia', blared the *Sun*, was running the country. Next, Westminster gossipers blessed 'statesman-like' Mandelson and mentioned him as Blair's heir apparent. In a rush of mad fury, Routledge was let off his leash. On 17 December, Mandelson heard that Robinson's secret loan to him would be exposed within four days. 'A sort of mutually assured destruction,' was his description of the Brownite plot that now spread across Westminster.

'Why didn't you tell me about the loan?' Scholar asked Mandelson, with genuine sorrow.

'Because it is confidential,' came the reply. 'It's not an interest or an asset but a loan.'

Scholar laughed at the absurdity of Mandelson's interpretation of the rules.

In Downing Street, Blair 'exploded'. He was in the midst of a bombing campaign in Iraq, his first military engagement, and his own cover-up of Robinson's dishonesty had come back to haunt him. Restless newspaper editors urged journalists to investigate other allegations of Labour sleaze and cronyism. Blair asked Richard Wilson for his opinion. The Cabinet secretary replied that the loan was undoubtedly a conflict of interest and Mandelson should have declared it.

'I can't see what the problem is,' Mandelson told Blair. 'You and Alastair are overreacting.'

Blair agreed. He urged Mandelson to brazen out the storm and quickly repay the loan, ignoring the minister's failure to register a benefit in the Commons – the same sleazy sin he had hounded Tory MPs over. 'The prime minister does not consider it a hanging offence,' Campbell said on Blair's behalf. Both overlooked the journalists' lust for vengeance against Mandelson for his undisguised disdain towards them over the years.

'A wall-to-wall disaster area,' admitted Campbell after five days of unremitting hostility.

'Scandal is an absolute nightmare in politics,' Blair would write. 'It was a political assassination to destroy Peter and damage me.'

On 23 December, Blair decided that Robinson, Whelan and Mandelson would all have to go. 'I blame myself,' he admitted. 'We should have got rid of Geoffrey earlier.' This time he telephoned Robinson in person.

'The PM', Robinson later wrote, 'did not convey any sense that he blamed me for what happened. Rather he was annoyed and dismayed about the press reaction to the private arrangement.'

Blair next rang Mandelson. There's been deception, he said. Resign, learn from your mistake and you can return. Mandelson cried. The arch-manipulator, renowned as a bully, was surprised that Blair, who owed him so much, could be so ruthless. And he blamed Campbell, his rival, for seizing an opportunity 'to see my wings clipped'.

Disappointed at seeing such a talented minister reduced to jelly after just 150 days, Scholar urged Mandelson to stay.

'I must protect the honour of my grandfather,' replied Mandelson, referring to Herbert Morrison, a leading figure in Clement Attlee's government.

That day, Blair attempted to minimise what the media saw as 'the corruption of cronies'. 'It was a silly thing to do,' he said, 'but there was nothing illegal about it . . . This is nothing more than a moment of madness.' Mandelson was presented as an honourable man whose misfortune was to become a casualty of appearances.

The Tory criticism of a 'cancer at the heart of government' was mocked by Blair, but in *The Times* Libby Purves saw the end of 'this sweet, sticky web of mutual admiration' among a coterie of politicians, PR men, journalists and tycoons. The powerful magic of the New Labour family was wrecked. Most damaged was Blair's relationship with Brown. 'Thereafter,' wrote Mandelson, 'everything achieved in government was forged in combat.'

He was consoled by a note from Cherie Blair after a dinner at Chequers. 'I have no doubt', she wrote, 'that you have been the victim of a vicious and selfish campaign. My only consolation is that I believe that a person who causes evil to another will in the end suffer his returns.'

For the Tories, the sight of Labour's halo turning into a noose was a godsend. 'It's a government without any principles,' said Michael Howard on Radio 4, highlighting the fact that it had taken Blair six days to ditch his friend. 'They're obsessed with newspaper headlines.' Mandelson, the king of spin, had been brought down by the same public outcry against sleaze that he had ruthlessly deployed against John Major's government. The victor was Campbell. His indispensability in Downing Street was sealed.

Blair was determined to regain the initiative. 'This must be the year of delivery,' he told Richard Wilson after returning in January 1999 from a Christmas break in the Seychelles and a ragged official visit to South Africa. 'Once the taps are turned on, things will happen.' More money, he believed, would switch the public's attention from sleaze. Every department was urged to announce new spending, especially for the NHS. The government had already increased its budget by £5 billion a year and was due to add another £4 billion the following year.

Yet the waiting lists continued to grow. Philip Gould's focus groups were criticising the government for failing to deliver any improvements. 'They had no idea about anything we had done,' noted Campbell, fearful of Labour losing the next general election. Blair was puzzled why, despite spending so much more than in 1997, there seemed to be so little to show for it. 'Modernise or die' became his battle cry.

Dutifully, the Cabinet listened to Derry Irvine's list of new legislation: the decriminalisation of homosexuality; the removal of most of the hereditary peers from the House of Lords; the promotion of fairness at work; the creation of a disability rights commission; reform of the justice system; and enacting the right of freedom of information. In part, the list satisfied the government's agenda to modernise Britain, but Blair's predominant concern was winning the next general election. Yet the irritating stories never stopped. The tens of thousands from the countryside planning to march through London in February to protest against the ban on fox-hunting were the same middle classes whose support for New Labour Blair had secured in 1997. Now, to retain his party's support, he was proposing a ban that risked losing theirs. And those same marchers were appalled by Irvine's purchase of expensive wallpaper for his government apartment. Blair gasped when he heard about Irvine's conduct. 'There's a real sense we are losing our grip,' admitted Irvine. The government risked being ridiculed as a soap opera. One day, Blair complained to the Press Complaints Commission about newspapers probing into his children's education in their pursuit of 'trivia', but some twenty-four hours later he was sitting in a TV studio with Richard and Judy answering intimate questions about Cherie's clothes, whether his children took the mickey out of him, and sniping that Glenn Hoddle's belief in reincarnation was 'very offensive' and should bar him from being coach of the England football team. The people's politician was getting a little desperate.

Blair asked Wilson for a plan for delivery, especially on reforming welfare to 'make work pay'. Wilson's gospel, written by Brian Bender, was enshrined in 'Modernising Government', a White Paper developed over six months. To satisfy Blair's prejudices, Wilson focused on curing the civil servants' failures by recruiting independent experts and training people who were more talented. Civil servants, he wrote, should take 'more pride in what they do' – an odd admission. In March 1999, two weeks before the paper's publication, Blair dismissed the draft for lacking 'excitement' and 'impact'. A lexicon of new phrases was inserted. 'Joined-up government', 'integrated government', 'diversity', 'globalisation', 'the removal of regulation' and 'targets' conjured up the Blairite vision. Science was blessed with unlimited investment and £2.5 billion was committed to computerising Britain's 'information-age government'.

In the foreword, Blair wrote, 'Modernising government is a vital part of our programme for the renewal of Britain ... It is modernisation for a purpose – modernising government to get better government – for a better Britain.' Licensing laws, roads, waterways and even wages were to be 'modernised'. And updating the NHS was at the heart of this ambition. 'We will be forward-looking', Blair promised, 'in developing policies to deliver outcomes that matter, not simply reacting to short-term pressures.' His publicists, keen to find a suitable showcase, organised a summit of cancer experts in Downing Street. Among those invited was Professor Karol Sikora, the head of the World Health Organisation's cancer programme. Welcomed by Blair and Dobson, the nine experts posed for photographers. Labour, Blair told the cameras, would treat 60,000 more people suffering from cancer by 2010.

Shortly after the first presentation began, he apologised and departed. 'We were left talking amongst ourselves,' said Sikora, 'and two hours later we're back on the street. We thought this was silly ... It was clearly orchestrated hype and there was nothing at the end to show for it.' Cancer survival in the UK was worse than in Estonia. Blair omitted mentioning Dobson's decision to abandon the Tory scheme targeting cancer. The White Paper was quickly forgotten, and cancer treatment did not improve.

Centralised commands and collaboration were evidently not working. Blair expected Alan Langlands to resolve the problem. One morning, he summoned the chief executive to meet Bill Gates.

'Bill can make the NHS paperless in five years,' Blair said.

'How can I help?' asked Langlands, bemused by the prime minister's credulity. After a pointless exchange, Langlands departed.

The next day, he met Blair after a meeting chaired by John Prescott to discuss seventy-seven NHS targets. 'All this is nonsense,' Langlands had exclaimed during the meeting. 'The NHS is too complex for this.' The meeting had ended in disarray. Blair gave a wry smile. 'I hear that David Sainsbury saved you,' he said, implying that the official's job depended on the support of one junior minister, albeit one of the party's wealthier benefactors.

'The current system's broken,' said Langlands. 'There needs to be another way.'

Raising his eyes, Blair agreed that 'There are too many targets,' but as so often he offered no solution.

Langlands subsequently told a conference of NHS accountants, 'Blair, Brown and Dobson could not agree what to do.'

Those three politicians were united in ignoring one reality: the majority of Britain's mentally ill and elderly citizens had been placed under the good care of the private sector, while some patients in NHS institutions were complaining about abuse. Private care did not necessarily mean exploitation. The market was producing the best health care for the richest members of British society for approximately the same cost as the NHS, so why should the private sector not provide a similar service for the poorest? Labour's stock answer was that fragmentation would fatally undermine the NHS, but by July Blair's dissatisfaction with Dobson overrode that ideological riposte. To protect the sacred principle that health treatment should be free, he once again considered the NHS partnering with the private sector. 'I've got the feeling,'

Dobson told a trade union leader, 'that Tony is in favour of a mixed economy in health care, but I'm not sure.'

Nor was Blair. Already under fire from the British Medical Association for conjuring gimmicks rather than funding improvements, in mid-1999 he was lambasted for waiting lists that had again risen above the 1997 level. Blaming the Tories was one option, but it did not explain why the extra billions of pounds were making no difference.

The authority of the premiership, Blair persuaded himself, was illusory. Taxpayers' money was being poured into health and education, laws were being passed and there were speeches explaining the new world, and yet real influence clearly lay somewhere else. 'A new prime minister', wrote Jonathan Powell, 'pulls on the levers of power and nothing happens. That feeling of powerlessness goes on. The centre of government is not too powerful but too weak.'

Blair's anger with Richard Wilson's breed exploded when he addressed a group of venture capitalists on 6 July. 'You try getting change in the public sector and public services,' he told his audience. 'I bear the scars on my back after two years of government.'

'Scars' dominated the next day's media. In a noisy world, the prophet was thrilled by the headlines, despite the evidence being so thin. He was comfortable with humiliating civil servants. The staff in Downing Street were less excited. Some feared he had alienated too many public employees and politicised the NHS just as the country's health authorities were being increasingly run by Labour supporters (in 1998, Labour had appointed 288 party activists and forty-nine Conservatives). Blair dismissed their criticism. He needed to redefine The Project, he said, with 1997 set as year zero.

'Just think,' Langlands told Blair soon after the 'scars' speech, 'who are the people who work in the NHS? Ideologically, they must be those who support the NHS. You've just demoralised a million people.' Blair did not reply. In his opinion, he had identified a convenient enemy.

Some in the party were unconvinced. 'The speech wasn't true,' said Tom McNulty, a Labour MP. 'He just wanted a good line. So he set up a straw man, a bogey. Foolishly, he alienated the public-sector workers. His speeches were substitutes for action.' Only later would Blair confess, 'I knew nothing about how tough it really was, nothing about how government really works.'

Too many of his ministers were making 'a mess'. On the eve of leaving for his summer holidays, he decided on a reshuffle. John Prescott was mismanaging transport but, as deputy prime minister and Labour stalwart, he was untouchable. A raft of more junior ministers would be fired, but that still left Dobson, Beckett, Cook and others.

On 28 July, Blair sat with Jonathan Powell, Anji Hunter, Alastair Campbell, Richard Wilson, Sally Morgan, Downing Street's political director, and David Miliband, a special adviser.

'The chancellor has his tanks parked on your lawn,' said Wilson, surprised by Blair's unwillingness to reduce Brown's influence.

'I know,' replied Blair. 'I want to appoint my people but I'm not spoiled for choice. There's so little talent.' Even his few good ministers were struggling. Each person in Blair's office was given a sheet of paper. On the left was the department and the existing minister; the right side was blank. By the end of the session, the pack had been reshuffled and a few deadbeats removed. Blair departed for his holiday feeling depressed. He seemed unaware that the only unqualified loyalists supporting his government were those he most disparaged – the civil servants.

TEN

Frustration

'You need to dismiss bad teachers,' Chris Woodhead said firmly. He was urging Blair to cross the Rubicon and support him against David Blunkett, Michael Barber and Michael Bichard. 'You must confront the poverty of expectations in the classrooms and the abysmally low performance of schools. Choice is essential. Bad schools should be allowed to go to the wall.'

'Absolutely,' replied Blair.

Bichard gave the opposite view. 'People want quality, not choice.'

'Yes,' replied Blair.

Choice was only possible, Bichard continued, if there was spare capacity – and spare capacity meant a waste of resources.

Woodhead despaired. Blair was facing every possible way, looking for excuses to avoid the bottom-up battle, classroom by classroom, school by school. Although Blair spoke about addressing parents' concerns, not only did he refuse to dismiss bad teachers, close bad schools or neutralise the LEAs, but he had agreed that disruptive pupils should not be expelled from classrooms, bowing to the new Social Exclusion Unit's demand that troublemakers should be protected. In Woodhead's opinion, Blair flinched from an outright battle both with the trade unions and with the educational establishment.

In reply, Blair denied cowardice. Success, he said, would be delivered by persuasion. The eighteen task forces established by the Social Exclusion Unit mirrored his conviction that poverty and other social disadvantages like debt, addiction, mental ill health and bad housing caused poorly educated children, not bad teachers. Reflecting his confusion, Blair also agreed with his senior education officials that 'great' head teachers should be supported by removing bad teachers.

His inconsistency was repeated in his annual speech to Labour's new National College for Teaching and Leadership. He urged his audience to improve teaching by using his party's new performance assessments, an initiative that allowed head teachers to reward good teachers with bonuses and sack bad teachers. His hopes would be dashed. During 1999, no teacher lost their job and most were paid a bonus. Annual salaries would increase by 6.6 per cent. Blair fell back on his only weapons to cure underperforming schools: Blunkett's directives and Barber's targets.

He still wanted to tinker. 'Should we do more phonics?' he asked Barber at a meeting also attended by Bichard and Blunkett in which he mentioned the success of phonics in teaching reading in Scotland.

'No,' said Barber.

'It's not right to force schools,' agreed Blunkett, deferring to Barber.

Bichard also agreed, favouring the so-called 'Trendy Wendy' methods. Although the former director of the benefits agency lacked expertise in children's learning processes, he recognised Blair's detachment about phonics. 'We all know so little about how to expedite learning,' he said. Blair did not disagree.

'I think you should challenge teachers to use phonics,' countered Woodhead, angered by their complacency.

'They assumed', he would recall, 'that everything was perfect and they just needed to bang on a bit longer.' The chief inspector of schools' persistence irritated Blair. With a hectic schedule, classroom activities distracted him from making headlines about hitting targets. The others, Blair knew, wanted the intransigent Woodhead dismissed. He expected the tough-talking Blunkett to solve the fallout.

The tension increased after an argument about A-levels. With Blair's agreement, Barber and Bichard had made these exams easier. Studying for them, Barber and Bichard believed, should be a pleasure. Children should not be limited to 'just one chance and then you're out'. Modules had been introduced to replace one-time examinations, and schoolchildren could endlessly retake these new forms of examination to improve their marks.

'You need to release children's potential,' Bichard told the chief inspector. In his view, Woodhead did not want education to be enjoyable, but to his distress Blair failed to recognise that he, Bichard, was not an educationalist but a polemicist preaching equality.

'So you want every child to do a *bit* of an A-level?' Woodhead asked the prime minister. Blair's engaging smile concealed his confusion. His mantra was 'standards, not structures', but by supporting Bichard he was pursuing the opposite.

Unexpectedly, Blunkett was also critical of Blair. 'It's no use,' he told Bichard, 'to keep on hitting my head against a brick wall.' They argued about structures and what happened in classrooms. 'Tony wanted speedy results and relied on centralisation and directives,' Blunkett observed. 'As a teacher, I wanted to rely on improving teachers' skills and leadership.'

Blair's mixed messages were compounded by the fact that his two sons attended the London Oratory. In 1999, John McIntosh, the school's head teacher, asked the parents of his 1,340 pupils to donate £30 a month for the 'extras' because Blunkett had cancelled the additional money paid to schools that enjoyed grant-maintained status. Like all England's 1,198 grant-maintained schools, wrote McIntosh, the Oratory's unique achievements in music and other activities were 'in jeopardy'. Blair paid the money to solve a problem he had created. More directly, to avoid a battle with the Left, he agreed with Andrew Adonis, his education adviser, that new grant-maintained schools should be created, labelled as academies and given extra money and more independence. The Tories dismissed Adonis's 'invention' as simply a rebranding of their city technology colleges, introduced in 1988. Once again, Blair was tinkering with structures.

One day, he agreed to Blunkett's suggestion that failing schools in Bradford and Rochdale, if they were to survive, should be transferred to the private sector, and soon after agreed that the seventy-three schools branded as Education Action Zones should be abandoned as not worth saving. Despite financial support, educational standards in the EAZs had not improved and truancy remained 'disturbingly high'. EAZs were replaced by 'beacon schools' – another of Blunkett's gambits – to spread the standards of the best schools around a locality. 'Blair's taken in by Blunkett's and Barber's whacky initiatives,' complained Woodhead. 'Some men', he said, quoting Max Beerbohm, 'are born to lift heavy weights and some are born to juggle golden balls. Blunkett and Barber were born to do neither.'

The mish-mash of conflicting ideas among the five men was aggravated by two innovations. Before the election, Blair had been persuaded by Blunkett and Tessa Jowell to upgrade his interest in pre-school education. Both wanted a manifesto commitment to launch Sure Start, a plan to finance mothers to create and run groups for children from poor families. Sure Start supported their ambition to halve the number of children in poverty by 2010, so that 'everyone has an equal chance to achieve their full potential'. The civil service, they agreed, could not be trusted to pioneer the new idea. Blunkett appointed Naomi Eisenstadt, an independent expert, to establish Sure Start and summoned a conference of interested parties.

Some 250 people representing thirteen Whitehall departments, government agencies and pressure groups demanded representation to plan 'a completely new way of working'. 'I want to smell the babies,' said Jowell, hoping that mothers from poor backgrounds would flock to learn how to nurture their children. Blunkett presented the report, describing 'partnerships' and 'trail-blazing districts' to Blair, and sensed the prime minister's interest wane as he flicked through the conference's working papers. Blair was willing to announce that child poverty would end within a generation and would happily speak about stopping teenage pregnancy, but the detail was too much.

The vacuum was filled by Gordon Brown. To take control of social policy, in July 1998 the chancellor announced that the government was advancing £452 million for 250 Sure Start programmes. To Blunkett's dismay, Brown 'watered down the idea of creating child centres. It became a numbers game'. Eisenstadt gave each self-appointed group about £1 million to design a local service for children up to the age of three. In the rush to meet Brown's target of 250 groups, those who suggested trials to test how the money should be spent were ignored. By October 1999, only two groups had been created.

At that moment, Blair moved Tessa Jowell, a passionate supporter in the health department, to the Department for Education. Instead of letting her keep control of Sure Start, Blair bowed to Brown's insistence that Yvette Cooper, the new health minister, take control. To Eisenstadt's disappointment, Cooper started a tug of war. Jowell wanted to concentrate on poor children, while Cooper, on the Treasury's behalf, wanted Sure Start to provide childcare for single mothers seeking work. Jowell was sidelined, while neither Blair nor Blunkett offered to protect the original idea. 'The honeymoon is over,' Eisenstadt reflected.

Encroaching further into Blair's territory, Brown had seized upon the government's promise to increase the education of poor eighteen-to-thirty-year-olds by 50 per cent in 2010. To 'develop in everyone a life-long commitment to learning', he came up with Independent Learning Accounts. One million adults, he said, would be entitled to receive £150 in cash from the government if they subscribed to a recognised education course. He spoke about putting individuals 'in control of realising [their] potential and destiny'. With Barber's endorsement, Treasury officials were ordered to launch the scheme by September 2000 – without ever running a pilot.

Blair did not object. Uppermost in his mind was his fear of losing the next election if the public were not persuaded that Labour had delivered all-round improvements. He had two years in which to achieve good education results.

In his monthly presentations to Blair during 1999, Michael Barber presented graphs with the lines all going the right way. His delivery unit showed that the government's targets were being met. In 1998, the number of eleven-year-old children achieving level four in maths had risen by 10 per cent.

'Why haven't they gone up more?' Blunkett asked.

'They will next year,' Barber replied.

In public, Blunkett took the credit for this small success. Newspaper headlines splashed that Labour was making a difference. Seventy per cent of schools that had instantly adopted Labour's daily numeracy hour, said Blunkett, had met the target. He failed to mention that nearly all English schools had introduced the same numeracy-hour scheme in 1996, or that Barber was using the national pupil database set up by the Conservatives.

'Targets and glowing announcements,' snapped Woodhead in frustration. Blair's reliance on Barber drove him mad with rage. Barber relied only on tests. His data ignored whether the quality of teaching was improving children's education. 'Blair is gullible thinking that Barber's initiatives will make a difference,' Woodhead carped, before echoing Blunkett: 'It's like banging my head against a brick wall.' Once again, he urged Blair to challenge the unions and change the teaching profession. Once again, Blair demurred.

'We can't be in a permanent war with the teachers,' Blunkett told Blair. 'I don't want to take on each school and teacher.'

Blair feared where this was leading. 'If you go against Woodhead,' he cautioned Blunkett, 'the public won't understand. Go soft on him.'

Bichard disagreed. He disliked Woodhead's right-wing attitudes and in his annual appraisal refused to award him an 'A'. In a personal confrontation, he blamed the chief inspector for failing to improve conditions in the classroom. Woodhead angrily appealed to Blair, who refused to overrule Bichard. With Blunkett's encouragement, he began to engineer Woodhead's departure.

The argument over Woodhead's fate triggered a discussion between Blair and Bichard about the government machine. The two men had become close after Blair had closeted himself with Bichard in the Cabinet room. While ministers waited noisily in the lobby, Blair expressed his concern over Bichard's health. That genuine interest persuaded the civil servant that he might eventually be appointed as the new Cabinet secretary, tasked with resolving Blair's frustrations about the government machine. 'You missed your opportunity in 1997,' Bichard thought, 'and the "scars speech" sent mixed messages.' They could continue the conversation, he hoped, after Blair's return from Italy in September 1999.

The family holiday in a villa on the Tuscan coast attracted media criticism about the Blairs' extravagance, which saw other tourists excluded from their beach to protect the prime minister's security. Then news leaked about the refurbishment of the Downing Street bathrooms with marble. Philip Gould reported at the regular Monday-morning meeting that his focus groups had complained about the government's arrogance and about Blair's misunderstanding of their lives. Mandelson blamed Campbell's spin for ruining the message with repeated exaggeration that reflected 'the shallowness of our approach'.

To repair the damage, Blair agreed to speak to the *Observer* about the 'moral purpose' of his own life, but in the interview he admitted that he was troubled by something bigger: should the change in Britain's public services be gradual or fast and radical?

His indecision perplexed Richard Wilson. Like so many others, the more he observed the prime minister, the harder he found the task of identifying what Blair represented. Besides generalities, there was no defined objective. Unlike Thatcher's fundamental transformation of capitalism, Blairism proposed no monument other than 'reforming the public services'. By contrast, Brown's agenda was indisputable: to redistribute wealth by stealth.

At that moment, Brown was introducing the £3.6 billion New Deal to help unemployed youth into work. Although he was continuing mostly Tory programmes (including the Jobseeker's Allowance) established since the 1980s, he was flying blind by refusing once again to run a pilot scheme to test the new system. Filling the news grid with announcements caused even the most complicated measures to be rushed. To raise an extra £5 billion every year, he also abolished tax credits on dividends for pension funds. Blair called that single move 'brilliant', making Britain 'fair, modern and strong'. He did not understand how this single change would shatter Britain's enviable private pension system, with Treasury officials warning him that pension funds would lose £100 billion. Hitting the thrifty English middle classes suited Brown's redistributive agenda, despite glaring contradictions that reduced his control over Britain's fate.

The chancellor's new tax rates favoured speculators, tax-avoiders and the super-rich. Tilting to the other side, he also now opted into the EU's social chapter, agreeing to new controls on employment and increased health-and-safety rules. One unforeseen consequence was an unnoticed limitation on using the trust laws to accumulate wealth and bequeath property. As a result, British taxpayers began selling expensive property to foreigners and would gradually be less able to afford British assets in the face of competition from the oligarchs whom Brown welcomed to London. 'I wanted to preserve Thatcher's competitive tax rates,' he wrote. 'I wanted wealthy people to feel welcomed in the UK.'

Blair was unaware of the consequences of Brown's intensive financial juggling, later conceding that he regretted giving the 'damaging impression that I had vacated economic management'. His principal focus was on spreading social equality. To make Britain fairer, he defied employers' predictions of doom, imposing a statutory minimum wage and giving employees more rights when it came to holidays and maternity leave. Younger people were attracted by his promise to remove the stigma of disability, homosexuality and racial differences. Having set his staff to realise those aspirations, he now focused on his global ambitions to change the world.

ELEVEN

The War Project

The possibility of using Britain's military as a 'force for good' was raised by Michael Pakenham, the chairman of the Joint Intelligence Committee, in early 1998: 'I must tell you, Prime Minister, that there are new problems in Kosovo.'

'Right,' replied Blair. 'You'd better give me a full note, starting with: where is it?'

Pakenham described the intention of Slobodan Milošević, the Serbian president, to invade neighbouring Kosovo and expel the Muslim population. The new threat mirrored Milošević's attack on the Muslims in Bosnia seven years earlier. That war had been misjudged by John Major, who had relied on the Foreign Office's belief that the Balkans were enveloped in an old-fashioned religious dispute. Despite reports describing Serbia's army and militias murdering thousands of Muslims in ethnic cleansing reminiscent of the Nazis, Douglas Hurd, the foreign minister, had urged Washington and Paris not to intervene but instead allow 'a level killing field'. Hurd's strategy was supported by other Western governments, who, instead of stopping the atrocities, appeased the Serbs. Across the House of Commons, politicians were prejudiced and misinformed. The Labour Party, in common with Europe's left-wing politicians, supported neutrality. Those urging military intervention to stop a blatant land-grab in the wake of Yugoslavia's break-up were condemned as imperialists who were no different from the warmongers responsible for the carnage in Vietnam.

Those opinions changed after eyewitness reports of the massacres emerged. Labour supported Major's belated support for a UN peace-keeping mission and humanitarian help. The full truth dawned in July 1995. Some 8,000 Bosnian Muslims in Srebrenica were abducted by the Serbs under the eyes of Dutch soldiers attached to the UN and murdered. All European politicians were tarnished. Only America's threat to intensify its bombing of Serbia persuaded Milošević to sign a peace agreement negotiated in Dayton, Ohio. President Clinton's success embarrassed Blair, Robin Cook and others about their mistake.

Four years later, Milošević's threat to invade Kosovo convinced Blair that the Serbs might repeat the Bosnian massacres. 'We can't let it deteriorate to that,' he said, acting at that moment as the president of the European Union. With remarkable self-belief, he wanted to take control, 'convinced that he could resolve the problem'.

His resolve hardened after he delivered an agreement in Belfast on 10 April 1998, Good Friday, to start negotiations to end the civil war in Ireland and share government between Catholics and Protestants. Patient negotiations had been rewarded with international acclaim. Forging close personal relationships with all the leaders of Irish terrorism fed Blair's conviction that men of evil would succumb to his persuasion or, if necessary, be forcefully removed.

Ignoring the Foreign Office's reluctance, he flew across Europe urging other leaders to join in military action in Kosovo rather than rely on America. Most were not persuaded; even President Chirac of France, a sceptical rival, agreed only that 'something must be done'. Despite the rebuffs, Blair enjoyed the spotlight. International diplomacy was more engaging than battling to reform the public services or arguing with the chancellor. The media headlines were more flattering too, as British journalists succumbed to Campbell's image of Blair winning the argument as Europe's most popular leader. But, by the autumn, Blair acknowledged the truth: Chirac and the other Europeans were unwilling to join a military adventure involving ground troops.

Clinton, however, would consider air strikes. Blair's close relationship with the White House had been tested ever since the president faced impeachment for lying about his relationship with an intern, Monica Lewinsky. Any foreign intervention would be damned by Clinton's enemies as a deliberate diversion from his answering for his conduct. In August 1998, US bombs would be dispatched to destroy alleged al-Qaeda camps in Afghanistan and Sudan in what were called the 'Lewinsky raids'. The bombs hit a pharmaceutical factory in Sudan, but that didn't shake Blair's support for the bombing of Serbia.

The possibility of a new Balkan war arose on the eve of Operation Desert Fox, the proposed aerial bombardment by the Americans of buildings in Iraq where Saddam Hussein's scientists were suspected of developing chemical and biological weapons. 'It really is pretty scary,' said Blair, adding hawkishly, 'We can't let him get away with it.' American intelligence had reported in late 1997 that Saddam, after expelling the UN weapons inspectors, was exploiting ineffective UN sanctions to restart the development of weapons of mass destruction (WMDs) in breach of a 1991 UN resolution. Both Blair and Clinton knew that the weapons inspectors had been expelled after the Iraqis discovered they were operating as agents for the CIA, a clear breach of UN rules. Although Clinton's bombing operation had not been approved by the UN, Blair committed the RAF to the unlimited operation. He did not disguise the fact that his ultimate ambition was to overthrow Saddam.

In early February 1998, he flew to Washington. 'I can't tell you how good it is to have you guys in town right now,' Clinton told his visitor. The Lewinsky affair had ruptured his relationship with his wife Hillary. Standing near by, she was icily ignoring her husband. At their joint press conference, Blair emphatically closed down questions about the scandal, then agreed with the president that Saddam would be told 'the threat of force is real'.

Around this time, Blair had read, at the 'memory-soaked table' in Chequers, Neville Chamberlain's 1938 diaries, handwritten following his meeting with Hitler at Berchtesgaden. On his return to Britain, Chamberlain had waved a piece of paper bearing the German chancellor's signature that promised 'peace in our time'. Blair saw this as weakness: Hitler should have been confronted. In his opinion, Chamberlain had misunderstood the threat and produced the wrong answer. Less than two years later, Winston Churchill was Chequers' new occupant. The convergence of appeasement and Churchill in the same country house roused Blair. 'Having read widely, I knew a lot about history before becoming prime minister,' he would write. Blair was casting himself in Churchill's mould – the indefatigable champion against tyranny. One part of his justification at least was flawed: contrary to his assertion, he had read remarkably few works of history.

As late as 1996, Roy Jenkins, a former Labour home secretary and chancellor, had thrust upon Blair two biographies he had written about Herbert Asquith and William Gladstone, both Liberal prime ministers. Each of the books was a readable, heroic account based on secondary sources. Blair, wrote Jonathan Powell, 'devoured' Jenkins's life of Gladstone, 'on whom Tony modelled himself to some extent'. He had also read a biography of Henry Campbell-Bannerman, an unexceptional Liberal leader, and was influenced too by John Macmurray, a moral philosopher who at first sought to combine Christianity and Marxism, later shedding Marxism and politics to preach about the virtues of 'community'. Otherwise, Blair's understanding of history was unusually thin. He lacked any hinterland regarding politicians, social movements and conflicts before 1939. He was uneducated about the Reformation, the French Revolution, the eruption of European nationalism and socialism during the nineteenth century, the causes and conduct of the First and Second World Wars, and the collapse of the European empires across the Middle East and Asia after 1945. He had never read the biographies of the architects of modern Europe's fate – Napoleon, the Pitts, Bismarck, Stalin and Hitler – nor those of any American president, nor the classics relating to the machinery of government and international finance. He was even uninformed about the Labour Party's history and its leaders. Clement Attlee, Harold Wilson and Jim Callaghan were names he knew, but the details of their tribulations remained unknown to him. There wasn't one statesman he praised as an outstanding guide.

While all his predecessors had come to office with some experience of government or had read the classic textbooks at Oxford, Blair's three years at St John's College were mainly spent playing football in the quad and rock music in a hall. He was rarely seen in the library. The instinctive politician was a master of concealing his lack of education. 'I only know what I believe,' he once said. He admitted his ignorance about contemporary foreign affairs and accordingly did not understand his mistaken comparison of Chamberlain versus Hitler with himself against Saddam. Modern European history had little in common with the religious and imperial conflicts across the Muslim world.

Gladstone's attraction for Blair was his conviction that he was sent to do God's will on earth. With self-righteous indignation, Blair excluded those whose personality and recommendations conflicted with his own convictions – thus Robin Cook, who would push for diplomacy rather than bombing Iraq, was dismissed for playing 'silly buggers'. But General Charles Guthrie, a devout Catholic, was embraced as a loyalist, and beyond his trusted inner circle Blair relied on him to persuade the doubters in his government.

On 11 November 1998, Guthrie set out his estimate of the effects of a bombing campaign to the Cabinet. Britain would be responsible, he said, for about a tenth of the 2,500 deaths, especially if a tank containing anthrax exploded. If the destruction were successful, said Guthrie, Saddam would be compelled to readmit inspectors. Blair glanced around the room for any critics. Since all knew that the decision had already been taken, opposition was pointless. Blair now waited for Clinton to say 'go'.

One month later, bombing was imminent. In Cabinet, Robin Cook questioned the RAF's participation. Britain, he said, would be isolated among EU countries. Blair ignored him. A week earlier, in St Malo, Blair had signed a defence agreement with Chirac for closer co-operation between their military services. In his mind, it symbolised a new era reflecting his passion for European unity and Britain's new influence in Europe. In the future, he hoped, despite the alliance with NATO and the US, Britain would lead a European army of 60,000 troops. Although Chirac had purposefully, in the words of one eyewitness, 'overlorded' Blair during the signing ceremony, the prime minister expected the president would drop his opposition to bombing Iraq.

In the Commons, Blair went further. He was, he said, seeking ways of 'improving the possibility of removing Saddam Hussein altogether'. That first unequivocal mention of regime change was supported by Clinton's pledge of $97 million to any opposition group minded to 'topple Saddam', and then by Robin Cook speaking in a similar vein on CNN, where he explained that Saddam intended to develop WMDs. Not everyone was convinced. Writing in *The Times*, Simon Jenkins ridiculed these 'paper tiger' threats, adding that 'neither Britain nor America really minds enough about Saddam to fight him to the death'.

Britain's military machine was purring. Guthrie asked for explicit authority for the RAF to hit particular targets. Blair was visibly anxious. This was real politics without the dreary process of legislation. Nothing had prepared him for his first life-or-death opportunity to kill and change history. The Cabinet agreed to the bombing.

On 14 December 1998, Clinton ordered the B-52 bombers to fly. At the last moment, he feared domestic uproar. The impeachment hearings were imminent and a pernickety lawyer questioned whether the legality of a formal deadline had been observed. Clinton instantly terminated the mission. Then, within twenty-four hours, he reordered the bombing, but without British involvement. Blair called Guthrie for help, whom he reached while the general was driving to the opera.

'We can't let this happen,' said Blair. 'They're breaking our agreement.' Clinton, he feared, had lost faith in his ally.

'I believe I can do something, Prime Minister,' replied the general. Minutes later, he was speaking to General Hugh Shelton, America's senior military officer. The problem was solved.

Blair's admiration for Guthrie was shared by Campbell. 'I sensed him', wrote the publicity chief that night, 'as someone who was a great ally and a terrible enemy, and I liked him instinctively. You would certainly go into the jungle with him.' The bombing was delayed until 10 p.m. on 16 December. 'We act because we must,' Blair told the media as bombs fell on Baghdad. 'We had no other choice.'

He had passed a milestone. He thought about the loss of life and the danger for the pilots. 'I think if you ever lose that,' he told Campbell, 'you risk making the wrong decision and you cease to do your job properly.' That night he read the Bible.

During those tense hours, Blair called his confidants for relief. The phone rang in Peter Mandelson's office while he was speaking to officials. 'Have you taken your cough medicine and vitamins?' asked Mandelson, after noting that Blair was suffering from a cold. Mandelson's audience loved the sight of their minister enjoying such a close relationship with the prime minister.

That evening, Blair watched *Air Force One*, starring Harrison Ford. The following day, he made a statement in the Commons. His ambiguities foreshadowed his attitude towards Iraq over the following years. The RAF, he told MPs, had hit their targets, even though Guthrie had reported that the Tornadoes had missed most of theirs. Blair also spoke of 'the risks if we do not halt Saddam's programme of developing chemical and biological WMDs'. His emphasis on the word 'developing' reflected the intelligence reports' silence over whether Saddam actually possessed usable weapons. Finally, he concluded, 'It is a broad objective to remove Saddam . . . If we can find a way to remove him, we will.' Despite criticism by some Labour MPs, he had taken his first step towards regime change. Over in Washington, the Republicans decided to resume impeachment hearings.

Two days later, during the third night of bombing, David Owen was invited for dinner in Downing Street. Blair told the former Labour foreign secretary that his early nerves and insomnia had disappeared. As a result of the bombing, the Americans estimated that at least 75 per cent of Iraq's WMDs had been destroyed. The action against Saddam appeared to be justified, leaving Blair feeling relaxed. The two discussed the relationship in Iraq between the Shias, Sunnis and Kurds. Owen noted that Blair did not seem particularly knowledgeable.

In the midst of the bombing, Geoffrey Robinson's loan to Mandelson was at last exposed and was followed by their resignations. On Christmas Eve, Mandelson was invited to Chequers. Blair was adept at separating business and friendship, and he encouraged Mandelson to feel undamaged, although the resignation had strained relations among Blair's team. Cherie's jealousy over Anji Hunter's importance was unabated. Once again, she had burst into Blair's office while the two were speaking and demanded, 'When are you leaving?' Hunter said nothing, and later Cherie attacked her husband for ignoring her feelings. Blair retorted that she was ridiculous and could damage the government; she would have to accept that Hunter was staying.

Soon after Christmas, Blair received verified reports that the Serbian army was murdering Kosovans. 'I saw it essentially as a moral issue,' he would write, one that had to be resolved by the military. 'God, had we learned nothing from Europe's history? It was shocking.' More shocking still was the absence of similar outrage in Paris or Berlin. Both governments resisted involvement and were prepared, Blair believed, to 'abandon the people'.

The fate of the Balkans was irrelevant to Britain's national interest, but being a 'force for good' had been conceived by Blair for precisely these circumstances. 'This is something Britain should be doing,' he said. The bombing of Iraq had reinforced his self-confidence.

The traditional format for government meetings to consider major military interventions, honed over previous centuries, would have triggered a cast of ministers and officials to gather in the Cabinet room, each having read thick files outlining the background and options. The discussion of the Overseas Policy and Defence Committee would have been minuted and available for posterity. Blair disliked that formality, not least because he wanted to exclude Gordon Brown. Powell and not the Cabinet secretary was told to organise an informal conversation in Blair's new, larger office, or 'the den'. In that ambience, any official record of the discussion was intentionally limited.

The scene for the arriving military and intelligence officials was unusual. 'Jonathan Powell', noticed Guthrie, 'was sitting at a desk outside Blair's office like a dog in a basket. He was no more a chief of staff than a monkey. We all knew by then that he couldn't co-ordinate government affairs.' If only, he thought, Blair had retained someone like General Hastings Ismay, Churchill's invaluable wartime assistant. But mentioning Ismay would have confounded Blair.

Inside the room, seated on chairs or perched on a sofa were David Manning, a solid foreign-affairs expert who had been ambassador in Warsaw, New Delhi, Paris and Moscow before returning to London; defence minister George Robertson, who smiled a lot but would say little; John Kerr, the unremarkable head of the depleted British foreign service, who had given up arguing with Cook; John Sawers, the prime minister's new gung-ho foreign-affairs adviser, who had recently returned from the British embassy in Washington; and Robin Cook, whose manner sapped Blair's patience, not least because he often telephoned Robertson before meetings to alleviate his indecision. Finally, lurking at the back, stood Alastair Campbell, firing himself up for another self-declared war against the media to 'show who was boss'.

The focus was on Guthrie. Sending the military on a moral mission to the Balkans made him cautious. 'I'm dead against bombing,' he said. 'With bombing, you're bound to make mistakes and risk alienating the local people. We must have a Plan B to move in on the ground.' He was also wary of Kosovo's mountainous terrain, the poor roads and the warring nationalities. 'The army', he explained, 'is overstretched for a sustained commitment.' The Americans, he added, opposed sending troops into an inhospitable environment.

By the end of an hour, some were unsure whether Blair had grasped all the problems, but he directed the army and intelligence agencies to check the environment around Kosovo, while the Foreign Office and Blair's personal team negotiated with Paris, Berlin and Washington to agree on a plan to compel Milošević to withdraw. Afterwards, he agreed that he was obliged to consult the Cabinet for an engagement that would cost hundreds of millions of pounds.

When the politicians assembled again in the Cabinet room, the scene was surreal. Gordon Brown, finally present, was noisily scrawling huge black letters across endless pages, interrupted only by his murmuring, 'I don't agree'; John Prescott, mispronouncing Milošević, 'blathered rubbish'; Cook spoke portentously about morality; Robertson went on at length but pointlessly; while Clare Short repeated, 'Tony, it's more dangerous than you realise.' Blair smiled, concealing his dislike of this perpetual irritant. Short was tolerated in the Cabinet so that he could preserve his relationship with Labour supporters around Birmingham. He allowed everyone to speak without interruption, limiting his own contribution to platitudes. As soon as the meeting was over, he expected Cook and Short to telephone their media friends, and he was keen to keep any reports about his 'minority view' from those he did not trust. But it was obvious to some that 'Cook clearly wanted to nail the bogeyman'.

The reports of Serb savagery preoccupied Blair, but finding allies was difficult. Despite the St Malo agreement, Chirac was still unwilling to commit to a war (Blair did not understand Chirac's warning that Milošević's fate would be decided in Moscow), while attempts to secure German chancellor Gerhard Schröder's agreement would climax in an argument, with Blair sighing, 'I thought he was going to hit me.' Getting Clinton's approval in the middle of his impeachment hearings was fraught, not least because the president recalled John Major's vehement resistance to bombing. But without Washington signing on, Blair had discovered, Britain's army could do little.

Then Clinton relented, and on 24 March the first American bombs fell on Serbia. Five hundred bombers had been committed to the battle, plus a naval war group armed with missiles. The transformation of Michael Foot's pacifist Labour movement into a Labour government launching an aggressive campaign shocked many. In *The Times*, under the headline 'The Real Catastrophe', Simon Jenkins warned: 'No amount of NATO bombing will make Milošević see sense in Kosovo.' Sending in the bombers, he wrote, was 'madness posing as morality . . . what is inconceivable is that the Serb leader will suddenly withdraw'. The criticism attracted support across the country.

At the end of that first day's operations, Blair descended three floors below Whitehall for a briefing in the MoD's Crisis Management Centre. In the sterile atmosphere, he learned that the RAF's Harriers had all missed their targets, while a missile fired by a British submarine had nearly sunk a French frigate. His questions were 'bright and sharp', thought Guthrie, but the replies were discouraging. Bad weather was hampering the bombing and more refugees were flooding into neighbouring Macedonia.

The negative report hit Blair's self-confidence. He was due to appear on television to broadcast a success story that would win public support. Since the final bombing reports were not ready, he was given estimates.

'Is that OK?' he asked an official about his script.

'No,' he was told, 'you've exaggerated everything I've said.' A few words were altered.

His return to Downing Street from the depths of Whitehall sparked a sense of unreality. The contrast of switching from bombing missions in Serbia to half-heartedly seeking to resolve Donald Dewar's mismanagement of Scottish devolution, the EU's shrill demand to reduce Britain's rebate and the quicksands of negotiating peace in Ulster, combined with Brown's refusal to discuss the Budget, was an awkward precursor to more bad news.

Two weeks after the bombing started, the RAF was still missing its targets, NATO headquarters was mired in bureaucratic mayhem, the refugees' plight was dire and, instead of surrendering, Milošević was more resolute than ever. To compound these setbacks, Blair was uncertain about the proper response to the British public's 'pathetic' disengagement from the 'monstrous and unpardonable outrage' of human misery.

He was equally upset about the continuing media criticism. Favourable publicity was his lifeblood. He needed instant results and, unused to the fluctuations of war, despaired about success after reading reports of Belgrade in flames and high civilian casualties. 'This is not moral,' wrote a newspaper columnist, 'it is megalomaniac.'

'This could be the end of me,' Blair sighed.

'If we ran our election campaigns the same way NATO do their press,' he told Clinton, 'we would not have been elected.' Alastair Campbell was sent to Brussels to deploy his wiles. In his instructions to NATO's spokesman, Jamie Shea, he described how to manipulate the media. 'Your job', he told Shea, 'is not to help the reporters. We decide what the news is. If you don't like the news, put something else in the news. If there's a hole, fill it. It's an open goal to fill, otherwise you're at the media's mercy. It's your fault if the media reports are bad.'

Blair's distress about bad publicity was compounded by the continuing deaths of refugees. Milošević, he believed, would surrender only if he feared an invasion by allied troops, but NATO's nineteen governments were divided, disorganised and resistant. Even Clinton, a man struggling for his own survival, opposed the threat to send troops. Controlling foreign adventures, Blair discovered, was as difficult as modernising Britain's public services.

To satisfy the prime minister's ambitions, Guthrie stuck a map above a fireplace in Downing Street. With his leader's rapt attention, the general described a plan to expel the Serbs from Kosovo that would require 150,000 troops – 50,000 Britons and 100,000 Americans. The army's size surprised Blair. Fighting in the mountains, said the general, was a risk. There was also a procedural obstacle: 'If there's no legal justification for war,' Guthrie had told Robertson, 'the British military will not get involved.'

Blair was told by Edgar Buckley, a senior policy adviser in the MoD, that intervention without a UN resolution would be illegal. 'I'm not interested in your analysis unless I can change the premise,' replied Blair. 'There are many views on international law and we'll ask when it is necessary.' The following day, an American pilot mistakenly bombed a convoy of fleeing refugees, killing at least seventy-two people.

Guthrie was told to prepare for the invasion, while Blair took it upon himself to persuade Clinton. First, he planned to shuttle around Europe to galvanise NATO's leaders. 'We are going for broke,' he told Campbell. He would risk his government's survival by intensifying the war, but he would not risk discussing his options with his ministers. Without Robertson's knowledge, MoD officials were summoned to Downing Street. During one meeting, he used Cook's unexpected dash for the lavatory to take a decision he knew the foreign secretary would oppose.

Both Robertson and Cook were left in London when Blair flew with Campbell, Powell and Guthrie to Washington on 21 April. 'If we don't win this,' Blair said, 'it's curtains for the government.' His melodramatic prediction reflected his fear of losing face among his confidants, humiliation by Milošević and, worst of all, souring his relationship with Clinton.

While driving to the White House with Guthrie and Sawers, Blair rehearsed his arguments about tipping the odds to guarantee success. 'We cannot afford to lose,' he repeated. 'We must do whatever we have to do to win.' After greeting Clinton, he sensed an unexpectedly embittered mood. None of the three had appreciated how America's fatal involvement in Somalia in the early 1990s had created a reluctance to fight for liberal ideals rather than exclusively in the nation's defence. Campbell's earlier depiction to American journalists of Blair's flight across the Atlantic to 'stiffen Clinton's resolve' in the midst of the impeachment battle had angered the president.

In those circumstances, Blair's performance was unimpressive. The moment Clinton challenged that bombing would be enough, Blair backed off. 'Blair at his worst,' thought Guthrie. 'He's mesmerised by the Americans. He's caved in.'

During the drive back, Blair was downcast. 'I'm deeply disappointed by how you folded over with Clinton,' said Guthrie.

'Oh well, it's politics,' replied Blair. Later, he admitted to Campbell, 'I think I failed in my mission tonight. I am starting to panic.'

Hours later, Blair's mood changed. Clinton's negativity was derided by Republican politicians, who praised Blair's championing of humanity. In the capital's piranha bowl, Clinton's critics snatched any opportunity to embarrass their prey.

Even Blair forgot his loyalty to the president during his flight from Washington to Chicago. He arrived at a packed hotel ballroom to address a Republican group with a speech drafted by Professor Lawrence Freedman, a London academic who specialised in war studies. Freedman had provided the arguments to justify removing Milošević by force. In finalising his doctrine of liberal intervention, Blair did not consult the civil servants in Whitehall. They would read the revised meaning of 'force for good' in their newspapers. Idealist or Superman, Blair would invoke the authority of a power greater than a mere politician, one who knew the ideal outcome for the world better than mortals.

Speaking to big audiences energised him. In preparation, he found Gladstone to be his ideal model, a principled politician who irrevocably defined an era. In particular, Blair was attracted to Gladstone's campaigning speeches in 1876, which damned the Turks for committing widespread atrocities in Bulgaria. Gladstone's outrage, so similar to his own about the slaughter in Kosovo, had won over Britain's electorate. Blair hoped Chicago would similarly mark the beginning of a new age.

His conservative audience echoed his strengths. An articulate, handsome Englishman passionately describing the 'unspeakable things happening in Europe – ethnic cleansing, systematic rape, mass murder' – touched many in the fevered auditorium whose forefathers had fled to America to avoid similar suffering. Appeasement, exhorted Blair, did not work – not only with Milošević, but also with Saddam Hussein. Thunderous applause interrupted his plea for global co-operation against 'an evil dictator' who could not be allowed to 'range unchallenged'. For the British diplomats accompanying Blair, the contrast between the star lapping up the audience's chant of 'Blair for president' and his timid performance the previous day in the White House was 'astonishing'.

There was also incredulity at his naivety. Alarmed by the rise of Islamic extremism, Blair had searched the Koran for passages distinguishing moderate from extreme Islam. His argument exposed a misunderstanding. Modern Islam, unlike Christianity or Judaism, was morphing once again from a suppressed secular religion into an international political movement reminiscent of Soviet communism. Islam was not reinforced by history books and academic studies because until recently many Muslims had been illiterate; nor did it tolerate critical discussion. Believers believed, full stop. Blair's audience did not grasp his misunderstanding. Instead, they rose to his emotional appeal for armies of morality to intervene against evil regimes across the globe. 'This is the moment to seize,' he cried. 'The kaleidoscope has been shaken. The pieces are in flux. Soon they will settle again. Before they do, let us reorder the world around us.'

Labour's leader attracted some unusual admirers. 'The most eloquent leader in the Western world,' gushed Senator Jesse Helms, a veteran of America's unyielding conservatives.

The American media's reports about Blair's 'Churchillian tone' and his simplification of the Balkan crisis irked White House aides. Blair was mocked for 'overdoing it' and 'sprinkling too much adrenalin on his cornflakes'. Guthrie provided the antidote. Other Americans, said the general on the eve of the next day's NATO summit in Washington, were critical of Clinton. Emboldened by his popularity, Blair privately pressed the president to commit troops. Clinton declined frostily.

At least ten people had just died after a NATO missile hit Belgrade's TV centre. Blair justified the attack as hitting Milošević's 'apparatus to do the ethnic cleansing in Kosovo'. Three days later, Jill Dando, a well-known BBC presenter, was shot dead in front of her house in London. Some speculated wildly that she was the target of a Serb. Blair returned home on the same day with a reputation as a hawk among NATO's leaders, behaving as if Britain possessed the military capability to win single-handedly.

To maintain the momentum, on 3 May Blair flew to visit General Mike Jackson, a former paratroop commander, at his headquarters in Macedonia. Kosovan refugees were streaming into the nearby Stanković

camp. For ninety minutes, watched by a group of accompanying journalists, Blair sat under a camouflage net with Jackson and Guthrie,
discussing the options. Both reassured Blair of their support because
Kosovo was 'a messy business'. An invasion by 150,000 troops, they
explained, would require two months to prepare, and it would take at
least another month for the troops to arrive in Belgrade. 'Worst-case
scenario', said Jackson, who had never fought in a war, 'would be several
hundred British dead.' Blair was given a deadline: the invasion would
need to be completed before November. His fear, he confided, was TV
pictures of corpses and defeat if Milošević were not persuaded to resign
before the winter. Having mutually seduced each other, the discussion
ended with more questions than answers, not least Blair's refusal to
consult the attorney general about the legality of an invasion. Instead,
he relied on Charlie Falconer's unscripted advice that a sovereign state
could be invaded to avert a humanitarian catastrophe.

On the second anniversary of his election, he had every reason to
fear the worst. Labour MPs resented the war, and even William Rees-
Mogg, the right-wing columnist who up until then had supported the
operation, turned against 'NATO's arrogant, ill-judged Balkan campaign [which] has produced a disaster'. Repeating the familiar criticism, the former *Times* editor damned the belief that bombing could
produce peace.

That same morning, Blair, together with Cherie, visited the Brazde
refugee camp ten miles from Kosovo for TV pictures aimed at Clinton.
The bombing had aggravated the 29,000 inhabitants' plight. 'Tony,
Tony,' chanted the crowds of Kosovans. Cherie burst into tears and
Blair's voice cracked as he told the destitute hordes, 'This is a battle for
humanity. The butchers of Belgrade will be defeated.' He promised that
more refugees would be allowed to enter Britain.

At the next Cabinet meeting, Blair's declaration about 'the right
thing to do' recruited few allies. Cook was a snake murmuring that
Blair wanted to 'fix the world rather than running Britain'. Brown mentioned the combined cost of the bombing and help for the refugees as

a reason for the Treasury's kitty being empty. Other ministers offered little support for Blair and, compounding the difficulty, eighty Labour MPs intended to defy the whips and vote against the government on a welfare reform bill.

Blair was dismissive. Most of his Cabinet ministers were disagreeable, and at the end of the day all of them would obey him. His anger was directed at his supposed foreign allies who resisted his exhortations. The bad news didn't let up: allied bombs were killing innocent civilians and also hit the Chinese embassy in Belgrade, while their foe appeared unbeatable. Clinton was plainly antagonistic and, on 13 May, finally exploded in 'real, red-hot anger' during a one-hour telephone call. He rejected Blair's protestations of ignorance that Campbell was 'deliberately briefing' the *Wall Street Journal* to build up Blair at his expense. Campbell, Blair later admitted, was 'exposed . . . and we had to fly by the seat of our pants' to avoid irreparable damage to the relationship. Yet finally, on 26 May, Clinton announced that 90,000 American troops would be sent to Kosovo. Blair claimed the credit for the switch.

Over the following five days, there were intense conversations between Washington and Moscow. At the top, Clinton persuaded President Yeltsin that the threat of invasion was real but that Russia's involvement in peace negotiations would avert the danger. At the ambassadorial level, American and Russian diplomats agreed that Russian troops could participate in a multinational peacekeeping force to protect Milošević. At the end of the dialogue, under Russian pressure and with bombs thought to have been dropped by the Americans obliterating a Serb battalion, Milošević hinted that he might withdraw from Kosovo. Blair was excluded from the negotiations.

On 3 June, after seventy-two days of bombing, Blair heard about the Serb surrender from Campbell, who had learned the facts from a Reuters newsflash. Milošević had agreed to pull back. British and allied soldiers were readied to move into Kosovo without the risk of Serb opposition. Taking the media by surprise, Campbell commandeered the headlines. Blair's 'resolve and determination' were credited for the victory. Elsewhere, his critics were unwilling to be as generous. The bombing, wrote Simon Jenkins, 'did not bring about yesterday's deal'; he doubted that Milošević would be prosecuted as a war criminal, and he anticipated a third Kosovan war. Others were more self-critical. 'It was a gamble,' wrote Matthew Parris. 'We peaceniks should grit our teeth and admit: it paid off.' But he feared future jingoistic wars in pursuit of the 'Blair doctrine'. 'So much is still hazy,' he wrote, listing many countries that could be the target of Pax Americana. Iraq was not on the list.

Blair adopted Campbell's propaganda as the truth. Presidents, he told audiences, needed his advice, and needed him as the bridge between America and Europe. Non-intervention, he went on, would have led to 'unforeseeable' consequences.

After the eulogies faded, Blair told Robertson and Guthrie, 'I want a small team to review the lessons to be learned.' A post-mortem, he implied, would prevent mistakes in the future. Out of Blair's and the military's self-interest, no report was produced, although estimates of the war's cost ranged from £1 billion to £10 billion.

Unlike the rejoicing in Downing Street, the end of the bombing was a reality check for the MoD. Kosovo, agreed the military chiefs, was not a military victory but, as General Jackson would concede, 'a procedural drive-in' by the armed forces that was unopposed by the Serbs. No VCs were won because, as Guthrie said, 'Milošević caved'. No one on that side of Whitehall disputed Blair's doctrine of liberal intervention or mentioned that Kosovo was an American, not a British, victory.

One week after the Serb surrender, the British did at last have the chance to shine. Unexpectedly, General Jackson found himself competing with a Russian brigade for the occupation of Priština airport. On the insistence of General Shelton in Washington, Jackson ignored orders from NATO headquarters to deploy British troops and directly confront the Russians to prevent their presence in the airport. Instead, he held back while the Russians advanced. Downing Street propaganda portrayed the general as a hero for preventing a third world war.

Less dramatic but more serious was the British occupation of Priština itself. Eight hundred and fifty British troops commanded by Colonel Paul Gibson had entered the town as peacekeepers. The Serb army had withdrawn before the deadline. As the standard-bearer of the 'force for good', Gibson was ordered to unify everyone in the city within a multinational authority. With 'God on our side', Gibson exhorted his soldiers, 'your duty is to protect the Albanian good guys from the murdering Serbs'. By July, the town was peaceful for Blair's visit. He was lionised by the huge crowds as a hero. Streets had been renamed after him. Basking in the cheers, Blair had good reason to believe that by keeping his nerve he had saved the population from genocide. He had taken a gamble and won.

Days after his visit, Albanian thugs began murdering Serbs. The lawlessness, Gibson would write at the end of his tour, was the British military's fault. Their intelligence was wrong, the rules of engagement never arrived and the right questions about the political plan for Kosovo's future were not asked. Like all military post-mortems, Gibson's indictment was sanitised as it moved up the chain, and his review became meaningless. Blair's halo remained undimmed.

Blair believed he had discovered new qualities within himself. He had been right about so much. 'The Kosovo conflict', he wrote, 'taught me many things, about government, about leadership, about myself . . . It also completely changed my own attitude to foreign policy.' He had, he believed, understood diplomacy and the importance of Britain's alliance with America, and was confident that in the future his skills would carry him to even greater success. Andrew Turnbull, the Treasury's permanent secretary, would date that moment as the birth of Blair's Messiah complex: 'He is into saving the world from evil.' Others would say that he had become addicted to a life-or-death gamble to get away with more and to change history. One lesson he rejected was that military power alone rarely solved political problems. He drew the opposite conclusion.

TWELVE

A Demon to Slaughter

The black-and-white outcome of warfare fed Blair's exasperation about modernising Britain. Compared to Charles Guthrie, the civilians were not delivering results. The civil service, he decided, would not count among his allies. 'TB seemed lost at the moment,' noted Campbell on Blair's return from his summer holiday. Blair admitted a lack of self-confidence. The desultory Monday-morning meetings mirrored his forlorn search for a silver bullet. Beyond Westminster, resentment festered about 'spin', Brown's double and triple counting, the 'scars' speech and a prime minister surrounded by on-message ultra-loyalists who lacked authenticity.

Blair's conversations aggravated the despondency. 'I don't want to take on the civil service,' he told Charles Clarke, who had been promoted to the Home Office. 'I don't think it's worth the effort. I'm not going through the battle of getting rid of that kind.'

'That's a terrible mistake,' replied Clarke.

Rather than reform Whitehall, Blair's substitute ploy was to express his anger at the annual Labour Party conference. He wanted to rebut the Tory complaint that he lacked beliefs. His speech's theme would repeat New Labour's promise of 'giving everyone the chance to fulfil their true potential'. To prove his commitment to that promise he would identify those to blame for the obstruction.

Chequers was his ideal place to formalise his thoughts. Sitting in the September sun and served by Wrens, he struggled to find different words for the same theme: building a fairer, modernised Britain based on New Labour's values. His problem was the absence of an ideology. New Labour's 'triangulation' – taking the best and denigrating the worst of competing philosophies – had disarmed the Tories and the hard Left but provided no answer to his perpetual quandary: how should he change Britain? Labour had adopted the Tories' ideas to give more freedom to banks and businessmen. Further, thanks to John Major's Lottery, the party could finance the growth of British culture and sport, while Labour activists were enacting laws to enhance minority rights. But reform of the public services – health, education and welfare – remained stymied. Although he had no road map to help him reach his destination, Blair knew he needed a big catchphrase for the media headlines – what Mandelson called a 'washing line' on which to hang memorable slogans.

In anticipation of meeting Blair at Chequers, Philip Gould, Peter Mandelson, Alastair Campbell and David Miliband discussed his forthcoming speech in a conference call.

'People don't have a clear sense of Tony's direction,' said Gould. 'We have a huge majority yet we appear to be struggling to make change happen quickly. We're drifting.'

Campbell agreed: 'The media are not as excited about Tony any more. They think Tony is losing his bearings.'

Another voice added, 'Tony has lost his radical cutting edge.'

'How can we make Tony sound radical?' asked Campbell.

Having promised to rebuild the world, they were failing, and they needed a scapegoat. The agonising ended when the discussion finally produced the answer: Blair should attack 'the forces of conservatism'. No one, Mandelson admitted later, could identify the 'forces', and Campbell would agree that '"forces of conservatism" was the right concept but the wrong language'. The best justification for New Labour as the answer to Britain's problems would come by creating a demon to slaughter.

By the time Blair's team met at Chequers, the 'forces of conservatism' had been identified as cynics, elites, the Establishment and unscrupulous vested interests. Like any tabloid journalist, his speechwriter Peter Hyman had overbilled a shallow headline. Adapting well-worn socialist clichés, he offered a draft full of colourful phrases. Plucking at those, Blair wrote in longhand, 'Power, wealth and opportunity should go to the many and not just the few.' He promised to lead those 'who have the courage to change' against 'the forces of conservatism [who] have to be taken on and defeated'.

Blessed with a theme, he repeatedly revised the speech, crafting the image of a leader articulating the people's courageous insistence that a 'progressive' movement – 'the patriotic party' – would sweep away discredited conservatism and give the people liberty. The result, he promised, would be 'a new Britain of true equality . . . free from the closed doors of snobbery and prejudice'. The casualties would be the 'old elites [who] held people back. They kept people down. They stunted people's potential. Year after year, decade after decade . . . [they] chain us to an outdated view of our people's potential.' He pledged to end the class war, make the Tories redundant and lead a government of national unity. The result would be a community working together in a fair society. Individuals would have a 'responsibility' to work but could depend on the state to provide welfare.

Unexpectedly, when he arrived at the conference in Bournemouth his theme was illustrated by a group in favour of fox-hunting who were protesting outside the building against the government's proposed ban. They were excluded from New Labour's tolerant culture. While Blair, in his hotel suite, continued to refine phrases about 'enabling' a citizen's self-fulfilment and rejecting Whitehall's bureaucracy, his ministers were promising delegates endless directives from a centralising government. Throughout the four days of the conference, Blair was darting in and out of lunches, £350-a-plate dinners, and receptions organised by Lord Levy and the party's fund-raisers to tap rich bankers, hedge-fund managers and property developers. Using what he called 'my Rolodex memory', Blair could summon the perfect questions and comments for conversations with miners or multimillionaires.

Thanks to Brown, the managers of the investment companies at the conference would be paying less tax than their cleaners. Those trim, well-dressed chief executives, each personally worth tens of millions of pounds, intrigued Blair. The wealthy and their ostentatious lifestyles would evoke his refrain about whether his mistake was to have headed for Westminster rather than the City. 'I love aspiration,' he would say. 'I adore the notion of coming from nothing and making something of yourself.' At a rich men's jamboree in Davos some years later, he would sit next to Bill Gates and confess, 'Coming here reminds me of what a bad career choice I made earlier in my life.' During private dinners, many fat cats – including George Soros, the speculator, and Matthew Harding, the mercurial businessman – had answered his questions as he sought to understand the source of their fortunes. He invariably came away bewildered at how men who apparently lacked exceptional intelligence could create such huge personal wealth. At the end of his premiership, he promised himself, he would not return to a house in Islington burdened with a high mortgage.

To the party faithful, the money-makers counted among those damned by Blair for hiding behind the 'closed doors of snobbery and prejudice'. But he was comfortable circulating among the rich and took an interest in his patronage. Labour loyalists, he ensured, emerged with titles befitting their friendship and finances. In Blair's vision, those were proper rewards for contributing to 'modernisation'.

Three months before the coronation of 'Cool Britannia' at the Millennium Dome, Blair seemed determined to label anything that had existed before the victory in 1997 as redundant. He snatched at the phrase 'We live in a new age but in an old country' to win applause.

Spouting slogans to the party faithful was easy; explaining the message was not. Just twenty-four hours before delivering the speech, Blair became flummoxed. 'What's the argument?' he asked his team. They were not surprised. Moments of panic always preceded his most effective speeches; his crisis of confidence would produce the performance. But on this occasion he was struggling more than usual. Conquering the old elite was the easy bit, but what followed? New Labour was not promising to liberate the downtrodden masses, nor had it pledged to redistribute landowners' wealth to the workers. Blair was modernising, not subverting.

Delegates had been passing the noisy pro-hunting demonstrators as they entered the packed auditorium in Bournemouth. Blair's own opinion about hunting was uncertain. He gave the impression that he wanted to avoid both fighting the Labour Party and annoying Middle England. The masquerade was irrelevant to his audience.

Soon it was time for him to take to the podium. Those watching him pace in the gloom behind the stage, his face contorted and his hands clenched, feared disaster. But as the music signalled his entrance into the spotlight, they witnessed a transformation. Within seconds, the crumpled wreck metamorphosed into a colossus. The actor smoothed over the inevitable imperfections of his speech with a wondrously theatrical presentation. He loved the sound of his own voice. He had a deft line to soothe the activists: 'Realism and idealism at last in harmony.' Wild cheers greeted his attack on the 'forces of conservatism', a phrase repeated seventeen times. The delegates assumed his target was the hunting lobby and the Conservatives, but in reality he meant anyone who opposed his ideas, including old-fashioned supporters of Scottish independence and the defenders of the NHS's dreaded internal market.

Afterwards, Matthew Taylor, the director of a left-wing think tank, wrote that the speech was a 'turning point' that 'goes to the heart of New Labour's diagnosis of the country's ills'. Noting Blair's enjoyment of manipulating his audience, Richard Wilson observed 'the cold eyes behind the chummy exterior', while his ministers seated beneath him in the hall were bemused by the meaninglessness of 'setting our people free' and his commitment to lead Britain towards 'national salvation'. Some thought his target was the trade unions.

'I don't understand "forces of conservatism",' Brown told him later.

'It defines us against the Tories,' Blair replied. 'Reformers against extremists.'

'Not great,' said Mandelson.

Blair shrugged off the criticism and told another critic, 'I have re-defined The Project.'

'It's government by assertion,' concluded Tom McNulty, the Labour MP, 'and hope that the facts will catch up. Then hope it works.'

In the aftermath, Gould admitted, the 'cynicism was dreadful beyond belief'. Newspaper headlines included 'Mad King Tony', 'The Cult of Blair' and 'This Man Is Dangerous', but the public loved it and Labour's lead in the polls rose to 27 per cent.

To relieve the Tories' dismay, their new leader William Hague fer-ociously attacked Blair's sanctimony at his own party conference the following week. The Labour leader was ridiculed as the public-school barrister from Islington who, despite a Commons majority of nearly 200, was admitting to being powerless to usurp the so-called Establishment that was holding the country back. 'Tony Blair', mocked Hague, 'thinks he's a Napoleon Bonaparte figure who's taken near total control of the levers of political power.' Listing all the contradictions uttered by 'the man [who] is a fraud' and the author of 'the Great Labour Lie', Hague attacked him as the leader of 'vindictive, mean-spirited, class-obsessed' activists who were 'a bunch of hypocrites'. To laughter, he contrasted the Labour Party magazine's description of 'Tony's favourite food' as fish and chips, which he bought as 'a takeaway from his local chippie', with what Blair had told *The Islington Cook Book*, a constituency publica-tion, was his preferred meal: 'fresh fettuccini garnished with an exotic sauce of olive oil, sun-dried tomatoes and capers'.

Blair ignored Hague's brickbats. His nervous dislike of his own party was reflected by his agent's advice on his first visit to a working-men's club: 'Don't ask for Perrier.' But the party's rapturous response had restored his self-confidence and, since the Tory corpse was heading fur-ther to the right, as reported by Gould, he could tell his colleagues that the Conservatives were no longer an electoral threat.

Privately, however, Blair knew that Hague's speech had exposed his limitations, and he feared that his ministers were insufficiently courageous to overcome Whitehall's neoliths. Beyond the core of his team, he lamented, few genuinely understood how New Labour's success depended upon slaughtering those 'sinecure cynics who despise anything modern and are made uneasy by success'. New Labour making good on its promises depended on his own relentless willpower.

The Dome in Greenwich, where the arrival of the new millennium would be celebrated, reflected those weaknesses. There was no reason why Blair's ambition for the Dome to project Britain as young, confident, relaxed, dynamic and diverse should not have been realisable after the Cabinet had agreed, in June 1997, to continue with the project inherited from the Tories. With two and a half years before its opening, there was sufficient time to hire Disney's expertise and prepare an entertaining show that, predicted Mandelson, the then minister for the Dome, will 'make a powerful statement to the world about Britain's new-found pride and self-confidence'. The only necessity was appointing a creative manager. Selecting the right person for any task ranked high among Blair's weaknesses, and instead of luring a Disney executive, he chose Jennie Page, a callow bureaucrat. The result would be a financial and cultural disaster. The estimated cost was heading towards £828 million, double the original budget. If New Labour's 'modernisers' could not even produce Disney-by-the-Thames, how could they transform Britain's public services, which were already consuming nearly 35 per cent of the nation's revenues?

THIRTEEN

Saving the NHS

Blair would write that his conference speech of 1999 reflected his anger at the entrenched interests within the NHS and its trade unions. In hindsight, he blamed the NHS managers who supported Labour for preventing change. That could not have been true. At the time, he offered no radical plan to reform the health service, instead repeatedly urging his inner circle, 'We need a strategy.' Civil servants were asked to produce a solution for a politician searching for a spiritual identity. They duly examined Blair's speech for clues. Replacing 'conservatism' with 'modernisation', they decided, was not a policy.

With Blair's support, Frank Dobson had repudiated the Tory reforms, issued commands and waited for the extra billions of pounds to save the NHS. 'We will run from the centre and govern from the centre,' Blair had often said, but he also complained that his message about 'change' was failing. The NHS, he acknowledged, was 'underfunded, under pressure and unappreciated' – and was not delivering. A Mori poll showed that public satisfaction with the NHS had fallen from 72 to 58 per cent during the previous year. Blair was baffled.

He had inserted into his conference speech 'the dreaded internal market' would be 'banished for good', words that Dobson had applauded. Blair knew that this wasn't true, but with similar hyperbole he had also promised his audience that his plan to improve cancer treatment would save not 60,000 but 100,000 lives. Winter would test his veracity.

To find a solution, he engaged in circular conversations with health experts, always starting with the same two problems: Dobson had not yet saved the NHS; and money was not proving to be a quick fix. Some visitors told him that effective reform depended on breaking down vested interests and ending centralised control. Blair's charm convinced them that their arguments had made an impression. They were mistaken. George Alberti, the respected president of the Royal College of Physicians, was taken by Blair's manner but understood the reality after advising Blair that ineffective A&E departments should be closed.

'You can't close A&Es,' protested Robert Hill, Blair's special adviser. 'They are in today's towns what churches were in the nineteenth century.'

'Treating a hospital as an icon', replied Alberti, 'is not an excuse for unsafe care.' Hill, he concluded, was 'a bit thick. Not up to standard.'

Blair confessed some doubts. 'We were wrong to end GP fund-holding, weren't we?' he asked Alan Langlands.

'Yes,' the chief executive agreed.

Not mentioned was Blair's impatience with Dobson. In reality, both men were floundering. Neither understood that officials were unable to solve a crisis perpetuated by politicians.

Circumstances altered Blair's assumption that Dobson should remain responsible for the NHS. There was no intention to remove the minister, but the left-winger Ken Livingstone unexpectedly threatened, despite Blair's efforts, to stand as Labour's candidate in London's first mayoral election, a successful Blairite innovation. In the prime minister's opinion, the party's only suitable contender was Dobson, a London MP, although, as the candidate improbably recalled, 'It wasn't significant for Blair whether I stood or not.' The health minister volunteered to take the risk in exchange for Blair's assurance of a return to the Cabinet if he were defeated.

Dobson was replaced by Alan Milburn, who in late 1998 had been moved from health to the Treasury.

'Put your foot on the accelerator,' Gordon Brown advised.

'We need to modernise,' Blair told him.

'Yes, Tony,' replied Milburn, who would recall, 'I returned to find a burning platform, which was a blessing rather than a curse.'

Waiting lists had not been cut but instead had increased by 150,000. The waiting time for heart and hip operations was still two years. Over the previous three years, despite Brown's freeze, spending on the NHS had increased annually by about 3 per cent, yet only 2 per cent more patients were being treated. One explanation was that since 1997 the service had recruited more administrators than nurses.

'The NHS has imploded,' Milburn told Blair soon after his move. 'The situation is grave, especially for Labour.'

Blair summoned the department's senior civil servants to ask why the party's assumption that it would deliver remarkable achievements had not materialised. The NHS, he suggested, not for the first time, required a new plan. 'The 1997 White Paper', he told the officials, 'is unfinished business.' They in turn silently registered that the White Paper was now discredited. Few dared to volunteer the full truth. Health care was a Byzantine jigsaw without straightforward solutions. Pushing one button caused unexpected repercussions, and the complexity was increasing. Blair wanted 'modernisation', the officials understood, but he failed to grasp that managing change required special skills.

While academics were ripping apart research into the past and proposals for the future, Blair's refusal to consider any departure from Dobson's orthodoxy, especially Labour's partisan opposition to 'choice', presented an unusual log jam.

'Right, we're going to sort this out,' he said, believing that words themselves would guarantee delivery. He still expected extra money to resolve the crisis, and Milburn agreed. One solution both excluded, for the umpteenth time, was to use the private sector. 'That', Milburn declared, 'would be a Trojan horse for privatisation.'

Getting extra money depended on the chancellor. At a meeting in Downing Street on 19 November 1999, Gordon Brown sulked. Despite his boast that the state's finances were robust, he refused to allocate any additional new cash for hospitals. Blair did not understand why. Thanks to the inheritance from the Tories, the budget was running a surplus, the debt was still falling and, as he told supporters in Newcastle, 'We've introduced literally a revolution in economic management.' Brown's pieties about 'ending boom and bust', 'prudence' and 'the abolition of the economic cycle' enhanced the government's reputation as public-sector debt continued to fall to historic lows, offsetting damaging publicity about the chancellor's stealth taxes, an increase in national insurance and a self-destructive 75p rise in the weekly pension.

'He sees himself in opposition to us,' said Blair, infuriated when Brown, without any consultation, and after refusing extra money for hospitals, announced a plan to cancel the Third World's debt to Britain. His contempt towards Blair had become brazen. 'Don't ever speak to me like that again,' snapped Blair in fury after another insulting incident. 'We might be better off without him,' he told Campbell. 'He has flaws.' His chancellor's bachelor lifestyle – chaotically untidy homes and tormented relationships with women – reflected his awkward psychology. In his relationships with the public, civil servants and those beyond his intimate circle he was devoid of emotional intelligence, though he still attracted many admirers. In his bid for the leadership, for instance, Brown adroitly wooed Murdoch's newspapers and the *Daily Mail* group, which would revere him as blessed by 'a mantle of greatness'. By contrast, the Blairs' dinner with the *Mail*'s editor and proprietor would end amid mutual loathing. The problem, as Blair conceded, was the absence of a replacement for his chancellor. 'You always think Gordon speaks for the party,' Charles Clarke told Blair. 'He hasn't got the pull.' Blair disagreed. He knew Brown had assiduously courted support among MPs and the trade unions. Fearing that the NHS could become a negative issue at the next election, Blair was convinced that the only solution to Brown's sabotage was to override him in some way. But circumstances gave him scant opportunity.

A new storm was growing over NHS waiting lists. Once again there were reports describing the sick waiting on hospital trolleys for twenty-four hours before being admitted. Among the victims was Mavis Skeet, a cancer patient whose long wait had possibly condemned her to a premature death.

Then, on New Year's Eve, a new disaster materialised. Poor organisation meant hundreds of guests and journalists hoping to celebrate the new millennium were left fuming outside the Dome, unable to pass through the sole security control. Inside, Blair and the Queen awkwardly held hands, obviously wretched. Cherie looked even worse. Inside and out, the Dome was an unmitigated flop. And it got worse. Ten days later, after returning from a break as a guest of Cliff Richard in the Algarve, Cherie was stopped at Blackfriars station for travelling without a ticket. She was fined £10. The media headlines fed Blair's overriding conviction: 'In the fast changing world . . . one must communicate at the speed of light compared to the speed of sound.'

The same applied to the NHS. On 14 January, the *New Statesman* revealed that Professor Robert Winston, a pioneer of *in vitro* fertilisation and a Labour peer, blamed 'a conspiracy of silence' for deceiving Blair about the parlous state of the health service. He also accused Blair of deceit about closing down the internal market when he hadn't. To illustrate his case, Winston described the treatment his mother had received in a London hospital. He had found her lying abandoned and unfed – after waiting thirteen hours in casualty – on the floor of a mixed ward, where she later caught an infection. The exposure of such negligence by an eminent doctor was aggravated by the sight of Winston leaving his home the next day looking 'beaten and dejected' following a conversation with Alastair Campbell. In his briefing to journalists, Campbell blamed the Conservatives for the poor treatment received by Winston's mother.

To break the cycle of misery, Blair needed to deflect the criticism. Repeating once again in the Commons that Brown's 'extra £21 billion is real money' was certain to rebound. The public knew the truth about the chancellor's triple counting. 'It's time to stop fighting the last war,' Blair agreed. Among those close to Milburn, the questions from Downing Street suggested that Blair was finally taking a serious interest in the NHS. As usual, he did not ask experienced civil servants for advice. As Andrew Turnbull put it, 'He's charming but deep down he has no respect for us.'

To stage a counter-coup against Brown's withholding of funds, Blair's office arranged for a television interview with David Frost on Sunday morning, 16 January 2000. 'In the hours before his appearance', reported an eyewitness, 'Blair's office was chaotic.' Closeted with Milburn, the health secretary's assistant Simon Stevens and his own special advisers, Blair was preparing a bombshell to capture the headlines. A telephone call the previous night from Downing Street to the Department of Health's chief economist had revealed that while Britain was spending 6.9 per cent of its GDP on health, Germany and France each allotted over 10 per cent, with the European average at 7.9 per cent. 'Tin-helmet time with Gordon,' an adviser chuckled. Brown was not told about the plan.

In the course of his interview, Blair admitted there were 'problems', but he ruled out the NHS's use of the private sector. His masterstroke was to announce an unprecedented 5 per cent annual increase in spending for the next five years so that the NHS would match the European average. In effect, the NHS budget would rise from £34 billion in 1997 to £76 billion in 2006. In the hours after the interview, spending extra billions of pounds was presented as a triumph. Brown had been outsmarted, but Milburn and Stevens were struggling to understand precisely what Blair had promised. No video recording had been made in Downing Street, and the requested transcript from the BBC got stuck in a faulty fax machine. 'It was the most important battle of his prime ministership,' Jonathan Powell would write.

'He's stolen my fucking budget,' screamed the chancellor as soon as he heard, accusing Blair of thinking the solution to every problem was 'always more money'. In their first conversation after the broadcast, Brown flatly told Blair that the NHS's budget would not be increased before the election, and then only after a Treasury review. His refusal was followed by other Cabinet ministers demanding their share of the chancellor's fabled war chest, built out of the accumulated surplus.

The 'crisis' for both the NHS and the government dominated the week, and the afterglow of the promised bonanza faded within days.

The public and media were unconvinced that money alone would cure the problem. Opinion polls showed a majority were now dissatisfied with the government. 'The headlines are a nightmare,' an adviser briefed *The Times*. 'It is turning into a disaster.' The blame was placed on an 'overenthusiastic briefing' by Robert Hill that suggested the extra billions would indeed prove to be the panacea. Nevertheless, despite the dissatisfaction 50 per cent of those polled said they would vote Labour, compared to 29 per cent for the Tories.

In Parliament and elsewhere, Blair was caricatured by some as an autocrat or control freak, but in truth he was struggling to make an impression. Standing on the stage of the Old Vic theatre to celebrate the Labour Party's centenary, he addressed the disillusionment of his followers. In front of him were Ken Livingstone supporters, who were contemptuous of the Downing Street smear squad's attempts to blacken their man's reputation in the forthcoming mayoral election. After Blair left, the audience sang 'The Red Flag'. New Labour's roots were thin. His struggle to find a meaning for 'modernisation' seemed fruitless.

'We're putting money in,' Milburn told Blair, 'and nothing is happening. Everything is flat, except waiting times. The NHS is the last great nationalised industry that is an untenable model for the twenty-first century.'

Blair agreed: 'The NHS should be a system of care, not a nationalised industry.' Researchers had discovered discrepancies in care between the best and worst hospitals. Some employed twice as many nurses for the same number of critically ill patients; there was a 200 per cent difference between the cost of the most and the least efficient hospitals; some GP surgeries gave patients an appointment within twenty-four hours, while others expected their patients to wait five days; and the top 25 per cent of trusts used their consultants twice as productively as the bottom 25 per cent. The variation in performances and costs was as intolerable as the BMA's obstruction to change. 'This is the last-chance saloon,' Milburn told a group of doctors at a dinner in Downing Street.

But other than identifying enemies in the public services and spending money, Blair and Milburn were stuck.

Fundamental changes were needed. Blair and Milburn's dilemma was that they lacked an acceptable solution. Like all party loyalists, both had ridiculed the six years of John Major's government, when Ken Clarke had challenged those very same vested interests. Their mockery bequeathed vacuity. Harping on about 'modernisation', 'reform' and 'New Labour' as the route to a better NHS was meaningless. 'We didn't have the same sort of prior intellectual ferment to build on,' admitted Powell in a backhanded compliment to Thatcherites. 'To a large degree we had to make up our philosophy as we went along.' Their struggles led to Labour politicians being ridiculed. Rory Bremner's parody on his weekly television shows of Blair as an empty vessel buffeted by Brown and under Campbell's control was too close to the truth.

'Gothic quadrangles were his territory,' observed Andrew Turnbull. 'Oxford, the Inns of Court, Parliament. As a small-organisation man, he completely misunderstood that one man cannot run the government machine. He needed systems and specialists.'

New Labour's skill was to discover what the electorate wanted and promise to deliver it. Blair was still struggling to discover how to move from shadow to substance. He explained his failure to Milburn as him being 'terrified of the past'. The crowds cheering him as he drove from Islington to Downing Street on 2 May 1997 were crying out for maximum change, yet while his rhetoric matched their aspirations, his paralysed government was providing the minimum.

Ferocious arguments finally cajoled Brown into opening the purse strings. At the same time, Milburn persuaded Simon Stevens, by then Blair's health adviser in Downing Street, to rethink the NHS before spending the extra billions. 'There can be no parameters,' he told his senior officials. In his opinion, most of his department's staff were inflexibly resistant to change. In too many meetings he listened to officials reciting numbers proving that targets had been missed, but he still feared that new policies would destroy the essence of Nye Bevan's

1948 dream. 'I need to mount a coup against the department,' Milburn decided. He recruited six advisers to staff a new strategy unit led by Chris Ham, a senior civil servant, and Stevens. His starting point was radical: the NHS was too big to succeed. 'I took a blank sheet of paper,' he would later say, 'and the new NHS plan wrote itself.'

To Blair's frustration, while Milburn sat composing, Brown established his own review of the NHS's future. To counter that challenge, Blair asked Richard Branson, a favoured supporter, to investigate. Virgin would report that the NHS was badly managed, offered abysmal patient care and should use the private sector. Although none of this could have surprised him, Blair was unsure about the suggestions. More money, he remained convinced, was the answer, and that was now due.

To Blair's relief, Brown finally agreed to announce in his Budget speech on 21 March that the government would spend £63.5 billion on the NHS in 2003/4, nearly double the amount spent in 1997. Downing Street buzzed with genuine excitement at the commitment. At the last moment, Milburn's office invited the leaders of England's health professions to watch Brown in the House of Commons. Among those telephoned that morning was George Alberti. 'I'm at my investiture at Buckingham Palace,' he replied. 'I'll come over afterwards.'

Brown delivered a virtuoso performance. Billions of pounds were promised as the reward for 'prudence with a purpose', a winning slogan that pushed the Tories further to the right. Like the other NHS leaders looking down from the Commons gallery, Alberti was thrilled. 'It's the opportunity of a lifetime,' he told Milburn, as they walked along Whitehall to celebrate with a cream tea in the minister's office.

Later, to cap their euphoria, they crossed the road to meet Blair. 'I'll be in charge,' Blair told his visitors, before repeating the mantra, 'This is real money' – unlike, he implied, the triple counting and other phoney cash announced in the past. In exchange, he wanted all NHS staff to commit to significant changes that would cure the list of woes.

'What you're saying is, no more excuses,' said Alberti.

Blair nodded. The changes, he speculated, could be driven by contracting private providers, setting targets to monitor performance and paying incentives. But, he insisted, all those present would be expected to sign their agreement to reform on the document he flourished.

Blair's reassurances were undermined by Milburn. In his haste to change the NHS, the minister argued with several officials, including Alan Langlands, who resigned. Neil McKay, his temporary successor, was 'disappointed' by Langlands's departure. The NHS's performance, he told Milburn at their next monthly meeting, was 'getting worse', not better. Julian Le Grand added to Milburn's grief. The NHS, said the professor, had experienced decentralisation, recentralisation, internal markets and inquiries by management consultants, but none had cured poor-quality care by staff and unnecessarily long waiting times. 'The only clear explanation', said Le Grand, 'is that more money is not the only answer.'

Nor was the spin. In the days since the Budget, Jeremy Heywood, Blair's high-flying principal private secretary, had scrutinised the small print of the Treasury's Red Book, the bible of the Budget, and discovered more examples of Brown's exaggerated claims. An ITV programme had revealed how the chancellor had double counted the number of new nurses. Rather than admitting shame on Brown's behalf, Alastair Campbell complained that the revelation was 'all part of an effort to poison the well of debate and make it look like we couldn't be trusted'.

The issue, Blair agreed, was indeed trust. Why, he wondered, did the public distrust the government about the NHS? In his mind, the answer was New Labour's image. Instead of the party appearing classless and representing everyone, Brown was championing the poor against the middle class. He had, for instance, made a catastrophic attack against Oxford elitism based on the university's rejection of the comprehensive-educated Laura Spence, who had applied to study medicine at Magdalen College. Not only were Brown's facts about Spence wrong, but his tirade also echoed provincial old Labour's hatred of excellence. By championing the poor, overtaxing the middle class and deriding those who aspired to be wealthier, the resentful Scotsman was dividing the nation.

On the eve of the election, Blair feared that, in a conservative country, Labour was portraying itself as anti-family, anti-tax cuts and anti-strong defence, while being weak on crime and promoting all rights and no responsibilities. The idealism of that sunny morning on 2 May 1997 had been dented by derision, isolation and a lust for laudatory headlines. That was electoral folly. Burying the Tories for ever depended on New Labour being all-inclusive and sticking to the centre.

Brown believed the opposite. Endlessly tinkering with taxes, he planned to continue raising billions of pounds to spend on welfare. 'Community, not individualism,' was his slogan to entrap the nation in universal dependence on the welfare state. That, in his eyes, would secure permanent electoral support. He had even signed up with Europe's left-wing politicians to integrate the continent's economy according to socialist principles. However, his passion for 'community' did not extend to Blair and Robin Cook. For personal reasons, and to set himself apart from their support for Britain joining the euro, he loathed them both. In that poisonous atmosphere, on 23 March the three politicians flew on three separate planes to the EU summit in Lisbon, destined to sign a treaty to end Europe's stagnation and endorse a ten-year plan to make the community 'the most competitive and dynamic knowledge-based economy in the world'. The political leaders' optimism was infectious.

Blair returned to London determined to resolve his dispute with Brown and decide the fate of the NHS. In his lexicon, that required a speech to redefine New Labour as a 'radical' political movement advancing 'new, modern patriotism', and to present a threatening image of Tory Britain. Ken Livingstone's overwhelming victory in the London mayoral contest – an embarrassment for Blair – and other bad results in the local government elections in May made a 'mission message' relaunch vital. The ideal moment appeared to be an address to 10,000 members of the Women's Institute in Wembley Arena, fixed for 7 June, fortuitously close to the birth on 20 May of Leo, the Blairs' fourth child. The prime minister's appearance was billed as a major event – an opportunity to spell out his philosophy of 'equal worth, responsibility, community', and his ambition to soothe the anxious middle class by renewing old values. He had been warned to steer clear of politics. That message was forgotten.

The result was torturous. Blair's audience wanted to hear about Leo, not Labour. His polemic was interrupted by jeering and slow hand-claps. Deflated, the 'strong' leader hurried from the hall, a loser with a bloody nose. Over the following days, he felt isolated – then furious about a note from Philip Gould saying that 'he wasn't believed' because 'he is pandering, lacking conviction, unable to hold a position for more than a few weeks and lacking the guts to be able to tough it out. He is all things to all men, he's all spin, TB has not delivered. He is out of touch.'

Recriminations, loathing, humiliation and more poison were shared between Blair, Brown and Mandelson. Matthew Taylor, the director of IPPA, a left-wing think tank, wrote, 'Yes, Labour's love affair with the electorate is definitely over,' but that it could be saved by refining its message and dropping 'naked gesture politics'. Blair responded by announcing that delinquent teenagers should be marched by the police to a cashpoint to pay an instant fine. Six days later, his drunk son Euan was arrested in Leicester Square after celebrating the end of his exams. Cherie was enjoying a subsidised holiday in Portugal as the guest of John Holmes, the British ambassador who became a friend of the Blairs while serving in Downing Street. Cherie's critics noted that she had been visiting America while Euan was sitting his exams. Parental delinquency plus cronyism: nothing was working.

Battered, Blair called a press conference. 'I feel fine,' he smiled, before being humiliated by Campbell's decision to admit the BBC into Downing Street. Michael Cockerell's film portrayed Blair as an out-of-touch prime minister without a credible voice, especially among his own MPs. Later, in a memorandum to his inner circle headed 'Touchstone Issues', Blair lamented that he was 'out of touch with gut

British instincts' and ordered that he should be 'personally associated with the action taken to remedy the problem'.

One of the key complaints highlighted by Gould was that Labour 'were too late with the NHS'. Milburn offered some relief. On 11 July, he and Simon Stevens completed their draft NHS Plan 2000. Three years after ravaging their inheritance, Milburn quietly restored the scheme set out by Stephen Dorrell in 1996 to devolve health services to a hundred primary care centres. Even Dorrell's language was resuscitated. The scorn heaped on John Major's government had blinded Blair to its achievements. Labour supporters would be shocked by Milburn's mention of 'choice' and 'competition', but after the disastrous winter and the indignity suffered by Robert Winston's mother, the politician had reconsidered the Tories' ideas.

'The existing system is unsustainable,' he told Blair. Finding the answer had required endless conversations. Among the experts were Don Berwick, an academic, and Alain Enthoven, an American health expert who had advised Margaret Thatcher to introduce the internal market. Over the following months, Milburn had been persuaded that choice would help the poor to get the same treatment as the middle classes. The private sector would be contracted to reduce waiting times and challenge the NHS staff and trade unions. In targeting cancer, Milburn realised, the lack of money to buy better equipment was only part of the reason for the NHS's poor record. Another was the doctors' failure to recognise many illnesses' symptoms early enough. The errors were due not to a lack of money but to the profession being resistant to studying developments in other countries. The NHS's inflexibility would be best challenged by the state subcontracting some services to private doctors. All the care provided by the service would be free, but the NHS would cease being the monopoly provider. That was Milburn's wish list for the future but it was impolitic to include it in his draft plan. Rather, the headlines would be dominated by the pledge to rebuild a hundred hospitals and recruit an additional 9,500 doctors and 20,000 nurses.

'What do you think, Peter?' Blair asked Mandelson after reading out parts of the draft.

'It has the appearance of an untidy washing line,' replied Mandelson, putting aside his BlackBerry.

'Right,' said Blair, 'there's still work to do.'

Introducing private treatment centres into the NHS along with competition and 'patient choice' was unacceptable to most Labour supporters, not least the 1.3 million employees of the NHS. To blame those staff for the service ranking among Europe's worst, Blair knew, risked jeopardising over 2 million votes. He directed that the White Paper should be rewritten to explain that in France 'choice' had proved to be 'wasteful'.

He read the revised draft with unusual care while flying to a summit meeting in Japan on 19 July. Combining command, control and partnership with passing mention of 'choice and competition' riddled the White Paper with confusion. Milburn had satisfied Blair's demand for headlines of 'reform' and 'modernisation', but how much could the prime minister accept?

Blair's annotated copy, faxed back to London, revealed his indecision. He could not digest the idea of a private company providing a public service. Accordingly, a patient's 'choice' would be limited to selecting a GP, the time of an appointment and the food offered in hospital. Providing real choice was beyond his prerogative, as was any 'partnership'. Whitehall would still control everything. To enforce better standards, new modernisation action teams would scour the NHS to subject hospitals to more regulation, more targets and more inspection.

On 27 July 2000, Blair presented the plan to the Commons. To defuse any criticism that the Labour Party was embracing the market, he condemned the Tories' internal market system as 'a weak lever for improvement'. He spoke of wanting to 'redesign the NHS around the patient' but, as Milburn said, without noting the Orwellian irony, 'devolving power depends on command and control from Whitehall'.

With the exception of the BMA, NHS employees and the trade

unions were ecstatic about this apparent rejection of the Tories' plans. Finally, they cheered, the NHS would be rescued. None of them knew that Brown was still refusing to release the billions of pounds promised both by himself and by Blair.

The agent who would mastermind the revolution, Milburn decided, was Allan Leighton, the chief executive of Asda supermarkets. However, after researching the realities of management in Whitehall, Leighton rejected the move. The next stage was to compile a shortlist of six candidates, a chore that was entrusted to the civil servant responsible for Scottish affairs. George Alberti saw his list. 'They're all deadbeats,' declared the doctor to Milburn and promptly added Nigel Crisp, the manager of NHS hospitals in London. Crisp was duly selected.

The burden of revolutionising the NHS was thus handed to an impassive former charity manager known to revere the NHS's traditions – the exact opposite of what Milburn was seeking.

FOURTEEN

Everything Is PR

'I'm sending you Stephen Byers,' Jonathan Powell told Michael Scholar, the permanent secretary at the DTI, after Peter Mandelson's resignation. 'I think you'll like him. He's a first-rate Blairite.' In Blair's opinion, Byers ranked among his most trusted and talented ministers.

Scholar did not interpret the appointment in similar terms: 'I nearly fell off my chair. Byers was not recommended because he was good and honest but because he got on with the prime minister and not the chancellor.'

The third secretary of state at the DTI within nineteen months was even more resentful of his civil servants than Margaret Beckett. The feelings were mutual after Byers appointed Jo Moore, an undisguised Labour activist, and Dan Corry, an unexceptional economist, as special advisers. 'Outrageous,' complained one DTI official. 'He's giving power to low-calibre, unqualified people who are unreliable. It's more like the government of a banana republic.'

As if to prove their own disdain for the 'lazy' civil servants, Nigel Griffiths, a newly appointed junior minister, left a message on Scholar's desk at 6 a.m. that his printer had run out of ink. Byers's department, predicted a Labour MP, would mirror himself – 'rude, self-obsessed and not clever'.

Byers did not trouble himself with the problems besetting Helen Liddell, the new minister responsible for energy. She inherited from John Battle the department's assumption that prices would remain low and that the benefits of cheap energy were permanent. The market was assumed to be working.

Unnoticed by Blair's team, Labour had effectively abandoned the simplicity of competition. With the prime minister's support, Battle had protected coal mines and banned the construction of more gas-powered electricity generators. 'There's too much gas in the world,' he had insisted. Neither Battle nor Blair had listened to experts warning about the world's increasingly complicated energy market. Taxes to protect coal and reduce carbon emissions – and soon a climate-change tax to encourage industry to use less energy – were distorting the market, and the complications intensified as world oil prices unexpectedly began to double during 1999.

Britain suffered a further shock. Because of the country's open market for energy, prices rose just as supplies from the North Sea began permanently to decline. British consumers became the victims of Europe's state-controlled, subsidised schemes. On a tilted playing field, Britain was paying more for gas and electricity than the Europeans.

Soon after taking over, Liddell mentioned that the security of Britain's energy supplies was threatened. 'Eyes glazed over,' she observed. She watched Derek Scott, Blair's special adviser, allude to energy, only to be dismissed as 'too geeky'. There was, she realised, 'a national malaise leading by default to a lack of strategy'. Without leadership from Downing Street, she found 'so many subplots going on about gas, coal, nuclear'. Then Brown began disparaging Blair's interest in climate change. 'No one', she discovered, 'was considering the possibility of interruption of supply.' Instead of planning for the future, Liddell was firefighting to prevent European countries artificially fixing high prices.

Britain's plight was aggravated by Labour's decision to merge all the energy regulators into one, Ofgem. Staffed by fanatical pro-marketeers, the new regulator focused solely on the consumers' immediate interests, opposed 'the green crap' and refused to consider whether Britain's supply of energy was secure. 'After Ofgem was created,' a Blair adviser would later reflect, 'the DTI had a lobotomy on energy. They deferred to Ofgem.' Downing Street did not reprimand the DTI for abandoning any original thinking about the issue. Blair was uninterested. In his big picture, he favoured commissioning the next generation of nuclear power stations, but he was uncertain how to consummate his idea and was also reluctant to pursue his argument.

Forever anticipating the next election, he seized on climate change as *the* issue. The weather had become political during the 1980s. In a lecture to the Royal Society in 1990, Margaret Thatcher had offered her government's White Paper, 'This Common Inheritance', as an endorsement of using economic instruments to deal with atmospheric pollution. Seven years later, John Prescott had arrived at the Kyoto conference on climate change with an ambitious brief prepared by his Conservative predecessor that alerted the world to danger.

By 2000, Downing Street advisers had noticed that Blair's enthusiasm for international summits had overtaken his interest in domestic issues. In anticipation of a G8 or Euro summit, Blair spent a disproportionate amount of time considering how to present himself to the world rather than grapple with his policies on energy, agriculture or housing. The opportunity to appear at the Earth Summit in New York in 2000, a year before the election, was irresistible. Speaking before a huge audience, he praised his own government for being 'a world leader on protecting the environment'. Britain, he said, would place conservation at the heart of the decision-making process.

Blair's commitment was enshrined in the Utilities Act 2000. Renewables, pledged the government, would generate 5 per cent of electricity by 2003 and 10 per cent by 2010. Officials asked ministers to reconcile the new targets with the unquantifiable investment required to generate electricity from renewables. The only source of finance was taxes, and Blair refused to argue with Brown about assigning more money. Accordingly, few took the government's pledge seriously. After all, the 5 per cent target had first been set in 1997 and could not be met until at least 2008; and no one was sure when the 10 per cent target would be achieved (by 2010, it had reached 7 per cent). The DTI's energy section appeared to be suffused with unreality.

As energy prices rose, Blair was persuaded by his special adviser and the few experts at the DTI that oil and gas prices would soon fall by 30 per cent, so he could rely on market forces to reverse the increases. Blair never questioned whether those predictions were reasonably safe. Those were peripheral issues for a man focused on the big challenges. Accustomed to living day by day, he relied on Byers and Liddell and endorsed his ministers' distrust of their civil servants.

By chance, DTI officials discovered that Blair, Brown and Byers, together with Byers's political advisers Dan Corry and Jo Moore, were secretly considering the sale of the Post Office to Deutsche Post. 'How can they discuss this without someone who knows something about this being present?' Scholar asked Jeremy Heywood. 'I'll see what I can do,' replied Blair's principal private secretary. Invited to the next meeting, Scholar further discovered that the politicians had ignored the mechanics of a sale, and never asked how a German-owned Post Office would be regulated. Once the realities were explained, the idea died.

Next, Byers was offered a substantial briefing paper by his officials outlining how the sale of five licences for the 3G radio spectrum could raise in excess of £500 million. Byers, the officials complained, did not discuss the paper with them or refer it to the Cabinet. Instead, he deliberated with Corry and Moore on how to promote the sale to the media. After an auction arranged by officials, the credit for an unexpected windfall of £22.5 billion was taken by Byers.

Soon after, he decided that the DTI should encourage four businessmen, self-styled the 'Phoenix Four', to take over the Rover factory in Longbridge, near Birmingham. The unprofitable company was 'sold' by BMW for £10. To rid themselves of all legal obligations, BMW also gave the Phoenix Four a long-term loan of £427 million. DTI officials complained that Blair and Byers were warned about inadequate consultation across Whitehall and that both politicians ignored the concerns aroused by the deal.

Blair's dislike of his DTI officials initially blanked out another of their warnings: not to rescue a bankrupt ship-building company in north-east England by ordering an unwanted luxury liner. 'It would be illegal,' he and Byers were told.

'Why do you say that?' asked Byers.

'Because I've looked at the Act,' replied the official.

'But you're not a lawyer and I have a degree in law,' said Byers.

'I've taken advice from the department's seventy lawyers,' retorted the official.

'But they're bound to agree with you. And I've looked at the Act and I do have the powers.'

To resolve the stalemate, the official announced the nuclear option: 'I won't act unless you formally instruct me, and if you do I will set out in writing the reasons why you cannot do this, and it'll be sent to the Public Accounts Committee, who will publish it.'

Appearing undaunted, Byers scoffed, 'I've no problem with that. You'll look foolish.' He never issued the instruction.

Byers's conduct did not trouble Blair. His advisers preferred not to bring bad news about such remote events. Rather they added to the turmoil in the Queen's Speech by committing the DTI to produce a bill providing cheap energy for small businesses. When one of Blair's advisers asked to read the draft bill, the response from the DTI was incredulity. Downing Street had not informed the department about the proposed law.

In turn, Blair was criticised by civil servants for clogging up the system with too much legislation. He replied that making new laws sent the signals that forced the system to change because, as Jonathan Powell agreed, edicts from departments 'didn't do the trick'. In Blair's opinion, laws were the substitute for management. Eventually, to satisfy the perennial quest for media headlines, the DTI's badly drafted bill struggled through the Commons with endless amendments and statutory provisions to proclaim regulations in the future, and was then forgotten.

'This is a dysfunctional government,' concluded Scholar. To Whitehall's old guard, Blair's approach lacked intellectual coherence and core beliefs. The DTI was floundering.

And then the government was stung. In September 2000, crude oil prices hit $33 per barrel, up from $10 in 1998. Petrol prices rose automatically and a slew of government policies crashed. For three years, John Prescott had been urging people to abandon their cars and use public transport. Predictions that his 'integrated transport' policy would aggravate road congestion had materialised and yet he still refused to build new roads. Instead, he supported Brown's idea of an annual 6 per cent increase in fuel duties above inflation to deter motorists and protect the environment. To rescue his reputation, Prescott announced a 'Ten-Year Transport Plan' costing £80 billion. When this initiative was greeted with derision, Blair shook his head. 'There's nothing a government can do about transport,' he told Charles Clarke.

As petrol prices soared, commuters who relied on cars felt unfairly penalised. Unexpectedly, the drivers of fuel-delivery lorries also felt aggrieved and in protest against the fuel taxes began to blockade the oil depots. Within hours, six of the country's eight refineries were besieged by a thousand protesters, and within two days half the country's petrol stations were closed. TV pictures of motorists queuing in a panic portrayed a country in chaos.

Blair was warned by the police in Hull that his plans to celebrate Prescott's thirtieth year in Parliament in a Chinese restaurant were endangered by protesters. Five days later, he realised the country faced a shutdown. No one had told him that for days the TV news had been showing long queues of cars outside every garage, nor that the daily evening news had been filled with pictures of panic-buyers emptying supermarket shelves. Britain was threatened by paralysis.

Blair did not blame Prescott, Brown or himself for the emergency, but Alastair Campbell could not find a minister prepared to take public responsibility for the lack of fuel. The first meeting of civil servants in the Cabinet Office had ended after ninety minutes in what David Omand, the chairman, called 'disaster'. Whitehall had plans to cope with OPEC countries refusing to sell oil, but there was no civil contingency plan for a blockade of Britain's refineries. Ministers swapped anecdotes and agreed nothing. 'Why don't we run this as a counter-terrorism operation?' asked Omand. 'Let's use the Cobra room' – Cobra being the acronym for 'Cabinet Office briefing room A', where government ministers and officials meet during a crisis.

The walls of that room were covered with maps of Sierra Leone, the focus of a British military operation. Blair was invited to attend. 'Gosh, I didn't know this existed,' he said, as he watched representatives of the military, police, oil companies and government officials running around like scalded cats. Men and women were racing up three floors to make telephone calls because the Cobra room, set up for a nuclear attack, lacked facilities for video and telephone conference calls. The correct equipment, Blair was told, would take a week to install. On his introductory visit, he hesitated to take charge. For those gathered, the prime minister's mismanagement of his first domestic crisis left an uncomfortable impression.

Reports in the press described diminishing petrol stocks and police refusing to confront the truck drivers – a marked contrast to the robustness that served Thatcher against the miners. The spokesman for ACPO, the Association of Chief Police Officers, explained that police were barred by health-and-safety laws from entering lorry drivers' cabs. Frightened by intimidation, the oil companies were pusillanimous. 'We're not far off a crisis,' murmured a senior official.

Richard Dearlove, the head of MI6, declared that 'This is the most serious threat to the country in my career.' Richard Wilson, embarrassed by the chaos, was missing in action. As for Blair, he asked a few questions and departed. He was not seen in the Cobra room again. Jack Straw took charge.

As so often, Blair named those he blamed: the Tories, the media who had turned their guns on the government in revenge for Campbell's distortions, and Wilson. He summoned Omand and Wilson to his office. 'Your jobs are on the line,' he warned. 'If you fail, you're out.'

His desperation spread among his ministers. Anna Walker, the DTI's director of energy, was summoned by Byers. 'You are my senior energy official,' he told her. 'I will hold you to account to get solutions to solve the crisis.'

Blaming officials was understandable, but it did not solve Blair's isolation. Brown denied his taxes were to blame and absented himself, wondering whether there would be an opportunity to seize the leadership. Prescott, an excitable liability during a crisis, stayed in Hull. Straw listed problems but offered no immediate solutions. 'He's hopeless,' Blair told a Cabinet colleague. 'He's like fighting blancmange.' Yet it was Straw, together with Blair, who over the next few days pulled the levers to persuade the police, oil companies and trade unions to end the dispute. Finally, with the country on the precipice, Brown agreed to abandon the tax increase. The blockades were lifted.

Blair declared victory. 'Why', he asked David Omand, 'can't all government be as successful as settling this crisis?'

'Because, Prime Minister,' replied Omand, 'during the fuel crisis we were all on the same side, working together. Your government doesn't have a common objective. Your government is split in two: between yourself and Brown.'

In reply, Blair held an 'off-site' of Cabinet ministers and their permanent secretaries at the Commonwealth Club near Whitehall to discuss how to run the government as successfully in normal times as it was run during the emergency. 'He wants to be saved in the same way,' thought Omand.

To disprove his officials, Blair dispatched an emissary to the MoD. 'The prime minister wants 5,000 drivers permanently trained so this cannot happen again.'

'That's impossible.'

'But the PM wants it,' the official insisted.

'No,' he was told.

Historically, Britain's energy policies were always created after a crisis. The aftershock of the fuel blockade was compounded four months later by energy blackouts in California. Electricity supplies in the Golden State were provided in a competitive market similar to Britain's.

In the Enron era, Blair and others still assumed there was an irrefutable benefit that came from replacing the monopoly of the nationalised utilities with dynamic competition, but the Californian crisis showed that markets could fail. Overnight, the assumptions on which Britain's energy policy had been based since 1982 were undermined.

In the name of an open market, Blair had allowed the purchase of many of the country's power stations by state-owned German, French and Spanish companies. Those takeovers had terminated any chance of new British businesses challenging the foreign monopolies, and this, combined with the blackouts in California, reinforced the warnings by a few experts that reliance on the market was failing to protect the security of Britain's energy supplies.

With neither interest nor urgency, Blair approved the chore of reviewing Britain's vulnerability to blackouts. Since he had no confidence in the DTI, the review was handed to Downing Street's policy unit. Those assigned to the task were not scrutinised for their expertise or prejudice. His expectations were low.

FIFTEEN

Clutching at Straws

In 2000, Blair was in the midst of yet another argument with Richard Wilson. 'I want change,' he repeatedly told his senior civil servant. The Home Office, he complained, was failing to meet targets to reduce crime. Wilson told Blair that his problem was that he had never managed anything.

'I managed the Labour Party,' said Blair stoutly.

'You didn't manage them. You led them,' replied Wilson.

The chill aggravated the division between the two men. Wilson's attempt to appease Blair with proposed reforms, written in business jargon, about targets, performance-related pay, benchmarks, minority quotas and 'appraisals with 360-degree feedback procedures' had not impressed his 'client'. The prime minister did not seek his advice. Instead, he commissioned John Birt to deliver some 'blue-sky thinking' about Jack Straw's department.

'Unleashed by Number 10,' Straw would write, '[Birt] began to interfere in the Home Office's work for no good reason so far as I could see, and even less understanding.' In reply to Blair's conviction that Straw 'had been captured by the department', Straw thought Birt's arrival proved that Downing Street had 'been captured by the fairies'. Birt presented his conclusions to Blair, Straw and David Omand, illustrated by eighty slides. At the end of his presentation there was silence.

'No one had thought what we were meant to do with Birt's results,' Omand later recalled. 'There was no vision. And there was no money to effect change. Blair never understood what went on outside his office.'

Blair broke the silence by expressing frustration that Birt had not presented a clear set of levers to pull. He was equally annoyed with Straw and Omand, whose reputations were tainted for predicting that crime rates would rise. 'If the economy is doing badly,' said Omand, 'there'll be more burglaries. If it's doing well, they'll steal laptops.' To his surprise, 'Blair lost his cool because either way he was losing.' Both minister and department head had failed to present him with an initiative or good results to publicise. His solution was to insert five anti-crime bills into the Queen's Speech.

Blair was also frustrated because 'nothing' had been done to reduce the number of bogus asylum-seekers. He blamed Mike O'Brien, the junior immigration minister, for lacking an instinctive interest in the problem. Some would judge that harsh, but just what Blair meant could be seen by his choice of Barbara Roche, a north London MP, as O'Brien's replacement. In common with so many of his appointments, Blair did not discuss immigration with Roche. Straw was also unaware that Roche was the daughter of a Jewish émigré family brought up in London's East End and had entrenched opinions. His brief instruction to her about bogus asylum-seekers was, 'Deport them.' Immigration was still not a priority for either Straw or Blair.

In her first conversation with a senior IND official, Roche was candid: 'I think that the asylum-seekers should be allowed to stay in Britain. Removal takes too long, and it's emotional.' She also dismissed Straw's vouchers as 'not dignified'. Every asylum-seeker, she believed, should receive full benefits. Thanks to a threatened rebellion by over a hundred Labour MPs, the benefits were 50 per cent higher than Straw had proposed. Roche also openly criticised IND staff as being uniformly white males. 'I was angry that it was all bound up in race,' she would say. 'It was polarised and unpleasant. The immigration policies were racist. The atmosphere was toxic.' She wanted to see black faces in Croydon. 'I know our asylum policy,' she told IND head Stephen Boys-Smith, 'but what's our immigration policy? I cannot understand why I cannot say that immigration is a good thing. I want a progressive, non-racist immigration policy.'

Roche shared her frustration with Sarah Spencer, an academic who specialised in the subject. For years, Spencer had been a lonely voice urging the Labour Party to treat immigration as a benefit to the country. 'Legal migration', the softly spoken woman told Roche, 'is a good thing.' Like Spencer, Roche believed that keeping the number of migrants down was 'misguided' because 'immigration and multiculturalism brought positive good'. British cities, they agreed, should enjoy large non-European communities.

Asylum-seekers, Spencer told Straw, were not benefits-hogging fraudsters but people in need of protection. Even the use of the word 'bogus', she said, created a negative feeling. Straw's vouchers, she believed, exposed the government's intention to use enforced destitution as an unjustified deterrence. 'The old approach', she told Straw, 'of simply keeping people out is no longer tenable.' Straw rejected her criticisms, but Roche's objections, he realised, were different. To avoid alienating the party, he did not openly contradict her, although he did not grasp the direction in which she and Spencer were heading.

In the midst of celebrating 'Cool Britannia' in the Dome, Spencer stood among Labour's progressives, who embraced their own brand of modernisation. They disdained white Britain's glorification of British history and identity. British society could be transformed, she hoped, by relaxing the Home Office's immigration controls. Roche offered Spencer the chance to realise that ambition and fortuitously discovered a kindred spirit in Boys-Smith. 'It was clear that Roche wanted more immigrants to come to Britain,' he recalled. 'She didn't see her job as controlling entry into Britain, but by looking at the wider picture "in a holistic way" she wanted us to see the benefit of a multicultural society.'

Boys-Smith agreed with Roche that Britain should welcome more foreigners in what he called 'managed migration'. Introducing such a dramatic change should not be too difficult, he thought, because the government's policy was half-baked. Blair and Straw discussed asylum but never immigration, meaning that more migrants were entering Britain than was being formally acknowledged in Whitehall. A policy vacuum existed because Blair refused to create a Cabinet committee dedicated to the topic, and nor would he appoint a Downing Street adviser who specialised in immigration.

That omission, suggested Roche, was the opportunity to 'signal a change'. On Spencer's advice, she pondered transforming bogus asylum-seekers into legally admissible citizens. Over the following months, she sketched out a speech outlining the advantages of immigration and reducing controls, and portraying asylum-seekers in a positive light as skilled labour. She intentionally avoided giving any numbers, and did not discuss her speech with Straw: 'He wasn't interested. And nor was Blair.'

During her two visits to No. 10 for presentations about entry into Britain, Roche found Blair impatient. As usual, he did not mention immigration. Instead, he complained about the increasing number of asylum-seekers and the slow rate of removals. 'He didn't understand the process and wasn't interested in the detail,' recalled Roche. 'All he wanted to hear was the good news, and in his terms there was none. He was shallow. He had no grasp of immigration policy. There was no policy.' Liz Lloyd, Blair's special adviser, confirmed that he was interested only in responding to public anger and reducing the number of asylum-seekers to minimise media criticism. He demanded the removal of '30,000 failed applicants' in 2000, out of the 90,000 who had applied over the previous year. In 1999, only 7,645 had been removed. Blair's target was unattainable.

Straw seemed to be similarly irritated by Blair's lack of focus. 'The man's a lawyer, surely he understands the problems?' Roche commented after they left Downing Street. Straw did not reply. Every person and institution had a limit of nervous energy. Blair, Straw knew, was interested in crime, prisons and the aftermath of the Metropolitan Police's inadequate investigation into the racist murder of black teenager Stephen Lawrence – not immigration. Ed Owen, Straw's special adviser, sympathised with the home secretary's dilemma, one he shared with other 'progressives'. Even the mere mention of an immigration policy was castigated as an unsavoury association with the prejudices of the racist Tories. Resolving the quandary fell to Spencer.

The academic had been asked by Jonathan Portes, an economist in the Cabinet Office, to write a paper for the Policy and Innovation Unit advocating an increase in migration. 'I was saying the kind of things that they wanted to hear,' recalled Spencer. Both she and Portes emboldened their cause by naming Blair as the authority who commissioned their report. To impress the prime minister, both relied on Labour's favoured 'evidence-based policies' to show the benefits of economic migration. Naturally, they were attracted to evidence that matched their argument. That suited Andrew Turnbull, the Treasury's permanent secretary. Labour, he knew, believed in the 'globalisation package', which meant welcoming people, capital, goods and investment into Britain.

An early draft of Portes's own paper, 'Migration: An Economic and Social Analysis', was given to Roche to help her write her speech. In his report, Portes emphasised the economic benefits of migration unreservedly. Migrants, he wrote, were not a burden on the public purse but increased the government's income through taxation. He focused on French entrepreneurs setting up high-tech ventures and earning jackpot salaries. 'It would be counter-productive to constrain the growth of migration,' he recommended, because the British economy would grow by an additional £2.6 billion in 1999/2000.

Although his report was to be published in 2001, Portes based his arguments on statistics collected in 1997, the year Michael Howard's Act had reduced migration markedly. Without fear of contradiction, he wrote that most migrants were white – omitting the 510,000 immigrants who arrived from the Indian subcontinent during the first three years of Blair's government.

In the same manner, he downplayed any adverse consequences of immigration. With Spencer's support, he asserted that 'in theory' there was no 'evidence' that migrants would 'increase the pressure on housing, transport . . . and health services'. On the contrary, he praised migrant children for bringing 'greater diversity into UK schools' and assured Blair that migrants had not caused any overcrowding in London – which was true in 1997. 'There is little evidence', he wrote, 'that native workers are harmed.' He added, 'Migrants will have no effect on the job prospects of natives.' Nine years later, a report by the Migration Advisory Committee found that twenty-three British workers had been displaced for every hundred foreign-born workers employed in the country.

Portes's enthusiasm was reinforced by his relying entirely on pro-immigration groups for information. He failed to consult Migration Watch, a group critical of unrestricted migration that, he assumed, supported the entry of white Christians but not Muslims. Although the government clearly could not discriminate on the basis of colour, it could distinguish between migrants by country of origin. Purposefully, Portes avoided the word 'integration', which offended the Labour progressives' embrace of multiculturalism. Instead, he advocated that migrants should be helped to become a 'cohesive' part of society. He ignored any damaging consequences to British life by not mentioning the reluctance of the growing Muslim and Hindu communities to integrate. His solution to reducing isolation was for a race equality grant scheme to distribute money that would help 'connect communities'.

Spencer admitted later, 'There was no policy for integration. We just believed the migrants would integrate.' Her assumption that the British would unquestioningly accept hundreds of thousands of migrants was underpinned by the BBC's general categorisation of critics of immigration as racist, which had censored a public debate, thus concealing any problems. Accordingly, Portes's assurance that the number of migrants entering Britain could be 'totally controlled' appeared incontrovertible.

Numbers, Portes knew, were critical. He relied on Spencer's 'evidence' to predict that net migration of non-EU nationals into Britain would rise from 100,000 in 1997 to 170,000 in 2004. He and Spencer were wrong. In 2004, 500,000 migrants entered. No fewer than 370,000 stayed – 200,000 more than Spencer had predicted. The cumulative effect over five years was that there were a million more migrants than Portes had anticipated.

Portes's report was ideal material for Roche, who also drew on her previous job as a junior minister at the DTI. Employers had frequently complained about red tape preventing their recruitment of skilled foreign workers, despite the dearth of equivalent British labour. To overcome that bottleneck, Roche argued that Britain should 'modernise the work permit system'. Instead of migrants posing as asylum-seekers, they could enter Britain legally with permits. By then, the number of such permits had already risen from 25,000 in 1997 to 40,000.

In drafting her speech, Roche avoided the phrase 'asylum-seekers'. Migrants were described as 'entrepreneurs, the scientists, the high-technology specialists who make the global economy tick'. She also avoided setting target figures, which, she said, would be a 'foolish' mistake. Once her script was completed, she asked Andy Neather, a speech-writer for Blair, to give her text 'a gloss'.

It was a memorable experience for Neather: 'I remember coming away from some discussions with the clear sense that the policy was intended, even if this wasn't its main purpose, to rub the Right's nose in diversity and render their arguments out of date.' Later, in an interview, Neather also allegedly disclosed that Blair supported migration as it would increase electoral support for Labour. He would later claim to have been misquoted.

Next, Roche showed her speech to Straw. Over the previous months, the two had argued. Straw wanted more deportations, but Roche had refused and nothing was resolved. She found Straw's manner 'hard to read'. When offered her draft speech, he said nothing. Roche suspected that Straw was keeping his head down to avoid being labelled in the argument, a conclusion he did not later deny. Straw's silence did not surprise IND officials. The minister, they had noticed, was also avoiding any discussion about the accession of eight countries, including Poland, into the EU. In Boys-Smith's opinion, Straw left them leaderless.

Finally, the speech was sent to No. 10 for approval. Roche was uncertain whether she would receive Blair's support. While the prime minister did believe that Britain needed skilled migrants, he also blamed 'liberal' judges and 'out-of-date' civil servants for not accelerating the deportations of bogus asylum-seekers. Roche's own experience suggested that, despite media reports, Blair was still not entirely focused on the surge. She was mistaken. He was principally worried about the electoral risk but, unknown to her, Gordon Brown had warned him, 'Don't mention immigration, it's a Tory issue and should be ignored.' Accordingly, her draft elicited no comment from Downing Street. But David Blunkett and Charles Falconer, having spotted that Roche was using 'economic migrants' as an apparent smokescreen for increasing immigration, did suggest that Portes's report should be modified. Falconer was more forthright: Roche's speech should not be delivered. His advice was ignored. The silence from Downing Street encouraged the pro-immigration lobby to believe that Blair endorsed the chancellor's and the Treasury's argument about the economic advantages of increased migration.

On 11 September, Roche delivered her speech to 'a gathering of the converted' in a hall owned by the British Bankers' Association. Boys-Smith was in the front row. Other than the invited guests and members of the left-wing Institute for Public Policy Research, few were aware of Roche's speech. No backlash materialised. 'Well done, Barbara,' Blair told her soon after. Although he would not read Portes's report nor attend its presentation in Downing Street, his office did approve its publication in 2001. Blair had embraced a fundamental change in Britain's immigration policy.

Few white Britons were ever aware of Roche's speech, but after hearing about her sentiments on the grapevine, migrants in Britain certainly grasped its importance. Successful asylum-seekers told their friends and family across the world about the new mood music, and that Britain provided benefits and state housing unavailable in other European countries. Few in Whitehall understood the implications. Since the advocates of increased migration denied that migrants would put pressure on any services, there was no discussion among civil servants about providing additional homes, schools or hospitals. 'It was a policy, not a plan,' said Roche. Shortly after, she was moved from the Home Office. According to Blunkett and Clarke, she was 'muddled' and 'incompetent', but her legacy was regularly broadcast by television news.

Hundreds of migrants camped in squalor in Sangatte, outside Calais, were trying to smuggle themselves onto lorries heading for Britain. News reports showed them jumping from trucks in Kent, punching the air in victory. The broadcast media blandly sympathised with the victims, reflecting Blair's pride in his 'diversity agenda'. That year's Race Relations Act imposed on local authorities a duty to promote racial equality and, at the request of Muslim pressure groups, criminalised discrimination on the grounds of religion. Some Muslims interpreted the new edict as Blair's approval of Sharia law, arranged marriages, polygamy and even female genital mutilation. Since Blair never convened an interdepartmental discussion to consider Muslims' apparent preference for living apart from their fellow citizens, the government's silence encouraged some Muslims to deduce that multiculturalism placed no expectations on them to integrate into British society.

Stephen Boys-Smith welcomed that tolerance. The torrent of asylum-seekers arriving in Britain, he noted, never provoked a summons from Straw with the reprimand, 'I've had a roasting from No. 10 about this.' He assumed that, unlike the media, Blair was uninterested in the increasing numbers, or else approved their arrival. Both conclusions were accurate. Although Blair feared that negative media reports might endanger his re-election, he did not order Whitehall to stop the 350,000-plus foreigners arriving every year. On the contrary, he criticised Straw for failing to provide adequate care. To improve the migrants' conditions, he summoned a meeting with Straw and Brown to implement Derry Irvine's proposal that asylum-seekers should be given sufficient welfare benefits and housing. The Treasury, he ordered, should allocate money for all asylum-seekers to be properly treated.

Brown remained silent. Afterwards, a Treasury official telephoned Irvine's office. Brown, he announced, had vetoed any allocation of additional money. Blair did not challenge his chancellor.

News about the new liberalism – or, as Blair called it, 'the change agenda' – combined with welfare benefits in particular attracted Somalis who had settled in other EU countries. Although there was no historic or cultural link between Somalia and Britain, over 200,000 began to cross the Channel. Initially, most applied to settle in Britain on humanitarian grounds rather than as asylum-seekers. Since most were untrained and unemployable and would be dependent on welfare, the Home Office could have refused them, but Boys-Smith directed that they be granted 'exceptional leave to remain'.

They were not the only ones. On 9 February 2000, Blair was told that over a hundred Afghans had arrived at Stansted airport aboard a hijacked aircraft. Most were seeking asylum. 'If I hear from the Home Office that their applications will be processed like any other,' said Blair, 'I'll go out onto Horse Guards and scream.' The Afghans, he said, should be sent home 'within hours'. His orders were ignored. Britain's judges, explained Straw, would prevent their immediate return to their homeland. 'It's the civil servants,' said Blair, convinced that Straw had once again been manipulated by Whitehall. Six years later, a judge would grant the nine hijackers asylum, in protection of their human rights. Although they were criminals without any connection to Britain, the nine men had by then received £10 million in welfare benefits and legal aid. The judge would insist that he was applying the law. Blair always overestimated Parliament's control over the judiciary.

Two months later, he became rattled by one of Philip Gould's regular reports. The previous September, Gould had predicted the demise of the Conservative Party. Now, the pollster reported that asylum had become his focus groups' prime issue in the local elections. In the polls, there was a 14.9 per cent swing from Labour. 'The Tories are using asylum to run the race card,' said Straw, blaming the previous Tory government for the embarrassment he now faced. Although he spoke confidently to his senior officials about 'keeping the lid on asylum-seekers', Home Office officials knew that for the fourth year running their department was battling with a chaotic backlog of applications.

Straw's assurances about reversing the tide were no longer convincing. Asylum, Blair finally conceded, was 'going to be really difficult for us'. His response was to describe the crisis as 'a Tory mess', with Labour deflecting the blame by 'hitting the Tories hard on opportunism and hypocrisy'. The Tory rebuttal, he knew, would not be believed. Although the Conservatives' ammunition was compelling, the combination of the electorate's star-struck wonder of Blair, Labour's election machine and Tory leader William Hague – not least his folly of wearing a baseball hat at a theme park, making him look foolish – undermined Tory credibility. Nevertheless, at his Boxing Day party for his confidants at Chequers, Blair fretted that Straw was failing to defuse the threat of the Tories taking their votes.

The home secretary was flummoxed. After four years, he was grappling for a reply to Hague's attack that, if re-elected, Labour would turn Britain into a 'foreign land'. The Tories proposed that Britain should be 'a safe haven, not a soft touch'. All bogus asylum-seekers, said Hague, should be sent back to France immediately or incarcerated in new detention centres. Britain had only one such facility, which could hold just 400 people and had cost £8 million to construct. To build new centres for 40,000 people would cost billions. Blair accused Hague of being 'opportunistic' and left it to the media to unravel the Tory plan.

To Blair's distress, Straw's silence was followed by Robin Cook extolling the virtues of more migration and multiculturalism. The British, he said, were a gathering of countless different races whose national dish was no longer fish and chips but chicken tikka masala. 'RC had definitely got us into the wrong place on race,' noted Campbell after Blair complained about 'a catastrophic intervention'. Labour, the prime minister directed, needed to acknowledge that there were 'genuine concerns'. Brown again disagreed. Any mention of immigration or asylum-seekers, he repeated, 'would fuel rather than calm public anxiety'.

As they continued to wade through uncertain territory, Blair and Brown were caught out by the eruption of race riots in Oldham. In anticipation of Labour's uncontrolled immigration being blamed for the riots, Blair blasted the Tories for waging a cultural, racist war. To prove his own anti-racist credentials, Straw volunteered to praise asylum-seekers and immigrants for their contribution to British life. Blair vetoed the idea. Straw, he had decided, would be replaced after the election by Blunkett, whom, he felt, he could trust to navigate through the contradictions. Unlimited immigration was acceptable, but the number of asylum-seekers needed to be either curtailed or relabelled. And that had to be done before the election.

SIXTEEN

Class Conflicts

Ever since Blair had returned from his summer holiday in Italy, Charles Clarke noticed, 'he was frightened about losing the election'. In four areas – education, crime, health and transport – he wanted ammunition to announce 'successes'.

Education did give Blair headlines. Thanks to Labour's numeracy and literacy hours, Michael Barber told him, the results of the key stage two tests for primary schoolchildren in 1999 and 2000 showed a 'big leap'. The rises of 5 per cent in reading and 10 per cent in maths were beyond even Barber's dreams.

Barber credited his Standards and Effectiveness Unit for Labour's 'most conspicuous delivery success'. England's eleven-year-olds had been placed 'among the best in the world' in an assessment survey of literacy and numeracy conducted by PISA, a respected OECD organisation. 'In just over two years,' Barber would write, 'the face of primary education had been changed forever.' With an acute sense of his place in history, Blair did not question Barber's opinion that England's primary schools had suddenly leapt in quality to rank third in the world. Labour could also take the same credit, said Barber, for PISA's glowing report on England's fifteen-year-olds, although the government had left secondary schools untouched so far. Insiders quipped half in jest that the triumph should satisfy Alastair Campbell's lust for the newspaper headline 'Sir Gets a Sir'. No one mentioned that Labour's literacy hour was just one year old and the numeracy hour had not yet started.

Money, Blair believed, was curing his appalling inheritance from the Tories. No fewer than 424 failing schools, he told the public, were being closed down. In 2000, spending on education increased to £56.9 billion, 8.3 per cent more than the previous year. The figure in 2001 would be £62.4 billion, up 9.5 per cent in a year. Since the number of schoolchildren was falling and classes were getting smaller, the government could boast that spending per child would rise within the first parliament by 78 per cent. Pertinently, in 2001 Labour spent less on education as a percentage of GDP than John Major in 1995.

The good news provided Blair with a smokescreen to break an election pledge. He was again tinkering with structures. Two years after the 424 condemned schools had been reopened under Fresh Start, a rebranding programme, Estelle Morris, the junior education minister, told Blunkett that none of those schools was improving. To rescue them, Blair could have adopted Chris Woodhead's proposal to dismiss failing teachers. Instead, he approved a Tory plan to hand the schools over to private sponsors and a board of governors, naming them 'city academies'. He agreed to the same rebranding for failing comprehensives. They were to be recategorised with a designated speciality and given extra funds.

As usual, Blair's espousal of structures, not standards, dissatisfied Woodhead. The chief inspector also criticised Blunkett as 'a table-thumping bully'. The tension between them, Blair decided, had finally become too destructive. 'It's time for Woodhead to leave,' he pronounced. Fortunately, revelations about Woodhead's allegedly inappropriate relationship with a young woman some years previously had surfaced and would limit any political damage. So Woodhead left – a relief to Blair's educationalists and causing no harm politically even when, three months later in the *Daily Telegraph*, the deposed chief criticised Blair for 'not seeing anything through, especially the reforms'. Woodhead also blamed Blunkett for 'wasting taxpayers' money' on endless initiatives that 'encapsulated the worst of the discredited ideology with educational claptrap and wacky initiatives'. His worst moment, the educationalist disclosed, was a serious discussion to rename teachers 'learning professionals'. Blair's defence was Barber's statistics. They were Labour's trump card.

Woodhead's successor at Ofsted, appointed by Blunkett, was Mike Tomlinson, a former chemistry teacher who had been an inspector of schools for twelve years. Aligned to the left, Tomlinson agreed with Blunkett that Ofsted's rigorous inspections of schools should be softened. His priority, he said, was no longer to focus solely on inspections but to work in partnership with teachers. 'Inspections', he told the schools, 'will be done with you rather than to you.'

Blair remained displeased. The primary-school key stage tests, he knew, did not reflect improvements across the whole of education. He demanded 'results'. Blunkett urged patience. 'It was deeply frustrating that progress was so slow,' he would admit. 'We couldn't accept in our heads that it would take so long.' Only later did both men understand the cause of their disappointment. 'We'd started out in 1997 with a real sense of momentum,' Blunkett reflected, 'but we weren't ready for the next step. We'd thought of stage one but not thought of the next stage, of reinforcing primary and secondary schools.'

Michael Bichard agreed. After four hectic years, they had hit the buffers, with no new ideas. Millions of pounds had been poured into 'process' and, like the rest of Whitehall, the education department had fought ferociously over structures and relationships, but too little time had been spent discussing the quality of the service. 'You can't run the system with targets from Whitehall', Bichard realised, 'because you often set the wrong targets.' The department had spent money on new buildings and on raising teachers' salaries. They had spoken about schools being accountable for standards, but too little had been achieved.

Blunkett half agreed. Aware that he would go to the Home Office after the election, he regretted that Blair was irrevocably glued to targets and regular inspections. The prime minister, he thought, had been sucked into centralised intervention; after all, he had refused to abolish the LEAs' supervision of education, and still spoke about the advantages of collaboration and against the Tories' promotion of competition and autonomy. Blunkett had moved on. 'For the second stage,' he realised, 'we needed an exit policy.' To ease the change of policy, embracing Tory ideas without admitting any mistakes, required deft management.

Unknown to his minister, Blair had arrived at a similar conclusion. Just as 'choice' had been introduced into the argument about the NHS, he had been converted to actually embrace 'the parents' right to choose' from a range of schools. But he was nervous of publicly mentioning markets. That would confirm his critics' suspicions that he was heading towards both private education and American-style payments for health care rather than continuing the NHS's free treatment.

Influenced by his experience at the Oratory, Blair acknowledged that the destruction of grant-maintained schools had been a serious mistake. Good schools had been sacrificed to please ideologists. He decided to change course. He had been persuaded that 2,000 comprehensives (nearly half the total) should be converted from schools offering a general education to providing special courses in arts or science by 2005; and although 7,000 of the country's 25,000 state schools were faith schools, he would create even more of them. At a Christian Socialist Movement conference, he preached the virtues of church schools as a pillar of the education system 'valued by very many parents for their faith character, their moral emphasis and the high quality of education they generally provide'.

In 1997, a quarter of England's primary schools (that is, 6,384) and one in twenty secondary schools (589) were run by Christian churches. The Church of England was urged to open another hundred secondary schools within five years. Blair's enthusiasm was opposed by many Labour MPs. Faith schools, he was told, would inevitably lead to Muslim establishments with segregated classrooms teaching Islamic studies and embracing Muslim values. They would separate themselves from the community. The first two Muslim schools approved by Labour in January 1998 had been condemned by the Church Society as 'a foot in the door'. Blair was unimpressed by the protests of what he called 'entrenched interests' who wanted to return to old Labour rather than loosen the government's monopoly and devolve. Schools have to stop treating all the children the same, he told Campbell. His spokesman went public, and immediately incited an argument by disparaging 'bog-standard comprehensives'.

Blair's attitude to education was hardening. 'What gives me real edge', he told an adviser, 'is that I'm not as Labour as you lot.' Thatcher, he was not afraid to admit, had been partly right. The solution was to mix the best of socialism with Thatcherism. There would be top-down directives to meet targets and, at the same time, he would introduce market mechanisms. Adding to that confused ideology, he now advocated changing structures. He made no pretence of being consistent. Prime ministers were allowed to change course, he felt.

Just before the election, there came another shift when Bichard was replaced by David Normington, a skilled Whitehall operator. In an early conversation with Blair, Normington sensed that the prime minister no longer believed in centralisation, and so Blunkett's departure would remove a barrier. He was mistaken. Blair passionately believed in Whitehall's control over local education by using targets. Blair also agreed with Andrew Adonis that the governance of schools should be decentralised, yet both men insisted on keeping centralised control over teachers. They did not trust school principals to dismiss bad teachers, nor did Blair want a battle with the unions about standards. To his senior civil servants, the position made little sense, but Barber, with limited interest in the ideological battle, said nothing. He believed that his new delivery unit – the epitome of centralisation – would solve all the problems.

SEVENTEEN

Unkind Cuts

'This is what we can do,' General Charles Guthrie told Blair in the Downing Street flat just after Leo's birth. Wearing a nightdress, Cherie sat silently near by. Bored by his paternity leave, Blair was nervous.

In March 2000, Sierra Leone, an impoverished former British colony, was in chaos. Rebels were usurping the civilian government, and an inept UN force was unable to protect the population. Blair had agreed that General David Richards should lead a small military group to secure the airport and organise the evacuation of about 400 British citizens.

In a war for blood diamonds, marauding rebels were cutting off limbs as punishment for voting, and murdering helpless civilians. 'I am morally outraged by the amputations,' Richards reported to London from Sierra Leone. In a direct conversation with Robin Cook about imposing an ethical foreign policy, he asked for permission to kill the rebels. The foreign secretary's status, as the army knew, had been dented by his messy divorce and an embarrassing statement to the Commons about his officials' misconduct in allowing Sandline, a private British company, to supply weapons to Sierra Leone; an inquiry would show that Cook had distorted the truth about his officials' proper conduct regarding the arms sale. Cook embellished his ready agreement with Richards by mentioning Blair's interest in a country where his father had worked.

'It's the right thing to do,' declared Blair to a meeting of excited officials. Some 5,000 heavily armed soldiers were dispatched in a naval task force – including a frigate, an aircraft carrier with Harrier jets and an amphibious assault ship with helicopters – that would assemble off the coast of Sierra Leone and confront an ill-disciplined gang of marauders. Within days, the troops had killed the rebels without losses. Richards returned to Britain, leaving behind a group of Royal Irish Rangers to train the Sierra Leone army. Shortly after, some soldiers carelessly allowed themselves to be caught by the West Side Boys, a murderous gang of drug-dealers, and were hauled off into the jungle.

'We must do something,' Guthrie told Blair.

'Will there be casualties?'

'If we do nothing, they'll all be killed or skinned and tortured,' said Guthrie, fearful that the prime minister might go 'limp-wristed'. 'If we try and rescue them, there might be a few casualties, and there could be forty if the helicopter is shot down.'

Blair flinched but, to his relief, the SAS rescue mission was a success. Most of the gang were killed, all the hostages were saved and just one SAS soldier died. Soon after, Blair was given a pop star's welcome in Freetown, the country's capital. Few in London disputed the proportionality of 5,000 troops and a naval task force combating a small group of drug addicts, or questioned Cook's ethical imperialism. Rather, Blair was praised for another military success.

And there would be another. In the wake of Kosovo and Sierra Leone, 300 Gurkhas and a group of SAS troops under Richards's command had policed a peace agreement following riots in East Timor. Blair had found a useful ally in the military. In particular, he liked how the army welcomed a challenge and appreciated leadership. Orders were given, the ranks obeyed and results were delivered. His respect for Guthrie and General Mike Jackson and his suspicion of civil servants gave the armed services an unusual advantage in Whitehall's turf wars.

In the aftermath of these minor engagements, countless position papers criss-crossed Whitehall articulating Blair's doctrine of military intervention to save humanity. No one voiced doubts about the British military's capability or compared the triviality of those engagements with any serious operation. The euphoria of success silenced scepticism. By the end of 2000, the Foreign Office had produced a strategy for a foreign policy that described the military's enhanced capability to execute Blair's blueprint for intervention. Beneath the title, the authors' script failed to anticipate the nature of the conflicts Britain might be fighting. Since there was no precise plan, there was no description of an objective. There was only 'strategy', that frequently misused word in Labour's lexicon.

The new review empowered the generals to become proactive, influencing Britain's foreign policy rather than awaiting orders. Without anticipating the consequences, both the Foreign Office and Blair encouraged the military to accept their ascendant influence. In a government driven by overpromising, any voice of caution was made to feel unwelcome. The change was signalled by the reduced status of Kevin Tebbit, the new permanent secretary at the MoD. His predecessors, such as Frank Cooper, had been Whitchall giants, intellectually equipped to guide and challenge the military and politicians with their recognised expertise. During the Second World War, Cooper's RAF plane had been shot down over Italy. Within twenty-four hours, he had escaped imprisonment and returned to his base. Such bravery counted in the MoD. Tebbit was not in the same position to question ambitious generals like David Richards, who evangelised about Blair's 'force for good' turning Britain into a global troubleshooter. 'Once the military became used more regularly,' Richards believed, 'the civilians could not second-guess the military.' Others rejected that explanation – but silently.

In 2001, Guthrie, fed up with his minister, refused to extend his service as chief of the defence staff, despite Blair's efforts. 'Hoon's a lightweight,' the general declared, and retired. His disenchantment with Geoff Hoon, Robertson's successor as defence minister, was duplicated by his replacement, Admiral Mike Boyce, a taciturn submariner. Despite playing squash with Hoon, Boyce scorned him as 'a bearer of little brain'; he also disliked Tebbit for protecting Hoon rather than championing the military's interests. Neither man, in Boyce's judgement, appreciated the absolute nature of war: risk was endemic, men would die, and nothing should be allowed to obstruct total victory.

With hindsight, Hoon understood that Boyce was 'too straightforward and didn't like the confederation of politicians'. The unusually intelligent admiral agreed: 'I don't do chummy.' Unlike Guthrie, he made little effort to disguise his rational, unemotional approach. The solitariness of submarines was not the best preparation for charming the prime minister, and in turn Blair was displeased at how Boyce chilled rather than warmed the room. The whirlpool of fraught relationships was further complicated by Jonathan Powell's antagonism towards Tebbit ever since the two men had served together at the embassy in Washington. Powell's sentiments influenced Blair, a misfortune for the permanent secretary at the MoD.

Boyce took over in the midst of a Whitehall storm. Gordon Brown's underfunding of the defence budget, the chiefs had discovered, was worse than the £200 million shortfall they had concealed in 1998. 'We are £900 million short every year,' they were told by a vice air marshal reporting to the chiefs. The result was shortages of manpower, equipment and training. 'Blair's championship of "prevention diplomacy" as described in "Defence Planning Assumptions"', the vice air marshal continued, 'doesn't stand the reality test. The question is whether there is a political will to fix it.'

Admiral Nigel Essenhigh, the financial architect of the defence review, suspected the worst. The annual budget, he estimated, was in reality '£2 billion light'. At Blair's request, the chiefs were making plans based on assumptions that Britain could not afford. The army was funded to prepare for war but not to fight one.

In 2001, Brown directed that the MoD should make further cuts. Officials began compiling a 'cut list' of equipment, frigates and planes. Disturbed that the 1998 defence plan would be fundamentally undermined, Essenhigh urged Tebbit to consider 'less damaging savings' by 'smart procurement' and identifying waste. 'Cutting the front line is a flawed approach,' Essenhigh told him. 'We should aim for the flabby costing.'

Tebbit did not agree. He had already made substantial efficiency savings, but Essenhigh was unconvinced and turned to Hoon. 'You're being poorly advised,' he told the minister. 'You're being misled by your officials that we can make savings only by cutting the front line – frigates, RAF squadrons and the army. There are huge savings in the soft underbelly – the bureaucracy, management and procurement.' In Essenhigh's opinion, he was regarded by Hoon as an embarrassment for having the facts at his fingertips.

The minister didn't want to listen and wished Essenhigh would go away. As a last bid, the admiral urged Hoon to tell the prime minister. Hoon refused. Blair, he knew, 'had little control over the Treasury'.

It was Boyce who agreed to confront Blair. Their conversation was predictable. 'You can have all the money you want,' replied Blair courteously, 'but you'll have to ask Gordon.'

The outcome of Boyce's meeting with the chancellor was similarly preordained. 'The military needs at least an extra £500 million every year,' he told Brown, but he had hit a brick wall. 'He offered £150 million,' he recalled later.

Blair asked no questions about what would happen now. Detaching himself from the consequences of underfunding the military, he was preoccupied by the forthcoming election, having received a reprimand from Philip Gould, his trusted adviser: 'You are not focusing on the domestic agenda. Your language is wrong.'

Unmentioned in that message were the fractured relations among the New Labour family.

EIGHTEEN

The 2001 Election

The mood inside Blair's own home had been poisoned by a ninety-minute argument between himself, Cherie, Alastair Campbell and Campbell's combative partner, Fiona Millar, who had told Blair that his government was too right-wing and that he should no longer employ Jonathan Powell or Anji Hunter. Blair replied that he would decide on his staff rather than be subject to Millar's diktat. Her rant spurred Campbell to snap that he would resign after the election, due in spring 2001.

The festering disagreements among Labour's top echelon were stoked by Geoffrey Robinson's newly published memoirs, which offered a gloriously prejudiced description of his service in the Labour government, laced with a disparaging account of Blair's lapses as compared to Gordon Brown's genius. 'I have a real sense of foreboding,' Blair told Peter Mandelson. 'I feel very insecure. It's just not going to work.'

The test of leadership, Blair knew, was to stay in power. In the wake of the petrol crisis, the polls had put the Tories temporarily ahead. Newspapers reported the fading of 'Teflon Tony'. The bad news was compounded by Hunter announcing that she would definitely leave No. 10 after the election. Blair pleaded with both her and Campbell to stay. Without them he felt even more vulnerable, especially because Brown was being 'vile and rude', according to Mandelson, about the election campaign. Blair's charm and popularity enraged the chancellor, who shrugged aside Blair's warning that, if his vitriol did not stop, his expectations for the succession would be stymied. If he were fired, he threatened, there would be war. Blair recoiled. He fulminated about the risk of 'Gordon on the back benches' rousing his considerable army of supporters.

His fears had become profound. Without Brown, he could not fight the election. Only his chancellor had the intellect and political savvy to rout the Conservatives with beguiling slogans and the thunder of competence. Unlike most other ministers, including John Prescott, Stephen Byers, Harriet Harman and Jack Straw, Brown, despite his dubious counting, retained the appearance of running his ministry flawlessly. Somehow he concealed his dithering over decisions, his volcanic temper and his propensity to blame others for his own mistakes, like the award of a 75p pension increase. Brazenly, however, in his quest to become leader he also threatened to destroy the government. 'The two clowns', Alan Milburn told Blair unceremoniously, referring to Brown and Mandelson, 'are harming the government.' Blair's best weapon against Brown, and his only defence against the *Daily Mail*'s latest attacks against Mandelson, was Campbell, who was soon to be deployed when the New Labour family's troubles increased markedly on 21 January 2001.

Norman Baker, a Lib Dem MP, was alleging that Mandelson, by then employed as secretary for Northern Ireland, had interceded with the Home Office to help Srichand Hinduja, an Indian billionaire, obtain British citizenship. Baker knew that, two years earlier, Mandelson had persuaded Hinduja to finance the Millennium Dome's Faith Zone. Mandelson denied Baker's allegation, a denial that was repeated by Campbell to journalists.

Mandelson's answer surprised Mike O'Brien, the immigration minister at the time. Referring to his notes, he recalled a telephone call from Mandelson asking about the application's progress, and mentioned the contradiction to Jack Straw. At that stage, Straw could have remained silent to protect Mandelson and the government. Instead, he telephoned Blair and subsequently appeared on television to say that Mandelson had 'told an untruth'. Not only had Mandelson telephoned O'Brien, said Straw, but he had also asked for his name to be omitted from any parliamentary answer.

Blair was trapped. Mandelson pleaded his innocence – 'I never used my position to help anyone get a passport,' he said – but the media were demanding the resignation of a man who aroused suspicion. While Mandelson fretted, Hinduja was bathing in the Ganges during a festival. To enquiring journalists he denied placing any pressure to obtain British nationality other than asking Mandelson to make 'purely a casual query'. Blair approved an official inquiry into the allegations, but the media were unsatisfied. Mandelson's honesty was widely disputed. The fate of a controversial politician could have awaited an independent report, but Blair was feeling even less secure than usual. At the best of times, holding together a government threatened by the passion of personal rivalries was difficult but, as he well understood, cynicism always triumphed over sycophancy. After four days of torrid headlines, the foundations of his government appeared to have become unusually fragile.

Campbell reckoned that Mandelson had been lying. He had indeed telephoned O'Brien, Campbell decided, and 'had misled us'. Although Richard Wilson told Blair it was all 'a minor mix-up' that should be ignored, Campbell pronounced the opposite and pressured Blair to dismiss Mandelson. In choosing between his two closest aides, Blair surrendered to his overbearing spokesman. 'Peter Mandelson is at this moment upstairs discussing his future with the prime minister,' Campbell told journalists at a briefing on 24 January, implying the minister's departure even before Blair had requested a formal resignation.

Mandelson was outraged by Blair's disloyalty: 'I was simply not worth the trouble and was dispensable.' He also felt 'betrayed' by Campbell, who in turn suggested that Mandelson was 'mentally detached'. Blair absorbed Mandelson's outburst about an unnecessarily ruined career. Although his minister was a gambler, Blair had allowed Campbell, declared by a High Court judge in a recent libel action to be an 'unreliable witness', to destroy an invaluable confidant. His only concession was to describe his doomed adviser's fate as 'tragic'.

On his last morning in office, Mandelson had been served breakfast by his butler at Hillsborough Castle, his official residence in Northern Ireland, and by lunchtime was opening the door of his London house in Notting Hill to take delivery of a 'Mermaid Queen' pizza. Over the following days, he would admit his mistake, then deny his confession and finally repudiate the investigation. 'I came briefly to be persuaded that my recollection was entirely wrong,' he would say, 'that I had erred, and that I should resign. Downing Street sentenced me to political suicide without a fair trial.' No one could have imagined that a consequence of creating a Faith Zone at the Dome would be the termination of a career on account of a 'forgotten' telephone call two years earlier. But, in Blair's judgement, he could not afford to ignore Campbell and take gratuitous risks so close to the election.

In one breath, he had dumped Mandelson and, with Campbell's encouragement, embraced Richard Desmond, a publisher with a background in pornography and other murky business ventures, including a contract in 1991 to supply pornographic magazines to the Gambinos, New York's mafia family.

Blair's interest in the abrasive millionaire was sparked by Desmond's purchase on 22 November 2000 of the Express group of newspapers. Although no longer the dominant influence it was in the Beaverbrook era, the *Daily Express* was still read by over a million people. Its new owner's expectation of respect from Britain's power brokers was instantly rewarded. Within an hour of his arrival at the *Express*'s headquarters, he was telephoned by Blair, who offered his congratulations and an invitation to visit Downing Street the same afternoon.

Blair seemed unaware that in 1997 Desmond had donated £5,000 to the Conservatives and, on that year's election night, had watched with Barbara Windsor – 'wearing our blue badges' – the news of Labour's landslide victory. 'We were crying,' Desmond recalled. Nor did Blair know that, a few months before, Desmond had ordered the editor of his pornographic magazine *Readers' Wives* to 'put Cherie Blair on the front cover'.

On his arrival in Downing Street, Desmond snatched Blair's out-stretched hand and volunteered, 'I'm a socialist.' After some excited small talk about their shared interest in guitars, Desmond agreed that Margaret McDonagh, the Labour Party's general secretary, should visit him to discuss a donation. A day later, he agreed secretly to donate £100,000 to the party.

To cement the new relationship, McDonagh invited Desmond to visit the party's headquarters in Millbank. His appearance shocked Lance Price, a Downing Street spokesman. With Blair's approval, said Price, 'a sleazeball was allowed to run around' the secret sanctum. Days later, Campbell addressed the Express group's editors as members of Labour's election machine rather than independent journalists.

'Can you get Posh Spice to say, "Vote Labour"?' he asked.

'She's Tory,' he was told.

'Beckham?' chimed in Campbell, laughing. The footballer, he was informed, might be a more likely bet, but could not be relied upon to say the right thing.

'I like Blair,' Desmond recounted after his next meeting with the prime minister. He prided himself on having dictated his lunch menu to Downing Street – asparagus, steamed fish and berries – in order to satisfy his diet. 'I can talk to Blair about anything – asylum-seekers, pensions and music. He and his wife are what modern Britain is all about. They are typical *Express* readers, self-made, liberally minded and down-to-earth.' Shortly after, Blair met Anthony Bevins, who had just resigned as the *Express*'s political editor. 'Why did you leave?' Blair asked. Bevins placed in front of him *Horny Housewives*, *Mega Boobs*, *Posh Wives*, *Skinny & Wriggly* and other magazines owned by Desmond. One year later, Blair was asked by Jeremy Paxman on televi-sion whether he knew Desmond published pornography. 'No, I don't,' he replied with doe-eyed innocence.

The new partnership would be tested after the *Mail on Sunday* revealed Desmond's £100,000 donation to the Labour Party and jux-taposed it with Byers's formal approval of the takeover of the *Express* and Desmond's recent employment of McDonagh as general manager of Express Newspapers.

'Richard Desmond', said Alice Mahon, a Labour MP, 'is the last person I would want to support and finance the Labour Party.'

Baroness Kennedy, the Labour lawyer, added about the donation, 'I do think this is tainted money.'

In response, John Reid, the secretary of state for Northern Ireland – his fourth job in the government – retorted, 'If you're asking if we are going to sit in moral judgement on those who wish to contribute to the Labour Party, the answer is no.'

Blair damned all his critics for being part of a 'systematic attempt . . . by some parts of the media to undermine politicians and undermine the political process'.

Events interrupted the flow of Blair's spleen towards his critics. On 19 February, Brian Bender, now the permanent secretary at the Ministry of Agriculture, told Blair that foot-and-mouth disease had been discovered among pigs at an abattoir in Essex. The ministry's policy in such cases assumed that the neighbouring ten farms were at risk. Restrictions on animal movements were imposed and the ministry's staff were deployed to resolve the outbreak. 'You'll have to sort out that mess,' Blair told Bender. His priority was preparing for a meeting at Camp David with George W. Bush, the new US president.

After weeks of turbulence, Blair's critics watched his arrival with Cherie in Washington on 22 February 2001 with particular scepticism. Taking his wife to meet Bush was a risk. Quite possibly she would not conceal her dislike of the Republicans, but rejecting Bush's invitation was impossible. The right-wing president seemed uninformed but safe. 'At Last a US President Who Won't Meddle in Foreign Intervention' was one British newspaper's headline. By the end of their first day in Camp David, Bush's charm had melted Cherie's antagonism. Despite their different political allegiances, the two leaders also bonded over shared philosophies towards terrorism and religion.

Few beyond his inner circle had realised Blair had developed a genuine interest in religion since his days in Oxford with Peter Thomson, the Australian chaplain of St John's. Unlike his predecessors, Blair made no secret of his Christian worship, which Matthew Parris in 1998 perceptively predicted would end with his conversion to Catholicism. Thomson, a lifelong friend, encouraged Blair's conviction that religion lay at the heart of human existence, but sensibly Blair rarely discussed his faith, unless it was with like-minded people, including Bush. Both had read the scriptures, especially with regard to the importance of providence. Among their shared values was a hatred of Saddam Hussein. Blair opposed the dictator in the name of social democracy, while Bush wanted revenge against Saddam following the Iraqi president's failed attempt to assassinate his father, former president George H. W. Bush. During their conversations, Bush reassured his visitor of their union in a moral crusade.

In the press conference at the end of the visit, Bush blessed Blair as 'our strongest friend and closest ally'. The two leaders were asked about sanctions against Iraq. The previous week, American and British planes had attacked targets around Baghdad, the first bombing in nearly two years, evoking protests from many Labour MPs but justified by Robin Cook and the Foreign Office as necessary to prevent the development of WMDs.

'Don't be under any doubt at all', Blair replied, 'of our absolute determination to make sure that the threat of Saddam Hussein is contained and that he is not able to develop these weapons of mass destruction.' Blair's emphasis was on Saddam 'developing' the weapons. After conversations with Bush and the CIA's director, he did not state that Saddam actually 'possessed' them.

He flew back to London exhilarated, but any feelings of triumph soon evaporated. New outbreaks of foot-and-mouth disease had been discovered in Northumberland and Devon. Fifty-seven farms in sixteen counties had been infected even before the first discovery in Essex. The unexpectedly large number of animals being transported around the country was overwhelming the government's outdated contingency plan. Whitehall's leaders had allowed the organisation created during the Second World War to manage civil emergencies to disintegrate. The replacement Cobra machinery, Brian Bender discovered, was 'antiquated. We were making it up as we went along. Everyone was out of their depth.' 'You may be looking for leadership,' Helene Hayman, a junior agriculture minister, told a group of officials in the Cobra room, 'but I'm completely untrained for this role.' In their slow, uncoordinated response, officials were closing down rural areas and culling thousands of healthy animals. Smoking pyres were beginning to cover Britain, as Blair searched forlornly among the civil servants for a solution. In this major battle to save the countryside, he shrank from assuming the mantle of commander-in-chief.

At that moment, Nick Brown, the minister for agriculture and an ally of the chancellor, told David Frost on his television programme, 'I'm absolutely certain we have it under control.' Simultaneously, David King, the government's chief scientific officer, was offering data to Downing Street showing that 'It's all out of control.' The culling of animals, recommended King, would need to be intensified. Notably indecisive, Nick Brown failed to respond. Relations among fearful civil servants became tense and the machinery of government stagnated. Critics, especially in rural areas, accused the government of dithering, while farmers accused metropolitan politicians of disliking the countryside. The public's confidence, as well as Blair's, disappeared as newspapers reported irrational decisions to cull healthy animals.

During visits to infected areas, Blair encountered incompetence, mismanagement and a shortage of trained experts. In London, his principal private secretary, Jeremy Heywood, told Bender to employ sixteen Spanish vets.

'They don't speak English,' Bender replied.

'They can use translators,' said Heywood.

'No,' ruled Bender. 'I can't have a Spaniard telling an English farmer that all his animals must be killed. This is all nasty work.'

The Department of Agriculture, Blair saw, was irretrievably broken.

Healthy animals could have been saved by vaccination, but because of opposition by the farmers' union, King's cull was transforming the countryside into a killing zone. Six and a half million animals were being slaughtered, meat exports were banned and the rural economy was being crippled. The government was spending £8 billion to save the farming industry at the expense of tourism.

This was not an ideal backdrop for an election, even though Labour was still some fifteen points ahead in the polls. Despite the lead, Blair was sufficiently nervous that he postponed the election from May until June.

William Hague calmed the public's anger. The army, he suggested, should take over. In a video conference, Blair's face visibly eased as Brigadier Malcolm Wood provided the solution. Nick Brown was pushed aside in favour of Geoff Hoon but, though the army was critical to the nation's salvation, Gordon Brown was infuriated that his ally had been sidelined. Alternating between sulking and verbally assaulting Blair with demands for his resignation, he refused to allocate additional money for the public services.

'Life is a living hell,' Blair told Powell, and questioned why he would even want to be re-elected. Organising the campaign had become fraught. None of his Downing Street advisers, Blair admitted, including David Miliband and Andrew Adonis, could invent 'a sufficiently compelling vision of a second-term government to engage the electorate'. He summoned Mandelson as the one person with the ingenuity to express 'Blairism' in slogans and ideas.

During his visit to Downing Street, Mandelson found Blair isolated and distracted, 'unsure exactly what his message should be'. One proposed slogan – 'A lot done. A lot still to do' – barely disguised the Labour leader's disappointment about his achievements so far. Blair mentioned his desire for his next government to be 'more radical, more ambitious', especially when it came to health and education. Too often over the previous four years, he volunteered, he had approved government by assertion: spokesmen uttered seat-of-the-pants announcements in the hope that the facts would catch up. Mandelson, on whom Blair relied despite his dismissal from the government, offered reassurance. The theme, he suggested, was New Labour as 'a party of aspiration and compassion'. Blair was relieved, but the respite was brief.

In the midst of their brainstorming, Anthony Hammond, a former Treasury solicitor asked to investigate the saga, delivered his report about Mandelson, who, he concluded, was not dishonest, although a call probably had taken place about Hinduja's application for British nationality. Briefed by Mandelson, Andrew Marr announced on BBC TV that the minister had been cleared. That was untrue, Blair said, and an argument erupted between the two men. Blair drew the line: Mandelson would never return to government.

In the midst of this recrimination, Gordon Brown told a sympathetic journalist that Blair was about to resign. 'You're a crap prime minister,' he raged at Blair to his face, 'and it's time you moved over and let someone better do the job.' Egged on by two aggressive advisers, Ed Miliband and Damian McBride, Brown encouraged Ed Balls to speak to Blair 'like something on a shoe'.

Not discussed amid all the abuse was Hammond's description of the absence of checks on Hinduja by the Home Office. Despite warnings by MI5, the ministry did not ask the police, Inland Revenue or other agencies about the probity of a man who was under investigation in India. Suspicion now fell on Keith Vaz, a junior minister for Europe. His wife ran a company that advised on applications for British citizenship, and it had received money from the Hinduja Foundation. But Blair's self-interest guaranteed that they all survived – except Mandelson.

'I love his deviousness,' sighed Blair's loyal friend, 'the way he is able to turn everything to his own advantage. His genius as a politician is his understanding of people, but also the fact that he is totally selfish and people either don't see it or, if they do, they don't seem to mind because of what he brings to them and the job.'

In the final weeks before the election, outsiders rarely witnessed Blair's doubts. At the launch of the campaign on 8 May in a London school, he appealed to his audience in a relaxed speech, portraying himself as a middle-class evangelist, 'still basically someone who believes in the power of politics to change things'. The opening campaign advertisement was negative: 'The Tories Present "Economic Disaster II". Coming to a home, hospital, school, business near you.'

'Last chance to save the pound,' shouted Hague, leading a faltering party. Oliver Letwin, the shadow chancellor, revealed a proposal to cut taxes by £20 billion, then disappeared in order to avoid the merciless media hounding him to explain which public services he proposed to cut. Mocking the invisible Tory was the ideal backdrop for Brown to warn the country about the impending disaster of the Tories' 'Mr Boom and Mr Bust'.

Yet victory could have been jeopardised on 16 May, the day the Labour manifesto was launched, when Straw was slow-handclapped by the Police Federation, John Prescott was photographed punching a protester, for which he refused to apologise, and Blair was harangued at a Birmingham hospital for two minutes by Sharon Storer about her partner's inability to get a bed the previous night for cancer treatment. 'He suffered terribly,' she told the prime minister in front of the TV cameras, blaming the government and not the hospital. 'You are not giving them the money to give them the facilities. All you do is walk around and make yourself known, but you don't do anything to help anybody.' Supremely polite, Blair did not let his mask slip. Even the succession of disasters did not dent Labour's poll ratings, which showed them up to 26 per cent ahead of the Tories. Blair had faith that Campbell, plying his trade, would drown out the negatives.

True to form, his *consigliere* revealed to the *Mirror* that Blair's hidden strength was his Calvin Klein underpants, and that at the Blackpool party conference in 1996 he had worn a pair specially adorned with a red rose. He even supplied the words for his old newspaper: 'cool men' who wore CKs were men of 'confidence, poise, good sense, sound judgement and style. CKs oozed class and statesmanship.' The following morning, Campbell attacked the tabloid for 'trivialising' politics.

By election day, 7 June, the result was not in doubt. Labour were at least 11 per cent ahead of the Conservatives in the polls, and would win by a margin of 9 per cent. Blair's new majority of 167, losing just six seats thanks to the weak opposition, a sound economy and his own personal magnetism, provided another blank cheque to re-energise his revolution.

At Myrobella, his home in Sedgefield, Blair appeared exhausted and not noticeably joyous. He felt misunderstood and isolated within his own Cabinet. There was a human limit, he decided, to anxiety and responsibility. Political life was not always a pleasure, and he anticipated resigning before the next election. In explaining his moodiness at the moment of glory, he would write, 'I did lack courage.'

In London the following day, the public accolades failed to lift the feeling of anticlimax. Neither his party nor many Cabinet ministers showed genuine gratitude for his achievement. The Brownites scowled and Blair's confidants in Downing Street were at war. Cherie and Fiona Millar renewed their demand that Anji Hunter be dismissed. While Hunter remained, said Cherie, she would feel sidelined. Her jealousy may have been irrational but it was ineradicable. Cherie was 'being ridiculous', declared Blair, startled by the vehemence of the ultimatum. Millar sent a 'vile' email to a friend about Hunter, before Hunter finally offered to go. Only his praetorian guard – including Estelle Morris at education, Stephen Byers at transport and Patricia Hewitt, a former civil rights campaigner sent as the senior minister to the DTI – were unconditionally loyal. He sent them a message radiating positivity. With age and experience, he said, he had learned how to focus on important matters and work the system. New Labour would be reincarnated.

During the upheaval, Blair delayed calling Brown, spending four days hoping to summon up the courage to send him to the Foreign Office. He knew the ensuing argument would be ferocious – not only with Brown, but with John Prescott, Neil Kinnock and other old Labour supporters. 'The decision I didn't take', he would write, 'was to move Gordon . . . the combination of the brilliant and the impossible.' Without the benefit of having studied how predecessors such as Robert Peel, Benjamin

Disraeli, Harold Macmillan and Harold Wilson had shrewdly sidelined their Cabinet rivals, Blair lacked the imagination to exploit his landslide victory. On Monday 11 June, he finally called Brown.

'I assume you want to carry on as chancellor.'

'Yes,' replied Brown stiffly.

Nothing more was said.

PART 2

A SECOND CHANCE

JUNE 2001–MAY 2005

NINETEEN

The Same Old Tale

The day after Labour's re-election, David Blunkett arrived for dinner in the private room of Shepherd's restaurant in Westminster, where he would be briefed by his senior Home Office officials. His two priorities were to reduce crime and stop the rising tide of asylum-seekers. Television pictures from Calais regularly showed men from Iraq, Afghanistan and Zimbabwe plotting to hide on lorries destined for Britain. Their success was highlighted by there being 97,000 applications for asylum in 2000, another record number, only 10,185 of which were recognised as genuine. 'My inheritance from Jack [Straw]', cursed Blunkett, 'is a mess.'

Stephen Boys-Smith confirmed that judgement. 'We are not going to meet our targets for removing failed asylum-seekers,' he told the home secretary, referring to the bogus asylum-seekers from Albania, 'even though we are chartering planes to the Balkans.' Only 4,870 had been deported, half the previous year's number, against a target of 30,000.

'I'll have to clear it up,' Blunkett replied. Labour's liberalism, he added, would not change. Immigration from the Indian subcontinent would not be reduced or even discussed. In 2000, 210,000 immigrants had arrived as 'family members', compared to 70,000 in 1998. He supported more migration, but the controls on bogus asylum-seekers 'need to show we were getting a grip'.

During those days after his victory, Blair focused on the problem – for the first time, Boys-Smith would say – after witnessing Labour's vulnerability during the election. At an early crisis meeting in Downing

Street, Blunkett arrived with John Gieve, his permanent secretary, and Boys-Smith. Blair's 'big issue', Blunkett knew, was the quick removal of anyone with an unfounded claim. His anger was directed at the unjustified welfare demands by the Roma and other benefit tourists.

Blunkett waved that aside as a minor issue. 'Our real problem', he said, 'is that controls over immigration into Britain have broken down. The asylum-seekers are economic migrants who want to work and live here.'

'I understand why they want to come,' came the reply, 'but they can't come as asylum-seekers.'

Knowing that Blair supported managed migration, Blunkett summarised Sarah Spencer's opinion. 'You can't shut the door,' the academic had explained. 'No government can control the number of economic migrants, neither by keeping people out nor by removing them. The government's strategy is wrong because it's failing to manage the public's expectations.' The general hostility to asylum-seekers, Blunkett was persuaded, could be reduced by admitting them as skilled migrants and giving them work permits.

Obeying his political director Sally Morgan's advice that he should not upset Labour supporters, Blair approved the ruse. 'Right, this is what we'll do,' he said, his eyes tightening to suggest his determination. Blunkett would issue 150,000 work permits in 2002. Most of those migrants, including the unskilled, would become British citizens.

As usual, the rising number of legal immigrants arriving every year from the Indian subcontinent was not mentioned. 'Lifting the primary purpose rule', Blair admitted to Blunkett, 'was a mistake. It seemed the right thing to do in opposition, but I never thought that Afghanis, Iraqis and Somalis would take advantage of the change.'

'Nothing can be done any more,' replied Blunkett, who had also supported removing the rule. Neither politician, their civil servants and special assistants knew, wanted to discuss the new problems of polygamy, phoney marriages and the thousands entering Britain using invented relationships.

Convinced that his first term had been damaged by ineffectual officials, Blair appointed the educationalist Michael Barber to head a new Delivery Unit. Civil servants would be directed to meet specific targets on 160 policies. With targets, Blair sensed, would come results.

One month later, Blunkett and Gieve returned to Downing Street for Barber's stock-take. Applications for asylum, Barber reported, were still rising. In reply, Gieve assured Blair that IND officials were making quicker decisions. Blair nodded. He was aware that these quicker decisions were not hastening the removal of failed asylum-seekers or halting the numbers. On the contrary, Boys-Smith had made the decision-making process faster in order to allow asylum-seekers to remain in Britain. No one volunteered to tell Blair that the new regulations were encouraging migrants. As Matt Cavanagh, a special adviser in the Home Office, would confirm, Blair 'shared a conviction that immigration was good for Britain and the British economy'. The Cabinet was still not asked to discuss the principle.

As the weeks passed, Blunkett failed to get to grips with the IND. 'God knows what Jack did for four years,' he complained, adding later, 'I am simply unable to comprehend how he could have left it as it was.' His spleen was directed at his staff in particular. Despite more officials having been recruited, the organisation was not improving. Blunkett blamed Gieve, whom he viewed as aloof and no better than the 'hopeless' Richard Wilson. He also condemned Boys-Smith as 'incompetent'. For their part, Boys-Smith and his colleagues were not enamoured of Blunkett's 'bullying and aggressive style'.

'It's abysmal,' Blunkett told Blair. 'Nothing had prepared us for this. It's worse than any of us imagined possible.' He wanted Blair to approve Gieve's dismissal. 'We made a mistake of not reforming the civil service in 1997,' he cursed. Blair's response was more diffident than during the old days when they had discussed education. Now, he urged Blunkett to find a solution but offered no ideas of his own. Their discussions, Blunkett lamented, had become 'always fraught'.

By the time of Barber's next stock-take, in early September, IND officials had already come up with a ruse to win approval. By ticking the right boxes in Barber's questionnaire, Gieve could give the impression of 'limited progress'. Blair and Blunkett were not convinced. To secure some political advantage, they directed Gieve to draft new legislation. 'We need to show that we have the numbers under control,' repeated Blair.

After the meeting, rather than introducing new laws to strip asylum-seekers of their legal rights and welfare benefits, Blunkett agreed that Nick Pearce, his special assistant, should write a White Paper to be called 'Secure Borders, Safe Haven – Integration with Diversity'. Pearce's intention was to improve foreigners' conditions in Britain. The fevered media reports from Sangatte, he believed, were inciting anti-immigration sentiment. Asylum-seekers, he agreed with Spencer, deserved the benefit of new citizenship rules to help their settlement. They knew that Blair supported the principle. If only, Pearce lamented, they could get rid of the poisonous headlines.

TWENTY

The Blair 'Which?' Project

'We need to see how we can break the monochrome,' Blair told Alan Milburn, his health minister, soon after the 2001 election.

The campaign slogans about closing the health gap between rich and poor, the pledges about building 'a world-class public service', recruiting 80,000 extra nurses, reducing waiting times from eighteen to six months and cutting waiting lists by 100,000 were meaningless when some health authorities, it was revealed, were massaging lists by removing names. The NHS Plan 2000 had produced headlines but still no profound solution, not least because Gordon Brown still refused to fund the expansion. The promise to build new hospitals and appoint thousands of new staff, Neil McKay, a senior official in Richmond House, the NHS's headquarters in Whitehall, told Milburn, was not enough: 'You need to change the way NHS people think.' Milburn's answer was to give Nigel Crisp, his new NHS chief, whom he barely knew, additional power.

In an unusual breach of precedent, Blair and Milburn had decided not only to remove Christopher Kelly, the permanent secretary at the Department of Health, but also to scrap his job. Crisp would be simultaneously the permanent secretary and the NHS's chief executive. Crisp arrived convinced there was 'a real doubt whether the NHS could survive'. His melodramatic assumption reflected his professional bias. 'I was always interested in NHS staff and not politicians,' he said. The suspicion was mutual. Milburn blamed NHS executives like Crisp for blocking Blair's modernisation ambitions. NHS managers, he told

Blair, were culpable for the long delays and dirty wards. Now, the two politicians were dependent on another civil servant similar to all the others they disdained.

The politicians' distrust of the bureaucrats was mirrored by the public's shock over medical negligence. A report had confirmed that, during the late 1990s, doctors at the Bristol Royal Infirmary had caused the deaths of twenty-nine babies; another report disclosed that Dr Harold Shipman, a GP in Manchester, had probably murdered over 200 of his patients. 'This year must be the turning point for the NHS,' Blair impatiently told NHS executives. He resented the experts' warning that, despite the billions of pounds spent since 1997, they would need ten years to effect an overhaul. Ten months rather than ten years was his timetable, and his guests' protests were unwelcome. The experts' reaction, he wrote, was 'a betrayal of public service ethos. I began to look for ways of getting business ideas into public service practice.'

In reality, he was stumped. Other than spending money on new buildings and employing more people, he had no new ideas. Yapping at his ankles, Roy Hattersley, an old Labour stalwart, was deriding his 'free-for-all philosophy' for shifting the party to the right with 'vacuous platitudes'. And Brown was still refusing to allocate the extra money.

'We have to cut the waiting times for operations,' Blair was told by Simon Stevens, his trusted adviser. 'That's the key to improving public satisfaction.'

Blair agreed. He despairingly compared civil servants to the army and its successful response to the outbreak of foot-and-mouth disease. 'Why did the army succeed?' he asked rhetorically. 'Because they didn't take "no" for an answer. They used rules as a means to an end.' If only civil servants became social entrepreneurs taking risks to 'achieve change', many problems would be solved.

Once again, he trusted one of Britain's self-publicising businessmen to deliver salvation, although like Richard Branson and Richard Desmond, his latest hero, Stelios Haji-Ioannou, the founder of easyJet, had orchestrated several unsuccessful ventures. Unaware of his failings,

Blair invited the Greek to map out the path for reform. The honest answer was disappointing. 'You can't have an entrepreneurial civil service', Haji-Ioannou explained, 'because you don't have any competition.' Milburn's snap advice, after returning from his constituency with a litany of complaints about the NHS, was, 'We must get back to choices.'

Blair liked 'choice' as a slogan and had embraced it for education, but was resistant to adopting it for the NHS – as Julian Le Grand discovered when, during a conversation, the professor revealed a statistic. Productivity in the NHS, he told Blair, had peaked in 1997 and ever since had been flat. In 2001, it was beginning to slide back. Although the measurements were controversial, the trend as monitored by the reputable King's Fund was embarrassing. The crunch statistic was 'activities'. Despite all the extra money – £5 billion more in 2001 – spent on additional staff, higher wages and drugs, the number of patients being treated had risen by less than 1 per cent since 1997. Targets were intended to place NHS professionals under pressure to deliver, but they were failing in their efforts.

'Is this true?' asked Blair, clearly surprised.

'Yes,' Le Grand replied. 'Productivity increased with choice and the internal market.'

'Well, if that's what the data shows . . .' said Blair, unsure about his next step. He knew the Labour Party's limits. Unlike the Tories, his supporters were not suspicious of the state. He had ostentatiously jettisoned Thatcherism and old Labour's socialism, but the Third Way had not provided an answer. Nor had discussions with the trade unions. He never mentioned productivity to Nita Clarke, his special adviser liaising with the unions. Aggressive incentives were one solution, but Brown prevented their introduction. Milburn's answer was five well-funded regulators and the Modernisation Agency, another quango that armed the regulators with 'targets and terror' to improve the NHS through rewards and warnings.

Blair was still searching for a speedier cure. The NHS was absorbing money like a sponge, yet failing to treat the anticipated numbers of additional patients. He invited Le Grand to return to Downing Street. In successive conversations, the professor explained that a better alternative to targets was the market. 'Markets don't distort like targets,' he said. 'Patients' pressure through patients' choice, or patients' screams, will improve the NHS. Hospitals will have to be nice to patients.' Blair was not wholly convinced but agreed that Le Grand could stage a PowerPoint presentation in Downing Street.

Among the seven in attendance, Ed Balls and Ed Miliband challenged the academic scathingly. 'What are the ideological foundations of choice?' they asked.

'They tried to intimidate me,' Le Grand said later, 'but I could not understand their ideological reasons.' He did not give up, describing to Blair the solution based on payment by results, which effectively restored GPs as fund-holders.

'How do we know it will work?' asked Blair. Le Grand resisted the obvious answer: because the scheme had succeeded under the Tories.

Milburn, however, was a convert. Money and targets alone, he conceded, could not improve the NHS. 'The simple truth is that the NHS cannot be run from Whitehall.' The absurdity of such command and control had struck him after he was called upon to dismiss a hospital executive in Bedford for mismanaging a mortuary. In his search for solutions, during a brainstorming session with Loraine Hawkins, an expert on health systems, he was told: 'Do you realise that in Australia they got 20 per cent more activity in hospitals by using payments by results?' Milburn liked that idea and another proposal put forward at the same time by Simon Stevens, who was advocating the advantages of the Swedish health-care system, which allowed patients to choose the hospital where they would be treated, using the state's money. 'Right, let's do that,' Milburn said, without mentioning the resemblance to the Tories' derided 'patient voucher' scheme. 'Don't even go there,' he warned a smiling civil servant who was clearly tempted to make the point.

In a moment of epiphany, he next told Blair that the answer was to decentralise decision-making to local communities and 'empower' individual patients. Choice and a market culture, he said, would cleanse the NHS of the 1948 relics so entrenched within the party, especially the dogmatism of both the trade unions and the NHS staff. Blair liked the sentiment but, as always, disliked the word 'market'. Labour voters would assume a lurch towards the American system of payment for health treatment, and that would be bad politics. As usual, no one fully understood Blair's intentions, not least because, despite his enthusiasm, he obviously remained undecided on which direction was best.

Undeterred, Milburn urged Blair to revive the internal market, but in a more radical manner than the Tories. Blair asked Chris Ham to recruit fifteen people for a new strategy unit, using the code name 'rainbow project', to pave the way for another White Paper. To protect the project's secrecy, civil servants in the Department of Health were excluded. Hostile officials, Blair feared, would tip off Brown and Balls about the plan. The results were delivered in early summer 2001. The project recommended moving the NHS towards the market and choice. 'A fundamental wake-up moment,' said John Hutton, the junior health minister.

By then, Blair was admitting that his appointment of Frank Dobson had shown 'how little I understood' about the modern world. He was ready to think about a health 'market', but the appropriate cosmetics were vital. He had come to accept that patients' treatment could only improve if the NHS embraced the private sector. The money should follow a patient to a hospital. He liked the artificial distinction made by Stevens between the 'patient's passport' or 'voucher', a Tory idea, and the unlabelled 'patient's right to choose'. Similarly, he nodded through Milburn's proposed foundation hospitals, which would be independent and free from Whitehall control, even though they were a development of the Tories' hospital trusts, which Labour had opposed.

The battle lines were drawn, only Blair was hazy about the implications. 'He wasn't an economist,' noted Le Grand, 'so he didn't understand markets. He didn't know where he was heading.' His plight was not helped by the lack of a senior economist as an adviser at No. 10. Unlike Ken Clarke, who had delighted in challenging vested interests,

Blair sidestepped conflict. He ignored one of Peter Mandelson's rules: 'If a government policy cannot be presented in a simple and attractive way, it is more likely than not to contain fundamental flaws and prove to be the wrong policy.' A new plan was only workable if it could be sold.

To test the Labour Party, in July 2001 Blair spoke at the Royal Free Hospital in north London, advocating the privatisation of some services. The NHS, he said, should employ the private sector to perform non-emergency surgery, hire foreign surgeons and allow NHS patients to be treated in France. Sixteen months earlier, he had made the same suggestions but had been ignored. This time, he was attacked instantly by the trade unions and Labour MPs. 'If the unions want a fight,' he countered, 'they can have one.' One moment he recoiled from confrontation, and the next he threatened battle. The inconsistency reflected his vacillation, unlike Milburn: 'I welcomed a fight,' the minister recalled, 'but I wanted to win. I didn't want to do fifteen rounds in one round. I needed to stretch the elastic to move on.'

One principal adversary was Nigel Crisp. In an unexpected blast of criticism, the NHS's chief executive opposed the private sector receiving public money. Blair knew that too many NHS executives were institutionalised, but he had not expected fossilisation to encroach at the very summit. Crisp, he discovered, typified the conviction within the profession that the NHS Plan 2000 was the Bible and, beyond spending additional billions, nothing should undermine the sanctity of the national monopoly. The problem, as Neil McKay, the Richmond House official, observed, was that Crisp was not managing the disbursement of the money. 'There was a sense that Crisp had no grip on the finances,' thought McKay, but nothing was said to Milburn – or to Blair.

With the prime minister's blessing, Milburn presented a White Paper entitled 'Shifting the Balance of Power in the NHS'. Ostensibly, he was replacing the top-down command system with local groups. In reality, a flurry of contradictory changes reflected his indecision about who should manage the NHS. First, the eight regional health authorities were cut to four. Soon after, these four were demolished and resurrected as twenty-eight strategic health authorities and a hundred health authorities. The differences were imperceptible. To remove dud managers, Milburn started a carousel of executives being dismissed from one post only to be re-employed by another health authority, and that continued when those authorities delegated their power to 481 primary-care groups, heralded as 'the front line', under new directors. In the process, over 30,000 administrators were shunted around, reflecting the disagreement between Crisp, Milburn and Blair about the ideal size and structure of the NHS's management. Should it be big or small? Dictated from Whitehall or devolved?

Over the summer, Blair's talk about the market continued to inflame the opponents. Milburn fed the dispute by speaking about 'a self improving culture' at local levels, but no ministers or civil servants understood his plans. The dilemma was not surprising: other than advocating 'choice', Blair was no more certain about the principles on which the NHS should be reconstructed than he had been when he first took office. Resolving the conundrum required a leap of political conviction – that competition could reduce waiting times – and he was reluctant to make that jump.

To help resolve matters, a few Blairite ministers were invited to Chequers on the eve of the summer holidays. In unusually nonchalant mood, Blair urged his supporters to praise choice for both parents and patients. Their response was not enthusiastic. Educating his party to somersault and embrace choice as 'progressive' required proof of his sincerity. 'It's going to be hell for a large part of the time,' he told Michael Barber. 'But I don't see any point in being prime minister unless we take risks.'

The issue was still not resolved when he left for a holiday at the Mexican seaside, where he and Cherie underwent a 'rebirthing experience', which involved covering themselves with watermelon, papaya and mud and screaming loudly to signal the pain of birth. They travelled on to Egypt, where the proposition of bowing to Brown's new demand for his resignation before the next election disappeared. 'I'm not going to be pushed out,' he told Mandelson on his return. He also decided that Anji Hunter should finally leave. Her continued presence was aggravating his relationship with Cherie, and he could no longer resist Hunter's own insistence that she resign in order to take a senior post at oil giant BP. Relations between the two old friends appeared to have deteriorated to such an extent that Blair would fail to attend her farewell party.

Enjoying the September sunshine at Chequers, he redrafted his conference speech about – yet again – modernising Britain. He also handwrote a note advocating more cash for schools and hospitals. His target was Brown. Before Blair's summer holiday, the chancellor had reasserted his refusal to advance additional money for either ministry. Instead, he sidelined Blair's priorities to highlight his own flagship scheme: means-tested tax credits that would capture most of Britain's population as recipients of state benefits.

The idea of such credits had been introduced to Brown by Ed Balls. The scheme, designed by Larry Summers, a Harvard professor, was aimed at helping the poor and accelerating social engineering. Blair had discovered that the introductory cost was over £2 billion, four times higher than Brown's original estimate. 'They basically lied to me about it,' he complained. In reality, Brown's tax credits were costing £4 billion a year and, financed by loans, were rising remorselessly (by 2015, they would cost £30 billion a year). And because the programme was unsupervised, the payments had become chaotic.

Dithering and meddling as usual, Brown had become the unsuspecting victim of incompetent computer programmers. He had also not understood that many poor people were incapable of completing the application forms for credits, leaving thousands of genuine claimants penniless. Nor did he grasp that the Inland Revenue was not set up to administer a welfare scheme. To Blair's misfortune, none of his own advisers realised that the scheme, organised by the Treasury without consultation, was turning into a debacle.

On that Sunday night in Chequers, he ordered that a copy of his memorandum about the NHS be sent to his chancellor. 'We thought he was crazy to think that Brown would be converted by his note,' recalled a Downing Street adviser. Regardless, Blair summoned a meeting on 6 September. At the outset, the discussion was about the gap between rhetoric and policy, and the huge cost of more change in the NHS. Blair waved the objections aside. His message was 'deliverology', a new word heralding a new vocabulary for the structural reforms to health, schools and universities. The agent for change would be targets administered by Michael Barber.

Flattered by the spotlight and Blair's trust, Barber did not offer complete reassurance. The civil service, he explained, required clarity, leadership and a sense of urgency, and without being told any plans, officials lacked confidence in the government. He did not complete his indictment. In his unsuccessful search for 'coherence at the centre of government', he blamed Blair for creating the problem by establishing competing quangos and targets.

Nearly two years after his commitment on David Frost's TV show to increase spending and change the NHS, Blair was still floundering.

TWENTY-ONE

Instinct and Belief

For many, the appointment of Estelle Morris as education minister was a surprise. Morris had failed her A-levels and, although she was a popular teacher, her nail-biting and shyness suggested a lack of self-confidence. During a brief conversation in Downing Street after her appointment, Blair did not discuss his expectations, while Morris did not mention her concern over his shift towards choice and diversity for schools. 'Market mechanisms to accommodate choice don't work with education,' she believed. She also disputed Andrew Adonis's bold assertion that he had contributed to the expansion of good schools. Blair was unconcerned. As ever, he gave little weight to what Cabinet ministers said.

Morris's department was suffering ideological turmoil when she arrived. Under Blair's new agenda, nearly a third of all comprehensives had been converted into specialist schools and, since he was persuaded that faith schools 'add to the inclusiveness and diversity of the system', more of that kind were expected. Labour MPs opposed to this mentioned the recent riots by Asian youths in northern England. In his report about the disturbances, Sir Herman Ouseley would identify Muslim-populated schools in the inner cities, which effectively had a single culture, as potential breeding grounds for intolerance and racism. Under the Tories, faith schools had been integrated into the state system but were empowered with state funds to develop a distinctive ethos, morality and curriculum.

Blair was unimpressed, and approved a £12 million grant to build a secondary school for Muslim girls in Birmingham. Forty-five Labour MPs revolted against the legislation backing faith schools, forcing the government to accept that such schools would have to admit 25 per cent of non-faith children. Blair blamed left-wing ideologues and not fears about Islamic extremists for the opposition. The same critics rejected his decision to privatise more state schools. Opinion polls showed that two-thirds of the public wanted only the state to provide education. Blair's ideas encouraged trade-union leaders to conjure up images of greedy capitalists charging parents and the sick for schools and medical care. 'I feel my persuasiveness is slipping,' Blair told Peter Mandelson 'For the first time, I felt they were not buying into what I'm saying. They are listening and rejecting.'

At a dinner for his 'delivery ministers', Blair was noticeably depressed by his party's criticism. Coming so soon after he had delivered a second landslide victory, he was barely consoled by the jolly mood and the loyal people he had placed in key departments. Gordon Brown, he realised, was telling his supporters that the prime minister was stumbling, losing his touch and planning Thatcher-style privatisation. The dissenters were encouraged to sabotage his ambition for public-service reforms. Brown was personally insisting that every department abide by public-service agreements imposed by the Treasury. Blair despaired. 'It's intimidation in order to dislodge me,' he complained. 'I asked him all the right questions about the 1998 Comprehensive Spending Review,' he told a confidant, 'but I was lied to. I'm ready this time.'

His new armoury consisted of three divisions based in Downing Street: Michael Barber's Delivery Unit; a Strategic Unit under Geoff Mulgan to advise on future policies; and the Office of Public Sector Reform under Wendy Thompson to transform Whitehall into a centre for entrepreneurs. Thompson was delegated with pioneering 'choice and diversity' and overcoming the civil servants' uncertainty about Blair's intentions. In the exuberant language favoured within No. 10, Mulgan was asked to produce 'strategic policy challenges' that would make society work better by 'enhancing the individual, the market and the society with security and a stable sense of being'. The elaborate wording was adopted to disguise the reality of government.

A major fissure appeared during the summer. Morris was hesitant about the contents of her new White Paper and asked for a delay. 'Flaky,' Alastair Campbell noted. Sensitive about Morris's hesitancy, Blair realised how many in the party disliked New Labour. Even the Blairites were split. Morris's White Paper, 'Schools: Building on Success', did not resolve the disagreements.

Brown continued to create problems. First, he had seized control of Sure Start and, without waiting for proof of success, announced that the number of centres would double to 500, with the annual budget increased from £184 million in 2000/1 to £499 million in 2003/4. Although Naomi Eisenstadt, the director, protested that confusion, acrimony and disputes between constantly changing ministers and officials made it too early to evaluate the programme, Brown demanded the creation of a sticker declaring 'success'.

Such haste troubled Eisenstadt. In an unexpected turf war, Sure Start found itself contending with a glut of other big-budget government programmes, announced with great fanfare, to cure poverty, including Health Action Zones and the 'New Deal for Communities'. All those armies of social workers would produce limited benefits. Then Eisenstadt discovered that the teenage single mothers targeted by Sure Start were uninterested in the programme, which as a result could not find sufficient children to rescue from poverty. Instead, middle-class mothers were taking millions of pounds to finance their own niche groups.

Brown's more serious problem was the Independent Learning Accounts (ILAs), which provided government grants for free adult education. In May 2001, the government handed out £273 million to a million of these accounts. By September, 2.5 million of them had received over £500 million and 8,910 companies were registered to provide the education. Morris's senior officials rejoiced, unaware that those responsible for the programme had become suspicious that the ILAs were a honeypot for fraudsters, with 6,000 applications being received from just one address. By then, at least £100 million had been lost to fraud.

The programme was suspended. Some ministers blamed their officials for naivety; others said that the fraud showed that Labour could not trust the civil servants, who lacked any incentive to tell the truth. Blair despaired that here was yet another example of Whitehall's failure to deliver. At the same time, in his familiar language, he wanted to cast aside cautious government and, with 'radical thinking', drive 'modernisation' from the centre. His tangled message for the annual meeting of the trade unions would be that they should end their 'outdated thinking', especially those trade unionists who said that 'education is for children, not for profit'.

On 11 September 2001, Blair arrived in Brighton to address the TUC Congress. His sour relationship with the unions, he knew, was unlikely to have been altered by the election victory. John Edmonds, the union leader for local authority workers, had predicted in that morning's newspapers 'a bumpy ride. This is Tony Blair's last chance to step back from the brink.' Blair's speech advocating public-service reform was certain to reinforce their mutual dislike. His loyal supporter Patricia Hewitt, he knew, had been received in sullen silence the previous day. Blair did not enjoy the twists and turns of his relationship with the unions. 'They could not understand why I was doing what I was doing, and I could not understand why they could not see it was the way of the future,' he would write.

He had built his career on attacking the unions, challenging the closed shop in 1989, then winning the vote to abolish Clause Four. Rewriting that clause in modern terms, replacing the pledge for mass nationalisation of industry with a meaningless promise to welcome 'power, wealth and opportunity in the hands of the many, not the few', was Blair's coup against the party. His polished revision rebuked the committed socialists but preserved a fig leaf to distinguish Labour from the Tories. To the Congress's additional dismay, he had refused to repeal Thatcher's anti-union laws and defied those left-wingers pledged to save the party's soul. To continue fighting the class war, Blair retorted, was pointless. He had won the leadership with 57 per cent of the total vote, without needing the unions' support. Ever since that victory, he was convinced that with unwavering willpower he would always triumph.

Just after his first general-election victory, he had spelled out in the same hall in Brighton his belief that the unions were partly to blame for preventing the modernisation of Britain. In 2001, his prepared speech again defined himself against those stubborn forces of conservatism within the Labour Party.

Just before he was due to step on stage, two hijacked passenger planes crashed into the Twin Towers in south Manhattan. A Pearl Harbor moment for America would change Blair's destiny for ever. Abandoning his speech, he headed back to London on a commuter train. During the hour-long journey, he appeared transformed, even traumatised. The warnings by the intelligence services after the recent fatal Islamic terrorist attacks in Kenya and Aden had proven to be understated. The world, he convinced himself, had fundamentally changed on his watch. Islam was no longer a benign religion but one that was being usurped by extremists to destroy Western values. In the battle between good and evil, his responsibility now was to save civilisation. Rather than contemplate how normality might be restored, he was planning to embark on a worldwide crusade.

London felt eerie as Blair was rushed to Downing Street to prepare a speech committing him to stand alongside President Bush. 'It was not America alone who was the target,' he later wrote, 'but all of us who shared the same values. It was war. It had to be fought and won. It was a battle for and about the ideas and values that would shape the twenty-first century.' Unmentioned was his new conviction about the threat from Islamic fundamentalists.

In years to come, he would admit his misunderstanding of Islam but would deny that his ignorance was to blame for his response. 'The only course', he wrote, 'is to follow instinct and belief.' Even after reflecting for nine years, Blair ignored the importance of acting on the basis of expert knowledge gained through reading and listening. During the summer of 2001, he had read the Koran rather than a series of new books describing recent conflicts in the Middle East. The nuances of the schism between Sunnis and Shiites and the tribal antagonisms embittering relations across the Muslim world were not reflected in the Koran. Blair never questioned the inherent dangers of relying on 'instinct and belief'.

He repeated his view that this was 'an attack on America but also an attack on our values' to the group awaiting him in the Cobra room. 'We shall support America in anything they do,' he told them. The senior military officer present was surprised by Blair's 'excited rant' and welcomed Blunkett's intervention – 'Provided we check the intelligence first.' Blair ignored his home secretary, and no one else spoke. That night, he publicly committed Britain to 'stand shoulder to shoulder with our American friends in this hour of tragedy, and we, like them, will not rest until this evil is driven from our world'. The label of 'evil' was not fixed on any one person in particular. 'Are we bombing Baghdad?' an official in Downing Street asked the liaison officer in the Ministry of Defence.

Elsewhere in Westminster that day, Jo Moore, the special adviser trusted by Stephen Byers at the DTI, sent out an email: 'It's now a very good day to get out anything we want to bury. Councillors' expenses?' Her email was later leaked to the media. Also that day, Byers quietly made a series of telephone calls to begin the appointment of administrators for Railtrack, the privately owned and solvent company whose unknowing shareholders were about to lose their money.

On the same day, Blair called Brown to discuss the crisis. 'When are you resigning?' was Brown's response. Speechless, Blair slammed down the phone.

Within twenty-four hours, there was no doubt that the attack had been plotted by Osama bin Laden, the leader of al-Qaeda, from his base in Taliban-controlled Afghanistan. In Blair's conversation with Bush on 14 September about those responsible, the American president mentioned Iraq's possible relationship with al-Qaeda, which had never previously been associated with the country. At the time, Downing Street's spokesman relayed Blair's reply that they would need to find the evidence for that link, and the immediate focus should be on the Taliban. In 2010, Blair admitted that 'at the forefront of my mind' immediately after 9/11 was his fear that terrorist groups would gain possession of weapons of mass destruction.

One of the sources of his conflation of Osama bin Laden, international Islamic terrorism, WMDs and Iraq was Richard Dearlove. Accompanied by the MI6 chief during his flights around Europe as the self-appointed broker gathering support for American retaliation in the newly named 'war against terror', Blair took in Dearlove's conviction that Iraq possessed WMDs. He also heard that a suicide bomber could possibly trigger a nuclear explosion in London. Dearlove's warnings were not dismissed. On the contrary, he was telling the prime minister what he expected to hear and, in the can-do manner beloved by Blair, highlighting his new priority of killing bin Laden.

On the morning of 20 September, just before flying to New York for a memorial ceremony for the 3,000 victims of the attack, Blair attended the regular education stock-take in Downing Street. 'I might be preoccupied for a while,' he told the small group, 'but I don't want you to forget how important education is for me.' In an emotional farewell, everyone shook his hand in what the education department's permanent secretary David Normington would call 'a heart-stopping moment'.

During the flight, accompanying journalists were informed that Blair was reading the Koran. Taut and sombre, he later told them that he bore a 'huge and heavy responsibility'. At the same time, Foreign Office officials were working hard to persuade Bush to emphasise that Afghanistan was the danger, not Iraq. They took comfort from the fact that the president's speech to Congress on 21 September avoided linking Iraq with the New York massacre. Cool heads cut through the emotion.

Twelve hours later, raw passion convulsed the congregation in New York as they listened to the address, which included a message from the Queen to the bereaved: 'Grief is the price we pay for love.'

TWENTY-TWO

Hither and Dither

Towards the end of November 2001, Blair was discussing with his foreign-affairs advisers the bombing campaign against the Taliban in Afghanistan. A small contingent of British SAS soldiers was support-ing the American special forces, who were guiding the US air force's bombing raids and cruise missiles. Out of the blue, he asked, 'Is there any danger that America will bomb Iraq?'

'No,' was the unanimous reply.

Blair's question was surprising. No one had found a link between Saddam Hussein and Osama bin Laden. 'I'd like a strategy paper on Iraq,' he concluded.

Unknown to those advisers, Blair had heard from President Bush that in January he would name Iraq as one of the 'axis of evil' countries whose reigning government should be toppled. He was not entirely surprised. The Iraq Liberation Act passed by Congress in 1998 empow-ered the president to remove Saddam, and ever since their meeting in February the two men had been discussing the continued risk of Iraq developing WMDs, despite the Anglo-American bombing raids. Blair knew that the mood in Washington had changed fundamentally. Before 9/11, American policy had been to contain dangerous dictators, but Bush now supported confronting them.

Blair's thoughts since September had moved in the same direction. An ideological war, he concluded, had broken out, a 'fundamental struggle for the mind, heart and soul of Islam'. More accurately, he reduced the conflict to 'our values versus theirs'. As he had told his party conference later that month, 'There is no compromise possible with such people – just a choice: defeat it or be defeated by it.' He persuaded himself that the battle of values 'required interventions deep into the affairs of other nations', as well as 'nation-building' to promote democracy and freedom. 'I thought we had to provide a comprehensive strategy for changing the world,' he would write. 'Not fighting until victory would have been cowardice.' The 'force for good' would wipe terrorism and all the other evils off the face of the earth. Purposefully, he offered to 'lead the world' in restoring order and building a 'coalition against terror'. 'Mission creep and we haven't even started,' Simon Jenkins had noticed just two weeks after the attack. The same government that could not prevent a few handfuls of asylum-seekers creeping through Dover was ready to wage a global war against terror.

Even the White House noted that Blair was more hawkish than its president. Only later did Blair acknowledge, 'I misunderstood the depth of the challenge.' At that moment he was fired up to take on all his foes, and his speech to the party conference included among the villains both those who denied global warming and trade unionists who obstructed reform of the public services.

Of those who did formally warn Blair about the perils of his planned crusade one of the best informed was Admiral Mike Boyce. Boyce knew that the British military's contribution to America's war on terror would be minuscule. Even the government's offer to send 6,000 troops to Afghanistan had been rejected by the Pentagon. Blair's commitment was driven entirely by an untested philosophy, and he could not provide a definition of 'victory' that would end the war. In October, Boyce had described the fight against the Taliban as no different to the global war against communism after the 1917 revolution. Just as that war had been waged for seventy years, the one in Afghanistan would end up going 'nowhere' and could last fifty.

The first bombs and missiles had hit Kabul on 7 October. Within hours, bin Laden, dressed in a combat jacket and with a Kalashnikov rifle propped up against a wall behind him, had appeared on television to boast of his responsibility for the attack on New York, which had 'split the whole world into the camp of the believers and the camp of the unbelievers'. On the second day of the bombing, John Negroponte, the American ambassador to the United Nations, wrote that, in self-defence, America could decide to extend its attacks to other organisations and states. Blair acknowledged Negroponte's code for Iraq and agreed that after victory in Afghanistan 'the job is not over'.

In Baghdad, America was accused of using the bin Laden attacks as a pretext for settling old scores. In Britain, the public understood the effect of 9/11 on their lives, with 81 per cent telling a Mori poll that the world had 'changed for ever'. On 13 November, six weeks after the bombing had begun, Kabul was taken over by American-sponsored warlords. Contrary to the scepticism of critics, the campaign had worked. Exhausted after his fifth foreign tour, Blair briefly expressed his satisfaction at a Cabinet meeting and anticipated Boyce's frown. The admiral was indeed a pessimist, not eager to accelerate the hunt to find bin Laden or to combat militant Islam. He cautioned against hysteria. Pursuing the Taliban in the caves, he said, was a forlorn effort. The bombing, Boyce went on, had triggered fury in Muslim countries against America, yet Donald Rumsfeld, the American defence secretary, was talking about a war 'sustained for a period of years'.

The prime minister did not welcome a passive chief of the defence staff. Such an attitude risked opening up a debate he disavowed, and Boyce was not offering any ideas on how to prevent the Taliban remaining in Afghanistan. Blair wanted a plan to rebuild that country led by Britain's military, even if Washington was against nation-building.

'I think we need a strategy on Iraq,' he told Richard Wilson on 1 December. Three days later, he sent David Manning, his foreign-affairs adviser, and Richard Dearlove to Washington to hand over a personally drafted letter setting out his ideas about regime change. Wilson and other senior officials did not see the message. Inside his den, Blair's trusted advisers did not judge the prime minister to be Bush's poodle. On the contrary, he appeared as an equal, advocating the interventionist doctrine he had spelled out in Chicago two years earlier, albeit subject to UN approval. Notionally, Britain could escalate from bombing to an actual invasion only if there were legitimate reasons under international law.

These weeks formed a seminal moment in Blair's life. Before 9/11, he had shown no deep interest in the intelligence community and had rarely met Dearlove. In the aftermath of the attacks, he allowed the 'seductive spook' to come very close. Within Whitehall's and Washington's tight circle of security chiefs, Dearlove had already won respect for organising blood-and-guts operations using mercenaries in Afghanistan. That success appealed to Blair, who now took Dearlove with him as he flew around the world to build a coalition to support a war against the plotters. 'Dearlove seriously swam into Blair's life,' noticed Wilson. Not surprisingly, the spymaster was puffed up by his unprecedented access and sought to satisfy his master's requirements. 'Dearlove was a buccaneer who had lived in the shadows, and it was flattering for him [to be] exposed to a politician,' observed former Cabinet secretary Robin Butler, who would scrutinise these events three years later.

During those flights, Dearlove emphasised his conviction that Saddam still possessed WMDs and rockets. When he and Manning arrived in Washington, he would discuss with the CIA the orchestration of a coup to remove Saddam, knowing he spoke with special authority; after all, he enjoyed an unusually 'close relationship with the prime minister'.

Previous prime ministers, especially Harold Macmillan, Harold Wilson and Margaret Thatcher, had allowed Whitehall's institutional filters to cast automatic scepticism over MI6's reports. By its very nature, the secret service obtained information from thieves, liars and traitors. That danger had been understood sixty-six years earlier, when the Joint Intelligence Committee (JIC) was created to rigorously assess the information collected by Britain's intelligence agencies. John Scarlett, the current chairman of the JIC, was qualified to lead that task in the Cabinet Office. As a former MI6 officer, he had participated in a successful operation in Soviet Russia and masterminded its bloodless conclusion.

However, his operational experience in the Middle East was limited. Given their relationship, Blair would not have perceived that vulnerability. By the nature of his previous job, Scarlett had not become closely involved with politicians and would not have considered warning the prime minister to engage with caution in direct discussions with MI6's chief. Remarkably, in his punctilious manner, Scarlett's rigid interpretation of the JIC's formal task to 'assess' the intelligence supplied by MI6 and the other agencies excluded natural scepticism. 'We didn't see it as our job', he would say, 'to second-guess the agencies on the reliability of their sources.' Unaware of that unusual self-denial, Scarlett's reassurance gave Blair confidence in the JIC's judgements and Dearlove's reports.

Unlike previous Cabinets, which had included wartime military officers whose personal misfortunes during action in Europe or Britain's colonies had occasionally been caused by incorrect intelligence, Blair lacked the experience to penetrate the polished bluff of the intelligence community. Accordingly, Blair never probed the reasons for the failure by the British and American intelligence agencies to predict the 9/11 attacks; nor did he invite a vigorous debate about the nature of the Islamic threat. Pertinently, he never encouraged Whitehall to challenge the interventionist doctrine described in Chicago. One dominant memory of that speech was the resounding applause, the same approval received by the Good Friday agreement in Ireland. That success had owed much to his patient diplomacy with stubborn enemies and his understanding of their contradictory interpretations of history. He assumed that his expertise could be carried over to the Middle East.

No one warned him about the complexities of the Middle East's history. He did not request an independent analysis of Iraq, a country artificially created by Britain and France in 1916 that Saddam ruled by controlling the irreconcilable divisions between languages, religions, tribal clans and family loyalties. Previous British prime ministers had relied on the Arabists in the Foreign Office, who understood the suppressed violence between the Sunnis, the minority led by Saddam, and the Shias. That experience was diluted after the Foreign Office switched its focus from the Middle East to Europe. Without an embassy in Baghdad, the Foreign Office and MI6 had gradually lost their Iraqi experts; simultaneously, the foreign department lacked an authoritative ambassador in Downing Street. Sir Michael Jay, the permanent secretary, was disliked by many in his department for being a 'politically correct' time-server incapable of representing the Foreign Office's arguments and interests with real authority, although he was to become its head in 2002. Having failed to protect the department's finances from the Treasury, Jay represented a diminishing influence, which was not helped by Jack Straw, the new foreign secretary. Reflecting Blair's attitude, Christopher Meyer, the smooth British ambassador in Washington, welcomed David Manning's request that his reports should be sent direct to Downing Street, without copying in Straw.

The seeds of fate were sown during Blair's discussions with Dearlove and Scarlett. The two intelligence officers knew each other from MI6 but were not friends and showed little mutual respect. Dearlove belonged to the 'camel drivers', a group of derring-do adventurers whose James Bond projects won either praise or suspicion. By contrast, Scarlett was 'Moscow school', trained to run meticulously orchestrated operations to outwit Russian counter-intelligence surveillance. In Scarlett's opinion, Dearlove was a cowboy, while Dearlove regarded Scarlett as boring. In theory, the deep-rooted tension should have produced an ideal combination; in fact, they united to lead Blair astray.

'What if he gets nuclear weapons?' Blair asked about bin Laden. A rogue state, he speculated, might supply a fanatic with the means to destroy the world. The scenario was validated by his two intelligence chiefs, despite the absence of any information to justify that fear. Both echoed their patron's conviction that Islamic terrorism needed to be destroyed to protect democracy.

One unknown was whether bin Laden was associated with Saddam. In Blair's judgement, if there were a relationship, Saddam would supply the terrorist with WMDs. Dearlove lacked a prime source who could supply eyewitness accounts on Saddam's thoughts and activities.

He could only speculate, drawing on second-hand and, more usually, unverifiable third-hand informants with questionable motives. For an MI6 chief to discuss raw intelligence alone with a prime minister was most unusual. The established tradition was for the Cabinet secretary to be present. 'I would always insist on sitting in,' recalled Robin Butler. 'I wanted to provide the counterbalance to the enthusiasm of the heads of the agencies, to prevent the prime minister being misled.' His successor, Richard Wilson, was excluded by Blair and Jonathan Powell. By downgrading him, they had cast aside a safety net, which meant that one discrepancy, instantly spotted by Blair, was not properly explained by Dearlove.

In 1998, the JIC concluded that international agencies had 'succeeded in destroying or controlling the vast majority of Saddam's 1991 weapons of mass destruction capability'. The Anglo-American bombs and UN inspectors had also destroyed Iraq's Russian-built rockets with ranges of less than 150 km. The JIC's only reservation was that Iraq had probably hidden some stocks of WMDs and possessed the ability to resurrect its WMD programme, but the JIC admitted there was no evidence to support that assumption. Thereafter, the JIC regularly minimised the likelihood of Iraq running an active WMD programme. Six years later, even that possibility was described as a 'worst-case scenario'.

In 2000, the JIC reported that Iraq's WMD programme had been further reduced, although a limited research facility might exist. Based on inconclusive reports, the committee speculated that Iraq was restarting a nuclear programme. If Blair had read the JIC reports during that year, he would have noticed that Michael Pakenham, the committee's chairman, omitted any reference to such a project. One year later, the JIC's assessment had not changed, yet Blair ignored the committee's last evaluation, not least because of Dearlove's emphatic certainty and Saddam's refusal to deny the existence of WMDs. Blair could not imagine that a murderous despot would disguise his weakness. The momentum grew.

In late November 2001, Whitehall's foreign service was unprepared for reports that General Tommy Franks, the American chief responsible for operations in the Middle East, was drafting plans for an invasion, dubbed 'Phase Two of the war on terror'. Ever since 1997, Blair had supported the toppling of Saddam. The removal of Milošević had broken any taboo, but he also believed that threatening force was a deterrent. Like Milošević, Saddam might eventually succumb and co-operate fully with UN inspectors. If not, then a rogue dictator could not be allowed to threaten the world. Those minded to contradict that assessment were excluded from Blair's den, while David Manning, a mild career diplomat, lacked the independent spirit to explain to Blair with any real force the risks of Britain engaging in the widening 'war on terror'. Success in Kosovo, Sierra Leone and, more recently, Afghanistan had reinforced those who spoke about Britain being able, in Douglas Hurd's phrase, to 'punch above its weight'. Only the military chiefs were disturbed.

Admiral Boyce in particular was troubled by Blair's promise to commit thousands of extra British soldiers to Afghanistan. He understood the risk of waging war against ideologues. During his early life in South Africa, Boyce had learned about Britain's ragged campaign against the Boers. Now, he feared that an engagement in Iraq would end in a quagmire like Vietnam. That wretched conflict had proven the inability of a superpower to defeat defiant nationalist guerrillas.

The admiral used one of his regular meetings with Blair to explain the pitfalls of Western counter-insurgency operations in Third World countries. As so often, Blair nodded politely. His instinct, he replied, convinced him that Afghanis and Iraqis would embrace Western-style liberal democracy once the ruling dictatorships had been destroyed. Uneducated about Vietnam, Blair was unaware of how America's involvement had escalated from a handful of advisers in the late 1950s to an army of 550,000 men under President Johnson. He never asked why the communists were victorious, despite the US air force dropping 7 million tons of bombs onto the country.

Frustrated by the prime minister's disregard of history and the limitations of Britain's armed services, the admiral decided to publicise his warnings. On 11 December, Boyce's public speech to a respected military audience in London fired a broadside at Downing Street. Bombing, he warned, would not defeat terrorism but would radicalise the Muslim world against the West. A conventional invasion of Afghanistan and Iraq, he added, would fail to win 'hearts and minds' and would drag on for the next ten years. 'The world', he said, 'cannot afford non-states, black-hole states or failed states because such states breed terrorism. Therefore, we have to attack the causes, not the symptoms, of terrorism.' He went further, parodying Bush's policy against terrorism as 'a high-tech twenty-first-century posse in the Wild West'. It would be in Britain's national interest, he suggested, for Blair to lay down red lines in his relationship with America and not be unequivocally associated with Bush's putative adventure.

The instant reaction from an irritated Donald Rumsfeld was to ridicule Boyce's prediction that allied troops would still be fighting in Afghanistan the following summer. America's high-tech war, he said, would crush the Taliban within weeks, and his country's soldiers would all return home before the spring.

Unknown to Boyce, Blair was also irritated. He did not understand the admiral's argument, but he did appreciate that annoying Rumsfeld was not in Britain's interest. Boyce, he complained privately, had form. Some weeks earlier, in a joint press conference with Geoff Hoon, he had contradicted the politician about the military's preparedness for war. 'The army's killing cows and we've got 20,000 on stand-by to fight fires, so we're not ready,' he told journalists, alluding to foot-and-mouth disease and the army preparing to cover for firemen who were threatening to strike in pursuit of a 40 per cent pay rise.

'Is Boyce looking for a reason to quit?' noted Alastair Campbell after the speech. 'CDS [chief of the defence staff] doing nothing but giving TB headaches.' But, despite his anger, Blair said nothing to Boyce. The admiral, he knew, would snap back that the government should increase the spending on the military to the agreed sum and avoid letting the annual deficit amount to £2 billion.

A week later, Blair committed British troops to the International

Security Assistance Force (ISAF), a UN operation in Afghanistan. The deployment was criticised in the House of Lords by General Charles Guthrie and other former chiefs of the defence staff. The British army, they complained, was being overstretched to serve Blair's desire for media coverage. He ignored their complaints, being more concerned by European leaders opposing ISAF if it fell under the control of America's hawkish commanders.

By Christmas, with Boyce's help, those concerns had been soothed. Exhausted by arguments and ceaseless foreign travel, Blair celebrated Christmas at Chequers with his family, then headed for the sunshine in Egypt. On 5 January 2002, he and Cherie arrived in India from their holiday to speak about being proud of Britain's role as a 'pivotal player' in the new world order. Two days later, he flew to the Bagram air base near Kabul to emphasise Britain's commitment to transforming impoverished Muslim tribes into liberal democrats. He departed three hours later, having visited his twenty-second country in six months. Ostensibly, Blair was committed to nation-building, while Bush, he knew, was focused on the hunt for bin Laden – and Saddam.

On 28 December, Bush had received a memo from Franks outlining plans for invasion. Five days later, he made his 'axis of evil' speech, identifying Saddam as an architect of international terror. In the aftermath, Washington's newspapers reported that the president was preparing to invade Iraq.

Blair returned to London excited about the new challenge. Joining with America in another battle against evil was a worthwhile cause but, he decided, it was best considered in secret. Richard Wilson and other senior officials were not told that the Cabinet Office had prepared an 'Options Paper' outlining how the existing containment policy based on sanctions could escalate to a ground offensive.

Foreign Office lawyers had anticipated Blair's response to Bush's speech, and the Whitehall machine delivered a formal legal opinion, should Blair decide to join America's invasion. War, wrote the lawyers, was legal only on three grounds: in self-defence; to prevent ethnic cleansing; and to enforce UN resolutions following the first Gulf War. Blair received the advice with indifference. As a lawyer himself, he knew that legal opinions are not cast in stone but are subject to interpretation. Nevertheless, political realities required any invasion to be justified. The best option would be to prove that Saddam had broken UN resolutions to protect his WMDs. To satisfy Blair's requirements, MI6 intensified the search for the evidence.

On 16 February, President Bush set off on a tour that would include Japan, South Korea and China. Under the headline 'The Countdown Starts for Operation Saddam', William Rees-Mogg predicted in *The Times* that Bush intended to invade Iraq. Rees-Mogg's mistake was to assume that Blair would give the White House 'some support . . . but without the enthusiasm he showed over Afghanistan'. Nine days later, Downing Street confirmed to journalists that Blair was 'bolstering' Parliament and the country for an invasion. A dossier on Iraq's responsibility for international terrorism was being drafted. In preparation for US vice president Dick Cheney embarking on an eleven-nation tour, officials in Washington were openly debating regime change. 'This is something we've got to deal with,' Blair told Australian TV. On 11 March, the same day Cheney met Blair for lunch in London, Bush told 120 ambassadors in Washington that there could be no neutrality in the next battle against Saddam.

In early March 2002, the tenor of the JIC's reports altered. Scarlett's assessors described an 'intent' by Saddam to pursue a WMD programme and, although 'hindered' in his ambitions, reported on the possibility of a 'break-out' to develop WMDs. The JIC admitted the intelligence was 'sporadic and patchy', but it believed that Iraq intended to acquire WMDs by reconstituting its 1990s programme and creating a delivery system to reach Israel and the Gulf by 2007. Scarlett admitted there was 'very little intelligence' relating to chemical warfare, and 'no intelligence' about biological warfare. In summary, he was speculating. The intelligence services had failed to find a scrap of reliable information, let alone a silver bullet.

Blair recognised the conundrum in a message to Jonathan Powell on 17 March. 'The immediate WMD problems don't seem obviously worse than three years ago,' he wrote, going on to complain that 'I don't have a proper worked-out strategy' either to force Saddam to prostrate himself to the American and British governments or forcibly remove him. Facing that dilemma, he said, 'We have to reorder our story and message. Increasingly I think it should be about the nature of the regime.' As he would later admit, even if Iraq did not possess WMDs, 'I would still have thought it right to remove him. You would have had to use and deploy different arguments about the nature of the threat.'

Christopher Meyer received a briefing from Manning – a 'chunky set of instructions' – explaining that Blair favoured regime change. On reflection, the ambassador, who had been personally chosen for Washington by Blair, considered that his prime minister had become 'more neocon than the Americans. This was not the poodle being pulled by the leash.' Manning reflected the same judgement in a letter to Blair after a dinner with Condoleezza Rice, then Bush's national security adviser, on 14 March: 'I said you would not budge in your support for regime change but you had to manage a press, a parliament and a public opinion that was very different than anything in the States.'

To clinch Blair's desire of proximity to Bush – or, as Meyer would later describe his orders, 'to get up the arse of the US government and stay there' – the ambassador arranged to meet Rice. Repeating Manning's script, he told her, 'We backed regime change, but the plan had to be clever and failure was not an option.' Rice was not surprised. By then, Manning had established a regular telephone dialogue with her pledging Blair's support. Meyer repeated the script on 18 March, over lunch with Paul Wolfowitz, the US deputy secretary of defence.

Blair kept those discussions secret from Wilson and Boyce. Similarly unaware but suspicious of Blair's ambitions, Robin Cook and David Blunkett insisted that the Cabinet should discuss Iraq. Blair agreed, but told his staff that the 'Options Paper' should not be revealed. 'I don't think it's necessary for them to have it,' he said. 'They can rely on the media.' The Cabinet was flying blind. In Blair's opinion, the alternative to his position was the enemy's position, and there was no reason to help his critics by engaging in a debate.

'Can we have some papers on Iraq?' Alistair Darling, the transport minister and former Treasury official, belatedly asked Blair to his face before a Cabinet meeting in March. There was no reply. Ministers would not be provided with a single policy paper on Iraq for eighteen months. Having dominated his party for nine years, Blair had haughtily told a confidant, 'They know the score.' Darling reflected that Blair, the global star, gave the impression on his occasional visits to London that, at best, he tolerated the Cabinet. 'Before one Cabinet meeting,' recalled Darling, 'ministers joked that we should give him a full explanation about the function of that big hall with green benches facing each other.'

The Cabinet's first substantial discussion that year about Iraq started on a false premise. On 7 March, Blair spoke only about 'bombing Iraq'. Invasion was not mentioned. Curiously, not a single minister asked whether any secret papers had been prepared or why no papers had been presented for Cabinet consideration. Andrew Turnbull would call the deception 'a mismatch'. Blair, he noted, was telling the Cabinet that 'all options were still open, including peaceful ones, while telling Bush, who had already decided on military action, that "You can count on us whatever."' Twelve years later, Turnbull noted, 'I wouldn't call it a lie. "Deception" is the right word. You can deceive without lying, by leaving a false interpretation uncorrected.' At the end of a robust two-hour discussion, Blair was even more suspicious than at the outset. Several around the table did not trust Bush or believe in the gospel of Britain's unbreakable alliance with America. Robin Cook had pointedly warned that Europe's leaders would oppose the use of military force against Iraq. Gerhard Schröder, the German chancellor, had openly denounced an American invasion without a UN mandate. Blair's belief, continued Cook, that 'we saw attacks on the US as attacks on us' was dangerous, and his black-and-white conviction that he could reshape the Middle East ignored the facts.

To defuse the tension, Blair quipped, 'I do want to assure you that the management has not gone crazy. The problem is, I really believe this stuff.'

Alastair Campbell understood his apprehension. 'Not exactly division but a lot of concern,' he wrote. 'Where is it going?'

'The party', Blair told a confidant, 'wants me not to believe Bush on Iraq, but I believe it more than Bush.' Unknown to the Cabinet or across Whitehall, Blair was in constant telephone and video contact with Bush. With the notable exception of Powell, Manning and a handful of other advisers, those intimate conversations establishing the timetable for regime change were kept secret.

The following day, 8 March, the Cabinet met again in Chequers for a stock-take. Gordon Brown looked venomous. His sour mood was aggravated by that day's newspaper reports describing the Cabinet's divisions over Iraq and the various threats of resignation. The leaks confirmed Blair's fears. Labour Party members, he knew, needed to be educated about Iraq. His distrust extended to Richard Wilson. During monumental arguments on the eve of his retirement, Wilson had prevented Blair appointing an outsider as his successor. In the choice between Michael Bichard, David Omand and Andrew Turnbull, Blair chose the latter. Many were surprised by the decision, as Omand was considered the best candidate. Some assumed that Blair's choice had been guided either by impatience or by ignorance; others gossiped about Blair's hope that Turnbull, the permanent secretary at the Treasury, would help improve his own relations with Brown; still others, with hindsight, suggested a rather less wholesome explanation.

Before applying to become Cabinet secretary, Turnbull knew that Wilson was being excluded from Blair's meetings with Dearlove and Scarlett, and even from Blair's meetings with Boyce. He interpreted the prime minister's abolition of the constitution's checks and balances as the result of 'a man in a hurry who didn't want to be bogged down by having to carry people along'. Rather than attempting to restore the Cabinet secretary's traditional role, Turnbull had set out a winning prospectus to secure his new job. He pledged to focus on managing the civil service and reforming Whitehall and the public services, and further suggested that the prime minister should appoint a security co-ordinator to manage defence and intelligence. Blair agreed, and appointed David Omand. The former director of GCHQ assumed that he would be present during the prime minister's defence and intelligence briefings.

During his last months, Wilson's penalty for protecting the traditionalists was further exclusion from the inner circle. Although he was based in Downing Street, he was unaware that on 2 April Blair was at Chequers being briefed by Boyce and the intelligence services about Iraq. Hoon and Straw were also absent. Dearlove fed Blair reports about Saddam's brutalities and his development of WMDs. 'I didn't know what was going on,' Wilson would admit. 'It is humbling.' To an extent he blamed Jonathan Powell, who 'despised him'.

Amid that small group, there was no secret that the invasion of Iraq was being planned for the new year. Everyone also knew that Blair wanted to stand alongside Bush. Dearlove was in no doubt, as he later said, that Blair 'wanted to lead, not just support the process of regime change'. Or, as 'C' explained, 'It's keeping our hands on what's going on and not letting the Americans run away with the ball.' At that stage, the notion of Blair acting as Bush's poodle was fanciful to Dearlove, Manning and Powell.

'I resolved to be part of the planning from early April,' Blair would write, adding in self-defence, 'But war was not decided.' Boyce suspected that Bush had already committed to the invasion and, to his mind, that was against Britain's interest. To avoid the admiral's objections, Blair hid his intentions behind a facade, replying to Boyce's protest that regime change would be illegal, 'Well, it's both regime change and his WMDs.' With time, Blair calculated, Boyce would be assuaged or manipulated into obedience.

Blair's ambition was fixed. 'I had resolved in my own mind', he would write, 'that removing Saddam would do the world, and most particularly the Iraqi people, a service.' But he also admitted that 'I knew that regime change could not be our policy.' Pertinently, he continuously mentioned 'strategy' but never asked in London what would follow Saddam's removal.

Those secret discussions with his restricted group in Chequers and Downing Street prepared Blair for his meeting in April at the Bush family ranch in Crawford, Texas. He was seeking reassurances over the president's intention to protect the sanctity of Britain's alliance with America. In advance, Manning and Meyer were tasked with describing the mood among Bush's confidants. They discovered an unbridgeable division between Colin Powell at the State Department and Donald Rumsfeld at the Pentagon, and between Condoleezza Rice and Dick Cheney. Since Rumsfeld and Cheney were unapologetic sponsors of American power and unfriendly towards Britain, the British diplomats attached themselves to Powell and Rice. Their choice made no real difference after Rice revealed that she too was committed to regime change. 'Fuck Saddam. We're taking him out,' Bush had reportedly told her. In Crawford, Blair would be meeting the 'reasonable' Bush, who only turned 'aggressive' after spending time with Cheney and Rumsfeld. But, regardless of his company, as Bush would admit before Blair arrived, 'I made up my mind that Saddam needs to go.' After Colin Powell's conversations with Meyer and Manning, he reported to Bush that Blair agreed. 'On Iraq,' Powell wrote on 28 March, 'Blair will be with us should military operations be necessary' and would expect Bush to behave as if 'Britain and America are truly equal partners in the special relationship'.

Mindful that the Labour Party was suspicious – 140 MPs had signed a Commons motion expressing 'deep unease' after Blair refused to allow a parliamentary debate on Iraq – and that the country as a whole was not convinced that war was in Britain's interest, Blair needed Bush to present the invasion as part of a commitment to promoting the Middle East peace process. Since chairing an unsuccessful summit in London in 1998 between Benjamin Netanyahu and Yasser Arafat, Blair's success in Ulster had convinced him that he could now broker a deal between

Israel and the Arabs. More recently, Ariel Sharon, Israel's prime minister, had encouraged him to remove Saddam. 'You're saving the Middle East from a madman,' Sharon told Blair. 'He could wake up in the morning and decide to invade Israel. His army of one and a half million needs just an hour to reach our borders. In the Middle East, nothing is predictable. If you have a problem, deal with it. Get rid of Saddam.'

Blair would also explain that Britain's participation would depend on Saddam being proven to have broken the UN's 1991 resolution about inspections. He needed Bush to maintain the impression that America supported Britain's diplomats finagling agreements with disparate governments, especially the French, Germans and Russians, in order to legitimise the invasion with a UN resolution.

To win the call to arms required tenacity. Blair appeared to possess the necessary self-confidence, but the bewildering contradictions between his public and private life eluded even Delphic interpretation. There was the public politician preparing for a momentous journey; there was a media outcry about his office becoming embroiled in an ugly spat about the protocol for the Queen Mother's funeral; and there was the private man in his Downing Street flat dressed in yellow and green underpants and greeting Alastair Campbell with the question, 'How many prime ministers have a body like this?' When he was in the apartment, he would don footballer's kit or lilac pyjama trousers and a blue smock, or appear with a nude woman emblazoned on his shirt cuffs.

Just before his transatlantic flight to meet Bush he wrote to George Carey, the Archbishop of Canterbury, saying, 'I am one of the Western leaders the US will really listen to on these issues. That carries a price. It means that I don't grandstand; I don't negotiate publicly; and I don't list demands. It's a very difficult and delicate line to tread . . . My objective must be to pull the Americans towards a strategy that is sensible in Iraq and contemplate military action only in the right circumstance.' As so often, he implied the importance of protecting Britain's special relationship with America. He was unaware that Harold Wilson had refused President Johnson's request to send British troops to Vietnam, without fatal consequences.

Blair's prejudice, noted Omand, was highlighted by the final intelligence brief presented before his departure. Its authors admitted there was no connection between Saddam and al-Qaeda or any other international terror group. They also highlighted the absence of any evidence about Iraq's development of WMDs. Finally, they revealed that the successful Islamic attacks on America had increased the radicalisation of Muslims. The message from Manning was that, on the advice of the hawks in Washington, Bush had moved from containment to confrontation. Those key advisers dismissed the UN route.

To other European leaders, Bush gave the impression that he remained undecided. 'I have no war plans on my desk,' he told the media. But to Blair, during their walks alone across the Texan countryside, he described his intention to remove Saddam regardless of WMDs. Mindful of their common attitude towards good and evil, Blair echoed his companion's ambition, so long as Bush understood Blair's domestic obstacles. Britain, he said, 'would support military action to bring about regime change' if attempts were also made to negotiate a Middle East peace settlement, and only after the UN route was exhausted. 'The thing I admire about this prime minister', Bush told the media in Crawford, 'is that he doesn't need a poll or focus group to convince him of the difference between right and wrong.' Blair agreed: 'Leaving Iraq to develop WMDs is not an option.' As a believer, he had decided to join Bush in the cockpit.

'What happened?' Meyer asked Jonathan Powell soon after the prime minister's party left Crawford.

'We'll debrief him on the plane,' replied Powell, whose antagonism towards the ambassador was unhelpful.

Meyer interpreted everything he heard as proving that Blair had pledged 'in blood' to topple Saddam.

To eyewitnesses in Texas, Blair appeared to be a calm adventurer seeking close involvement in a historic drama to change the world. But the keen observer noticed something more. Travelling in long motor cavalcades accompanied by well-drilled protection officers was a prime minister who appreciated the privileges of office. Private jets, limousines and hassle-free travel were the perks of premiership, and in America the trappings of power were particularly congenial. Regardless of the cost, switching from helicopters to jets seemed appropriate for a leader discussing war. Not once did Blair question his advisers over whether Britain's taxpayers would thank the government for spending billions of pounds on a distant war.

On his return to London, he did not reveal to his Cabinet any details about his discussions. He did not trust his ministers, especially Brown, Short and Cook. He was particularly distrustful of Cook's blustering, because in 1998 Cook had issued a gung-ho warning to Saddam that the dictator would be 'making a grave mistake' if he doubted Western resolve to bomb the country and stop WMDs being produced. Four years later, Cook appeared to have forgotten those words.

Even Blair's supporters were naive. Patricia Hewitt's warning that an invasion of Iraq would 'cause a lot of tension among the Muslim communities in Britain' evoked a cursory nod from her leader. More disrespectful was Blair's silence towards Hoon, Straw and Boyce. But he was careful not to lie outright. Instead, he reported that no action was imminent and that Bush had been persuaded to avoid an invasion while UN inspectors searched for WMDs. Britain was committed, they were told, to working through the UN. Blair's ministers left his briefing convinced that an invasion was far away.

In early July, Colonel Paul Gibson, the British army liaison officer in Tampa, reported that the US military's preparatory work for the invasion had suddenly intensified. Since Britain was not officially committed to the war, Gibson was excluded from any discussions. 'The shutters are firmly down,' he added. At the same time, Kevin Tebbit returned from Washington and, in a memorandum to Blair, wrote that there was a 'sharp shift in attitudes' among the Bush administration, which now intended to 'topple the regime by military action'. Tebbit was surprised not to receive a reply.

After clarifying Washington's position, Boyce told Blair, 'Bush is going ahead,' and described how Franks had been ordered to 'gear up for action'. Blair waved the admiral's assertion aside. 'I knew Bush had not decided,' he would write. In a bravura performance on 16 July, he told a Commons committee the same: while he supported Bush's general policy of pre-emptive action, no decisions had yet been made.

To clarify any misunderstandings, Richard Dearlove flew to Washington. His journey coincided with the arrival of a letter from Blair to Bush that began, 'You know, George, whatever you decide to do, I'm with you.' As Blair's special emissary, Dearlove was told the truth. He returned to London, and an ad hoc meeting was convened in Blair's office for 23 July. For the first time, Hoon, Straw, the attorney general Peter Goldsmith and Richard Wilson squeezed into Blair's office alongside Scarlett, Powell and Boyce to hear facts that could no longer be confined to Blair's confidants. The cosy atmosphere of the meetings among Blair's friends was fractured by the inclusion of outsiders. Dearlove explained that 'Bush's public statements that war would be a "last resort" were untrue. Military action was now seen as inevitable.' The invasion would go ahead with or without Britain. All that was missing was finding a way to sell the war so that 'the intelligence and facts' would be 'fixed around the policy'.

Scarlett agreed. 'It seemed clear', he would later say, 'that Bush had made up his mind to take military action.' He asked Blair whether the reason would be Saddam's link to terrorism, WMDs or the need for regime change. Blair was adamant: whatever the reason, Britain had to stand alongside America. Regime change was necessary to end the problem of WMDs. 'It's worse than you think,' Blair told a sceptic. 'I actually believe in doing this.'

Unhappy about the direction of the conversation, Straw, in his customary long-winded manner, mentioned that the case for war was 'thin' because Saddam was not threatening anyone with WMDs. That comment was unwelcome to Blair. Although he had told the Commons committee on 16 July that 'Hussein is still *trying* [my italics] to develop weapons of mass destruction', he wanted to draw dramatic conclusions from Saddam's refusal to co-operate with the UN. Britain could not show 'weakness in the face of a threat from a tyrant'. In Blair's opinion, Straw was a process merchant rather than a constructive thinker. He also lacked the courage to resign.

Blair moved the discussion on to the 'Options Paper' that had been prepared in March but not shown to the Cabinet, which outlined how sanctions could escalate to a ground offensive. If Britain participated in the invasion, the military's commitment was graded at three levels, or 'packages'. Boyce, asked to describe the alternatives, did not conceal his disdain for all the politicians in the room, especially Hoon. The secretary of state refused to endorse Boyce's advice to Blair that the British military was underfunded for an invasion. Even the Commons Defence Committee had criticised Hoon six days earlier for allowing Britain's military to become dangerously overstretched. Boyce made special mention of Hoon's invisibility in that discussion. Alone against Blair, he also recommended that Britain should choose package one, the smallest commitment, and even that would require extra funds. Blair replied that additional money would be granted after Britain's commitment was formally approved. Boyce suspected that he was making an important distinction between preparing for war and the official declaration, and the prime minister's calculated delay further strained their relations. Nevertheless, Blair counted on Boyce's discretion not to reveal his intentions.

'Right. Thank you,' said Blair, wrapping up the meeting. The authority of his office had suffocated any questions about possible failure. The Americans would be told that Britain would join the invasion. All those in the room were sworn to secrecy. The Cabinet would not be told, as too many ministers were untrustworthy. Blair would consider how to win the public's support over the summer. His emphasis on concealment prevented Whitehall from mounting the traditional Red versus Blue military exercise to scrutinise the risk.

Boyce departed the meeting with neither additional funds nor Blair's decision about the packages. Richard Wilson departed feeling 'very startled' about the prime minister's secret progress towards war. 'I was taken aback,' he would say. 'There was a gleam in his eye. I was worried that he was getting into a position which was dangerous. And I told him.' Blair gave Wilson one of his wry grimaces. The Cabinet secretary clearly did not grasp that the decision had been taken.

Admiral Alan West, the commander-in-chief of the fleet, did understand. He immediately ordered the dispatch of mine warfare ships to the Gulf and signalled that the fleet and marines should be prepared for war by the end of the year.

Meyer called Manning to ask why Blair was giving Bush unconditional guarantees. 'We tried to stop him, but he refused,' Manning replied.

On 25 July, Blair appeared at his monthly press conference. Asked about Iraq, he answered, 'I think we are all getting a bit ahead of ourselves on the issue of Iraq. As I have said before, action is not imminent, we are not at the point of decision yet.'

TWENTY-THREE

The Bogus Students

Towards the end of 2001, David Blunkett was told that over 500,000 migrants would have arrived in Britain during that year. 'We're going to be tougher,' he told his officials, bearing in mind the government's original estimate of 100,000. After twelve weeks of focusing totally on security in the wake of the Islamic attack on America, the Home Office resumed normal business.

The media pressure started again. Blunkett responded by publicly warning immigrants to 'become more integrated by being more British'. The headlines dismayed Blair. He was not disturbed by warnings about the effect on housing, schools and the NHS of an additional half a million people. The actual numbers never concerned him. The majority of immigrants, he was told, would arrive 'legitimately' as members of a British family. His only interest was bogus asylum-seekers, and he chivvied Blunkett to enforce deportation orders. 'We need to build fifteen detention centres,' Blunkett replied, who expected the funding would be personally negotiated with Andrew Smith, the chief secretary at the Treasury.

On the day, he was met instead by Gordon Brown and Ed Balls. Blunkett began describing the problems caused by the uncontrolled arrival of asylum-seekers. 'We'll only be approving the money for three centres,' the chancellor said brusquely. The undertone was his personal support for large-scale immigration.

Unexpectedly, Blair then turned up. 'It's too much money,' Brown repeated, at which Blunkett became irate.

'Let's go to a room without officials,' interrupted Blair.

After a prolonged argument, Brown shouted, 'Right, four centres.'

'We've been shafted,' screamed Blunkett in turn, snapping a pencil in half.

In the end, only three centres for just over a thousand people were built. In the face of his chancellor's intransigence, Blair was powerless.

He was also irritated. At their next monthly stock-take, he complained about the asylum laws being 'perverse and dysfunctional'. They prevented the Home Office from finding the asylum-seekers, holding them in centres and deporting them. 'What more powers do you need?' he asked the officials. 'Tony ignores the fact that the Human Rights Act created grounds for new appeals,' noted Nick Pearce, a special adviser.

Blair was facing in several directions at once. To persuade the wider electorate about the government's tough stance and to prevent those who did arrive from obtaining work, he endorsed Pearce's new White Paper foreshadowing harsher controls. At the same time, he considered abandoning the vouchers he had approved in August. 'You could be reducing your armour,' Stephen Boys-Smith warned Blunkett. 'The vouchers have only just been introduced.' Eight months earlier, Boys-Smith had told Jeff Rooker, the new immigration minister, that vouchers had limited the number of asylum-seekers that year to '80,000. With cash benefits 180,000 would have arrived.' But Blair insisted that the vouchers were disliked by both asylum-seekers and trade union leaders. Blunkett agreed with him.

To win the public's trust, on 24 April 2002 the home secretary endorsed his constituents' complaints in the Commons, while introducing the latest Nationality, Asylum and Immigration Bill. Asylum-seekers, Blunkett blurted out, were 'swamping' schools and doctors' surgeries. Despite a request from Downing Street, he refused to apologise for the outburst; but at the same time, with Blair's agreement, he reduced the backlog of asylum applications by 'quietly' approving the entry of 50,000 people. More unannounced amnesties would follow.

Asylum, Blair privately admitted, had become 'the toughest issue', one with 'the capacity to explode at any moment'. Sarah Spencer, the academic who specialised in immigration, was told that Downing Street had held 'fifty meetings' about cutting the number of asylum-seekers by 50 per cent because Blair blamed himself for failing to focus on domestic issues.

The message to Spencer was wrong. Blair was in fact congratulating himself on the increase in the number of foreigners in Britain, especially students. Britain's education industry, he boasted in a speech, had attracted 24 per cent of the global market, producing £1.2 billion in income. In 2000, an additional 75,000 students had arrived, and the numbers would rise every year from then on. But he omitted to mention one aspect of that increase: after relaxing the rules for granting student visas in 1999, a flood of bogus students had registered at phoney colleges to gain permanent entry. When a newspaper exposed the racket, Blair cursed the Home Office's lack of 'cutting-edge policies' for those illegals. The culprit, he agreed with Blunkett, was Boys-Smith. Regardless of the justice of the complaint – and there were good reasons to dispute their judgement – he had to go.

'This is a mess,' Blair told Bill Jeffrey, a civil servant he trusted after they had worked together in Northern Ireland. 'It's out of control and needs sorting out.'

Jeffrey replaced Boys-Smith as the head of IND in July 2002. His briefing from Blunkett was unambiguous: 'I want people to come here freely and I want them to work.' Two months later, Blunkett criticised Asian immigrants for failing to learn and speak English, and was attacked as racist. Blair was not disturbed by the contradictions. Blunkett had negotiated the closure of Sangatte, and his new Immigration Act restored several of Michael Howard's barriers, including the denial of benefits to asylum-seekers if they failed to register on arrival. Both events, Blair knew, attracted good publicity, but they were mere gestures. Since 1997, at least 67,000 foreigners had passed through Calais as illegal migrants, and during 2002 over 100,000 would apply for asylum, up from 92,000 the previous year.

Michael Barber's report during that month's delivery meeting about improvements in Calais was used to brief Jeffrey. The new IND chief, said Blair, should sharply reduce the number of illegal migrants and chase the bogus students. On the other hand, he added, 'I'm all for good immigration.' Jeffrey appeared to be unaware of 'managed migration' and how controls had been relaxed under the guise of work permits. 'Don't mention the advantages of immigration in public,' Blair cautioned a meeting that included Andrew Turnbull, 'because they won't even want that.' The electorate, he went on, should be told only about the government's efforts to stop bad immigration. Jeffrey nodded. Since the IND head was Blair's personal appointment, Blunkett did not reveal his doubts about his 'detached' official. He had, after all, reached an understanding with Blair that summer.

The two had discussed whether the citizens of eight European states (known as the A8 nations) due to become members of the EU in May 2004 should be allowed to enter and work in Britain immediately. Other EU countries, including Germany, planned to delay such privileges for seven years. Initially, Blair was wary about lifting all the restrictions on migrants from the new EU states. His misgivings were addressed during a trip to Warsaw, where his hosts in the British embassy described the virtues of allowing unlimited numbers of Poles into Britain.

'Let's be good Europeans,' Blair was told by the Foreign Office's senior representative.

'Yes,' he replied. 'We shouldn't worry about numbers.'

In London, Turnbull agreed. The Germans, he thought, were 'crazy' to pass up the opportunity of employing hard-working East Europeans. The only concern was public opinion. Too many people were alarmed by what some Blair aides called 'the immigration tinder box'. Arguments in support of the unrestricted admission of A8 nationals, Blunkett noticed, made Blair 'jumpy'. The solution, everyone agreed, was to avoid mentioning numbers.

'Is this handleable?' Blair asked.

'Yes,' replied Blunkett. 'It's legal migration which we can control.'

The truth, both knew, was the opposite. The IND had already lost control over those East Europeans ostensibly coming to Britain as students or tourists, and many of the A8 nationals, especially those from Poland, were already working in Britain, often illegally. Deporting them, Blunkett had decided, was expensive and pointless. Since the IND could not even guess at the numbers intending to come after their countries' accession, Home Office officials seized upon a report produced by Christian Dustmann of University College London. Dustmann's research for the European Union estimated that 13,000 Poles would arrive in 2004. IND officials were dubious about Dustmann's investigation, but the report's academic label suppressed any controversy. 'We didn't spell it out', Blunkett would later say, 'because of fear of racism. We were on the side of the angels.'

Unknown to the public, the 'angels' in the government did not know how many foreigners would be coming into Britain, or how many would be legal, or from which countries they would come. No civil servant in the Home Office was even asked to make an inspired guess.

TWENTY-FOUR

Groundhog Day

The best antidote to a cycle of negative news, Blair believed, was an announcement of the government's intention to spend billions of pounds. The blowback came when such a promise failed to materialise. That was Blair's burden twenty-two months after he had pledged on David Frost's show to save the NHS.

Gordon Brown was still refusing to hand over the money. Insiders' reports about the two men's arguments were repeated by Mo Mowlam, a retired and disappointed Northern Ireland minister. Their disputes, she told a newspaper, were 'crippling the government'. On 18 November 2001, Downing Street summoned journalists to insist that the relationship between Blair and Brown was 'closer and better than any of their predecessors'. Simultaneously, a Treasury spokesman denounced the 'same old gossip' as 'malicious tittle-tattle with absolutely no foundation'. To confirm the message, Brown told *The Times*, 'Tony Blair is the best friend I've had in politics.' Three days on, he denied that he had ever left their meetings 'shouting and screaming'. Then, five days later, on 27 November, he launched another attack against Blair.

Brown's weapon was a report by Derek Wanless, a banker and statistician. To present himself as the defender of the traditional NHS, Brown had asked Wanless how Labour could save it. The result did not match Brown's expectations. The service, wrote the banker, suffered from poor productivity and, compared to other European countries, provided inferior treatment. The NHS's budget should double over ten years, but going by past history the additional money would increase rather than solve the problems. Brown, convinced that the NHS was 'the envy of the world', was horrified by Wanless's conclusions.

Just before presenting the findings to the Commons, Brown was summoned to No. 10. In retaliation for the Wanless report, Blair had commissioned Adair Turner, a former head of the CBI, to review the NHS's management. Turner's conclusions confirmed Alan Milburn's contention that the bloated ranks of NHS managers 'have never saved a life'. The health service's survival, Blair told Brown, depended on money and also deep-rooted changes. A bitter argument erupted. Blair wanted the money without increasing taxes, while Brown feared that, if too much was spent now, no money would be left when he became prime minister. 'This is bollocks', Alastair Campbell pronounced in a reconciliation session. The bruiser urged both to embrace each other as Christians, but the peace was short-lived.

Wanless listened to the chancellor's presentation of his report to the Commons on his car radio. To his horror, Brown was distorting his conclusions. Wanless had praised 'choice' and the NHS's use of the private sector, but Brown announced that the banker opposed both those policies. That very day, he had also told the *Sun* that the NHS would not receive 'an extra penny' without reforms. Those did not include 'choice and diversity', which, he told the newspaper, was 'all crap'. He quite happily stymied Blair without offering any alternative. On the sidelines, Wanless was outraged by the misrepresentation.

Two days later, the mood in Cabinet was unusually fraught. Blair put forward his argument about the NHS in terms of 'wreckers against modernising reformers', while Brown presented himself as substance versus style – the chancellor's code for Blair's ideological misconduct. In dictating the terms of the war, he classified Milburn as a Blairite enemy. 'This is the same man', countered Milburn, 'who in 1998 asked me to plan the privatisation of the Royal Mail.' As usual, Brown refused to discuss his differences with Milburn face to face. 'It did sometimes feel', noted Campbell, 'like there were two governments.'

That weekend, Brown invited himself to appear live on David Frost's

TV show. To the inevitable question about the leadership and the deal for the succession, he offered a surprise answer: 'What Tony Blair and I have said to each other really is a matter for us.' Frost was speechless. Brown was implying that the two had agreed a timetable after all.

Blair's anger soared. Over the past months, he had toyed with the idea of resigning just before the end of his second term. After Brown's cryptic comment, he told his chancellor over dinner before Christmas to forget about a smooth succession if a bid were made to force him out. Blair's ultimatum was succinct: unless he could create a legacy as the NHS's champion, he would not leave Downing Street before the next election.

Their argument seeped into every Whitehall department and beyond. An effective chief of staff or Cabinet secretary would have sought to reconcile the two men, but Jonathan Powell was not qualified to navigate through the warring factions, and Richard Wilson was impotent. 'The mood in the media', Campbell noted, 'was now pretty nasty.' Newspapers were also reporting disputes among Cabinet ministers. Reflecting his personal antagonism, John Prescott took a sideswipe at Robin Cook, calling him 'a little red gnome', and then blasted a warning at Blair that any further privatisation of NHS services would not be accepted by the party. Defending his reforms, Milburn ignored Prescott but attacked Brown. In retaliation, Brown's supporters openly mocked the Blairites.

Seven months after his landslide victory, any awe about Blair's wizardry had evaporated. In early 2002, the London *Evening Standard* reported that ninety-four-year-old Rose Addis had been found by her family crying in bloodstained clothes in a north London hospital. Her maltreatment at the Whittington hospital was compounded by Blair revealing personal details about Addis, and the Labour-supporting medical director of the hospital accusing Addis of racism.

Blair was agitated. No one had yet produced a blueprint to reform the NHS. He despaired that 'delivery' was being frustrated. Senior civil servants blamed the paralysis on the contradictory advice he was receiving from his advisers. In turn, David Blunkett and John Reid, the secretary of state for Northern Ireland, charged the civil service with disloyalty and incompetence. 'We'll put the best people in to monitor delivery,' Richard Wilson had said, 'and civil servants will be rewarded for success.' Blair was unconvinced. Bad civil servants, he knew, were protected, while the good ones were not promoted and, once disenchanted, lost their flair.

The farrago was intensified after the sudden death of Brown's newborn daughter. Brown's tragedy evoked sympathy for a man whose unconventional personal life appeared to have stabilised after his marriage to Sarah Macaulay in August 2000. Encouraged by the advice that a bachelor could not hope to become prime minister, with fatherhood the fifty-year-old chancellor had embraced the whole domestic package. The effect of his daughter's death in Scotland on his conduct in Westminster, however, was short-lived. After his return to London, his impatience for the leadership intensified. He planned to use the party's spring conference to renew his aggression against Blair. 'He hasn't changed,' Blair said after meeting Brown in Downing Street. 'If anything, he's worse.'

Blair's predicament, as always, was aggravated by problems with financial donors. In 2000, Labour had passed legislation ostensibly to prevent corrupt contributions to political parties and, in 2002, had claimed the moral high ground by outlawing anything that could be interpreted as a bribe by corporations to governments to win commercial contracts. But, on 10 February, a newspaper revealed that Lakshmi Mittal, an Indian billionaire living in London, had given £125,000 to the Labour Party. After the donation, negotiated by Lord Levy, Blair had written privately to the president of Romania endorsing the tycoon's bid for a local steel mill. At the same time, he encouraged the British ambassador in Bucharest to endorse Mittal's business activities. The letters had been organised by Powell following Mittal's introduction to Blair at a high-value donors' party organised by Levy in June 2001. The original draft presented by Powell for Blair's signature had described Mittal as 'my friend', but the endearment was judged to be excessive and was removed. In the aftermath of the donation, the DTI also supported

Mittal's application for a £70 million loan from the European Bank of Reconstruction and Development.

The DTI's patronage of an offshore company that paid little tax and employed fewer than a hundred people in Britain was unusual. When questioned, a Downing Street spokesman denied that Blair had known about the donation before signing the letter. That statement contradicted Levy's memory. The spokesman could also not explain why Blair should support a foreign-owned company against the rival bid for the steel mill by Corus, a British-owned steel-maker that was struggling to survive. 'Cash for influence' mirrored the 1997 Ecclestone affair, and the sleaze associated with Geoffrey Robinson a year later. The prime minister's judgement appeared permanently warped by money.

At the outset, Blair refused to be embarrassed by his association with Mittal. With no reason to fear Iain Duncan Smith, the Tories' new leader, he praised Mittal's business as good for Britain. Campbell told the media their enquiries were 'boring'. The calculated indifference imploded after Campbell's repeated changes to the narrative were headlined by the *Sunday Times* as 'Lies, Damn Lies and Labour Spin'.

Unexpectedly, more allegations of sleaze entrapped Stephen Byers at the Department of Trade and Industry. Jo Moore, his special adviser, had again become enmeshed in allegations of distorting news to the government's advantage. Martin Sixsmith, a DTI spokesman, revealed that he had forbidden Moore to publish unfavourable statistics about the railway network's poor performance during the funeral of Princess Margaret, who had died on 9 February. Moore denied that had been her intention, but the throwback to her suggestion on 9/11 to 'bury bad news' confirmed the cynicism at the heart of the government.

Until then, both Blair and Campbell had protected Moore. Both approved of her conduct after 9/11 and blamed disloyal civil servants for the original embarrassment. In the macho male culture shared by both men, manipulating the media was not a sin. This time, however, she was asked to resign. Her belated departure failed to protect Byers from other allegations of misleading the Commons or, as the headline-writers pouted, being a 'Liar for Hire'. Byers, a prized Blairite, had attracted torrid headlines alleging he had misled the Commons about Railtrack, had even found himself accused of smearing a survivor of the 1999 Paddington rail crash, and was now lying on TV about Sixsmith's conduct. He survived, but Campbell admitted, 'We are swimming through treacle.'

Instead of questioning his own judgement, Blair once again blamed his misfortune on the 'feral beast' that was the poisonous media culture. On the first anniversary of his rise to power, he had been warned by Matthew Parris that while he could take comfort from the fact that most sleaze stories sink like rocks, apparently without trace, 'slowly the whole foundation rises towards the surface . . . because [while] you can get away with a lot for quite a long time, while the love affair lasts . . . the old scandals never die'. Then comes the reckoning.

Among the list of government-inspired 'distortions' were reports about the NHS. Blair was relying on the targets set by the new Delivery Unit. In the first months, Michael Barber's 'name and shame' had produced improvements and good media headlines, and Barber gave himself a pat on the back since departments were turning the extra money into desired outcomes – 'unlike 1998,' he would write, 'when money disappeared into black holes'. Yet, in 2002, the government's auditors discovered the opposite, with some health authorities running huge deficits. To avoid censure and dismissal for missing targets, their senior managers had seriously overspent.

Driving change from Downing Street by setting highly ambitious targets, Blair realised, had its limitations, but he could not think of an alternative. To clear his mind, he wrote a memorandum over a weekend at Chequers. Having finally persuaded Brown to announce increased NHS funding in the next Budget, he questioned why, despite the extra money already spent, waiting times were not falling and the number of patients being treated was not rising. It was the same disappointment he had suffered throughout his premiership. Would things never get better?

Milburn replied that his own ideas had once again changed radically. The NHS Plan 2000, he said, was a revitalising shopping list. The government needed finally to cross the Rubicon and embrace choice as a cornerstone of the NHS. The heart of Milburn's plan was to resurrect competition as the gospel, which meant reintroducing the Tories' internal market. Blair agreed, and Milburn began drafting a new White Paper, 'Delivering the NHS Plan: The Next Steps'. Ten years of policy in opposition and government was being jettisoned.

In Blair's new NHS, all hospitals would compete against each other to win contracts from private care trusts (PCTs). England's best hospitals would be liberated from central control. Those so-called foundation hospitals would be run by local organisations and would have financial and managerial independence from Whitehall, although they were subject to targets. NHS managers who failed to perform would be dismissed. 'It's Groundhog Day for you, Andy,' said Milburn to Andrew McKeon, the department's director of policy and his internal ally. McKeon had helped Ken Clarke shape the reforms in 1991 and had contributed to Stephen Dorrell's White Paper in 1996. Having watched Labour rip it all up, McKeon now witnessed Blair returning to the original philosophy. However, a decade later, one difference was critical: while the Tories had developed the reorganisation slowly, Milburn refused to commission pilot schemes to test his ideas. Blair wanted instant results – and numbers became important. 'It will be heavy-duty and ruthless,' observed McKeon.

To seal the devolution of health care, Milburn started another round of reorganisation. The primary-care groups were transformed into 302 PCTs, funded by a new system of payment by results and supervised by twenty-eight strategic health authorities.

Blair finally believed he had reached the beginning of the future. In that new dawn, the NHS would be equipped with a giant new IT infrastructure. One computer system would give instant access to the records of 50 million patients across the country, compiled by 30,000 GPs and 300 hospitals. Accurately described as 'the world's biggest civil information technology programme', the unprecedented technical ambitions matched Blair's search for a legacy. In February 2002, he hosted a seminar to approve the scheme. No critics were invited. To those querying the estimated cost of £2.3 billion, Milburn replied that the finances of the NHS were being monitored by an inspectorate reporting to Parliament. Blair praised Richard Granger, hired to supervise the project, as a man 'with a demonstrable professional track record' in Internet technology, something that was unavailable within the civil service. Recruiting Granger, John Birt told Blair, was a triumph over risk, establishing 'a more strategic and innovative approach to policy' than civil servants could achieve.

On 'Devolution Day' (but also April Fool's Day) 2002, Milburn's White Paper was published. Politicians spoke about 'building capacity', 'transformational change' and the 'big bang' of health reforms. Blair mentioned that NHS employees should feel part of the 'culture of the community'. NHS pressure groups dismissed such jargon as gibberish intended to conceal the ultimate betrayal of the service's ideals. Others scoffed that Blair was not devolving authority because Whitehall retained control. Unsure about his final destination, Blair could not spell out a complete vision. In a display of ideological contradiction, he spoke about 'empowering the individual', but also said that 'the weaknesses of free markets are clear'.

A key adviser in Downing Street realised that Blair 'was muddleheaded. He could not describe a coherent and complete model of what he wanted to achieve. So he could not explicitly tell Nigel Crisp what to do.' But for the moment his team – Barber, Milburn, Stevens and Paul Corrigan, a special adviser on the NHS – were all agreed on the same 'line of travel'. They would push through the first changes from Whitehall, then decide on the next step.

Two weeks later, Gordon Brown delivered his Budget. Conscious that the image of Blair was fixed behind him in the TV camera's frame, Brown's publicists presented the occasion as the coronation of the king-in-waiting. To Labour's cheers, the chancellor flourished a record

8.6 per cent increase on that year's NHS spending. The Tories' glum faces helped cast Brown as the hero.

Blair did not question the chancellor's claim that, despite the extra spending, he would stick to his 'golden rule' of balancing the budget over the economic cycle; nor did he query his pledge to keep government debt below 40 per cent of GDP. He seemed unaware that the Budget broke both assurances. Knowing that there was no prospect of financing the additional spending by private wealth creation or by increasing productivity in the private sector, Brown borrowed money from China and other countries, without any prospect of immediate repayment. To protect himself from criticism, he redefined his 'golden rule' for balancing his budgets.

The technical terms fooled Blair. But, unlike Barber, who praised Brown's 'new discipline established over public expenditure', he suspected chicanery. Although he could not master economic detail and thus prevent Brown's overspending, he did understand that the electorate would damn the chancellor's latest stealth taxes on savings, pensions, petrol, stamp duty and allowances as 'broken promises'. To avoid an argument, he retreated. 'I have a floppy PM on NHS costs,' Simon Stevens told Julian Le Grand.

Nor had Blair understood Milburn's reorganisation. In the nature of his government, well-meaning but fearful civil servants did not dare mention their foreboding. Suspicious ministers, they knew, disliked being told to 'read the game'. Within months, however, Milburn came to recognise his errors. He should have approved ten strategic health authorities instead of twenty-eight, fifty PCTs instead of 302 and eleven ambulance authorities instead of forty. He started another wasteful bout of restructuring, propelling 30,000 administrators into a merry-go-round of expensive redundancies.

During his regular meetings with Barber about the NHS, Blair never asked about these costly mistakes. Targets focused on crude numbers, not fundamental policies. The sessions gave Blair the opportunity to pose questions prepared by his staff that reassured those summoned about his being in full command. Although Jonathan Powell liked to boast that Blair possessed the 'barrister's ability to soak up vast amounts of paper while at the same time remaining focused on the big picture', the experts could see through the performance.

Improving the NHS depended largely on Nigel Crisp, but by then he and Milburn were arguing regularly. Milburn disliked Crisp's attitudes and upper-crust style, while Crisp resented Milburn's persistent questioning, which he regarded as interference. Others had become disillusioned with the NHS chief, not least George Alberti, who had originally nominated him. 'He was affable and smooth,' recalled Alberti, 'but I realised after two weeks that nothing was going on.' The health chief, he suspected, was 'anti-clinical'.

To Crisp and his departmental team, the NHS Plan 2000 was sacrosanct. Billions of additional pounds to erect new hospitals, hire additional staff and improve regulation were a nirvana, but to revolutionise the service according to the plan devised by Stevens and Milburn was, Crisp believed, unacceptable. The chief executive resented Blair's reintroduction of the internal market, but he did not oppose the 2002 White Paper outright. Instead, he cherry-picked from the new plan by approving 'limited choice'.

Inevitably, his tactics created contradictions. On the one hand, he criticised the lack of incentives for hospitals to treat more patients, which caused 'a sense of drift', but then he scorned incentives because 'there are limits to markets'. Not that he was blind to his Janus-like pronouncements. Rather, in his heart Crisp resented the politicians for generating the problems. Blair and Milburn, he observed, failed to understand 'the difference between wanting to change things and making things happen'. He went further: 'The NHS Plan was a plan of action which I could implement, while the 2002 White Paper was just more political developments.' To stymie any return to the Tories' blueprint, he created an unbridgeable chasm between the two plans. With the help of John Bacon, his deputy and the director for performance, he gathered the traditionalists in Richmond House to entrench top-down controls, prevent the devolution of powers and sabotage the loathsome internal market.

Crisp's rejection of profound change incensed Milburn, a volatile politician. The official was accused of being 'too laid-back, wishy-washy and not on top of his brief'. 'I had a simple and rather unsophisticated management model in my head,' Crisp would later explain. Blair, he believed, had 'a naive notion that you can change things from the centre. The problem with politicians is they're restless and push things on.' He spoke with pride about remaining remote from the political battles, biding his time, watching Blair and Milburn steel themselves to outwit Brown. He could count on the chancellor to stymie Blair.

In Crisp's portrayal, Milburn was not a true moderniser but was 'still very wedded' to the model of a centrally controlled NHS and 'very nervous' of going beyond old Labour's orthodoxy. 'There's already enough political blood on the floor,' Crisp recorded Milburn saying in an argument about change. Milburn denied that recollection but admitted being caught in the middle between Blair and Brown. In frustration, he appealed to the public by writing in *The Times* that Labour needed to seize diversity and choice from the Tories, just as it had taken over traditional Tory territory on the economy and crime.

As Crisp anticipated, Brown opposed the NHS contracting any privatised services or there being any dilution of Whitehall's control. He picked on foundation hospitals as his battleground, refusing to allow them to borrow money. These hospitals, he said, would fragment and eventually destroy the NHS. By contrast, an inflexible, monopoly NHS with no competition, no devolved powers and no patients' choice would preserve the values established in 1948. He rejected the evidence that competition was producing positive results in other countries.

By the beginning of June, Blair's self-confidence was being pummelled. Two days before a Cabinet meeting, he asked his close advisers whether he should announce that he would not contest the next election. 'Tony has to face up to the fact that Brown is killing him,' said Milburn. Blair was persuaded to fight. The showdown at an unusually dramatic Cabinet meeting on 13 June exposed the fractures. 'Our mettle is being tested,' Blair told his ministers during a discussion described by Richard Wilson as 'a big bad moment'. Brown brooded silently, stoking the division he had created.

Over a weekend at Chequers, with the help of officials Blair wrote a twenty-page note explaining the advantages of foundation hospitals. For once, his endorsement of Milburn's disdain for Whitehall's micro-management showed a better grasp of the detail than that shown by officials in the Department of Health. Brown ignored the note. He never engaged with Blair over ideas on how to improve NHS treatment. In retaliation, an eyewitness observed, Blair 'egged Milburn on to fight Brown'. 'Don't hold back,' he told the minister. Foundation hospitals, he stipulated, would be independent of the Treasury's control. 'If independence is good enough for the Bank of England,' Milburn had said brazenly to Brown in Cabinet, 'then it's OK for schools and hospitals.' His audacity, other ministers rightly assumed, had been blessed by Blair.

Unknown to Milburn, at that delicate moment Blair was preparing for war in Iraq. Over the following three months, his appetite for a power struggle over foundation hospitals disappeared. His weakness was revealed at the confrontation on 9 October with Brown, Milburn and Prescott. Brushing Milburn contemptuously aside, Brown refused to surrender the Treasury's control over every hospital's budget. His hatred for Milburn, sitting right next to him, was undisguised.

Blair retreated. In what one eyewitness called 'split the baby', he ruled, 'Your hospital plan and Gordon's financial plan.' Contrary to Milburn's blueprint, hospitals would not have their own budgets or benefit from financial incentives for good performance. Of course, in his remarks to the media Campbell would present 'new-style foundation hospitals', but they would not be financially independent nor would they embrace choice and competition. 'They'll be free to innovate,' was the best the Downing Street spokesman could say. Simon Stevens wrote out the agreement, with Andrew Turnbull looking over his shoulder. In a prearranged move, as soon as Brown left the room

Campbell issued a press statement praising the plan but omitting any hint that Brown had won. The chancellor was furious. Blair was consoled that, although the policy was lost, he had at least scored a victory with the press release.

Half a victory did not thrill Milburn: 'Once again Tony had said he would get rid of Gordon and endlessly, as usual, he didn't.'

TWENTY-FIVE

Targets and Dismay

At the end of Michael Barber's first year as head of the Delivery Unit, Blair was still excited by the regular stock-takes about the 'performativity' of the five priorities – crime, health, transport, immigration and education. Barber was basking in the glow of a Progress in International Reading Literacy Study about the reading standards of ten-year-olds in 2001. English primary schools had been ranked third out of forty countries. Part of the credit, eulogised Barber, was owed to Labour's 'excellent' reforms of Britain's teacher-training programme. His own credibility, Barber hoped, would be further enhanced by the 2002 results. But there was a hiccup. In June, on the morning of a critical World Cup match, he walked into Estelle Morris's office. 'It's a disaster,' he cried. 'England are playing a crucial match tonight and they'll go to bed too late.' The following day, eleven-year-olds were due to sit their SAT examinations, and Labour's political reputation would suffer if the targets were not met. Barber's fears were justified. 'Panic in the Department of Education,' was the eyewitness observation of Margaret Brown, a professor of mathematics education at King's College, London. That one day's results showed there had been no improvement in maths or English. The government's target of 80 per cent of eleven-year-olds achieving level 4 in maths was missed.

In his subsequent post-mortem with Blair, Barber fluently recited the disappointing statistics supplied by the schools and test boards. He heaped the blame on teacher training and on teachers failing to understand Whitehall's strategies. In searching for other culprits, he even blamed Chris Woodhead's resignation and Whitehall for 'losing its edge at every level'.

'The results will improve next year,' said Blair with conviction.

'I'm more worried that the media will rubbish the process,' said David Blunkett.

'Should we change our strategy?' Morris asked.

'No,' replied Barber. 'It worked with the previous children, so we'll do more of the same.'

Barber was in denial about the research presented by the statisticians. The dramatic improvement in level 4 maths had started in 1996. The best results were in 1998 and 1999 – before Labour's £80 million programme began – and the results would remain static after 2002 for another six years. 'We could not understand why the results plateaued,' said David Normington, the education department's permanent secretary. 'We never got an answer.' The standards among the poorest children, who did not benefit from the government's strategy, actually declined.

Margaret Brown knew the reason. She criticised cheating teachers and Labour's introduction of 'whole-class teaching'. Maths teachers trained under the Tories had divided classes into sets by ability. In those schools where numeracy skills had jumped between 1999 and 2002 from 33 per cent to 45 per cent of children meeting the high grade, many children had been specially coached for the tests. In 1998, Blunkett had ordered a dramatic change. Maths was now taught to mixed-ability classes by teachers who pitched their lessons at the middle, dragging down the results for those at the top. Innumeracy among children, Brown discovered, was growing. Even the best students no longer showed a deep understanding of maths.

Margaret Brown's criticism was particularly directed at Barber and his political masters. With Blair's agreement, Barber had ordered teachers to follow 'lesson plans' drafted in a rush and, in part, by a non-mathematician, just as schools faced an unexpected shortage of maths teachers. Labour had ended teacher training in universities, and the new intake was not specially trained in maths. The chance to improve teaching, Brown wrote, was being wasted by the politicians' distortions. 'In some cases, research evidence was disregarded for political reasons,' she said. 'Barber even suggested that computers should replace bad teachers,' she recalled.

Barber was particularly dismayed by the literacy results. His target had been for 80 per cent of eleven-year-olds to reach level 4 by 2002. He failed. In 2000, 75 per cent of children reached that level, but standards would rise no further. Indeed, many children could not sustain their progress and their reading skills deteriorated. Barber struggled to find an explanation. He had underestimated, he pleaded, the power of the educational establishment and had forgotten to champion parents. He also blamed the slowdown on 'a failure to understand sufficiently the nature of the challenge'. 'Too often', he wrote, 'it felt like a revolution without enough revolutionaries.' Bemused by his verbosity, others blamed the guru himself. They were suspicious of the tests and realised that a credulous prime minister had misunderstood how Barber's graphs failed to measure the human factor.

During those monthly stock-takes, Blair asked probing questions, but disappointing answers did not lead to any recriminations. In his world, post-mortems were rare. Neither Blair nor Barber would admit the reason for the plateauing – namely, that the snap improvement was a reflection of the Tories' achievements, which Labour's policies had stymied.

'Should we do more phonics?' Blair asked once again.

'No,' replied Barber.

'What's next?' asked Blair, referring to the day's agenda. Dabbling with statistics and passing over phonics in a brief sentence suggested little appreciation of pedagogy.

In public, he never challenged teachers' skills or questioned the slide in standards. Some assumed he was avoiding political pitfalls, while others sensed his obliviousness to the educational establishment's passion for 'child-centred' classrooms that followed the National Literacy Strategy (NLS). In his newspaper commentaries, Woodhead blamed the NLS for perpetuating illiteracy.

Blair also preferred to ignore those who scorned Barber for using data produced by educational institutions that was likely to confirm his own success. The critics suspected that he disregarded data collected from eleven sources by Professor Peter Tymms of Durham University that contradicted Barber's statistics showing 'success'. Tymms questioned whether Barber understood the discipline of statistics, as his own research showed schools were failing to improve literacy and numeracy. 'Barber's world is in the shadow between the idea and reality,' commented Michael Little, another academic critic. 'We can never be sure what happened.' Such criticism made no impression. Barber had won respect across Whitehall. His energy and organisational skills were admired, and that counted in a zone where, in Blair's assessment, talented officials were rare.

Blair's approval lulled Estelle Morris into not questioning Barber's target for secondary schools to improve their GCSE grades from D to C, especially in maths and English. No official warned Morris that setting such targets was complicated. When the teachers complained that the new demands would cause chaos in school tests, they were ignored. Morris was focused on enacting the 2002 Education Bill, an important landmark for Blair.

Under the bill, schools would be given more freedom, more faith schools would be approved and private sponsors would be welcomed for the new academies. The change reflected Blair's abandonment of 'standards not structures'. Structures – whether the school was a comprehensive, a city technology college or a specialist school – were important, he now acknowledged. After the first three academies were opened, Morris urged Blair, 'You must take the teachers with you. We need their support.' He ignored her advice but approved Andrew Adonis's search for more sponsors for the academies, a 50 per cent increase in teaching assistants, the recruitment of 25,000 more teachers, and Teach First, an innovative scheme to encourage graduates to teach in disadvantaged schools. With over 600,000 teachers and assistants employed in English schools – now better paid in a profession that had become more popular – the odds were stacked in favour of outstanding results. The doubters included senior officials in the Department of Education, who were not convinced that money would buy success. And Morris herself had become depressed.

Adonis was another problem. 'Andrew's as bright as a button', Morris told her confidants, 'but a nightmare to work with.' Many in the party, she knew, disliked him as a right-wing, self-aggrandising nerd.

Adonis was criticising Morris for being 'nervous' about taking on the left-wing educational establishment. 'That is untrue and makes me furious,' she retorted. He also questioned her understanding of education after she allowed, with Blair's agreement, fourteen-year-olds to abandon learning foreign languages.

The two officials were moving in opposite directions. Behind Morris's back, Blair told Adonis to ignore her and just secure the support of the department's officials. Without her agreement, Adonis regularly visited the department to give orders that contradicted her own. 'You can't do that,' he was told by the senior civil servants. With Blair's blessing, Adonis ignored their instruction, blatantly challenging Morris's authority.

'Adonis is running his own education policy,' a senior official told Morris.

'What shall I do?' she asked Barber.

'Just listen to him,' he replied enigmatically. Morris was powerless to challenge Blair.

Overseeing the bureaucracy was proving too much for a fragile woman with low self-esteem. Blair rarely engaged with her personally. He was unaware, she complained, of her anguish over failing schoolchildren and his refusal to meet teachers or understand their complaints. Isolated from Blair and irritated by Adonis, she was also critical of her 'inadequate' civil servants. Vulnerable, she winced about the imminent parliamentary battle to introduce tuition fees for university students, which had been explicitly excluded from the party's election manifesto. Finally, she wilted, overcome by the failure to meet the government's literacy and numeracy targets.

In 1997, Blunkett had promised to resign if his numeracy and literacy targets were not met by 2002. In March 1999, Morris had subscribed to the same pledge. On 24 October 2001, she unconvincingly denied that commitment. Months later, as a stream of negative headlines erupted about the A-level results, her undertaking was thrown back at her. She had become the target of blame for Blunkett's failed ambitions.

In 2000, Blunkett had been accused of downgrading standards by rushing in changes to A-levels. The following year, the A-level pass rate jumped by 4.5 per cent. The disparity between examinations, course work and modules reignited complaints about fixing exams and falling standards. Researchers showed that, since 1988, high grades in the gold-standard exam had become progressively easier to obtain thanks to less demanding questions, grade inflation and the opportunity granted by Labour to take AS modules repeatedly. In anticipation of even more students passing in 2002, the fearful examination boards unexpectedly employed stricter marking to fail an unusually high number of A-level candidates. Newspaper headlines described a pass rate that had been fixed to prevent embarrassment, and an official report would later confirm limited 'grade manipulation'. Academics appointed by Morris to resolve the problem engaged in a public dispute, then turned against her. Battered, the minister who had failed her own A-levels was accused of giving a 'misleading' assurance to the Commons and of undermining the authority of Mike Tomlinson, Ofsted's chief inspector.

Blair was unaware that his minister was crumbling until about 11 p.m. on 18 October 2002, when he was told that the following day's newspaper headlines would report a 'fiasco'. Just after midnight, he telephoned Morris while she was being driven to her home in Pimlico.

'Are we in trouble over A-levels?' he asked.

'Yes,' she replied. 'We are.'

There was a long silence, and then Blair tersely ended the call.

'I knew at that moment that I had lost the confidence of Downing Street,' Morris would later say. In truth, Blair still trusted her and had no reason to be suspicious when he was told three days later that she was returning to London from Birmingham for an immediate meeting. After brief pleasantries, Morris delivered her bombshell.

'I want to resign,' she said.

'What?' Blair exclaimed. 'Why?'

As she listed her failures – not least the imminent publication of the official report that fraudsters had stolen over £100 million from the Independent Learning Accounts – Blair became adamant that she shouldn't resign. 'You're doing a good job,' he repeated. The reforms she had started would work and her problems were a legacy from the first term. 'I want you to go away and think about it,' he said. 'Tell me tomorrow morning that you will not resign.' Alastair Campbell's calls over the next hours encouraging her to stay intensified her anguish. Blair, she felt, was blind to her plight.

She returned to Downing Street two days later. 'I'm going, Tony,' she said.

Charles Clarke was appointed education secretary in her place. The experienced political operator, characterised as corpulent, clever and occasionally boorish, was expected by Blair to trample on Morris's critics, not least by reassuring teachers that the education budget would increase annually by 9.2 per cent, raising expenditure to £70.9 billion in 2003/4. In their brief conversation, Clarke and Blair did not discuss standards. In Clarke's opinion, doctrines about education attracted obsessives. Phonics was unimportant. He would even decry studying classics at university and tell a parliamentary committee that blaming a child's poor performance on the parents 'makes me weep'. His response to bad teaching would be to refuse the invitation to attend the teaching unions' annual conferences. The differences between him, his predecessors and Adonis undermined those attempting to explain Blair's education policy. Like health and welfare, the only consistency was constant change.

The undisputed result of the turmoil in education policy was the growing dissatisfaction of the aspiring middle classes. Although Labour had built new schools, appointed a record number of teachers and reduced class sizes, more children than ever were going to private schools or receiving private tuition to improve their chances of entering Oxbridge, including the children of the prime minister's friends, advisers and ministers in his government. Blair's two sons would also apply for Oxbridge from a specially endowed school. Many inner cities had become immigrant ghettos, and a large number of young parents who could not afford school fees were fleeing from the cities to state schools in the shires. In response, Morris had launched London Challenge, a successful programme to reverse that trend through extra money and better teachers, but other cities had not followed suit. Neither Blair nor Clarke identified that as a priority.

Both, however, were horrified by the slowdown of Britain's economy. Gordon Brown admitted his forecasts were worthless. The country would need to borrow an additional £20 billion over two years to pay for increased welfare benefits and the pay hikes for public-sector workers, including increases of 21 to 40 per cent over three years for some NHS employees. Others would have to pay for that largesse. Later generations would have to repay the PFI debt, already fixed at £15 billion and heading higher.

'Will you push through university top-up fees?' was Blair's only question to Clarke during their first meeting. Neither mentioned the breach of the manifesto pledge that Blair cursed as short-sighted. Soon after the election, the leaders of the Russell Group, Britain's best universities, had asked him to introduce the fees to prevent Britain's leading colleges fading in the world's league tables. Blair agreed that 'co-payments' – the government's euphemism for tuition fees – would, in his words, 'modernise' Britain's education system. He hoped to rely on Clarke to persuade Labour MPs to support the government.

'I'll go through it and let you know,' replied his education minister. Blair, he found, was always willing to discuss problems. The glitch was whether anything happened thereafter. Two days later, as a warning to Clarke, and sensing Blair's weakness after Morris's resignation, Brown sent a forty-four-page letter to Cabinet ministers attacking foundation hospitals and opposing university tuition fees. With little effort, he made John Prescott 'furious'. Blair tried to reason with Brown, but the chancellor adamantly opposed anything provided by the private sector. On reflection, Clarke agreed that compelling wealthy graduates to pay for their education retrospectively seemed sensible. He also agreed with Blair that the alternative – Brown's proposed graduate tax – was unworkable because universities would need to wait fifteen years for their money. As anticipated, his conclusion provoked a battle with Brown. Clarke won the first round, but Brown kept on coming. Ignoring the chancellor's behind-the-scenes manoeuvring, on 22 January 2003 Clarke published a White Paper advocating tuition fees. In retaliation, on Brown's initiative 160 Labour MPs pledged to vote against the bill. 'People have been licensed by Gordon to rebel,' Blair told Peter Mandelson.

'Don't worry,' Clarke reassured Blair. 'Gordon's a paper tiger. I don't think he's got the support on the back benches.' Blair looked at the signatures on the opposition list and disagreed. His tolerance for political pain was inconsistent. Mindful of Alan Milburn's fate, Clarke told Blair, 'I won't give in to Gordon.'

Blair was struggling to understand why, since the start of his second term, he had been stuttering, failing to recover from the disappointment of the first. He had publicised his conversion to abandoning state monopolies in the NHS and education, and had declared his support for 'the consumer' and 'diversity of supply and choice', but little was happening. He wrote about building 'New Labour around the ideas of traditional values – solidarity, social justice, opportunity for all – applied entirely afresh to the modern world', but Labour stalwarts were scathing. He even advocated a debate about his support for 'greater interdependence plus greater individuality', a baffling proposition that was greeted with silence. What more did he have to do?

TWENTY-SIX

Broken Vows, Part 2

In July 2002, Blair hosted a generous farewell dinner in Downing Street for Richard Wilson, the retiring Cabinet secretary. Over the course of the evening, both men ignored the consequences of their fraught relationship. Wilson did not mention his regret that the traditional machinery of good government had been abandoned, while Blair showed no guilt for regularly humiliating Wilson by excluding him from meetings. On the contrary, he intended to also exclude David Omand, the newly appointed security and intelligence co-ordinator, from any involvement in Britain's defence and intelligence operations.

Within weeks of his appointment, Omand realised that he was not invited to Blair's meetings with Richard Dearlove or the other intelligence chiefs, or those with Admiral Mike Boyce. Instead, Jonathan Powell would sit with Blair. 'Powell regarded us with contempt,' noted Andrew Turnbull.

'The system of government was obviously corrupted,' recalled Omand. 'Turnbull and I tried to get it changed, but we were blocked by Manning.' David Manning would deny the accusation: 'I had no say over who had access to the prime minister.' The other possible culprit was Powell. In either case, the exclusion of representatives of honest government from critical meetings resulted in what Omand later called 'a failure of statecraft'.

The newcomer's fate was not surprising. During his last days in Downing Street, Wilson's suspicions had grown. At one point, he noticed Blair was writing a conversation note for a forthcoming telephone exchange with President Bush about Iraq. 'We will be with you come what may,' was the summary. Wilson's surprise was shared by Manning, who advised Blair, 'You can't say that because you're committing the British army to an invasion which no one else knows about.' Blair appeared unmoved.

Those who assumed that the prime minister had been seduced by Bush in Crawford misunderstood his attitude. Blair was not the president's poodle but his partner. However, unlike Bush, he could not legally reveal their joint plan to pursue regime change. Iraq's possession of WMDs could be the only justification for Britain's participation. Manning, a reporter rather than an innovator, resisted raising the alarm by appealing to Turnbull for advice. Instead, he moved closer to Blair's inner circle alongside Powell and Dearlove, excluding any potential critics. 'I got "keep out" vibes from Manning,' recalled Turnbull. 'He had the Stockholm syndrome – complete loyalty.'

Boyce was struck by the prime minister's unyielding conviction. 'I don't want to look at myself in the mirror in ten years', said Blair, 'when he has used WMDs again and know I could have stopped that.' He did not welcome the admiral's scepticism, especially his questions about what would follow Saddam's defeat.

In his report in July, Dearlove had highlighted the absence of any American plan for post-war occupation, a warning that was repeated by Jack Straw. The foreign secretary now introduced Michael Williams, a Middle East specialist, to Blair. Williams explained that Iraq's stability owed everything to Saddam forcibly keeping the Shias and Sunnis apart. Once this control disappeared, peace was unlikely. 'That's all history, Mike,' said Blair. 'This is about the future.'

Another warning was delivered by Peter Ricketts, the director of the Foreign Office's Middle East department. He predicted Saddam's overthrow would lead to turmoil. He also cautioned that the scramble 'to establish a link between Iraq and al-Qaeda is so far frankly unconvincing'. Since Ricketts's advice did not appear to be endorsed by either Michael Jay, the Foreign Office's chief, or Straw, Blair avoided any response. He also sidestepped the legal advice offered by Peter Goldsmith, the attorney general, that regime change without the approval of the UN would be illegal. 'Well . . .' Blair replied, his voice trailing off. He had decided to accept his lawyers' advice that in public statements 'we focus on WMDs and we do not mention regime change'. Any suggestion that this amounted to deception would be fiercely denied by him.

On 24 July, Blair met David Owen, the former Labour foreign secretary, for dinner. Although restless, he spoke with certainty about war, despite the difficulties. His enthusiasm was explained by some as a way to sabotage Gordon Brown's attempts to make him resign; others, like Peter Mandelson, anticipated that a victory would seal his reputation, as the Falklands had for Thatcher. Few could understand why he was so focused on Saddam, whose rule posed no risk to Britain nor an immediate threat in the region, on top of which there was no proof that he possessed WMDs. Yet Blair had brushed these factors aside and told Bush that Britain was committed to the invasion. Nothing could interfere with his crusade against evil.

One result was immediate. 'The Americans are raising the shutters,' Britain's army liaison officer in Tampa reported to military headquarters in Northwood, north London. Shortly after, a team of American planning staff arrived at Northwood to describe the invasion plan. Boyce and the chiefs intensified their discussions about the size of Britain's commitment, or 'package'.

Britain could enter the war, Blair knew, only with the public's support. Putting British lives at risk and spending billions of pounds could be justified by defining the military and political objectives as vital to the national interest. He realised that 'force for good', the original policy, would meet those criteria, so long as Saddam's WMDs threatened world peace. The JIC, he decided, should publish a dossier bringing together all the intelligence. Giving the public what Powell called a 'sort of Rolls-Royce information campaign' would be judged as honourable.

JIC chairman John Scarlett started assembling the material, but then Blair reassessed the implications. Publication would trigger speculation. Daylight was dangerous. After a press conference in late July, his astute performance led Simon Jenkins to write, 'Mr Blair has no clue what America intends to do in Iraq. This is understandable since, as yet, nor does America.' By keeping his plans in the shadows, even his most cynical critics could be controlled, as Blair discovered on the eve of his summer break. Towards the end of July, he agreed to meet Clare Short.

'I really think we should have a discussion about Iraq,' she said.

'No decisions have been made,' replied Blair, 'but I do not want it to come to Cabinet because it might leak into the press and hype things up.'

Short appeared satisfied, and Blair left for his summer vacation resolved not to publish the dossier Scarlett was assembling.

The holiday, which included a stay at the home of Alain-Dominique Perrin, the French billionaire owner of the luxury-goods company Richemont, ended with a hike in the Pyrenees with a friend. Blair stayed overnight in a mountain hotel. At breakfast the following morning, he was tense. 'He said he'd been up all night', the friend told the *Financial Times*, 'because he couldn't get to sleep. And then he said, "I've made some big decisions."'

Blair returned to London at the end of August. Dick Cheney was agitating for war and declaring that Iraq was undoubtedly amassing WMDs. In Britain, Labour Party activists were threatening revolt, but Blair had decided. Any lingering doubts about his support for Bush and his fear of the Labour Party and public opinion had been resolved in favour of war.

By then, the chiefs had read the JIC's first draft of the dossier about WMDs. Scarlett's committee admitted that their conclusions were based on just one source and that there was 'very little intelligence' about Saddam's WMD programme. 'An overlong and rather poor cut-and-paste job,' concluded Admiral Nigel Essenhigh. The source of the 'intelligence' seemed to be information drawn from the 'red books' – the intelligence summaries distributed among senior military staff – and material already in the public domain. Based on historic information, the draft lacked any compelling new evidence.

'I think this is all ghastly,' said another chief. 'Rubbish. We don't need this.' The three chiefs told Boyce they were puzzled as to why the government needed a dossier. Essenhigh in particular argued that Blair could go to war on the basis that Saddam had breached UN resolutions. 'If the government insists that a dossier be published,' said Essenhigh, 'this confused version is as good as anything.' Boyce did not repeat those messages to Blair.

By 28 August, the chiefs' comments were redundant. Blair decided that an intelligence dossier should be published after all. Scarlett's team under Julian Miller, the chief of the JIC's assessment staff, began rewriting the draft. At a press conference in Sedgefield, Blair announced, 'America should not have to face this issue alone. We should face this together.'

Since the informal decision in July, a small team in the defence staff had been compiling three options for Britain's participation. Package one was limited to air, maritime and intelligence support of the American invasion. The second package committed ninety planes and twenty ships employing about 13,000 personnel. Package three was full-blown involvement by 42,000 personnel, including infantry and tanks, all totally integrated within the American command. Half the British army, comprising a third of the invasion force, would be committed to the full brunt of war. In September, Boyce told the army to assume its involvement would be limited to package one. The generals regarded Boyce's decision as 'profoundly unsatisfactory'. The army, he was told, wanted to be involved from start to finish.

One obstacle was the army's decay, mainly as a result of Brown's refusal to provide extra money to replace equipment. The fallacy of the 1998 strategic defence review was exposed. Essenhigh told Geoff Hoon that the budget was inadequate. 'It's like talking to a wall,' he complained. Without influence over Blair and his confidants, Hoon refused to become involved. Essenhigh's request for a meeting with the prime minister was refused.

The military's fate depended on Boyce making a direct appeal. Late one afternoon in Chequers, he stood in front of maps of Iraq explaining to Blair the different scenarios, packages and problems of an invasion.

'I'm told repeatedly', he said to Blair, 'that we are not sufficiently funded. We are committed to do our best but we cannot do the whole mission.'

Blair nodded. The Treasury, he knew, would in the event of war fully fund an operation, but for the moment he resisted the army's request that he commit himself to package three, and pointedly refused to permit the purchase of new equipment. 'If you want more money,' he said, 'speak to Gordon.'

Following the familiar path, Boyce approached Brown twice. 'I got no traction,' he reported wearily.

The quickening pace posed Blair with a dilemma. Although he believed that his 'force for good' philosophy justified removing Saddam, none of the senior politicians in his Cabinet shared his unqualified passion or his trust of Bush. To justify Britain's participation, he needed the president's continued support in building a coalition of nations working through the UN ostensibly to seek a peaceful resolution with Saddam. Certain of his power to persuade America to follow his path and not alienate other countries by focusing only on an invasion, he sent Manning to Washington to convince Bush to 'stick to the UN', meaning that an invasion needed to be authorised by a UN resolution in order to be legal. Manning reported back that the UN was 'not a lost cause' and that Bush wanted to meet Blair.

During a quick trip to Camp David, where he met Bush and, to his surprise, Cheney, Blair laid out his plan to achieve disarmament through the UN. If that happened, he said, Saddam would find survival difficult. If the process were exhausted and shown to have failed, then an invasion could be justified. 'If we get disarmament through the UN,' said Bush, 'we would have crated the guy.' However, his sympathy was crushed by Cheney's antipathy towards the British. Cheney wanted disarmament delivered by regime change, nothing less. Blair returned to London fixed on an implacable truth: regardless of Britain, Bush and Cheney were going to war.

On 23 August, the JIC had reported that we 'know little about Iraq's chemical and biological weapons since late 1998'. On 9 September, the team hardened their opinion, with the latest draft stating that 'Iraq could produce more biological agents within days . . . and nerve agents within months.' This new conclusion was reached without any new proof. Despite the 'relative thinness' of the existing evidence, an inquiry would later decide, the JIC applied 'greater firmness' in their judgement.

The evidence had been sharpened after Alastair Campbell's intercession. Four days earlier, during a committee meeting to consider the JIC draft, he had told Powell that it required 'a substantial rewrite . . . It had to be revelatory and we needed to show what was new.' Campbell relied on Scarlett, whom he called a 'mate', and Dearlove, who was praised as 'really helpful', to deliver the goods. Both met Blair in his den rather than in an austere committee room surrounded by sceptics. And both were keen to oblige.

As chairman of the JIC, Scarlett had to assess the information provided by all the intelligence agencies and present an uncorrupted conclusion. Blair was entitled to expect a judgement based on forensic examination of MI6's sources. Accordingly, when the chairman spoke with conviction about Saddam's WMDs, Blair in theory had no reason to harbour doubts. But what Scarlett actually said did raise questions. The intelligence agencies, he conceded, lacked hard evidence. The latest information from the European intelligence services confirmed that judgement, and some early sources on whom Dearlove depended had already been reclassified as 'fabricators and fantasists'. Those circumstances had persuaded the Cabinet defence committee to conclude that 'our intelligence is poor'.

Scarlett's solution was to offer a compromise: Saddam did possess WMDs, yet intelligence to that effect was 'sporadic and patchy'. His words of caution, he would later explain, did not carry their normal meaning. He was not challenged over his vagueness. Blair could choose what suited him. For others, the confusion Scarlett sowed was complete – not least for the defence chiefs.

Regardless of their personal opinions, Blair could depend on the chiefs' loyalty never to challenge a prime minister's legal order. The only fly in the ointment of the 'can-do' spirit that Blair so admired was Boyce. 'He says everything is too difficult,' complained the prime minister. 'He's too negative and monosyllabic.' The admiral reported 'problems' in a dry manner, without making himself amenable.

'Why do you have to be so gloomy?' Campbell asked him. 'So half full?'

Surprised by Campbell's anger, Boyce looked back at him with contempt. 'I don't tell people what they like to hear,' he replied.

'He had an arrogant style and was irrelevant,' Boyce, with intense dislike, would later say about Campbell, unaware of the publicist's bouts of clinical depression. 'He was trivial, not interested in real outcomes.' Curiously, Campbell had earlier judged Boyce as possibly 'a fellow depressive'. Providing erroneous explanations for Boyce's suspicions about Blair's intentions was natural to Campbell, and for those same reasons Blair preferred to avoid speaking to the admiral.

The antagonism between Blair and his chiefs highlighted one of several handicaps blighting the British military. For an army to launch an invasion across a desert under the command of a former submariner exposed the inexperience of all British officers in this kind of land warfare. Unlike the American army, no senior British army officer had commanded a battle group or even obtained a PhD. Unaware of that deficit, Blair was also heading towards war without a network of civilian defence specialists providing critical advice. Not only had he excluded Andrew Turnbull from the discussions, but Kevin Tebbit too, the permanent secretary at the MoD, whom Jonathan Powell disliked. He had also abandoned the traditional OPX Cabinet committee that in the past had scrutinised all combat plans. He had constructed what Manning described to the Chilcot committee as 'a ring of secrecy'.

Whitehall had not previously prepared for a war on the exclusive basis of intelligence rather than reasoned arguments written and discussed by senior officials in the Foreign Office, MoD and Cabinet Office. Never before had the Cabinet secretary, the fulcrum of the government machine, been excluded from such vital discussions. Blair's innocence about the fallibility of intelligence officers could have been remedied by the secretary but, during his transfer of responsibilities to Turnbull in the summer, Wilson did not mention his belief that the dossier was being 'overcooked' by Scarlett; nor did he comment about Blair's pressure on the intelligence services. On the contrary, Wilson said, 'It's a good thing.'

Blair's diktat of exclusion also applied to David Omand, the former head of GCHQ, who had been specifically appointed as the co-ordinator of security and intelligence in the Cabinet Office. His repeated requests to Manning for access to Blair were rebuffed. Instead of having a well-oiled bureaucratic machine heading towards a common objective, Blair had fragmented Whitehall between a handful of trusted advisers and the majority, who were alien. Leading the loyalists, Scarlett was scurrying around the intelligence agencies in search of convincing evidence to justify the reason for war, and his pickings were meagre.

Since GCHQ could offer no intelligence from its intercepts, the pressure to come up with conclusive evidence was on Dearlove. He was convinced that Saddam possessed WMDs, but his agency lacked trustworthy Iraqi agents with access to the leader. Without those direct links, he relied upon information traded from foreign agencies.

An Italian source was proffering a letter that showed Saddam had attempted to buy yellowcake uranium in Niger, West Africa, in order to eventually manufacture enriched plutonium, a redundant process discarded by the Israelis in the 1960s. MI6 had obtained a separate tip about an Iraqi enquiry for uranium in Niger that did not lead to a subsequent purchase. Then there was Rafid al-Janabi, an Iraqi chemical engineer, who arrived in Germany in 1999 and claimed to have worked in a mobile biological warfare laboratory. Code-named Curveball, he was interrogated by German intelligence (BND) for two years. Prevented by the BND from asking the Iraqi any questions directly, Dearlove accepted his eye-witness account of there being WMDs, as did the JIC assessors, without any additional scrutiny. Finally, there was an assortment of information supplied by the Jordanian and French intelligence agencies that had been gleaned from high-ranking Iraqis who had either been debriefed in Europe or had flitted across the border to Jordan. Among the dissenters was Hussein Kamel, related to Saddam by birth and marriage. He and his family had arrived as fugitives in Amman in 1995. During debriefings, Kamel told MI6 officers that as Iraq's minister of industries he had supervised the development of WMDs since 1987. Crucially, he described how Saddam's WMD programme had been destroyed in 1991. In 1996, Kamel and his family were lured back to Baghdad and murdered. Ever since, the intelligence agencies could not agree on whether Kamel was reliable or had been planted by Saddam.

The stories told by all these sources were unverifiable because every Western intelligence agency, including America's, lacked agents within Saddam's entourage. But, in 2002, there was also a prejudicial mindset that Saddam was concealing his WMDs, which therefore meant that the low-level Iraqi informants who confirmed that conclusion were classified as 'reliable'. The professional's instinctive suspicion of deception was abandoned.

Dearlove's interpretation of the reports was challenged by some middle-ranking analysts in MI6. Their voice had been weakened by Dearlove's reduction of MI6's 'Requirements' section, which no longer employed the most experienced officers to scrutinise incoming intelligence. 'Dearlove removed the checks,' Omand realised with hindsight, 'and left some in his team who were too eager to believe in WMDs.'

Dearlove's certainty was disputed by Brian Jones and his fellow intelligence analysts at the MoD. Despite Jones's expertise, Scarlett took comfort from the fact that the official was sidelined because of his low security clearance. In Scarlett's view, Jones was not an 'authoritative' expert 'within the system', and therefore could be ignored.

All the material was collated and tested for credibility by Julian Miller, a senior official seconded to the JIC from the MoD, who then presented a considered opinion for Scarlett. The system worked only if Miller and his staff treated MI6's reports with robust scepticism. For that independence, he needed Scarlett's support. In September 2002, the JIC assessors faced serious hurdles.

In the scenario offered by high-ranking Iraqis, Saddam's programme of weapons development had been effectively curtailed by the bombing campaign in 1991, then terminated by UNSCOM inspectors in 1995. An attempt to restart development in 1996 had been stopped two years later by Operation Desert Fox. Thereafter, Saddam delayed setting up the programme again while he negotiated the end of sanctions. That truthful version was not believed by the British and American intelligence agencies. Neither grasped the dictator's unwillingness to admit his weakness.

Conditioned by the errors of their predecessors in 1991, Dearlove, Scarlett and Miller wrongly believed that Saddam's weapons programme was more sophisticated than it really was. In unison, the staff of the intelligence agencies in Britain and America fell victim to a familiar flaw: convinced that Saddam possessed WMDs, they interpreted any 'intelligence' as supporting their prejudices. They even disseminated false intelligence to the media to generate the notion that Saddam possessed the terrible weapons they wanted him to have.

In the countdown to the dossier's completion, Scarlett was under intense pressure – or 'unduly influenced', as Robin Butler's subsequent inquiry would conclude – from Campbell to produce the most convincing case. As a believer, he did not raise any doubts about compromising the intelligence agencies' independence. In fact, he deliberately omitted from the final dossier his damning summary that the evidence for WMDs was 'sporadic and patchy'. Instead, he wrote in his draft in early September that Saddam 'continued to produce chemical and biological weapons'. He must have known that there was no real evidence for that conclusion. His staff also knew that the 'new' intelligence describing Saddam's al-Hussein rockets was as old as the weapons themselves, and there were serious doubts as to whether he possessed a missile that was actually usable. Desperate for something new, on the eve of publication Scarlett made what he called a 'last call for any items of intelligence that agencies think should be included'. That produced what his staff believed was a golden nugget belatedly discovered by MI6. Based on information from an Iraqi informant, Scarlett included in the dossier hard new evidence alleging that Saddam possessed 'weapons' that could be armed with chemical or biological warheads.

According to the JIC report inserted into the dossier, 'The Iraqi military are able to deploy these weapons within 45 minutes of a decision to do so.' Scarlett never publicly explained the genesis of that account or described the weapon. Butler's inquiry would describe the original 'vague and ambiguous' report to MI6 as 'based on a single, uncorroborated source'. Scarlett ought to have known that MI6's second-hand contact was an Iraqi brigadier who was passing on gossip about a short-range artillery shell and not, as was later assumed by the media, the 'regional' al-Hussein rocket. Blair's critics would refer to the omission of that detail as an example of 'sexing up' the dossier. According to Butler's inquiry, 'More weight was put on it than the intelligence was strong enough to bear . . . The interpretation [of the intelligence report] was stretched to the limit.' Scarlett would subsequently blame the litany of errors on Miller's team and expressly excused himself of responsibility. By nature, he was not of a mind to question the collective wisdom. His role, he believed, was to represent the consensus rather than to encourage counter-intuitive debates. The JIC machine reached conclusions without dissenters.

On 11 September, the latest draft of Scarlett's report was passed around Downing Street's media specialists and government spokesmen. Several submitted unflattering comments. Phil Bassett emailed that it was 'reading like the *Sunday Times* at its worst'. He wanted 'more in officialese'. Godric Smith wrote, 'It's a bit of a muddle,' while Tom Kelly lamented the absence of any proof that Saddam 'could pull the nuclear trigger anytime soon'. Boyce and the chiefs were similarly unconvinced.

Their jeers were squashed by Dearlove. In a meeting that same day in Downing Street with Blair and Powell, he disclosed that MI6 had found a new source. He declined to share the new intelligence with

Brian Jones and the specialists in the MoD. At Blair's insistence, every traditional safeguard that might have led to a warning about any potential danger was excluded. Omand was unaware that the prime minister had invited Dearlove and MI6's Iraq specialist to return to Downing Street on 12 September for what the MI6 chief called a 'heads-up'. With Campbell watching, Dearlove would describe 'a pretty rare event . . . a silver bullet moment'. Blair never questioned the validity of the new intelligence, encouraging the MI6 chief to bypass Omand, Turnbull and Scarlett. 'Blair loved his close relationship with Dearlove,' Turnbull would observe. Even the MI6 chief recognised his position was 'fragile and dangerous'. Omand would call it Dearlove's 'Icarus moment', when he crashed to his death by getting too close to the sun.

At the meeting, Blair was told that MI6 had received confirmation from a source in Iraq that Saddam had accelerated the production of chemical and biological agents. Blair had the impression that the information was connected to the mobile laboratories that could produce WMDs, thus reinforcing Curveball's credibility in London.

On the basis of Dearlove's briefing, Scarlett became more assertive. As he himself recalled, the new information 'did famously influence what was in the dossier'. Among the changes now made was the removal of Scarlett's prediction that Saddam would need 'at least five years' to produce a nuclear weapon. Overnight, the wording became: 'Iraq could produce a nuclear weapon in between one and two years.' No new verified intelligence existed to justify the change.

When Blair read Scarlett's draft, as Campbell noted, he 'felt it was pretty compelling stuff'. This self-congratulatory diary note was premature. Six days later, Powell emailed Scarlett that the draft failed to demonstrate any imminent threat. 'We must make clear', he wrote, 'that Saddam would not attack us at the moment.' As previously, such dissent was unwelcome. Blair's reply to Powell's question 'Why now?' was that Britain's priority was to maintain its alliance with America.

Over the following days, the JIC's blurs and smudges came to be viewed as conclusive proof that Saddam possessed WMDs. Conditional words, including 'indicates', 'probably' and 'could be', were removed from the draft. On 17 September, Campbell emailed Scarlett, telling him that, after reading the latest draft, Blair was pleased, but asked whether a 'might' and a 'may' could be replaced in the draft with concrete assertions. No sooner asked than done. Scarlett also removed the sentence, 'We have little intelligence on Iraq's chemical and biological warfare doctrine and know little about Iraq's CBW [chemical and biological weapons] work since 1998,' and refined his assertion that Saddam possessed rockets with an 'extended range'.

In his own defence, Scarlett would later describe how he had prevented Campbell from exaggerating the intelligence community's conclusions. Two exclusions undermined his defence. First, at the very last moment Powell had objected to seventeen words that portrayed Saddam as using WMDs only in self-defence. They were removed to give the impression that Iraq would use WMDs as part of his offensive threat. Second, Scarlett did not object to the exclusion from his own summary of the admission that the intelligence about Iraq's WMDs was 'sporadic and patchy'. Instead, he omitted any serious qualifications in the published dossier about the weakness of his intelligence. He wrote that everything he had learned 'points clearly to Iraq's continuing possession after 1991 of chemical and biological agents'. Saddam would, on 'refurbished sites', be 'able to manufacture these agents, and to use bombs, shells, artillery rockets and ballistic missiles to deliver them'.

To reinforce the dossier, Blair decided to express his own opinion in a foreword (written by Campbell) to the JIC's report. It contained his view that 'I believe the assessed intelligence has established beyond doubt that Saddam has continued to produce chemical and biological weapons, that he continues to develop nuclear weapons, and that he has been able to extend the range of his ballistic missile programme.' He added, 'I am in no doubt that the threat is serious and current . . . and he has to be stopped.'

The foreword made mention four times of 'WMDs to be ready within forty-five minutes of an order to use them'. Blair's words were reviewed and approved by Scarlett, but no subsequent inquiry has asked Blair whether he actually read the final report.

Blair knew publication was a risk, but the odds, he believed, were stacked in his favour. 'Moral luck' would conceal the risk once the WMDs were found. ('Moral luck' is if two drunken men drive away from a pub and one kills a pedestrian. The other driver had 'moral luck'.) Scarlett's silence about the foreword deceived Whitehall insiders. 'We didn't realise how misleading the first dossier was,' said Omand.

Despite the certainty of war in Washington, the prospect was dividing public opinion in Britain. To show their strength, many of Blair's British opponents joined a 400,000-strong protest march through London by the Countryside Alliance on 22 September. The demonstration showed the deep schism between the metropolitan Blairites and those Britons who inhabited the countryside. The marchers detested Blair's betrayal of British values. To them, the encouragement of immigration and the criminalisation of fox-hunting pandered to English self-hatred. Leaked minutes of a meeting between Prince Charles and Blair recorded Charles repeating a farmer's complaint that 'if we as a group were black or gay, we would not be victimised or picked upon'. For opposite reasons – the betrayal of British values and of Labour's core values – the antagonism towards Blair came from the right and the left. To his credit, Blair had been persuaded that a hunting ban would damage the countryside, and had relied on Anna Walker, a civil servant, and Alun Michael, a non-confrontational Labour MP, to find a third way, with the help of a report by Terry Burns. But, faced with his party's opposition to the war, he decided after the march to drop any compromise solution on hunting.

One hurdle in his plan for war was the Cabinet, which met the following day, 23 September. This was to be the ministers' first serious discussion about Iraq since March. Once again, Blair forbade the Cabinet Office to prepare any papers with the latest assessments. 'The Cabinet will be informed by the media,' he told Turnbull, confident that his decision would not be challenged. Reports by Campbell that Straw and

the Foreign Office were particularly 'paranoiac' confirmed his calcu-
lation about a possible backlash. There were to be no leaks until the
public were persuaded that his cause was valid. Blair's passion for speed
and secrecy, Turnbull realised, was 'not a bad habit he and Powell had
slipped into, but how they wanted to operate from the start'.

The Cabinet meeting was desultory. 'They never asked for a discussion on the options for war,' observed Turnbull about the approximately
twenty-five ministers in the room. 'They bought into Blair's challenge
to Saddam.' Following that tune, his ministers regarded the dossier as
one more step to persuade Saddam to allow UN inspectors full access.
They agreed to focus on the legitimacy of the UN route as their best
method of justifying the war – if it occurred – to their constituents.

The highlight of the meeting was a question from Robin Cook
about the military options. Blair replied that no decision about joining the invasion had been made. Manning and Powell, who were both
in the room, knew this was not the complete truth, as did Hoon and
Straw, but the overwhelming majority of ministers remained unaware
that Blair was committed to invading Iraq the following year. Turnbull,
attending his first meeting as Cabinet secretary, was surprised by the
denial. Cook himself suspected Blair had decided to go to war but few,
he knew, would accept his own conviction that his leader was 'deluded'
and 'a fantasist' pursuing some higher moral purpose. To Blair's good
fortune, Cook was a loner who played his cards close to his chest. He
sought no allies, nor did he challenge the dossier's authenticity. No one
asked Blair whether he believed the intelligence, and any discussion
in what Cook would later describe as a 'grim meeting' was kept to a
minimum. At Blair's request, the few critical questions were removed
from the official minutes. Cosmetics concealed the meagre trace of a
dispute. In hindsight, Cook pinpointed that meeting as the birth of
Blair's Messiah complex, while others would call the moment the collapse of proper government. Blair could run his domestic agenda relying on Powell, Sally Morgan and other cronies, but those were not the
people to manage the machinery of a democracy undertaking a war.

On the eve of the dossier's release to the press, Powell had asked, 'What will be the headline in the *Standard*?' He was answered at 10.30 a.m. on 24 September, as the London paper was distributed across the capital. At eight o'clock that morning, Charles Reiss, the *Standard*'s veteran political editor, had been allowed to read the dossier, thirty minutes before the deadline for the first edition. After a speed-read, Reiss was left in no doubt that '45 minutes' to deploy a weapon carrying WMDs should be the tabloid's lead. After all, it appeared in the text four times, and a preceding section mentioned Iraq's 'strategic missile systems'. He juxtaposed the two and sent his copy to the newspaper for instant publication, without speaking to Campbell. The newspaper's editor supervised the front-page headline, '45 Minutes to Attack', above a map showing the rocket's range, which stretched across Israel to British troops in Cyprus.

The effect was as dramatic as Blair had anticipated. Taken in conjunction with official advice that Britons should store tinned food and new batteries for their torches, the majority of the population was convinced that Saddam possessed deadly weapons. At Downing Street's eleven o'clock briefing, Reiss was not approached by a government spokesman to correct the mistaken impression he'd given of a long-range rocket armed with WMDs. 'They'd have come fast enough if I'd got it wrong,' observed Reiss, a veteran eyewitness to Campbell's intimidation.

Blair's masterful speech to the Commons later that day reflected Dearlove's assurance about the strength of a new source of intelligence: 'His weapons of mass destruction programme is active, detailed and growing. The policy of containment is not working. The weapons of mass destruction programme is not shut down, it is up and running ... Documents show that some of Iraq's WMDs could be ready for use within forty-five minutes.' Going further than the dossier itself, and far beyond the JIC's 'sporadic and patchy' evidence, Blair told the country that the intelligence reports describing Saddam's WMDs were, 'I believe ... extensive, detailed and authoritative'. The public were assured that the dispatch of UN inspectors to specific locations in Iraq would protect them from the deadly missiles. While most Tory MPs approved the dossier without criticism, the professionals reacted coolly. In their opinion, Scarlett's report revealed nothing new.

Eight years later, Blair would write, 'The infamous 45-minute claim was taken up by some of the media on the day but not referred to afterwards and was not mentioned by me at any time in the future . . . So the idea that we went to war because of this claim is truly fanciful.' He added, in an unintended self-revelation, that after publication the '45 minutes' was universally ignored. Blair had forgotten the million anti-war protesters who marched through London on 28 September. The forty-five-minute claim was alive for them – as it was for Dearlove. During those days, the MI6 chief was feeling, he later said, 'extremely uncomfortable' because he knew that the dossier had misrepresented an artillery gun as a rocket, but he remained silent. He would also discover that the new source of intelligence personally revealed by him to the prime minister in Downing Street was bogus. But he did offer Blair another trump card: MI6 and the CIA hoped to persuade an Iraqi general to kill Saddam and take control of the country in a swift coup. Blair voiced no doubts about the scenario.

The protest in central London was mirrored by opposition to the war at the Labour Party conference in Blackpool. As usual, Blair spoke fluently, but his passionate sentiments about dictators fell flat. The audience packed into the Winter Gardens had not devoted their lives to the party in order to approve an imperialist adventure. But without Brown, an Atlanticist who would not want to oppose the American president, or even Cook offering themselves as alternative leaders, they were powerless.

Not that Brown was quieted. Once again, he was demanding a date for Blair's departure, with foundation hospitals his new battleground. His rallying cry in his conference speech was, 'We're best when we're Labour.' Overnight, Blair's team invented the riposte, 'We're best when we are boldest,' and recited that the reforms were not 'the betrayal of the public services, but their renewal'.

For the first time, Blair failed to inspire passion among the faithful. His magic had faded. Five years earlier, he had shaped a moment in history, speaking for the majority of Britons about responsibility and honesty. Since then, dozens of quangos had been established to transform Britain into Blair's image of a fairer country. In his moral equivalence, creating fairness in Britain was no different to doing so in Iraq. His conscience acquitted him of wrongdoing for secretly planning a potentially illegal war. His miscalculation was underestimating his audience's anger.

This error was illustrated by the appearance of Bill Clinton on the Blackpool stage and a colourful story in the media about the former president eating a McDonald's hamburger late at night in the deserted seaside town. Clinton excited the party faithful, but others wondered why Blair, at the moment when his credibility was to be tested, would want to stand alongside a proven liar whose alleged abuse of state funds in Arkansas, association with high-profile criminals and receipt of kickbacks for favours cast him as an irrefutably corrupt politician. 'He's the only man', a wag sniped, 'who can cry out of one eye.' Blair replied that Clinton's presence showed that 'I counted, was a big player, was a world, not just a national leader . . . Our alliance with America gave Britain a huge position.' In turn, Clinton queried why Blair had aligned himself so closely to Bush, a question that Boyce was also asking. Answering Clinton was easier than responding to the admiral, not least because Blair had been told that the army was dissatisfied by Boyce's 'marked reluctance' to commit beyond package one.

Under that package, the British army would enter Iraq after Saddam's defeat to act as peacekeepers. That scenario, General Mike Walker, the chief of the army, told Tebbit, was 'profoundly unsatisfactory'. Following Operation Swift Sword, the army's recent training exercise in the Omani desert, Walker was insistent that 42,000 British soldiers supported by ships and planes should be integrated into the US forces according to package three. 'This is what we have to do if we are to deliver,' he said. Britain needed to share the risk with the Americans and bear the casualties. The global status of the country's military depended upon close involvement with the US. Without full collaboration, the British would be denied future access to American intelligence, new equipment and planning.

In response, Blair quibbled. He did not reject Walker's opinion but wanted to delay his decision until the last moment. He agreed to the purchase of some equipment for an invasion. He also agreed with Walker's criticism of Boyce. Tebbit had been agitating against the admiral, who had been complaining about the permanent secretary's failure to secure sufficient funds to re-equip the military. 'I hadn't hidden my contempt,' Boyce admitted. Blair had no reason to defend an officer critical of the war.

Hoon's invitation to Boyce to 'drop in for a cup of coffee' seemed unremarkable to the admiral. Soon after the first cup was poured, Hoon delivered the bombshell: 'We've decided not to extend your tour of duty beyond two years, and in fact would like you to retire by February.' He noticed the admiral's usually inscrutable face registering shock. 'I was surprised,' admitted Boyce later.

Boyce's reply, when it came, was categorical. To dismiss a chief of the defence staff on the eve of war would be careless, even irresponsible. 'You would be making a mistake,' he said, explaining the complications of a handover in the midst of preparing the army for an invasion 3,000 miles away. Hoon was easily persuaded that neither he nor the prime minister had thought through the consequences, and agreed that Boyce should remain until the end of the war.

Blair's position was unprecedented. No other British prime minister had planned to start a war while distrusting his chief of defence, the permanent secretary at the MoD, the Cabinet secretary, the foreign minister, the defence secretary and most of his Cabinet ministers.

TWENTY-SEVEN

Lights Out

For Blair, relying on Margaret Beckett was particularly distasteful. In July 2002, the minister responsible for the environment and agriculture had been summoned to Downing Street to discuss Dr Iain Anderson's report on foot-and-mouth disease. Blair's successful resistance to demands for a public inquiry had been vindicated, as Anderson's conclusions were devastating. Each chapter's headlines, including 'panic', 'erratic' communications, 'haphazard and messy' decision-making and criticism about Blair's thirty-one-day delay while he reorganised the Cobra machinery, punctuated the chronology, which described the successive mistakes that ended up costing the country £8 billion.

Fortunately, unlike the £30 million inquiry into BSE, which had triggered a witch-hunt against named culprits, Anderson had been persuaded not to pick out individuals. Instead, he blamed incompetent civil servants for being 'insensitive' towards farmers and paralysed by a 'fear of personal risk-taking'. By default, Blair had failed the test of leadership by allowing the crisis to run out of control for the first month, but he himself escaped criticism.

He had resisted commissioning an inquiry until pressure from Brian Bender, the permanent secretary, overwhelmed his objections. The result matched his fears. Clearly nervous, Blair told Beckett and Bender, 'I don't want any leaks.' Looking at Alastair Campbell, he then 'read the riot act'. All the potential political pitfalls were to be covered, he ordered. 'No one was to misbehave,' was the message. There was to be no mention about the waste of £8 billion. 'Well, Margaret,' said Blair as

Beckett rose to leave, 'I've got great confidence in you. You're the safest pair of hands in the government.' He spoke through gritted teeth.

Bender had already reported that the merger of the Ministry of Agriculture into the Department of the Environment had overstretched Beckett's skills, and the department had become 'messed up', just as Blair's relabelling of the DTI, her old stomping ground, had proved a costly embarrassment. 'Reorganisation won't magically make anything better,' Bender noted. Rearranging departments, like changing ministers, Blair discovered, made little difference.

Beckett's opposition to nuclear power remained the biggest obstacle to the security of Britain's energy supplies. Until September 2001, Blair had ignored warnings that the country could face future blackouts. Convinced it was safe to continue relying on the market, the government praised itself in its 2001 manifesto for having 'brought full competition to the gas and electricity markets'. The reality was the opposite.

The original privatisation of the electricity-generating companies had been the idea of Stephen Littlechild. Later, as the first electricity regulator, Littlechild had encouraged the generating companies to earn big profits, in the hope of attracting more competition into the market. However, after 1998, his model crumbled. With the government's approval, several of Britain's energy companies were bought and integrated into three giant foreign electricity suppliers. The DTI had not protested over the fact that EDF, the state-owned French energy monolith, now dominated the supply of electricity in southern Britain, or that privatised British companies had been renationalised by foreign-owned corporations, or that British industry was being stripped of the engineers needed to design and build future power stations. Simultaneously, as the independence of British companies diminished, cheap French energy was being imported through cables beneath the English Channel and undercutting British electricity.

Competition was shrinking, but Blair's staff appeared unconcerned. Geoff Norris, the prime minister's adviser in Downing Street, and the DTI's energy experts were convinced that an energy market would permanently guarantee low prices. The department approved the creation of NETA, a new regulator to supervise the trading of electricity. NETA's rules were too complex for any politician or civil servant to understand, an incomprehension that pleased the accountants of the electricity companies, whose increasing profits went unquestioned by Ofgem, the new regulator created to protect competition.

Blair had not understood the problems he was entrusting to his new team of ministers at the DTI under Patricia Hewitt. His instructions to her in 2001 had been perfunctory: 'You know about business. Just do what's to be done and build the economy.' He remained uninterested in energy. His distraction extended to forgetting to tell her that she was also the minister for women.

In the weeks after the election, oil prices rose and gas supplies from the North Sea fell. For the first time in a decade, Britain was a net importer of energy. Reluctantly, Blair considered the implications. He was persuaded by David King, the government's chief scientific adviser, that Labour's 1997 moratorium on new power stations had diminished the safety threshold that protected Britain from blackouts. The country, said King, could not rely in the future on wind and solar energy, which together contributed only a small fraction of its needs. Nuclear power, Blair knew from his time as Labour's shadow energy minister, was the only environmentally safe way to guarantee Britain's electricity supplies over the next fifty years, but building new nuclear stations would require complicated negotiations and guarantees for private investors.

Blair's commitment was supported by Brian Wilson, his new pro-nuclear energy minister. Norris convinced Wilson that, as 'Blair's vicar on earth', he should deliver 'the tablets of stone on nuclear'. One obstruction, Wilson knew, was Hewitt, who, like Robin Young, her permanent secretary, was anti-nuclear. Further down the chain, Wilson believed the DTI's energy directorate was unqualified to steer the argument in the direction Blair wanted. But the major problem was Beckett. Wilson and Norris attended a succession of ministerial meetings with the minister. 'We went round and round in circles', recalled Wilson, 'watching

Beckett, supported by Peter Hain, killing off nuclear energy, which had become her life's work.'

While concentrating on Northern Ireland's problems in Belfast, Blair accepted Norris's suggestion that, instead of entrusting a Cabinet committee to reconcile the differences within his government, he should ask Nick Hartley in the Policy and Innovation Unit to discover whether Britain was permanently guaranteed cheap energy and how soon the country could reduce carbon emissions by 60 per cent. Five months later, on 22 February 2002, Hartley published a sanguine report. Blair's adviser saw no reason to abandon the policy enshrined by Nigel Lawson in 1982. 'The process of privatisation and liberalisation', wrote Hartley, 'seems to have succeeded well.' Britain's competitive energy markets, he enthused, 'should continue to form the cornerstone of energy policy'. Relying on markets, he predicted, was not a risk. In any future crisis, high prices or shortages would be benignly resolved by 'efficient . . . price shocks', which, thanks to the perfect operation of the market, would reduce consumption. The government, Hartley advocated, should remain detached and 'monitor' events while Britain increasingly relied on imported oil and gas.

Hartley's faith chimed with Blair's championing of competition. During summit meetings with his fellow European leaders, Blair urged them to depoliticise energy by relying on the market. Gas prices across the EU, he argued, would be kept down in liberalised markets. His arguments were universally rejected. Europeans regarded electricity as a political, not a private, business. Blair's energy advisers in Downing Street noticed his lack of interest in such nuances. Distracted from domestic policies by frequent trips abroad, he misunderstood how Labour was interfering in Britain's energy market and had inadvertently politicised the country's energy. New environmental taxes and government subsidies for coal, wind farms and solar panels had distorted the market, while the proliferation of additional agencies that enforced laws to fight climate change had deterred the generating companies from building power stations. As energy prices slowly increased, the government was indecisive. Blair accepted Hartley's conclusions but ignored the author's myopia regarding the dearth of private investment.

Brian Wilson took the opposite view. If an energy policy were not developed, he believed, Britain would face a serious shortage. The solution to Hartley's blind optimism, he suggested, was a White Paper – the first since 1989 – in which the DTI should advocate nuclear power. With Blair's support, Wilson presented drafts to Hewitt. 'The meetings went again round and round in circles, with Hewitt doing nothing,' Wilson complained. 'It's ridiculous,' he told Hewitt. 'This White Paper will have a huge hole in it – which is nuclear energy.' The problem returned to Downing Street.

Previous governments had discussed the issue in a Cabinet committee supplied with briefing papers to support a structured debate. Blair disdained that forum. First, Downing Street talked to journalists to produce suitable headlines like, 'Blair Set to Put Nuclear Power Back on Line'. Next, to overcome Beckett's opposition, in late 2002 he invited Gordon Brown for another 'chat' in his office. Blair hoped that Brown would broker a deal with Beckett and Hain.

The chancellor arrived in a thunderous mood. As usual, Blair did not reckon on Brown's self-interest. Most recently, they had argued once again over his refusal to share Blair's enthusiasm for the euro. Blair suspected that Brown's stubbornness was the prelude to a coup. 'He's behaving outrageously,' Blair had told Mandelson. 'This time he's gone too far.' But as usual, he had resisted dismissing his chancellor. Although the abuse was as bad as in 2001, when Brown had called him 'a crap prime minister', he had not organised his supporters effectively. Fearful of the party and of Brown himself, he had refused to strike.

Now, Brown fumed while Norris and Joan MacNaughton, the DTI's director of energy, explained that, without new nuclear stations, by 2020 Britain would rely on gas for 70 per cent of its power, and 90 per cent of that gas would be imported. Britain's energy security would, therefore, be jeopardised. At the end of the explanation, Blair hoped that Brown would pledge his support. Instead, he got up and walked out without revealing his intentions. To those left in the room, Blair appeared to underestimate his authority as prime minister. But he could only blame himself. He was semi-isolated within his own government.

To conceal his embarrassment, Blair summoned Hewitt to hear her proposals. Like Beckett and Wilson, she was unaware of her leader's latest fracas with Brown. 'Do you want a row in Cabinet about nuclear?' she asked. 'Do you want a fight with Beckett?' Since any new nuclear station required fifteen years to plan and build, she continued, he should abandon the idea. Instead, she described her passion: a carbon-trading scheme operating across Europe that would commit governments to lowering carbon emissions and encourage the greater use of renewable energy.

'I'll think about it,' Blair replied.

Even before Nicholas Stern, a civil servant, published an error-strewn review in 2006 warning about the dangers of climate change, Blair had been hooked on the political importance of controlling emissions. Labour's 1997 manifesto had pledged to reduce carbon dioxide emissions by 20 per cent by 2010. No other country burdened itself with a mandatory law on climate-change targets. A law like that in a country like Britain, which refused to plan its energy supplies, was particularly dangerous without nuclear energy. And Brown was vetoing that development.

The deadlock gave Blair every reason to ponder Brown's obstruction to reform. The chancellor's track record was transparent. Contrary to his assertion that the New Deal's £3.6 billion welfare-to-work programme was helping 1.2 million young people find employment, by February 2002 just 3 per cent of unemployed youths had found jobs. Two years later, at a total cost of £5.2 billion, only 130,000 young people had moved into unsubsidised employment.

Other indicators exposed the poor value of Brown's redistribution of wealth. The number of people claiming incapacity benefits rose by 1 million to 2.7 million in 2004, costing taxpayers £19 billion a year. Unemployment was also rising: 7.8 million people of employable age – a fifth of the total – were not working, not least because since 1997 a million jobs had been lost in manufacturing. Despite all the new skills councils, development agencies and apprenticeship schemes, British industry invested less and produced less than its competitors. Brown's forecast of an economic miracle was not materialising. Instead, the country was being transformed by his relentless increase in welfare benefits.

The proportion of the population receiving more in welfare than they paid in tax was rising towards 53 per cent, 10 percent higher than in 1997. Quite intentionally, the Blair government was overseeing the creation of a nation dependent on state welfare. Not only was work made less attractive than government handouts, but Downing Street's task groups encouraged the disadvantaged to expect an equal stake in society. With the government's blessing, a new majority of Britons classified themselves as victims. In Blair's opinion, the growth of welfare dependency confirmed Britain's transition towards a fairer society. His satisfaction was shaken only by his chancellor's stubbornness.

On Brown's instructions and with Blair's support, John Prescott had begun the part privatisation of the London Underground. The Tube's managers are 'useless', declared Brown, convinced that private companies would perform better. While the network would still be owned by the state, he proposed that private companies take over the maintenance and renewal of the track, rolling stock and stations. Incapable of mastering his brief, Prescott quickly lost control of the process to a group of businessmen, consultants and lawyers whose fees would total over £1 billion. Prescott was replaced by Shriti Vadera, a favourite banker close to Brown. Lacking any experience in such ventures, Shriti 'the Shriek' Vadera produced a 28,000-page contract that allocated the profits to the private companies and the risk to the state.

Suspecting that Vadera's solution was chaotic and costly, Blair summoned Bob Kiley, the American manager of the Tube, to Chequers. Kiley arrived to discover the privatisation contract strewn over Blair's desk. He confirmed the prime minister's fears. Brown's hubris 'would cost', said Kiley. The disaster, Blair was told, could have been averted by issuing bonds to borrow the money. Neither man could foresee that the final bill for taxpayers would be about £30 billion. Instead of confronting Brown with that considerable waste of money or highlighting the contradiction of his positions on the Tube and the NHS, Blair supported his chancellor's scheme 'as the only way to get massive investment into the ailing network'. He spoke with genuine conviction. Out of similar ignorance – or fear – he would also break a manifesto pledge in support of his chancellor and sell Britain's air-traffic-control system to private owners.

It was not just that Blair had a complicated relationship with Brown; rather, after five years as premier, he had still failed to recruit a colossus to challenge the Treasury on his behalf. Instead, Downing Street employed about eighty special advisers running units focused on strategy, research, social exclusion, innovation and delivery, but not concentrating on the management of the economy – and not least on producing a coherent energy policy.

It thus fell to Blair to fret about the fate of British Energy, the privatised nuclear company sliding towards bankruptcy. To support coal mining, the government had reduced the subsidies for nuclear energy, but no one in Downing Street had anticipated the consequences of slashing the income of the company (which generated a fifth of Britain's electricity) or the company's unforeseen liabilities in cleaning up Sellafield. Bankruptcy risked Britain's lights immediately going out. Blair asked Norris to distil the crisis into bite-size options – 'not too much detail', he insisted – and a solution. Norris's alternatives were to renationalise the company, bail it out or allow its sale to profiteering vulture funds. He favoured the sale. 'There's no point wringing one's hands with Blair,' he decided, and asked James Sassoon, a banker, to reassure Blair that a bail-out and a later sale would be 'honest'. The crisis passed, but there was still no energy policy, and no agreement on nuclear power.

Admitting his failure, Blair accepted Hewitt's advice to adopt a carbon-trading scheme with a 5 per cent carbon cap. The result was a commitment to spend billions of pounds on subsidies for installing generators powered by renewables and energy efficiencies such as home insulation, and to switch from coal to gas generators. The additional cost of electricity for consumers was unquantifiable but would be enormous. Even after those changes were made, carbon emissions were still destined to increase, which made the commitment to reduce them substantially by 2050 impossible without nuclear energy, and that was ruled out.

To keep Beckett's support and maintain the government's unity in the weeks before the invasion of Iraq, Blair sacrificed Britain's energy security. Wilson's draft White Paper, 'Our Energy Future – Creating a Low Carbon Economy', was changed and nuclear energy was condemned outright. 'Its current economics', stated the paper, 'make it an unattractive option for a new carbon-free generation capacity.'

'Blair tried to balance Beckett,' raged Wilson, 'whom he should have ignored. We ended up with a stupid White Paper filled with wrong assumptions about gas to dodge the nuclear issue.' The media were briefed that Blair was against nuclear power 'because of the terrorist threat' and because nuclear would have 'undermined the drive for renewables'. Instead, gushed the White Paper, thanks to Labour the UK was committed to 'cleaner, smarter energy' and would reduce carbon dioxide emissions by 60 per cent in 2050. At the age of ninety-seven, Blair would know whether the target had been hit. In the short term, he asked John Birt to draw up a secret nuclear plan that could be implemented in 2005, when Beckett had less influence and Hewitt was no longer the minister at the DTI.

Until then, improving the nation's infrastructure was delayed by the party's division over Iraq. 'I was as isolated as it is possible to be in politics,' Blair would write about those weeks, referring to the countdown to the war. 'My isolation within the Cabinet let alone the PLP and large parts of the media and public opinion was colossal.'

David Blunkett talked to him about this, touching on Iraq and also the tenor of his leadership. He blamed Blair's impatience to forge alliances. 'I can't do organisational matters,' Blair admitted, meaning that he had no patience to manage Whitehall or even to successfully direct the whips to win over the doubters.

The home secretary then made a second visit, this time accompanied by Alan Milburn. 'This is not anti-Gordon,' said Blunkett, 'but you've got to sort out the government. This is the moment to lay down the terms for him to move on from being chancellor.'

'Things are very difficult,' replied Blair. 'I don't want to divert my attention from Iraq. If I fire Gordon, the consequences on the government would be too great.'

The management of the country was being ignored not only because of Iraq and Blair's dilemma over Brown, but because of the prime minister's domestic life. At the beginning of December 2002, a volcano erupted in Downing Street. The *Daily Mail* published a story claiming that Cherie had bought two flats in Bristol worth £270,000 with the help of Peter Foster, the boyfriend of Carole Caplin, her lifestyle adviser. Foster had been convicted in Australia of fraud. Further, he had negotiated a £40,000 discount on the flats by dropping the Blairs' name to the developer. Cherie was known to seek discounts and free services from businesses – and even a piano shop – by using her name, but this unprecedented allegation fuelled a media frenzy.

Blair asked his wife whether she had had any contact with Foster, 'No,' she replied. That was the answer Campbell repeated to the *Mail* and the rest of the media. It was untrue. The *Mail* had copies of emails between the two, including Cherie's thanks to Foster for his help. 'You are a star,' she wrote.

The unfavourable publicity was exacerbated by Blair's peculiar relationship with Caplin. Staff at Chequers reported her staying for extended periods to massage the prime minister, and occasionally Blair went to her London home for anti-toxin rubbing treatments. Inevitably, there was gossip. Ever since 1994, when she was first included in the Blairs' lives, Campbell and Fiona Millar had disliked Caplin and had warned Blair that her presence would end badly. But, mindful of Cherie's needs, Blair rejected their warnings.

Part of the problem was his unworldliness. After a jar of honey fell and broke on the kitchen floor, he grabbed a brush and pan to clear up the mess. On another occasion, when water came pouring through a living-room ceiling from a bathroom above, Blair was found standing by the bathtub, without having turned off the taps or pulled the plug, using Virgin Radio mugs to shift water from the bath into the nearby basin.

Then there was his own relationship with Cherie. She soaked up the exaggerated media descriptions of herself as a 'brilliant lawyer'. She was undoubtedly intelligent, but she was far from brilliant. Beset by thin-skinned fragility, she could be gregarious and warm towards those she trusted, but as Anji Hunter discovered, she could also deploy bitchi-ness that crushed like a Centurion tank. Her legal onslaught against Ros Mark, her children's nanny for four years, after a misunderstanding about a sympathetic book Mark had written for a children's charity, was regarded by lawyers aware of the circumstances as vindictive. Her aggressive protection of her privacy when no violation had occurred sat oddly with her own detailed description of the contraceptive methods she had failed to use during a visit to Balmoral.

Her attraction to Blair was often debated, and the host of explan-ations was as unsatisfactory as the business of unravelling Blair him-self. Among the worst that could be said was that their marriage rested on mutual irritation. Some praised Cherie for transforming a geeky youth into a calm socialite able to pacify her hysteria. She could claim credit for contributing to his political success and calming his out-bursts of insecurity. Together, in the midst of any crisis, they lacked any sense of how long they would remain in the building or their own future after Downing Street. Both feared rejection by the rest of the cast and the audience.

Among Cherie's many misfortunes was the presence around her husband of people she disliked, not least Gordon Brown, who was for-bidden to enter her private flat. Of the other miscreants, she most sus-pected Campbell, and the sentiment was reciprocated. The ex-alcoholic became venomous towards those he disliked, and after the *Mail* showed

Cherie had lied about Foster – the lies of a Labour lawyer using a convicted fraudster to buy flats as an investment was a gift to the Tory media – there was no sanctuary from Campbell's venom for anyone in Downing Street.

Without hiding his anger, Campbell now briefed journalists against Cherie, openly scorned Caplin and failed to defend Blair. In the meltdown that followed, Blair raged at everyone, not least the media. The crisis was ended with the help of Blair loyalists, especially Peter Mandelson. Cherie made a tearful apology on TV, Fiona Millar stayed in Downing Street and Carole Caplin left.

In those moments of stress, Blair read either the Bible or theological books. He knew that his Christianity was an unpopular subject. However, his belief had guided him since Oxford. He appeared regularly for Mass on Sundays at Westminster Cathedral, occasionally wearing a T-shirt and jeans. The discretion surrounding his beliefs, preferring the rigour of Roman Catholicism over Anglicanism, baffled those who could not reconcile his religion with his support for ungodly activities like marriage for homosexuals, freer gambling and the liberalisation of the alcohol licensing laws. His religion and poor judgement of people coalesced in the choice of Rowan Williams, an eccentric leftish cleric, over Richard Chartres, the charismatic and purist Bishop of London, as Archbishop of Canterbury. Blair's pick, based on a recommendation by a commission, was odd. As usual, he would eventually regret another delinquent appointment and the waste of the power of his patronage.

The time had come to grasp the nettle. 'I'm going to sack him,' he told Jonathan Powell in January 2003 about Brown. Jack Straw, he said, would be the new chancellor. Then he dithered, before finally retreating. The nettle remained untouched.

TWENTY-EIGHT

Countdown

'The military', Jonathan Powell had emailed Blair in early October 2002, 'are making another effort to bounce you into a decision on Option 2.'

Blair was prevaricating. In his opinion, the longer he waited, the better. The army chiefs, he knew, wanted Britain's unconditional pledge of support for the invasion in order to win the confidence of General Tommy Franks in Florida. So far, Blair was committed to package one, the smallest commitment. The outcome of any battle against Iraq's impoverished army was not in doubt. Alongside America's technological advantages, the British forces could be trusted to deliver, but dispatching half his military to the desert was an irreversible gamble. To clear his mind, he began a round of rhetorical conversations. On the one hand there was his relationship with President Bush and his own dazzling success as an interventionist; on the other were his critics in the Labour Party and his European antagonists, Gerhard Schröder and Jacques Chirac.

'Where does Britain stand in the world?' he asked a civil servant in the MoD. 'If I agree to join the invasion, then I'll be in a position of command, influence and regular conversations with the president. We have all these military people,' he continued, 'why not use them?'

'Why not?' replied the official, observing Blair work his way towards a Faustian pact.

On 16 October, the conversations became more difficult. In a televised speech after Congress had authorised him to invade Iraq, the president explained that war would, he hoped, 'not become necessary' once Saddam surrendered his WMDs, but was inevitable if he refused. Hours later, Saddam's spokesman replied that all of Iraq's WMDs had been destroyed years earlier. The neocons around Bush were unimpressed. Although the American intelligence agencies could not prove that Saddam was lying, Dick Cheney and Donald Rumsfeld remained intent on his removal. In London, Blair repeated his demand that Saddam allow the UN inspectors to visit nineteen sites where WMDs were allegedly being developed. If he agreed, the invasion could be avoided.

The next day, Admiral Mike Boyce addressed the prime minister. General Franks, he told Blair, wanted to know by the following week whether Britain was choosing package two or three. The army, Boyce added, wanted package three. Blair's patrician inscrutability deterred serious questions. He was inclined to choose package two but was tempted to go for broke after the latest JIC assessment, based on Curveball, 'confirmed' that Saddam possessed a mobile biological-agent production facility. Neither Richard Dearlove nor John Scarlett mentioned the refusal of the BND, Germany's intelligence service, to allow MI6 officers access to Curveball. In hindsight, the BND's intransigence was judged a ruse to leverage influence over the CIA and MI6. In any circumstances, taking such 'war or peace' information on trust was a gamble.

Fickle confidants surrounded Blair while he considered the most momentous decision of his life. Powell and Alastair Campbell spoke decisively but lacked experience in foreign affairs; the Foreign Office's leaders hesitated to cross the road to warn of the dangers; Dearlove and Scarlett peddled misinformation like Warren Street spivs selling second-hand cars; and finally there was David Manning, the loyal diplomat who, though lacking accurate insight into the Arab world, criss-crossed the Atlantic beneath the radar to represent Blair's interests. Manning's only escape from the conspiracy would have been an appeal to Andrew Turnbull, but it was a call he never made.

Towards the end of October, Blair arrived in the MoD's bunker with Campbell and Powell for a briefing by Lieutenant General Rob Fry, a

Royal Marine. During his presentation, Fry took considerable effort to explain the timetable for transporting 42,000 personnel and equipment to the Middle East, the preliminary plans for the invasion and the outline for occupation after Saddam's defeat. Blair's lack of interest was spotted by Fry and Geoff Hoon. Clearly, Hoon realised, Blair did not appreciate the importance of his visit to the military and the officials. At the end, the prime minister asked no questions. He did not intend to debate the virtues of the presentation and, after an embarrassed silence, he departed.

On 31 October, Blair summoned Jack Straw and Hoon to Downing Street, where they agreed on package three without protest. Later, he would credit Boyce for persuading him to make that choice. That was unlikely: Generals Mike Walker and Mike Jackson were the lobbyists for all-out involvement. Blair was not unhappy, though, as package three confirmed his relationship with Bush. Boyce did, however, protest once again about the lack of money. 'Yes, we must fix that,' replied Blair, without any intention of arguing with Gordon Brown. Once again, Boyce was left on his own. Walker resisted issuing an ultimatum that there could be no war without proper funds, and instead made his plans on the presumption that the British forces would be first in and first out and that the Treasury would pay all the costs. Brown allocated £1 billion for the war. Such a small provision did not trouble Blair, but he instructed that knowledge of his decision was to remain within the ring of secrecy. 'Keep it all tight,' Hoon told Boyce. 'Only twelve people should know what we're doing.' Even the chief of defence logistics was to be excluded from the planning staff, and no additional equipment for the war could be ordered.

'That's crazy,' said Boyce.

'We cannot let the world know we are working for war', explained Hoon, 'and at the same time say at the UN we want peace.'

Dissatisfied, Boyce went straight back to Downing Street.

'Well, that's how it is,' Blair replied, accepting responsibility for delaying the military's mobilisation.

The winning team in 1997: (seated from left) Peter Mandelson, Alastair Campbell, Blair and Gordon Brown.

The Blairs move into Downing Street, 2 May 1997.

Blair's first Cabinet.

Blair and his mentor and friend, Bill Clinton, with Cherie Blair and Hillary Clinton during a visit to Washington, February 1998.

Blair meeting soldiers in Macedonia, May 1999, during the Kosovo war: his trust in General Sir Charles Guthrie (left), his first chief of the defence staff, and General Sir Mike Jackson encouraged his belief in military solutions to political problems.

Celebrating the millennium at the Dome on New Year's Eve 1999 was an embarrassment.

Three disappointed Cabinet secretaries: Robin Butler (served until 1998), Richard Wilson (1998–2002) and Andrew Turnbull (2002–05).

Camp David, 2001: George Bush unexpectedly became Blair's soulmate and trusted ally.

Blair was unusually dependent upon three advisers: chief of staff Jonathan Powell, director of communications Alastair Campbell and director of government relations Sally Morgan.

The relationships of three chiefs of the defence staff – Admiral Mike Boyce, General Mike Walker and Air Marshal Jock Stirrup – with Blair provoked disappointment and criticism.

Contrived smiles during the 2005 election campaign concealed a turbulent alliance between Blair and Brown. Only weeks later, Blair was humiliated at the Sedgefield election count by Reg Keys, an independent candidate, who questioned the legality of the war in Iraq after his son was killed there.

While he was prime minister, Blair campaigned against dictators but later served their interests: (top) with Sheikh Mohammed bin Zayed al-Nahyan, the crown prince of Abu Dhabi; (centre left) with Paul Kagame, president of Rwanda; (centre right) with Nursultan Nazarbayev, the president of Kazakhstan; and (bottom) with Libyan leader Muammar Gaddafi.

27 June 2007: the Blairs leave Downing Street after ten years.

Among Blair's new close allies was Rupert Murdoch, but their friendship collapsed when Murdoch suspected Blair of having an affair with his wife, Wendi Deng.

Blair has denied mixing his philanthropic ventures with business in Africa, and yet, in November 2010, after meeting President Goodluck Jonathan of Nigeria – accompanied by Jamie Dimon, J. P. Morgan's chief executive (who paid Blair a retainer) – Blair tried hard to develop his business interests in Nigeria.

Blair's eulogy at Ariel Sharon's funeral in Jerusalem, in January 2014, combined with his alleged affair with Wendi Deng, finally undermined his hope of retaining his lucrative role as Middle East peace envoy.

Hoon, too, appealed to Blair. 'We need to order machine guns, body armour and other equipment.'

'No,' replied Blair. 'I've got to keep the UN negotiations going and I can't act as honest broker if it's clear we're planning to go to war.' The death of soldiers because they lacked sufficient body armour would become a sensitive issue.

'Getting to Baghdad will be a doddle,' Jackson told author Max Hastings when the two met in Washington around that time, 'but the Americans haven't a clue what to do once they get there.' The British were relying on the Americans' plan for the invasion but were puzzled about the aftermath. On the orders of Rumsfeld and Cheney, the US army was not expecting to police post-war Iraq. Nation-building did not feature in the Pentagon's calculations. The MoD assumed the British army would stick to the policy spelled out in the 1998 strategic defence review – 'Go first, go fast and go home.'

The countdown to war accelerated on 8 November, the same day the UN passed resolution 1441 authorising the weapons inspectors to return to Iraq because Saddam had breached resolution 687, passed in 1991. Despite the ambiguity of the wording, Blair's hunger for a resolution had been satisfied by Jeremy Greenstock, Britain's ambassador to the UN. Blair was further rewarded by Bush ad-libbing during his speech to the UN General Assembly his personal support for the organisation's involvement.

The knife-edge drama in New York was followed by an unusual twist in London. Blair told Turnbull that he refused to appoint a war cabinet 'because we are trying to avoid war'. Even the Cabinet's committee on defence and overseas policy – the group that traditionally discussed foreign wars – was to remain moribund. And, ordered Blair, no special committee would be dedicated to Iraq. Instead, Powell would invite officials to ad hoc meetings. Brown was automatically excluded.

To his surprise, Kevin Tebbit discovered that he was apparently excluded too. He called Manning, asking, 'How can you plan a war without the head of the Ministry of Defence?' Manning agreed to ask Blair.

The reply, which appears to have been concocted by Manning and Powell with Blair's blessing, was incomprehensible. 'We can't have you', Manning told Tebbit, 'because we would then have to include the permanent secretaries of the Foreign Office and DFID [the Department for International Development], and we don't want Michael Jay and Clare Short involved.'

Powell's vendetta against the Foreign Office and his contempt for Whitehall's officials had created a unique situation. By excluding the MoD – and Tebbit's background included seventeen years in the Foreign Office, then GCHQ – Blair denied himself direct advice about the movement of manpower and the supply of equipment before and after the invasion. Hoon could have challenged Blair, but everyone knew that the prime minister did not want to hear about problems and details from Tebbit, who, he complained, spoke too much – in other words, the MoD man would challenge him. 'I was rebuffed,' said Tebbit. 'I was embarrassed, humiliated that they would not have people like me.'

Blair also preferred to avoid speaking to Hoon about the war or about the pitfalls set by officials in the MoD. 'Blair didn't care who the minister was,' Hoon had realised. 'Everything was run from the centre, No. 10.'

Unlike education or the NHS, Blair cared little about defence and, as Hoon discovered, 'never discussed detail'. After approving package three, he never questioned the preparations for moving 42,000 men, tanks, ships, planes and tons of equipment to Iraq's borders. 'This is what I want, go away and do it,' Hoon was effectively told. Conversations with Blair, Hoon discovered, were invariably undermined by the prime minister's attention shifting elsewhere. For some time, he assumed Blair was thinking about something more important. Later, Hoon confessed that 'I've never had a conversation with Blair about the war.' Others had the same experience. Blair's detachment, combined with both his and Hoon's indifference to Boyce and Tebbit, meant he resisted providing the services with sufficient money to fulfil their task, thus scuttling the military's inviolability.

'You cannot send the armed forces on adventures without paying for it,' Admiral Nigel Essenhigh told Hoon. The military, he added, had insufficient money to maintain an army in Iraq after Saddam's defeat. Labour was fighting a war to win prizes on the cheap; the corruption of 'punching above our weight' would be exposed.

Hoon ignored the criticism. 'The MoD's budget has actually gone up,' he replied. The admiral was incredulous.

On the eve of his premature retirement, Essenhigh wrote to Blair warning that the estimated additional cost of raising the standard of the three armed services to Blair's requirements would be £2.6 billion a year. He urged Blair not to choose the favourite ruse of inflicting cuts on the front line. Rather, he should save money after first rigorously investigating the issue of waste in the military. In the nature of Blair's government, Essenhigh's negative message was intercepted and never reached the prime minister. Instead, Hoon replied. Major cuts to the front line, he told the admiral, would be made after the war.

'I was disappointed that Blair was not moved by my warnings,' Essenhigh said later, 'and that he lacked the stomach for more struggles with Brown.' With Essenhigh's retirement, the military had lost the only chief who could master the financial minutiae of its budget. Walker, a typical soldier, could only challenge Blair and Brown about the size of the total budget and not the details, although that would have been sufficient for his immediate purpose. He rejected that option. 'That was playing politics and would not be honourable,' the general explained.

Blair appreciated Walker's aloofness. The amiable, solid soldier, whose bluff exterior reflected his unchallenging intellect, was a comfort. The combination of General Charles Guthrie and the army's skill during the foot-and-mouth outbreak had enhanced Blair's confidence in the military's discipline, which stood in direct contrast to that of his own government.

The casualness of the ad hoc meetings in Blair's office belied the gravity of the discussions about Iraq. Officials leaning on walls, perched on arm rests and squeezed onto sofas dispelled the rigour of formal committee gatherings. Often, during over twenty-five meetings about the war, no official was summoned to write the minutes, and the papers submitted by the Cabinet Office outlining the options remained unread. The untroubled mood concealed Blair's quandary. He spoke about WMDs and the UN but never 'regime change'. He rarely requested informed debates involving Arabists from the Foreign Office. Straw, it was gossiped around Downing Street, was being treated with contempt. To the amusement of those present, the foreign secretary had once been told to sit in a deep sofa while Blair stood over him. Straw's status was not enhanced by Blair's repeated decision that Christopher Meyer, the British ambassador in Washington, should report directly to the chosen few in Downing Street rather than to the Foreign Office. 'I'm sure we received those messages eventually,' Straw said later.

In mid-November, Blair could no longer ignore the debate about what should happen in Iraq after Saddam's demise. Until then, he had eschewed the wisdom of those with an understanding of the Middle East's history since the end of the First World War. In Blair's opinion, Saddam's fate was black and white. Regardless of history, intervention for the reasons he had explained in Chicago was justified. Nevertheless, at Professor Lawrence Freedman's suggestion, he agreed that three academics – all Arabists who opposed the invasion – should be invited to Downing Street. Led by Toby Dodge, who had recently returned from Baghdad, the experts were asked to describe to Blair, Straw and Manning what would happen after Saddam fell. The fourth person invited to listen was Edward Chaplin of the Foreign Office's Middle East section, who had not visited Iraq for several years.

Blair walked into the Cabinet room rubbing his hands. 'Thank you for coming,' he said, exactly as parodied by Rory Bremner. 'I really appreciate it. I want to listen to your opinions about Iraq', he continued, looking tense, 'but, first, don't tell us not to invade, because we must and will; and, second, don't tell us it'll be bad after Saddam, just tell us how bad.' He then described his vision. As the invasion unfolded, he expected Iraqi officers to execute a successful coup before the Americans arrived in Baghdad and to replace Saddam by an unknown leader, who, in turn, would appoint trusted followers to take over the functioning government. The new president, continued Blair, would champion liberalism and capitalism, changing Iraq into a proper democracy. 'We will hand power to the people,' he said. The region, as he later wrote, was 'urgently in need of modernisation, fundamental reordering, [because] the chance of steady evolution was not good'. Thus the 'modernisation' of Islam was equated to the modernisation of Britain's public services.

'Well, I've just been speaking to Tariq Aziz,' said Dodge, referring to Iraq's foreign minister, 'and he warned that there'll be a civil war if Saddam is deposed.'

'And what do you think?' asked Blair.

'There'll be a lot more violence than you imagine,' replied Dodge, who nonetheless did not envisage the unprecedented slaughter that would occur.

'You know it could take a generation to build a new country?' another expert told Blair.

'I'm committed to that,' replied Blair, before adding, 'but isn't Saddam uniquely evil?' Silence followed as his visitors wondered, 'What does he mean?' To justify a war on the grounds of 'evil', without understanding the profound complexities of Iraq, mirrored Blair's conviction that a brief conflict would be followed by the overthrow of the tyrants ruling Syria and Iran. He offered no further illumination of his optimistic scenario.

Practically unmentioned throughout the three-hour briefing were WMDs. To the visitors, Blair was using the mention of such weapons in public as the excuse for removing the dictator. In hindsight, one of the guests regretted not being tougher towards his host. He would have been wasting his time. After the war, Blair was asked about the influence of that meeting. He looked blank. He had no recollection of it.

The final decision to invade was taken by Bush in December. 'We invaded Iraq', said Paul Wolfowitz, the neocon deputy secretary of defence, 'because we could.' He predicted there would be no sectarian violence.

In Iraq, the UN inspectors began visiting the sites identified by Western intelligence agencies as the locations for the manufacture of biological, chemical and nuclear weapons. The inspectors would be able to detect any trace of WMDs better than any clandestine agent reporting to MI6. In London, weight was placed on satellite photos showing the teams arriving at suspected facilities and Iraqis departing quickly from the other side of the compound. The inspectors regularly reported back on their failure to find the evidence. 'He's stored the WMD material in a bunker under a hockey pitch,' Dearlove told Boyce. 'We'll find it.' Ground-penetrating radar was dispatched to help. David Omand reported 'tense discussions' at JIC meetings as the repeated failures were logged. In reply to Desmond Bowen, a trusted civil servant in the MoD, challenging MI6's reliability, Dearlove blamed the inspectors' lack of success on Saddam's skilful deception and their own incompetence.

Uppermost in London was the fear that inspectors would report that there were absolutely no WMDs. 'That would have been bad news,' admitted Omand, 'because we had set our reputations on Saddam possessing the weapons.' Instead of pushing the button for a fundamental reassessment of their previous reports, Scarlett said stoically, 'Let's see what we get over the next few days.' He did not consider cautioning Blair about the implications of the inspectors' negative reports. An independent official with a sense of civic duty would have been expected at that point to make such a challenge. Scarlett and Manning, however, both knew that WMDs were Blair's legal excuse for regime change. To question their existence would have undermined the entire plan. The traditional means of self-protection would have been an appeal to Turnbull, but Blair had cut off that safety valve. Scarlett's eventual explanation for failing to alert his prime minister was calculatedly bland: 'I see that as a policy issue.'

Dearlove, however, was placed firmly in a vice. At the Wednesday-morning meetings of all the most senior civil servants, he was asked to explain the inspectors' reports of finding no WMDs. 'It's going to take us longer,' he replied, 'but George Tenet [the CIA director] tells me there's no problem.'

No one challenged him. 'Once you're on the outside,' admitted one permanent secretary, 'you're on the outside.' With the prime minister's support, Dearlove had single-handedly hijacked Whitehall's safeguards for preventing a rogue decision. 'Blair loved all that,' said Turnbull.

'SIS [MI6] had over-promised and under-delivered,' concluded Omand, 'and when it became clear that the intelligence was hard to find, they really had to bust a gut to generate it.'

Blair gave the impression of hoping to call Saddam's bluff. He spoke of the dictator surrendering rather than suffering inevitable defeat, like Milošević. In the real world, while urging Bush to allow more time for Britain to organise support for another UN resolution that might legitimise the invasion, Blair was under pressure from Boyce to author- ise proper preparations for war. The continued concealment of his intentions, said Boyce, was risking soldiers' lives. Blair resisted. Before announcing the war, he needed more legal cover. Political cover relied on him displaying his involvement in domestic politics.

TWENTY-NINE

Juggling the Figures

On Saturday 25 January 2003, Blair telephoned Michael Barber. That week, applications for asylum had reached a new peak, and he was irritated that, despite new laws and threats, the problem had not disappeared. He was sure Home Office officials were to blame, as usual. Barber agreed to give a presentation the following Monday. Next, Blair rang David Blunkett. The Home Office, he cursed, was still failing. Only the previous week he had visited front-line staff in Croydon with Bill Jeffrey, who was responsible for the immigration department at the Home Office, and asked why so many bogus asylum-seekers remained in the country. 'You've got so-called Iraqis claiming asylum,' Blair told Blunkett, 'and they can't even speak the language.'

The focus of blame was on Jeffrey, the convenient scapegoat. He was accused of vacillating between those in his department who advocated ruthlessly removing illegal migrants and those who feared legal objections. 'Why can't we just sort this out?' Blair asked Jonathan Powell. He called Blunkett: 'Do you need more legal powers?' Together, they cursed the judges for overruling a new law denying benefits to undeclared asylum-seekers and raged about incompetent Home Office officials. Both felt powerless. To conceal Blair's frustration and rebut the media's attacks, a senior official heard Alastair Campbell encourage Labour supporters to damn critical journalists as racists.

On Monday, Barber presented his latest graph. In 2002, 110,700 people had applied for asylum. He predicted that, while in November 2002 there had been 8,000 applications, by June 2003 they would fall to 4,000 per month. He credited the decline to the closure of Sangatte and to the 2002 Act. But the fall was for a very different reason: it was the direct result of the increase in the number of work permits being issued, which would rise to 90,000 during 2003, compared to 25,000 in 1997. Despite his fluent jargon, Barber's unit could not cure the Home Office's failures.

In mid-January, Blair's frustrations had boiled over. Four Algerian asylum-seekers living on welfare benefits had been arrested in north London and Manchester on suspicion of manufacturing a chemical bomb using ricin, a deadly poison. In the Manchester raid, a police detective – a father of three teenagers – had been stabbed to death. The tabloid headlines – 'Hundreds of Terror Suspects on the Loose' – plus Tory complaints that 'the asylum system is a complete shambles' were followed by the discovery of an arsenal of weapons and forged passports at the Finsbury Park mosque in north London. Britain's Muslim community was under pressure, as was the government after a Taliban fighter claimed asylum in Britain. Amid the hysteria, Blair held a five-hour summit, and Blunkett lamented that, despite issuing 200,000 'temporary' work permits, the number of bogus asylum-seekers was still rising. The media highlighted not only the thousands of foreigners working illegally in Britain, but also the tens of thousands who, thanks to well-organised criminal gangs, were unlawfully receiving benefits.

To put pressure on the Home Office, Blair deployed surprise. Early in the evening of 6 February, he telephoned Blunkett. 'I've made a commitment on BBC TV about cutting down the number of asylum-seekers,' he said. 'I hope you understand.'

'What!' shouted Blunkett. 'By how much?'

'By half within six months,' replied Blair, ending the conversation.

Blair knew Blunkett would be furious. That was his intention. 'Using the media to tighten the screws on us,' was Blunkett's reading. Blair, he knew, governed Britain via the media. Broadcasting a shock on TV was like throwing a ball across the room, watching the scurrying and then advancing.

After the programme, Blunkett reflected that Blair was 'under pressure to do something instead of waffle. He thought he could wave a magic wand and it would happen.' He called Blair: 'It's best if I sophisticate this. I'm going to reinterpret this as an aspiration rather than a policy.'

'Tony's driving the policy now,' the home secretary told his officials the following morning. 'The facts show that such a reduction is impossible within one year.' Nevertheless, under pressure from Downing Street, IND officials were told to fast-track asylum applications, speed up the approval of work permits and announce tougher sanctions against people-smugglers.

Four days later, Blair and Blunkett met for a delivery meeting. 'TB was looking more worried and harassed than I had seen him for a while,' noted Campbell. 'TB could barely be in a more exposed place now.'

'What's happening?' Blair asked Bill Jeffrey.

'Asylum applications are falling,' replied Jeffrey (the number of applications would decline from 84,000 in 2002 to 49,000 in 2003). Blair looked satisfied. Pertinently, he ignored the increase in migrants entering Britain using work permits, the continuing annual arrival of 230,000 immigrants from outside the EU who were joining their families, and the imminent arrival of an unknown number of nationals from the A8 countries due to join the EU. He had other matters on his mind.

THIRTY

The Collapse of Baghdad

At the Cabinet meeting on 9 January, Blair's plans for Iraq were not discussed. Nor were they mentioned at the following week's reunion, although by then he was regularly seeking information from Admiral Mike Boyce, David Manning, Jack Straw, Geoff Hoon and Richard Dearlove. 'Richard, my fate is in your hands,' he said to Dearlove after their first meeting that year. Their relationship, the MI6 chief thought, had the negative effect of arousing Straw's jealousy.

By then, some officers in both the BND (the German intelligence agency) and the FBI had unofficially classified Curveball as 'unreliable', and Curveball would later admit that he had fabricated his story about a mobile WMD programme because he wanted asylum in Germany and Saddam deposed. The account of Iraq's interest in buying yellowcake in West Africa, accepted by Italian intelligence, was shown to be exaggerated and would subsequently be exposed as an attempt to earn money. Then, in the midst of those tremors, a senior Iraqi employed by Saddam told French intelligence officers while travelling through Paris that Iraq no longer possessed WMDs. Nonetheless, at no stage before the war did Dearlove or John Scarlett warn Blair of any reasons for doubt.

The military commanders were less amenable. In a series of meetings in Downing Street between 15 and 18 January, Blair did not disguise his intention to join the invasion. His decision would be made without considering all five of the tests he had listed in Chicago in 1999 to justify intervention. Although loyal, Hoon knew that the chiefs were dissatisfied. Since Iraq was not a war for national survival, they wanted a genuine reason why servicemen should risk their lives. Similarly, they wanted Blair to stop posturing in public by saying that he was focused entirely on seeking a peaceful resolution. Maintaining the illusion, complained Boyce, would lead to the troops fighting with obsolete equipment. Blair needed to lift the last vetoes on the purchase of arms. Finally, the chiefs wanted to know the politicians' plans for post-war occupation.

The opportunity to answer all these points came in January, shortly after the Turkish government had refused the British army permission to cross its territory as the soldiers made their way into Iraq. Blair was at the MoD for a briefing by Boyce about the latest plan for invasion. Britain would now join the amphibious and land invasion from the south as an integrated member of the American forces. Also present were the three chiefs, senior officials and Hoon. The atmosphere was tense – not because of the imminent war but because of the antagonism among those gathered deep below Whitehall.

To Boyce's fury, Blair had brought Campbell. 'How dare he come to a meeting in the Ministry of Defence,' Boyce said to Admiral Alan West, 'an unelected spin man who's had a mental breakdown?' Blair's and Campbell's dislike of Boyce had broken a threshold, and Blair now wished that Boyce would be replaced by Walker as soon as possible. Their antipathy spread to West, who was irritated by Blair's games-manship and resented his refusal to meet the three chiefs to discuss the invasion and its aftermath. On 7 January, without waiting for Blair's approval, he sent a fleet with 3,000 marines to the Gulf.

'What about phase four?' West asked during a rare meeting soon after, referring to the post-war occupation.

'The Americans have it all sewn up,' replied Blair.

Boyce had repeatedly pressed for the same information. He had also raised the problem directly with Donald Rumsfeld and the American chiefs. 'The Americans' eyes just shut down,' he reported after a trip to Washington. 'They didn't want to hear what I was saying.'

Boyce's was not an isolated voice. Since November, several delegations of Whitehall officials from the Cabinet and Foreign Offices had flown to Washington to impose conditions on the American government about post-invasion Iraq and the importance of a role for the UN. They returned to London with assurances. 'I was told we should rely on the Americans,' Walker would later say. General John Reith, responsible for directing the invasion from the permanent joint headquarters in Northwood, knew there had been no post war planning.

'Are we ready for war?' Hoon asked Boyce.

'We're not,' replied Boyce, making no attempt to pander to a 'malleable Blairite' whom he did not respect.

On 15 January, Boyce again told Blair that post-war planning was 'immature'. The chiefs, he said, had offered to co-ordinate the post-war occupation with the American army, but discussions had fizzled out. 'There could be trouble.'

'I'll talk to Bush about this,' replied Blair.

Even Kevin Tebbit could understand Boyce's judgement that 'the government didn't understand what they were getting into, and they weren't providing the means for their ends'. He could not help Boyce, however. His exclusion from Downing Street by Jonathan Powell, he acknowledged, 'put me in a weak position against the CDS [chief of the defence staff]'.

Blair had isolated himself from Whitehall's machine, unaware of the air of ambivalence. Military preparations were restricted, diplomats were chasing a mythical second UN resolution, the JIC was providing Blair with false information and Scarlett had not yet established a reliable back channel to the Iraqi government. Senior officials in the MoD hesitated to record their thoughts over whether Britain should sacrifice its independence in an American war. An Iraq unit established in the Foreign Office under Dominic Chilcott, an assistant secretary, was derided by defence officials for 'having no bite except to pick around'. Michael Jay, mocked for being childishly excited by the rare invitations to Blair's den, still spoke about avoiding a war. During his appearances in Downing Street, he failed to confront Blair with the opinion of the Arabists that the fall of Saddam would be followed by chaos.

British officials in Washington knew they were being ignored. 'Do it right, don't do it fast,' Christopher Meyer advised Downing Street about allowing Hans Blix, the Swedish head of the UN Monitoring, Verification and Inspection Commission, sufficient time to do his work. But Blair was hitched to Bush's timetable for the war to start in mid-March. Other governments were less easy to corral. Based on their conversations with trusted Saddam officials, there was growing scepticism among French, German and Russian intelligence about the existence of WMDs.

Hoon's announcement to the Commons on 20 January that 26,000 troops and a fleet would be sent to the Middle East had followed a deliberately pointless Cabinet discussion – except that, according to Stephen Wall, the civil servant who had sat through most of the previous year's Cabinet meetings, Hoon's statement did provoke most ministers to actually realise for the first time that Blair did intend to go to war. Hoon's speech reflected the government's euphemisms. The dispatch of the forces, he said, did not 'represent a commitment of British forces to military action'. No decision to invade Iraq was 'imminent or inevitable'. Blair told heckling Labour MPs that, after Iraq, 'we have to confront North Korea'. The noisy response forced his concession that, at the mercy of events and people beyond his control, he was 'risking everything'.

To reassert his influence in Washington, he arranged a quick visit on 31 January. The day before, Lord Goldsmith, the attorney general, had sent Blair a memorandum stating that a war without a second UN resolution declaring that Saddam had failed to disarm would be illegal. 'I don't understand this,' Blair wrote in the margin of Goldsmith's note. On the same day, a *Daily Mirror* poll recorded that only 2 per cent of Britons believed that war with Iraq would make the world safer.

During the flight to Washington, accompanied by Powell and Manning, Blair was briefed about the two issues to be discussed with the president. The most important was securing a second UN resolution; the other was the plan for post-war Iraq.

In previous meetings, Britain's military inferiority to America had been masked by Bush's warmth towards Blair. Their understanding suggested equality based on their personal relationship. But the countdown to war noticeably changed their rapport. With some 300,000 American servicemen preparing to travel to the Gulf, Bush had wholeheartedly embraced his moment of destiny. Blair was still struggling, preparing for war but still appearing to fight for peace.

During their two hours together, Blair did elicit some sympathy from the American president. US diplomats, Bush agreed, would support Britain's search for a second resolution but, regardless of the outcome, America would start bombing Iraq on 10 March and the invasion would follow soon after. The British prime minister was no longer an equal partner.

Before Blair left London, Boyce had warned him that the US army was psychologically unprepared for ruling post-war Iraq. The Pentagon was unwilling to act as a nation-builder and was ignoring the detailed plans for post-war government, as prepared by Colin Powell and the State Department. Condoleezza Rice, the ineffectual security adviser, had tried to push the issue in the White House, but had failed. Bush had been persuaded by Rumsfeld that the Iraqis would welcome the invaders as liberators and was already planning for his servicemen to return after securing their trophy – Baghdad.

Blair was pumped up by several advisers to challenge Bush. 'George, shouldn't we do something about the aftermath?'

'We've got that in hand.'

'Good.'

'There won't be any civil war,' insisted Bush, dismissing the possibility of Sunnis and Shias fighting each other.

'Good,' said Blair again. Seated beside him, neither Powell nor Manning suggested that Iraq would collapse.

Blair returned to London to face a fractious Cabinet. Clare Short and

Robin Cook were outright opponents of the war. Short succumbed to self-interest to remain inside the tent. From his period as foreign secretary, Cook knew of the doubts about Iraq's WMDs but was, as Helen Liddell, the Scottish minister, realised, 'too arrogant to build an alliance around the Cabinet table'. His resignation was inevitable once Britain was formally committed to war. Blair was fortunate. If Cook had persuaded two other ministers to resign with him, he would have been vulnerable, but Cook went quietly. 'A wasted opportunity,' said one dissenter.

Blair's support from the other ministers was fatalistic. None doubted that Saddam possessed WMDs and, even if critical of a war, they were restrained out of loyalty towards a leader who had won two landslide victories and by their loathing for the alternative – a government led by Brown. They would remain unaware that an MI6 officer had flown to Jordan to meet the head of Iraqi intelligence, who had travelled from Baghdad. The British officer, assumed to be Nigel Inkster, was assured that Iraq possessed no WMDs. The conversation was discounted by MI6 as 'a provocation'.

Blair's staunchest ally was Hoon. The minister supported a just war against Saddam, despite his loyalty being tested by Powell. During his presentations describing Boyce's recommendations, Powell would repeatedly interrupt, saying, 'I've spoken to senior army officials in the MoD and they say the opposite.' Blair's blushing chief of staff, his audience assumed, wanted to emulate his brother Charles, who had served Margaret Thatcher.

Powell's interference was a minor irritation for Hoon compared to the battle between the generals and Boyce. The admiral's unlikely ally was Tebbit. The permanent secretary sent a message to Hoon expressing reservations that 'we're running into this without full consideration. There should be a full Cabinet discussion because all the criteria cannot be met.'

'Can we pull out of the invasion?' Hoon asked.

'It's too late,' Tebbit told him. Neither man could gauge whether Blair was troubled by Washington's obduracy.

At the MoD, General Tim Cross, who was involved in preparations for the war and its aftermath, was frustrated by his meeting with Blair. The post-war planning for Iraq, Cross had patiently explained, was incoherent. 'The plan was we did not need a plan,' he would write. 'I don't think he understood what the possible consequences could be.'

Blair's lack of awareness was shared by Boyce and all the chiefs. Neither the Foreign Office nor MI6 had predicted the quagmire around Basra, in southern Iraq, which had been allocated for occupation by the British. No one could imagine the consequences of the local Iraqi Shias' allegiance to Iran. So far as the army was concerned, that was irrelevant. After the victory, control of the southern region would be handed over by the British to other NATO armies.

Post-war reconstruction of the area had been allocated to the DFID under Clare Short. Rob Fry had approached Short's senior official about his plans after the army withdrew.

'We should not be doing this at all,' the official replied with moral disdain.

'But you're part of the government,' protested Fry. 'You must help.'

'No, we don't,' replied the official.

'You're acting like the provisional wing of the government,' concluded Fry.

The inevitability of war was strewn with challenges. The first was the public's opposition. Its distrust gnawed into Blair's self-confidence. He did not see himself as a career politician but as a hero making the moral choice to save mankind. To head off an anti-war march planned for the middle of February in London, he approved the publication of a second dossier compiled under Campbell's supervision, 'Iraq – Its Infrastructure of Concealment, Deception and Intimidation'. Blair presented the intelligence in the new dossier as further conclusive evidence of Saddam's deception, but within days the contents were exposed as unreliable. Campbell had mixed a plagiarised and distorted ten-year-old PhD thesis taken without permission from the Internet with more unreliable intelligence collected by the JIC.

Scarlett had not agreed to Campbell's publication of the JIC's assessments. 'It was a bad own goal,' the PR man noted in the uproar, 'especially as we didn't need it, given the very good intelligence and other materials we had.' Although Campbell's second dossier was a fabrication, Blair did not consider dismissing his spokesman. Losing his master of the dark arts would have removed an invaluable shield. Secretly, he admired the gall of the quixotic risk-taker.

In the Home Office, Stephen Boys-Smith reflected on the debacle. 'Deliberate obfuscation', he observed, 'requires considerable clarity of mind. But if you're not careful, you deceive yourself.'

The argument against Saddam was barely improved by Colin Powell's presentation of the evidence of WMDs to the UN two days later, on 5 February. Shaped to copy Adlai Stevenson's dramatic demonstration in October 1962 of conclusive photographic evidence of Soviet missile sites in Cuba, Powell's submission lacked conviction. Despite being directed by the CIA to suspected sites, the UN inspectors had still not found any evidence of sarin, mustard gas, anthrax or other weapons of mass destruction. Contrary to Blair's assurances in September that 'present intelligence confirms that [Iraq] has got such facilities', inspectors had not even found a mobile laboratory, nor any trace of WMDs in machinery. The inspectors were raising doubts about MI6's and the CIA's reports and asking for more time. Pertinently, Blair did not ask Scarlett or Dearlove to reassess their intelligence. Instead, he was furious with Blix, the messenger delivering bad news.

'I have to decide for war or peace,' Blix told Blair.

'No,' replied Blair, 'just give us your honest assessment.'

At that stage, Blair did not want to be told there were no such weapons. Manning even deluded himself that Blix had gone to ten out of nineteen identified sites 'and found some interesting material'.

While the Anglo-American army was being deployed along Iraq's borders, Blair embarked on a tour of foreign capitals, sustained by the Koran, books about Islam and the Bible. 'I'm acting on the say-so of a greater power,' he told journalist Trevor Kavanagh. 'I feel the hand of fate on my shoulder.' His powers of persuasion, he was certain, could deliver the vote in New York, despite the opposition of France, Germany and Russia. The unusual spectacle of a prime minister globetrotting between capitals misjudging other leaders did not enhance his image.

'He didn't get it,' Blair scoffed about Chirac's refusal to support the invasion.

'Blair never listened to Chirac or took his warnings seriously,' realised Stephen Wall, the senior civil servant responsible for Britain's relations with Europe. The breakdown of his relations with the French president revealed Blair's misinterpretation of history. In the 1960s, Chirac had fought in Algeria against Muslim nationalists. He had witnessed a bitter colonial war that scarred France and could foresee the turmoil in Iraq after Saddam. Blair swept his warnings aside as a personal insult.

Looking nervous, the prime minister arrived in Scotland on 14 February, on the eve of Labour's spring conference in Glasgow and the anti-war protest in London. One million were expected to march, including Labour MPs who had pledged to vote against the government's motion to join the invasion. Outside the conference hall a major anti-war protest was taking place. Donald Dewar's devolution arrangements had unexpectedly empowered the Scottish Nationalists, which Blair was ignoring. Inside were the representatives of a disintegrating Labour party. The heavy make-up could not conceal Blair's gaunt appearance and bloodshot eyes, and the usual excitement was missing as he strode onto the stage. His speech contained one memorable thought: 'Ridding the world of Saddam would be an act of humanity. It is leaving him there that is inhumane.' Recited with passion, the exhortation was received in silence. Blair successfully concealed his fear of humiliation. A week later, he flew to Rome for an audience with the Pope, who advised him to avoid war. Blair ignored his vows of obedience.

Mesmerised by the lessons he drew from Neville Chamberlain's policy of appeasement, Blair had his 'moment of truth' highlighted by David Margolik during an interview in London for *Vanity Fair* in anticipation of his fiftieth birthday. Talk drifted towards Blair's Christianity and his audience with the Pope in February. 'As a private individual,' Blair said, 'I find prayer a source of solace.'

'We don't do God,' Campbell interrupted sharply.

'I do not want war,' Blair told the Commons on 25 February. 'Saddam should comply with the inspectors.'

To be certain of his arguments, he asked Dearlove to come to Downing Street, with Hoon as an eyewitness.

'Are you sure Saddam has WMDs?' he asked.

'Yes, absolutely,' replied Dearlove. 'Categorically.'

The public's hostility and Blair's failure to gather international support for a second resolution encouraged Admiral West and General Jackson, who was designated to take over as head of the army, to query whether the war would be legal. 'I don't want a marine to appear in the International Court accused of war crimes,' said West.

After visiting a City law firm for advice, West told Boyce that the military required a specific opinion from the attorney general about the legality of the war. So it was that, at the beginning of March 2003, Boyce, dressed in an admiral's uniform, visited Blair, who greeted him in jeans and an open-necked shirt. The admiral demanded a formal assurance that Britain's invasion of Iraq was legal.

This was an unprecedented encounter. Boyce was questioning Blair's honesty. The mutual trust between the prime minister and the chief of the defence staff had vanished. Five years earlier, Boyce had formally opposed placing British servicemen under the jurisdiction of the International Criminal Court. His protest, he believed, had been ignored by Goldsmith and Hoon, while Straw and Michael Jay had written a joint memo stating that the prosecution of a British officer could not happen. 'I was told to "shut up",' Boyce said, 'but now I feared an illegal war. If the invasion of Iraq was not legal, then all the military could go to jail. I told them, "If I go to jail, then Blair, Hoon and everyone else will be going with me."'

He demanded from Blair the attorney general's written opinion that war without a second UN resolution was legal. Without that document, Boyce made clear, he would resign, just as he would if there were any suggestion that the objective of war was regime change.

'I understand,' said Blair, not concealing his surprise from Hoon about the consequence of a fractured relationship. Forty-two thousand British soldiers would not advance an inch without Peter Goldsmith's signed approval.

To Boyce and the military, Goldsmith's previous advice was complicated by conflicting legal arguments and was inconclusive. 'He [Boyce] wants a straightforward certificate ignoring the legal difficulties,' was Hoon's interpretation. Boyce, he acknowledged, 'was not well-suited to present the case for war to the public as we required'. The admiral was too honest.

Blair had good reason to fear disaster. Goldsmith, in his first legal opinion, presented on 31 January, had expressed doubts about the legality of war without a second UN resolution unless Blair was satisfied on 'strong factual grounds' that Saddam had failed to comply with the UN resolutions to disarm Iraq of its WMDs and rockets. Since the JIC had failed to prove its case, Goldsmith could not approve the war. To be crystal-clear, he warned that an 'unreasonable' veto in the UN of a second resolution would not legalise the war. This, Blair knew, was too complicated, so he asked Goldsmith to reconsider. The attorney general agreed. Lawyer to lawyer, Blair and Goldsmith discussed how a different opinion might be produced. Their answer was for Goldsmith to consult those involved in passing resolution 1441, especially Jeremy Greenstock and the US government lawyers. The attorney flew to Washington.

On 7 March, a week before the unpredictable Commons vote, Blair considered resigning. Without his knowledge, Andrew Turnbull was investigating the mechanics of a handover of power. His preparations appeared justified after Clare Short invited herself onto a BBC radio show and, after describing Blair as 'reckless', threatened to resign herself if the UN failed to pass a second resolution. Blair jettisoned plans to fly to Chile, Moscow and Washington to gather support for the UN vote, and instead sent Manning on another hapless mission, while he contemplated defeat in the Commons, the return of the troops and the end of the special relationship.

His foreboding was not helped by a telephone call from the American president on 9 March. 'Don't come if it's too much,' Bush entreated Blair after listening to the hurdle the prime minister faced to win the Commons vote. Bush anticipated the answer. This was the challenge that Neville Chamberlain had botched. Two days later, Rumsfeld publicly dismissed Britain's participation as unnecessary. Blair was embarrassed. The neocons, Jonathan Powell told Straw, didn't care about Britain.

Sullenness and a sense of crisis pervaded Downing Street. The chance of a second UN resolution was dead, and there was no likelihood of neutralising the opposition within the party. War was unavoidable.

'You don't have to do it,' Manning told Blair.

'No, David, I really do have to do this,' came the reply.

'I was wrong on every count,' Manning would later admit, referring to his anticipation that the conflict could be delayed.

Either complicit or cowardly, Manning did not separate himself from the decision. Additional relief came for Blair after he persuaded Short not to resign. Her unique skills in managing humanitarian aid in Iraq after the war, he urged, demanded that she remain. The time and passion he devoted to an awkward woman suggested that the cause was no longer freedom but Blair himself. On the edge, he was focused on his survival.

Before Goldsmith returned from America, the lawyer let it be known that he would change his advice. He now said that Blair's global dash to produce the second resolution was unnecessary. The British people, Blair would write, had 'assumed wrongly' that the government needed a second resolution. He forgot to mention that he was the author of that assumption, until Goldsmith changed his mind.

This new advice was given to Blair on 14 March. Goldsmith's legal duty was to give his revised opinion to the whole Cabinet. Instead, in what was interpreted as a clear breach of the ministerial code, he sent his new document directly to Blair, whom, he would later say, he regarded as his exclusive 'client'. Blair showed the full thirteen-page version only to Hoon and Straw, while the Cabinet and Boyce were given a nine-paragraph précis that omitted the conflicting legal arguments. Based on previous UN resolutions, wrote Goldsmith, 'Authority to use force against Iraq exists' if Blair possessed 'strong factual grounds' that Iraq was in 'material breach' of the previous resolution. Fortuitously, Dearlove, citing Curveball's latest offering, had produced those 'factual grounds'. Goldsmith's somersault persuaded Elizabeth Wilmshurst, a Foreign Office lawyer, to resign in protest.

To ensure that no minister complained about being misled, Blair held four unscheduled meetings to keep ministers onside. His Cabinet was shackled. The record would show that it had discussed Iraq twenty-four times over the previous year (including a gap of six months during which it was not debated), but without any of the authoritative papers prepared by Whitehall's experts there was no ammunition to raise objections. To Blair's satisfaction, at the formal Cabinet meeting on the eve of war on 17 March no minister 'rose to the level of events', as Roy Jenkins observed, and asked Goldsmith to explain why his advice had fundamentally changed since 31 January. Six years after Blair dismissed Robin Butler's assumption that the system of collective government would continue, his docile ministers approved war without asking for the truth. The only person with the power to stop Britain's involvement was Gordon Brown, but like Blair he was convinced about the importance of the special relationship with America.

Despite his dislike of the Commons, Blair could be an unrivalled performer at the Dispatch Box. In defence of war, his passion flowed. To neutralise his Labour opponents, he recited Saddam's repeated deception of the UN inspectors. And then came the call to arms. With trembling hands but a steady voice, he asked, 'Who will celebrate and who will weep if we take our troops back from the Gulf now? I believe passionately that we must hold firm.'

Persuasive and courteous, his battle cry was Churchillian: 'This is the time . . . to show that we will stand up for what we know to be right, to show that we will confront the tyrannies and dictatorships that put our lives at risk, to show at the moment of decision that we have the courage to do the right thing.' He was assured of the Tories' support but was opposed by 139 Labour MPs, one of the biggest revolts by a governing party in parliamentary history. In the rebels' opinion, the sincerity of Blair's opinions did not make them less dangerous. Several dissidents were reminded of a play review in the Fettes magazine, in which the school was described as being 'very fortunate in having so experienced an actor as Blair for the central figure'.

The majority for war was 263 votes. Blair looked relieved, the Tories cheered and Margaret Beckett was seen to cry. The prime minister's brilliant oratory had won a majority in the House but had deeply divided the country. Among the outraged was Fiona Millar, who chose the start of the bombing campaign to announce to Blair that she intended to resign.

Britain's war was being directed from Northwood, an hour's drive from Downing Street. To the military's surprise, Blair never visited the headquarters. 'He's not collegiate,' General Walker noted. 'Maggie even had the chiefs down to Chequers. This prime minister doesn't want to meet them.'

Just as he rarely visited Whitehall departments or Parliament, Blair was uninterested in the machinery of war. Until WMDs were found and Saddam overthrown, he preferred to summon Boyce and Walker into the intimacy of his office. Daily, Powell gathered the ad hoc group for morning meetings, excluding the gossip-prone Cabinet critics. Daily, assessment papers and reports were prepared by the Cabinet Office and MoD, but few appeared to be read. To his military visitors, Blair displayed emotion over soldiers' deaths and frustration at his powerlessness to make things happen. 'Have they found the WMDs?' he would ask Boyce every day. Daily, he was disappointed by the reply.

Walker would leave Blair's office perplexed. 'I couldn't work out why the UK was not on a war footing,' he recalled. 'No decisions were taken during the meetings. Ad hoc meetings were ad hoc in name and ad hoc in nature. We never seemed able to grasp this slippery bar of soap which was Iraq properly.'

Boyce was similarly puzzled: 'We had no war cabinet, and if I'd asked half the Cabinet, they would not have known we were at war.'

After ten days, the British advance in the south was halted to allow the Iraqi army to retreat and avoid unnecessary death and destruction.

'Can't we get on?' Campbell asked Boyce during the halt.

His impatience irritated Boyce, who would again complain that 'We lacked any sense that we were at war.' Across the country, however, the public supported the troops. An ICM opinion poll found that 84 per cent of those questioned believed that the war should be fought to a successful conclusion, although two-thirds replied it would be justified only if WMDs were found.

On 2 April, twelve days after the invasion began, the American army reached the perimeter of Baghdad. Among the news items was the shooting of seven Iraqi women and children by American soldiers at a checkpoint. In his office, Blair looked at Peter Stothard, the former editor of *The Times*, who had been shadowing him during the invasion. 'It does really get to you,' he said. He added he was ready 'to meet my Maker' and answer for 'those who have died or have been horribly maimed as a result of my decisions'.

Five days later, American soldiers entered the capital. The city quickly slipped into chaos but, under orders from Rumsfeld, the army did not intervene. 'Stuff happens,' he said. 'Freedom is untidy.'

Blair's daily routine was similarly a succession of struggles for power. Overnight, he had been fighting against the neocons to keep Bush's support for the UN taking a major role in Iraq and to ensure he did not abandon his announcement of a new initiative for a Middle East peace plan. At the same time, he was recovering from another blistering argument with Brown, ostensibly about the euro. In between, Campbell was moaning that Fiona Millar had called him 'a bastard' that morning and thrown a cup at him; he had decided to resign. Blair could cope with warfare but not with Campbell's departure: his spokesman was the one person he trusted and needed. At the end of the day, he flew to Belfast to meet Bush. By any reckoning, the president's agreement to endorse Blair's Ulster peace plan was an extraordinary climax before another storm.

Blair returned to London certain of victory in Iraq. The British army controlled Basra and southern Iraq and had lost only thirty men. In the north, the Americans were crushing the last bursts of opposition and searching for Saddam. At about 8 a.m. on 9 April, Boyce arrived for his daily briefing. Blair was slumped in a sofa. The walls of his office were covered with maps.

'We can say officially the war has ended,' Boyce announced. Blair registered no joy. There was no sign of emotion. The admiral could just as well have announced that a number 24 bus had broken down in Whitehall.

'Any news about WMDs?' asked Blair.

'No, Prime Minister,' replied Boyce. 'They'll probably be found in a bunker.' The civility was ice cold. After his retirement, Boyce would criticise the Labour government's 'trade' on the armed forces' loyalty and indomitable can-do spirit without providing adequate money as 'wrong and immoral'.

Later, Blair met his ad hoc group of ministers and officials. The UN inspectors and the American army, he said, were searching for the buried WMDs. 'I wonder why the WMDs weren't used during the war,' piped up one voice. After a murmur of agreement, nothing more was said.

In the Commons that day, Blair enjoyed his moment of glory. The 'Baghdad bounce' was propelling his approval ratings upwards. To prove his righteousness, he had rejected an invitation to meet Vladimir Putin, Gerhard Schröder and Jacques Chirac at the weekend in St Petersburg. Blind to the consequences of Saddam's fall, he classified the three as deflated rivals rather than potential allies. 'I suppose I have toughened,' he told *Saga* magazine in anticipation of his fiftieth birthday. Iraq was his Falklands. He had come of age. He could even spare a moment to record a cameo appearance for *The Simpsons*.

Back in Downing Street, the television screens were reshowing a small crowd in Baghdad toppling Saddam's statue. With exquisite symmetry, Fiona Millar walked into Blair's office to announce that since she neither liked nor respected him any more, both she and Campbell would definitely be resigning. At eleven o'clock that same morning, just hours before he delivered his Budget speech, Gordon Brown was needling Blair in a Cabinet meeting. Blair was stung by the absence of any praise from his colleagues or the media.

THIRTY-ONE

Knights and Knaves

The latest battle for control of Downing Street had been raging for about ten days. The victory in Iraq, Gordon Brown feared, might persuade Blair to reconsider his resignation. He needed to act. For his part, Blair felt isolated. The constant altercations with his chancellor were wearing.

On 1 April, Blair sat through Brown's long presentation on Britain's readiness to join the euro. To provoke Blair, who, Brown knew, had still failed to master the technicalities of what membership would mean for the British economy, he declared that his decision would be revealed in the Budget. In a heated exchange, Blair, who knew that the chancellor was still against Britain joining the euro, forbade him to terminate the option publicly.

Their argument continued the following day. Blair raged. Some would recall him telling Brown to resign, while others would say the chancellor was dismissed; a third group would describe Brown storming out of the room having agreed to resign. Overnight, both men stood at the precipice.

In the morning, Blair considered the folly of losing a chancellor while British soldiers were risking their lives. Trust in the government was precarious. With the party split, he had limited the damage within the Cabinet, but the divisions over the euro could not be similarly concealed. He had failed to forge the alliances recommended back in 1998 by Richard Wilson. But, as the Cabinet secretary also observed, Blair usually anticipated the troublemakers and manoeuvred appropriately. In this case, he encouraged Jeremy Heywood to negotiate a truce.

Brown agreed to say nothing about the euro in his Budget and prepared instead a lengthy assessment for a future Cabinet meeting.

Just as one fire was extinguished, another burst into flames. In the tit-for-tat to prove his power, in the days before the Budget Brown refused to disclose how much money he would allocate to the NHS for the following three years. 'I went mad,' recalled Milburn, although as he wasn't even allowed to enter the chancellor's office, he was unable to vent his anger to Brown's face. Awareness of Milburn's anger and Blair's impotence emboldened Brown. This was the moment to exact his revenge for being outwitted by Milburn seven months earlier over the press release describing the compromise over foundation hospitals.

Just before the Blackpool party conference, Brown had circulated to the Cabinet a forty-page paper that attacked choice, competition and foundation hospitals. 'That was an apocalyptic moment,' Milburn reflected. 'Brown had distributed his paper without Blair's knowledge. It was deliberate subterfuge.' Brown had co-ordinated his revolt with Bill Morris. The trade union leader was due to raise the flag during the conference.

'This is the end,' Milburn told John Prescott in a telephone call from Durham.

'I agree,' said Prescott. 'I'll tell Gordon that if this leaks, that'll be the end of it' – meaning the final straw for his brokering of Brown's bid to become prime minister.

Remarkably, Brown's mutiny evaporated without a whisper. His paper was suppressed. 'Tony should have sacked Gordon there and then,' thought Milburn.

But he didn't. In the battle between principle and a phoney prophet, Blair had incited Milburn to lead the charge against Brown, but when it came to sacking his chancellor, he ducked for cover. Hopeless or helpless, this was the wrong time to fight, he decided. Compared to securing Brown's continued support for Iraq, Milburn's muscular loyalty could be taken for granted.

At midday on Wednesday 9 April, Blair was sitting on the front bench beside Brown for the Budget speech. No outsider could have imagined the tumult he had endured during the day. His cheers for his chancellor masked his anger – and also his nonchalance towards the economy. In a quick-fire speech, Brown was admitting that his optimistic predictions of 2002 were wrong. The public-sector net debt, which had been falling steadily from 42 per cent of GDP in 1997 to about 31 per cent in 2000, was rising remorselessly, as he borrowed to pay for public services and tax credits. Public spending had increased by 5 per cent in 2003/4. Brown had assumed that the debts would be repaid by increased taxes, but the combination of the dot-com bubble bursting and increased oil prices had suffocated economic growth. He shrugged off forecasts that Britain's deficit would soar, while Blair sneered at the Tory taunts. Preoccupied by conflicts in Iraq and Downing Street, he did not flinch as Brown increased taxes and raised borrowing in one year from £11 billion to £20 billion, breaching the 40 per cent of GDP mark. He seemed oblivious that Brown's 'golden rule' limiting borrowing exclusively to investment was being broken. He even cheered Brown's announcement that tax credits, or 'progressive universalism', were expanding – immune to the fact that the welfare programme was veering out of control.

Brown originally intended to give the poor means-tested cash credits, financed by loans, to augment their incomes. By 2003, he was giving credits to nearly every citizen, including those in employment, regardless of their wealth. The cost was about £10 billion a year, twenty times more than originally estimated. The Inland Revenue was struggling to cope. A hundred million telephone calls swamped the Revenue's centres in 2003 as hundreds of thousands of poor people could not get their cash. Nearly 2 million would eventually be penalised for receiving too much money, losing the Exchequer over £2 billion in a single year. The tax-credits system, Nicholas Montagu, the chairman of the Inland Revenue, admitted, has 'gone spectacularly wrong'. Despite the rising bedlam, he was barred from the chancellor's office.

Brown's personality generated dysfunction. Civil servants in the Treasury had become afraid of him, and because in order to control the process he rarely made a decision until the last moment, they were wary of correcting obvious errors without his approval. Even Blair apologised for the 'hardship and distress'. But Brown, knowing that Blair did not dare challenge him about the chaos or the cost, admitted nothing. 'He told me there was no more money,' Blair whispered to a Labour minister in the Commons chamber about the extra billions of pounds being spent. 'They basically lied to me to get it through me,' he said later.

Worse, with the exception of the very poorest poverty levels in general had not fallen, and some people were getting poorer. Brown's claim in 2001 to have taken a million children out of poverty was discredited by the government's own statistics. Only half that number had benefited, and his programme's fate was dire. Blair was flummoxed.

Two weeks later, Blair and Brown met to discuss a route towards joining the euro. For months, Downing Street had been briefing journalists on how Blair was determined to join and would hold a referendum to win public endorsement. The scenario, conjured up by his media fixers, of a meeting between Labour's two leaders was overshadowed by newspaper reports that Cherie had exploited an offer by a Melbourne shop-owner to 'take something' as a gift. She had grabbed sixty-eight items. 'I wish she didn't have this thing about a bargain,' Blair told Peter Mandelson. On her return home, he pleaded, 'When we leave we'll have lots of money. We'll have enough. You've got to stop this.'

His wife was chastened but could not help herself. Her lack of self-control had seen her asking the Queen whether Queen Victoria had had an affair with John Brown, and matily telling Princess Anne, 'Call me Cherie.'

'I'd rather not, Mrs Blair,' Anne had replied.

Thinking only of his own position, Brown arrived at the euro meeting expecting another showdown. 'I know what you're up to,' he told Blair. 'I know your plans.' He expected to be fired, but Blair ducked for cover as usual. He was too distracted by Iraq to seize the opportunity.

An example of his distraction came at an NHS stock-take. 'What's on your mind, Tony?' asked Milburn as Blair entered the Cabinet room.

'What *is* on my mind, Alan?' Blair replied, looking absent-mindedly over his glasses.

'NHS workforce?' prompted Milburn.

'Ah, yes,' said Blair, and uttered hardly another word.

'There's finally progress,' Michael Barber told the meeting. Emergency waiting times had fallen and access to health care was easier and faster.

Blair later sent his congratulations. Rigidly enforcing targets, he was sure, had worked. But he had one reservation. 'Do we have to crack down on hospitals like this every year?' he asked Julian Le Grand. 'Is there no other way to keep this going?'

The professor sympathised. Targets were draconian and caused ill feeling. Over the course of a year, he replied, they did shake up the system, but in the long term could be toxic and would fail. 'It's like a macho culture that demands instant delivery.'

Many NHS executives were being bullied after failing to meet a target. To avoid dismissal for breaching the four-hour wait in accident and emergency units, ambulances were parked outside hospitals until the staff were ready to treat the patients. Bureaucrats were 'gaming, cheating and misreporting' their results. In Scotland, administrators changed their system of measurement to prevent embarrassing comparisons. No one mentioned that similar practices in the private sector would be a criminal offence. 'Hit the target and miss the point' had become the shorthand for the flaws in the Delivery Unit's operation and the NHS's performance. Yet Blair was not persuaded by these negative reports. Despite the unpleasant culture, he believed there was no other way. Nevertheless, to resolve the doubts over targets and markets, command and control, choice and competition, he asked Le Grand to join his Downing Street team of advisers.

New arrivals in Downing Street noticed an omission in Blair's lexicon. Unlike Margaret Thatcher, he never said, 'I want the money well spent.' Relying on Barber's targets had replaced any interest in seeking value for money. In contrast to executives in the private sector, Blair never asked whether Nigel Crisp could cost a patient's cancer treatment. Nor did Barber. Both aides were focused on numbers and waiting times, not finances. Blair failed to realise that Crisp's passion for 'shovelling in the money' made him disregard the complexities of incentives, improvements and prices.

To satisfy Blair's fixation with modernisation, Crisp had created a unit actually called the Modernisation Agency, at an annual cost of £230 million. Some 760 staff spoke about 'change' produced by 'inclusivity' and 'collaboration', but not about 'productivity'. 'They're tinkering at the edges', complained a senior adviser, 'because Nigel wants to hold on to the NHS's traditions.'

'It's flabby,' agreed Neil McKay, the senior NHS executive.

Le Grand's outsider's view offered an explanation. His book *Knights and Knaves* challenged the civil servants' mantra that they were serving the public interest. Many officials, he suggested, were knaves working in their own self-interest. The monster derided as the Blob – the one-third of civil servants at the Department of Health who were former NHS managers – resisted reforms. Those officials, disdainful of Downing Street, ploughed their traditional furrow, rarely recommending changes. Even Simon Stevens, Blair's special adviser, acknowledged that the NHS had 'gone from the trust to the mistrust model'. For those NHS employees, like Crisp, who had been praised for their altruism by Brown, Le Grand's book was the satanic outpourings of a heretic.

Crisp regarded the NHS as stately. He loathed those who described it as a real-time business – one that generated about 10 per cent of the British economy. At the end of 2002, his anger was directed particularly at Ken Anderson, the experienced hospital manager recruited from Texas to introduce cost controls. The American had asked an irritating question after he arrived in Richmond House: if 90 per cent of the economy is based on choice and competition that works, why not the NHS? Anderson represented what Crisp disliked: an independent disrespectful of the Establishment.

The health department, Anderson announced, was 'obsessed' by buildings. NHS Estates was a huge organisation that focused on the size of rooms, car parks and the construction of new hospitals as the way to improve patient care. 'Abolish it,' he told Stevens. 'To get change, you can't nickel-and-dime. The NHS is filled with folk trying to block change. You need to offload billions of pounds of work.'

Anderson was introduced to Blair, who was sympathetic to his lament that the NHS was being run in the interests of its employees and not the patients. 'They believe 200 per cent that the NHS belongs to them,' said Anderson. 'They don't want to change it.' Crisp, he added, 'hates talking about money. He loves talking cerebrally about "change". He oversees forty-two NHS quangos employing ten times more staff than the department's headquarters in Whitehall. And nothing happens. He ignores that he's running the biggest business in the world.' (Anderson did not count the Chinese army as a business.)

'How do we change it?' asked Blair.

'You've got to use the private sector.'

Anderson assumed that 'Getting Tony to land on a decision will be difficult. The problem for him will be a political bridge too far.'

For four years Blair had relied on Milburn and Stevens as agents of change, but they were not guided by either an ideology or a master plan. Everything was hit or miss; even the anticipated showdown with Brown about foundation hospitals was undirected. 'Progress is always heavy lifting,' a Downing Street adviser told Blair, 'but your problem is that you've no clear sight of your destination.'

Blair had no answer. So much was piecemeal, even haphazard, with disappointment the inevitable outcome. The latest disillusionment came in the form of Wendy Thompson, the new head of public-service reform tasked with ensuring Barber's NHS targets were met. Blair's choice was not a success. Thompson complained about excessive expectations and was accused of impolitely asserting her authority. Matthew Swindells, a respected health adviser in Whitehall, was among several who resigned rather than experience her conduct. David Omand called her 'a complete disaster because she didn't understand government'. Resolving the problem was Jonathan Powell's job, but he could neither manage people like Thompson nor co-ordinate policies with Brown, who steadfastly ignored him. Once again, everything depended on Blair.

After another argument with Brown about the NHS, he resolved, once again, never to retreat. His Alamo was a breakfast in Downing Street for Britain's top forty private health executives.

'I know you've been duped in the past,' he told them, 'but now we do want to co-operate with the private sector.' He then declared: 'I no longer care who provides the service so long as patients receive the right treatment at the right price.' No one at the end of the seductive speech doubted his commitment to the NHS contracting treatment from the private sector.

First, Milburn needed to seek Crisp's agreement. 'We must give these poor buggers a choice,' he said.

'Patients don't want choice,' replied Crisp, convinced that Milburn, to avoid alienating Brown, 'wasn't yet ready to come out in favour of the private sector'. In his distrust of politicians, he dismissed the minister for 'playing both ends'.

'Well, let's test that hypothesis,' Milburn retorted.

Some 200,000 patients were treated for cataracts every year. All waited about eighteen months, and Milburn blamed the doctors and bureaucrats for the delay. 'They're taking the NHS for a ride,' he told Blair. The elite consultants were especially to blame. Their work practices were riddled with abuses, in particular keeping their NHS patients waiting for treatment until they switched to pay the same consultant for private care. Targets could not cure the exploitation. 'We must shift from "NHS delivery" to "NHS reform",' agreed Blair. The removal of cataracts was offered to the private sector. Confronting the forces of conservatism would be a question of carrots and sticks, agreed Stevens's team.

The first stick with which to beat the doctors came in the form of privately owned clinics, known as independent sector treatment centres (ISTCs), which were created to provide a free alternative service. Competition would shame the NHS into change. The next step was to sign new contracts with the BMA. Milburn reported to Blair that his negotiations had been completed. To end their abuse of the system, the consultants' annual starting pay would be increased from £52,000 to a maximum of £110,000.

'Alan, I like what I hear,' said Blair, 'but is it truly radical?'

'Yes,' replied Milburn, knowing that Blair was interested only in the headline, not the details.

The doctors needed to vote their approval. Milburn's offer was rejected. The consultants resented risking their private income and allowing NHS managers to fix their working hours. But Milburn refused to compromise. The dispute was black and white: the government against greedy doctors. Negotiations resumed.

Other negotiations were equally complicated. Under the Agenda for Change, Milburn's detailed plan for all the NHS's staff with the exception of doctors, the government agreed to give a million NHS employees big pay increases in exchange for their learning new skills. Better-educated staff appealed to Blair in his quest for an improved society. Focused on daily performance statistics, he welcomed the headline that, to 'modernise the NHS', nurses' pay would increase by 5 per cent. He did not ask whether their productivity would improve, nor whether pay increases could be equated with modernisation.

Blair also failed to question Milburn's agreement with the GPs. In 2001, they had threatened to resign if their demands for more money, more autonomy and less work were not met. Instead of rejecting their demands outright, Milburn delegated the negotiations to the NHS Confederation. Two years later, there was a stalemate. The BMA was demanding that GPs be able to opt out of working unsocial hours, including weekends, in exchange for reducing their annual salaries by £7,000. The government demanded a reduction of £12,000. 'I've got to make a decision,' John Hutton, the junior minister, told an official. 'I know it's the wrong decision but I've got to take it for political reasons.' The GPs won. They received a 26 per cent annual pay increase plus a large rise in their pension in exchange for giving up well-known, lucrative abuses of their contracts, and at the same time their working hours were dramatically reduced.

Blair was happy to buy them off. Ever since he had been ambushed during a TV interview in 2001 by angry patients complaining about the failure of the policy of giving a £5,000 reward to every GP practice that guaranteed to see a patient on the same day they rang for an appointment, he believed in buying peace. 'We pointed out the risks to Milburn and Hutton of giving the GPs too much money,' said Rob Webster of the NHS Confederation, 'but it was ignored.' In 2005, the concession would cost an extra £392 million, 22 per cent more than anticipated, and create a crisis of access by patients to GPs. 'We made a mistake,' admitted Hutton. Blair, he noted, was untroubled by the excessive costs.

At the monthly stock-takes, Blair never asked Crisp whether he was monitoring expenditure. Neither he nor Milburn realised that Crisp shared their fondness for good headlines. At the regular NHS board meeting, Crisp beamed about newspaper reports describing 'panic' among the private health insurance companies because their business plans were 'going up in smoke' as NHS waiting lists fell. During those meetings, he did not question the NHS's accounts, which revealed that some hospital operating theatres remained unused for 43 per cent of the week, or that staff in some A&E wards were grossly inefficient. Andrew Foster, responsible for human resources, noticed that Crisp usually listed pay negotiations at the end of the board's monthly agenda – and the meetings ended before personnel contracts were discussed. Such managerial habits were, naturally, unknown to Blair. To secure a headline about saving a small sum of money, Blair would approve reducing staffing levels at Richmond House by 38 per cent in order, he explained, to have less 'unproductive interference in the day-to-day management' and to direct civil servants to be 'focused on strategic leadership rather than micro-management', but he did not engage in forensic discussions about NHS finances.

During his regular meetings with Barber and Milburn, Blair rarely discussed the changing skills required from doctors and nurses. New drugs, keyhole surgery and revolutionary diagnostic equipment ought to have prompted Crisp to revise the job descriptions in the new contracts awarded to NHS employees, but the technical revolution was ignored. Crisp's mistake, he would later admit, cost hundreds of millions of pounds every year.

Blair also never questioned whether the new medical gospel of dispatching patients as fast as possible from hospitals might not contradict Brown's £12 billion PFI scheme for 107 new hospitals. 'We created over-capacity,' Crisp would later acknowledge, 'so we had waste.' He blamed the politicians for lacking the 'political appetite' to close unnecessary buildings.

By then, the Princess Royal in Bromley, one of the first PFI hospitals to be completed, was crippled by debt. Undeterred as ever, in 2003 Blair opened the new Hexham General Hospital to display his commitment to PFI. His publicists mentioned that the rebuilding had cost £51 million. They omitted to disclose that the hospital trust would need to repay a debt of £249 million over the following thirty-two years, including £114 million to the private financiers. The total PFI debt was heading towards £100 billion, yet the burden was not recorded in the national accounts.

Borrowing, Blair and Brown agreed, should increase to create a positive legacy for the 2005 election. Brown now posed as the protector of NHS spending. While Treasury officials devoted inordinate time to scrutinising the cost of widening a single road or ordering the sale of an embassy's wine cellar, they never challenged Crisp's accountants about reducing the cost of hospital care, and the additional £8.7 billion allocated by Brown in 2002/3 was soon spent.

Blair's tool for changing the NHS's culture remained foundation hospitals. The legislation had been delayed by the Iraq war and compounded by media storms about gun crime, the A-levels fiasco and a strike by firemen seeking a 40 per cent pay increase without any change to their work practices. To keep the flag flying during these storms, Blair continued to speak about the modernisation of the NHS. Brown, he knew, would lead the opposition, despite the facts.

Anderson's plan for some cataract operations to be treated privately had proven the value of the private sector. Phaco, the ISTC contractor, used a much faster American procedure that NHS doctors had resisted, one that took twelve minutes rather than nearly two hours. Fearful of losing their jobs, NHS doctors quickly adopted the new method and immediately increased their workloads. Although barely 4 per cent of the operations in Britain were conducted by Phaco, the NHS's waiting time for cataract removal contracted from eighteen months to near zero within the first year. '75 per cent of patients with the opportunity did make a choice,' Milburn pointedly told Crisp.

'The NHS got a huge jolt from the private sector,' noted John Hutton. 'It was a fundamental wake-up moment, because the private hospitals' treatment was so much better than the NHS's.'

Not everyone was pleased. Among the critics was Crisp, who accused private contractors of being overpaid and of 'draining the NHS of funds'. He was supported by Brown and the chancellor's media sympathiser, Polly Toynbee of the *Guardian*. To prick that bubble, Milburn took Toynbee to a hospital in Peterborough to meet an NHS doctor who specialised in cataracts. 'I'm absolutely against these ISTCs and choice,' the doctor told her. The journalist glowed sympathetically before the doctor continued: 'It's absolutely ruined my private practice.' Milburn watched Toynbee's astonishment with pleasure. However, experience had taught him not to expect the facts to influence her journalism, and she continued to support Brown's opposition to foundation hospitals.

Brown had reopened hostilities on 3 February 2003. In a speech in London, he condemned talk about choice, markets and foundation hospitals. 'The consumer can't be sovereign,' he said. He wanted collectivism and co-operation in the NHS rather than competition. The state and its servants, especially doctors and administrators, knew better than patients. Milburn, he complained, had not delivered any real improvements. The following day, Ed Balls, Brown's *consigliere*, described foundation hospitals as deliberately divisive. Blair was the party leader despite the party, implied Balls.

'Tony felt cornered,' noted Mandelson. To counter that impression, Downing Street leaked to *The Times* that Blair intended to revive the argument in favour of foundation hospitals by organising a Commons vote in May. The following day, 1 March, Brown's spokesman retaliated by briefing the media against Milburn. An investigation was launched over whether the existing foundation hospitals were disobeying the Treasury's financial rules. Then the Iraq war forced a stand-off between the two ministers.

In Blair's interpretation, Brown was pitching old Labour against New Labour in a Commons revolt organised by his lieutenants. As many as two-thirds of Labour MPs threatened to vote against foundation hospitals in a debate arranged for 7 May. Here was another example of Blair's folly. Political success depends upon bartering, exploiting the weaknesses and strengths of both opponents and supporters to tilt the balance and win a vote, but Blair never fully understood pork-barrel politics. He engaged in confrontation without preparing the ground to guarantee victory, or else participated in an argument without the certainty of a safe exit before defeat.

To Milburn's dismay, despite the victory in Iraq Blair still appeared hesitant about taking on the Labour rebels. 'It's fucking not on,' Milburn told him after a fractious Cabinet meeting on 30 April, when the government appeared destined for defeat in the Commons. 'Tony, you can't just stand there and take it. You have to do something.'

Blair stared. 'I am,' he replied. 'I know I am right about this.'

Blair recognised his minister's weakness. Since his conversion to supporting competition, Milburn had become intolerant of his Labour critics and was unloved by the NHS establishment. To push his agenda, he had bullied his path through the opposition and had lost support. In one reluctant concession, he agreed to establish Monitor, an agency to protect the NHS's values inside the foundation hospitals. 'The best politics,' he had announced combatively, 'is the best policy. Labour will get the benefit.'

Brown badgered Blair to silence Milburn. In response, Blair questioned

Brown's ability to become prime minister. In a throwaway comment, he even gave the impression he could replace the chancellor with Milburn. Then, fearful as ever of Brown on the back benches, he backed away and summoned Milburn and Stevens for an hour to seek reassurance.

'If we lose the vote,' threatened Milburn, 'I'll resign.'

'Don't be foolish,' replied Blair. 'If we lose, I'll bring the legislation back without the Brown compromises.'

'I didn't believe Tony,' recalled Milburn. 'He wasn't a coward but he was pragmatic. Brown had too much support in the party, and there was Iraq.' But he did not reiterate his scepticism. He nodded as Blair repeated that foundation hospitals were of 'monumental historic importance', and then volunteered that he had surrendered too often to Brown; now he, Blair, needed to draw a line. Politically, he would test Brown's motives by announcing more innovation and competition in the NHS and other public services. His reforms required new ministers, so there would be changes once the crisis had passed.

But first he needed to end the revolt. After telephoning some rebels to avoid defeat – and he counted over a hundred opponents – he called Brown over the weekend at his home in Scotland. As usual, the conversation, punctuated by threats and blackmail, ended without resolution. Many of his Labour opponents, Blair knew, were influenced by the continuing failure to find WMDs. Other critics in the party sensed that Blair's support for foundation hospitals was not ideological. Blair could not accept that introducing the market into the NHS meant, if the circumstances arose, allowing a foundation hospital to become bankrupt. He did not rebut Brown's spectre of abandoned patients suffering in a failed hospital with the natural answer – that a failed hospital would be automatically taken over by a successful group. Blair's silence reflected his drift.

On Sunday morning, 6 May, he telephoned Milburn. 'We're going to have to find a way through this,' he said.

'What do you mean?'

'We're going to have to compromise with Gordon.'

Milburn was outraged. Blair had travelled to the turning point but refused to change direction. The wise politician, Blair had decided, is a trimmer, not a destroyer. 'It's the right thing to do,' he said.

'I had told Blair in 2001 to get rid of Gordon,' Milburn said later, still feeling betrayed. 'I got fed up with hearing, "Something must be done about Gordon." I realised nothing would be done. He had tried to manage Gordon rather than pull the trigger. Brown blocked every reform. I was in a cul-de-sac and there was no way out.'

Blair's fate was precarious. On Monday, Brown refused to return from Scotland to vote. At last, Blair grasped the nettle: if the government were defeated, he told Brown, he would be sacked. His chancellor returned to London and ordered his supporters to make an about-turn. Despite his speeches in the Commons and his calls to individual MPs, Blair was nevertheless faced with a revolt by sixty-five of his party. Victory had come at a price. Even more MPs were expected to join the rebellion in later votes.

Trust in their leader had fallen further. Chris Smith emerged from the mist to denounce Blair as a man who 'never claimed to be part of the heart and soul of the Labour movement'. Blair was again torn over whether he should run for a third term or fight Brown by throwing himself into 'truly radical' change for the NHS. He was persuaded by Cherie to trounce his rival. 'I've been driving with the handbrake on for too long,' he exclaimed. Finally, he would wholeheartedly embrace the revolution. He would prove that he could turn lemons into lemonade. Milburn, he assumed, would be delighted.

His health minister's request for a meeting in early June, he reckoned, was routine. That morning's *Sun* newspaper had reported – to Milburn's surprise – that Blair was to appoint him home secretary. 'I don't know if that's true,' he thought as he walked into Blair's office. His own vision of the future was very different. After weeks of turmoil, he told the prime minister that he was resigning. Blair was 'shocked' as Milburn blamed disruption to his family life as the reason. 'Blair made it easy,' he recalled. 'He didn't roll his blue eyes and he didn't offer me another job. He had a lot of empathy. In any case, I was unpersuadable.'

Some judged Milburn's departure as seismic. Once again, Blair had been delinquent with a relationship. Not only had he forsaken loyalty and bowed to an enemy, he had also failed a test of leadership by sacrificing a potential successor. Carelessly, he had not considered the consequence of tilting against the standard-bearer of everything he held precious. Having championed Labour as Britain's natural party of government, Blair was undermining his own ambition. Jack Straw and John Reid may have looked into the mirror and seen themselves as Blair's successor, but neither possessed Milburn's potential. Blair appeared to care more for his enemies than his friends, and his concessions to Brown had tipped the balance. 'Your problem', he told Milburn, 'is that you're too rational for politics.' Milburn would see himself as principled. By contrast, Blair had equivocated too long and was then short-sighted and selfish.

Across the NHS there was shock and anger. There was predictable gossip about Milburn's 'family life', while others accused him of betrayal. Blair they accused of folly: he had gone to war against Saddam but not against Brown. 'He [Brown]', Blair would write, 'was a brake, not a brick wall . . . I believed he was the best chancellor for the country.'

Blair's own sense of his debt to Brown could not be overestimated. On arriving in the Commons in 1983, he had volunteered, 'I was very non-political in my view of politics.' While he governed by instinct rather than analysis, Brown's strength was to develop slogans from analysis. After he gave Blair the phrase 'tough on crime, tough on the causes of crime' for a speech, Blair admitted, 'I really never looked back.' But, in his opinion, Brown had mistakenly assumed that Blair remained 'an empty vessel into which the liquid that was poured was manufactured and processed by him'. His illusion, continued Blair, was that 'I was just a front man . . . incapable on my own . . . [but] no matter how good an actor you are, in the end it's not an act.'

Driven by instinct, Blair's flexible showmanship always trumped Brown's addiction to convention. Their endless arguments about the succession would lead Powell to write, 'His way of managing Gordon was to string him along indefinitely without ever addressing formally the difficult issue of who was in charge.' Others would say the opposite. Blair was clear that he was the commander but acknowledged that, if sacked, Brown would be able to mobilise sufficient MPs and trade union leaders to destabilise the government from the back benches and deprive Blair of support.

Blair never examined similar rivalries in history to understand how powerful challenges to his predecessors had been defeated by careful preparation. Successful leaders like Harold Macmillan and Margaret Thatcher survived by marginalising opponents. Dismissing the big beast would have outraged Neil Kinnock (still a force), John Prescott and the trade unions, but eventually they would have put party ahead of personality. By sacrificing Milburn, Blair put his own security ahead of principle. He did not seek to understand how Clement Attlee, Hugh Gaitskell and Harold Wilson had disarmed their opponents. He lived in ignorance of history by believing that his successful fight in 1995 to ditch Labour's Marxist Clause Four was world-shaking. In truth, the vote was a signpost. His power was based on his electoral victory and was challenged only by the defeated Brown. Blair's weakness was to shy away from spilling blood when he was guaranteed victory, without understanding the strength of the truism that cemeteries are filled with indispensable people. Instead, he consoled himself that the advantage of Brown's presence outweighed the cost of his absence.

As usual, Blair's survival gene suppressed any self-blame. Despite his surprise at Milburn's departure, he refused to look back in self-recrimination. His resilience was fed by focusing on the future. While he acknowledged Iraq as one reason for his weakness, he failed to recognise something more profound. Kevin Tebbit, a seasoned Whitehall warrior nearing retirement, identified the flaw: 'Blair didn't own his policy. He didn't understand that you have to stick to it all the way like a gadfly. He was like a barrister who came and then walked away. He should have dipped everyone's fingers in the blood to get delivery.'

Milburn's departure was followed by Simon Stevens accepting a post in America. 'You're leaving,' Ed Miliband, a Treasury special adviser, told Stevens, 'so we won't pay any attention to you.' Within a short period, Blair had lost his two agents of change. Nigel Crisp was empowered to be in sole charge of the NHS – and he did not believe in the prime minister's reforms.

Blair retaliated by appointing John Reid as Milburn's replacement. Born in Glasgow, Reid's early life of whisky, womanising and membership of the Scottish Communist Party had permanently alienated the Presbyterian Brown from the sinful Catholic. As a shrewd political operator during the 1970s, Reid had proved himself to an admirer as 'remorseless, unremitting and practical. Just like Stalin.' To defeat Labour's left wing, he had advised Neil Kinnock, 'Get the synthesis right, pick the moment and then kick the shit out of them.'

In compensating for his lack of political substance, the muscleman had become Tony Blair's 'Mr Fixit' – 'a semi-polished pearl among a lot of mud'. Known as 'a safe pair of fists', Reid was more than just another minister; he was the remaining Blairite who could be nurtured to challenge Brown for the leadership.

In the reshuffle following Milburn's departure, Reid was given his fourth job within a year. 'Oh fuck, health,' he cursed in an eruption that echoed across Whitehall. On his first day in Richmond House, he assured officials that his period in the building would be short. He would rely on Paul Corrigan, a former academic and his special adviser, to supervise Nigel Crisp.

Among Reid's visitors that day was Dame Carol Black, the president of the Royal College of Physicians. In advance, Reid was given a list of ten issues Black wanted to raise and a 300-page briefing about the problems, in the manner Milburn preferred. 'I don't fucking understand the point of these ten fucking points,' Reid screamed to Andrew Foster, a senior official. 'I just want one page. And when fucking Black comes into the room, you can fucking answer her questions.' There was a pause, and he then asked, 'What is a physician?'

'Well, a surgeon cuts and a physician doesn't,' he was told.

Reid greeted Black with charm. To prove his expertise, he said, within the first moments, 'I realise that physicians don't cut people up.' Black looked baffled throughout the remainder of the meeting.

Next, Reid prepared for his first radio interview. His questioner, Foster advised, would ask about the MRSA bug infecting hospital patients. Dirty staff were causing widespread illness, but Reid did not ask about the bacteria or the treatment. Instead, the new minister sat with a piece of paper reciting the bacteria's full name. One of his talents was to 'wing it' by delivering soundbites to the media, so when he appeared on Radio 4, Reid spoke confidently: 'I know the public are worried about methicillin-resistant *Staphylococcus aureus*, known commonly as MRSA, and believe me, we are going to defeat this problem.' His audience, Reid knew, would be impressed by his fluent enunciation and unaware of his ignorance. Blair's minister was skilled at managing the message. Corrigan, the department would come to recognise, was more interested in caring for Reid's image than supervising the NHS's management.

Reid's first challenge was to resolve the consultants' contracts. Nine months earlier, the doctors had rejected Milburn's offer, which would have terminated some profitable abuses. A presentation to Blair by the health department on 4 November had revealed an ugly scenario of a war between ministers and doctors. For a politician who preferred to be liked, this was a prospect to avoid. The antagonism with the consultants, Blair declared, should end. He wanted Reid to make the NHS a vote-winner for the election. There was nothing 'progressive' or Third Way in the instruction; all that mattered was crushing the 'wobble' to win a third term. As usual, Blair did not ask about the financial cost.

Foster gave Reid a thirty-two-page brief and an equally thick appendix describing the disagreements. 'Far too much,' snarled Reid. 'Two pages. Nothing more.' The detail was irrelevant. He called Paul Mitchell, one of the BMA's negotiators: 'We'll do six tweaks and have a deal in forty-eight hours.' The tweaks included abandoning two of

Milburn's demands: that the consultants work exclusively for the NHS for the first seven years; and that they be available for work after normal hours and over weekends.

'If you give that away,' Reid was told by his senior official, 'the costs will increase by many millions.' The minister wanted headlines confirming him as a problem-solver. He surrendered. Blair approved the increase in costs while travelling abroad after a telephone conversation with Brown, but he and his Downing Street advisers did not understand the consequences. Neither Reid nor Corrigan asked Crisp whether the right contracts had been drafted for the health authorities to present to the doctors. For his part, Crisp, with limited interest in human resources, left individual hospital managers to accept the contracts offered by the BMA. Not surprisingly, the BMA's version favoured the doctors.

'The BMA don't have the patients' interests at heart,' George Alberti, the former president of the Royal College of Physicians, warned Blair. The government's three pay settlements had rewarded NHS staff with an average 9 per cent pay increase, without any improvement in productivity. Within a year, British doctors and nurses ranked among the highest paid in the world. After taking account of the pay awards and rising drug costs, only 2 per cent of the annual 10.8 per cent increase in the NHS budget would be spent on patients. The estimated cost of the NHS's new computing system, which had been approved by Blair in 2002, had risen from £2.3 billion towards £10 billion. The prime minister said nothing. 'We changed the doctors' contracts', Powell would write, 'so that they were better paid and had to work more hours for the NHS.' Two years later, Blair discovered that, despite their higher income, they were working fewer hours.

'The boss says I should see you first,' Reid told Ken Anderson soon after arriving. The new minister's self-introduction was appealing: 'I believe that if we don't change the NHS, it will become a poor service for poor people.' For Anderson, Reid was a breath of fresh air. The minister had no stake in the NHS Plan 2000. Milburn and his bullying was replaced by a politician uninterested in policies. 'Foundation hospitals', said Reid at the outset, 'are important.' His commitment to the market was unquestioned.

Blair had defiantly announced plans to double the number of foundation hospitals after the enabling bill was passed by MPs in July with a majority of thirty-five, before heading for further trouble as it passed through the parliamentary process. 'Does it mean that a hospital could close?' he asked the House rhetorically. 'Yes, it does.' Brown's opposition was Reid's incentive to make foundation hospitals work. He assumed that Crisp would compensate for his own meagre knowledge.

Blair's misfortune was that the NHS's chief executive had little interest in building the infrastructure to implement his reforms. 'The rats are returning to the ship,' Milburn observed, surveying the dismemberment of his ambitions as civil servants in the department resurrected old attitudes.

Blair was fighting on every front: the NHS staff, the trade unions, the civil service and a third of the Labour Party, led by Brown. Signalling his weakness, he had capitulated to allow the anti-hunting bill to pass through the Commons, provoking ferocious demonstrations in Parliament Square. His only weapon was his oratory, and he chose the NHS as the theme of his speech at the 2003 party conference in Bournemouth.

In anticipation of his appearance in front of a huge audience, Blair's eyes sparkled. After endless rewrites and fraught rehearsals, the perfected tone enhanced his quest to crush his critics. His overriding ambition, or the 'supreme fulfilment of my mission', as he would write, was to show 'how progressive politics, itself modernised, could modernise the nation'. In other words, he wanted to establish New Labour as the natural party of government by burying the distinction between left and right.

Achievements and adversaries were at the heart of an impassioned speech to a divided party. Cardiac deaths, said Blair, had fallen by 19 per cent since 1997, and cancer deaths by 9 per cent. 'We should be proud', he told his audience, 'that we have increased public-service pay.' But, he added, obstructive civil servants were preventing more improvements. Putting power in the hands of the patient and ending 'one size fits all', he said, were vital to 'change the system . . . The reason I bang the drum for change is I get so angry that it takes so long, restless at how much there is to do. I want us to go faster, further.' Few in the hall understood his accusation: they were the conservatives obstructing modernisation.

His critics outside the party dissected the hyperbole. Rates of death from cancer and heart disease had been falling 'at similar rates' since 1971, and cancer treatment across Europe was better. Britain's survival rates were improving, but not by comparison to neighbouring countries. Much of the extra money spent on the new cancer programme, an audit revealed, was being wasted on bureaucracy and on unused technology because too few specialists had been trained. Targets were being shown to be meaningless. No one, for example, could identify how long a patient had waited at different stages in the treatment process. More waste was uncovered at the Modernisation Agency. The 760 employees were accused of causing disruption and the agency was closed. Other units created in Downing Street to modernise the NHS had caused confusion, and they too were shut down. To confirm his reputation as a cost-cutter, Reid also terminated the Health Action Zones as aimless and expensive. But, at the same time, he approved the employment of more doctors, nurses and managers, and rubber-stamped the creation of Transferring Community Services, another new programme designed to redirect 250,000 NHS employees towards improving a wide range of treatments – all without questioning the self-defeating complexity and cost of the growing number of services. The ever-increasing budget spent on more staff was justified by a fall in waiting times for inpatient treatment from 12.9 weeks in 2000 to 8.2 weeks in 2008. Few wanted to notice that the productivity of the workforce was deteriorating. The extra staff were working less. The solution, Julian Le Grand told Blair again, was to make a fundamental change in the NHS.

'Our aim is full choice,' he said.

'Why aren't we doing it now?'

'We'd be pushing the bulge around the system,' replied Le Grand. 'We need to be gradualist.'

Even after Ivan Rogers, Blair's private secretary, enthused, 'I think the boss will go further,' Le Grand held back. 'Blair feared institutions and didn't know how to take them on,' he would say. Inhibited by Brown's opposition, Le Grand never dared to say, 'Our final destination is a full market for the NHS.'

The start, in anticipation of the implementation of the new legislation, was momentous nevertheless. In the unheralded return to the 1991 blueprint, the NHS partially reintroduced GP commissioning under the disguise of the Quality Outcomes Framework. Twenty per cent of a GP's income would be linked to incentives and special payments. Reid handed out contracts for twenty-four additional ISTCs to the private sector. Then he hit an obstacle. 'Your job is to put forward radical reforms,' Crisp's deputy John Bacon told Le Grand. 'My job is to slow them down.'

In that cause, Bacon unexpectedly discovered in late 2003 that the NHS had 'sufficient capacity'. Crisp agreed: 'We don't need extra capacity from the private sector.' He added later, 'We had too much capacity in the NHS.' He objected to wasting and even closing NHS resources to help private companies earn profits and, to his delight, believed that 'the politicians had very little room to manoeuvre'.

Some were surprised by Crisp's misunderstanding of the market. Despite attempting the hard graft of 'lever-pulling' to outwit the civil servants, Le Grand found himself stymied. He needed Reid's support. Unexpectedly, the headline-chaser was a good ally. 'You deal with the technicalities,' the minister told Crisp, 'I'll deal with the politics.'

'Reid didn't care how hospitals worked,' concluded Alberti.

As a populist, Reid favoured everything opposed by Brown. He had already refused to endorse the proposal put forward in 2004's NHS Improvement Plan to reduce some waiting times to nine months. 'I cannot defend this,' he said. 'Eighteen weeks maximum.' He also liked the idea of 'real choice' in a patient-centred NHS. Care would be quicker because patients would be allowed to choose free treatment in a private centre if the NHS hospital was unsuitable. He agreed with Blair that if the target for treatment by private providers was substantially increased to 15 per cent of all patients, NHS hospitals would be under pressure to perform.

The challenge, Le Grand noticed, made Blair 'wobble'. As always, the prime minister feared Brown.

'You're the only person who can drive through the reforms we need,' Le Grand told Blair.

'I might not be here for long,' he replied.

Reid himself glowed as Blair's fireman and protector, not as his mechanic. In the midst of another row with Brown, he met Niall Dickson, the chief executive of the King's Fund, Britain's pre-eminent health think tank. After discussing the market incentives Reid was considering for the NHS, Dickson asked casually, 'But what will happen when 11 moves to 10?' Reid looked surprised that the question about Brown becoming prime minister was relevant. 'That is not going to happen,' he replied apoplectically.

At that moment, Blair was losing his appetite for the fight. Dismayed by the aftermath of Iraq and irritated by his failure to push through membership of the euro, he was also thinking about the 2005 manifesto. He issued an order: the NHS's vocabulary needed to be sensitive to the Labour Party's criticisms. Private contracts were to be called 'co-terminosity' agreements; competition was 'contestability'; and 'markets' should not be mentioned. Promises of choice should be buried, not least because Blair still could not decide whether a patient should be able to choose a hospital or even a surgeon. 'The pace became too leisurely,' noticed Norman Warner, a junior minister of health. 'Tony had bet the farm on targets and money going to the workforce, and then had other things on his mind.'

The NHS had reached a crossroads. At the end of 2003, George Alberti had recommended that the government should measure whether the extra billions of pounds were being properly spent. Michael

Barber's target system, some believed, was redundant. Gaming by managers had partially corrupted the system, advised Andrew Turnbull. Even Crisp recognised there were 'too many targets, some badly conceived'. 'It's too crude,' Anderson told Blair. But a stock-take of Barber himself was regarded as a step too far, and Crisp, supported by Blair, rejected Alberti's suggested review. Any survey that could potentially embarrass the government was resisted. The King's Fund stepped in, and Derek Wanless, the banker originally hired by Gordon Brown, agreed to undertake the investigation.

The headlines, nevertheless, were positive. Even the Tories pledged higher taxes to pay for the NHS. The proof of good news, said Crisp, was the steady increase in the number of employees. The NHS payroll was rising by 2.5 per cent a year and totalled nearly 1.5 million people. Reid never asked why more staff meant better care, and unquestioningly accepted Crisp's reports that the billions were being well spent and performance was improving. Corrigan also rarely probed. He simply passed Crisp's headlines on to Downing Street.

Both Corrigan and Reid were unaware that 130,000 people employed by the PCT managers through agencies did not appear in the records submitted to Crisp. The chief executive had not introduced an accounting system that would reveal how the PCT managers responsible for 80 per cent of the NHS's budget were allowing cash to disappear. As the money ran out, they relied on Crisp's executives to juggle the accounts to hide the discrepancies. Reid was allowing the NHS to accumulate a £1 billion deficit.

It was not just Reid. No one in Downing Street or the Treasury questioned the NHS accounts. The compartmentalisation installed by Blair and Powell had built a wall around the prime minister's office. 'I didn't realise until later', recalled Turnbull, 'that Blair didn't want mandarins to tell him what he didn't want to hear.'

THIRTY-TWO

Restoring Tradition

During summer 2003, senior officials in the Department of Education became increasingly aware of racial segregation in schools in some parts of England. David Normington, the permanent secretary, spent a day visiting some schools in his home city of Bradford and vividly noticed the extent of the separation. Some were 90 per cent Asian, while others were 90 per cent white. In the predominantly Asian primary schools, children were arriving for their first year after growing up in homes where little English was spoken and where Asian television was watched via satellite. Normington returned to London pondering the policy conundrum of how to encourage more integration when communities were so separate and radical solutions like busing and rehousing were not possible practically, ethically or politically.

Although over 450,000 immigrants were arriving in Britain annually and birth rates among those unable to speak English were rising, the civil servants knew that race was a sensitive issue for Labour's educationalists. Normington had inherited from Michael Bichard an unspoken departmental convention not to discuss the effect of immigration on schools. Teachers, Whitehall knew, resisted interference, so the issue had been delegated to local councils to solve. The few officials tempted to speak were silenced by Blair's support of immigration and his enthusiasm for multiculturalism.

Beyond that soft toleration was a hard core of educationalists who condemned Britain's policies for stipulating standards and targets that discriminated in favour of the white middle class. For them, education in Britain was wrongly promoting pro-business 'white supremacy' instead of egalitarianism. Any mention of 'ability' was condemned as 'racist educational inequality' or undesirable 'colour-blindness'.

Only Blair could have quashed that prejudice outright. But, while rejecting extremism, he never contemplated organising cross-departmental discussions in Whitehall. In deciding which battles to fight, his priority was to promote 'choice' and ignore race. He saw no reason to give security clearance to Normington and his officials so that they could attend Whitehall's meetings about the dangers of Islamic radicalisation. Education remained, senior officials realised in hindsight, 'not sensitised to Islam'. The department did not discuss the consequences of multiculturalism in schools with Blair until after four bombs exploded in London in July 2005.

One casualty of the silence was the fate of white working-class children who were failing in school. That embarrassment was hidden under the noise of the Iraq war. The number of white children classified as NEETs – not in education, employment or training – was rising. In 1997, 8.5 per cent of older teenagers were NEETs. In 2004, despite spending millions of pounds to encourage sixteen-year-olds to stay at school, that figure rose to 9.6 per cent. By 2006, 10.4 per cent of the young would be NEETs. Exhaustive research by Professor Robert Cassen and his team of Oxbridge professors of education showed that inadequate teachers were the principal cause of poor educational standards. But, once again, Blair blamed the civil service for pushing back reform. The 'forces of conservatism', he believed, were preventing delivery. 'I've been driving with the handbrake on for too long,' he repeated in May 2003. The cure, he decided, was to be 'truly radical'. He would abolish the LEAs and give schools independence. He would create a mixed market that embraced the private sector and promoted competition. He would resurrect his inheritance from the Tories.

In a succession of White Papers, the government emphasised both autonomy for schools and teachers and parental choice. Blair signalled a return to traditional values. Schools were encouraged to impose

discipline, reintroduce the house system and require pupils to wear uniform. Another batch of White Papers – 'Excellence and Enjoyment:
A Strategy for Primary Schools', 'Five-Year Strategy for Children and
Learners', 'Choice for Parents, the Best Start for Children: A Ten-Year
Strategy for Childcare' and 'Every Child Matters' – extolled the new
vision and how it might be achieved. David Blunkett's plans were
replaced by other initiatives, regardless of the waste. One followed
another, each lasting a few weeks before being forgotten. As with health,
as with the military, as with immigration, Blair never questioned the
cost of so many abandoned programmes – including £50 million on
a behaviour-management course for teachers. He was, in every sense,
going for broke.

Billions of pounds were spent on extra pay for teachers, supplying
them with support staff, reducing class sizes and refurbishing or building new schools. Hundreds of millions were allocated to hiring teams
of advisers to help minorities and poorly performing schools. Again,
high-concept titles flowed like water into the debate. The programmes
included 'New Deal for Communities', 'The Neighbourhood Renewal
Fund' and 'The London Challenge and Building Schools for the
Future'. The latter, a fifteen-year programme costing about £45 billion,
was promoted as a way to remedy Tory negligence. Any challenge from
Gordon Brown about the additional spending was quashed by Blair.
Education was uniquely his domain. He was particularly proud that
Labour had 'realised the potential of new technology' by equipping
classrooms with computers and replacing blackboards with electronic
whiteboards.

In the monthly stock takes, Blair was reassured by Michael Barber
that, despite Iraq, the domestic agenda was not being ignored. He was
encouraged by David Miliband, the junior education minister, that targets and scrutiny were enabling him to 'get his way'. The simplicity of
the process was appealing. Barber's graphs and headline judgements,
honed into digestible soundbites, presented what appeared to be an
accurate snapshot of performance and progress in schools. Only those

on the sidelines, observing Barber being inundated with statistics about the punctuality of trains and the tapestry of roadworks across Britain, wondered whether 'deliverology' could reflect reality in classrooms. Maths and English tests for eleven- to fourteen-year-olds (Key Stage 3) had been abandoned as unworkable without any discussion with Blair, but then again he was not expected to confront detailed problems.

Among those who experienced the routine of his stock-take was Naomi Eisenstadt, Sure Start's founder and director. In January 2003, Barber invited her to address Blair. 'We'll need good data,' he told her. Sure Start was still being praised by Tessa Jowell and other women supporters as one of Labour's flagship policies, but Eisenstadt sensed that No. 10 had become mystified about a programme costing £680 million a year, which the following year would rise to £921 million. There was also the feeling in some quarters that its original intention of helping poor children had become diluted by the middle classes' capture of the programme, and that under the Treasury's influence the educational purpose was being submerged to provide basic childcare centres.

No one even knew if Blair was genuinely interested. Ever since Blunkett had sensed that Blair's eyes were wandering during the original presentation in 1998, Sure Start had been mentioned only occasionally in his hearing. His aides appeared to be keener on branding the scheme as a success in order to win political kudos rather than caring about its content. Signalling his own mindset about securing immediate results, Blair had quipped, 'Won't all this early years' funding only bring benefits long after I'm PM?'

At the stock-take, Barber summarised his assessment of Sure Start's achievements and ambitions. Then Eisenstadt read out her presentation. 'How many centres are there?' Blair asked. 'And what are the costs?'

Eisenstadt became tongue-tied, and Blair was clearly irritated. She got the meeting, she confessed, 'wrong... We were short on quick wins. The government liked having new things to announce.' Even so, Blair failed to ask the key question: was Eisenstadt's ambition of encouraging social mobility succeeding? The answer would have been negative. The old inequalities, she knew, stubbornly remained.

Research by academics at Durham University would confirm the absence of any proof that, after seven years at school, children had materially benefited from a programme that would eventually cost £1.1 billion annually, and a National Evaluation report in 2007 would show that Sure Start had failed to deliver. Her ambitions, Eisenstadt would admit, 'have not yet borne fruit'. She left Downing Street depressed, and was not invited to discuss the programme again. Nevertheless, in 2010, Blair would acclaim Sure Start as 'one of New Labour's greatest achievements'.

Beyond Sure Start, Blair's attention was focused on the academy programme, based on the city technology colleges inherited from the Tories and replacing the grant-maintained schools. The beacon was Mossbourne Community Academy, which would be built on the site of Hackney Downs School, once an outstanding grammar school in north London. Instead of converting the existing building for a cost of about £15 million, Blair encouraged the construction of an entirely new school designed by Richard Rogers, one of Britain's most famous architects, and costing about £30 million. Of the seventeen academies to be opened during 2004, Mossbourne would count among the best.

Forty-two more academies were planned to meet Blair's target of 200 by 2010. The standard cost of a new school was about £23 million; the Business Academy in Bexley that Blair opened cost £31 million. He was not worried by the civil servants' reports that sponsors who had promised to contribute £2 million were slow in producing their cash. Money was still not his priority; he wanted a legacy. At the very moment of yet another battle with Brown, Jonathan Powell told a journalist, 'It's a Shakespearean tragedy. Gordon Brown is like the guy who thinks he's going to be king and never gets it. He's never going to be prime minister.' At the same time, the prime minister's spokesman was telling journalists, 'Blair will stay to fight and win the battle of ideas.' The only problem was that he was struggling to make any idea come to fruition.

Unlike the health unions, he was prepared, out of his passion for education, to confront the teaching unions and ignore the warning by David Bell, the new chief inspector of Ofsted, that parental choice should be revoked. Bell, a left-wing educationalist, complained that choice was dividing rich from poor, propelling unpopular schools even further behind. Blair had given up trying to persuade the Left about the benefits of private finance and selection, and was deaf to the protests that choice in education would cause the 'social destruction' of deprived communities or even that the new academies would not improve education. Instead, he finally demanded that inadequate head teachers be fired.

All that activity concealed the bad news about children's numeracy and literacy. The results had not genuinely improved since 2001. Charles Clarke naturally claimed that the numeracy strategy 'has made huge progress since 1997'. The very next year, the top 4 per cent of eleven-year-olds, said Clarke, had achieved a 7 per cent improvement. Professor Margaret Brown of King's College, London, disagreed strongly with Clarke's announcement. Ofsted's results, she argued, had been distorted by focusing on small groups of pupils and excluding unhelpful results from their reports. The inspectorate's inadequate figures, she concluded, cast doubt on politicians saying 'we know what works'.

The teaching unions identified Barber as the culprit. Too many primary schools, anxious to satisfy his demand for successful data, were coaching children to pass the tests, and the consequent good results inflated the eleven-year-olds' abilities. Those children arrived in secondary schools lacking a proper understanding of maths and, once deprived of additional coaching, could not catch up. 'Deliverology' was corrupting education.

Blair was uninterested in that argument. In his view, Margaret Brown was an outsider. For the most part, he trusted Barber, who, despite his eccentric party piece of walking barefoot across two metres of broken glass without suffering any cuts, produced apparently verified results.

But there were doubts. Six years after his election and more than half-way through his premiership, Blair's declared priority of improving Britain's education was faltering. He could not blame the chancellor. There were no conflicting orders about education. Success or failure depended entirely on him.

Not enough, he feared, had changed. Officials in the education department appeared to be detached as they lurched from success to calamity without achieving firm control. Blair's telephone call to Charles Clarke in the midst of another disaster confirmed his worst fears. The education secretary was on holiday striding through an Estonian turnip field when his leader called.

'You must come back immediately,' implored Blair. 'We have an £800 million schools' funding crisis.'

'I'm not returning,' replied Clarke, suggesting that, viewed from Estonia, the shortfall was not an emergency.

'You must understand, Charles,' continued Blair, 'I have a relationship with the people, and the people are angry. It's urgent and it will explode if we don't settle this.'

'I'm not coming back.'

'OK,' said Blair meekly.

On his eventual return, Clarke met with Blair, Gordon Brown and John Prescott. For thirty minutes, a slanging match rich with expletives filled the Downing Street room as Brown refused to sign off any additional money.

'Right, this is what we're going to do,' said Blair, readjusting his armour with an expressionless face. 'If Gordon won't approve it, then the permanent secretary will authorise it.'

'Fuck off,' screamed the chancellor, and he stormed out of the room. To Clarke's satisfaction, Blair had for once smothered his chancellor's ill will, and the crisis passed.

THIRTY-THREE

Lies and Damn'd Lies

The army's plight in Iraq – both financial and political – could not be solved as easily.

Just days before becoming chief of the defence staff, General Mike Walker discovered that he could not get £10 million from the Treasury to hire engineers. Gordon Brown and his department had become, in his view, 'a drag on our system'. Trying to find the money to provide water and electricity in Basra, Walker stumbled onto a stalemate between the military, Whitehall, the politicians and the aid workers, a situation that only Blair could resolve. He was determined that on this occasion the prime minister's struggle with his chancellor should not be allowed to interfere with the fate of 42,000 servicemen and women.

The army had not been greeted as liberators by Basra's 1.3 million inhabitants, yet the city was relatively peaceful. Since there was no mandate for nation-building, British soldiers were seen sunbathing and body-building while awaiting UN or NATO forces to take over from them. On the basis of the original plan – 'first in, first out' – General Mike Jackson ordered that the army should start to return on 19 April. By August, 32,500 soldiers would be back in Europe, leaving just 9,500 troops in southern Iraq until 2004. Walker doubted whether the plan would endure, but he was receiving no guidance from Downing Street.

Just before the war ended, Blair had finally agreed to Andrew Turnbull's suggestion that a committee should direct Britain's aid to Iraq. Jack Straw chaired the first meeting of the Ad Hoc Ministerial Committee on Iraq Reconstruction. From the outset, he found himself embroiled in a turf war between the army, the Treasury and DFID, Clare Short's department, which was directly responsible for overseeing the reconstruction of southern Iraq. Straw blamed Short for its inactivity. 'Short and DFID didn't come to meetings,' Admiral Mike Boyce discovered during his last days as chief of the defence staff. 'She showed no will to support the army either with money or in human terms.' Blair's intense efforts to prevent her resignation had been counterproductive.

Because of her disapproval of the war, Short encouraged her officials to be semi-detached from the government and reluctant to use soldiers for civil work. Suma Chakrabarti, DFID's permanent secretary, rejected Kevin Tebbit's request for money to train the Iraqi police and dispense aid. 'It doesn't fit our poverty criteria,' he told him. Without either the finance or the organisation, British experts were not dispatched to Iraq. 'It was a breakdown,' Boyce realised within the first week of occupation. 'I don't know why they didn't come.'

Short revealed her anger on 15 April, six days after Saddam's statue was pulled down. In a BBC interview, she listed the humanitarian plight, the disorder in Baghdad, America's 'illegality' and finally condemned Blair's conduct once again as 'reckless'. 'Treachery,' was Blair's verdict on both her and Brown.

Blair was fretting. Still no WMDs had been found, and reports from Paris, Berlin and Moscow were discouraging. Those governments emphasised their belief that Saddam did not possess the weapons. Facing the Commons in the past, Blair's confident delivery would have brushed aside his critics but, in the debate on 18 April, he played for safety and, rather than mentioning the WMDs, boasted of Saddam's fall as being comparable to Hitler's.

During the third week of peace, ministers heard that Curveball's so-called 'mobile laboratory for the manufacture of biological agents' had been found. American soldiers then reported that the machine in fact manufactured meteorological balloons. 'Bollocks. Where does this leave us?' asked Geoff Hoon. Others in Whitehall shuddered nervously.

No minister, transport minister Alistair Darling noticed, dared to raise the subject of WMDs in that week's Cabinet.

Just as some newspapers were accusing Blair of having blood on his hands, Richard Dearlove rushed into No. 10. 'Bits and pieces', he reported, had been found, meaning old Russian Scud rockets. 'A scientist has just come over with his laptop,' he told Blair, referring to an Iraqi fugitive, 'so we should get the hard intelligence soon.' No more credible promises were heard from Dearlove and, with those words, the curtain was finally lowered on his reputation.

During that last week of April, the failure to find WMDs was 'like a bucket of cold water' for Lieutenant General Rob Fry, the chief of staff in Northwood. Although Kevin Tebbit could not recall 'a moment of collective embarrassment or confession' within the MoD, Desmond Bowen, the senior policy adviser, admitted to Tebbit that 'We're dumbfounded, amazed and horrified.' In public, Blair maintained his customary cool performance. 'Before people crow about the absence of weapons of mass destruction, I suggest they wait a little bit,' he said. At that moment, Air Marshal Brian Burridge, the commander of the British invading forces based in Qatar, sensed that Blair's grip over the machinery of government was faltering. To prevent the public sensing any wobble, Alastair Campbell encouraged *The Times*' Tom Baldwin, one of his trusted journalists, to write the opposite. Under the headline 'Blair Has Emerged Bolder and Braver from War in Iraq', Baldwin described 'Blair the Bold's' intention to gamble against Brown's obstruction on foundation hospitals and tuition fees.

In early May, Mike Jackson toured Basra, the first of over twenty British generals who visited the city without speaking any Arabic and without any special training in the unique circumstances of the region. Jackson was horrified. The British army lacked experts and money. Because of Short's 'complete lack of direction', none of the non-governmental organisations expected to rebuild Iraq had arrived. Without the necessary equipment and expertise to restore essential services, the army was struggling. 'It is startlingly apparent', Jackson reported to London, 'that we are not delivering that which was deemed to be promised and was expected.' Nothing was to be said in public, Jackson ordered his staff: 'This is a good-news story. Our political masters are happy. We're not rocking the boat. Don't start a bad-news story.' He would subsequently be accused of being 'General Hypocrite' for failing to publicise the truth.

Blair followed Jackson to Basra. There were no Iraqis shouting 'Tony' to welcome the celebrity liberator. He was cheered by British soldiers, but in private he heard about their frustration and the sabotaging of their efforts by the locals. On his return to London, Blair told Turnbull to put Whitehall on 'a war footing' to dispatch experts. Turnbull mentioned the army's complaints about Straw's committee. 'We were cross', said Walker, 'that departments would not get focused and refused to take Iraq seriously. At the meetings, people arrived, gave their fiver and then disappeared.' To relieve the tension among ministers and create harmony in Basra, Walker asked Blair to appoint a Cabinet minister uniquely responsible for Iraq. Without a special government department that would 'make sure that everyone is steaming in the same direction', he warned, the British position would deteriorate. Blair refused and asked Straw to energise his committee.

Soon after, civil servants noticed Blair's reluctance to attend the committee's meetings. His absence, some speculated, coincided with the failure to find the WMDs; others marked the moment his eyes glazed over when Patricia Hewitt, according to one general's swipe, 'banged on about women's rights in Basra'. Even Hewitt noticed the general's disdain over her contribution. The army, she thought, was foolish not to recognise that only with Iraqi women's engagement could the country be transformed. But the army wanted £10 million to provide water, not to engineer a social revolution.

Without Blair demanding action from his ministers to promote 'vital British interests', Straw's own enthusiasm waned and Hoon became angry. The army's budget, he told Blair, was falling, while DFID's was increasing. Yet Short's department still refused to dispatch teachers, currency experts, engineers or policemen to Basra. 'Blair was in charge of the system but, with the lack of focus, the system was failing,' observed Bowen from the MoD. Once Blair stopped attending the committee, Straw would make his own excuses after thirty minutes, and soon Hoon became reluctant to attend at all. 'The Ministry of Defence could not do anything,' said Tebbit. 'I found it embarrassing.' Short's fiery resignation on 12 May made no difference other than to cause Blair to curse his timidity for not dismissing her earlier. She was replaced by Valerie Amos, a professional quangoist born in British Guyana who was ennobled in 1997.

The stagnation in London continued, reflecting the faltering conditions in Baghdad. Blair sent John Sawers, a Foreign Office adviser, to the Iraqi capital to discover the reasons. His report, 'Iraq: What's Gone Wrong?', delivered in early May, described a breakdown of law and order. He blamed Jay Garner, an ineffectual general who was a personal friend of George Bush. His appointment as America's director of reconstruction had confirmed Washington's lack of any post-war plans for Iraq other than to dispense suitcases of cash.

Sawers recommended that the American command's request for British troops to be sent to help in Baghdad should be approved. In particular, he wanted the 16 Air Assault Brigade to be dispatched from Basra. The 5,000 battle-ready commandos, he wrote, were ideal for patrolling Sadr City, a volatile area in Baghdad. Blair approved the plan, but Walker objected.

'There's only so much we can do,' he told Blair. 'We have limited resources. It would be a logistical nightmare.'

'Can't we increase troop numbers in Iraq?' asked Blair.

'No, we cannot, Prime Minister,' replied Walker. The government's plan, he explained, was to withdraw the army out of Iraq as quickly as possible. To support a brigade in Sadr City would require another 10,000 back-up troops and rotation for men who had spent too long on the front line. Blair, Walker realised, did not understand that military plans could not be changed on a whim.

Walker also found a new gripe. Sawers was earning a reputation for excessive interference by continuing to contradict the general. 'We don't want to get involved in another Fallujah,' said Walker, referring to an American assault that had devastated an Iraqi town. At least 5,000 British soldiers, summarised Walker, would be lost in the mayhem of supporting the Americans in Sadr City. 'I didn't think they were going to change the price of fish,' he would say. The military, Walker said, adapting Rab Butler's famous phrase, 'is the art of the possible'. Blair was disappointed, but concealed his exasperation over the fact that the British refusal to dispatch the troops would irritate the Americans. He did not overrule the military's advice.

Towards the end of May, Walker returned to Downing Street to brief Blair about his first visit to Iraq, which coincided with the arrival from Washington of Paul Bremer as America's governor, replacing Jay Garner. Without understanding the complexities of Iraq's divided society, Bremer used his vice-regal powers to demobilise the Iraqi army, allowing ex-soldiers to disappear unpaid with their guns. He also abolished the Ba'ath Party. Since most civil servants were Ba'athists, Iraq was effectively deprived of a civilian government.

Bremer's decision initiated a civil war for which the American army was unprepared. Walker, similarly lacking experience of the Arab world, admitted that he had not grasped Bremer's 'complete misunderstanding about Iraq's psychology'. However, he could not mistake Bremer's disdain for the British. 'We got cold-shouldered by Bremer,' he reported. Blair did not react. The situation in Basra, Walker continued, was worse than he had anticipated. He had arrived with 'no thoughts that it would go wrong', and was pleased that British soldiers were patrolling there without flak jackets among supportive Iraqis. But, he told Blair, showing him what he called his 'optimistic charts', the army was stumped. Not only was the reconstruction package delayed, but the army's training of Iraqis to be policemen – a priority for Blair – had been unsuccessful. He cautioned that, in a city riddled with corruption, British policemen found training the locals 'most difficult'. The British intelligence agencies, he added, had been 'clearly misinformed'. The JIC, in a pre-war report, had predicted that the Iranians were 'unlikely to be aggressive'. The reality, he reported, was that they 'are exploiting the situation, but we cannot find anyone'. Army intelligence officers could not find the Iranians fomenting revolt and, even with the SAS's help, the military could not seal the border with Iran.

This was the moment when rigorous questioning of Walker would have extracted hard truths about an underfunded army. But Blair did not welcome precision, and Walker, who had risen to the top by going with the flow, saw no point in imitating Boyce and irritating Blair. Even had Blair asked, Walker could not have offered any perspective regarding the consequences of the government's decisions. He was a loyal servant rather than a sage, chosen by Hoon because, as a member of the Royal Anglian Regiment rather than the upper-class Guards Regiment, 'he was not a social snob but a breath of fresh air; a man who, unlike Boyce, understood how to operate in the political context'. Hoon had not considered that the historic antagonism between Jackson and Walker undermined a considered discussion among the army chiefs.

Others recognised that Blair's predicament was self-made. He had excluded Hoon, Tebbit and any Iraqi specialists from his meeting with Walker, choosing to rely on a plain soldier who was, like himself, unversed in history. A man of few words, the general believed that the military should not interfere in politics or discuss with the prime minister whether his judgement 'made sense'. He left Downing Street satisfied with his honest report. Blair's mask did not reveal whether he recognised that he had just moved closer to the precipice.

On 28 May 2003, the prime minister flew to Kuwait. From there he planned to hop across into Iraq to visit British soldiers and hear briefings from Paul Bremer. The month had been turgid. The Tories had won impressively in the local elections, and Brown's renewed warfare was dousing his self-confidence about a third term.

Subverting the mood throughout Downing Street was the continuing failure to find WMDs. The chance of their discovery some six weeks after the invasion began, Blair and his advisers knew, had become remote. Surrounded by those complicit in his blunder – David Manning, Alastair Campbell and Jonathan Powell – Blair underestimated the anger across the country about going to war on bogus intelligence. After sixteen months' proximity to Richard Dearlove and John Scarlett, he realised they had committed an 'error' but believed they were innocent of 'deception'. In any case, in his mind the weapons were irrelevant. The invasion was still 'the right thing to do', regardless of WMDs. Or at least that was the argument he adopted in public. Giving Hans Blix more time would have been pointless, explained Blair, since the inspector 'would have yielded . . . the [wrong] conclusion that because Saddam had no active WMD programme, therefore he was not a threat'. Blair was uninterested in reconciliation with his critics. Digging in to defend his belief in 'regime change', the accusation he faced across the country was of 'deception'.

Blair's shield was punctured soon after he stepped into the desert heat of Basra on 29 May, alongside Campbell. After earlier telling journalists that he remained 'absolutely confident that the weapons would be found', he was informed that Donald Rumsfeld had publicly conceded that Saddam's WMDs would probably never be discovered because he possibly never possessed them. Campbell noted about Bush's hardman, 'What a clot . . . really irritating.'

Another irritation was a report on the BBC *Today* programme that morning. Andrew Gilligan, an experienced BBC reporter disliked by Campbell for his critical dispatches from Baghdad, had broadcast that the government 'probably knew' that the dossier's assertion about intelligence showing that Iraq could prepare and fire WMDs within forty-five minutes of any order 'was wrong even before it decided to put it in'. Gilligan added: 'Downing Street, our source says, a week before publication [of the dossier], ordered it to be sexed up, to be made more exciting, and ordered more facts to be discovered.'

In later broadcasts that morning, Gilligan altered his narrative, saying that the government knew the 'forty-five minutes' claim was 'questionable' rather than 'wrong', but he repeated his central allegation that Blair and Campbell conspired to falsify the assertion against Scarlett's wishes. In fact, Scarlett had wholeheartedly approved the dossier, although he knew that the 'intelligence' did not describe a rocket but an artillery gun. Gilligan assumed that Campbell and Blair were aware of Scarlett's mistake.

The dam had broken. In Washington and London, military and intelligence experts conceded that the WMDs may not have existed. In Westminster, seventy Labour MPs demanded an inquiry. Many were briefed by friends in Whitehall that the September dossier was based on flimsy evidence. Over the next three days, Gilligan's 'sexed-up' allegations were repeated across the media. Critics described a common thread running from Blair's macho protection of Jo Moore after she had suggested 'burying bad news' on 9/11 to Gilligan's allegations about the manipulation of intelligence.

A journalist accompanying Blair to Iraq and then on to Poland was told by the prime minister, 'The idea that we authorised or made our intelligence agencies invent some piece of evidence is completely absurd.' Blair also told the journalist about the discovery in Iraq of 'two trailers which were used to make biological weapons'. Blair was repeating Curveball's invention, which had been accepted by Dearlove.

During his onward flight to St Petersburg for an EU–Russia summit, Blair read in the *Mail on Sunday* an article by Gilligan in which he spelled out his allegations under the subhead, 'I asked my intelligence source why Blair misled us all over Saddam's weapons. His reply? One word – Campbell'. Gilligan described how Downing Street had 'sexed up' the dossier and how the intelligence officers responsible had become distressed by Campbell's distortion of the 'forty-five minutes' report. The combination of Campbell, Iraq and the dishonesty about the dossier created a frenzy of lurid headlines that fuelled the public's loss of trust in Blair and, eventually, all politicians.

Campbell was incandescent. Tired and ready to resign, he understood the damaging effect of even a partial truth. Blair was equally dismayed. 'It's another attack to go to the heart of my integrity,' he told his PR man, knowing that the dossier's foreword, which had been written by Campbell, misrepresented the 'sporadic and patchy' conclusions in the original JIC report. 'It is grotesque,' continued Blair. 'There is no story here at all, but it is being driven by the BBC as a huge crisis for us.'

Neither had survived for nine years in the spotlight without the skills to deflect the truth. They were helped by Gilligan's two principal mistakes: Blair and Campbell had not distorted the 'forty-five minutes' intelligence; and Gilligan's source was David Kelly, a weapons expert employed by the government and as a UN inspector in Iraq who had no role in compiling the dossier. Authorised by his superiors to brief journalists, Kelly had cautiously repeated a complaint he had heard from Brian Jones, an analyst at the MoD. However, even Kelly was convinced before the invasion that Saddam possessed WMDs.

Under pressure to shame Gilligan's unknown source, John Reid blamed 'rogue elements' in the security services, and a hunt was launched for a disloyal senior officer in MI6 or the JIC. 'John believes you should go for the throat when you're in a corner,' said one of his allies. Reid's mistake horrified Blair. Clinging onto Dearlove's and Scarlett's loyalty was important for his own survival. They would sink or swim together. Campbell for his part took comfort from Dearlove's support, forgetting that the MI6 chief was vulnerable himself.

Blair's initial instinct was to allow the media frenzy to burn itself out. His misfortune was that Robin Cook and Clare Short joined the debate to denounce him for 'duping' the country. Both the party's and the public's anger grew. Loyalist Labour ministers accused the intelligence services of skulduggery. In retaliation, anonymous voices said Blair was paranoid. The public's trust in him dived. To his irritation, the parliamentary Intelligence and Security Committee opened an inquiry into the 'forty-five minutes' claim. At least he could be confident that, under the chairmanship of Labour MP Ann Taylor, the committee's Labour majority would be sympathetic towards the government. His dependency upon Campbell was less secure.

Blair's good fortune since 1994 was to be supported by outstanding political operators. None was better than Peter Mandelson or Alastair Campbell. His misfortune was that neither could satisfy the public's expectations of probity. For nine years, Campbell had successfully shaped and misshaped the news to promote and protect Blair. In that time he had become infamous as a bully and a liar. His misleading descriptions about Blair's relations with Brown, the fate of a hapless minister or government achievements were trivial compared to the two dossiers that persuaded many Britons to support the Iraq war. By the end of May 2003, both were known to be untrue.

As he returned to London from St Petersburg, Blair failed to assess his principal defender dispassionately. Ever since Fiona Millar had told him that she and Campbell wanted to resign, Blair had noticed his ally's instability. The obvious solution was to bid both farewell and start afresh. He resisted. He needed the comforting support of his *consigliere*, for Brown was once again agitating for his resignation, citing their disagreement over the euro.

As agreed, Brown had submitted the Treasury's studies to the Cabinet. To Blair's dismay, the eighteen massive volumes made normal scrutiny impossible. But, with the Cabinet's support, he still proposed a referendum in which he would advocate membership. Brown appeared on television to say he was against joining and, among several other obstacles, could wield a veto. The following morning, Blair told Campbell while eating toast with marmalade in his flat that 'The best way would be to get out a gun, shoot the obstacle and then have a reshuffle.' Once again, Blair was urged by Alan Milburn, Reid and others to dismiss the chancellor. He refused. 'Removing Brown', he wrote, 'would have brought the entire building tumbling down around our ears.'

When, three days later, Milburn announced he was resigning, Blair mishandled the reshuffle. After several emotional arguments, Derry Irvine was replaced by Charles Falconer as Lord Chancellor. Irvine's sacking was quoted as another example of Blair's disloyalty, and the resulting reorganisation of the justice system was chaotic. Blair was vulnerable on so many fronts – except against the Tories. Iain Duncan Smith had failed to exploit Labour's divisions both on tuition fees and foundation hospitals, and, having given unequivocal support for the Iraq war, was perplexed about how to lead the charge over the intelligence flaws. Blair had no reason to fear the lame leader of a demoralised party as an alternative prime minister. His chancellor was the only serious threat. Under attack from Ed Balls and other Brown supporters, Blair feared life without Campbell.

Hating any journalist who failed to show obedience, Campbell used his appearance before the Foreign Affairs Committee on 25 June to defend the September dossier and assault Gilligan: 'I simply say, in relation to the BBC story, it is a lie, it was a lie. It is a lie that is continually repeated, and until we get a public apology for it I will keep making sure that Parliament, people like yourselves and the public know that it was a lie.' Blair congratulated Campbell without grasping the truth: his great protector had lost his self-control.

Two days later, Campbell walked unexpectedly into the *Channel 4 News* studio during its live broadcast, sat down and launched a vitriolic attack against those who accused him of 'sexing up' the dossier. He was looking for scalps – Gilligan's in particular, then the BBC's editors' and that of anyone else whose demise would resurrect his reputation for probity. That night, even Blair realised his spokesman was unbalanced. Yet Campbell's mental state was unimportant compared to the thrust of Gilligan's report. The public, Blair understood, would excuse an 'error' but would not forgive 'a deception' or that he himself 'had deliberately misled the House of Commons'.

Blair's fate – possible 'resignation and disgrace', as he would later write – depended on how his representation of Scarlett's summary was judged. The JIC had originally described the intelligence on WMDs as 'sporadic and patchy', yet Blair represented it as 'extensive, detailed and authoritative', and pleaded that any discrepancy was an 'error'.

'The intelligence was wrong,' he would write. 'We admitted it. We apologised for it.' That was inaccurate. In June 2003, he emphatically insisted that the Iraq Survey Group, a thousand inspectors under American command, would eventually find the WMDs. In the meantime, he needed to deflect criticism, and agreed with Campbell to launch a broadside against the BBC. 'Alastair was concerned by the lowering of the standards at the BBC', recalled Hoon without irony, 'and wanted to fight against that.' To their relief, the 'chaff' who, like the metal fired into the sky to disorientate guided missiles, could deflect the public's criticism unsuspectingly offered himself on 1 July.

David Kelly, an honest, loyal and troubled man, wrote to his manager at the MoD to reveal that he had spoken to Gilligan. However, he explained, he could not be the journalist's source because Gilligan's story did not match what Kelly knew nor his contribution during their conversation.

As the news spread in Downing Street that Gilligan's 'source' was known, Blair's confidants and top security officials, including Scarlett, were summoned to discuss how Kelly could be used to discredit the BBC. Campbell was agitating for retaliation. 'The biggest thing needed', he noted, 'was the source out.' That would 'open a flank on the BBC'.

On the afternoon of 8 July, Blair was under pressure. Instead of recalling the humiliating retreat the previous year after Campbell had complained about a newspaper's allegation that Blair had sought to promote his own role in the Queen Mother's funeral, he succumbed again to his lieutenant's impetuosity. In what Tebbit would call 'a decisive meeting' that included Campbell, Powell and others, Blair agreed that the MoD should announce that Gilligan's source had revealed himself. Gleefully, Campbell ordered that the government machine be mobilised 'to fuck Gilligan'. The only complication was that Tebbit arrived in Downing Street just after the meeting had broken up.

'Alastair will explain to you what we've decided,' Blair told him as he disappeared into an education stock-take.

Tebbit found Campbell completing a press release. 'We're going to leak the name,' Campbell told him.

'You can't do that until I have spoken to him,' said Tebbit. In the meantime, the press release, he said, should state that 'someone has come forward'.

'OK,' replied Campbell, without betraying his emotions.

Tebbit agreed that the government statement could describe Kelly's background to hasten his identification. That had been authorised by Blair, even though such an announcement was unprecedented. Kelly's outing, Blair would later write, was 'handled' by Tebbit 'at my insistence'. He drew a distinction between 'leaking' Kelly's name and 'confirming' enquiries.

In reality, at Campbell's behest Hoon directed spokesmen at the MoD to confirm Kelly's name whenever a journalist correctly identified him. Soon after, a ministry official told Kelly that his name would be released. Kelly was mortified. Blair would subsequently deny 'the brutal media allegation' that Campbell had 'leaked' Kelly's name. 'He hadn't,' wrote Blair, which, strictly speaking, was true because the revelation of Kelly's identity, as Tebbit agreed, matched the commitment by the MoD to 'provide as much information as we can', albeit with Campbell's encouragement. To aggravate the smear on Kelly, he was described by Tom Kelly (no relation), one of Blair's spokesmen, as a 'Walter Mitty character'.

Both then and later, Blair confused the true nature of the dispute. He described Kelly as Gilligan's 'source'. That was inaccurate because Gilligan had misrepresented Kelly. More importantly, the dossier was more than 'sexed up' – it was wholly inaccurate.

The one weak point was Gilligan's focus on the forty-five minutes. Kelly had mentioned to the journalist Scarlett's inaccurate description of an artillery shell and how the public misconception of rockets carrying WMDs had not been corrected. Blair bore the responsibility for that mistake. To deflect the media's attention from the phoney intelligence, Blair joined Campbell's roller coaster. 'I was outraged by the BBC's position,' he would write about the corporation's refusal to apologise. He agreed that Kelly should testify before the Foreign Affairs Committee. Kevin Tebbit protested that Kelly, a reticent scientist, was unsuited to the parliamentary spotlight, but Hoon overruled him. The summons to Westminster aggravated Kelly's distress. Under intense questioning by petulant MPs on 15 July, he was pummelled, leaving the public puzzled and the scientist agitated.

Blair was preparing for a glory trip to Washington. He was to address both Houses of Congress, receive the Congressional Gold Medal and be feted by Bush. He was exhausted. Distrusted and disliked by so many Britons, he was undecided about the theme for his speech to the party conference in two months' time. An election victory would depend upon rebuilding trust and reasserting the party's values. Endless slogans, targets and announcements had contaminated the New Labour brand. His hope of re-establishing a relationship with his supporters was being torpedoed by the Kelly row. The public's attention had returned to Iraq just as relief over the victory was vanishing. The worst offenders were Labour MPs. Their constant criticism had galvanised the ineffectual Iain Duncan Smith to surprise everyone by accusing Blair and Campbell of creating 'a culture of deceit and spin', provoking even Tory MPs to call for moderation in order to avoid damaging the morale of British troops.

During July, General Jackson witnessed the first security problems in the British zone. A roadside bomb had killed a British soldier. Some blamed Rumsfeld's order for American soldiers to return home for encouraging rival religious groups to bid for power in Basra. Others highlighted Bremer's decision to disband the army and remove Ba'athists from the Iraqi government for fomenting defiance in the north. A bomb had destroyed the headquarters of the UN mission in Baghdad, killing over twenty officials, including the admired chief officer. With one blast, Blair's insistence on a UN solution evaporated. Iraqis watched helplessly as their country slid into chaos.

Blair denied what was happening. 'There was no inevitability about the violence,' he would write. Even when he wrote this – seven years later – he did not recognise that a power vacuum was the predictable consequence of Saddam being deposed. Without a dictator, few Arab nations have remained peaceful. The pre-war intelligence failure about WMDs was all one with Blair's misunderstanding of Iraq. In 2010, he denied that the country's violent collapse 'lay in planning failures [before the invasion] to rebuild Iraq. It isn't true . . . It's a delusion.' He explained that 'The truth is that we did not anticipate the role of al-Qaeda or Iran' in organising an insurrection. In actual fact, he had been deaf to loud warnings of exactly those dangers.

No other foreign leader could have expected more applause than Blair received in Washington on 17 July. 'Our ultimate weapon is not our guns but our beliefs,' he told his congressional audience. 'We are fighting for the inalienable right of humankind to be free.' He charged America to 'listen as well as lead . . . because destiny put you in this place in history, in this moment in time, and the task is yours to do'. The nineteen standing ovations, Blair noted, were partisan. Some parts of his speech were cheered by Democrats, others by Republicans. 'The problem was that this, in a way, describes my political weakness,' he would write. 'The right agreed partly, the left agreed partly. But very few in whole!'

After dinner with Bush in the White House, Blair and Cherie flew on in a celebratory mood to Tokyo, the first of seven cities to be visited over the following eight days. The journalists at the back of the plane, he hoped, would repair the image created over three pages of the *New Statesman* under the headline 'What's the Point of Tony Blair?' The lead-in stated that Blair 'doesn't really know who or what he is. More technically, he is diagnosed as a psychopath capable of reinventing himself with remarkable dexterity, like an actor.' The magazine's owner was Geoffrey Robinson, the disgraced former paymaster general.

During the flight, David Manning woke him. 'Very bad news,' he said. David Kelly had been found dead in woods near his home. Suicide was suspected. 'It was truly a ghastly moment,' Blair reflected. A firestorm was inevitable. Within an hour he had agreed with Charlie Falconer, his friend the Lord Chancellor, that any inquest should be chaired by a judge rather than a coroner. The judge would consider all the circumstances, including the compilation of the dossier that might have contributed to Kelly's suicide.

Lawyer to lawyer, Blair and Falconer knew that no judge was impartial. Both recalled John Major's folly in 1992 of appointing Richard Scott to investigate the export of arms to Iraq. From the outset, Scott conducted an exhaustive inquiry aimed pointedly at humiliating Major's government. Four years later, his report provided invaluable ammunition for Robin Cook to demolish the Conservatives' reputation. To avoid that fate, Blair and Falconer agreed that the ideal choice would be someone sympathetic to Labour's cause. Three hours after Kelly's death, while Blair was still flying towards Japan, Falconer personally interviewed and then appointed Brian Hutton, a former Lord Chief Justice of Northern Ireland, to start work within three weeks. Hutton had a reputation as a steadfast bastion of the Ulster Establishment whose judgements had favoured servants of state rather than the media, but he had also once ruled against the armed services. 'His sobriety guaranteed that he would do no favours to the clamour,' noted Andrew Turnbull. With that agreed, Blair walked to the back of the plane to announce the news to the accompanying journalists.

To scotch his branding as a 'liar' manufacturing spin and deceit, he would portray that moment in the arena as an example of him being 'utterly transparent'. However, in that contest he fell at the first hurdle, and to the newspaper he feared more than any other – the *Daily Mail*.

'Why did you authorise the leaking of the name?' he was asked by Paul Eastham, a political reporter.

'That is completely untrue,' replied Blair, apparently forgetting his comment to Kevin Tebbit on 8 July that 'Alastair will explain to you what we've decided.'

'Have you got blood on your hands?' Eastham went on.

Blair's face froze and, without saying a word, he terminated the interview.

In subsequent speeches, he characterised the media as a 'feral beast just tearing people and reputations to bits'. The greater transparency introduced by him since 1997, especially the Freedom of Information Act and his regular press conferences, had, he believed, only increased distrust. He was oblivious to the backlash by *Daily Mail* journalists over Campbell's manipulation of the newspapers and also their irritation at the pro-Labour bias in the BBC's newsroom, a direct legacy of John Birt's eight years as director of the corporation.

The television pictures of Blair arriving in Japan portrayed a shattered man who, the unkind would observe, was clinging to the wreckage. In London, Campbell's staff blamed the *Daily Mail*, the BBC and the rest of the media for provoking Kelly's suicide. Privately, Campbell was angry that Blair 'dropped us in it like that' for hinting that it was he who had released Kelly's name.

Blair was realistic. In a telephone call to Lord Levy, he 'sounded utterly devastated'. 'When will all this end? What am I going to do?' he asked. His chief fund-raiser offered no answer.

Blair returned to London intent on changing Downing Street. Those who were writing him off would discover that he was to be relaunched. At Carole Caplin's suggestion, Cherie had allowed *Marie Claire* magazine to publish photographs of her in her bedroom having lipstick painted on, with her knickers, cosmetics and tights scattered about the dressing table. Few could understand what impression the prime minister's wife intended to convey. Fiona Millar's scorn had provoked an argument, and Cherie decided that Millar, always dithering about the date of her departure, should finally leave.

After urging Campbell to stay and fight, Blair realised his spokesman's tenure was also coming to an end. 'It's gone too far,' he told Mandelson. 'He's totally headstrong. In the end, I think he's just got too big for his boots.' In the future, Blair would be relieved that Campbell no longer had the opportunity to 'rampage through the media like a mad axeman'. Next, he summoned Tebbit. He wanted the permanent secretary to know, he said in a five-minute conversation, that the MoD had been 'wrongly put in the frame as part of a conspiracy'. He added, 'You acted honourably, and I take full responsibility.' Tebbit did not place a cynical interpretation on Blair's expression of faith. On the contrary, he was grateful for the recognition.

Michael Howard, the former Tory home secretary, would recall Campbell's era without nostalgia. Blair's publicity king, he said, looking directly at his target during a television discussion, 'lied and bullied his way across our political life and has done more than anyone else to lower the tone of British politics in the last ten years'. Campbell did not flinch. Blair, he knew, had changed the nature of British politics and won. The result was what mattered.

For six years Blair's instinctive savvy had dominated the Labour Party, humbled the Tories, charmed Fleet Street and enthused the electorate enough to bring him two landslide victories, but now he needed a new team to fashion a major revival. Campbell was replaced by David Hill, an unemotional operator. To find new strategies that would reunite the party, Blair also appointed Geoff Mulgan to replace Andrew Adonis. The prime minister had difficulty in harnessing all the ideas offered by the dozens of task forces and policy units, and the irrepressible Mulgan was eager to deliver what he called a 'long-term strategy on policy' to restore people's trust. But the bad news kept on coming.

Areas of northern Iraq had become an inferno. Every week, rival religious armies – Shias against Sunnis – were killing hundreds of civilians. Across Whitehall, officials reflected that Blair had relied on an ideological American president who had deluded himself about the aftermath of war. The assurances to Bush by his military chiefs, intelligence agencies and secretaries of state were dust. Yet, in exchange for supporting America, Blair's influence was waning. His huge risk, officials noted, had produced nothing in return. On the contrary, Britain's relations with leaders in Europe and the Middle East were suffering.

In 1999, Blair had protested that in the past the West had talked too much about exit strategies: 'But having made a commitment we cannot simply walk away once the fight is over.' Now, despite diminishing influence in Washington, he refused to restore Britain's status by funding any more than 9,000 British troops stationed in southern

Iraq, compared to Washington's deployment of 130,000 soldiers in the north. He was ignoring Colin Powell's homily that 'If you break it, you own it.' Contrary to a pledge he had made in November 2002 to the three Iraqi experts he had consulted, he was unwilling to spend the additional billions of pounds required to stabilise southern Iraq. His only concession was to consider delaying the final withdrawal. In Westminster, Blair appeared to be isolated, standing practically alone.

THIRTY-FOUR

Sabotage and Survival

Governing meant being able to defuse any media outcry, not least over how many people should be allowed to enter Britain. To Blair's relief, David Blunkett was finally bringing the immigration controversy under control. Not by reducing numbers – more migrants were arriving than ever before – but by announcing raids on bogus colleges, exposing sham marriages, closing Sangatte and converting illegal asylum-seekers into legitimate employees with work permits. In 2003, the official number of asylum-seekers had fallen by 40 per cent from the previous year to 61,050, but this was still three times higher than targeted and was costing the country over £2 billion every year. Naturally, Blair would not mention that the amnesty for 50,000 asylum-seekers had been quietly extended during the year to include over 150,000 foreigners living illegally in Britain. Managed migration was working.

His next step was to allow entry from the eight countries that would be joining the EU in 2004. Other EU countries had decided to place a seven-year delay on allowing A8 nationals entry to work. Blair and Blunkett decided to ignore that restriction. In October 2003, Beverley Hughes, the new minister responsible for immigration, directed IND officials in Sheffield to 'wave through' applications for work permits, even on the spurious grounds that the migrants intended to establish a business in Britain. This lack of proper scrutiny, Hughes believed, had been approved by Bill Jeffrey, who was still IND's director. He would later deny knowing about his department's decision.

As thousands of East Europeans arrived, Blunkett embraced immigration expert Sarah Spencer's argument, hoping to 'shift the debate into positive attitudes towards migrants'. That November, he arranged to appear on *Newsnight*. For the first time, he would not pander to the public's anger. 'There is no obvious upper limit on migration,' he told his astonished audience. Britain, he said, was always 'crowded' and the net inflow of 172,000 was sustainable. In fact, that calendar year the net increase was 350,000. An uproar followed. 'I made a mistake going on *Newsnight*,' he would later admit.

At the time, Blunkett's appearance reflected an unseen crisis in Blair's relationship with his chancellor. Gordon Brown expected the combination of the failure to find WMDs and Brian Hutton's report to terminate Blair's premiership. Despite the growing economy and improvements in the NHS, he planned finally to dispatch the besieged leader. His punchline during a subversive speech at the 2003 party conference – 'We are best when we are Labour' – had electrified dissatisfied loyalists. Blair's evangelical performance the following day – 'We are best when we are boldest' – and an appeal to support modernisation sealed their irreconcilable schism by starkly omitting any reference to Brown. The polls, for all Blair's personal unpopularity, showed Labour's lead rising. So long as Blair led the party, the economy remained strong and Iain Duncan Smith remained the unimpressive alternative prime minister, the Tories had little chance of success.

On 5 November, Blair excluded Brown from the party's national executive, which would be planning the 2005 general election campaign. He also telephoned Alan Milburn and, in the ex-minister's words, 'started playing footsie with me to get me back' to replace Brown. Blair was set on demoting or, if necessary, dismissing Brown from his government after the election. Yet, the following day, he agreed to meet him over a dinner hosted by John Prescott to hammer out an agreement on the handover.

Brown had good reason to arrive at the meeting suspicious of his colleague's intentions. After the fracas in 1994, Blair had agreed to leave after two terms. Now, worn down by office, the aftermath of war and by Brown himself, he appeared to be persuaded that his rival was entitled to fight the next election. At the end of their conversation, Blair agreed to resign in 2004 if Brown 'became a better Gordon' by fully supporting the reforms for the NHS, academies and tuition fees. Plus Brown was required to guarantee not to mention their agreement to anyone else, especially Ed Balls and Ed Miliband. Brown agreed to the conditions. Prescott, who had been absent during the haggling, was told on his return of Blair's agreement to depart within one year. The terms, Prescott would recall, were 'ambiguous and on condition'. Some time later, Peter Mandelson heard from Blair 'that a deal had actually been done'.

Thirteen days later, on the next stage of the legislation to introduce foundation hospitals, the government's majority in the Commons fell to seventeen. The media's portrayal of Blair as weak seemed to be justified. He was also blamed for the death of soldiers in Iraq because they lacked body armour. Unable to conceal his fatigue, he admitted to the media that his plight was caused by 'a thousand people kicking your backside morning, noon and night'.

The new blows of attrition, Blair suspected, were the result of Brown failing to keep to their agreement. Both Balls and Miliband clearly knew about the pact, and were openly encouraging Brown's supporters to oppose the prime minister. The final test of the chancellor's loyalty would be the vote on tuition fees. In principle, the Tories should have supported the government, but they could not resist being party to the anti-Blair plots. Although Brown had conceded that his alternative graduate tax was flawed, his lieutenants were marshalling the anti-government vote among those Labour MPs not concerned about universities' finances but who wanted to demonstrate their distrust of Blair.

Looking at the numbers, Blair needed Brown's support to survive. The vote was set for 27 January 2004. 'Better to fight, lose and go down than give in,' said Charles Clarke. Blair half agreed: he would fight to win. 'Make or break' was the sentiment around Westminster, and Blair's nervousness was obvious to those listening to his 'back me or sack me' conversations as he fought for his survival. One hundred and sixty Labour MPs had threatened to rebel, wiping out his current majority of 161. 'There will be absolutely no retreat,' he told a press conference. 'Of course my authority is on the line.' Until the last moment, he wondered whether Brown would go over the top to defeat his own government. 'I think politicians who cave in are weak,' said Clarke, who had helped Neil Kinnock confront Labour's left wing.

Although surrounded by sympathisers, Blair stood alone. Only a fellow leader, he reasoned, could understand his plight. How, he asked Bill Clinton, had he survived facing impeachment? The essence, replied the former president, was that he didn't 'let it dominate his view of his presidency'. Blair commented, 'This is where [Clinton's] resilience was so fundamental to his success and survival. He used to tell me that every day he got up, determined to carry on governing.' He intended to copy his mentor.

On the morning of the vote, Brown discussed with Balls and Miliband whether he should defeat Blair. On the same day, a Downing Street spokesman persuaded Alice Miles of *The Times* to write that 'relations between the Chancellor and the Prime Minister are said to be very good at the moment'. In the event, Blair won by just five votes. The Tories were jubilant. Overhanging Blair's fears was the certainty that his fate in the Commons would be on the line again the next day. To his good fortune, having their divisions exposed had assuaged his party's anger, and his MPs returned to Westminster the following day in less venomous mood.

Hutton was due to publish his report that day, 28 January. The witnesses' testimony indicated that Blair and Alastair Campbell would be pilloried. Exactly five months earlier, Blair had returned from his summer holidays in Cliff Richard's villa in Barbados to give his evidence. Astutely, Charlie Falconer had retained Jonathan Sumption QC, one of Britain's most accomplished lawyers, to represent the government. He would be helped in preparing the government's case by David Omand.

By contrast, reflecting the carelessness with which the BBC had treated the David Kelly saga from the outset, the corporation's case was argued by a workhorse lawyer burdened by lackadaisical BBC executives offering ill-considered testimony. Blair was assured that Hutton would be presented with a convincing argument that his administration had behaved with exemplary behaviour in exposing Kelly, a man guilty of breaking the trust he owed to the government. Regarding the dossier, Blair turned to the judge and said, 'hand on heart', it had not been sexed up.

Sumption's presentation transformed the inquiry into a trial of the BBC. In cross-examination, the corporation's executives – in particular Greg Dyke, the pro-Labour director general, and Andrew Gilligan – undermined their own case. Nevertheless, the oral and written evidence presented to Hutton by the civil servants conclusively established the corruption of the JIC's intelligence by the authors of the dossiers to suit the government's purpose. After Kevin Tebbit testified that at a meeting on 8 July the 'prime minister wanted something done' about identifying Kelly to the media, Blair had reason to fear Hutton's judgement.

To the surprise of those who had sat through the hearings, Hutton ignored Tebbit's testimony. In his report the judge ruled, contrary to the evidence, that 'There was no dishonourable or duplicitous strategy by the government covertly to leak Dr Kelly's name to the media.' In a similar vein, Hutton disregarded the written and oral evidence describing an intense relationship between Campbell and John Scarlett. The intelligence chief, declared Hutton, had only been 'subconsciously influenced' by Campbell. The judge also discounted the evidence from other intelligence officials – especially Brian Jones at the MoD – that Scarlett had been warned not to exaggerate the evidence. Hutton's only criticism about the dossier's distortions focused on the fictitious long-range rockets armed with WMDs. That intelligence was 'unhelpful' but unimportant to his inquiry. In his opinion, he had to decide only whether the government, as alleged by Gilligan, 'probably knew that the intelligence was wrong'. By focusing entirely on that narrow question, Hutton avoided the more important issues – namely, why the intelligence described in the dossier was mistaken and whether Blair had ordered Kelly to be named. To have recalled Blair to answer Tebbit's revelation, he said later, would have been 'simply playing to the gallery', resulting in 'glaring headlines'.

By wholeheartedly accepting Sumption's narrative of events, Hutton concluded that Blair and Campbell had not deliberately 'sexed up' the dossier. To justify his bias that the two men had not exaggerated the intelligence, the judge used a definition of 'sexed up' that did not tally with the meaning intended by Gilligan. In conclusion, he praised the government, Campbell and all the civil servants for behaving with the utmost honour, honesty and professionalism, while Kelly, Dyke, Gilligan and the BBC management were excoriated. 'Too good to be true,' Blair said after reading an early copy of the judgement. Some were suspicious about his sanguine reaction, and became more so when the report was given to the *Sun* on the day before its publication. Many suspected the source of the leak to be one person in Downing Street: Campbell.

Blair had good reason to be relieved. On the same day, David Kay, the former chief UN weapons inspector who before the war had energetic-ally broadcast his conviction that Iraq possessed huge stores of nuclear and other WMDs, broke his silence. As director of the Iraq Survey Group, he had dispatched a thousand inspectors across the country to find the weapons. But now he shakenly confessed, 'It turns out we were all wrong.' Saddam, reported Kay, had effectively stopped production in 1991. That truth was irrelevant to Blair. Instead of acknowledging that he and others had made errors and moving on, he preferred to slay his critics.

His final hurdle that day was a vote in the Commons. Iain Duncan Smith had been replaced in October by Michael Howard, an accom-plished lawyer seen by some as a transitional choice. Blair risked being cornered by Howard about Hutton.

Twenty years earlier, Howard had been puzzled by Blair's member-ship of the Labour Party. In 1983, he had invited Blair and Cherie for dinner at his home. His purpose was to prise an explanation from Blair as to why he had not joined the Conservatives. After all, Blair's father would have been a Conservative MP had he not suffered a stroke, and Blair himself would admit to the *Guardian* in 1995 that he understood the Labour Party only after he became its leader. Blair clearly enjoyed the evening, while Cherie hated every moment. She was the reason why, Howard decided, her husband had opted for Labour.

Since then, Howard had grown to like his fellow lawyer. While prime minister, Blair had sent a generous handwritten note to the mother of Jonathan Aitken, a Conservative MP, after she suffered a fall, and an endearing personal letter of condolence to the widow of Alan Clark, another maverick Tory politician. Both had been grateful for his thoughtfulness. While Blair regarded Howard as an old, grating right-winger, the Conservative leader was charmed by his rival's genius at the Dispatch Box. Those personal considerations influenced Howard while he considered his response to Hutton's conclusions.

Given just over an hour before the debate to read the massive report, Howard had insufficient time to translate what he called Hutton's 'mandarin language' and identify 'a whitewash'. He was also compromised: as a lawyer he disliked challenging a judge's honesty; he had supported the war; and his staff, especially David Cameron, who read the report next to him, dismissed Iraq as a non-issue. The combination muted a normally aggressive politician as he listened to Blair's defiance: 'The allegation that I or anyone else lied to this House or deliberately misled the country by falsifying intelligence on WMDs is itself the real lie. And I simply ask that those that made it and those who have repeated it over all these months now withdraw it fully, openly and clearly.' Blair threw down the gauntlet. 'Opportunism', he scoffed at Howard, 'is not the same as leadership.' Watched by Cherie from the gallery, he gracefully deflected the serious and true allegations against him with humour. Loudly supported by the same Labour rebels who twenty-four hours earlier had sought to bring down his government, he offered a challenge: would Howard dare call him a liar?

The Tory leader ducked the opportunity. Presenting an inconsistent

argument and throwing wild punches, he cast discord across the opposition benches. Hisses and boos interrupted his lament, while Blair's
grin destroyed any remaining self-confidence. But Blair's respite was
short-lived. Campbell had summoned a press conference to mark the
victory and, in his naturally brutal manner, he demanded retribution
from the BBC. His vitriol produced the immediate resignation of both
the chairman of the BBC's board of governors and the director general.
'I really didn't want that,' wrote Blair.

Instead of the report and Blair's parliamentary triumph concluding
the matter, Hutton's endorsement of the dossier's credibility – wrongly
asserting that it was based on the 'available intelligence' – aroused new
suspicions of an Establishment fix. The media's criticism of Hutton's
'whitewash' spread the existing public distrust of Blair to the judiciary
and across Whitehall. Bringing MI6 and the JIC to account for their
manifest failure remained unfinished business. Days later, Blair agreed
that Robin Butler should chair an inquiry into the accuracy of the
intelligence. After all, if he survived Hutton, there was no reason to be
concerned about a third report. On the contrary, its existence should
release the pressure on himself and guarantee a soft landing.

Surviving two critical votes within days – first tuition fees, then
Hutton – infused Blair with renewed self-confidence. All his enemies
in Parliament had been repulsed – except Brown. The two had been
arguing throughout that week. 'You've got to work with me,' Blair
urged Brown.

'Let's talk about the handover,' Brown screamed back. 'Are you fucking going or not?' Labelling Brown as psychologically flawed was an
understatement.

His promise in November, Blair admitted, had been 'unwise because
it was never going to work . . . It was an act of cowardice.' John Reid,
Mandelson and Milburn urged him to stay. All three, along with Blair,
feared a lurch to the left under Brown and, in the election war with the
Tories over tax-and-spend versus lower taxes and controls on immigration, Labour would lose. 'I knew we would be finished,' wrote Blair.

'The folly of retreat was unthinkable and precipitate withdrawal – a disaster.'

Politics was trumped by the human factor. 'Why are you still sitting here?' Ed Miliband brusquely demanded of Sally Morgan, Blair's adviser. 'Why haven't you packed up to go? There's a deal.' Blair, outraged by that discourtesy, had another consideration. He loved political power, attracting the spotlight and being surrounded by celebrities. Downing Street provided an enviably privileged lifestyle. The absence of chores, the easy travel in limousines and private jets, and the large support operation would vanish overnight. And for what? To allow an unbalanced sociopath responsible for seven years of misery to occupy the spotlight. He told Brown unequivocally their deal was off – and there was an explosion.

Blair's battle to survive produced another casualty. Blunkett's revelation about unlimited immigration had angered IND officials in Sheffield. Repeatedly, they were reprimanded for failing to deport asylum-seekers, while Beverley Hughes was obeying Blair's directive to open the door to those wanting to enter Britain. Anonymously, several IND officials contacted David Davis, the Conservatives' shadow home secretary, expressing 'disgust' at their inability to prevent mass immigration. Their alleged incompetence, wrote the officials, was not to blame; thousands were entering Britain every week because of the government's policy. Other officials told the *Sunday Times* how migrants were abusing the system to acquire welfare benefits.

Before the newspaper exposed the deception, Davis was told by a British embassy official in Bucharest that the government's own rules were being disregarded by IND officials in Sheffield. A 'one-legged Romanian who described himself as a roof tiler' had been granted a work permit. Davis wondered whether Brown and Blair were ignoring the rules to secure the migrants' votes. On reflection, he decided that the two politicians were not gerrymandering but pursuing a misguided economic strategy for growth. Neither of them seemed to realise that the low wages paid to migrants reduced the wealth of native Britons.

The *Sunday Times*' eventual report detailing the chaos in the Home Office caused uproar. Blunkett blamed Straw and the Foreign Office: 'At the beginning, Jack said everybody was welcome to come from the A8 countries and draw benefits. Now he tells Tony that we shouldn't have anyone here at all.' As a smokescreen, Blair publicly demanded new restrictions.

In the Commons, Davis probed for 'inconsistencies and lies' in the Home Office's response to his questions about fraudulent applications by Bulgarians and Romanians. Hughes replied that she was unaware of any misconduct. To her embarrassment, she was reminded that Bob Ainsworth, a Labour MP, had sent her written warnings that IND staff had been told to fast-track visa applications from specifically those countries. Similar advice had been sent by the IND to the British consul in Bucharest. Hughes denied receiving any notification that work permits were being granted contrary to the guidelines, but her statement was undermined by an internal investigation in Sheffield. Caseworkers at the IND's office, it was revealed, were assuming that applications should not be refused. 'They're over-interpreting the Bulgarians' and Romanians' entitlement to come,' Hughes was told by Bill Jeffrey. 'They're passing them on the nod. It's a surprise to me that it is being handled this way.' In the Commons, Hughes blamed her senior IND officials for being overcome by 'an excess of zeal'. 'This came out of the blue,' she said. Her misfortune was the paper trail in her office showing that she had indeed been warned.

'It's sod's law,' Blunkett told Blair. 'She's the victim of inept management and confusion.' Jeffrey, he said, was the culprit. Blair disagreed. He appreciated Jeffrey's work in Ulster. Instead, he blamed Hughes. She resigned on 1 April 2004 and was replaced by Des Browne, a Scottish supporter of Gordon Brown with limited experience of politics who now became Blair's fifth immigration minister.

In the run-up to the election, Blair knew that Labour's biggest weakness was the public support for the Tories on immigration. In that year, 589,000 migrants would be registered, the third year running that over half a million foreigners had settled in the country. Those numbers would continue until reaching a peak of 591,000 in 2010. Net immigration was five times higher than in 1997. Blair's pre-election claims in 2001 to have imposed controls were proven untrue. Tory research showed that 85 per cent of the electorate condemned the government's policy. Unusually, the Tories were supported by Trevor Phillips, the chairman of the Commission for Racial Equality, who condemned Labour's policy of multiculturalism. With the polls showing that 75 per cent of the public wanted stronger controls, the Tories were eating into Labour's lead.

To restore himself alongside the majority, Blair convened a 'work party' to produce an initiative. Des Browne anticipated his role as Blair's punchbag. 'Christians fed to the lions', was his observation as the former barrister interrogated the new minister at another immigration summit. It was a blood sport for the other participants, but there was nothing Browne could say. All the policies were in place: Sangatte had been closed; some trucks had to pass through port-side X-ray machines; and new laws had supposedly made asylum less attractive. The problem now was the judges, many of whom were lenient to those who had destroyed their identification papers or claimed to be Chinese or Iranian, making deportation impossible.

At the end of his asylum summit, Blair admitted there were 'real abuses of the immigration system' and that Britain was at a 'crunch point'. Blunkett promised a crackdown on sham marriages and bogus students – the same script he had used seven months earlier. And, to ingratiate himself with European leaders, Blair secretly decided to surrender Britain's veto over the EU's asylum policy.

THIRTY-FIVE

Confusion in the Ranks

On 18 March 2004, John Scarlett sent an email to Rod Barton, an Australian weapons inspector employed by the American Iraq Survey Group based outside Baghdad. The message reflected Blair's burden: the failure to find WMDs.

Later that month, Charles Duelfer, the leader of the Survey Group, was due to deliver a report to the US Congress. Duelfer intended to record the truth: the Iraqi weapons programme had ended in 1991 and nothing new had been produced for the next twelve years. To reduce the embarrassment, the CIA had placed Duelfer under pressure to report that Saddam's WMD programme *could* have been active in 2003, and the group would continue to search for the evidence. Scarlett joined that chase.

In his email to Barton, he urged that nine 'nuggets' be included in Duelfer's report to reinforce the belief that Saddam had been pursuing a WMD programme in 2003. 'He's trying to sex up our report,' thought Barton, a former intelligence officer. 'We cannot accept any of these.' He said later on Australian TV, 'I thought it was dishonest.' Barton resigned and watched on 30 March as Duelfer delivered an inaccurate report to Congress.

The deception failed. President Bush was compelled by Congress to initiate an investigation into the errors committed by America's intelligence agencies. This ended any hope Blair had of putting an end to the controversy. Unable to quash the continuing complaints about Brian Hutton's distortions, he had announced on 3 February that

Robin Butler, the former Cabinet secretary, would review the whole affair.

Blair's lack of respect for Butler, particularly for his willingness to accommodate his critics, was the mandarin's qualification. During John Major's premiership, Butler had probed allegedly dishonest statements by Neil Hamilton and Jonathan Aitken, two Tory MPs. As a trusting man, he acquitted both of any wrongdoing. Subsequently, both were exposed as liars. Butler had many qualities, but he was neither a sceptical nor a forensic investigator. The star schoolboy who led Harrow's Bible society would not, Blair suspected, overtly embarrass Scarlett, Richard Dearlove or himself. His safeguard was to appoint Ann Taylor, a Labour MP and chairman of the parliamentary Intelligence and Security Committee, as a member of the inquiry.

Taylor's committee had published its own report on the WMDs in September 2003. Few were surprised that she had exonerated the government, the intelligence services and Alastair Campbell. MI6 and the JIC, Taylor declared, had provided 'convincing intelligence' that Iraq was pursuing an active WMD programme, and she refused to rule out the possibility that WMDs might still be found. Blair, her report concluded, had not misled Parliament.

Blair knew the truth but remained suspicious. 'Why did he [Saddam] allow his country to be devastated to protect a myth?' he wrote in 2010. Seven years after the war, he still could not understand Saddam's self-delusion. As he later acknowledged, Saddam had destroyed his WMD capability in 1991 and intended to restart his programme once sanctions were removed. The Anglo-American bombing in December 1998 had hit worthless facilities. Possibly, Saddam was misled by his intelligence chiefs, but certainly in 2003 he was in denial about the American invasion.

The following year, Blair similarly refused to admit the truth. Instead, he repeated that the JIC's reports over many years 'assumed an active chemical and biological programme ... [and] no one seriously disputed it existed'. That inaccuracy was trivial compared to his misinterpretation of why he went to war. 'At stake', he wrote in 2010, 'was the whole future of Islam.' Iraq, he suggested, was invaded to crush 'the forces opposed to modernisation'. He failed to say that, both in 2003 and seven years later, he had continued to misunderstand that the 'liberation' of the Iraqis meant something different to him than to the Iraqis themselves. Iraqis – Sunnis, Shias, Kurds and Christians – did not yearn to replicate Westminster's liberalism. And the Sunnis feared Shiite Iran.

To protect his vulnerability in the aftermath of the war, Blair took care of his core group. In particular, he approved Scarlett's appointment as Dearlove's successor. The selection of a retiring JIC chairman to head MI6 was unprecedented. More surprisingly, Scarlett was appointed before Butler had completed his inquiry. To some, the choice appeared to be an inducement to secure Scarlett's loyalty during Butler's inquiry, while Whitehall insiders said that Scarlett had the field to himself once Nigel Inkster, the alternative candidate, performed badly during the interview.

Regardless of his managerial qualities to reform MI6, Scarlett had shown manifestly poor judgement before the war. Among Butler's tasks was to establish why Scarlett had excluded his conclusion that the evidence for WMDs was 'sporadic and patchy' from the published dossier. To bury the inconsistencies, Blair directed Butler to limit his inquiry into the mundane techniques of intelligence gathering. This restriction was successfully challenged by Michael Howard, and the inquiry's remit was extended to include the 'use of intelligence'. These three extra words empowered Butler to look carefully into Blair's relations with Scarlett and Dearlove. Whether Butler was minded to embarrass the three protagonists was unknown – as was whether Blair understood the growing crisis enveloping Iraq.

On 10 October, the prime minister attended a service of Thanksgiving at St Paul's Cathedral for Iraq's war dead. Years before, there had been a parade through the City of London to commemorate the Falklands war, but Blair knew that similar triumphalism would be inappropriate. At the reception after the service, he encountered Air Marshal Brian Burridge.

'Is this all doable in Iraq?' he asked.

'Yes,' replied Burridge, 'but this is a three-brigade war and we're down to one.'

Blair looked blank. With hindsight, Burridge realised that his advice was wrong. Even three brigades of soldiers – about 15,000 men – could not have resolved the festering violence around Basra. Burridge had witnessed the irreconcilable divisions of Iraqi society. No one in London, he realised, had understood the loyalty of the local Shias to the Iranian government or their enmity towards the Sunni government in Baghdad. Blair still believed that those religious differences could be smoothed over by the British military. Burridge, like other senior officers, recognised the impotence of soldiers when it came to reconciling political enemies.

Such insight was not unique. Four years earlier, Colonel Paul Gibson had warned about the army's mistakes in the Balkans. His sanitised post-operation report had been ignored but, in the aftermath of the invasion of Iraq, he noticed the army make similar mistakes. 'Soldiers only see as far as the horizon because that's how far they can walk,' reflected an admiral anticipating the consequences of serial miscalculations.

The visit to Downing Street by General John Abizaid, the American commander responsible for Iraq, highlighted that unfortunate truth.

'The overall situation is getting bad,' he told Blair and General Walker.

'I'm sorry about that,' Blair replied. 'What will you do?'

He listened to Abizaid's fears about violence spiralling out of control, and his concerns over the torturous restoration of water and electricity and the struggle to impose a representative government. To his visitors, Blair appeared to be either embarrassed by the failure to find WMDs or nonplussed by the slide towards lawlessness. Abizaid's departure was followed by an awkward conversation between Blair and Walker. Both men were groping for an explanation.

On 11 March, in a sign of what was now in store for Europe, 191 commuters were killed after Islamic terrorists set off explosions on the

Madrid rail network. In the general election three days later, Spain's governing People's Party unexpectedly fell. Blair had reason to fear similar retribution. To reassure the British public that there was a reason for the war, he flew from the funerals in Madrid to Libya to meet Colonel Muammar Gaddafi. The dictator responsible for financing terrorism in Ulster and planting a bomb on the Pan Am flight to New York that blew up over Lockerbie had been persuaded by MI6 to accept Western aid in exchange for surrendering his WMDs. The TV pictures for what was called 'the deal in the desert' gave Blair much-needed credibility.

As a show of goodwill, just before Blair arrived in Libya MI6 and the CIA organised the kidnap of a Libyan jihadi and his wife, who were living in Thailand, and arranged their transportation to Libya for interrogation. The couple's evidence was to be used in British courts to obtain the deportation to Tripoli of other Libyan dissidents. Simultaneously, MI6 and Libyan intelligence began joint operations against Libyans living in Britain who were members of the Libyan Islamic Fighting Group. Letters sent by Mark Allen, the head of MI6's counter-terrorism section, to Moussa Koussa, the head of Gaddafi's intelligence, included the warning that their agreement needed to be kept secret and not be 'discovered by lawyers or human rights organisations and the media'. Despite Jack Straw's later denials, the operations would have required his approval and, by implication, Blair's too, although he would deny 'any recollection at all'. The aftermath of the war was proving to be as murky as the fifteen months before the invasion.

Blair was now challenged by Labour's left wing over his loyalty towards Israel. Tony Benn and his followers argued that 9/11 was the direct result of the Israeli occupation of Palestine. Their scenario, developed since the Iraq war, described Blair's support of Israel as justifying the Islamic grievance against the West. In reply, Blair argued that al-Qaeda was using Palestine as an excuse to destroy Western liberalism. His reasoning was echoed by Israeli politicians. Like Blair, they argued that civilisation could be protected only by defeating Islamic terror – which simply evoked more anger towards Blair among Labour's left wing. So many countries, tribes, sects, armed groups and politicians were fighting for power within Iraq that Blair's regular refrain of the war being a battle of 'good against evil' baffled his military advisers.

The prime minister was struggling to come to terms with a mini-lecture from General Mike Jackson. 'Without a political objective', Jackson had told him, 'the army cannot define their enemy. And the army cannot offer a solution in Iraq because you're resisting the chiefs' request to define "victory".'

To avoid that question, Blair danced around 'conditions' and 'solutions' and steered away from asking Walker for detailed plans on the army's fate or his view on the consequences of Gordon Brown's refusal to provide more money. Since British casualties were still low, Walker in turn resisted asking Blair to clarify the government's long-term ambition. 'What good would it do to whinge?' he reflected. 'Blair had his divided interests, between Britain and Iraq, and we had to deliver what we promised.' The general's perfunctory briefings always ended with Blair's solicitous question, 'And how are the men and women in the armed forces?' Walker realised later that Blair never asked about the civilian disturbances and deaths. The mismatch partly stemmed from the unreliable predictions by MI6 and the JIC on whether the violence in Basra would escalate. The continuing poverty of intelligence reflected the agencies' inability to penetrate the Iraqi groups causing the violence. Ill prepared for the mayhem, British soldiers were haphazardly shooting back at attackers, inaccurately describing the hostilities as the actions of criminals rather than correctly identifying them as the result of political attrition between religious militias.

That misinterpretation undermined the debate in London. During his discussions with both David Manning, Blair's trusted envoy, newly posted as ambassador in Washington, and his replacement in Downing Street, Nigel Sheinwald, Blair rarely focused for long on the government's inability to impose its will on Basra. He preferred to ramble across topics rather than host aggressive arguments about identifiable follies. Since Andrew Turnbull, David Omand, Kevin Tebbit and other senior officials were excluded from Downing Street's discussions about Iraq, the army's fate languished and a new crisis unfolded.

Just as Admiral Nigel Essenhigh had predicted, the shortfall in the military's budget in 2004 was £1.9 billion. George Robertson had created an unaffordable dream in 1998. Only Blair could end the day-dreaming, but after Anji Hunter's departure Walker and Geoff Hoon found access to Downing Street much harder. Both blamed Jonathan Powell for being 'very difficult', while in their opinion Sheinwald had already proved to be 'unhelpful'. Then Gordon Brown demanded more cuts in what Walker called 'all big-ticket items', including 38 per cent from the helicopter budget. For some weeks in spring 2004, Walker tried to negotiate with Blair but found him 'inattentive'.

He was not the only one to feel frustrated. Vice Admiral Rory McLean, responsible for resources in the MoD, finally got Powell's agreement to demonstrate to Blair the Network Enabled Capability programme, a sophisticated communications system that would enable marksmen to identify enemy positions. The Treasury had cancelled funding for its development. At the end of a twenty-minute presentation, Blair asked, 'What's the effect if you don't have the money?'

McLean realised that the prime minister had not read the single-page brief. 'Our military cannot operate without this equipment,' he replied.

Soon after, Walker was told that Blair had approved more funds, but then nothing happened. 'The mattress mice would get at it,' quipped Walker, politely blaming civil servants rather than Blair for the lack of action.

One Friday afternoon, after Whitehall's mechanisms to settle the financial dispute had been exhausted, Blair was told that Walker had issued a draconian ultimatum: matters would have to improve or he would resign. Blair invited the general to Chequers for Sunday lunch. Other than General Charles Guthrie, he found all military personnel a strange breed. He could not grasp that, once committed to an oper-ation, a soldier willingly faced death in pursuit of success. Nor could

Blair appreciate that the military found politicians incomprehensible.

'I've never been able to work Mike out,' he told the general's wife at a dinner in Downing Street.

'We've been married thirty-three years,' Lady Walker replied, 'and he's the most straightforward person you can want to meet.'

Blair smiled the Blair smile.

Over the lunch at Chequers, Walker showed the prime minister the government's list of proposed cuts. 'I've drawn a line halfway down the page,' he explained. 'We'll accept the cuts on top. If you go further, you'll have to look for a new set of chiefs.'

'We can't have that,' said Blair. 'You're going to have to see Gordon.'

'But he's your man.'

'Well, there's nothing I can do.'

'I wouldn't put up with my officers behaving like that.'

'I can't do any more,' replied Blair, without noticeable embarrassment.

The following night, over a glass of whisky, Tebbit answered Walker's question, 'What should my resignation figure be?' Armed with the critical amount that the MoD needed, Walker met Brown in the Treasury. A small, spartan room had been allocated, with one table and two uncomfortable chairs.

'Chancellor, I must tell you that the armed forces don't like you,' were the general's opening remarks. 'You've never once visited a military base, and they don't like it.'

Brown did not reply. In the recent Budget, he had announced a spending and borrowing spree to win the election and pave the way for his premiership. To prevent Walker's resignation, he had no choice but to surrender; he also promised to visit the military. Over the following two years, Walker regularly sent Brown invitations; none was ever accepted.

Walker did not trust Brown's concessions. To underline that his ultimatum was still in place, McLean called Jonathan Powell. General Walker, he said, would not stand on a rostrum with Hoon at the parade the following Wednesday unless the government agreed to provide an additional £1.9 billion over the following three years. On a Sunday afternoon, Hoon sat in his office holding one telephone receiver connected to Blair to one ear, while listening to Brown shouting his refusal to reduce the cuts into the other. 'Blair', said Hoon afterwards, 'had lost control over the government's spending.'

So it fell to Hoon to repeat to Brown the political consequences of Walker leaving. Early that evening, McLean was told that Brown had ordered, 'Get that fucking bearded admiral here now.' McLean aborted a visit to the theatre and drove to the Treasury. By the end of the evening, Brown had agreed to hand over some real money and, by 'some financial tricks', had conjured up other funds. Late the following night, with the chancellor threatened by the chiefs' resignations, a settlement was finalised in a conference call between Brown, Hoon and Tebbit, who was driving back from a weekend in Buckinghamshire. Just minutes before the printer's deadline for producing the Budget statement, Brown bad-temperedly agreed to extra money, although it fell woefully short of what was needed.

The Budget speech on 17 March was hailed as a triumph for the chancellor. That evening, Brown again demanded Blair's resignation, threatening that otherwise he would, as Powell noted, 'bring down the government immediately after the next election'. Campbell advised Blair to go, while Peter Mandelson said he should stay, although he would write, 'I wasn't sure that Tony had the spirit to fight on.' To scotch a coup, Blair told Brown he would announce his departure immediately: he would go in the autumn. Brown feared that would allow sufficient time for a rival for the leadership to emerge and urged Blair to delay his announcement.

Brown's worries momentarily became a sideshow. On 28 April, photographs appeared in the press of American soldiers humiliating Iraqis in Abu Ghraib prison. Simultaneously, the first accounts emerged of the CIA transporting suspected Islamic terrorists through Britain to Poland and other countries, where information was being extracted under torture. Despite the conclusive evidence of the flights landing in Britain, Blair and Straw denied any knowledge of such 'secret renditions'. Official documents would challenge their denials.

Torture, terrorism and violent massacres in Iraq, and no WMDs: Blair badly needed to reassert his authority. His solution was his meeting in the Libyan desert with Colonel Gaddafi in March 2004. Not everyone was convinced about the distinction between Gaddafi, Saddam and Osama bin Laden, but Blair felt triumphant. Nevertheless, still insecure and preparing for his resignation, he agreed that a friend of Cherie should look for a house for them in London. Angry with himself even now for having sold his Islington home for a mere £615,000 in 1997, he would buy a house near Marble Arch for £3.65 million, financed almost entirely by a mortgage. For the prime minister to be indebted to a bank was a conflict of interest, but the impropriety was never raised by Turnbull. It was at this point that Blair again told Brown he would 'probably' not fight a third election.

Blair was not sleeping and was suffering from an irregular heartbeat that required a minor operation. Stripped of his make-up, he looked haggard, with greying hair and falling weight. His children were also suffering, and a crisis involving his daughter was concealed by the media. Those who believed Iain Duncan Smith had been unwise to criticise Blair's exposure of his children to the spotlight in 2002 – 'I think Tony Blair uses his children ruthlessly,' he had said, 'I think it is wrong' – reconsidered their opinion.

In the tumult, Cherie reinforced her husband's survival gene. At the end of April, Blair told some Cabinet ministers that he intended to serve a full third term. Then he said the opposite. 'I am not seeing Tony give way to that man,' Cherie countered. 'I will stop him moving in here with everything I've got.' At her behest, on 11 May, over dinner at Wiltons, the fish restaurant in St James's, Michael Levy urged Blair not to resign. Four days later, his pleas appeared to have been rejected when John Prescott, in his clumsy manner, volunteered that 'the plates are shifting' – meaning that Blair was resigning.

With so many trusted loyalists gone, Blair's remaining supporters were beset by fatigue, disillusion and distrust. 'He's in a fight for his political life,' commented David Blunkett. But, at the end of May, Blair bowed to Cherie's exhortations and decided to fight on. Curiously, in September, Cherie would tell *Richard & Judy*, while promoting her book on television, 'There never was a moment when he was going to resign. I can assure you if he had done, I would have known.' Many witnesses, including Levy, were surprised by her assertion but understood the reasons for it.

The omens seemed good. The local and European elections in early June were bad for Labour but not good enough for Michael Howard to be confident of victory. In the election year, Brown would bribe the electors. The Tories, Blair knew, could not overturn the 2001 landslide unless the middle class preferred Howard to himself. For many reasons, including Howard's recent support for the Iraq invasion and his own declaration of war against Islamic terror, that was unlikely. Despite all the horrors, there was hope for a third term. And then another Iraqi time bomb ignited.

On 24 June, six British military policemen were murdered by a mob in Basra. Their deaths ended the army's 'light touch' policing. This was the moment for Blair to reconsider the 1998 strategic defence review. The shortage of money had denied the army a range of essentials, including cooks, communications equipment, hospitals and bomb-proof vehicles. If informed advisers had been allowed access to Blair, he would have been persuaded to commission a new review and abandon the construction of two aircraft carriers. But his military leaders were squabbling.

The mutual dislike between the chiefs was professional and personal. Air Marshal Jock Stirrup's RAF had been criticised for missing most of its targets during the Iraq war; Admiral Alan West was being pilloried for letting no one get between himself and his mirror; while General Walker, himself characterised by another chief as 'a plodding infantryman', disliked General Jackson, the chief of the army. And Tebbit was disliked by Blair for his continual demands for more money.

Aggravating their distrust was Powell, proudly preventing them access to his master.

Among the excluded was Admiral West. After three and a half years as head of the navy and marines, he had never been invited to Downing Street. 'If I'd been a member of a pop group, I would have been invited to Downing Street,' he said, stung by Blair's refusal to engage with him as an individual. However, he eventually found himself invited there by Cherie. His misgivings were resolved when she explained that she wanted to launch a ship. Twelve Type 45 destroyers had been commissioned in 1998. West knew that the government wanted to cut the number to eight, so he wrote to Downing Street that Cherie had been nominated to launch the twelfth ship. The destroyer was not built.

Blair's detachment screened him from the confused chain of command that was debilitating the military. 'There's a fifth wheel on the car,' complained an admiral to Walker. Effectively, the three chiefs, their headquarters staff and senior officials at the MoD were excluded from directly influencing any operation, including Iraq. The responsibility for wars was assigned to the head of Northwood (the headquarters for military operations), reporting to Walker. As the chief of the defence staff, Walker had no obligation to consult the heads of the three services. Blair was uninterested in both that institutional muddle and another deficiency among Britain's military: compared to the American army, the intellect of British officers was unimpressive. One crippling consequence of that was the army's blind trust that operations in Iraq would be identical to their policing of Ulster. That error could have been identified had Blair met officers other than Walker and had he also realised the necessity of a robust government machine to direct the military. Accordingly, he seemed to be unconcerned that General Jackson, the army's chief, had no direct control over the commanding officers posted to Iraq on six-month tours. Before leaving, none of those men was adequately briefed about the growing insurgency, and none was exposed to Arabists outside Northwood. None of the senior officers in Northwood had studied Iraq's history, nor did they speak the local languages. That casual approach was mocked by the American commanders in Iraq. Without exception, they were higher ranked and better educated than their British counterparts, and each decision made in Baghdad was subject to approval from headquarters in America. By comparison, communications between Northwood and Basra were slipshod.

The British suffered another weakness. Like Jackson, the commanding officers dispatched to Basra were fixated on drawing from their experiences in Ulster. None had fought in a foreign country or killed an enemy in battle. The army's inexperience would have been less onerous had Blair not decided to increase Britain's military obligations.

Blair arrived at the G8 summit at Sea Island on the American east coast on 6 June, dismissive of the criticism that he was blindly supporting Bush's policies without having any influence on their outcome. Over the previous weeks, the MoD had briefed journalists that the army would stay in Iraq 'for however long it takes', but then briefed them about plans for a 'speedy exit' under the banner 'Mission Accomplished'. The contradiction reflected the decisions being handed down from No. 10.

Blair's response to American criticism was an agreement to send 3,000 more soldiers to Iraq. On his return, he consulted Walker, who told him that the army's plight had worsened. He doubted that he could send the additional troops and he had been 'shocked' by the technology developed by the Iraqi militias to make bombs: 'They had taken six months compared to the IRA needing thirty years.' As the violence escalated, more British soldiers had been killed. Facing an unknown future in Iraq and the certainty of reductions in the defence budget, Walker reckoned that the British army had 'reached a fork in the road'. The troops were unable to maintain security and were fighting to survive. They were on borrowed time, he told Blair, so the best policy was to cut and run. 'That was the plan at the beginning,' Walker said. 'But now . . .?'

Blair was obdurate. Regardless of money and men, he intended to stay in Iraq at least until the end of 2005. The extra soldiers did not materialise, yet three weeks later he announced another commitment. Despite the public's disenchantment with war, out of the blue he pledged to increase Britain's forces in Afghanistan.

Over the previous two years, NATO's involvement there had become diffuse. After the defeat of the Taliban in November 2001, American special forces had continued their search for Osama bin Laden in the Tora Bora mountains. Shrewdly, Washington had followed the advice of the hawkish Paul Wolfowitz. 'One of the lessons of history', he said, 'is if you go in, don't stay too long because they don't tend to like foreigners.' Separately, in the remainder of Afghanistan, some NATO countries, including Britain, had deployed Provincial Reconstruction Teams (PRTs) to suppress the narcotics trade. Playing on Blair's antagonism towards Afghanistan's heroin traffic, George Robertson, the NATO secretary general, had urged him in front of Jackson to 'do better in Afghanistan and put a footprint across the whole country'. Otherwise, said Robertson, NATO's reputation was in danger because so little was being achieved. His enthusiasm for NATO to run the war in Afghanistan involved the dispatch of more PRTs to build a prosperous modern state. Europe's division from America, Robertson told Blair, could be bridged if Britain played the honest broker and increased its participation.

Robertson's proposal was not perfunctory. Some 2,400 soldiers, mostly British, were attached to NATO's rapid reaction force. The symbolic group had been unemployed and marooned in Germany since 1999. Moving the Allied Rapid Reaction Corps (ARRC), the British army's jewel, as well as NATO's mobile headquarters to Afghanistan with the aim of strengthening the International Security Assistance Force satisfied Robertson's ambition and would please President Bush. The British army was also keen.

To reinforce the army's status in Downing Street, the generals promoted the deployment of the ARRC as an invaluable opportunity to place a British three-star general alongside the Americans, and to restore relations damaged in post-war Iraq. The proposal had not been properly debated within the MoD and Foreign Office by the time that Blair arrived in Istanbul in June 2004 for a summit of NATO leaders. Nor had those around the sofa in Downing Street bothered to consult Whitehall's traditional channels regarding Blair's decision to shift the focus of Britain's army away from Iraq's rich oil fields and the commercial opportunities around Basra and into the hostile Afghan mountains. Blair's explanation mentioned only providing the headquarters staff to stabilise Afghanistan and 'finish the job'. He seemed driven by instinct rather than informed argument to satisfy Robertson.

Tebbit was 'angry that Blair made the commitment'. His complaint about the deployment to a two-star female officer was rebutted. 'It's our turn,' she replied. Tebbit urged Hoon to challenge Blair, but the politician was reluctant. Walker joined in. 'If you're not happy,' he told Hoon, 'we must say no.'

Shortly after Blair returned to London, he summoned Hoon, Walker and General Rob Fry, the deputy chief based in Northwood. 'I want to go to Afghanistan,' he announced.

'It seemed to just come off his head,' observed Fry.

'The chiefs say it's overstretch,' Hoon told Blair.

'We're doing it,' insisted Blair, without asking for more information.

'Yes, Prime Minister,' said Walker, loyally.

THIRTY-SIX

Managing the Mess

A third election victory depended more than ever on restoring the trust of the aspiring working and middle classes. Blair could rely on John Reid to soothe concerns about the NHS, but Charles Clarke at education was truculent – he was even, to Blair's dismay, sympathetic towards Mike Tomlinson's recommendation that A-levels should be replaced.

Tomlinson, the former chief of Ofsted, had been appointed to investigate the fiasco of inflated A-level grades and examinations for fourteen- to nineteen-year-olds. His radical proposal was encouraged by David Miliband, a junior education minister. Like Clarke, Miliband believed that Blair could be persuaded to replace A-levels, education's so-called gold standard. Both were wrong. In Blair's opinion, their abolition would inflame the middle class's growing distrust over education standards and lose votes. To avoid a high-noon confrontation, Blair listened patiently to Clarke's argument in favour of Tomlinson's recommendations while he considered a bloodless solution.

The problems were accumulating. Just at that point, David Normington, the education department's permanent secretary, told Blair that the government would miss its target of 85 per cent of eleven-year-olds reaching the required standards for English and maths by 2007. About 30 per cent of children would still enter secondary school either innumerate or illiterate. Even the Labour-dominated Commons Education Committee chaired by Barry Sheerman, an independently minded Labour MP, reported that there was 'no measurable improvement in standards', despite all the extra billions of pounds spent since 1997. 'Links between expenditure and outcome', added the report, 'remain difficult to establish.'

An Ofsted document made even more discomfiting reading. Blaming bad teachers, David Bell, the chief inspector of schools, declared that almost half of all boys and a third of girls were leaving primary school unable to write properly. After eight years of Labour government, illiteracy was increasing.

Looking for explanations, many criticised the emphasis on targets and the accompanying exams for tarnishing standards. Ever since the spike in 2001, Michael Barber's graphs had plateaued. His Delivery Unit had exaggerated expectations. Although 21,700 more teachers had been employed since 2001, only 8,700 were qualified. The rest were trainees or unqualified assistants.

Blair did not recognise these flaws. Ignoring the statistics, he would write in 2010 that England's 'ten-year-old pupils were ranked third best in the world in literacy and the fastest improving in numeracy, with three-quarters of eleven-year-olds reaching high standards in reading, writing and maths'. Similar distortions kept the public's faith in Labour's education policies, until Tomlinson's report, which up till that point had remained private, was published. For several weeks, Blair hoped forlornly that Clarke would swing against Tomlinson's recommendation. Then a crisis offered a respite.

On 15 December 2004, David Blunkett resigned after compelling proof was produced that the award of a visa for the nanny of his one-year-old son had been accelerated by his staff. Surprisingly, the investigation found no proof that Blunkett had personally ordered the favoured treatment, while the minister himself denied knowing that the application for the visa was in his briefcase. Blair's prediction that Blunkett would be exonerated following what he had hoped would be a feather-light investigation had been proved wrong.

In the midst of another bout of 'Labour sleaze' and theatrical media exaggerations about Gordon Brown's latest bid to snatch the premiership, Clarke was summoned to Downing Street and told that he would move to the Home Office.

'Who is going to replace me?' he asked.

'Ruth,' replied Blair.

'That's a shocking appointment,' said Clarke. 'I can't believe it.' He doubted whether Ruth Kelly could lead any department, especially education.

Blair remained silent. The appointment, he knew, would dismay educationalists. Plucked from obscurity in the Treasury, where she had been ignored by Brown, the fourth secretary of state for education in four years had no administrative experience and enjoyed no political support. Like most new ministers under Blair, Kelly, a former journalist and employee at the Bank of England, was redundant even before her appointment and arrived at the department without an education philosophy or an agenda. However, there were, Blair believed, some advantages to promoting her that would help dispel the newspaper headlines deriding his government's 'soap operas', 'clowns', 'piggly-wigglies' and 'fairies': placing a thirty-six-year-old mother of four young children in the Cabinet before an election was helpful; and she would also obey Blair's orders to reject Tomlinson's report.

The new home secretary received a single instruction from Blair: 'Don't mention immigration, but sort it out before the election.' Clarke understood the reason: 'We feared it would dominate the election.' Michael Howard was scoring points by accusing Blair of 'pussyfooting' and 'sweeping immigration under the carpet'. Immigrants, maintained Blair, should continue to enter Britain according to a managed scheme, but bogus asylum-seekers were 'a real problem' that provided 'the Tories one good issue to beat us with'. He offered no new solutions.

Clarke was unimpressed by his inheritance. 'Blunkett left an enormous mess,' he said.

'It was a mess,' Blunkett agreed, acknowledging the complaint.

Clarke also blamed Jack Straw, noting that 'We had created a completely incoherent system.' He considered Bill Jeffrey to be complacent and 'no good', and after a few weeks demanded the departure of John Gieve, the permanent secretary, whom he blamed for taking too long to find a replacement for Jeffrey.

'Don't rock the boat,' cautioned Blair after hearing Clarke's proposals.

'There's no alternative,' replied his new minister. 'It will take five years to sort it out. So you must show your confidence in me and let me do it.'

Blair agreed unenthusiastically.

His leader's delinquency, thought Clarke, was his lack of interest in finding the right people for the job, be they civil servants or politicians. His strength was to resist agonising about the past. Self-criticism was rare. Although Labour had caused the migrant problem, Blair asserted his customary self-righteousness. 'Let's move on,' he told Clarke. 'Don't dwell on the causes. Forget it. Just look at how we can solve the problem.'

The familiar solution was a White Paper followed by new legislation. After five weeks' intensive consultation, Clarke proposed that Britain should introduce a points system that would guarantee 'better control than before'. Blair agreed but had no intention of closing Britain's doors. His mistake, he realised, had been to categorise his critics as prejudiced. He had even challenged Trevor Kavanagh, the *Sun*'s political editor, for questioning his record on immigration. 'Are you serious, Trevor?' asked Blair, forcing the journalist to deny that he was racist.

To regain credibility, Blair spoke about a new five-year plan. The deportation of bogus migrants, he pledged, would soon outnumber the approval of new applications. Making promises was easy but depended on civil servants. Clarke's dismal report about his Home Office officials reflected similar complaints by ministers about the departments of education and health. Eight years after he confronted Robin Butler, Blair still cursed the government machine. 'Changing a country was a whole lot harder than changing a party,' he wrote.

Switching from central control of schools and hospitals to devolving Whitehall's power was taking longer than he anticipated. Part of the problem was his lukewarm commitment to choice and competition; as the American hustler Mel Weinberg memorably said, 'Before you sell a deal you have to live the deal. You have to believe in it, because, if you don't believe in it, you can't sell it.' Another difficulty was his judgement about markets. Typical was his continuing faith in the energy market.

'Do you want to move to nuclear?' Mike O'Brien asked him during a chance encounter in the Commons lobby in 2004.

'What do you think?' Blair asked his fourth energy minister.

'I'm worried about an energy gap coming up,' explained O'Brien, 'which we will need nuclear to bridge. The problem is the very high cost of development.'

Blair moved on, leaving O'Brien puzzled. Blair had not revealed to him the reason for his indecision – an argument with Brown over whether to trust the market or impose new regulations. The confusion was compounded by the diverse characters contributing to the debate. Joan MacNaughton, the DTI's director of energy, had prepared a briefing paper in favour of nuclear energy. That was Britain's safest option, she wrote. After twenty years of self-sufficiency, the country had become a net importer of energy. Patricia Hewitt, relying on the assurances of Vicky Pryce, a newly recruited DTI economist opposed to nuclear energy, recited to Blair that the market was working. Low prices, both women chanted, would continue. 'Mysteriously, Pryce has become a force in the land,' commented Geoff Norris, Blair's energy adviser.

'The markets are not working in the consumers' interest,' O'Brien told Pryce.

'Yes, they are, because prices are coming down,' replied Pryce, pointing out that the cost of electricity had fallen to a new low.

'They'll go up soon,' replied O'Brien. In 2005, they would indeed begin to rise, and would nearly double by 2010.

Since there was no Cabinet energy committee to resolve the disagreement, Blair invited Hewitt and O'Brien 'for a chat in his office'.

'How are we planning to cope with the long-term problem of capacity?' asked Norris. 'The market has failed to encourage new investment. They've built no new generators.'

Hewitt repeated that the market would prevent an energy blackout.

Blair made no contribution. He voiced no concern over the fact that the regulator had allowed foreign state-owned corporations to merge Britain's independent power companies into six Goliaths, nor did he reveal that Brown had rejected his plea that only nuclear energy could guarantee Britain's supplies. The chancellor had cited the cost of disposing of the waste as his reason for opposing nuclear power.

Labour's manifesto for the 2005 election concealed the problems. 'We have reformed our energy markets', it stated, 'to make them open and competitive. We are a leading force in the campaign to make Europe's energy markets the same.'

Procrastination was making matters worse in other industries too. Just as he had postponed resolving Britain's energy needs, Blair had dawdled over the growing crisis at the Rover factory in Longbridge. The unprofitable company had been sold by BMW in 2000 to four businessmen, the self-styled 'Phoenix Four', for just £10. To rid themselves of all legal obligations, BMW had also given the Phoenix Four a long-term loan of £427 million. During 2004, Hewitt knew that Rover was running out of money. Six thousand five hundred jobs would be at risk in an election year. The only beneficiaries were the Phoenix Four, who had personally pocketed £42 million.

Once again, Blair first heard about the seriousness of the problem while passing Mike O'Brien in the Commons lobby.

'Give me more information,' said Blair, and walked on.

THIRTY-SEVEN

The Devil's Kiss

Obeying Blair's order, General Rob Fry was drafting the plan to reinforce the army in Afghanistan, but the 3,000 new troops would be dispatched with a fuzzy objective. Blair was committed to nationbuilding, while America was still bombing terrorists in the mountains. Once again, no Cabinet committee (embracing the key departments and the intelligence agencies) was convened to propound the purpose of the mission. Blair preferred to have Fry define his objective and describe the pathway to success.

Instead of questioning his brief, Fry snatched the blank cheque. Unlike most of his peers, he was educated in history and military strategy. He believed there was a convincing case that the allies should have either left Afghanistan for good in 2003 or stayed to destroy the Taliban. He now relished the opportunity to plan the return. His error, shared by Blair, was to ignore the growing chaos around Basra. One consequence of Whitehall's dysfunction was the prime minister's miscalculation that the same handful of ill-equipped soldiers could be relocated from Iraq to 'build the peace' in the Afghan mountains.

In normal circumstances, Blair would have had good reason to be nervous. Robin Butler was completing his report into the intelligence surrounding WMDs and he had naturally focused on the first dossier. Blair's fears were assuaged by Ann Taylor's regular discussions with David Omand in Downing Street. On Blair's behalf, she demanded amendments and exclusions. In particular, she opposed any direct criticism of the prime minister. John Chilcot, an undistinguished former civil servant and the member of the committee described as 'the prisoner's friend' for appearing to help Blair, negotiated the compromises with Omand. 'Omand dug Blair out of a hole,' noted Andrew Turnbull.

Omand judged that his task was to prevent any named person being blamed for the intelligence failure. The most obvious culprits were Richard Dearlove and John Scarlett. 'The intelligence community', he recalled, 'had suffered a severe blow by being proved to be wrong. We didn't want scapegoating of an individual. The collapse of the system was the real cause. The blame was the underlying failure of statecraft.' In his opinion, Blair was responsible.

The final negotiations between Taylor and Chilcot required a mandarin's compromise: either Dearlove and Scarlett would be damned outright for their errors or their culpability would be minimised as a sin of exaggeration.

The previous year, Dearlove had told Taylor's Intelligence and Security Committee that the intelligence reports stating that weapons carrying WMDs could be ready for firing within forty-five minutes were 'reliable'. MI6, he had said, had based its prized intelligence on three human sources. By the time Butler considered MI6's reports, the agency was admitting that all three were worthless. Some MI6 officers blamed the mistake of believing the bogus reports on a corrupted processing system within MI6, but Dearlove denied this.

After sifting through all the intelligence files, Butler could have judged that Dearlove's and Scarlett's mismanagement amounted to misconduct. Instead, his committee mildly reprimanded the two chiefs for issuing 'less assured' judgements and 'estimates' that became the 'prevailing wisdom', despite the absence of evidence. 'The dossier,' Butler wrote, by 'inferring the existence of banned weapons . . . went to (although not beyond) the outer limits of the intelligence available.' His most damning judgement was that 'More weight was placed on the intelligence than it could bear.' To seal the compromise, he criticised Scarlett for co-operating with Alastair Campbell, but accepted his excuse that he was simply obeying Blair's orders. He also endorsed Scarlett's self-congratulation for resisting Campbell's pressure to embellish his report.

Scarlett's lifebelt was his original description of the reports as 'sporadic and patchy'. He blamed his abandonment of caution on the new intelligence report disclosed to Blair by Dearlove in Downing Street on 11 September 2002. He switched the ultimate responsibility for the misinformation onto Blair, who, after all, had asserted in Parliament that the intelligence on WMDs was 'extensive, detailed and authoritative'. In his own testimony to the committee, the prime minister explained with charm and apparent candour that the contradictions were mere detail. He was justified in omitting the caveats because Scarlett sincerely believed that Saddam did possess WMDs. The dossier, said Blair, was an instrument of persuasion that merely provided information, and was not intended to make the case for war.

Butler did not pursue his witness forensically. He did not ask why, immediately after the dossier's publication, Blair had told Admiral Mike Boyce to plan for war. Rather, in response to Taylor's influence, he gave Blair the benefit of the doubt when he claimed that the dossier was not remotely connected with making the case for war. Recalling from his own experience how little the prime minister read, Butler also did not ask whether he had actually studied Scarlett's report. 'That would have been too insulting,' he would say. Instead of openly criticising Blair's distortions, he blamed him only for 'over-salesmanship' and 'sofa' government.

Dearlove could not make the same excuses as Blair and Scarlett. MI6's credibility was shredded. Yet even with him Butler's rebukes were mild. Dearlove was taken to task for allowing budget cuts to undermine the scrutiny of intelligence, but neither he nor Blair was criticised for forging unusually close relations. Those tepid words satisfied Taylor. Finally, at the insistence of other members of the panel, Butler agreed to express his 'high regard' for Scarlett's abilities and emphasised that he should remain MI6 chief, since he should 'not bear personal responsibility' for the flawed dossier.

Later, Butler looked at the transcript of Blair's interviews again. The prime minister's charm, he realised, had concealed how insubstantial his replies had been. 'Perhaps we were too polite,' Butler would later say. 'I'm a trusting fellow.' As a final concession to Downing Street, he also inserted into the report, 'We conclude that it would be a rash person who asserted at this stage' that WMDs and missiles 'will never be found'. This was seventeen months after the war. The civil servant's timidity, which Blair so disliked, was in this instance his protection.

President Bush did not enjoy that advantage. On 9 July, the US Senate Intelligence Committee published a similar report on the failure of the CIA. The agency was accused of overstating the threat of WMDs, relying on dubious sources and ignoring dissenting opinions. 'The biggest intelligence failure in our nation's history,' judged Senator Jay Rockefeller. To avoid the congressional missile, George Tenet, the CIA's director, had quickly resigned.

Five days later, Butler's report was published. Like Hutton's and Taylor's reports, his conclusions reinforced Blair's defiance of his critics. 'We found no evidence to question the prime minister's good faith,' wrote Butler. To assuage his own misgivings, he hoped that the media would draw damning verdicts by carefully reading the facts rather than the particular judgements. The report's annex compared the cautionary language in key passages of the JIC's original briefings with the modified version published in the dossier. In those pages, the reader would see the evidence of Scarlett acting under pressure to 'sex up' the dossier. Only by ploughing through the report to paragraph 458 and, more importantly, what followed would the diligent reader finally grasp the full chicanery that Butler was bursting to publicise. Butler anticipated that he would be asked at the press conference whether Blair should resign. He expected his intended reply to be explosive: 'That question is not for us, but for Parliament and the people.' The question was not asked and, to his regret, he was unable to cast doubt on Blair in public. The media's listless reaction to the report disappointed him.

In the subsequent Commons debate, Blair used the report as both sword and shield. 'No one lied,' he said. 'No one made up the intelligence. No one inserted things into the dossier against the advice of the intelligence services.' He admitted that Iraq did not have WMDs but, having 'searched my conscience', he said, 'I cannot honestly say getting rid of Saddam was a mistake'.

Once again, Michael Howard resisted exposing his rival's inaccuracies. He did not highlight the proof of Scarlett acting under pressure to 'sex up' the dossier. When he was asked by Patrick Cormack, a Tory MP, whether those who voted in favour of war had been deceived, instead of replying 'Yes' he fudged. Blair was safe.

Eleven weeks later, Howard regretted his uncharacteristic timidity. Tony Blair, he told the *New Statesman*, had 'lied' over Iraq. He would later accuse Blair on television of lying to Parliament about Lord Goldsmith's changing opinions.

Butler also abandoned his reticence. On 22 February 2007, the retired official told the House of Lords that Blair had been 'disingenuous' about WMDs in the first dossier by omitting the JIC's doubts. But it was too little, too late. Blair would gloss over the contradictions and accusations. To have failed to join America in Iraq, he would write, would have 'done major long-term damage to that relationship'. WMDs, he explained, were not the overriding issue: 'In the final analysis, I would be with the US because in my view it was right, morally and strategically.' Unburdened by curiosity, he displayed no spiritual struggle with Christian ideas of guilt, atonement or deception. Although he had solemnly apologised in Parliament for British heartlessness during the Irish potato famine that started in 1845 and expressed 'personal deep sorrow' for the slave trade, he would never apologise for the Iraq war.

The day after the publication of Butler's report, Labour lost a by-election in Leicester to the Lib Dems but retained a seat against the Tories in Birmingham. The polls again suggested that Howard would be unable to win the following year's general election. Blair was re-energised. Determined finally to forge his legacy, he snubbed Brown and encouraged Trevor Kavanagh to report in the *Sun*, in an article headlined 'Blair's Shock Blow for Brown', that he intended to fight the next election and serve a full and final five years as prime minister. After that he departed for his summer holidays, once again enjoying the hospitality of the rich, first at Cliff Richard's villa in Barbados, then at the Strozzis' estate in Tuscany and finally at Silvio Berlusconi's estate in Sardinia, which would become infamous for the owner's 'bunga bunga' parties with underaged prostitutes.

Soon after Blair's return from Italy, Rob Fry submitted his twenty-page report to General Walker and the chiefs, presenting the reasons why the military should strengthen its commitment in Afghanistan. The deployment, Fry foreshadowed, would be a bigger commitment than Blair's decision in Istanbul to dispatch the ARRC, the NATO headquarters staffed by British soldiers, to the country. Any reservations among the chiefs was silenced by the knowledge that Blair was already committed to Afghanistan, so Fry was told to develop the plan, even though he had never commanded a mission of the size he was writing about, nor did he have any familiarity with the country.

In January 2005, Mike Jackson decided that he should see at first hand how the NATO operation in Afghanistan could be revived. On his return, he told Fry, General Richard Dannatt, his successor as chief of the army, and others at Northwood that he was confident that the deployment could be executed without much danger. Moreover, he added, the engagement would be worthwhile because the Taliban were enjoying 'a free run'.

Smarting from their experience in Iraq, the generals discussed what the army could do, and those discussions continued informally between Jackson and the two other chiefs, West and Stirrup, and then with Walker. The two generals agreed that any involvement would be low risk, while Stirrup and West opposed the commitment. Nevertheless, the chiefs agreed that a British force would be dispatched to Kandahar in south Afghanistan the following autumn to satisfy Blair's orders for 'reconstruction and development', with the secondary aim of combating terrorism and destroying the local narcotics trade. Altogether that matched Britain's destiny as a 'force for good'. 'I didn't realise it was a hornets' nest,' Jackson would later say.

As Fry developed the plan in early 2005, he missed one contradiction: how could British soldiers committed to nation-building win the hearts and minds of the Afghan tribesmen if the opium crops – by far and away the main source of their income – were to be destroyed? Fry did, however, understand that Washington's attention was focused on Iraq and not Afghanistan, though he was unsure whether Blair was aware of that fault line.

Iraq, Blair knew, was becoming a war without a foreseeable end. He summoned Geoff Hoon and Walker. 'Tell me how to fix this,' he said to the general. 'What does the military need?'

Like Blair, Walker did not understand the complexities of the uprising in Iraq, and his presentation was reassuring. At the end of a series of platitudes, he declared, in the military's can-do tone, 'We'll get through this.' Blair thanked the general. Only with hindsight did Walker recognise the prime minister's unwillingness to devote time to understanding the army's predicament: a lack of men, equipment, intelligence and money. Even more corrosive was Blair's objective in Afghanistan – 'reconstruction and development' – a mirror of the army's woolly 'goal' in Iraq.

Sensitive to Blair's disillusionment about events in Iraq, the informal conversations around the water coolers in Northwood focused on the honourable circumstances in which Britain could leave. 'We're on a hammering to nothing,' the generals agreed. Those speaking to Jackson on his return from another tour in Iraq were struck by his pessimism: 'We're not doing any good. Our reputation is suffering. We have released forces we cannot control. I think there's the possibility of strategic failure.'

In discussions with his senior officers, Jackson suggested that the government needed to define how the army could withdraw with integrity. That required an approach to Blair. Walker refused to comment on Jackson's proposal, while Hoon resisted adopting any position, not least because there was no will or money to send reinforcements, nor to set a timetable for withdrawal. Paralysis hung over Northwood.

THIRTY-EIGHT

Towards a Third Term

'Tony is very gloomy. He's very miserable,' noticed Charles Clarke some months before the general election of May 2005. He followed Alan Milburn, David Blunkett and others into No. 10 to boost Blair's morale. 'You're tremendous,' Clarke told his leader. 'You're very important. You must stay. I'll support you all the way.'

'I'm grateful,' Blair replied unemotionally. Even at his lowest, he would conceal his true feelings from his Cabinet supporters. To serve his own interest, he toyed with their loyalty. 'Tony played footsie with me for nine months to get me back,' recalled Milburn, while Blunkett was assured of his return to the government after Blair pointedly presented his resignation as a charade by declaring that the former home secretary was 'a man without a stain on his character'. He needed his dwindling band of loyalists.

In the days before the party conference in Brighton, Blair was confident of victory in the election, with the polls showing a Labour lead of between 3 and 10 per cent. Yet he showed no excitement about the prospect of a third term. Gordon Brown's constant presentation of himself as the 'consolidator' offering 'stability and prudence' versus the Blairite 'transformers' was wearisome, but more troubling still for Blair was defining the reason for his re-election. Simply depriving Brown of the crown was hardly a rallying cry. Iraq hung over everything, especially during the conference, which coincided with the kidnapping in Iraq of Ken Bigley, a civil engineer, by Islamic terrorists. Following his capture, Bigley pleaded unsuccessfully in mournful videos for his life.

To insiders, Blair spoke about 'securing my legacy'; to the electorate he promised to 'serve a full third term', or at least bid a very long farewell, for the stock market was soaring.

After eight years, Blair listed his achievements: a more tolerant society, a minimum wage, multiple new schools and hospitals, a safer rail network, a Human Rights Act, a Civil Partnership Act to rid the country of institutionalised homophobia, laws to liberalise drinking, the encouragement of the arts and the embedment of the attitude that 'what you did in your personal life was your choice but what you did to others was not'. The hole was the absence of the enduring substance of Thatcherism or the Gladstone era. The former was symbolised by the transformation of Canary Wharf from derelict dockland into a global financial centre for over 100,000 professionals. It was not just the cynics who pointed to the appropriate symbol of Blair's legacy: the Dome.

Blair's solution was to get John Birt to solicit five-year plans from each government department. Similarly, Andrew Turnbull was tasked to deliver twenty targets for the public services. These would be distilled into 'A Fair Future for All', a paper written by Matthew Taylor, recently hired from a left-wing think tank. Taylor concocted six snappy election pledges, which, while hardly a legacy, did at least offer ideas for those scrambling to draft the new manifesto. With a few tweaks, they could also rely on the manifestos of 1997 and 2001, including the familiar pledge to 'unremittingly' reform the public services. The result was refashioned New Labour. Inevitably, selling the brand for a third term was difficult. The party's finances were also in dire shape: in early 2002, its debts were over £10 million.

In previous times, Blair would have automatically turned to Michael Levy, but his principal fund-raiser had upset many in the Foreign Office and the Middle East while acting as an intermediary between the Israeli and Arab leaders. Blair had been mistaken to entrust a former music agent with the task. The fault once more was his own naivety about the region, not least in thinking that the Arabs were likely to trust an Orthodox Jew as the prime minister's representative. Even Ariel Sharon, when prime minister, had shouted, 'No Levy!' and ordered the envoy to be thrown out of his office.

General Charles Guthrie was one of many who had found it 'odd that Blair trusted him as his envoy, because the Arab rulers hated his touchy-feely embraces and his kissing, and he had no merit because he didn't know anything'. Guthrie recalled some early advice from George Robertson: 'Get close to Michael Levy because he's very influential.' Accordingly, the general had invited Levy to visit Bosnia. 'He asked questions showing he didn't know the difference between Serbs and Bosnians,' he would report. During that trip, an army chef offered Levy a bacon sandwich.

Without telling Levy, Blair decided to rely on Ronnie Cohen, a private-equity investor based offshore, as the party's new principal fund-raiser. Cohen, a former parliamentary candidate for the Liberals, had switched to support Gordon Brown in the mid-1990s. Over the next decade, he had shown no particular flair for politics, nor did he prove able to entice previous donors to pledge £1 million each for the election campaign. Cohen's legacy, Levy complained, was a deficit of £12 million.

Blair needed an experienced hand to rescue the party's finances, but his old friend, he discovered, was incandescent. 'Tony had gone behind my back,' raged Levy. 'What I found so difficult to accept or forgive was that he hadn't been straight with me.' Nevertheless, against his better judgement that 'TB really was sometimes just in it for himself', Levy agreed to swallow his anger and resume raising millions.

The atmosphere among the donors, he discovered, had changed. Established friends of Labour were unwilling to be publicly associated with the party. Complicating the fund-raising was Labour's new law requiring the declaration of all donations over £5,000. However, an unintended omission did allow the legal concealment of loans. Knowing that the Tories were raising millions of pounds in this way, Blair urged Levy to follow suit.

Levy approached a series of businessmen and, deploying his talent, persuaded them to lend the party a total of £14 million, without receiving any publicity. Among those who agreed to lend over £1 million were Sir David Garrard, a property developer, Barry Townsley, a stockbroker, and Chai Patel, the founder of the Priory clinic. Sir Gulam Noon, known as the 'curry king', lent £250,000. Levy told Blair and the party's treasurer about those arrangements. In October 2004, showing little sensitivity, Blair nominated seven of the twelve who had given loans for peerages. They included Garrard, Noon, Townsley and Patel. The nominations were submitted to the scrutiny committee, which was under the chairmanship of Dennis Stevenson, a well-known corporate chairman. To vet whether the individuals would be suitable legislators, the committee's staff sought out any damaging information by circulating the names to the Inland Revenue, the police, the intelligence services and other state agencies. Blair and members of his staff who had compiled the nominations – principally Jonathan Powell and Ruth Turner, his trusted political adviser and close friend – did not expect any blowback despite the unusual desperation to raise money.

At the same time, Blair had also nominated Paul Drayson, the chief executive of PowderJect Pharmaceuticals. Within six months, Lord Drayson had contributed £1 million to the Labour Party and become a junior minister. Soon after, news emerged that, following his first donation of £100,000 in 2002, Drayson's company had been awarded a £32 million contract by the government for a smallpox vaccine. The relationship was denounced by a Tory MP as 'pretty corrupt. To describe Paul Drayson as a captain of industry is far from accurate. He is a young man in a hurry.' Drayson was forty-four. Unknown to his critics, the new minister had previously saved £3 million in tax by setting up offshore trusts before floating his company. After that saving was discovered, Drayson asserted that at all times he and his company had acted within the law, and there was no evidence to the contrary. Later, surveying Blair's record, a parliamentary scrutiny committee realised that twenty-five of the 292 peers Blair had created were donors to the party. They had given about £25 million.

With about £14 million secured and Labour enjoying a three-point lead over the Tories, Blair's pollster Philip Gould was predicting victory. Blair intended his surprise coup after the election to be Brown's exclusion from the Treasury. In retaliation for what he called Brown's 'no-holds-barred war of subversion' and 'Mafiosi skulduggery to get his way', his opening salvo was fired while the chancellor was flying to Washington: he revealed the appointment of Milburn as election supremo.

While Blairites cheered that their man had finally faced Brown down, the chancellor's allies screamed about a 'kick in the teeth' and 'an African coup'. Milburn announced his own coronation, publicly chortling about his return. 'That was the worst mistake I ever made', he would later say.

The result was predictable. 'Basically Gordon is on strike', said Peter Mandelson. 'Mad, bad and dangerous.'

Brown's vitriol festered until December. In an outburst, he called Blair a liar, a cheat and a fraud for not resigning. 'You can't talk about yourself as a Christian if you don't honour your word', he screamed, until Blair ordered him to leave his office.

The Blairs' new year holiday in Egypt was tinged by an apocalyptic mood. The couple had travelled to a seaside resort just as the world was coming to understand the huge death toll caused by the tsunami that had swept across the Indian Ocean and killed at least 150,000 people. Preoccupied by his own problems, Blair was isolated from the anguish across Britain. Appalled by harrowing pictures of the destruction, the public quickly raised £70 million. The government's first gift was £15 million. A journalist visiting the Blairs discovered that they had travelled without any books and that the prime minister was preoccupied with writing out a new year's message for the British public. The list of Labour's achievements – schools, NHS and reducing crime – was familiar. The surprise was his aggressive response to gossip that Brown was planning a new bombshell.

Once back in London, Blair called a snap press conference, deliberately timed to clash with a speech the chancellor was delivering on aid to Africa. Brown, he said, would play a full part in the election, but he pointedly refused to guarantee him the chancellorship in the next government.

The supposed bombshell was the publication of *Brown's Britain* by Robert Peston, a left-wing journalist, which portrayed Blair as an incompetent leader who had shown no gratitude for Brown's unwavering devotion. Peston's narrative, shaped by Brown, described the chancellor's dismay when he was 'cheated' of the premiership in 1994. The overwhelming evidence that he had withdrawn from the leadership contest in order to avoid certain defeat was ignored. But Peston did prominently insert, at Brown's request, the chancellor's damning exclamation to Blair in 2004: 'There is nothing you could ever say to me now that I could ever believe.'

'You should have worked with me,' Blair allegedly replied.

Blair was stunned by Brown's aggression. The media hype would burn itself out, but the venom could not be neutralised.

'Don't forget, Gordon's a paper tiger,' repeated Charles Clarke. Milburn echoed the same sentiment. Fearful of the damage, Brown summoned the BBC to declare on camera his passionate belief in unity.

The only credible riposte, Blair decided, was to launch a four-month campaign aimed at winning a majority of over seventy seats. With a new mandate, he could dismiss Brown and achieve in the third term what had eluded him during the previous eight years.

Over the next eight weeks, Brown sulked and the Tories' poll ratings rose. At the beginning of March, after Gould's warning that victory was only guaranteed if Brown and Blair stood together, Blair surrendered. Milburn, the party's media briefers whispered, was proving incapable of organising the campaign, so he was ditched and Brown resumed his role as election supremo. 'Tony's overriding concern', Mandelson observed, 'was to keep Gordon on board. He humoured Gordon and applied massive therapy.' Their reunion was sealed with a contrived photograph of Blair buying Brown a Mr Whippy ice-cream cone from a street van. Both laughed for the cameras.

Labour's electoral strength, Blair knew, was its reputation for economic competence. Brown had fashioned himself as the architect of economic stability and the social engineer who used tax credits to relieve poverty among children and pensioners. By 2005, the chancellor was boasting that Britain was booming and an additional 2.1 million people were in employment. Blair needed those headlines.

The truth was rather different. One million jobs had been lost in manufacturing since 1997. Most of the new jobs created by Brown were in the public sector, financed by taxes. As a result, the 2.2 per cent increase in productivity between 1997 and 2005 was 0.3 per cent less than in John Major's era. Even inequality was unchanged: despite the billions of pounds spent on tax credits, the gap between rich and poor remained static.

Thanks to Labour, Brown claimed, Britain had enjoyed the longest run of continuous economic growth since 1701. He overlooked the fact that a third of the last fifty-one quarters were under Tory rule. The benefits of the growth were not universally shared. The chancellor's much-vaunted 'investment' had cut the average incomes of Britons in 2003 and created a new £11 billion funding deficit because he had exaggerated the amount received from taxes. Thanks to his skewed financing, Britain's trade gap had risen from near zero in 1997 to a £57 billion deficit in 2004. Worst of all, the debt had risen from 34 per cent of GDP in 2000 – the last year directly influenced by the inheritance from the Tories – to 40 per cent in 2004, and the annual increase thereafter would be steep.

Blessed for introducing flexible labour laws and light-touch regulation for the banks, Brown posed as the master of the new capitalism and the godfather of private enterprise. Certain of his own genius, he had opened up British industry to unbridled competition with the world. Unnoticed, he had removed the statutory protection of British industry provided by the independent Office of Fair Trading. Without that law, Cadbury, ICI and other iconic British manufacturers could now be sold to foreign corporations, stripped and closed down.

Blair's grasp on the effect of Brown's policies on British industry, the

City or the economy was indiscernible. However, he showed no surprise when Clarke said, 'We're spending too much.'

'I know,' was his reply. 'I'll talk to Gordon about it.'

With limited interest in the financial world, Blair never questioned whether his sharing Bill Clinton's and Brown's hero-worship of Alan Greenspan, the chairman of the Federal Reserve, was wise. He didn't realise how ignorant Brown was of markets and balance sheets. Neither he nor Brown heard the warnings in New York and Washington that Clinton and Greenspan had inflated a property bubble and, by deregulating the trading of commodities, allowed speculators to wreck the markets. Only a few Wall Street insiders spotted the risks of complicated sub-prime loans on property and the speculation in oil prices, which were to cause the crisis in 2008. Just like Clinton and Greenspan, Blair and Brown regarded bankers and fund managers through starry eyes. The master spinners to the electorate could not imagine that the fluent money-men, self-styled as masters of the universe, were peddling false prospectuses and rigging the markets. Unable to see through the self-aggrandisement of Barclays' Bob Diamond or register the inexperience of Mervyn King, the governor of the Bank of England, neither Blair nor Brown queried whether Britain's Financial Services Authority was regulating the City adequately.

The illusion went unchallenged by a ragged Tory opposition. The electorate would not understand that Brown's seemingly healthy economy was built on sand. The Conservatives' simple battle cry was honesty, the caption of their election poster echoing the nation's dilemma: 'If he's prepared to lie to take us to war, he's prepared to lie to win an election.' Britain, the Tories and Blair realised, was split between haters and sympathisers. Facts, Blair knew, would not determine the outcome. In modern politics, he wrote, 'the mood trumps the policy every time'.

So it was that the prime minister of Great Britain sat happily on a sofa for daytime TV and let his hosts Ant and Dec proffer a pair of panties as a gift for Cherie and check people's reaction when he was asked about his 'ugly smell' in the bathroom. On other programmes, he exposed himself to hostile mothers who attacked him about the NHS, schools and Iraq. Little was off limits, including Cherie's boast to a *Sun* photographer in the Downing Street garden that her husband 'does it five times a night', followed by Blair's confirmation to the photographer and Trevor Kavanagh, who stood near by, 'At least. I can do it more, depending how I feel.' Labour's steady polling advantage showed the efficacy of such an unusual pitch.

The Conservatives panicked. Their negative campaign, directed at 900,000 swing voters and masterminded by Lynton Crosby, an Australian political strategist, rested in part on Labour's failure to control immigration. 'It's not racist to implement limits on immigration,' hushed the poster's caption. Blair's reply that 'Britain needs strict controls that work' raised questions about what Michael Howard called Labour's 'loss of control of the immigration system'.

Then the Tories made a mistake. They proposed to detain illegal immigrants on what shadow chancellor Oliver Letwin called 'a faraway island', although he could not identify its location. Blair seized on the 'fantasy island' as 'absurd, laughable opportunism' – although Blunkett had proposed a similar scheme two years earlier. Posing as the beacon of decency, he denounced Howard for exploiting people's fears. In a well-pitched campaign of contrition to rebuild his relationship with the electorate, Blair denounced Howard for appealing to racists, while simultaneously conceding that those who discussed immigration were not racists. Soberly, in a homily headlined 'firm, fair, fast', he praised the advantages that immigration had brought to Britain, from which Howard's own parents, the victims of persecution in Eastern Europe, had benefited. Even the leaked Home Office estimate that there were 570,000 illegal immigrants in Britain was convincingly dismissed as 'grossly inaccurate' by Blair's spokesman. In truth, the figure was an underestimate, because bogus asylum-seekers were not included. The Tories' best electoral weapon was lost.

Blair was pitching Labour as the architect of an advanced post-industrial economy in a globalised world. The Enron and WorldCom frauds in America, he assured enquirers, could not happen in Britain thanks to the Financial Services Authority. Labour, he said, had created the ideal foundations for his beloved countrymen to prosper. 'For me, simply,' he gushed, 'I believe in you, the British people, as much as ever ... I'm still the same person, older, a little wiser I hope, but still with the same commitment.' Howard could not replicate that performance.

Yet such self-assurance was threatened in the first days of April. After ignoring the warnings that MG Rover was heading towards collapse, Blair was told that a Chinese concern had refused to take over the insolvent company. Three weeks before the election, the employees faced unemployment and no pay, while the four chief executives were certain to walk away with £42 million. Concealing their self-enrichment, the Phoenix Four demanded that the government provide a £100 million loan to save the jobs. The trade unions accused the four of crashing the company to get more money. 'Give Rover whatever they need,' Brown shouted in a panic down the telephone at Patricia Hewitt. 'I've spoken to Tony. We have to save the jobs. You've got to put the money in. Just do it.'

Hewitt suspected it was throwing cash away and probably unlawful. 'They can't decide what to do,' Mike O'Brien told a friend. 'There's no grip.' Torn between the law and politics, the tearful DTI minister loaned the company enough money to pay the wages for one week.

Blair was grateful for Howard's failure to capitalise on the government's embarrassment. Instead, the Tory leader repeatedly accused Blair of being 'a liar' about Iraq. This line of attack did not survive after Howard told a TV audience on the eve of the poll that he still supported the invasion.

Blair's confidence grew. Flying in a helicopter with Alistair Darling at the end of the campaign, he asked, 'What's our majority likely to be?'

'Fifty to sixty,' replied Darling.

'Isn't that pessimistic?' asked Blair, convinced that the 10 per cent lead in the polls would produce a majority of nearer 130 seats. Relying on his consistent good luck and the bias of constituency boundaries, he expected the electorate's hostility would be overcome.

On 5 May, election day, his team gathered at his home in Sedgefield. Blair was nervous. 'We've lost,' groaned Alastair Campbell, a volunteer during the campaign, after hearing pessimistic reports from marginal constituencies. But, at 10 p.m., the BBC's exit poll forecast a Labour lead of 3 per cent and a majority of sixty-six.

'A minor miracle,' Blair would write five years later.

That was not his sentiment at the time. At his own count, Blair looked exhausted. A painful slipped disc and a heavy cold were aggravated by a withering speech by Reg Keys, the father of a soldier killed in Iraq, who had stood as a candidate in the constituency. Blair flew south aware that Labour was predicted to win with the lowest number of votes in history for any government. 'I have listened and I have learned,' he said unhappily on the doorstep of No. 10. 'And I think I have a very clear idea of what the British people expect from the government for the third term.'

Once inside, his misery erupted. On the main table were newspapers with headlines such as 'Blair Limps Back' and 'Time Is Running Out'. Across the country, Labour members were speculating about his early retirement. Beside him were Patricia Hewitt and Sally Morgan. Both saw a disappointed magician who was fearful that his wizardry was exhausted. Since 1997, Labour had lost nearly 4 million votes; worse, it had garnered the lowest share of votes for a winning party since 1832. Blair half doubted whether he had actually won. Party members were already being 'ungenerous' and 'grim' about the victory, blaming him for the poor result.

'I'd never seen him so low,' recalled Hewitt. 'Mr Calm', who rarely cried over spilt milk and moved on after a crisis, was distraught. There was no talk of 'progressive' politics.

'Should I get rid of Gordon?' he asked, starting the familiar hand-wringing, which ended with his voicing all his old fears about Brown on the back benches. The question, all three knew, was meaningless. The previous Friday, he had publicly anointed Brown as his successor. 'Gordon will make an excellent prime minister,' he had written in *The Times*.

Upstairs, Cherie was contemplating her future. In one month, she was due to fly with her husband to Washington. She intended to use that opportunity to be paid £30,000 for a lecture promoting her new book about life inside Downing Street. Also on her list was the chance to earn a fee at the opening of a shopping mall in Malaysia, another for a TV documentary based on her book, and a third for delivering a lecture as 'Cherie Blair' rather than 'Cherie Booth' in Australia. She had just submitted a bill for £7,700 to the Labour Party for her hair stylist's daily services during the campaign.

Half a mile away, Brown was waiting in his small Westminster flat.

PART 3

'NO LEGACY IS SO RICH AS HONESTY'

JUNE 2005–MAY 2007

THIRTY-NINE

Medical Mayhem

'Do health,' Blair told Patricia Hewitt at the end of their post-mortem following polling day. 'We'll talk about it later.'

As usual, he had not considered the appointment with any care, and Hewitt would need a year to understand her department. The ideal choice would have been John Hutton, Alan Milburn's deputy and former flatmate, but Blair had become disengaged. 'His door used to be open,' George Alberti had discovered during a thirty-minute discussion with Blair. 'It wasn't any longer. He was totally diverted.' Blair's preoccupation with the NHS had been reduced to a longing for headlines.

Hewitt left Blair in Downing Street and crossed Whitehall to her new office in Richmond House. Nigel Crisp, the permanent secretary and chief of the NHS, had left for home. Ever since being mentioned as a possible candidate to become the next Cabinet secretary, his confidence had grown. Hewitt found his briefing file on her desk. The summary described a super-class of confident administrators who, ever since 1997, had been improving the nation's health.

On Monday morning, the two met. 'He told me everything was marvellous,' recalled Hewitt. During the first weeks, Crisp's reports, especially after his regular Friday inspection tours across the country, were glowing. Every indicator was positive. Naturally, there were a few grievances. The IT programme was delayed by Accenture's failure to deliver on their contract, and the NHS needed to recuperate after the bruising employment of private contractors. Hewitt nodded. She was unaware of Ken Anderson's presence down the corridor, and Crisp did not enlighten her about the commercial section's mission to shame the NHS dinosaurs.

Hewitt entered Richmond House convinced by the party's election boast that Blair had transformed the NHS. Her presumption was, in Crisp's eyes, a blessing. In his briefing he did not mention the raging arguments over markets and choice; nor had Blair or Paul Corrigan, the prime minister's special adviser on health, forewarned her that those controversies remained unresolved. At least she was told that Milburn had created an excessive number of primary care trusts – 302. Too many were small, badly managed and wasteful in commissioning and providing care. Crisp agreed that the number should be halved. 'It's all in hand,' he told her. Without warning the new minister, Crisp had decided to remove the PCTs' authority to provide care – a revolutionary change – and to reduce the thirty-one PCTs in London to five. The publication of these proposals in 'Commissioning a Patient-Led NHS' provoked an uproar. 'It came out of the blue,' Hewitt would say. 'Crisp cut the PCTs' powers without any discussion, or telling Downing Street, because that was his policy.' London's Labour MPs led the outcry, and their complaints went directly to Blair.

'Get the MPs off my back,' he told Hewitt.

Until then, Blair had not mentioned that, despite all the changes, the NHS's structure remained unsatisfactory. The prime minister, Hewitt knew, 'did not do detail', but she was unprepared for his patchy knowledge. In the past, Corrigan, an other-worldly academic, had nudged Blair about 'strategy' but had rarely presented any pertinent insights on the NHS's performance. He was replaced by Ian Dodge, a civil servant. After it was discovered that the latest special adviser had a limited understanding of party politics, Dodge was reassigned and Corrigan recalled. The net result was that Hewitt was bereft of leadership from Downing Street.

'The PCTs don't have traction,' Blair told her. 'They're not entrepreneurial enough. Why have they not got enough bite? Why aren't we doing more with the market?'

Hewitt was bewildered. She was unaware of the hazardous journey since 1997 towards competition, nor had she grasped how Crisp and his lieutenants disparaged Blair's support for choice. The officials spoke about 'the difficulty of designing a market in health care'. None admired France's 'success' in providing faster and better health treatment, instead damning the internal markets operating there as 'wasteful'.

For five years, Blair had bit by bit opened the cage door to encourage NHS independence, but the bird had not moved. So often he would say, 'The reform programme is not going fast enough,' or, 'The department is not committed to the reform agenda.' Although he blamed civil servants in general for sticking to their traditional obstructive ways, he never identified Crisp and John Bacon, his deputy, as the culprits blocking his desire for modernisation. Accordingly, he did not consider removing them.

Crisp's proposed changes to the PCTs were instantly revoked, and the baptism of fire prompted Hewitt to reassess her inheritance. Her advisers completed the picture.

'John Reid did not dislodge the civil service opposition,' she heard from Norman Warner, the only junior minister with any expertise in health. Reid's murky legacy was concealed by Blair's praise for his troubleshooter, a misjudgement that pervaded Downing Street.

Corrigan gave a stark message about Blair's mindset to Matthew Swindells, Hewitt's new special adviser: 'We're stuck in halfway land on commissioning and choice. The department's unhelpful.' Swindells, an experienced NHS executive, was puzzled. Eight years after Labour first came to power, Downing Street still lacked a master plan for the NHS.

Blair did not wholeheartedly believe that 'choice' could reduce waiting times. His gospel remained targets and 'deliverology' – except there was a problem: Michael Barber, the godfather of the Delivery Unit, had resigned for personal reasons before the election. In Whitehall and beyond, no one could find a successor. There was a good reason: 'deliverology' had failed to win converts. Barber's bullying methods of command and control had, for example, reduced street crime but, once the unit's pressure moved on to another target, the old offences had increased again. 'Smoke and mirrors', was a familiar judgement. Blair was in an odd situation. He believed in delivery but lacked a deliverer. He drew the obvious conclusion: there was no alternative other than to close the Delivery Unit.

After hitting a brick wall about the NHS, he asked several experts for advice and changed his mind once again. Over a weekend at Chequers, he handwrote a memorandum spelling out the final reorganisation of the NHS. After all the targets and changes, he half understood his error. During the eight years since 1997, he had dismantled, then procrastinated and finally arrived back where he should have started – building on his inheritance from the Tories. He should never have placed his faith in centralised control. Only now did the sterility of his debate about reforming the public services begin to register with him. Naturally, he would not admit responsibility for the costly waste, even to himself.

Delivering his new wisdom required delicacy. To win Gordon Brown's agreement, he took the unusual step of creating a Cabinet committee, with himself as chairman. Among its members were Brown, Hewitt, John Prescott, Warner and Crisp. After the first meeting, Brown refused to attend and sent Paul Boateng, dubbed 'the ventriloquist's puppet', to oppose everything. Looking at Prescott's artless face while Blair described his ambitions, Warner contemplated how the NHS was again heading towards the buffers. Reform depended on inserting a team of like-minded supporters into Richmond House to challenge Crisp's prejudices. Blair's use of buzzwords like 'mechanisms' and 'organisation' showed a man talking a foreign language to the NHS staff. 'Tony doesn't know what he wants,' Warner concluded at the end of the first month. 'He's just looking around for a silver bullet to say "reform".'

Hewitt also grasped that 'Labour didn't have a road map. Tony hadn't caught up.' She turned to Crisp for help. 'Tell me, Nigel,' she said, 'how do you see reform progressing? Explain to me our "change" strategy.'

Crisp spoke, but Hewitt could make no sense of what he was

describing. 'Would you like to see the department's work programme?' he offered.

'Yes, please,' replied the minister.

The following day, Hewitt was shown a vast piece of paper – endless sheets of A3 paper sellotaped together – covering the length of a long conference table. 'This', said Crisp, 'shows 112 different work streams which the department is undertaking.'

Hewitt was bemused. The introverted chief executive defied understanding. Behind him stood John Bacon, his chief supporter brazenly showing that nothing had changed since Le Grand had discovered that 'he didn't care what ministers wanted'.

'We have a problem,' she realised. 'There's no narrative which explains what we are doing on foundation hospitals and markets.' Crisp, she suspected, 'didn't understand Tony's reform programme, politics or politicians'. She said nothing to Blair, who had appointed four new ministers to the department since the election. Other than Warner, none had yet mastered the NHS's complexities.

'There were no new ideas, no grip and no pushing forward,' observed the NHS's former chief executive Andrew McKeon. 'It was turgid drift.' Soon after, Corrigan departed for good. 'We need to decide what to do,' Blair told his replacement. The new adviser didn't take long to conclude what the others had realised – that Blair had no blueprint for the NHS, while 'Crisp supported his version of the NHS but not the real facts. He didn't get it.'

Crisp had also decided that Blair's latest initiative on 'choice' was just another of his quick fixes. 'The problem is always implementation. Real life doesn't happen in soundbites. It's hard work,' he later wrote. There was also institutional sabotage. Foundation hospitals, some NHS chief executives complained, were 'being strangled by bureaucrats introducing unexpected changes to the original vision'. The executives mentioned new red tape, interference in their finances and 'the reassertion of the old system of command and control'.

If Blair had heard Crisp's carping, he would have had good reason to feel resentment. At the Olympic summit in Singapore, his charm had tipped the balance during individual interviews with each delegation and, on 6 July, in Scotland, he heard that London's Olympic bid had succeeded. Gordon Brown, everyone knew, could never have achieved such a victory. Blair had flown on from Singapore to chair a meeting of the G8 leaders in Gleneagles. After intensive lobbying by Bob Geldof and Bono, Blair had persuaded the seven other leaders to place African debt relief high on the agenda. The 'Make Poverty History' campaign would write off Africa's debt.

In the early sunshine the following day, he walked with President Bush in the park before formally opening the summit. The forty Labour MPs known as the 'awkward squad', who had demanded his resignation after the election, had been silenced by his appeal for the party to unite and aim for a fourth election victory. By sticking by him they bene-fited not only from a charismatic leader, but also one blessed with luck. A week earlier, voters in Holland and France had rejected a proposed constitution for the EU. Those results saved him from holding a ref-erendum about Europe, and as he walked with Bush back to the hotel he had every reason to expect to remain prime minister for another four years. Minutes later, his life changed.

Just before 9 a.m., three bombs exploded in the London Tube. Soon after, another one destroyed a bus. The opening of the summit was inter-rupted as Blair was told about the attack. Clearly shaken, he chaired the meeting until midday, made a defiant TV address surrounded by the other leaders, then flew to London to attend a Cobra meeting. By the evening, he had returned to Scotland.

The security services assessed the outrage efficiently. Four Islamic bombers had killed fifty-two commuters and injured about 700 others. Blair was told that the emergency services were performing outstand-ingly – but those reports to Downing Street were not completely accur-ate. Incidents of poor leadership, an obsession by a few with health and safety, and lacklustre co-ordination among the services had led to a checkered performance. Nevertheless, Blair's status momentarily soared. In the crisis, even his most trenchant critics withdrew, while he dominated the airwaves talking about the dangers of terror. On the streets, Londoners nevertheless soon drew a direct link between the outrage and the invasion of Iraq. Initially, they were ignored by Blair. Later, he would say, 'What they want us to do is turn round and say, "Oh, it's our fault."' He refused to take the blame. He was back in the spotlight but under pressure.

Fortunately, Brown was similarly harassed to explain what the shadow chancellor George Osborne called 'the fiddled figures'. Britain's debts were rising, tax increases were inevitable and the public finances no longer looked so healthy. To maintain his reputation and secure an uncontested inheritance, Brown agreed with Blair a new spending limit for 2007, the date he assumed he would become leader. In anticipation, he did not give up his promotion of what he called 'Labour values' in the NHS.

Down the executive corridor in Richmond House, Ken Anderson, the commercial director, still felt ignored by Hewitt and was under pressure from the Treasury. The Texan was repeatedly summoned by Shriti Vadera, Brown's apostle, to justify the subcontracting of services to private companies.

Reflecting Brown's desire to undermine Blair, journalists were being tipped off by the chancellor's spokesman that Anderson's record in Texas was 'controversial' – a wholly unfounded allegation Brown was also sabotaging the stock-takes organised by Gus O'Donnell, the new Cabinet secretary. 'A disaster,' Warner concluded at the end of the first meeting on the NHS after the election. Brown left after twenty minutes and would never return, but Hewitt was untroubled by his absence. Unlike her experience at the DTI, the Treasury was, to her delight, 'shovelling money' into the NHS with no questions asked.

Warner, however, had misgivings. Just after the election, he had sent Hewitt and Crisp a memorandum warning that the NHS was heading for an unquantifiable deficit forbidden by the official spending rules. Hewitt accepted Crisp's assurances that such fears were groundless.

Ever since 1997, Blair had focused on staff numbers and buildings but not on productivity or value for money. Between 1998 and 2005, the NHS had hired an extra 307,000 people, the largest growth by a single employer in any country. Besides more doctors and nurses, it had employed 52,000 more administrators over the previous four years, increasing the managerial payroll by a third. 'There was overstaffing on a ministerial whim,' noted Rob Webster, the chief executive of the NHS Confederation. 'With so much money, they lost the plot and recruited more staff than was planned.'

Research by yet another organisation, the Office for National Statistics (ONS), revealed that staff productivity had risen until 1997, then flattened, and between 2001 and 2005 declined. Some, including Derek Wanless, the former banker employed by Brown, would describe the ONS's research as inaccurate because it failed to account for the quality and success of individual treatments. But even he acknowledged that unit costs in hospitals had increased.

A contagious malady handicapped NHS staff: from the most senior downwards, they seemed unable to embrace self-improvement. Too often, staff refused to read about medical innovations in other countries, and both hospital administrators and doctors stuck to outdated treatments. Many attempts to innovate failed. Under Frank Dobson, one NHS area was ordered to add 7,000 beds by 2000, but by 2005 4,518 of those beds had been withdrawn. The additional money and reorganisation was failing to treat proportionately more patients. Some blamed the culture of fear imposed by targets and inspection for undermining those managers who were minded to take risks and pioneer self-improvement. The Healthcare Commission reported that, if all hospitals were as productive as the best, the NHS could increase the amount of surgery performed by up to 49 per cent. None of these figures seemed to matter. Pressed on why productivity was falling by about 2.5 per cent a year – and by 4 per cent if the staff's high sickness rate was included – Crisp replied, 'The NHS is saving more lives.'

The traditionalists could always unearth ammunition to undermine

Blair's advocacy of change. Whatever flaws were exposed, the staff protected their benefits. Forty per cent of them were receiving annual pay increases regardless of performance. Milburn's rewards for employees who improved their expertise was proving as expensive as his concession of a 37.5-hour week. Half of the annual increase in the budget was spent on wages and ceaseless recruitment.

Reid's 2003 agreements with the doctors had also become a burden. Within three years, GPs' annual pay had doubled to £106,400, while consultants' pay was up 27 per cent to £109,974, which in 2005 cost the NHS an additional £220 million. The consultants' hospital car parks were like top-end car showrooms. In return for the extra money, GPs were working four hours less a week. 'John Reid paid out to GPs more than was anticipated, and that was after a 32 per cent pay increase,' admitted John Chisholm, the BMA's delighted negotiator.

Consultants were also working fewer hours on clinical care. 'The consultants' contract', said George Alberti, 'was insulting. The BMA created clock-watching doctors.' Weak hospital managers were failing to challenge the doctors to abide by the new contracts. The resulting higher pay, Wanless reported, failed 'to demonstrate significant benefits [for patients] from the pay deals'. Blair loathed the BMA but was powerless.

In sum, by 2005 the NHS was costing £43 billion a year more than in 1997. The country's health had improved (if not in proportion to the additional money spent) but, in terms of the number of doctors, the use of technical equipment, the number of patients being treated and the cure rates for cancer and heart disease, Britain still ranked near the bottom of the international league tables. Some argued that the improvement in the country's health, despite the growth of MRSA and other infections caught in dirty hospitals, owed more to the reduction in smoking, better drugs (especially statins) and a healthier lifestyle than the NHS's performance.

Despite his scepticism, Crisp was overseeing the applications for hospitals to become self-governing. Among the applicants seeking to become a foundation hospital in 2005 was the Mid-Staffordshire Hospital Trust. There was no opposition from the new regulators, which included the Healthcare Commission and the Care Quality Commission led by Cynthia Bower. All were satisfied that Mid-Staffs had consistently met its targets. Not one of those health professionals sifting through the hospital's data noticed the abnormally high death rates or that targets were being 'falsified outright to avoid non-compliance'. None of the experts visiting the hospital spotted that managers and nursing staff were being systematically cruel towards hundreds of patients; corrupted by the 'box-ticking culture', as a later inquiry would describe it, the carers were causing hundreds of patients 'unimaginable suffering'. Instead, the inspectors unanimously prided themselves on Labour having fulfilled its pledge to create 'a new tough independent health care regulator'.

A report by Professor Brian Jarman would estimate that malpractice at Mid-Staffs had caused more than a thousand premature deaths. Searching through the statistical records of fourteen other hospitals starting in 2006, he calculated that there could have been an additional 19,000 premature fatalities, an extraordinarily high figure. Compared to other European countries, Britain's premature death rates were higher and clinical outcomes worse.

A hint of the decay within the NHS had been highlighted in May 2005. Just after the election, Warner had sent Crisp and Hewitt a message about his 'serious issues of concern about how the extra money we have pumped into the NHS is being managed'. Crisp admitted that the NHS's accounts for the £76.4 billion budget were 'not meaningful', and he ignored the warning.

Four months later, Ken Anderson noticed that the accounts for the previous financial year had still not been produced. 'What's the deal with the finances?' he asked Crisp. 'Why haven't the accounts been presented to the board? They're six months late.'

'It's all very delicate,' replied Crisp.

Anderson asked a secretary in Crisp's office for the records. His examination revealed that 'Crisp had no control over costs and didn't have a clue what to do.'

Under John Reid, Crisp had allowed an unquantified deficit to grow. His Transforming Community programme, which had seen some employees' pay increase by as much as 50 per cent, was partly to blame. But the biggest culprits were the PCTs. Over half were serial over-spenders, guilty of misusing the payment-by-results scheme, yet their profligacy had been excused repeatedly by Crisp's officials. The NHS's financial checks were so poor that neither Crisp nor Richard Douglas, the financial director, had realised the extent of the overspending.

Anderson told Blair's adviser in Downing Street, 'There's a problem. We need to see the books.'

Blair was 'puzzled' after hearing the news. 'How can they be running out of money when they've had so much?' he wondered. He asked Hewitt to hold a meeting to scrutinise the finances.

She had limited expectations as twelve officials led by Crisp entered the conference room on 12 December 2005. Amid coughs and pauses, Crisp admitted that instead of the NHS enjoying a £1 billion surplus in 2004/5, there was a deficit of at least £700 million, and possibly £1.2 billion. The blood drained from Hewitt's face. 'Well, Sir Nigel, what do you suggest we do?' Crisp's reply was difficult to understand. 'This is a shambles,' she concluded.

'So basically', said Bill McCarthy, the director of policy, 'we are where we are, and we have no plan to solve it?'

Crisp – who would later say, 'I regarded myself as a problem-solver' – did not reply. Considering the NHS's budget, a deficit of 1 per cent was manageable, but more than money was at stake. Blair's reform programme was being threatened by officials who not only assumed there was unlimited money, but also that targets were pointless. 'We felt outraged by Crisp,' recalled Matthew Swindells. 'That's why we made a big thing out of it.'

Hewitt and Anderson told Blair that Crisp had been working with 'fairy-tale numbers which had been exposed as bullshit'. Some hospitals,

Hewitt explained, could not even accurately report how many staff they employed. She had also discovered that the department's 'indicative tariffs' – the costings for the entire NHS – had been 'wrongly calculated'. She ordered those responsible to her office. Three people arrived. All revealed they lacked the required expertise. 'The department's not fit for purpose,' Hewitt concluded. A qualified team was hired – in Australia, Hewitt's birthplace – to produce the first accurate tariffs.

The overspend, Blair heard, was only one difficulty. Another was that most of the additional £3.6 billion pledged to the NHS during that year would be spent on pay increases, drugs, buildings and negligence payments. Only £475 million would be directed towards improving treatment. Contrary to Richard Douglas's optimistic forecast promising productivity improvements in return for what he had called 'pay modernisation', the opposite had occurred.

Part of the blame, Crisp later said, was the use, despite his opposition, of independent sector treatment centres, which caused NHS facilities to be wasted. He ignored a report produced by his own department that admitted that the ISTCs had forced the NHS to become more productive. Crisp would only later concede, 'We lost clear direction.' Hewitt's conclusions were more explicit: Crisp and his team had lost control.

The truth was dismal. Under Crisp, the funding formula for the NHS had been changed four times since 2001, and each change had triggered costs and no benefits. The plans to incentivise quicker treatment – through choice, private providers, foundation hospitals and payment by results – had not been properly implemented.

Crisp's answer to all the complaints was that the NHS was the victim of its own success in treating more people. Bradford Royal Infirmary, a foundation hospital, was an example. In 2004, the hospital had treated 11 per cent more patients, but the improvement was cancelled out by the hospital's failure to get the cash from the PCTs to pay the staff for the additional work. Similar mismanagement had plunged a quarter of all hospitals into debt. The NHS executives had also failed to anticipate that the bureaucrats managing the 350 PCTs would increase their annual administration costs by £1.5 billion.

A study by Sir Tony Atkinson of the ONS provided the final judgement. Examining the NHS in 2004, he discovered that only £35 out of every additional £100 spent since the Wanless report had produced real improvements. Of the remainder, £56 had fuelled inflation within the service and £9 was lost through falling productivity, which had declined between 3 and 8 per cent each year since 1995.

The chaos built up over the previous five years was finally exposed. Talking with Hewitt, Blair was 'acutely aware how much had gone wrong'. As usual, he did not ask for a detailed explanation or the names of those who were to blame. 'We went backwards under Frank,' he lamented to Hewitt. 'It [reform] only started when Alan came in.' To Swindells, he looked demoralised. 'Probably I only found my voice on domestic reform in the last term,' Blair would write of his first eight years in power, but he was more candid when he also confessed, 'We shied away from deep systemic reform.' All the mantras – 'investment and reform', 'rights and responsibilities', 'hand up but not hand out' – had cut waiting times and improved some standards but had failed to prevent over a thousand deaths in the Mid-Staffs hospital, encouraged financial waste and stymied proper modernisation.

Blair was persuaded by Anderson that John Bacon, who was portrayed as a Soviet ideologue announcing the 'record production of tractors', was one obstacle. 'He's a wallpaper merchant,' said Anderson, 'putting up wallpaper over huge cracks.' Crisp was told that, unless Bacon resigned, there would be repercussions. Bacon agreed to depart, but denied any such shortcomings.

'You should under-promise and over-deliver,' Crisp suggested to his masters, 'but that's not the political way.'

'Is Crisp up to it?' Hewitt was asked by a Downing Street adviser. Blair did not ask the same question. Removing a permanent secretary was difficult, even for a prime minister.

The solution, Hewitt decided, was to hire McKinsey, the consultants.

'We don't want a report on the department,' the team was told. 'Just talk to people and tell us what you hear.' The result was ugly. A culture of bullying and innumeracy infected Richmond House.

'We need to get rid of Crisp,' Blair was told by his domestic adviser. He looked surprised but agreed: he was dispassionate about a man who had defied his quest for reform.

'You've lost the confidence of the health minister,' O'Donnell told Crisp. 'I think it's best if you retire.'

Crisp was surprised but understood the system. 'I had lost power and leverage,' he admitted later. 'The environment had moved against me.'

'Nigel will go,' O'Donnell reported. 'It will be quiet and dignified. You may need to get him a seat in the Lords.'

'If that's the way to get rid of him, do it,' Blair replied.

The prime minister summoned Crisp to bid farewell. 'I am particularly saddened', Crisp admitted, 'by the financial problems we are grappling with.' On 7 March 2006, he duly resigned – at the age of fifty-four – and was created a peer. No other permanent secretary had been rewarded in similar circumstances. Blair praised him as 'a superb public servant'. He had not, Crisp said, been pressured to resign.

FORTY

The Legacy Dims

The London bombings of 7 July 2005 permanently transformed the immigration debate. All four bombers were born in Britain, an unexpected phenomenon that challenged the virtues of multiculturalism. Overnight, Blair questioned his previous views. 'The rules of the game have changed,' he said in a declaration of war. He wanted more legislation to criminalise the extremists, an extension of imprisonment without bail of terrorist suspects and more money for the intelligence services.

Around the water cooler in the Home Office, officials and ministers discussed the pedigree of 'home-grown terrorists who sound like us'. Just why did people who found refuge and comfort in Britain turn against the country that was providing them with generous welfare benefits?

Blair offered no answer to those complaining that Abu Qatada and Abu Hamza, two Muslim preachers, were urging violence on the streets of north London. 'Multiculturalism is preventing their arrest,' said a security official who had formerly worked in the immigration directorate. 'We need to get inside the Muslim community to influence their opinions.'

General Jonathan Shaw, the director of Britain's special forces, watched Blair at the first Cobra meeting after the bombings. 'He didn't understand the machine of which he was the master,' he observed, 'so he got in the way of getting what he needed.'

Instead of demanding the two preachers' arrest, Blair listened to Jack Straw arguing that the Muslim community must not be alienated. 'Jack wants the Muslims to be uncritically indulged,' noted Tony McNulty, the new immigration minister.

Straw was supported by Robert Hill, by then a special assistant in the Home Office. 'It's incumbent on the host community', Hill told McNulty, 'to allow other communities to do what they want.'

Hazel Blears, the Home Office minister responsible for counter-terrorism, disagreed. 'We need to know why the Muslims have become radicalised.'

She was supported by Ruth Kelly. 'The Muslim Council', said the education minister, 'must adhere to Britain's common values and condemn Islamic violence.' There was a chasm between Muslims who refused to ostracise the so-called infidels and those advocating integration into British society.

'What does Tony think about the split?' McNulty asked Matt Cavanagh, Downing Street's new adviser on immigration.

'Tony refuses to take sides,' replied Cavanagh.

Since the election, Blair had sat on the fence about immigration, wrestling with a political minefield. The terrorist threat, he asserted, justified the invasion of Iraq. His critics said the opposite: the invasion had incited the outrage.

Just as he had relied on the army and intelligence services, in the aftermath of the explosions Blair trusted the police. His faith was misplaced. Their deliberate shooting of Jean Charles de Menezes, an innocent Brazilian, at Stockwell tube station proved that the Metropolitan force was flawed, and Scotland Yard had concealed their officers' mistake by lying. Combined with the violent corralling or 'kettling' of peaceful demonstrators in London, some police acted as if unfettered by the law. But by then the public's trust in all the state's institutions had become strained. Blair's answer to the scepticism was a speech focused on the continuing dangers of terrorism. Within days, the headlines were forgotten.

Before the London bombs, Blair had given Charles Clarke and Tony McNulty the impression that, with the election over, his concerns about immigration had evaporated. Only the extreme left and right, he believed, were 'peddling an emotionally attractive but practically foolish or even dangerous debate around immigration'. Discussion of the topic was to be shut down. McNulty was told in advance of a meeting in Downing Street that Blair did not want to discuss numbers, not even about the unexpected influx of European migrants. That was surprising. Rather than 13,000 A8 nationals coming to Britain, as predicted by Christian Dustmann, a London academic, the preliminary estimate was that 630,000 had arrived.

'I've just had forty-five minutes with Gerry Adams,' Blair said, as he walked into the room for the scheduled one-hour meeting, 'and I've got the Queen at five-thirty. So let's get on.' Clarke described his new immigration bill, the fifth since 1997. After thirty minutes, Blair stood up and ended the meeting. The latest wave of immigrants was not mentioned.

Three months later, Blair bowed to the public's anger over large immigrant families living on benefits in comfortable homes. Justin Russell, his special adviser, warned that media reports about the unending stream of 'foreign scroungers' unwilling to adopt British values was undermining support among Labour voters. The focus was no longer on asylum-seekers. By opening access through work permits, only 23,000 people would apply for asylum in 2006, the same as in 1996.

'We will meet the tipping point at the end of the year,' McNulty told Blair, meaning that the same number of bogus asylum-seekers would be deported as applied. 'You can hold me to that.'

'I will,' replied Blair.

The target would not quite be reached: 25,712 would apply for asylum and 22,654 applications were refused. McNulty could not remedy Blair's irritation that judges were still using Labour's human rights laws to prevent the deportation of foreign nationals, or offer any solution to the 520,000 migrants arriving that year. At least 200,000 people were leaving, which reduced the headline figures.

The articles generated before the election about 'crackdowns' had buried the research showing that a third of all new homes built in south-east England were inhabited by non-British people. The cosmetic treatment of statistics was discussed between Lin Homer, the new head of the IND, and Blair in September. 'There's a handling problem,' John McTernan, Blair's new policy adviser, was told. To improve the government's image, Blair announced the reversal of multiculturalism and the closure of the borders under the new slogan 'Prevent, Protect, Pursue and Prepare'. But the revival of his interest in immigration was short-lived, while Homer was soon regarded as being as hapless as her predecessor.

Blair was looking at the big picture. Finally, he believed that he understood the mystery of ruling. 'I really did feel absolutely at the height of my ability and at the top of my game,' he wrote. 'I was pushing hard on all fronts.' He would not be fighting another general election, he had already declared. The Queen's Speech would promise forty-five bills to create his legacy. Attitudes ingrained in 1997 about the NHS, education, pensions, welfare and immigration were jettisoned. In the best practice of the Third Way, he plundered the Tory manifesto. Nothing, he told his new team, would undermine his idealism. 'Every time I've ever introduced a reform in government,' he said shortly afterwards, 'I wish in retrospect I'd gone further.'

'I stand before you as the first leader of the Labour Party to win three full consecutive terms in office,' Blair told the party's annual conference in Brighton in 2005.

His emphasis on 'full' infuriated Gordon Brown, who had announced an immediate national tour to prepare for his premiership. 'You completely shafted me last year by ratting on our deal,' he shouted after they returned to Downing Street. 'You have to set a date.'

To fan the flames, Cherie told a BBC journalist that the corporation should dampen its speculation about her husband's departure: 'Darling, that is a long way in the future. It is too far ahead for me even to think about.'

In retaliation, Brown unleashed Damian McBride, a shrewd Rottweiler, to feed the media with anecdotes portraying Blair as a lame duck. Newspapers published accurate stories about Brown demanding

Blair's departure. Blair retaliated by asking Alan Milburn and Charles Clarke to question Brown's fitness to be prime minister, and even contemplated a leadership election. As increasing numbers of supporters asked about his intentions, Blair realised his error of pre-announcing his departure. 'We began to lose control of the party,' admitted Powell.

The proof of disarray was Blair's latest plan to protect Britain's security. Fearful of international terrorism, he decided that the police should be allowed to detain suspected terrorists for ninety days without charge. Not even Michael Howard supported such provisions. Rather than compromise, Blair staked his authority on success in the Commons. It was a miscalculation: forty-nine Labour MPs voted with the opposition, defeating the government by 323 votes to 290. Blair grimaced when told the result moments before the formal announcement. His luck had finally run out. 'Sometimes it's better to lose and do the right thing than to win and do the wrong thing,' was his rationale. No longer invincible, he immediately agreed to a compromise of twenty-eight days.

The Teflon was further scratched by the publication on the same day, 9 November, of an acerbic account by Christopher Meyer, the former British ambassador in Washington, describing Blair's subservient relationship with President Bush. Blair's sense of isolation may possibly have influenced his ungenerous farewell speech for departing Tory leader Michael Howard at the end of the month. Bitterness was capturing his spirit.

The seventh of December saw Blair make his debut against David Cameron, the thirty-nine-year-old new Tory leader. The Old Etonian's political bibles included *The Unfinished Revolution* by Philip Gould, a flattering accolade to Blair. Cameron had prepared a perfect soundbite for his first exchange at Prime Minister's Questions: Blair was 'stuck in the past and I want to talk about the future. He was the future once.' Blair's thin smile acknowledged the arrow had struck home.

Blair had also been persuaded that Brown was no longer a safe pair of hands: he had raised taxes too high, was spending 'massively' on

welfare credits to redistribute wealth and was failing to limit the deficit. Britons, Blair learned, were saving too little, and the government
was wasting untold amounts of money. He insisted on a Fundamental
Savings Review. Brown refused to co-operate until a formal letter
arrived at the Treasury. 'You asked for a fucking document, so there it
is,' shouted Brown, throwing the review papers on Blair's desk.

Both knew the exercise was pointless. Blair had long ago lost control of spending, while Brown assumed that the economy would grow
ceaselessly and refused to cut the budget. Instead, he would increase
borrowing, taxation and spending to win the next election.

Blair chose to concentrate on pensions. Ever since he had ridiculed
Peter Lilley's sensible reforms in 1997, he had ignored the consequences
of allowing Brown to wreck the balance between the social classes'
contributions to the welfare state, not least by levying an extra annual
£5 billion tax on private pensions. The chancellor had discouraged saving. Increasingly, only foreigners could afford to buy British corporations and expensive homes. Instead of praising his countrymen who
accumulated wealth, millions of Britons were encouraged to 'play the
system' by receiving welfare benefits rather than working and providing
for themselves. Belatedly, Blair recognised that Brown was ignoring the
abuses of the system and refusing even to protect the basic state pension.
The report by Adair Turner, commissioned in 2003, warned that people
were not saving for their retirement and intended to rely on the state.
The remedy, Turner advised, was to link state pensions to incomes. To
overcome Brown's opposition, Blair mastered the intricacies.

'We can't afford it,' Brown told him.

'Yes, we can,' insisted Blair, showing Brown the statistics.

'No,' said Brown, and stomped off.

Brown's first Budget had accelerated the end of Britain's private
pension schemes. Employees rapidly lost their traditional final-salary-
related pensions, but at the same time Blair surrendered to the trade
unions by allowing public-sector workers to retain their right to retire
at sixty rather than sixty-five with inflation-proof pensions.

Blair knew that the private sector paying for public-sector employees' advantages was unsustainable. Inevitably, Brown disagreed. Ignoring the Treasury's advice, he refused to abandon means-tested benefits and, as outlined by Turner, restore the link between earnings and pensions. Their argument became intense.

David Blunkett, the new pensions minister, understood the truth: 'Gordon wanted pension reform to be his achievement, his legacy, just like Beveridge. So he refused to arrive at our meetings.' Soon after, Blunkett resigned from the Cabinet for the second time after failing to declare payments and a share purchase from a private company.

In February 2006, John Hutton, the next pensions minister, gave a slide presentation in Downing Street. He did not get past the second transparency. 'Blair and Brown started screaming at each other,' he recalled. 'The row was terrible.' The argument lasted for what appeared to be 'a lifetime', but it had in fact gone on for about forty-five minutes when both men walked out. For the chancellor, pensions reform was just another weapon to destabilise Blair. He would not agree to any changes. He could not overthrow Blair, but he would make his life intolerable.

FORTY-ONE

The Great Game

After the election, Blair intended to 'settle Iraq and if possible get our troops on their way out before I left'. At the same time, the chiefs were obeying his order to send the army's ARRC headquarters, with over 2,000 soldiers, from its German base to Afghanistan.

John Reid was the new secretary of state for defence. 'I've come home,' he told one official, reminiscing about his happy period as a junior defence minister in 1997. With the cultivated image of the shrewd politician who delivered, he told his senior officials on his first day that at the top of the prime minister's list was 'put[ting] some backbone into the ministry'. Looking at Kevin Tebbit, he went on, 'Too many officials are not up for Afghanistan.'

'The army's too enthusiastic,' said Tebbit. 'This could be a mission too far.'

'The prime minister wants it,' Reid replied, having ingested Blair's suspicions about civil servants.

With Blair's encouragement, Nigel Sheinwald, his new foreign affairs adviser after David Manning had been sent as ambassador to Washington, spoke to senior officials in the ministry. Viewed by Tebbit as 'Blair's new attack dog', Sheinwald hoped in particular to persuade Desmond Bowen, responsible for the ministry's policy, to support Blair's commitment to Afghanistan. He found resistance. The snatch arrest of two undercover SAS soldiers in Basra in September 2005 by local police in alliance with Shia militias had exposed the army's plight. A large British operation to rescue the soldiers had provoked a firestorm. To embark for Afghanistan while British soldiers were still dying in Basra appeared to Bowen ill considered.

Soon after, apparently without General Mike Jackson's knowledge, a NATO meeting in Canada horse-traded a reassignment of British troops within Afghanistan as the price for securing Canadian partici-pation in the operation. Canadian soldiers rather than British would be sent to Kandahar, a traditionally quiet region, albeit one where the Taliban had been founded. The British army would head for Helmand, a centre of narcotics trading.

'Let's do some proper soldiering,' Jackson enthused to his fellow gen-erals. Afghanistan was attractive. Sending out patrols for a few days and returning to 'fixed' bases was a familiar routine, unlike the unpredict-able engagements in Iraq.

'Use it or lose it,' Generals Jackson, Richard Dannatt and Mike Walker chimed. Although the three men disliked each other, they agreed that supporting Blair might forestall the Treasury's abolition of certain regiments to save more money. Politics smothered the practical difficulties of relocating from Iraq to Afghanistan. Even under the best circumstances, the switch would be tricky, but to Blair's misfortune, the chiefs were divided on specifics. Despite Jackson's enthusiasm, Air Marshal Jock Stirrup believed that the army's withdrawal from Iraq would take longer than anticipated. Walker dismissed the airman's objections as worthless. To avoid an unseemly split, Stirrup allowed himself to be persuaded by Jackson and Dannatt's 'overenthusiasm' that the mission to Afghanistan was 'doable' and converted from opposition to ambivalence. 'We had to support the NATO mission,' he said. 'Other countries were relying on us, and I had no evidence against it.'

Only Admiral Alan West remained opposed. At a meeting between the chiefs and Reid, West mentioned his previous role as chief of defence intelligence for three years. 'I can tell you that there's a lack of intelligence about the truth on the ground in Helmand. This is a leap in the dark. Do we really want to get involved in this?' There was no evi-dence, he told Reid, that the Taliban had returned, and he questioned the reason for Britain's involvement in the operation. 'Why are we trying to cut poppy production and focus on counter-narcotics oper-ations?' he asked. The Americans, he added, had been combating drug operations in Colombia and that had 'dragged on for decades'.

'The prime minister wants to do it,' replied Reid once again, suspi-cious of the admiral. West found himself isolated – except that Kevin Tebbit privately expressed his agreement.

At a later briefing for the three chiefs at Fort Monckton, the MI6 training centre on the south coast, John Scarlett mentioned that only West opposed Britain's engagement in Afghanistan. To allay the ad-miral's grievances, particularly his unhappiness over the lack of any 'face time' with Blair, the prime minister agreed to host a dinner in Downing Street to discuss the fate of Britain's involvement in Iraq.

'What do you need to cope with this surge of violence?' Blair asked his guests, including Reid, Jonathan Powell, Sheinwald, Scarlett, the chiefs and General Rob Fry. As usual, the Foreign Office remained invisible, just as Powell and Blair wanted.

That evening, Blair, as a well-briefed lawyer, asked good questions. For their part, the chiefs had reached the pinnacle of their careers by telling any superior what he wanted to hear. Candour was not rewarded in the military, especially in an open forum. In return, Blair did not stir controversy by seeking unknown truths. Instead, he plucked at the answers that suited him, and no one was discomfited by penetrating follow-up questions. Drawn into the Iraqi war by a mixture of idealism, emotion and faulty intelligence, Blair once again failed to realise that none of his guests – each responsible for British policy in Iraq – could offer an original insight or a realistic solution. Despite eight years as prime minister, he did not grasp that none of his generals had fought in pitched battles and none understood Islamic societies. Nevertheless, he expected the military to produce an exit plan for the following year. Walker did at least volunteer that 'We need a minister to resolve this' – meaning Blair himself. The prime minister did not react. 'The gen-erals', observed one of the guests, 'could not offer a military solution to a political problem, and the Americans were not producing a political solution.'

Those at the dinner knew that, during a recent video conference with President Bush to discuss the chaos in Baghdad, Blair had 'bolted' rather than raise the difficult points with which he had been briefed.

'Why didn't you nail him on that?' Sheinwald had asked.

'I've got to play it long,' replied Blair.

To Fry, it appeared that Blair had convinced himself that 'If I believe hard enough and if I think hard enough, it will happen.'

The same sterile atmosphere re-emerged in Cabinet. 'What do you think I should do, Rob?' Blair asked Fry. 'How do we find our way through this? I'm really struggling.'

The general gave an anodyne answer.

'Great idea,' said Blair, concealing any doubts over whether his ministers understood the complexities. 'That's it.' The audience appeared to be impressed.

Progress for the withdrawal from Iraq and deployment to Afghanistan had been leisurely until the London explosions of 7 July. The British-born suicide bombers had been trained in Pakistan and had links to the Taliban. Like Bush, Blair wanted to minimise the danger in Britain by fighting the war against the terrorists as far away as possible. If the jihadists were defeated in Afghanistan, he calculated, the streets of Britain would be safer.

The violence in London coincided with Fry's submission of his proposal 'Why Helmand?' to the chiefs of staff. His answer was: because Britain could make a difference. With America battling terrorism in Iraq, and other NATO countries unwilling to enter the line of fire in Afghanistan, British troops would prevent the terrorists re-entering an ungoverned vacuum. Fry advocated dispatching troops to Lashkar Gah, the provincial capital. To reinforce his recommendation, Colonel Charlie Knaggs was sent to produce an intelligence report. After reading Knaggs's memo, Air Marshal Glenn Torpy, the chief of joint operations in Northwood, conducted his own survey. He confirmed that British troops faced no danger. His judgement was endorsed by Colonel Gordon Messenger, a marine who, like his predecessors, was not an intelligence officer.

'I had no sense from the military that Helmand was a hornets' nest,' Desmond Bowen would say after reading the reports. Sherard Cowper-Coles, posted as a British diplomat to Kabul in 2007, would claim that the intelligence agencies had distorted the information to avoid upsetting the politicians and generals, and that the Foreign Office's director for the region suppressed his own opposition to avoid being fired. '*Cognosco melior, facio taliter* [I know the best, I do the worst],' the official said.

No one paid attention to the negative report by Air Marshal Stuart Peach, the director of intelligence collection, who, as a former pilot, was deemed unsuited to assessing army operations in 'bandit country'. Nor, curiously, was much notice taken of the experience of the American intelligence agencies, or of Russia's fateful occupation during the 1980s. Torpy presented his plan to the chiefs without realising that, while Helmand was overrun with the Taliban, they remained relatively passive because the American counter-terrorist units bought peace from the local drug-traders with suitcases of dollars.

Fry proposed that the British army, as NATO's leader, should organise the transition from America's counter-terrorism strategy, which killed the enemy, to a counter-insurgency operation, which protected the nation-builders. 'Winning hearts and minds' was the sentiment, although it was not a term used by Fry because of its association with Vietnam. Just like in 2002, during the run-up to the invasion of Iraq, the Foreign Office's few specialists were muted. Blair relied on Nigel Sheinwald as his adviser, and Sheinwald knew no more about Afghanistan than did the military.

To avoid the familiar criticism of 'sofa' government, Blair agreed that Margaret Aldred, the deputy head of the foreign and defence policy secretariat, should chair a committee in the Cabinet Office to co-ordinate Britain's engagement. Aldred had been deeply immersed in the invasion of Iraq. Few regarded her as insightful, but her experience as a loyal supporter of the war was the ideal qualification for Afghanistan.

Known as the Reid Group, Aldred's committee oversaw the 'Joint UK Plan for Helmand'. Although it met without Blair, Aldred was guided by his motive: by leading the march into Helmand, Britain would expose the timidity of other nations. Ringing in the committee's ears was Mike Jackson's enthusiasm for the mission. 'Jackson was a dominant personality', recalled David Omand, 'with high prestige. He wanted to go. If he had opposed it, it wouldn't have happened.'

'The Americans and British could have declared victory after the Taliban's defeat in 2002 and departed,' observed Fry later, 'and Afghanistan could have continued to stew in its own juice with some PRTs [Provincial Reconstruction Teams] doing the nation-building.' Supported by his generals, Blair ignored that option.

Under the plan, the PRTs, protected by British and other NATO forces, would within three years transform Afghanistan into what was described as a 'mini-Belgium' by creating new education and legal systems and building a non-narcotic-based economy. Britain allocated a total budget of £1.3 billion. Eradicating the opium trade, one of Blair's favoured ambitions, was already a target of the Post-Conflict Reconstruction Unit led in Afghanistan by Major Mark Etherington, a Guards officer. Etherington was unimpressed by Aldred's plan. Whitehall, he cautioned at the end of 2005, was deluding itself. Afghanistan was a non-state governed by a corrupt elite of tribal leaders, financed and controlled by warring drug barons who were pretending to abide by an unsuitable constitution drafted by an ill-informed Frenchman.

Because Etherington's report contradicted Blair's intentions, the MoD ignored it. 'We know what we need to know about Helmand,' Etherington was told by an MI6 officer. An attempt by a Treasury special adviser to include Etherington on the Aldred committee failed. Aldred knew that Blair did not welcome contradictory opinions.

The lesson for other independently minded officers was that disloyalty obstructed promotion. 'Aldred's committee just stapled papers together,' despaired a Treasury official who watched the wheels grind.

By excluding the critics, Blair never heard from those who doubted the intelligence reports, or from those who questioned how Britain's under-resourced army could be effective 3,500 miles away, or from Whitehall's few Afghan experts, who were angered by DFID officials eagerly championing women's rights and seeking to impose 'liberal values' upon a feudal Islamic society. Despite the land-locked country's history, he believed that nation-building would defeat Islamic extremism. Confirming the prejudiced naivety in Downing Street, the politically correct Foreign Office had assigned a female ambassador to Kabul, despite the inevitable affront to the Muslim rulers.

Doubters were similarly silenced during a NATO conference in London in January 2006 aimed at encouraging participation in the operation. No one was allowed to mention the possible effect of NATO's presence on neighbouring Pakistan, a country that would eventually be destabilised by the war. Among those who would be ignored was General Graeme Lamb, who, following his exclusion by the MoD, would retire from the army after serving in Iraq and be instantly hired by General David Petraeus, the American commander, for service in Afghanistan.

The only dissident on Aldred's committee was Des Browne, the chief secretary to the Treasury. The notion of 'nation-building' in a medieval country that had never been ruled from Kabul, said Browne, was incoherent.

'What happens when we stop a convoy carrying heroin?' he asked Reid.

'We hand over responsibility to the sovereign government,' came the reply.

'Is there a sovereign government in Afghanistan?'

'These are sensible questions,' said Reid, adding with his familiar survivalist detachment, 'I'll ask the chiefs and come back with their answers.'

Browne said nothing more. He was familiar with the pattern of receiving unsatisfactory replies to questions. Criticising Reid would imply opposition to Blair himself.

To head off any disagreement, Afghanistan was listed on the Cabinet's agenda. While the chancellor remained silent at the meeting, Browne spoke against sending troops. 'We must go,' replied Reid, 'or the NATO mission will fail.' To end the argument, Blair assigned the decision to a Cabinet committee under John Prescott. The committee never met; Reid never answered Browne's questions; and Aldred's group was sidelined from the chain of command. The Cabinet Office, traditionally tasked with co-ordinating the prime minister's policies, was mocked as a 'Polo' – the hole at the heart of government.

Blair summoned Reid and Fry to his flat. 'Shouldn't we have a war cabinet?' Fry asked over a Sunday dinner. The lesson of Iraq, he implied, was the need for rigorous scrutiny. Blair rolled his eyes and pointed at the wall of 11 Downing Street.

To prove his meticulous shrewdness, Reid assumed the mantle of devil's advocate for his session with Walker to decide whether the army's enthusiasm for the new venture should be approved. Although he distrusted Tebbit, Reid relied on the permanent secretary to prepare a list of questions.

'Does going to Afghanistan make sense?' he asked.

'Yes,' replied Walker.

'Can we sustain two operations?' The 1998 strategic defence review had barred the army from engaging in two major wars simultaneously, so the move into Helmand should have followed the withdrawal from Iraq. Walker and his generals, especially Richard Dannatt, wanted to override that stricture.

'We've never been within the review plan,' Walker explained, meaning the defence review had been redundant since publication. Although there would be an overlap, he conceded, the army could cope. 'We want to withdraw from Iraq,' he said, identifying his quick cure to the stalemate in Basra. But since there was no date for the final withdrawal, he told Reid, 'We can do Iraq and Afghanistan.'

As he worked through his questions, Reid did not ask whether British officers could operate in a tribal society where they neither spoke the language nor understood the culture; nor did he query whether the

British would encounter resistance to nation-building, or whether the Taliban posed a danger. Despite the intelligence failure in Iraq, he did not question the reports stating that the army could perform well in Afghanistan. And since he favoured the deployment, Walker did not volunteer, as he admitted later, that 'we did not have any clear intelligence picture on Helmand. It was an empty hole.'

Reid was a bruiser who basked in the prime minister's trust, fortified by self-belief; he was not a counter-intuitive intellectual. One question did not dawn on him: had the army learned any lessons in Iraq? Accordingly, he never discovered that the army and the MoD had resisted a post-mortem to investigate their mistakes. In the military's mindset, not only did the generals and the MoD convince themselves that there would be no similarities between the two wars, but, pointedly, both had decided not to deploy senior officers with Iraqi experience to Afghanistan.

Not surprisingly, to protect his own department from embarrassment Tebbit did not prompt Reid to query the wisdom of Britain punching above its weight. Although the financial cuts since 1998 had denuded the army of reserves, Walker had stopped asking for additional funds. Knowing that Blair was addicted to using 'force for good', he said nothing more. At the end of the session, Reid thanked his guest for giving all the assurances he required. 'I acted on Walker's advice,' he would later say.

The two men visited Downing Street next. The passive mood in Blair's den did not reflect a government pondering another distant engagement. Walker was not surprised that Blair failed to ask, 'How badly wrong could it go?' or even ask for a comparison with the last three years in Iraq. The prime minister was not interested in the past. Since 2004, he had been eager to support NATO in Afghanistan, and General David Richards, the hero of Sierra Leone and the new NATO commander in Kabul, had assured him that nation-building was doable. For his part, Walker was not equipped to contribute to a discussion on foreign policy, and the general remained silent as Reid explained the plan devised by Air Marshal Torpy to send 3,150 lightly equipped troops, without surveillance drones and with only a few helicopters. Neither visitor mentioned that Brigadier Ed Butler, the mission's commander, had requested 10,000 men. That figure had been ridiculed by Walker. The number he had chosen reflected, in his words, 'what the market would bear' – not least to avoid an argument in Cabinet.

Relying on Torpy to decide the nature of the Afghan mission reflected the disorganisation of the British military. Torpy was a fighter pilot without any experience of land warfare. In his uneasy relationship with Butler, a seasoned forty-five-year-old former SAS commander and Old Etonian who first served in Afghanistan in 2001, Torpy never referred to the continuing flow of intelligence reports from the SAS groups that had been fighting the Taliban since 2001. 'Torpy didn't understand,' complained Butler long after. 'I was hugely frustrated and nearly resigned.' In 2005, Butler suffered Northwood's detachment in silence. Whitehall and Westminster relied on Margaret Aldred's committee to deliver the reassurance that Britain could safely engage in nation-building. Neither the contradictory intelligence reports nor Butler's request for at least 10,000 men were considered.

Reid was advised to suppress his own and Blair's gung-ho enthusiasm when he sought Cabinet approval, and instead to emphasise that it was a peaceful mission, with only 600 troops equipped for combat. Gus O'Donnell watched Reid make a 'this is all relatively straightforward and short-lived' presentation. Next, Blair went around the table asking each minister for their opinion.

Ruth Kelly stood up and gushed, 'Yes, we must go.'

Des Browne asked about the 'exit'.

'What are we getting into here?' asked Alistair Darling.

'This is essentially peacekeeping,' replied Reid, 'and we'll be surprised if there are more than a handful of British casualties.'

After the Cabinet gave its unanimous approval, Gordon Brown stopped his noisy scribbling and got up, saying, 'If that's your view, I'd better go and get the money.'

Five years later, Blair's recollection of the circumstances leading to that Cabinet decision did not match the memories of the others. 'As John made very clear, it would be a tough and dangerous mission [and] our military had a good plan for our contribution,' he wrote in 2010, contradicting Reid's suggestion that the mission would be peaceful. Jonathan Powell also provided a revisionist version. The military chiefs, he wrote, argued for going into Helmand in strength, 'although Tony and Reid were reluctant'.

A more accurate reflection of Blair's and Reid's intentions was the latter's statement in the Commons on 26 January 2006 announcing the commitment. 'This potent force', Reid said, was being sent 'to protect and deter . . . Afghanistan again becoming a sanctuary for terrorists', to guard the PRTs and to destroy the source of 90 per cent of Britain's heroin imports. The government's purpose was not to wage war. 'We would be perfectly happy', he fatally volunteered, 'if they returned without firing a shot.'

In April, as a final check before dispatching British troops to Lashkar Gah, Blair asked Bill Jeffrey, who had taken over as permanent secretary from Tebbit the previous November, for reassurance that the army's simultaneous engagement in Iraq and Afghanistan was 'manageable'.

Seeking Jeffrey's advice was bizarre. He had left the Home Office after being embarrassed by another immigration scandal. For the Cabinet secretary to appoint a man with no knowledge of defence as the senior official in the ministry highlighted the changing standards in the civil service. Previously, the new permanent secretary would have been an outstanding insider, and the disappointed candidates would have been dispatched to run other departments across Whitehall. The selection of Jeffrey, a taciturn man without any military expertise, just as Britain was about to enter another war reflected Blair's unusual management style. Having purposely excluded Tebbit from the inner councils, he by default deprived Whitehall of any senior civil servant able to scrutinise the logistics of the Afghan war – the manpower, equipment and plans. To no one's surprise, Jeffrey rarely emerged from his office, but he advised Blair that stretching the army between Iraq and Afghanistan was indeed manageable. The trick was for the troops to 'dribble' into Helmand over several months rather than all arriving together.

In his excitement, Reid ordered that a war room be set up in his suite of offices to follow the movements of the 'PRTs, plus a battle group in support and attack helicopters'. He was persuaded to desist.

On 23 April, Reid arrived in Kabul for his first visit to Afghanistan. Over breakfast, he was briefed by Ed Butler that, since the army's arrival in Lashkar Gah, the mission had gone pear-shaped. The intelligence reports had not identified the chaos and danger in Helmand, the Foreign Office and DFID officials were hopeless, and the 600 paratroopers were outgunned by the Taliban.

'What Taliban?' asked Reid. 'No one told me that there are any Taliban left. It's the first I've heard about this.'

Butler looked at the minister with surprise.

'What about nation-building?' asked Reid.

'It's always been a very complex security situation here,' Butler replied, unable then or thereafter to decide whether Reid was genuinely ignorant or just posturing.

Over the following four days, Reid saw the reality facing Britain's ill-equipped small army. 'We've got a serious problem,' he told Butler. 'I don't know how we got into this. Trust me, I'll sort it out. I'll knock a few heads together on this.'

The minister who had committed Britain to its fourth Afghan war spent the next five days hearing warnings about the possible consequences for Britain's inadequate force. He returned to London, but neither he nor Blair changed anything. And then he was gone, dispatched to the Home Office. His removal was followed by the departure of all the architects of the mission. Military officers, civil servants and politicians – all were replaced by men inexperienced in warfare or even defence.

FORTY-TWO

The Cost of Confusion

'Education is our best economic policy,' said Blair in 2005, but the truth about Britain's schools after his eight years in office was mixed. He had endorsed sixteen White Papers and eleven Acts of Parliament and had increased spending by 78 per cent, but the additional money, as David Normington was forced to admit to a parliamentary committee, had barely improved children's education. On the contrary, England's school examination results were poor, and had never been more controversial. In private, Blair accepted that failure.

In public statements, Normington occasionally asserted that 'school performance, both primary and secondary, is dramatically up, with a 17 per cent improvement in literacy since 1997', but he too acknowledged a different picture in private, with academic studies showing that there had been a decline in certain standards since 2000.

Research by the Curriculum, Evaluation and Management Centre (CEM) on 5,000 children across 120 schools had found no evidence of a rise in literacy levels since 1997. The improvements in the test results, particularly in literacy, owed everything to test preparation rather than an improvement in actual learning.

Blair had been misled by Michael Barber's graphs. Testing, the researchers reported, had been appropriated by the government to demonstrate an artificial rise in standards. To satisfy Barber, local authorities and schools were implementing *anti*-learning measures to boost results. Over 25 per cent of children were still leaving primary school without the required levels of reading and numeracy. Some studies would report that 33 per cent of school-leavers were deficient in the three Rs. 'National tests', admitted Andrew Adonis, newly appointed as junior education minister, 'show that progress is not being sustained across the board.' Blair knew that his original conviction that poverty was the principal cause of poor education was mistaken. Bad teachers were the main culprits. But, hooked by his slogan 'standards not structures', he had ignored the human factor and, like Adonis, he wanted to tell a good story.

Eight years after he had terminated the advantages enjoyed by pupils at 1,198 grant-maintained schools and introduced 'child-centred' classrooms, he reconsidered Chris Woodhead's homily that the only cure for England's inferior education was to remove bad teachers. Although his advisers had not shown him statistics indicating how well-trained American teachers had reduced the 'stubborn 20 per cent' of problem children in US schools to a mere 1.5 per cent, Ofsted reports sent to Downing Street did finally blame teachers for failing to improve education.

Records submitted to Downing Street showed that many of Labour's special programmes had been worthless. Some £885 million had been spent since 1998 to reduce truancy, but rates had increased, not least because of high illiteracy among secondary-school children. Schemes for eleven-year-olds had also failed. Those children targeted in one major project to improve literacy and numeracy costing £386 million still lacked the necessary skills. Most of England's disadvantaged children were not benefiting from the £1.1 billion spent annually on Sure Start, and even sympathetic politicians were disillusioned.

Blair's flagship policies giving schools greater freedom had failed. Just nine out of 21,000 had received the small grants that were part of a programme giving them the 'power to innovate', and none had won the status of 'earned autonomy' awarded under the scheme. Nine out of the eleven academies were ranked at the bottom of the 2005 national curriculum tests. The government was committed to spending £5 billion on 200 academies by 2010, without any certainty that standards would improve.

Blair lost faith in Whitehall's ability to improve education. 'I know what I want to do,' he told his special adviser. 'I just need to persuade my party to do it. I'll take charge because it has a political dimension.' His argument about education, he acknowledged, had been with the Labour Party and not the Tories.

In the race for his legacy, he once again changed direction. The state, he persuaded himself, should commission and regulate schools but not actually provide education. Competition was the answer and parental choice the best stimulus to improvement. 'The system', he said in a speech on 12 September decrying his failure to pursue well-grounded reforms, 'will finally be opened up to real parent power.' To complete the somersault, he advocated 'genuinely independent non-fee-paying state schools'.

The next day, the OECD reported that Britain had slipped down the league of educated nations. Stagnation over the decade meant that the country had fallen from thirteenth to twenty-second in the OECD's league. The government's own statistics confirmed a 'crisis' in state schools. Not only had truancy increased, but a hard-to-believe 25 per cent of students dropped out of university in their first year. Those 71,000 non-graduates wasted £500 million. Blair ordered initiatives to prove that the 37 per cent increase in the education budget since 1997 would not be wasted.

In an outpouring of headlines, new structures emerged: 'Trust Schools', 'Families of Schools', 'Primary Strategy Learning Networks' and 'School Improvement Partners'. In yet another White Paper, 'More Choice for Pupils and Parents', Blair further encouraged the fragmentation of the state system.

Blair's aspirations inevitably courted controversy. David Bell, the chief inspector of schools, had warned about the danger of segregating white and immigrant communities. Roman Catholic institutions had become 'white citadels', while Muslim schools were hindering integration. Traditional Islamic education, Bell told Blair, espoused intolerance and illiberalism, while it encouraged misogyny by subordinating

478

women. Ghettoisation in faith schools, he explained, would fail to equip Muslim children for life in Britain.

Bell was supported by protesting Labour MPs who demanded that Ofsted should force faith schools to promote tolerance. Others cautioned Blair that his priority of removing class inequalities would in turn create religious divisions. He ignored all that advice, as he did the threat of rebellion by about a hundred Labour MPs. A steely determination underlay his new philosophy.

The explosion of opposition reflected one anxiety. Unlike previous education secretaries, Ruth Kelly lacked the experience to dominate her officials. Her department also knew that Blair had unsuccessfully manoeuvred to demote her after the election in favour of Andrew Adonis. At least Barber's resignation had removed one hurdle to improving literacy, with Kelly encouraging primary schools to use 'synthetic phonics' to teach reading. The counter-revolution against the Left's passion for chaotic 'child-centred' classrooms using the National Literacy Strategy had begun, but the reading gap between children from advantaged and disadvantaged families was as wide as it had been in 1997. As Kelly admitted, 'It appears that we have not managed to narrow the gap between attainment of children from lower and higher income families.'

Her weakness suited Adonis. The junior minister was tasked by Blair with masterminding the fightback against Blair's own earlier policies. In the countdown to the prime minister's departure, he drafted 'Higher Standards, Better Schools for All', a White Paper calculated to upset Labour's vested interests in that it mirrored the Tories' 1997 proposals. The government revealed itself on 25 October 2005 as an unashamed supporter of parental power, selection, independent state schools, more private sponsorship, breaking the comprehensive model and reducing local authorities' powers. The focus, said Blair, was on excellent schools that were independent of 'politically correct interference from state or municipality'.

Approving the menu was, as usual, easier than delivering the product. Within days, his Labour opponents exposed flaws in the new scheme.

Even their own Westminster staff, complained MPs, found Adonis's system too complicated to understand. Blair's pontificating about delegation and independence, they concluded, was unrealistic. The paper was condemned as 'extraordinarily poorly written'. Beneath the headlines, the substance had been tailored by Adonis to match Labour's demand for centralised control. So, despite Normington's assurance that money would follow the pupil to finance the expansion of the best schools, Adonis's introduction of a minimum-funding guarantee prevented the closure of bad ones. Proper parental choice, a parliamentary committee confirmed, would be thwarted. The confusion was inevitable. Blair once again lacked the courage to disempower the local education authorities. School funds and teachers' salaries would still be controlled by the LEAs. Three weeks after his speech lamenting his past failures to reform, Blair was again fighting Labour MPs demanding his retreat.

John Prescott led the charge. 'Choice' was abhorrent to the uneducated, he said. Giving poor children the opportunity to choose a good school, he warned, was a risk: 'The trouble is, if you create good schools people will want to go to them.' Instead of allowing bad schools to wither, Blair's critics wanted to compel middle-class children to attend poorly performing schools. In the orthodoxy of social engineering, they imagined that the presence of such children would automatically improve failing academies. Prescott led the same charge against trust schools. The academies, he said, would be a revival of selective grammar schools. He could not take in the truth that the hurdle to good education was bad teachers.

One month later, at the end of January, Blair faced a revolt by ninety Labour MPs against his latest education bill's provisions for self-governing trust schools. He fought back hard. Eight years of New Labour, he said, had improved Britain's education system. The number of schools deemed to be inadequate by Ofsted, he said, had halved to 1,557, educating nearly a million children, while over 1,500 secondary schools had improved and the number deemed to be 'outstanding' had doubled.

In support of Blair, Normington had produced the government's statistics in front of a parliamentary committee, showing that, since 1997, with an additional 40,000 teachers and 260,000 more assistants and support staff – a 150 per cent increase – the quality of teaching and educational standards had soared. A-level pass rates had risen from 87 to 97 per cent. Over the same period, the number of candidates getting five GCSEs had zoomed from 45 to 76 per cent. 'There was a significant improvement in performance,' Normington said, contradicting the evidence of falling standards due to grade inflation.

In a speech to an academies conference, Blair praised his own success: 'English ten-year-olds are now ranked third in the world for literacy . . . and 96,000 more children can do basic mathematics than in 1997 . . . We have achieved the best-ever GCSE and A-level results.'

Research suggested the opposite. Blair was caught between propaganda and the truth. The Department of Education's senior official confirmed that exam scores were indeed being manipulated. 'It's the perverse effect of focusing on targets,' David Miliband was told by Normington. To satisfy Barber's target of five GCSEs and a rise in the GCSE pass rate to 76 per cent, many head teachers had directed pupils to take easy courses in subjects such as media, beauty and cooking. Coursework, which counted for up to 60 per cent of a pupil's GCSE score, was manipulated by some teachers to gain better marks. Hence, 21.7 per cent of pupils who managed to obtain what counted in the revised system as five good GCSEs did so without having demonstrated a reasonable knowledge of maths or English. Only 48 per cent of sixteen-year-olds passed GCSEs in those two subjects, and candidates could get a C grade in maths with a mark of just 16 per cent. In 2005, AQA, one of the country's largest examining boards, awarded an A* in business studies for marks of 47 per cent. That, reported the academics, was typical of grade inflation.

Studies conducted at Cambridge, Buckingham, York and Durham universities showed that examination standards had fallen since 1997, while schools could not produce evidence confirming any real improvements. Durham had tested 5,000 children in 120 schools every year since 1997 and had found no improvement in literacy.

The children faced a new problem: after they had been taught to pass the tests set in order to achieve Barber's targets, their cognitive and oral skills were harmed. Eleven-year-olds were entering secondary school damaged by Whitehall's pressure on local authorities and schools to 'teach to the test'. Although Blair emphasised 'the key to education today is to personalise learning . . . reflected in a distinctive approach also to every school', the opposite had happened.

Some research would report that teachers had not only lost their self-confidence, but also their honesty. Results were further boosted by allowing candidates to retake AS exams until they scored top grades. The statistical conclusions were controversial but there was no disputing the fact that Blair's target for 85 per cent of sixteen-year-olds to be literate and numerate had not been attained. Most surveys agreed that about 30 per cent of children were leaving school without those basic skills.

International surveys confirmed the failure. UNICEF reported that British children ranked at the bottom of twenty-one rich countries across a range of skills. The reading skills of ten-year-olds, according to the respected Progress in International Reading Literacy Study carried out in 2007, placed British children nineteenth, compared to third in 2001. The government blamed parents.

The studies could be challenged, but no one questioned the credibility of Professor Margaret Brown's conclusion that numeracy had also deteriorated. She blamed the government for spending too much time 'trying to change the wrong thing'. Regardless of whether a school was specialist, independent or an academy, she wrote, or whether the class was equipped with computers and interactive whiteboards, many teachers were not properly trained to explain the fundamentals of mathematics, and understanding basic maths was the foundation of all education, especially, to the surprise of many, literacy. Setting targets had failed to improve education and had undermined Blair's pledge to give the poor the opportunity of a successful life.

All that research was irrelevant to the Labour MPs opposed to Blair's education bill. In the debates, none of them mentioned falling standards or the misery of poorly educated sixteen-year-olds. They cared about political control of education and, more importantly, Blair's departure.

To enact his bill, Blair could rely on the Tories for support, but first, to reduce the rebellion, he half surrendered, withdrawing most of the freedoms he had originally granted to schools. In a quip favoured by City slickers, he chose his moment to 'amend and pretend'. 'He would rather sacrifice his leadership than back down,' noted Powell. The media was unrelenting, glorifying Labour MPs for deserting their prime minister.

On the night, to opposition taunts that 'This is a Tory bill', fifty-two Labour MPs voted against the government, but with the Tories' support Blair won with a majority of 343. The circle was complete, and he had restored the grant-maintained schools abolished in 1997. His success appeared to be trumped by Brown's snap promise to match the funding of state schools with the high income that supported private ones. Enquiries revealed that no money had been set aside for that expensive pledge, which was quickly relabelled by the Treasury as an 'aspiration'. A month later, Kelly silently resigned from the education department and became the new minister for equalities.

In 2007, the Rowntree Foundation reported that the opportunities for the poorest children – the targets of Labour's ambitions – had worsened. A paper by Robert Cassen blamed teachers in deprived areas for ignoring discipline and excellence. Other researchers recorded that the attainment of disadvantaged pupils had fallen because they were being supervised by unqualified assistants and ignored by the full-time teachers.

Despite the huge expenditure, some inequalities, while not worsening, barely changed. Forty-six per cent of school-leavers were going to university, nearly matching Blair's ambition of 50 per cent, but since 1997 the number of working-class students had risen by just 3 per cent. The number of state-school pupils going to the Russell Group universities, the best in the land, had not changed. Although Blair would say that 'primary schools in the poorest areas have improved at double the rate of schools in the more affluent areas', the gap between rich and poor had widened. 'The bad news', admitted David Miliband, the schools minister, 'is that when it comes to the link between educational achievement and social class, Britain is at the bottom of the league for industrialised countries.' The only children whose standards had improved were those educated in private schools.

Blair clung to academies as his lifebelt. 'You are the true change-makers in our country today,' he told the leaders of the thirty existing academies in 2006. 'You are lifting the sights of our young people, teaching them better, educating them more profoundly and to a higher standard than ever before.'

As so often, a series of reports, especially those by the National Audit Office, contradicted him. The exam results of academy pupils, reported the NAO, were below average and some academies were wasteful, weak and financially irresponsible. Blair would ignore such findings. In praising his own achievements, he would use inaccurate 2005 statistics, passing over poorer results published in later years.

In spring 2006, he promised to build 200 academies by 2010. Later that year, he upped his target to 400. In 2007, there were would be forty-six academies, costing on average £24 million each and educating less than 3 per cent of all secondary pupils. One had cost £40.4 million to build. The bill for refurbishing a normal secondary school was about £14 million.

Bringing the curtain down on a decade pledged to revolutionising education was the appointment of Christine Gilbert as head of Ofsted. The former director of education at Tower Hamlets believed in 'personalised learning'. She advocated that pupils should determine their own curriculum, mark their own work and rate their teachers, while traditional exam grades should be replaced by 'feedback'. From Woodhead to Gilbert, Blair had been defeated on his chosen battlefield.

FORTY-THREE

Cash and Consequences

On 26 April 2006, while enjoying the cheers of thousands of Hindus during a visit to a temple in north-west London, Blair was told about a new immigration crisis: the Home Office had failed to consider 1,023 foreign prisoners for deportation after their imprisonment. As a result, criminals convicted of violent and sexual offences had been released to continue living in Britain.

Charles Clarke was the vulnerable minister. In September 2005, he had discovered that 10,000 prisoners – one-eighth of Britain's prison population – were foreign nationals. He started discussions on how the number could be reduced. Two months later, he learned that John Gieve, the permanent secretary, did not know how many asylum-seekers had been released from prison without being deported. Relying on Gieve, Clarke had told a parliamentary committee that none of those allowed to stay in Britain was guilty of serious offences. But, as Gieve would admit, he had briefed the minister without knowing all the facts. The civil servants' excuse for the disaster was that they had followed the government's policy of being soft on immigration. In December, Clarke removed Gieve from the Home Office and told Blair that a number of foreign prisoners were being released without being considered for deportation. He reminded Blair of his earlier warning that clearing up the Home Office would take five years.

The bungle was forgotten about until April 2006, when, informed by hostile IND officials, David Davis, the Tory shadow home secretary, asked in the Commons for statistics about foreign prisoners.

Clarke could not provide them. To some, he appeared evasive and incompetent. There was uproar, but Blair hoped that Clarke could survive. In a meeting at the end of April, Clarke offered Blair his resignation, adding, 'Don't accept it, because my departure won't solve anything.' Blair agreed. Believing they were 'sticking together', Clarke revealed his exchange with Blair in a radio interview the next morning. He overestimated Blair's support because he misjudged the prime minister's own vulnerability.

Believing that he could still embed the reform programme before his resignation – planned, as he would later write, for summer 2008 – Blair was engaged in daily combat against Gordon Brown and his supporters, particularly Ed Balls and Ed Miliband. 'I was cornered,' he admitted, 'so it was either go down or fight . . . and I would not go unless Brown continued the reform programme.'

'What is to be gained by you staying on for another six months?' Miliband asked. His insults were encouraged by Brown, who would regularly walk past Blair's staff at 8 a.m., enter the prime minister's study and start screaming.

The battle reached a new climax on Wednesday 15 March 2006. Brown was due to meet Blair and Adair Turner to discuss pension reforms. For some days, newspapers, after receiving accurate information from a civil servant, had been reporting that eleven businessmen had been nominated for peerages, but four had been rejected by Dennis Stevenson's committee on the grounds that their financial activities while managing their businesses would bring the House of Lords into disrepute. Subsequently, however, the *Sunday Times* had interviewed one candidate, Sir David Garrard, a property developer, who admitted that he had loaned the Labour Party £2 million. Others would not deny their own loans. On 12 March, the same newspaper's front page led with a report about Chai Patel, who by then was attracting controversy over the deaths of residents at his old people's homes. Patel had earlier admitted to having made a donation of just £100,000. Now, he explained that Michael Levy had asked him to convert a donation of

£1.5 million into a loan, which could be changed back into a donation in the future. Patel's loan had coincided with his nomination for a peerage. Levy vehemently denied Patel's version of events.

The 'loans for peerages' storm erupted just as Tessa Jowell, Blair's closest supporter and the leader of a campaign to build super-casinos, was cleared by the prime minister of breaching the ministerial code. She had failed to reveal a 'gift' of £350,000 to her husband from his client Silvio Berlusconi, the Italian prime minister, money which was used to pay off their joint mortgage. Jowell claimed that, while signing the legal documents, she was unaware of the source of the money. To save her political career, she announced her separation from her husband. (Within months they would be seen together at Covent Garden.) Her exoneration attracted headlines about 'sleaze'.

Cash for peerages brought the same headlines. Levy had been asked by Jonathan Powell and Blair's special adviser Ruth Turner about those who had loaned the party over £1 million. Without knowing about the loans, Dennis Stevenson had decided that several of the donors were unsuitable for the Lords, despite their nomination by Blair. The revelation that the party had received £14 million from those same controversial businessmen aroused new suspicions. 'There were very good reasons for all of them being on the list,' Blair would write. Supporting the party with cash, he believed, qualified the donor to become a peer. He criticised the media for nurturing a scandal and refusing to debate government policies.

The day after the newspapers' revelations, John Hutton, the pensions minister, was waiting in No. 10 when he saw Brown enter Blair's office, ostensibly to discuss the proposed pension reforms. Ninety minutes later, Hutton was still outside, as Brown screamed that Turner's plan should be shelved and Blair should resign. 'You haven't heard the last about those peerages,' shouted the chancellor as he stormed off. Brown had threatened that the party's national executive would enquire into the loans. Since they had all been legally transferred to the party's treasurer, Blair was shell-shocked. 'For the first time, I'm scared,' he told Sally Morgan, his political adviser. 'He's going to bring me down.' Later, he told Gus O'Donnell, 'Gordon is going to do something very unconstitutional.'

That night, Jack Dromey, a trade union leader and the party's treasurer, toured the TV studios. Pleading that he had been unaware of the loans, he criticised the ability of the rich to buy peerages. 'No. 10', he said accusingly, 'must have known about the loans.' That, Michael Levy knew, was true. Not only did Blair know but, Levy believed, Dromey must have read the accounts (Dromey denied having done any such thing). However, Stevenson's committee, which had been responsible for vetting the nominations for the peerages, had not known about the loans, which had been arranged to protect the secret transfer of money by men who were simultaneously nominated. 'Cash for peerages' also generated acres of newsprint for Blair's earlier dodgy financial dealings, starting with Bernie Ecclestone's £1 million donation for changing the tobacco sponsorship law.

Dromey's posturing, complained Blair, reflected Brown's 'mafia-style politics'. The grim trade unionist was the husband of Harriet Harman, who had shifted allegiance to Brown in anticipation of his leadership. Dromey's accusations were a gift to the Scottish Nationalists. To boost their campaign against a corrupt Scottish Labour Party, Alex Salmond asked one of his MPs to lodge a complaint with Scotland Yard. The impression seeping out of Westminster portrayed Blair as hanging on.

FORTY-FOUR

Targets vs Markets (Take 8)

Big Ken Anderson gave it to Blair straight. 'There's been a lot of push-back by the civil service,' he said during a dinner at Chequers in 2006. 'Ultimately, however you measure it, it's all been a failure.'

Blair flashed silent dismay. Hearing the truth was unpleasant. With Elton John, another guest, seated near by, there was no opportunity for a proper discussion, but Anderson's views on the NHS were no secret. Blair's reforms were grinding to a halt.

Blair had taken his eye off the ball after the success of the private contract to treat cataracts in 2004. Ever since the Nigel Crisp debacle, he knew that his opportunity to limit Whitehall's control and empower patients was evaporating. 'We need to entrench the reforms to make it hard to reverse,' he told Patricia Hewitt.

Signs of lethargy in the reform programme were noticeable during the search for Crisp's successor. Blair, Hewitt and Anderson knew that there was no credible candidate among the NHS's board of executives. All those employed in Richmond House 'thought like Crisp'. Indeed, most were temporary appointments while headhunters searched for replacements. For the same reason, the chief executives of the strategic health authorities were unsuitable.

'It's a nightmare,' said Hewitt.

'We need an outsider,' agreed Blair. Headhunters produced two well-qualified Americans, but both were squeezed out by Whitehall's customary machinations against outsiders. Four months into the search, Blair failed to persuade Ian Carruthers, the temporary chief executive, to stay. Then, David Nicholson, the executive supervising the Mid-Staffs hospital, contacted Anderson.

Previously, Nicholson, a former member of the Communist Party, had been deemed unsuitable because, like Crisp, he opposed change. Nevertheless, over a drink, he sold himself as a reformer. 'He begged on his knees,' recalled Anderson, who finally recommended his appointment to Blair. 'Boy, do I regret that,' he would later say. 'He pushed the NHS further back.'

Eight months after her appointment, Hewitt had more reason to doubt her prime minister rather than the untested Nicholson. She finally understood Blair's irreconcilable ideologies: targets versus the market. He liked headline-grabbing targets to drive change from Downing Street; the downside was that such goals had never produced an efficient Russian economy under Stalin, and nor did they work for the NHS. Blair liked 'choice' but cautioned Hewitt not to mention 'markets', which he feared suggested to alarmed voters that his destination was America's system of payment for health. To avoid the problem of presentation, she was encouraged to say that 'The government is moving towards a self-improving NHS responding to patients' needs.' The snag, as she herself observed, was that 'He's been saying the same since 2000.' The prime minister's predicament was not that he couldn't raise his game but that he couldn't change it. Reassured by Matthew Taylor that the strategy developed since 2000 was 'in theory' right, he only half understood that in practice his ideas were malfunctioning.

At that late hour, Blair summoned a meeting at Chequers for ministers, advisers and permanent secretaries at the health and education departments to discuss their experiences. At the end of the day, all agreed the event had been enjoyable but somewhat odd coming in the twilight of his premiership. 'Are we basically on the right track?' Blair later asked Hewitt. He speculated about designing a scheme to monitor the progress of reform. The truth, he feared, was that the 'forces of conservatism' in the NHS had not been dislodged.

Traditional NHS administrators were still resisting. Economists in the Department of Health were able to show that competition had not improved efficiency. Even Chris Ham, a pioneer of choice in 2001, was unconvinced. Researchers, he wrote, had reported that doubling the budget and making the increased workforce subject to targets were the principal reasons for the NHS's improvement. Those researchers who reported the opposite – that markets were more important than managers – were derided. In the same vein, statistics showing how mortality rates were lower when two hospitals were in competition – because the incentivised managers demanded higher-quality care – were dismissed. Ever more money, the NHS establishment still believed, was the only route to improvement. Blair's revolution was teetering, the victim of what he called a 'vast network of special interests that have every incentive to defend the status quo vigorously, and virtually none to alter it or even adjust it'. He would make one last attempt to conquer their citadel, reverting back to something he had abolished in 1997: Hewitt was directed to resurrect the idea of GPs as fund-holders. Blair gave no hint that his renewed meddling would madden the medical profession, or that he feared Hewitt lacked the political nous to outwit the critics; nor did he give an explanation for his circular journey.

In 'Our Health, Our Care, Our Say', a White Paper about community care drafted by Hewitt, GPs were given control of over 70 per cent of the NHS budget to purchase treatment for their patients from the hospital they chose. Fifteen per cent of non-emergency care would be supplied by the private sector.

'We're not undermining choice and competition, are we?' Blair asked just before publication.

'No,' replied Hewitt.

On the eve of him announcing that the NHS would be spending more than ever in 2007 – £108 billion, or 9.3 per cent of the country's GDP – Blair was presented with a stark truth. The additional hundreds of billions of pounds spent on the NHS over the previous ten years had produced improvements, but the cost was disproportionate to the results. Attendances at A&E departments had increased by a third since

2002 because only 60 per cent of GPs were working full-time for the NHS, although GPs' wages had cost the NHS an additional £1.8 billion between 2003 and 2005. That unforeseen cost would contribute to the NHS's predicted deficit by 2010 of £8 billion. In addition, the cost of the IT project had escalated to £6.2 billion, with a final estimated price tag of £18 billion, eight times the original figure.

Although there were some positive statistics, Derek Wanless had reported that there was still no proof that all the extra money had markedly improved the nation's health, as the data, he discovered, was so imperfect. Health inequalities among the population had either remained the same or even increased. Without competition, the gap between the best- and worst-performing hospitals had not narrowed. In the former, operating theatres were used for 75 per cent of the time, while in the latter it was 35 per cent. Despite the NHS's interminable planning, Wanless wrote, everything had been for 'short-term imperatives [and] significant opportunities have been lost'.

Targets had distorted everything. The most damning statistics were the opinion polls. Although the NHS budget had grown from £34 billion in 1997 to a projected £127 billion in 2012, the electorate told pollsters they trusted the Tories and not Labour to care for the service. Powell's self-eulogy – 'No one will reverse Tony Blair's public service reforms' – looked as threadbare as his assertion that 'We succeeded in strategy but failed in spin.'

The love born in 1997 between Labour and, by then, 1.6 million NHS employees had truly ended. At the 2006 BMA conference, not only the nurses but also the doctors damned Labour for causing 'a real and imminent danger to the NHS'. That mischievous hyperbole revealed the doctors' hatred of the market for exposing their selfishness over income and work.

Powell's enthusiasm over 'Tony's fascination with technology' aggravated Hewitt's inheritance of a financial meltdown. To her alarm, no one in the department was planning cuts or controlling the public's insatiable demand for health services. To start getting value for money,

Hewitt froze recruitment and cut the number of new doctors. Contrary to Blair's promise that 'We'll put doctors and nurses in the driving seat,' the strategic health authorities were directing doctors to save money by either not seeing patients or by making them wait longer.

On 24 April 2006, Hewitt was the guest speaker at a conference of Unison health workers in Bournemouth. By then, the trade unions had spread familiar stories about Britain's health care system being endangered by mass redundancies and widespread privatisation. Newspapers were reporting that some GPs were earning £250,000 a year. The audience ignored that year's generous pay increase for nurses and instead, preoccupied by the NHS deficits, sleaze, Iraq and the Blair–Brown feud, were impatient with a speaker who represented a leader delaying his departure. In silence they listened to Hewitt deliver an incendiary message: 'The money isn't unlimited. It's not a blank cheque and we've recruited too many people.' To forestall angry interruptions, she added, '2006 is the NHS's best year ever.'

Two days later, she repeated her claim at the annual conference of the Royal College of Nursing. Orchestrated by the unions, the audience jeered until Hewitt was forced to quit the podium. In the aftermath, Blair said nothing to her. There was no opportunity. On the same day, Charles Clarke was under renewed pressure to resign from the Home Office over the failure to deport foreign prisoners, and John Prescott was exposed for having an affair with Tracey Temple, his diary secretary. Considering his costly failures as transport minister, including his waste of £600 million building unused regional fire stations and his expensive failure to create regional assemblies, Prescott should have been fired, but Blair resisted. The weakened deputy prime minister, Blair hoped, would be fodder to protect himself from Brown. Under their oral agreement, Prescott gave up most of his government tasks, although he retained his perks, including a flat in Whitehall and Dorneywood, a twenty-one-room country house in Buckinghamshire.

Three weeks later, during Blair's absence abroad, Prescott, the acting prime minister, was photographed playing croquet on the Dorneywood lawn in the middle of the week. The public anger reflected Blair's miscalculation. Back from his travels, he faced roaring Tories in the Commons, while Labour MPs sat glumly behind him. Just a year after his re-election, Black Wednesday was a battle for survival. 'A soap opera which you couldn't make up,' quipped critics after Tracey Temple sold her story to a Sunday newspaper allegedly for £250,000 and photographers snapped the delivery of a new porcelain lavatory to Prescott's home in Hull. 'We consciously decided', wrote Powell, 'to adopt a Micawber strategy of hanging on, hoping that something would turn up.' Survival meant no longer focusing on managing improvements in the NHS and education, but ensuring that Labour remained an electable party. 'Locking in the reform programme' was Blair's priority as he sought to secure Brown's understanding about the importance of Labour continuing to appeal to the middle ground. If he refused, Labour's fortunes would be threatened by the trade unions.

Blair's venom was directed at trade union leaders like Derek Simpson, who spoke about 'disinfecting the party of the Tory agenda dressed up in Labour clothes'. Any hope of preventing old Labour regaining control started with the local government elections in May 2006, and, with Labour trailing by about 10 per cent in the polls, the outlook was grim. Without speaking to each other, prime minister and chancellor travelled together to launch the election campaign. Over the following weeks, Blair ignored Brown's insults, including the chancellor's repeated denials on television that the two men had ever discussed a departure date.

Their division, Blair expected, would aggravate the party's defeat. Instead, although the Tories won key seats in the south, disaster was averted. The Tories were so disliked that the chance of rescuing his government and helping the party gain a fourth election victory was real. The weakness was not him but Brown. Sullen and unfriendly towards the aspiring English, the chancellor had to know that his chances of winning a fourth term for his party depended on him re-embracing New Labour. But, if Blair was going to box Brown into the 'renewal of New Labour', he would need to give his government a makeover.

His response to the election defeat was described by one newspaper as a 'bloodbath reshuffle'. In theory, he intended to promote Blairites and dismiss Brownites in what Brown called 'an act of war'. Inevitably, and true to form, the fallen included Blair loyalists. The first casualty on Thursday night, even before the polls closed at 10 p.m., was at the Home Office.

'I have to make a change,' Blair told Charles Clarke only forty-eight hours after steadfastly defending him in the Commons. 'It's just something I have to do.'

'I don't think I should go,' replied Clarke. 'I won't take the hit for the elections.'

'I think you should,' said Blair, knowing that Clarke was disliked for his authoritarianism.

'Do you realise sacking one of your senior supporters will make Gordon's putsch easier?' said Clarke.

Blair retreated. 'Well, have defence or another job,' he suggested. 'Anything other than the Foreign Office or the Treasury.'

Clarke's pride blocked the compromise. Over the following hours, Blair was advised by Mandelson to offer the Foreign Office. He demurred. Clarke would be too independent, he knew. Instead, that night, he summoned Clarke to his flat. 'Go to defence,' he said.

'No,' replied Clarke, as the tension rose. 'I won't be publicly scapegoated for the local election results and to please Gordon. I'll go to the Foreign Office.'

'You'll have to go altogether,' said Blair unemotionally.

He was a man in a hurry. He had campaigned to serve a full third term, yet now he was under pressure to resign within a year. To protect himself from a coup, others would be humiliated. As usual in such circumstances, he coolly detached himself from his decision.

The following morning, Blair called Clarke. 'Will you reconsider?'

'No,' replied Clarke. 'I'll only go to the Foreign Office.'

'No,' said Blair.

Clarke refused to send a resignation letter. 'I've been fired,' he told Blair's private secretary. A few hours later, he was 'shocked' by the news that Margaret Beckett had been appointed foreign secretary. By her own account, Beckett was even more surprised than Clarke. The minister for the environment had arrived in Downing Street expecting to be dismissed. Tens of thousands of farmers faced financial devastation because the Rural Payments Agency had collapsed, and she would be officially criticised for contributing to a blunder that cost over £1 billion in compensation.

'We were mired by scandal and controversy,' admitted Blair, 'and then I did a reshuffle which was the worst of all worlds.'

Foreign Office officials were even more appalled than Beckett. Blair clearly viewed their department with contempt. Jack Straw was demoted, as was Geoff Hoon. Neither was deemed worthy of loyalty. In Blair's helter-skelter world, he reckoned that he could ride out the familiar media ridicule.

It was at that point that Scotland Yard announced an inquiry into 'cash for peerages'. Ian Blair, the Metropolitan Police commissioner, was under attack for multiple misdeeds, including his alleged bias in favour of Labour. Ordering an investigation, as requested by the Scottish Nationalists, was an easy option for him, although acquiring the proof needed to obtain a conviction would be near impossible. John Yates, the deputy assistant commissioner assigned to the case, would need a full confession or written proof of an agreement to grant a donor a peerage in exchange for a £1 million loan. Since all the political parties had awarded honours to donors over the past century, Yates faced a difficult task.

Those who would be formally interviewed included Blair, Levy, Powell and Ruth Turner. Blair would be questioned three times, the first serving prime minister to suffer the indignity. 'There was a risk at one stage,' said Gus O'Donnell, 'that the prime minister would be arrested.'

Frustrated because no protest could be made over just how pointless the investigation was, Blair approved the handover of huge amounts of sensitive material. 'Eighteen months of absolute hell for all concerned,' he complained. 'It was a running sore of the most poisonous and debilitating kind.' His management of the crisis was not helped by Powell's nonchalance that all the accusations were 'frivolous . . . Unfortunately for [the police] there was nothing to turn up.'

Two weeks after his departure from the government, Clarke was invited for dinner at Chequers. 'I'm sorry to have lost you,' said Blair. It was the same, he added, as losing Mandelson and David Blunkett.

Not quite. Those two ministers were accused of breaking the rules. Clarke's mistake was to have relied on Blair's promise of support. His loyalty was not rewarded. Clarke was not even offered a peerage, unlike Chai Patel.

So much during those weeks was odd. No one in Westminster could understand why Ruth Kelly had become the new minister for equalities. After all, she was a noted Roman Catholic and a member of Opus Dei, and had purposely missed all the Commons votes on homosexuality and equal rights. She was not a natural advocate for equality. And there was something more: Blair knew that Kelly had secretly decided to send her son to a private school that specialised in dyslexic children. Her local authority in Hackney no longer provided the right facilities for that condition because Labour had closed those special schools and ended the assisted-places scheme in the name of 'inclusion'. Kelly had never protested about that policy. On the contrary, during the 2005 election she had criticised Maria Hutchings, the mother of an autistic child who was demanding the reopening of special schools, of trying to 'grab the easy headline'. Kelly knew she faced a charge of hypocrisy, but Blair was past caring. Hypocrisy was irrelevant. All that mattered was his legacy.

The exception was the Home Office. That citadel of cussedness, he decided, needed shock therapy. John Reid's self-portrayal as the tough guy sorting out the sinners had won his respect. The troubleshooter offered the exact opposite to Blair: he made a lot of noise and enjoyed giving officials a hard time. Even Elizabeth Filkin, Parliament's standards commissioner, had suffered his unpleasantness after finding him guilty of not co-operating in her inquiry into questionable payments he had made. Filkin criticised Reid for giving evidence that fell short 'of a candid and complete account' and placing 'pressure of various kinds' on witnesses to change their testimony. Allegations of wrongdoing no longer troubled Blair, who had long since disregarded his boast of being 'whiter than white'. Filkin resigned in December, complaining about the 'quite remarkable' vitriol from the Labour MPs she investigated, including Geoffrey Robinson and Keith Vaz, who were both suspended from the Commons for misbehaviour. This did not concern Blair either.

So Reid was drafted in yet again, his seventh Cabinet appointment in seven years. The prime minister stood in the Home Office's atrium to introduce him to his new staff. Reid's predecessors had struggled to organise the chaotic immigration department. All three had good reason to blame their civil servants, but no official had been told outright in 1997 that the government intended to open the doors to immigration.

'Your problem', Blair told his audience of hundreds, 'is that you are hated by your stakeholders – the prisoners, immigrants and asylum-seekers who do not want to co-operate with you.' He urged them to face the challenge. He charmed, he was cheered, and he departed. Reid did the opposite. He arrived with a single message. The Home Office, he said in a spurt of natural malice, was 'not fit for purpose'. In a single sentence, he successfully demoralised the entire department.

'You've brought the whole temple down,' observed David Normington, the new permanent secretary.

'Don't worry,' Reid replied. 'I've brought you down. Now you can only go up.'

In Downing Street, a senior official reflected to a colleague that 'Reid's Ratner moment has won him no support. He's not a leader.'

David Blunkett's reaction was the same: 'John bashed people on the head, and they rushed away.'

Reid's first order aroused incredulity. He demanded that the Home Office deport 30,000 illegal migrants a year – about a hundred every day. Like Napoleon, he loved the sound of his command and the smell of the grapeshot, even if his target was impossible. Worse, it was clear that he had not bothered to contemplate how his order would even begin to be achieved. He remained unconcerned even when Blair telephoned to remonstrate: 'John, I've looked into this. I've even been to Heathrow. It's quite difficult to get them out.' Reid was unapologetic. Denigration, he told Blair, was the only way to reform.

Stubbornness was their common currency. Neither was prepared to ease Brown's succession. 'Those dinosaurs are not going to win,' said Reid about the plots to remove Blair. To prevent Brown going back to an 'old Labour' agenda, Blair resisted renewed demands that he name a departure date. He also distanced himself from the NHS's problems – just as Hewitt's plight worsened.

Over the previous months, twelve different organisations had combined to produce a questionnaire that would help assign junior doctors to a new training scheme. The intention was to prevent consultants selecting their own juniors and, in so doing, discriminating against students lacking social advantages. The questionnaire went further and omitted to ask candidates about their exam results or medical experience. Instead, that year's 28,000 applicants were required to describe their lifestyle 'attitudes'. After nine years of Labour government, no one had noticed how political correctness had infected the Department of Health's staff. The dam broke after the applicants discovered they were competing for only 15,500 jobs. In the uproar, Hewitt could find no one in the department or the BMA who would admit responsibility. The consultants demanded that the new system be abandoned.

Blair hated the derogatory media headlines. 'I've been talking to a friend,' he said to Hewitt unsympathetically, 'and I think we should give the consultants what they want.'

'That's unacceptable,' she replied. 'That's the whole point. The system must be based on merit, not relationships.'

Blair shrugged. This was not the finale he wanted.

FORTY-FIVE

More Heat Than Light

Over those last months, the special advisers close to the prime minister watched as his diminishing attention to domestic politics was replaced by a growing enthusiasm for global travel. With gusto, he regularly flew off to meet world leaders at summits or for fireside chats. In hindsight, some of those journeys were influenced by his ambitions for a career after Downing Street. In particular, he was seeking to maximise his relationships with Europe's leaders. The negotiations to finalise an agreement for the union's energy market in March 2007 were an ideal opportunity to prove his European idealism.

Blair had convened an energy summit at Chequers soon after the 2005 election. It was his chance to repair eight years of indifference. While in 1997 Britain had been a net gas exporter, in 2006 the country would import 80 per cent of its gas. Within a year, the energy prices for British consumers would quadruple and rank among the highest in Europe. In the countdown to his departure, Blair sought to rectify his failed attempts in 1998 and 2003 to fashion a coherent energy policy. Liberated from antagonistic ministers, he wanted openly to advocate nuclear energy.

Alan Johnson, the DTI's new secretary of state, arrived with a briefing paper prepared by Joan MacNaughton. At the end of his presentation, Blair was unimpressed by what he believed was yet another attempt to thwart his ambitions. Next, he listened to John Birt and Geoff Norris. Both believed in the market but could not explain how the government could build nuclear plants if private corporations refused to risk their own money. Although Norris mentioned how Blair was 'eager to bite the nuclear option and embrace a love that does not dare speak its name', the representatives of the industry expressed their doubts over whether the prime minister and his advisers understood either the costs or the complications. The meeting ended with platitudes.

As usual, Blair fought back with a speech. In November 2005, he unfurled his ideas to the CBI. 'The issue back on the agenda with a vengeance', he told his audience, 'is energy policy. Around the world you can sense feverish rethinking. Energy prices have risen. Energy supply is under threat. Climate change is producing a sense of urgency.' Hence the need to look again at nuclear energy. Even so, few in his audience understood precisely where Blair was leading Britain. Indeed, even he was uncertain. Margaret Beckett may have said on TV, 'I've always accepted we can't afford to close the door on nuclear,' but Blair did not trust her. 'You need to persuade my Cabinet to sign up to nuclear energy,' he told a senior Downing Street adviser.

His enthusiasm was spoiled soon after by British Nuclear Fuels' sale of its stake in Westinghouse Electric Company to Toshiba for about $1.8 billion (£1 billion). With the break-up of the group, Britain lost its last source of expertise in building power stations that produced smaller amounts of radioactive waste. For those corporations being enticed by Blair to risk over £10 billion, Gordon Brown's encouragement of the sale cast doubt on Britain's commitment. To douse the uncertainty, Downing Street's spokesman explained that British ownership of a nuclear manufacturer would have complicated the open competition to find a contractor. Few were convinced, least of all Blair himself.

Despite spending £2.5 billion on consultants in 2004, 42 per cent more than the previous year, the government had received no worthwhile ideas regarding Britain's energy policy. Blair's weapon of last resort was yet another White Paper. Since he did not trust the existing DTI energy section to promote nuclear power, he appointed William Rickett, Whitehall's one remaining energy expert, as the new director. Rickett was surprised by his new estate. One hundred people in the

DTI's energy section were employed on weapons reduction and arms control, and the remaining 150 knew little about energy. Most would be reassigned, and the section rebuilt from scratch.

Rickett inherited the outlines of a review drafted by Norris and Vicky Pryce, the economist, to entice private investors. Their continuing faith in the market puzzled him. During the winter, energy prices had been lower in 'non-market' Europe than in 'competitive' Britain. Pryce blamed the irrationality of the market, although the circumstances causing the discrepancy were quite mundane. Responding to Europe's gas shortage, and to satisfy their own customers, Germany had held back supplies destined for Britain. In turn, Britain, without sufficient storage tanks, was forced to pay high prices on the open market – making it the only European country without secure supplies at stable prices. The result of Blair's latest slogan – a 'transformational energy policy' – was uncertainty.

Looking back over the previous nine years, Rickett understood the futility of Michael Barber-style stock-takes. As each successive DTI minister had proposed a new ten-year strategy, each 'plan' had replaced another 'plan', but nothing had happened except for Blair hankering for Europe to adopt liberal rules, without him understanding that any EU agreements on renewable energy and carbon emissions would sabotage the free market. Britain's target of producing 10 per cent of its energy from renewables by 2010 had been missed. So far, only 2.4 per cent of the country's energy was being produced in this way, while the cost of electricity for consumers had been increased by 5 per cent. Even higher prices would follow once Britain imported 90 per cent of its gas, as it would do by 2025. Despite all the obstacles, Rickett began composing a new policy.

Alan Johnson was baffled by the energy jigsaw, and Malcolm Wicks, the energy minister, could offer no help after Downing Street ordered him not to make any decisions. In May 2006, Johnson was replaced by Alistair Darling. During one of his early meetings in Downing Street, Darling heard John Birt volunteer to review government energy policy.

In that artless scenario, Birt said he could produce a plan to circumvent the chancellor by giving the DTI greater powers. Too embarrassed to decline the offer by his unpaid 'blue-skies thinker', Blair agreed. Others in the room were sceptical. Having experienced Birt's 150-slide presentation at transport – characterised by Rickett as 'a regurgitation of what was economically rational rather than politically realistic' – Darling decided that he would commission his own review.

Eleven days after the May reshuffle (Johnson became education minister and would languish there ineffectually until Brown became prime minister), Blair again addressed a CBI dinner. Five days earlier, he had finally persuaded Brown to accept Turner's pension reforms. With that success, he wanted to commit the chancellor to nuclear energy. His starting point to the CBI was that Britain's coal and nuclear power stations were 'coming to the end of their lives'. Without action, he warned, the country faced 'a dramatic shortfall in our energy capacity and risks to our energy security'. His short-term solution was the building of new gas plants – the same initiative that he had halted in 1997 – and he reannounced the construction of a new generation of nuclear power stations. Amid the predictable protests from the Greens, his nuclear ambitions were also criticised by Malcolm Keay, a British energy expert, as a 'fantasy-land' that was sure to flounder.

To head off criticism, Blair presented 'Meeting the Energy Challenge', a consultation White Paper, to Parliament on 11 July 2006. Inevitably, he ignored any responsibility for his past inactivity and the randomness of throwing nuclear, gas and renewables into the same pot. 'The government's preliminary view', he wrote in the introduction, 'is that it is in the public interest to give the private sector the option of investing in new nuclear stations.' He was assured, he wrote, of 'compelling' support for nuclear power – concealing the fact that for nearly a decade the uncertainty had left the government scrambling to find a suitable contractor, even with the offer of stratospheric price guarantees. But he did admit that too few new power stations had been constructed and, with the closure of old coal and nuclear stations, there was 'the (very small) risk of supply interruptions'. In truth, not a single station had been built. Steep price rises and possible blackouts were the reality. Even the government's initiatives to subsidise heating costs for the poor had been halted. The number of those suffering from the cold was rising and would nearly quadruple by 2010.

Blair's mind had strayed from such mundane matters. Noticeably, he began going for dinner with those who could help his career after Downing Street. Richard Desmond was no longer a member of that chosen elite. True to form, since Blair could offer him no further advantages, the controversial businessman had switched his allegiance back to the Tories. But there were others Blair had in his sights, in particular an even bigger newspaper proprietor: Rupert Murdoch.

In his preparations for his new life, Blair accepted, to the bemusement of Murdoch's executives, an invitation to News Corporation's weekend conference on 22 July in Pebble Beach, California. Until then, his relationship with the Australian had been professional rather than friendly, and was often conducted through Murdoch's employees. Their first introduction had come in 1995, when Blair was invited to deliver a speech to News Corp. executives in Australia. He flew there and back within three days. Thereafter, Murdoch's British newspapers switched their support from the Conservatives to Labour. The two men's communications centred on the *Sun*'s attitude towards the government. Blair had been delighted that David Yelland, his first *Sun* editor, had been influenced by Alastair Campbell's directives. Unfortunately for Blair, Yelland's successors were more abrasive. Throughout the decade, the dominant theme of their conversations with Blair was Britain's membership of the euro. As a Europhobe, Murdoch refused to support Blair's ambitions during his visits to Downing Street, but those differences were forgotten when Blair arrived for a night at Pebble Beach, along with Bill Clinton, Al Gore, Arnold Schwarzenegger and Nicole Kidman. In an interview conducted in front of his fellow guests, Blair spoke warmly about his host and was noticeably friendly in his conversation with Murdoch. That day, Murdoch's lieutenants noted, was the beginning of a deeper relationship, and the Australian's support became an important building block for Blair's future career.

Another, surprisingly, was Britain's energy policy. Ever since Blair had openly come out in support of nuclear power, William Rickett had been rebuilding the DTI's energy directorate and had begun composing another White Paper. Blair's waning interest in energy was momentarily revived by Birt's familiar slide-show presentation of his review. Darling and others in the audience were left disappointed. He offered no original insights and just repeated the DTI's own opinions. At the end of the presentation, Darling told Blair to restore energy policy to his department. Blair disagreed. Everything, he said, would be controlled from Downing Street. Although no investors in nuclear energy could be found, he would not trust the DTI at that late stage. And there Britain's energy policy languished.

In early March 2007, *The Economist* concluded that 'The UK is faced with a power crisis as a result of an almost criminal . . . planning failure.' The magazine's judgement was drawn partly from Blair's inactivity since his speech to the CBI, and partly by an apparently mundane EU summit. Unnoticed by *The Economist*, Blair arrived at the meeting pondering a critical concession that would destroy the very energy market he had championed for ten years.

On 8 March, eight weeks before Rickett's White Paper was published, Blair flew to Brussels for his penultimate meeting with the Council of Europe. In preparing briefs for what was billed as 'an energy summit', Rickett called around Europe's capitals to anticipate what might be discussed. He assumed that Angela Merkel, who had become the German chancellor in 2005, would as usual denounce Blair's championing of the market and deride Britain's notional 5 per cent carbon cap based on the trading scheme. Rickett knew that, as chairman of the summit, Merkel would push Germany's preference for paying subsidies to its coal industry and further subsidies to promote wind and solar energy. But instead of receiving confirmation of the traditional disagreement, he heard alarming news.

Merkel intended to propose that every European country should pledge to generate 20 per cent of *all* its energy from renewable sources – wind, solar and biomass – by 2020. In the world of subsidies for green energy, Rickett knew that for Britain such a pledge would be intolerably expensive. 'All its energy' meant taking into account the gas that heated most of Britain's homes, all the fuel used by vehicles, and nuclear power. Since the source of that energy was unalterable, the 20 per cent renewables target would require Britain to change the source of the remainder of its electricity. To reach that goal, more than 30 per cent of Britain's electricity would need to be generated by wind, solar and biomass, yet in 2007 only 1.6 per cent of Britain's energy needs was being generated by renewables. Engineering such a massive change would cost Britain's consumers billions of pounds every year and would wreck its energy market. To increase wind-generated power to the degree required would also disfigure Britain's countryside alarmingly. Rickett initially assumed that the German proposal would be rejected, but to his horror he heard from Downing Street that Blair intended to bow to Merkel's demands. He alerted Darling.

The minister approached Blair after a Cabinet meeting. 'Don't sign up to the European renewables targets in Brussels,' he said. 'It'll cost us an arm and a leg.'

'Right,' said Blair. 'I won't.'

'It's quite important.'

'I know that,' replied Blair.

On reflection, Darling was not sure whether Blair was even listening. As so often, although their conversation lasted only a few seconds, his eyes wandered. Later that day, Darling's officials regretted that their minister had rejected Gordon Brown's suggestion of sending Blair a joint formal letter.

'He won't be so stupid as to agree to it,' Darling told Rickett.

Blair's thoughts were clearly on Europe – and his chance to become the first president of the union. For years, he had scoffed at Britain's anti-European prejudice as 'hopelessly, absurdly out of date and unrealistic . . . a product of dangerous insularity . . . a kind of post-empire delusion'. Euroscepticism, he jibed at Cameron during a Commons exchange, was 'a virus' infecting the Tory party. During his premiership, he believed, he had put Britain at the centre of the EU, not least by preventing the appointment of Guy Verhofstadt, a federalist, as its president. In 2005, he had been applauded by the European parliament after urging the continent to adopt Third Way politics; and later, to prove his European credentials, he had agreed to forgo £1 billion of the annual rebate Margaret Thatcher had obtained from the EU. Notionally, he had given away £1 billion in return for France's agreement to reduce its receipts from the European agricultural support scheme. 'We got a good deal,' was his view. He was untroubled by France's subsequent reneging on the agreement. In that one-way traffic, Blair justified the sacrifice of £1 billion as necessary for building better relations in Europe. Rickett feared he was about to do the same over renewables.

Early in the morning of 9 March, Rickett telephoned Kim Darroch, Britain's representative to the EU, who was travelling with Blair. 'The 20 per cent renewable target', said Rickett, 'is inconsistent with the 5 per cent of energy from renewables which is the basis of the new policy in the White Paper to be published next month.' The cost to the consumer, he continued, of generating 20 per cent of Britain's energy from renewables by 2020 would be an extra £7.6 billion every year in subsidies. The issue was not the principle but the speed of the change. The amount of money involved was enormous. 'Britain's reliance on the market to produce the cheapest energy would be wrecked,' he explained. As an afterthought, he added, 'It will also crowd out much cheaper ways of reducing carbon emissions.'

'There's no danger of that happening,' Darroch replied. Rickett would never discover whether Darroch briefed Blair about the danger.

Blair arrived at the summit knowing his presence would count as a farewell appearance. By then, he had decided to resign on 27 June. Here was his last opportunity to seal his reputation as a good European. In that cause, Blair's self-interest triumphed over that of Britain. Oblivious as usual to money, he made no move to sidle his way out of the commitment and fully agreed to Merkel's demand. The British energy consumer would be paying £7.6 billion extra every year in subsidies to the power-generating companies.

'You're mad,' Darling told Blair on his return to London.

'Oh,' replied Blair, 'I got confused. I thought it was 20 per cent of all our electricity, not 20 per cent of all our energy.'

No one believed him. The briefing papers were absolutely clear. In the aftermath, Rickett and the DTI's economists calculated that Blair's giveaway meant that the cost to Britain of meeting its environmental obligations would be 'around three times higher' than the previous estimate.

Blair's look of shock was also less than genuine. As he later told a special adviser in Downing Street, 'There were lots of negotiations here. I couldn't stand out on that issue.' The bigger issues were not explained, but were assumed to be his bid for the European presidency.

'We're in a state of shock,' said Rickett after confirming the likely bill. 'That's not the sort of behaviour you expect from a prime minister. He's wasted eighteen months of work and it's delayed anything happening on the ground while we go back to the drawing board.' Nothing in the preceding months had forewarned Whitehall officials about Blair's opportunism.

'Blair', explained Rickett, 'has completely undermined the economics of nuclear power. The cost of a new nuclear power station has rocketed. Probably even higher than an onshore wind farm.' The astronomical cost was the result of the compulsory guarantee of prices for the electricity supplied by the developer of any new station. This guarantee would require huge subsidies from consumers. 'Overnight', said Rickett, 'our drafts of Britain's new energy policy for the next White Paper have been wrecked. He's undermined everything he wanted to achieve through the energy review.'

The following week, Blair arrived in the Commons to report on the summit. As he moved towards the Dispatch Box, the ministers on the front bench left the chamber. Only Tony McNulty, a junior minister, sat on the long green bench. 'You're not going to leave as well, are you?' said Blair, evidently distraught.

As a last throw, the government published a draft 'Climate Change' bill aimed at achieving a mandatory 80 per cent cut in the UK's carbon emissions by 2050 (compared to the 60 per cent already enacted). 'The time for market innocence is over,' said Malcolm Wicks in an unauthorised confession.

The 2007 White Paper ended the government's neutrality on nuclear energy. The first new station was predicted to be in operation by 2018.

FORTY-SIX

An Unexpected War

In the spring of 2006, a round of military musical chairs caused havoc to the army's adventures. General Rob Fry in Northwood was replaced by Vice Admiral Charles Style, and General Mike Walker gave way as chief of the defence staff to Air Chief Marshal Jock Stirrup. Neither Style, who struggled with details, nor Stirrup, a taciturn fighter pilot, had personal experience of land warfare. Then, in May 2006, Des Browne, a Treasury ally of Gordon Brown, became defence secretary. In the excitement of a particularly clumsy reshuffle, Blair never explained his expectations to Browne, an untested politician with no knowledge of defence and an outright opponent of Britain's involvement in Afghanistan.

Helter-skelter, Blair had committed Britain's underfunded army to two remote wars under the command of an air marshal, a vice admiral, a rookie minister, two brigadiers acting on their own initiative and Bill Jeffrey, the shy permanent secretary at the MoD who had no prior knowledge of his brief.

Browne's introductory forty-eight hours were a baptism of fire. At his meeting with Stirrup on his first day, he was told that the army wanted to quit Iraq. 'There's nothing more they can do,' said Stirrup, 'and they are under constant threat of attack.'

Browne volunteered that Blair's misunderstanding of the insurgency in Iraq had enmeshed the army in conflicting strategies. Stirrup agreed: 'Blair never understood that the military could not change the political process.'

The day after Browne's appointment, a British helicopter was shot down in Basra, killing five soldiers. Shocked by the deaths, Browne confessed he was unprepared for 'the daunting experience of people dying. I was deeply affected.' Thereafter, the stress of the daily routine and the incessant media attention was 'enormous and gave me no space to stand back'.

His burden was about to intensify. At that moment, unknown to him or to Stirrup, Brigadier Ed Butler was proposing to abandon the plans for his engagement in Helmand. Butler's orders, approved by Blair, had been explicit: as part of NATO, the British were to remain in Lashkar Gah, a safe town, and reinforce the peacekeeping effort in southern Helmand. Under their protection, the nation-building teams would attempt to civilise Afghanistan.

Five weeks after arriving, Butler was asked by Mohammad Daoud, the governor in Lashkar Gah, to send troops north up the valley towards Sangin, to protect Daoud's family and loyal tribal chiefs. Butler flew by helicopter to reconnoitre the region. He was sympathetic to Daoud's request and discussed the proposed change of plan with the newly appointed – male – British ambassador and the MI6 station chief in Kabul. In their reports to London, both men minimised the possibility of danger.

Butler returned to London at the end of May determined to set the record straight. In a room filled with over thirty people, including the chiefs and retired chiefs of staff, officials from the Foreign Office, MoD, MI6 and Margaret Aldred's committee, he spelled out the dangers in Helmand and the inadequacy of the British military force for nation-building. At the end of his presentation, no one suggested any change of policy or even started a discussion. His audience departed with barely a word. If anyone bore responsibility for reconsidering the mission, it was Aldred's committee, but Butler's presentation led nowhere. Aldred asked him nothing.

Butler had not mentioned at the meeting his proposed move to Sangin. Acting without accurate intelligence on the irreconcilable rivalries among the local tribes or the Byzantine relationship between the tribes and the corrupt government in Kabul, he was empowered to take the decision himself. 'I returned to Afghanistan', he wrote with hindsight, 'concerned that the senior leadership across government was still failing to grasp the enormity of the task ahead.' At the time, Butler also did not understand the implications.

Some generals, including General David Richards, the opinionated NATO chief in Afghanistan, encouraged the move up the valley as a tactical manoeuvre that did not require political approval. Others, including General Peter Wall, the deputy chief at Northwood, were told during a visit to Helmand that Butler proposed to change his mission but believed that local brigadiers were being entrusted to take the initiative without seeking permission from Northwood. Stirrup recognised that the local complexities in Helmand placed the military in a no-win position and deferred to Butler, while Browne remained silent, even after a visit to Afghanistan. Accordingly, on his own authority, Butler acquiesced to Daoud's request. The new adventure went ahead.

In June, small groups of British paratroopers landed in an unfamiliar environment. Their presence disturbed the American army's financial 'live and let live' relationship with the local tribesmen and drug-traders, and also irritated an aggressive American commander who was committed to hunting down the Taliban and who opposed Britain's nation-building plan. No official, general or politician in London thought of resolving the disagreement with the Americans. The expedition's fate depended upon Butler.

Hours after their arrival, the paratroopers met with incoming fire and duly retaliated. During the firefight some died. The escalation was instantaneous. After the tribal elders' exhortations to the paratroopers to leave had been ignored, the Taliban joined the battle and a 'series of Alamos' cropped up across the region. Groups of British soldiers, unable to communicate with the people they were protecting, were shooting at a mixture of drug barons and Taliban. To survive, the beleaguered platoons summoned air strikes. Inevitably, the pilots occasionally missed their targets and hit the homes of civilians. Villages and Sangin's thriving bazaar became rubble. British anti-narcotic teams, in accordance with Blair's instructions, began to burn the opium crop. 'You've just taken the food out of my children's mouths,' a tribal elder told the troops. By July, peaceful nation-building had transformed into war.

'Baffled' about the deployment to Sangin, John Reid telephoned Browne for an explanation. 'No one asked or told me,' replied Browne. 'I don't know when the decision was taken.' Later, he would tell an inquiry, 'I was not part of the chain of command to Afghanistan. I was never strategically in charge. I was never clear about the chain. There wasn't a proper structure to discuss the decision.' Even Blair would say that he was not told by Stirrup about the change of plan. Sofa government, it was said as an excuse, had allowed decisions to be taken in the field that should have been referred to Blair and the Cabinet. In theory, Richard Mottram, the new security co-ordinator, should have supervised the deployment to Afghanistan but, like David Omand, his predecessor, he was excluded from Downing Street decision-making by Blair. The lessons of Iraq were ignored.

Air Marshal Stirrup was stranded. Daily, he received reports about patrols dispersing around Helmand, shoot-outs, British fatalities and disagreements among the NATO powers. Without experience of fighting counter-insurgency wars, he could not judge the army's plight from London. Even after a tour of Helmand, he would explain that he never took personal responsibility for ground operations but, since Butler's duty was to protect Helmand and since the governor, Mohammad Daoud, did survive, the mission was deemed by him to be a success. In common with the army's chiefs, Stirrup could not identify who, other than Butler, had decided to change the mission and 'stir the hornets' nest'. At his request, Blair agreed to send an extra 900 combat soldiers – considerably fewer than the 10,000 troops Butler asked for. In the event, only a hundred were sent in June from Cyprus.

The scapegoating was aggravated by Mike Jackson. 'Search me, guv,' he would later say with surprise about the deployment. 'I thought we were going to Kandahar.' Northwood, Jackson would rightly add, was responsible for the army's operations, not the chief of the army. The same confusion over authority had arisen in Iraq, but neither the chiefs nor the officials in Whitehall and Northwood had considered resolving the ambivalence.

In Northwood, Air Marshal Glenn Torpy had handed over command to General Nicholas Houghton, who at the outset denied knowing about Butler's decision. He had not been alerted by Style to its implications, he said. His denial was challenged by the written records. An inquiry would conclude that Houghton 'had no grip on Butler', meaning that Butler should bear the blame for the change of policy. If Alice had observed Britain's military in Wonderland, she would have heard a chief admit, 'You'd have to be mad to dream me up.'

Des Browne received no special call from Blair to discuss the escalation. He read in a newspaper on 1 July a Downing Street spokesman's comment that al-Qaeda was using Afghanistan as 'a battleground. We have got to be victorious there.' Browne did know that Jackson was demanding more planes, helicopters and troops to satisfy Blair's judgement that the situation had become 'very dangerous'. Mission creep had infected Blair's interpretation of a monumental war within Islam, and between Islamic extremists and the West. Without proper discussion, Britain was slipping into a major conflict that would cost £38 billion, cause the deaths of 453 personnel and leave hundreds of servicemen suffering life-changing injuries.

On 12 July, Helmand became a sideshow, as Blair became preoccupied by developing hostilities between Israel and the Hezbollah army in Lebanon. He interpreted the initial destruction of buildings and civilian deaths along the Mediterranean as the continuation of the 9/11 attacks by militant Muslims, in this case supported by the Iranian government rather than Saudi zealots.

Israel's retaliation for a minor incident after two weeks of fighting in Gaza was widely condemned as disproportionate. Blair rejected the criticism. Although Lebanon was blockaded and the Israeli military had destroyed strategic installations, he believed the country, as the victim of Islamic terror, was justified in launching reprisals. Despite that partisan position, he still trusted himself to broker between the two sides. During his discussions with President Bush, launching a Middle East peace plan had been a condition for Britain's support of the Iraq invasion, and ever since he had taken an interest in the region.

On 14 July, he arrived in St Petersburg for a G8 summit, where he hoped to persuade Bush to endorse him as peacemaker. He first encountered the president in a common area. To his misfortune, a TV camera with live sound recorded Bush's greeting: 'Yo, Blair.' To viewers across the world, the president was disparaging the 'poodle'. Blair would reject that interpretation, insisting that the frivolous salute testified to their close relationship. But the damage was done, especially after Bush ,thanked Blair for a sweater.

'It's awfully thoughtful of you.'

'It's a pleasure,' replied Blair.

'I know you picked it out yourself.'

'Oh, absolutely – in fact, I knitted it.'

Both laughed. They became serious, and then Bush flatly rejected Blair's offer to act as Condoleezza Rice's advance man in the Middle East.

Compounding the embarrassment, Blair's renewed association with the president over another war outraged Labour supporters. The daily toll of deaths and destruction in Lebanon shocked Labour MPs, who expressed their disgust about Blair's refusal to condemn Israel's disproportionate attacks and his failure to call for a ceasefire. They were equally suspicious about his language. Unlike the diplomats, he spoke openly about 'Islamic extremists' and 'Islamic terrorists'. Israel, he implied, was on the front line in a war to protect civilisation against reactionary Islam. As a supporter of Israel, he ignored his advisers and the criticism by Labour MPs of Israeli excesses, criticisms that would be echoed by a commission chaired by an Israeli judge appointed by the Israeli government. He was unashamedly partisan.

The result was a growing number of his party demanding that he set a date for his departure – to little effect. Ever since his leadership 'coup' in 1994, he had sidelined the party's executives and public-sector trade union leaders. Twelve years later, he was not about to change the habits of his political career. He would go with dignity at a time of his own choosing. He seemed to have forgotten what he had said in a conversation in 1999 with the Lib Dem leader Paddy Ashdown: 'Going is the most difficult thing to do in politics. Too many people stay for too long. I would rather stop when people said, "Why is he going?" rather than "Why isn't he going?" Or worse, "When is he going?"' Seven years later, that wisdom was forgotten.

On 31 July, as the carnage in Lebanon escalated, Blair flew to Washington to persuade Bush to launch a peace plan. In advance, he knew from David Manning, the ambassador, that his trip would be pointless, but there was another purpose for the journey.

From Washington, he continued on to Los Angeles to meet Arnold Schwarzenegger. The governor of California was campaigning for re-election, and John Browne, the chief executive of BP, had arranged a climate change conference for billionaires in a specially constructed compound in the port of Long Beach. Among those assembled were the chief executives of DuPont, Timberland, Goldman Sachs, Swiss Re and American Electric Power, along with Rupert Murdoch's son James – whom he had met a week earlier at the annual News International gathering at Pebble Beach – and two hippy billionaires: Sergey Brin, the founder of Google, and Richard Branson. An organiser of the reception calculated that those gathered around the table managed companies earning half a trillion dollars a year and employing over 300,000 people.

Thanks to the American government's subsidies, the production of renewable fuels had become a profitable business, one that was promoted by Bill and Hillary Clinton, with Schwarzenegger's political support; even Branson had personally invested about $300 million in factories. In Blair's opinion, all these billionaires were worth cultivating.

'We're going to a baseball match,' Schwarzenegger told him at the end of the reception. To the guests who remained, Blair was America's heroic ally deserving of indefinite support.

One week later, the Blairs flew to the West Indies for their summer holidays. The following day, Britain's airports were reduced to chaos. Mass arrests had prevented a plot by Islamic terrorists to use liquid-based bombs to blow up seven planes flying to North America. Thousands of Britons suffered the ruins of their holidays while watching TV pictures of the Blairs in the Caribbean. Once again, critics drew a link between the terrorists and Britain's invasion of Iraq. Resentment was inevitable. The misadventure in Afghanistan was not mentioned by the media or the government. As the first coffins were driven from an RAF base through the ranks of retired soldiers lining the high street in Wootton Bassett before the private funerals, the summer was the perfect opportunity for a rigorous reassessment of Britain's commitment to the war.

Any one of five men – Blair, Des Browne, Jock Stirrup, Nicholas Houghton or Bill Jeffrey – was empowered to initiate the discussion. Orthodox and loyal, both Stirrup and Houghton lacked the experience. On his own account, Stirrup assumed that every plan collapsed on the first day. He could not have started a major review on his own; he would have needed support from Jeffrey Previous permanent secretaries in the ministry, like Frank Cooper and Michael Quinlan, had possessed the intellectual power and bruising personality single-handedly to question Britain's defence policies. Jeffrey's invisibility broke the mould. 'Bill opted out,' observed one minister. 'He stayed in his office and led the rest of the ministry's officials to opt out of decisions. All they did was type up orders.'

'Why are you not participating?' Matt Cavanagh, a political adviser in Downing Street, asked a senior civil servant in the MoD.

'From Blair downwards,' replied the official, 'you've all poured shit on us, so why should we?'

Browne later admitted, 'I managed circumstances instead of thinking.

I was constantly reacting to an overwhelming daily routine. I had no reason to doubt Stirrup.' On reflection, he identified his weakness: 'I was getting no help from No. 10.'

Nigel Sheinwald, the ministry's link to Downing Street, was regarded by his critics as inconsistent. To them, he blew hot and cold, and gave Whitehall no sense of direction. The responsibility for the policy vacuum led back to Blair, who could have challenged the military in the same manner as he questioned the 'forces of conservatism' across Whitehall. The idea never surfaced.

On his return from holiday at the end of August, the prime minister shrank back from the opportunity for a reassessment. 'Blair held workshops on education and immigration', recalled Browne, 'but never held a single day's conference on Iraq or Afghanistan.'

By September, the British army was facing a crisis. Soldiers in Afghanistan were dying, and those who were injured were receiving poor treatment from the NHS on returning to Britain. (One of Gordon Brown's cuts had led to the closure of the military's specialist hospitals.) The absence of American troops in Helmand and British reluctance to request help from other NATO armies aggravated the plight of the 1,500 British troops, who were fighting with insufficient helicopters and driving vehicles with inadequate armour. 'Whatever package they want,' Blair said about the army's demands, 'we will do.' Since Brown refused to approve additional money, the promise remained unfulfilled. At that moment, Britain's exit from Iraq – fixed for the end of 2006 – was being questioned by Washington. His country's continued presence there, Blair agreed without a proper explanation, was essential to protect national security. General Walker's assurance to Reid that engagement in two locations was 'doable' had proved to be mistaken.

And it got worse. Major-General Richard Shirreff had arrived in Basra for his six-month tour in July 2006. Faced by an uprising among the militia armies, Britain's 7,200 soldiers, alongside 7,000 NATO troops, were cowering. Some 150 British soldiers were available to patrol the whole of Basra, a city of 1.3 million people. Belfast had been controlled by a force of 10,000. 'It's like a self-licking lollipop,' said Shirreff. 'Everyone's just guarding themselves.' The army's effort was devoted to supplying and protecting their three bases in a lawless city plagued by corruption and Shia death squads. Acting as neither the world's policemen nor its social workers, British soldiers were risking their lives just to survive, without any chance of changing Iraq's fate. Stirrup, who prided himself on understanding that wars should be fought only to fulfil a strategy, as set out by Carl von Clausewitz, the famous Prussian militarist of the nineteenth century, looked to Blair to define the purpose of continuing their mission. He received no meaningful reply.

Before he left Britain, Shirreff had presented Operation Salamanca, aimed at removing Basra's criminal elements, to Generals Jackson and Dannatt over dinner at Bulford Manor in Wiltshire, the army chiefs' headquarters. Shirreff suggested a 'surge' to counter-attack the militias, retake control and build a 'better Basra'.

'Absolutely right, we'll go for that,' agreed Jackson.

The ambitious plan was presented to the two other chiefs and to Houghton in Northwood. Success would require money and more British troops in Basra, and also the support of Nouri al-Maliki, the Iraqi prime minister.

'We need a winning strategy to exit,' Shirreff told Houghton. The plan, noted Shirreff, went down with his superior 'like a lead balloon'.

Houghton was still seeking a policy from Downing Street, but instead of a reply there was only silence. Blair refused to decide on the fate of British troops. His only order to Stirrup was to bring peace to the British zone, but he offered no ideas on how achieve that Elysium.

Although Blair appeared to be fully engaged at their regular discussions, Stirrup sensed that Downing Street was languishing in a '*fin de siècle* atmosphere'. At one meeting, Blair agreed with the air marshal that the army should leave Iraq, then refused to name the date, as if he had no power to influence events. Adding to the confusion, Stirrup admitted, 'I didn't know whether Houghton supported Operation Salamanca.' Yet, before flying to Basra, Shirreff had the impression that

Blair had given his approval. The general arrived expecting 5,000 more British troops and additional funds. He had not anticipated a conversation in Downing Street between the chief of the defence staff and Blair.

'Prime Minister,' Stirrup said, 'it is clear that Maliki will not support the army's operation.'

Blair voiced surprise that Iraq's leader did not want the gangs wreaking havoc across Basra to be neutralised. 'Can't we do something about it?' he asked in the tone of a motorist looking at his flat tyre. Without Maliki's support, Shirreff's hopes would be dashed.

'I had kittens,' Stirrup admitted during his first visit to Basra following Shirreff's arrival. Sending reinforcements, he told the major-general, had not been approved. 'More British troops won't alter the strategic outcome.'

Shirreff's operation was duly watered down. Its replacement, Operation Sinbad, was a series of low-level hit-and-runs to protect the beleaguered British soldiers. The official policy was to protect the stalemate. Blair's decision to withdraw by the end of 2006 and in the meantime reduce the number of soldiers from 7,200 to about 3,500 was, Stirrup knew, 'not feasible'. He returned to London undecided on how to tell Blair that the position was hopeless.

'We need political involvement and a political solution,' he eventually reported. 'The army cannot fix the problem alone.'

Blair looked without confidence at the two ministers at the meeting: Des Browne, whom he disliked, and Margaret Beckett, whom he had appointed mainly to make ignoring the Foreign Office easier. 'Try and persuade Maliki to approve the removal of the Shia militias,' he told Beckett. Nothing happened.

'The levers of government and the Foreign Office don't deliver,' Stirrup discovered.

Shirreff's final orders were to 'give it a go'. He was to 'surge to get the Iraqis into a position to take over' and, at the same time, 'to ramp it down'. The attacks began in October. Within days, British soldiers were under heavy fire. In London, General Dannatt, the new army chief, was aggrieved. According to Whitehall rules, he was excluded from direct involvement in the Iraqi operations by Houghton and Stirrup.

Dannatt attracted mixed feelings. 'He's too Christian,' was a common complaint among his fellow officers.

'Dannatt never took advice except from God, and God isn't very good on defence,' observed General Charles Guthrie.

In theory, Blair should have found much in common with his new senior officer. 'God's on our side in Helmand,' the general told an RAF officer. 'We're doing the right thing.' But Dannatt had also told Desmond Bowen, the MoD's policy director, that 'We need to be shedding more blood to show that we're in there with the Americans.' That eccentricity caused Stirrup to dislike Dannatt, and the sentiment was mutual. 'When you're in a cockpit flying at the speed of sound,' Dannatt observed, 'you don't have to decide who lives and who dies and pick up the body parts.' At the chiefs' weekly meetings, at 10 a.m. every Wednesday, he found himself isolated. 'Stirrup's not prone to consultation,' the new chief complained, 'even though the army is fighting two wars.' He found that the two other chiefs 'played games'. Stirrup, he felt, spoke in bursts of 'grandstanding' and refused to discuss the detail of the war or the army's request for more money. 'When I need you,' Stirrup told Dannatt, 'I'll call for you.'

The mutual antipathy between the chiefs was aggravated by Dannatt's search through the formal minutes of his predecessors' discussions. He found no mention of their discussing the army's commitment to Afghanistan. Dannatt had himself supported the Afghan expedition, but his influence had become minimal.

The solemnity of the hearses regularly carrying fallen soldiers past guards of honour magnified media reports about the casualties and depressed morale in the MoD. Instead of the government following tradition and burying the dead where they fell, every soldier's death had become the focus of a coroner's public inquiry to fix the blame. Gordon Brown in particular was held responsible for ignoring the army's demand for reinforcements, helicopters and bombproof vehicles. 'War is not clean,' an official told Bill Jeffrey at the climax of a public storm about the army's lack of body armour. Neither Des Browne nor Jeffrey was suited to presenting to the public or the Cabinet the reality of modern warfare.

The politicians did not bear all the blame. The army had spent months inconclusively bickering among themselves about the ideal bombproof vehicle. On the other hand, Blair had agreed to allot billions of pounds to two unaffordable aircraft carriers, which automatically reduced how much the army had to spend. 'We have a huge hole in our budget,' Paul Drayson, the minister of procurement, had been informed by his officials. 'There's no money,' Browne had also been told. Britain could not afford the 'expeditionary' war set out in the 1998 defence review.

The officials in the MoD's logistics department presented their financial predicament to Jeffrey. 'You've got to ask for a formal direction,' he was told. That imperative would ultimately have forced Blair to justify the lack of money. 'Jeffrey stayed silent,' recalled one official. 'He should have asked for a formal direction from the minister, but he didn't want a public row. We were cheerleaders, and we were strongly discouraged from giving ministers unwelcome advice.'

Dannatt decided to rattle the cage. 'The army is running hot,' he told Browne. The 7,200 soldiers in Iraq, he explained, were part of the problem and not the solution. With limited resources, the British army would be defeated. 'We are fighting for our lives.' The army could retrieve its reputation only if everything were thrown into Afghanistan. Dannatt wanted a political decision. Until the army withdrew from Iraq, reinforcements could not be sent to Afghanistan. 'Browne could not understand,' he concluded. 'I got no positive outcome from him.'

In turn, Browne was irritated by his senior officer: 'It was always about Dannatt.' In the general's opinion, it was about soldiers risking their lives. 'I had to struggle in Whitehall to get the army's voice heard,' he said. 'It was very frustrating.'

Repeated attempts to arrange a meeting with Blair were ignored by Downing Street. The general was furious. The army, he believed, needed protection from a prime minister who was deaf to complaints and who was the begetter of dysfunctional chiefs.

Unwilling to listen to conflicting opinions, and weary of the generals' familiar antagonism, Blair would talk only to Stirrup. In his opinion, the more important battle at that moment was his own fight for survival against Gordon Brown and his supporters.

On his return from his summer holidays, Blair was told by Alastair Campbell, Jonathan Powell and Sally Morgan that support for him in the party was 'haemorrhaging'. With the party conference approaching, his support for Israel in Lebanon, he heard, was jeopardising his survival as prime minister. To reassert his authority, he invited Philip Webster, the political editor of *The Times*, to interview him at Chequers.

Eight times during their conversation Webster asked Blair when he intended to leave, and each time Blair refused to answer. He pledged only to give his successor 'ample time' before the next election and urged his party to 'stop obsessing' about the leadership. He arranged for himself to be photographed with a mug listing the traits of anyone with the name Anthony. Among them was, 'You're a man who's in charge, others follow your lead.'

To gauge the reaction of Labour MPs, Webster asked Blairite loyalists for their comments about their leader's silence. He heard that even they were 'demanding a timescale for his departure'. The newspaper's headline on 31 August was 'Blair Defies Party Over Departure Date'. There was uproar. Blair was accused of destroying the party by clinging on to power. Even Blairites were switching to Brown.

Brown was incandescent but, as always, dithered, resisting Ed Balls's demands for blood. He would not be seen publicly to wield the knife. Instead, he asked his closest supporters to organise the coup.

On 4 September, a group of MPs, with the chancellor's support, delivered an ultimatum to Downing Street: 'Sadly it is clear to us – as it is to the entire party and entire country – that without an urgent change in the leadership of the party it becomes less likely that we will win the next election. This is the brutal truth. It gives us no pleasure to say it. But it has to be said and understood. We therefore ask you to stand aside.' Over a hundred Labour MPs echoed the demand, led by Tom Watson, a junior minister, that he leave by summer 2007.

Instinctively, Blair wanted to fight back against what some insiders called a coup. While he sat in his office being consoled by political lightweights like Tessa Jowell and Charlie Falconer, his staff contacted Blairite MPs to sign a loyalist statement. 'We need to get people to start using the expression "blackmail",' urged Powell. The sympathisers' voices were smothered.

Through his own short-sightedness, Blair had lost his key supporters in the Cabinet. And his reliance on Stephen Byers and Alan Milburn to write newspaper articles criticising Brown, or David Miliband coyly suggesting that Blair would resign on his tenth anniversary as prime minister in May 2007, only fired the chancellor's anger. He wanted Blair to make a public statement, immediately.

At 7.45 a.m. on 6 September, Blair walked through the connecting door into 11 Downing Street and entered Brown's study. He implored Brown to be patient. They argued for an hour. Blair accused Brown of orchestrating an attempted coup, while Brown accused Blair of lying about his departure. Blair eventually left, unaware that Watson, a thuggish Brownite, had delivered a blistering letter urging him to depart 'for the sake of the legacy . . . I have to say that I no longer believe that your remaining in office is in the interest of either the party or the country.'

Blair was furious about the 'student's coup'. Watson, he spluttered, was 'disloyal, discourteous and wrong'. A meeting was arranged with Brown at 2 p.m. that same day in No. 10. Just minutes after their discussions began, the media were informed that four more MPs had resigned from junior positions in the government. They would describe their co-ordinated initiative as a 'spontaneous insurrection' aimed at obtaining a timetable for their leader's going. More resignations would follow, Blair was told, unless he announced his departure. 'He's got hours left,' said one rebel. 'He has been very foolish and arrogant. Tony is going to be told it is moving time.'

Michael Levy listened to his friend's woe: 'Tony got angrier and angrier. More furious than I had seen him. He kept saying that he had never realised how duplicitous Gordon was – and what a "liar".'

On David Hill's instructions, Downing Street told journalists that a coup orchestrated by Brown's cabal was under way. Derek Simpson, the trade union leader, was blamed for 'a disgraceful attempt to blackmail the PM from office'. Blair's nightmare scenario was departing Downing Street like Margaret Thatcher. To leave with dignity, he needed to regain control of events. In the City jargon, his choice was to bow to his attackers or 'catch a falling knife'.

That afternoon, he sat with Brown in the garden at No. 10. The common sentiment, he said with shrewd foresight, was that Labour risked being out of office for the next three elections if the succession were forced, in the manner of the Tories in 1990. Brown replied that removing Blair was the party's only hope; he was toxic.

By the end of their ninety-minute meeting, Blair had capitulated – but only partly. Rather than leaving quickly in order to allow his chancellor to establish himself at the autumn party conference and restore Labour's fortunes in the perilous Scottish and Welsh elections, he insisted on staying until he notched up a decade, which meant May 2007, at the earliest.

Brown agreed to Blair's compromise, which they settled should be announced the following day. He left No. 10 by the back entrance. A photographer caught him sitting in his car smiling.

Blair chose to make the announcement at Quintin Kynaston, a school in north-west London whose head teacher had been praised for exemplifying the best of Labour's education policies. (Eight years later, she was banned from teaching for life because of financial discrepancies.) Wearing heavy make-up, Blair was surrounded by fifty hand-picked children. With the media corralled as far away as possible, he apologised to a single camera for the party's behaviour: 'It has not been our finest hour, to be frank.' Then he confirmed that his speech to the party conference at the end of the month would be his last. And yet still he refused to give a precise date for his resignation.

While the Blairites, especially Charles Clarke, denounced the chancellor's behaviour as 'reckless', 'stupid' and 'madness', Brown himself denied there was a coup and pleaded, 'The situation is sad, regrettable and has caused us a great deal of grief.' Fearing a backlash, he whitewashed his participation: 'I said to him it is for him to make the decision.'

Blair's anger mounted. He felt that his loyalty to Brown had been rewarded by treachery. Stubbornly, Brown had ignored the polls that showed only 30 per cent believed Labour could win an election under his leadership, with 80 per cent of under-twenty-fives hostile towards the prospect of a Brown government. Ben Wegg-Prosser, the head of his Strategic Communications Unit, sent an email to the staff to say, 'There is no deal.'

That afternoon, Stephen Boys-Smith, working with the Independent Monitoring Commission responsible for disarming the paramilitaries in Ulster, visited Blair with the members of his team. Blair made no attempt to disguise his lack of interest. 'He could not even switch on his actor's performance,' noticed Boys-Smith. 'He didn't even try to look like being on the ball.' Two days later, Blair ordered his supporters to stop sniping at Brown. Without a ceasefire he feared the split would permanently damage the party.

At the end of Friday 8 September, Powell sent round another email: 'Very well done over the past week or so. A remarkable performance on behalf of TB, who is not very good at saying thank you directly. Thank you very much indeed for keeping the ship afloat.'

The TUC conference on 12 September was the dress rehearsal for Blair's farewell at the party conference. He enjoyed entering the bear pit to preach the truth. Labour's continuing dependence on the unions, he feared, still made the party 'the prisoner of the Left' and could terminate any chance of re-election. His own success owed everything to minimising their power. In return, the unions had vented their anger at the man who put the interests of patients and schoolchildren ahead of the self-interest of NHS employees and teachers. He was greeted with a hostile silence and placards of 'Time to Go'. Undaunted, he provoked boos and heckles by telling his audience the 'brutal truth'. If they refused to understand the problems of government and compromise, he warned, Labour would spend the future 'wasting our time in opposition passing resolutions which nobody will do anything about'. His message was rejected. Perfunctory claps was the reward for three election victories.

The party conference was held in Manchester. Brown arrived keen to solicit support, upset the polls showing the Tories ahead, and restore relations with Blair. In the middle of a clunking speech, he told the packed auditorium, 'It has been a privilege for me to work with and for the most successful ever Labour leader and Labour prime minister.' Outside the hall, Cherie watched a monitor and was heard by a Bloomberg journalist to remark, 'Well, that's a lie.' Her words dominated the media, suffocating Brown's emollient message. Cherie's denial seven hours later – 'Honestly, guys, I hate to spoil your story, but I didn't say it and I don't believe it' – was mocked.

That night, the Blairs hosted a party in their suite. One floor below, the Brownites sat in fury, 'feeling utterly sick', according to Damian McBride.

'She's killed us, she's killed us,' Brown wailed, slumping against a wall.

The next day came Blair's speech. It was a supremely confident finale. He started by thanking Cherie for her support and gave a flash of his showbiz genius: 'I mean, at least I don't have to worry about her running off with the bloke next door.' What followed was a captivating description of his successes and his hopes that the reforms would continue, and an admission that 'You make your own luck.' Having held his audience in thrall, he ended, 'In the years to come, wherever I am, whatever I do, I'm with you. You're the future now. Make the most of it.'

The standing ovation appeared endless. Biting his lip, Blair seemed set to shed a tear, but his emotions were torn. He craved an audience, but he did not love those who cheered. On the contrary, he hated their ingratitude. He had never loved the common man. For their part, many in the audience wanted him to stay on but realised that he was too damaged to win the next election. Sleaze and Iraq had stained him permanently. A Mori poll put the public's 'satisfaction' rating of Blair at 20 per cent, lower than Thatcher on the eve of her fall.

The following week, David Cameron asked Blair in a raucous Commons, 'Do you back the chancellor as your successor? Yes or no?' Blair did not reply.

During the whole of September, those engaged in the battle for Downing Street forgot the soldiers fighting in Iraq and Afghanistan. The 130th soldier had just been killed in Iraq, and a Nimrod surveillance aircraft had crashed in Afghanistan, killing fourteen crew. Their deaths were blamed on the government's refusal to provide enough money to service the plane. To the country, Blair was a lame duck repeating that the troops should remain in Iraq 'until the job is done'. Whitehall gossip did not restore any confidence.

In early October, during a visit to Downing Street to discuss the perils in Afghanistan, General Richards noticed that Blair was not listening. The war had been delegated to Stirrup. After their talk, Blair agreed to pose for a photograph. 'You sit down,' he said to Richards, 'and I'll stand behind you to show a coup.'

Dannatt's frustration boiled over. While Richards was standing on the Downing Street steps, he inhabited the shadows. Since Blair refused to listen about 'the army running hot', Dannatt turned to the *Daily Mail*. In the published interview, he said that Britain should leave Iraq 'sometime soon, as their presence was exacerbating the Islamic security threat to Britain'.

Blair was visiting Ireland when the general's words were reported. 'I wasn't best pleased,' he would write, understating his outrage. Dannatt, he complained, was a dogmatist scoring points at a politician's expense.

Senior army officers expected the general to be dismissed for breaching the constitutional code, and Shirreff spoke for many by criticising Dannatt's 'crass own goal'. Throughout history, rebellious American generals had been fired by their president, and an immediate decision to remove a maverick serviceman would have silenced the hubbub between the chiefs and the civil servants, and even resolved the breakdown between the military in Afghanistan and the politicians in London. Blair could have received that instant recommendation from Stirrup, but the air marshal held back.

In Blair's telephone conversation with Browne, Dannatt's dismissal was not seriously considered. Instead, Blair coyly anticipated the media headlines should the draconian measure be taken. 'If Dannatt's fired,' he reckoned, 'the *Mail* and the rest of Fleet Street will turn against me. Their headline will be "A Very Honest General".' Signalling his dislike of confrontation, he told Browne, 'I'm cornered.' His only request was that Dannatt should accuse the *Mail* of distorting his words and demand a correction. Then he invited the general and all the chiefs to a lunch of sandwiches.

The scene in Downing Street was surreal. The conversations at all social meetings between Labour politicians and the military were strained, but on this occasion the atmosphere of cordiality was particularly contrived. Energetically circulating the room, Blair went to pains to show that his distrust of civil servants did not extend to people in uniform. The chiefs would not be given ammunition to whisper any criticism of himself to the Tories. During lunch, no one acknowledged that the army was engaged in its biggest battle since the Korean war some fifty-five years earlier. No one reviewed the contradiction of launching two wars in the name of nation-building. Both the chiefs and the politicians shied away from mentioning that the army was unable to protect Iraqi and Afghan civilians from slaughter or discussing Washington's declining confidence in Britain's fighting ability. Blair and the military were united in their strategy of just muddling through.

The theme of Blair's short speech to his guests was, 'We must all work together' – or, as some quipped, 'We all must hang together.' He had admitted that Iraq was 'so far pretty much a disaster', but blamed Muslim extremists for preventing the majority of Iraqis from building a peaceful, democratic state.

That explanation was no comfort to Dannatt. With some justification he complained about his treatment, adding, 'Blair didn't look me in the eye,' and that he had not been invited to say anything. Powell's mistaken recollection was that the general did speak.

By the end of lunch, Blair had classified Dannatt as untrustworthy and unsuited for the job. But, assuming Powell is reliable, Blair's interpretation of his own dilemma was similarly skewed. 'We spent most of our time in government', Powell would write disingenuously, 'not fighting wars but trying to prevent them.' He added that Dannatt's use of the *Mail* would 'make politicians think twice if military action is proposed in the future'.

The written apology Blair expected from his outspoken general did not arrive. 'Dannatt's no fucking good to you lot,' Matt Cavanagh, Browne's special adviser, told General Richards. 'He's toast in No. 10.'

Animosities flourished among the chiefs. 'Everyone hated each other,' complained an official. 'Dannatt's made everything difficult.'

The politicians and commentariat would blame successive chiefs of the defence staff for failing to inform Blair and the secretaries of state for defence about awkward truths in Iraq and Afghanistan. Now, Dannatt was castigated for telling Blair just those truths. Newcomers like Cavanagh, a recent arrival at the MoD who witnessed the fractured relationships, blamed the military for having 'lost sight of strategy'. He also blamed civil servants for having 'simply opted out of the difficult arguments' between the military and the politicians. He was unaware of Whitehall's path to war in Iraq. From the outset, Blair had excluded those who offered unwelcome advice.

Even after nine years in office, Blair had a limited understanding of government. During a conversation with Stirrup while on a flight from Iraq, he referred to the importance of Europe's military defence agreements. 'It's a joke, Prime Minister,' said Stirrup. 'When the Europeans spend real money, I'll believe in it, but in the meantime it's a fig leaf for doing less.'

Blair looked discomfited. Despite the setbacks he had witnessed in

Iraq, he still believed passionately in intervention. He urged Stirrup to dispatch groups of special forces to solve humanitarian crises in Zimbabwe, Sudan, Darfur and other war zones in Africa. On each occasion, Stirrup replied, 'What is your strategic purpose? You don't know how this will turn out. No plan ever survives the first contact with the enemy. The unexpected will happen.'

Once more, Blair looked disappointed. He appeared to enjoy warfare.

In December 2006, the prime minister, while visiting Kuwait, darted across to Basra on a day trip. Operation Sinbad was in disarray. Not only was the army failing to defeat the Shia killers, but there was also a breakdown in relations between the military and officials from the Foreign Office and DFID. British civil servants were refusing to work together or share transport around the city. DFID's officials would not leave 'Basra Palace', while Foreign Office officials marooned themselves fifteen miles away. The antagonism that Blair had failed to resolve in London had erupted as a turf war in the midst of a real one.

The prime minister was greeted by the soldiers as a celebrity, and they were grateful when he posed with them for photographs. The odd man out was Shirreff. 'We're just dribbling,' he complained to Blair, the only person who could resolve the problem. Under Shirreff's command, nineteen British servicemen had been killed and 121 wounded. The casualties were higher than in the preceding months. 'More could be done if you'd help with troops and resources,' Shirreff told the prime minister.

'Why don't you write to me?' replied Blair, speaking, Shirreff thought, 'in a detached manner, as if he was a bystander chatting in a pub over a pint'.

Shirreff continued, 'And there's no co-operation between the army, Foreign Office and DFID. It's so dysfunctional.'

'Write to me,' repeated Blair, staring into the distance.

Shirreff duly wrote, but his letter was never acknowledged. He returned to Britain soon after.

On his final trip to Iraq in 2007, Blair was asked by a reporter, 'How long will it take for it not to be a mess?'

'I dunno,' he replied. 'You can't tell. It will resolve itself, it just will. People will get sick of the killing.' The health ministry in Baghdad estimated that 150,000 Iraqis had died since the invasion.

During this latter trip, Blair also met General George Casey, the US commander in Iraq. America had committed 140,000 troops to a 'surge' aimed at destroying the militias, while Britain's soldiers – soon to be reduced to 5,000 and embarrassed by the US's technical superiority in counter-insurgency operations – wanted to leave. But Blair was waiting for Washington's agreement. 'We're loyal supporters,' he told the general, 'and we'll do what you want.' For General Jonathan Shaw, Shirreff's successor, Blair's message symbolised the hopeless predicament he had created. To the public, in a television interview Blair declared that 'the progress in Iraq is remarkable'.

Stirrup decided that Shaw should reverse Shirreff's strategy. Rather than having to survive a further six months of attacks, the army would retreat to Basra airport, leaving the militias in control of the city. 'I was redeployed not knowing who was left in charge,' complained Shaw. 'The withdrawal was dishonest.' The British had been defeated, but Blair refused to admit it. Relations among the chiefs in London had deteriorated so badly that Stirrup refused to tell Dannatt that MI6 had brokered a deal with Muqtada al-Sadr, a terrorist leader in Basra, to protect the withdrawal. 'You're not security-cleared,' Stirrup eventually told the chief. 'It's not a military operation.' The one bonus for Dannatt was that more soldiers would be heading for Afghanistan, which, Blair belatedly recognised, 'was just beginning to be a bigger problem'.

Four years later, unrepentant about invading Iraq, Blair wrote: 'I was left with the feeling that had we believed in our mission more and not despaired so easily . . . we would have had a far greater part in the final battle.' He did not admit that, as the supreme commander, he bore the entire responsibility for the military's mood and resources.

FORTY-SEVEN

Self-Destruction

The deadline was agreed. During the countdown of the last nine months of his premiership, Blair demanded a frenzied schedule in order to prove himself as the master of his destiny. He would campaign in the May local elections, then announce his resignation and, on the eve of his departure on 27 June, attend two international summits. He would allow the curtain to fall only after his 'reform' agenda had been firmly established. This would both fix his legacy and tie Gordon Brown in to a winning programme for a fourth-term victory. The third, unspoken objective was to lay the foundations of a new career.

The mood in January 2007 was not conducive to a finale accompanied by rapturous applause. 'I want to get on with the job,' he said on television, oblivious to the hostility he was arousing. 'I want to finish what I've started.' With pride, he would describe himself as being 'on top form . . . The only meaning was in being true to myself.'

Labour's poll ratings were falling. In the media and the Commons, the government appeared indecisive about overcrowded prisons and whether Roman Catholic agencies should be banned by law from arranging adoptions because they discriminated against gay couples. Blair's vulnerability as an undeclared Roman Catholic illogically added fuel to another Commons rebellion by ninety-four Labour MPs against modernising the Trident nuclear weapons programme. Once again, Blair was saved by Tory votes. However, after another passionate debate, Labour MPs did support Blair and voted against a comprehensive inquiry into the Iraq war. A week later, Saddam Hussein was sentenced to death, a judgement Blair opposed.

In parallel, the police were providing a running commentary to journalists about their investigation into loans for peerages. Senior officers regularly stoked the public's anger. Ruth Turner was arrested in a publicised dawn raid, and certain members of the Downing Street staff were questioned under caution. To Gus O'Donnell's dismay, the police were given access to Downing Street's sensitive email servers. Soon after, a police source revealed the discovery of an email from Turner to Jonathan Powell. She had reported Michael Levy's request for her 'to lie for him' that he had no role in the honours system; for his part, he denied any wrongdoing. Journalists quoting 'police sources' said that at least three Downing Street staff were likely to be charged. In that febrile atmosphere, Blair was formally interviewed on 26 February by two police officers. It was the second time. Throughout the interview, Blair casually dismissed their questions.

True to form, to bury the bad news, on the day of the interview the government media machine issued fourteen announcements. They included the long-awaited report by Lord Stevens, a former Scotland Yard chief, into the death of Princess Diana in Paris; the closure of 2,500 post offices; and Blair's order to terminate in the 'national interest' a two-year investigation by the Fraud Office into alleged bribes paid by British Aerospace to Saudi Arabian power brokers to secure a huge weapons contract. Blair's helpmate in closing down that controversy was once again Peter Goldsmith, the attorney general. Blair also chose that moment not to renew the contract of Alistair Graham, the sure-footed chairman of the Committee on Standards in Public Life. The sleaze-buster was replaced by Rita Donaghy, a long-standing member of the TUC council. Her appointment symbolised Blair's swift descent from the moral high ground. In 2000, Labour had passed legislation to prevent secret donations to political parties; and, in 2002, the government had outlawed bribes paid by corporations to foreign governments to win commercial contracts. Both acts had been circumvented. The public were disturbed. To Blair's surprise, sleaze had made the British noticeably ungrateful for the benefits of his decade in power.

An hour after the police left Downing Street, their interviewee flew to Davos to mix with billionaires at the World Economic Forum, thence on to the Middle East, another certain location for his new life. He left behind an indignant party. Eleven weeks before the local elections, the opinion polls placed the Conservatives on 40 per cent and Labour on 29. The party was predicted to lose 600 seats and perform badly in Scotland. Blair urged Labour not to be rattled and told the public, 'I have taken absolutely no decision about my future at all.' Single-minded, he appeared oblivious to all the distractions, although the symmetry of his life, described as the 'final phase', was not exactly following the scenario composed six months earlier by his Downing Street staff.

Blair's farewell had been mapped out by Ben Wegg-Prosser, helped by Matthew Taylor and Philip Gould. Called 'Reconnecting with the Public – A New Relationship with the Media', the five-page memorandum proposed the orchestration of a glorified departure. Conjuring up images of a Hollywood melodrama, Blair was scripted to float on a wave of national euphoria. 'He needs to go with the crowds wanting more,' suggested Wegg-Prosser. 'He should be the star who won't even play the last encore. In moving towards the end, he must focus on the future.' In searching for high visibility, the author suggested, 'He needs to embrace open spaces, he needs to be seen to be travelling on different forms of transport, he needs to be seen with people who will raise eyebrows.' There would be many newspaper interviews and TV appearances on *Blue Peter* and *Songs of Praise*. The downside, Wegg-Prosser anticipated, was Brown's fury, while he described Iraq as 'the elephant in the room, let's face up to it'. He concluded, with remarkable honesty, 'His genuine legacy is not delivery, important though that is, but the dominance of New Labour ideas – the triumph of Blairism.'

The echo of Blairism's assumed permanence was Peter Riddell's judgement during the September 'coup' that 'Mr Blair has made Labour a party of government again. There is no going back to the 1980s.' That was precisely Blair's intention. His legacy was the continuous modernisation of Britain.

The obstacle, he complained, was Brown. At the end of their conversations about the transition, Blair had emerged to complain, 'Gordon has nothing. Nothing.' After a decade, Brown saw New Labour as a tactic to win elections, not an ideology. The chancellor, Blair knew, misunderstood why the middle class, especially in the south of England, had switched from the Conservatives to New Labour. 'Values to improve society', he emphasised, was the persuasive appeal. 'Once the values are fixed,' explained Blair, 'the policies would flow naturally.' To his despair, Brown resisted the lesson. His chancellor, Blair complained to his inner circle, had no ideas other than the reheated Bennism of the 1980s. Eager to reconnect the party with the trade unions and the working class, Brown still opposed Blair on foundation hospitals, academies and reforms to the welfare state. But beyond that antagonism lurked something deeper. Unlike Blair, Brown did not believe the New Labour brand could be regenerated. The problem was not marketing but the product. A section of the country harboured a deeply felt outrage towards Blair. Combined with their anger at Cherie, Alastair Campbell and Iraq, the poison could not be drained away by rebranding. Brown classified Blair not as a victor but as the victim of his own convictions.

Saving face had become a political necessity. Reluctantly, Brown agreed to accompany Blair to the Mossbourne Academy in Hackney to praise the success of the academy movement. Together, they pottered around smiling at the cameras and pupils, and for fifteen minutes served meals. Ofsted rated Mossbourne as the one outstanding academy out of forty-six. By the end of the year, Blair expected there would be about ninety-five in existence, and his ambition was for 400 by 2010, accounting for 10 per cent of all secondary schools. Brown refused to endorse that ambition, not least because David Bell, the permanent secretary at education, criticised academies for failing to improve basic skills. Too many were based in expensive, complicated new buildings. In one east London academy, no one knew how to open the windows after the maintenance man unexpectedly died.

A more searing indictment of the Labour decade was the enrolment of 40,000 more children in private schools than in 1997. Parents gave up their savings to avoid the bad discipline and poor teaching in state schools. Ignoring that 'vote' by dissatisfied parents, Blair would nevertheless praise his achievement, writing, 'In schools, standards up across the board.' Not for the first time, international statistics contradicted his self-congratulation. Writing for the Sutton Trust, a Blairite educational group, Alan Smithers reported that his research had unearthed 'a long trail of under-achievement' across all levels in primary schools, especially in maths. In 2009, PISA, the international monitor, placed English secondary schools twenty-seventh out of sixty countries in maths, and eighteenth in the three Rs and science.

To Brown, all that was irrelevant. Despite Blair's pleas, he refused to look beyond the Treasury. Blair acknowledged his impotence. As usual, on Budget day he sat on the front bench to cheer his chancellor, and found himself surprised by Brown's 2p cut in income tax and the abolition of the 10p band for the lowest earners. Blair's genuine praise placed him in good company. 'His stewardship of the nation's finances', gushed the *Daily Mail*, 'has been remarkable.' The newspaper's political columnist Peter Oborne hailed Brown as 'a great chancellor' and predicted that 'historians will look back at the Brown years and marvel'. As usual, the man himself had ignored warnings that the abolition of the 10p threshold would increase taxes for the poorest. Blair also discounted the alarm. Like the majority of the country, he assumed that Brown had stuck to his pledge of 'no more boom and bust' and did truly believe he had produced 'the longest period of economic growth for over 200 years'. The self-styled Iron Chancellor disregarded the rise of the public debt from 30.4 per cent of GDP in 2001/2 to 36.8 per cent, which was accurately predicted to soar the following year to 44.6 per cent, then 65.9 per cent in 2010/11, tipping Britain into recession. Those who forecast disaster were ignored.

In his Mansion House speech that year, Brown praised the City's 'ingenuity and creativity' in inventing new forms of finance. The banks' success, he boasted, was thanks in part to a decade of Treasury support for light-touch regulation. Brown's City audience applauded themselves. Blair appeared beyond caring that Britain's productivity remained poor and personal debts were increasing. He failed to catch that the cost of working tax credits was heading towards £20 billion, forty times more than Brown's original estimate. New Labour's achievement was not only the considerable redistribution of wealth so that poverty among children and pensioners had been reduced, but also that many people still appeared not to resent paying higher taxes to improve society. Yet Blair did appreciate that the limit would soon be reached. The cost of increased debt and ever-increasing stealth taxes contradicted New Labour's ideals. Brown's 'prudent' image was beginning to fade.

For the first time, Blair read the Treasury's official records recounting the abolition of the annual £5 billion tax credits on dividends for pension funds. In 1998, he had called Brown's edict 'brilliant' for making Britain 'fair, modern and strong'. The official records from that year revealed a different judgement. Released in 2007 after a long freedom of information battle, the papers recorded Treasury officials accurately warning Brown that Britain's unique private pension system would be wrecked by the loss of tens of billions of pounds. Nine years later, Blair publicly supported Brown's 'right decision to make for investment and the future of our pension system'. In private, his fears were reconfirmed.

Brown, he knew, was incapable of defeating David Cameron, but Blair had failed to nurture a network of party loyalists to support any alternative. In Powell's judgement, Blair was acutely sensitive that any 'mishandling' of the succession would attract 'bigger criticism of Tony than the Iraq war'. Out of either self-interest or a sense of obligation, he had tolerated Brown's destruction of any potential leadership rival. Alan Milburn, Charles Clarke and John Reid had been effectively undermined by Damian McBride's poisonous briefings to journalists. With Brown's tacit approval, McBride, who described himself as 'a cruel, vindictive and thoughtless bastard', had peddled stories about sexual affairs, alcoholism and personal peccadilloes. 'Tony never showed loyalty,' recalled Geoff Hoon. 'He spent no time to make sure there was a successor to entrench his brand of politics. He just looked after his enemies and damaged his friends.'

That left David Miliband as the sole Blairite flag-carrier. In some ways, back in 1992 the thirty-two-year-old had been similar to Blair – articulate, charming and intelligent. Hampered by Blair's refusal to make him education secretary in 2005 or foreign secretary in 2006, Miliband had limited experience of government, which made him a casualty of Blair's desire to control everything. Some believed that Blair feared the young man's opposition on schools and foreign policy. In truth, his misgivings went much deeper. After recognising Miliband's manifold weaknesses while he worked as the head of the policy unit in Downing Street after 1997, Blair had orchestrated his snap adoption as the Labour candidate for the South Shields constituency on the eve of the 2001 general election in order to propel him from his office. In those circumstances, he refused to encourage Miliband's challenge to Brown.

Miliband's own indecision exposed another serious defect: his lack of courage or, as Peter Mandelson would later put it, of 'lead in his pencil'. Accordingly, on 22 April, Miliband surrendered and pledged his vote to Brown. 'Then Tony handed over the government to the one man who hated him,' said Hoon. In the short term, by conceding the crown to Brown, Blair knew that the party would not split. But, beyond the smooth transition, he feared for its fate. The absence of influential Blairites at the head of the party threatened to bring about the demise of New Labour.

To exit in triumph, Blair used the long goodbye to fashion an image of his legacy. First, there was the Queen's Speech, which anticipated thirty-nine new laws that would pass before his departure. Everything was thrown in: crime, immigration, more private services for the NHS, more academies, tougher A-levels, more social housing and nuclear power. To the end, he believed that laws rather than good government would change the country, belying his own confession that it was only as the handover approached that 'I knew what to do and how to do it.'

Next he delivered 'Pathways to the Future', a series of lectures about public services, energy, defence and Europe. 'New Labour', he said at the outset, 'has set a new political course for our nation. Others now have to set variations on our basic theme.' However, his hope of changing the nation's mood was stymied by his inconsistent record. Over the decade, he had certainly helped the poorest and removed the intolerances suffered by minorities. The distress of the poor had been reduced by the minimum wage and higher welfare payments, especially for mothers. For those benefiting from the banking boom, especially in the south, Britain became a more comfortable, even happier place. Blair had caught the mood – enriched by the Lottery's money for the arts and the false impression of an improving economy – to transform London into a genuinely international city bursting with entrepreneurs and cultural icons. He described his paradigm as 'a new kind of politics in the new century. What you did in your personal life was your choice, what you did to others was not.' But improved lifestyles did not amount to a defined ideology. The regressive downside to 'modernisation' and 'progressive' politics, highlighted by his critics, was the rise in drug addiction and alcoholism, the decline of marriage, the fractures in social cohesion caused by immigration, the stagnation of educational standards, an Orwellian jungle of regulations, sleaze and the public's loss of trust in Britain's institutions.

His journey on health, education and energy had gone full circle, and at huge expense. Waiting times for treatment had indeed been dramatically cut, and the new schools and hospitals improved the atmosphere surrounding public services, but he offered nothing fundamentally new. After all his changes, he remained unconvinced and unconverted to real choice, competition and markets. New buildings were not the same as new ideas. His reforms had added little to his inheritance.

His valedictory speeches were either ignored or, as he admitted, greeted with 'cynicism'. The exception was the public's reaction to his passion for using Britain's military to crush international terrorism. 'Get real,' he told his critics. 'There is no alternative to fighting this menace [of a perverted form of Islam] wherever it rears its head. It has to be beaten. Period. Britain must be a player, not a spectator.' Few disagreed about the dangers of political Islam, but most questioned a messenger who still energetically denied that the wars in Iraq and Afghanistan had made life worse for the local people.

In 1997, as the champion of multiculturalism, Blair had labelled those who warned about the danger of allowing political Islam into Britain's mosques and opposed faith schools as racist. Ten years later, he was telling Muslims they had 'a duty to integrate' and should accept British values. 'So conform to it or don't come here,' he said. Wearing a niqab, he added, was 'a mark of separation'. Nevertheless, he did not believe that large numbers of Muslim immigrants rejected integration. In his opinion, immigration was not a harbinger of extreme Islam. On the contrary, he asserted, 'To an extent immigration [was] to me utterly mainstream and a vital point of what the government was about.'

The evangelist's sermon had become incomprehensible to the majority of Britons. He no longer presented his venture into Afghanistan as peaceful reconstruction. Helmand had become another front in the war on terror. Any defeat, he said, would be the fault of others for not sharing his self-belief.

Undeterred and led by General Charles Guthrie, the retired chiefs turned on Blair for dispatching a demoralised army to Afghanistan with insufficient money and equipment. From admiration to admonition within a decade, Guthrie's disillusion reflected the public's anger.

Blair's other-worldliness was noticed by senior *Guardian* journalists during a lunch in Downing Street.

'I was right to have gone to war in Iraq,' said Blair defiantly.

'But what if you're proved wrong?' a journalist asked.

'I am right,' Blair replied, and looking upwards continued, 'but someone else will be my judge.'

Afghanistan would be decided using the same criteria. His denial that British troops were 'stirring the hornets' nest' in a medieval society matched his incomprehension over how a decade of wars had degraded Britain's armed forces.

The litmus test was his reaction to the capture on 23 March 2007 of fifteen Royal Navy ratings and marines by Iranian guards in the Gulf. The men and women had behaved appallingly. Over the following days of their incarceration, the men whimpered and humiliated themselves on Iranian television, while British diplomats negotiated their release.

On 4 April, Blair stood in his study with David Hill, his media supremo, watching the live television coverage of Mahmoud Ahmadinejad, the Iranian president, announcing the ratings' departure from Iran. Constantly glancing at the mirror to check his tie, Blair was observed by an aide to be psyching himself as usual into the right mood for his choreographed exit onto Downing Street to address the waiting cameras.

The following day, the ratings emerged from a plane at Heathrow to be hailed by the navy as heroes. Instead of swiftly escorting the miscreants into oblivion, the navy chiefs encouraged a rating to sell her story to a national newspaper. Many were outraged, not least the heads of the army. To allow a rating to profit from humiliation symbolised the Blairist priority of placing the media before morality. Blair rejected the complaints as 'synthetic fury'. His principles had shifted sharply since 1997; alternatively, his true values had been concealed for ten years and only over the last weeks were they finally surfacing.

The public test of Blair's status would be the local elections on 5 May, his thirteenth election campaign as leader since 1994. He was ending his extended swansong with a calculated gamble against those who ridiculed New Labour as an ideology. He hoped his critics would at least acknowledge that electoral success was the glue that had held the party together. A good showing would confound the Brownites and make them admit, however grudgingly, that Labour was electable thanks to his championing of the centre ground.

His gamble failed. Labour lost over 500 seats in England, while the Scottish Nationalists became the largest party in Scotland. Labour's Scottish leaders feared eventual meltdown. The Tories won 40 per cent of the vote against Labour's 27 per cent. Blair once again blamed the defeat on those who refused to share his own belief in himself. To his disappointment, his long farewell had not provoked the crowds to ask for more but to cry for relief. He could no longer resist. The *Evening Standard*'s headline was percipient: 'Blair Quits to Make Millions'.

Five days later, he flew to Sedgefield, his constituency. In the Trimdon Labour Club, packed with local admirers, he made an emotional resignation speech, asking to be remembered as a visionary aiming for the stars – and getting there. Holding back tears, he apologised 'for the times I have fallen short . . . To be frank, I would not have wanted it any other way . . . I ask you to accept one thing hand on heart: I did what I thought was right.' Even before he returned to London, the New Labour logo had been removed from the party's website. That night's *Evening Standard* headline reflected the mood: 'I Am Sorry'.

Among the obituaries from his supporters, Peter Riddell wrote, 'Mr Blair may be widely reviled at present, but his influence will long outlast his departure.' Philip Gould concluded, 'New Labour rather than the Tories is the Establishment . . . The future remains New Labour, the only party of genuine change in Britain today.' One enduring success in those twilight days was a full peace agreement between the IRA and the unionists in Ulster.

Over the last six weeks, as Brown awaited his coronation, Blair embarked on a world tour using a Boeing 777, the world's largest twin-engined jet, which normally seats about 400 people and had been chartered by the government from British Airways. His first stop was Paris, after which, on 17 May, he flew to Washington to stand with President Bush in the White House rose garden for a public farewell. 'What I know', said Bush, 'is that the world needs courage, and what I know is that this good man is a courageous man.' World leaders, added Bush, listened to Blair. 'Even if they may not agree with him 100 per cent, they admire him.' Asked whether he had caused Blair's downfall, the president replied, 'I don't know.' The day ended with a party at the British embassy arranged by David Manning.

Next, Blair visited the Pope and formally revealed he would convert to Catholicism, before flitting across Africa, from Sierra Leone to

South Africa. In 2001, he had described the continent as a 'scar on the conscience of the world'. Since then, the successful organisation of debt relief had benefited some countries, while others had corruptly abused Britain's generosity.

The tour ended in Libya, where hints about the real Blair finally emerged. Over the previous year, MI5 officers, in co-operation with Libyan intelligence agents, had been targeting Libyans living in London who were opposed to Colonel Gaddafi's regime. In a letter Blair had written to Gaddafi one month earlier, on 27 April, he had thanked the dictator for the 'excellent co-operation' between their intelligence services, adding, 'As you know, I am determined to see that partnership develop still further.' He had also expressed his regret that an English judge had refused to deport two dissidents back to Tripoli. 'I am very disappointed at the court's decision,' he had written. To pacify Gaddafi, he had added 'a personal word of thanks for your assistance in the matter of deportation'. The 'assistance' was information possibly extracted from other dissidents by torture in Libya.

The presence of Blair's extravagant jet at the small dusty airfield in Sirte, set halfway between Tripoli and Benghazi, was exaggerated by the unrecognisable version of the British anthem played by the Libyan military band. In a scene reminiscent of Ruritania, Blair shook the hands of those summoned to accompany him on his visit to Gaddafi, including Peter Sutherland, the chairman of BP, and Mark Allen, the head of MI6's counter-intelligence. BP, the camouflage for the visit, had announced a £454 million plan to resume oil exploration after years of absence, but the company's gesture was quickly forgotten. The prime minister was secretly negotiating an agreement for an exchange of prisoners. Among Gaddafi's demands was that Abdelbaset al-Megrahi, convicted for his involvement in the Lockerbie bombing, be released from a Scottish jail. Why Blair, in the last days of his premiership, was keen to conclude such a controversial pact became apparent only after his resignation.

The contrast between Blair's public support for a murderous dictator and his private humanity was visible to only a few. During those final weeks, Peter Watt, the Labour Party's general secretary, asked for a favour. One of his father's dying wishes was to visit Downing Street. Blair readily agreed, and the fifty-three-year-old was welcomed into the Cabinet room. Few could beat Blair's expressions of sympathy. During the half-hour visit, their friendly conversation was recorded in a succession of photographs. In the aftermath of the millisecond flashes, Watt observed that his 'brilliant' leader 'did not allow a curtain to fall', reassuring his father that his visit was not a chore for the prime minister. The public, Watt feared, condemned Blair as a bogeyman rather than appreciating his genuine concern for those who suffered. The mismatch was Blair's tragedy.

On 6 June, a removal van arrived in Downing Street to start taking the Blairs' possessions. During a farewell dinner for financial supporters that week, the prime minister recounted that a Birmingham party official had called to explain how his local constituency had just completed a protracted discussion to decide whether to thank Blair for his thirteen years as leader. 'We've decided', the constituency chairman went on, 'not to give you a vote of thanks.'

The last Cabinet meeting was more generous. Brown congratulated his nemesis effusively and presented him with a painting of Chequers, paid for out of the £1,600 raised by the members of the Cabinet. 'It's the right time to go,' said Blair. And not just for him. 'I'm walking out of office with my head held high,' said John Prescott, who had also decided to retire.

In the dying days of his premiership, Blair crammed in two summits: a climate-change discussion with the G8 leaders, and an EU summit on the union's constitution. Everything was fashioned for a glorious farewell and a smooth transition into his new career. In Downing Street, his goodbyes to his staff were genuinely emotional. Buckingham Palace refused to agree to a dinner for the Queen in Downing Street on his last night, reflecting the monarch's dislike of the Blairs. Instead, the final piece of razzmatazz saw Blair welcoming Arnold Schwarzenegger for breakfast on his last morning. The governor of California was expected to help his friend earn an income as a global envoy combating climate change.

Just after 11 o'clock, Blair put on the same pair of Church's brogues he had worn for every Commons question time and headed for the chamber. In his pocket he carried a blank P45 form to wave as evidence of his imminent unemployment.

In an emotional, funny and solemn finale, the astute player paid tribute to the fears and the excitement of the past decade. 'I can pay the house the greatest compliment I can by saying that, from first to last, I never stopped fearing it. The tingling apprehension that I felt at three minutes to twelve today, I felt as much ten years ago, and every bit as acute.' With laughter and bathos, one of the great political performers at the Dispatch Box repeatedly bowed to a sceptical but charitable audience. To them, members of the world's greatest political arena, he offered the final credit amid a trace of tears: 'If it is on occasions the place of low skulduggery, it is more often the place for the pursuit of noble causes. I wish everyone, friend or foe, well – and that is that. The end.'

He froze. For a brief moment no one could quite believe that the curtain was falling. Labour MPs rose to their feet, and Cameron signalled for his side to follow as Blair made his way out of the chamber. Breaking convention, everyone was standing and clapping, except the Scottish Nationalists. 'We won't see his like for a long time,' said William Hague. 'In the Tory party, we are grateful for that.'

Back in Downing Street, Blair collected Cherie and their four children so they could pose on the doorstep for the photographers, then headed for the car to drive to the palace and formally resign. 'Goodbye,' Cherie said to the media. 'I don't think we'll miss you.'

Three weeks later, the Crown Prosecution Service announced that, after a lawyer had considered all the evidence collected by the police, no one would be charged for offering peerages in exchange for loans.

PART 4

REDEMPTION AND RESURRECTION

JUNE 2007–MARCH 2016

FORTY-EIGHT

Gun for Hire

Days after leaving Downing Street, Blair flew to Tel Aviv. The calling card for his new career had been negotiated during the closing weeks of his premiership. Emotional pressure on President Bush had secured his appointment as the unpaid envoy of the Quartet, the contact group established in 2002 to mediate in the Palestinian–Israeli conflict.

Blair would be based in Jerusalem, a post that could provide a glorious chapter in his new life. He had everything he enjoyed: sun, the Mediterranean lifestyle and status. As an envoy, he dictated his own conditions of work, which included his own home and an office in east Jerusalem for twelve members of staff – he would choose the whole top floor of the five-star American Colony Hotel for $1.3 million per annum – a fleet of black, armoured Toyota Land Cruisers awaiting his summons, access to a private jet and unsupervised expenses. Surrounded by intelligent people who praised his leadership in the 'war of salvation' to topple Saddam, he was empowered to continue life at the heart of international politics.

Ehud Olmert, the Israeli prime minister, embraced Blair's mission. Introduced by Ariel Sharon, the two had become friends, sharing banter about football and a common interest in a peace agreement with the Palestinians. In 2006, with Bush's support, Olmert had opened negotiations with Mahmoud Abbas, the Palestinian leader based in Ramallah on the West Bank, to create two states based on Israel's withdrawal from some of the occupied territories. Olmert's early optimism was undermined by his personal vulnerability. Heavily criticised for his leadership during the 2006 war in Lebanon, he was also accused of multiple frauds. Blair consoled Olmert by comparing the fraud investigation to his own cash-for-peerages saga.

Olmert's weakness was balanced by Ehud Barak, the defence minister and Israel's most decorated soldier. Blair and Barak were old friends. In 1997, Barak had arrived in London as the leader of Israel's beleaguered Labour Party, seeking help to win the 1999 elections. With the aid of Blair's Labour experts in Millbank, he won and remained prime minister for two years. After losing the next election to Benjamin Netanyahu, he became a successful businessman, until 2007, when he returned to Olmert's coalition government. Barak and Olmert both supported Blair's plea to Bush about the importance of America's engagement in a peace settlement. Bush's wishes had been frustrated by many in Washington, not least those in the State Department who had opposed Blair's appointment. Now, with the authority of his new position, Blair fed hope among Israelis and Palestinians alike, all exhausted by the war in Lebanon.

To Richard Makepeace, the British consul in Jerusalem who briefed Blair on his first visit, the new envoy radiated self-belief. 'I've solved Ireland, and this is just another problem,' said Blair, brushing aside warnings about the region's complexities. 'I've got unrivalled access to the leaders of all the parties,' he went on, 'and my relationships will bring success.'

'The Israeli occupation of the West Bank is near impossible to solve,' he was told.

'It can't be as bad as that,' Blair replied.

Towards the end of his first week, he was invited to a presentation by the head of the UN mission. A slide show started with an untouched map of Jordan's West Bank before Israel's occupation in 1967. Then one slide was superimposed over another, showing how land assigned to Israeli settlements, Israeli military zones, the security wall and special roads had transformed the region into a near wholly Israeli-occupied area. 'OK, I see what you mean,' said Blair, surprised but undaunted.

Brimming with self-confidence, he ignored the limitation placed on the envoy's task only to improve the economic conditions of the Palestinians and not become involved in the peace process. To prevent his encroachment into that delicate area, the State Department had assigned Robert Danin, a well-informed academic, as its representative on Blair's team. 'Danin was so lightweight, so junior,' observed one official, 'that he had no access to anyone senior in Washington or Jerusalem. He was appointed to be ignored.' The two British officials assigned by the Foreign Office and DFID were of similarly low rank. Blair disregarded that weakness. One telephone call from him was guaranteed to get access to Olmert and Bush. The presence of twenty Israeli security men and the local media's adulation confirmed his importance.

After a week in Jerusalem, Blair flew to meet Sheikh Mohammed bin Zayed al-Nahyan, the crown prince of Abu Dhabi. Like all the Gulf state rulers, Zayed al-Nahyan was flattered by the visit and grateful for Britain's contribution to Saddam's removal. The two men were not strangers. During his last months in Downing Street, Blair had cultivated their relationship and had bought the lease for his headquarters in Grosvenor Square from the sheikh's company.

The crown prince was also intrigued. During his decade as prime minister, Blair had ignored the Gulf states. New Labour had sponsored few trade missions to the region and had allowed historic military relationships to wither. As a result, French and German arms manufacturers had encroached into Britain's traditional territory. Blair was not visiting the country to rectify that; ostensibly, he was there to encourage Abu Dhabi to invest in the Palestinian economy and offer himself as an intermediary with Israel. However, both initiatives were misplaced. Firstly, the Palestinians rejected any interference by the Gulf states; and, secondly, Israel's relations with Abu Dhabi and most other Arab states were excellent. In Glilot, the Tel Aviv headquarters of Mossad, the office of the secret service's director was decorated with jewelled swords that had been presented by visiting Arab intelligence chiefs. Blair's offer to act as a messenger was superfluous.

During his visit, he mentioned other interests. With oil prices rising towards record levels, Abu Dhabi was seeking to invest in established states and corporations. Presenting himself as a consultant, Blair tapped that lucrative opportunity.

Aged fifty-four, he had an annual pension of £63,468 and a public grant of £84,000 to run an office, but he never intended to rely on these sums. He had constantly urged his wife to refrain from her embarrassing financial forays, promising her serious wealth once they left Downing Street. He assumed that a new world of fees and commissions would answer Cherie's familiar plea of 'Why can't we go by private plane?' From the outset, he was pushing at open doors and did not anticipate saying 'No' to financial offers.

The deals were already materialising. His American literary agent had secured over £4 million for his autobiography, and another agency representing celebrity speakers was attracting bookings for him to give a series of speeches lasting between thirty-five and forty-five minutes that would earn him at least $250,000, plus $150,000 in expenses to hire a private jet.

The downside was the public's interest in his activities. To head that off, he intended to avoid what he called the 'wall of noise' of media attention by operating in secrecy. One of his great regrets had been his own Freedom of Information Act. 'Three harmless words,' he would write. 'I look at those words as I write them and feel like shaking my head till it drops off my shoulders. You idiot. You naive, foolish, irresponsible nincompoop. There is really no description of stupidity, no matter how vivid, that is adequate. I quake at the imbecility of it . . . information is neither sought because the journalist is curious to know, nor given to bestow knowledge on "the people". It's used as a weapon.' On no other subject would Blair reproach himself so ferociously.

In anticipation of the media delving into his financial affairs, he had commissioned KPMG, the accountants, and his lawyers to erect unusual barriers to prevent an accurate assessment of his wealth. All his income would be channelled through a complicated legal structure. At the top was BDBCO No. 819 Ltd, a company that in turn owned a clutch of other companies called either Windrush or Firerush. Windrush Ventures No. 3 LP was part owned by Windrush Ventures No. 2 LP, which in turn controlled Windrush Ventures Ltd. The scheme's advantage was that the LPs, or limited partnerships, were not obliged to publish their accounts. A legal smokescreen had been cast.

Similarly, Blair hired only those with unquestioned loyalty. At the apex was Catherine Rimmer, who had been his special adviser at No. 10. Praised as a 'brilliant head of research with an extraordinary ability to master detail', she was devoted to him. Others brought from Downing Street included Matthew Doyle as his spokesman and Kate Gross, who would run his operation in Africa. Beneath them were young idealists recruited from McKinsey and the leading banks. All were obliged to sign an onerous confidentiality agreement punishing any unauthorised disclosures with severe penalties.

There was good reason for the secrecy. During the summer, Blair firmed up his plans. Modelling himself on Bill Clinton and his money-making operation since leaving the White House, he offered his experience of government and his network of relationships with political leaders and billionaires to corporations and governments. That commercial career would be incorporated as Tony Blair Associates (TBA), housed in Grosvenor Square. On the other side of the fence, occupying a floor of a tower block in Marble Arch, were those employed by his charities to promote the Africa Governance Initiative (AGI), based on Michael Barber's Delivery Unit, and his Faith Foundation encouraging tolerance between the religions. In Blair's description, the commercial work was a necessary burden that financed his more important charitable mission. Despite their interdependence, he ostensibly maintained rigid compartmentalisation between employees of the two branches.

The foundations for the charitable work had been laid in Sierra Leone during his farewell tour. That country's president had been delighted to insert AGI experts into his office. In early October 2007, Blair consummated his pitch with Paul Kagame, Rwanda's president, and then successfully offered the same help to the presidents of neighbouring

Liberia and Guinea. In those destitute countries, Blair was feted as a celebrity.

Shortly after flying through West Africa, he was welcomed in Kuwait by Nasser al-Sabah, the prime minister. Ever since the dispatch of British troops to the country's borders in 1961 to prevent an invasion by Iraq, the oil state had been grateful for London's protective embrace. The same thanks had been offered by al-Sabah in 2003, after the defeat of Saddam. Four years later, the Kuwaiti listened first to Blair's entreaty on behalf of the Quartet and, next, his offer to advise on the country's future.

Blair's principal contact, Ismail Khudr al-Shatti, the prime minister's senior adviser, revealed to Blair his interest in government structures, scientific decision-making and strategy. This was a man, Blair realised, with whom he could do business, despite al-Shatti's support for the Muslim Brotherhood. Kuwait had become a natural target for Blair's commercial advice. The country's health and education services ranked among the worst in the region and the government lacked any tools to manage the environment, technology or social welfare. 'This is a country in crisis but resistant to change,' Blair was told. He presented himself to al-Shatti as the firefighter who solved identical problems in Britain in 1997. His cure, he said, was the Delivery Unit attached to the prime minister's office. 'Kuwait's prime minister needs his own office,' explained Blair, 'to do the thinking the prime minister needs. In that way, Kuwait will become a state of the future.'

Fourteen months later, on 26 January 2009, Blair returned with Jonathan Powell rather than any Quartet staff. Powell would receive a substantial percentage of any commercial contract. Similar agreements had been fashioned between Blair and Alastair Campbell.

Blair and Powell left Kuwait with al-Sabah having promised a contract to produce a review of the country's economy. The work, to be called 'Kuwait Vision 2035', would be undertaken by young consultants again recruited from McKinsey. The fee was in excess of £20 million. The Kuwaitis persuaded the British Advisory Committee on Business

Appointments, a regulator established to monitor the commercial arrangements of retiring ministers, that the contract should be kept secret. No one in Europe or America had considered how Blair would support himself while acting as the Quartet's unpaid envoy. He trusted the Kuwaitis to protect that secrecy.

Selected Kuwaiti experts were hired for the project and flown to London for training, which followed a welcome by Blair at his home in Connaught Square. 'You need blue-sky thinking,' he told his visitors, 'and to think out of the box. Even if we get 5 per cent change, that will be progress.' They were directed to conduct exhaustive research in Kuwait to identify the country's problems – which confirmed exactly what they already knew – and were directed to visit Singapore to understand the best practice in education, and to South Korea for best expertise in health. No one mentioned any Blairite successes in Britain. 'You need a grid for long-term planning,' Blair declared to his visitors, unaware that traditionally Kuwaitis were resistant to thinking beyond the next day.

The Kuwaiti deal reinforced Blair's expectation of similar contracts. Financially secure, at the end of 2007 he spent £5.75 million on South Pavilion, a beautiful seven-bedroom house with a tennis court and swimming pool in Wotton Underwood, Buckinghamshire. The period furniture found by Cherie perfectly matched the house, which was formerly owned by the actor Sir John Gielgud. Blair also bought a mews building directly behind his London home in Connaught Square. He now had his own equivalents to Downing Street and Chequers. Over the following months, he bought homes for each of his three eldest children. The total spent on property, including a block of flats in Manchester acquired as an investment, was about £25 million. Most of the money was borrowed.

The purchases attracted public attention. The mixture of Blair's elegant homes, his Mayfair office and his frequent commutes between five-star hotels on private jets accompanied by his staff and up to six police protection officers, whose expenses were funded by the British taxpayer, angered his critics in Britain. Although he insisted that he was no longer accountable to the electorate, the government contributed £400,000 every year towards the three civil servants employed by the Quartet in Jerusalem. Put together, Blair's description of himself as a private individual when, at the end of January 2008, he was introduced as the co-chairman of the World Economic Forum in Davos lacked credibility.

His fellow speaker there was Jamie Dimon, the chief executive of J. P. Morgan, the American investment bank. Days before, the New York banker had formally hired Blair as an adviser for about £3 million per annum. Although Dimon would say that he and Blair were old friends, their first meeting had followed a call in June the previous year by Jonathan Powell to Martin Armstrong, a leading London headhunter.

'Tony needs a job,' said Powell.

Armstrong visited Matthew Freud, a PR man who represented Blair and was the son-in-law of Rupert Murdoch. Together they discussed their client's requirements.

'He's in charge of the Quartet,' said Armstrong, 'and the Middle East is oil and gas. He should also use his strong reputation in the US.'

Together they agreed on his ideal destination: J. P. Morgan. Armstrong's proposal was sent to Dimon in early July. The banker met the former prime minister at 8 a.m. on 11 July at Freud's office in Mount Row, Mayfair. Blair was in a hurry for another engagement, but for twenty minutes he listened to Dimon's offer of a seat on the bank's board. 'You'd take over from George Shultz,' said Dimon, referring to the ailing former US secretary of state. The annual fee was $100,000. Bluntly, Blair replied that he wanted 'a proper job' and expected $5 million a year, a five-year contract as an adviser and a percentage of every contract he initiated. Five minutes after he left the building, he asked his PA to send Dimon a message that he 'found the meeting incredibly useful and is looking forward to keeping in touch with him'. Long before the Davos conference, Dimon had offered Blair nearly all he wanted.

By the end of the summit, Blair's commercial tentacles had spread even further. Among those attending was James Schiro, the chief executive of Zurich Insurance, who hired Blair to advise on climate change for about $250,000 a year. Soon after, Blair was retained as an adviser by Bernard Arnault, the head of a French luxury-goods conglomerate, whom he had entertained at Chequers after enjoying a holiday on the Frenchman's yacht. His income was mounting up.

More pieces of the portfolio came together after he arrived in Rwanda on 23 February 2008 to meet 'my long-standing friend', President Kagame. Considering Kagame's association with mass murder, Blair was courting controversy by launching his philanthropic platform in Kigali. 'We don't tell the people of Rwanda what to do,' he explained, 'but to help get done what the president wants.' In 2009, with his support, Rwanda joined the Commonwealth.

The parallel wing of Blair's charitable operation was the Faith Foundation, established in America in May 2008. After his conversion to Catholicism, few doubted Blair's interest in religion. To enhance the foundation's credibility, Ruth Turner, his ultra-loyal Downing Street aide, recruited to the board Richard Chartres, the Bishop of London, the best-selling author and evangelical pastor Rick Warren and other leading American clergymen, as well as billionaires such as Haim Saban, an Israeli-born Hollywood producer, and Tim Collins, an American banker. Within a year, the foundation had over £4 million in funds and Blair had been invited by Yale to teach a course on faith and globalisation. 'Moral judgements', he said, were guiding his career. His speeches were raising millions of dollars, although their content was benign. 'When things are in the balance,' he told an audience in Beijing in 2008, 'when you cannot be sure, when others are uncertain or hesitate, when the very point is that the outcome is in doubt, that is when a leader steps forward.' His growing income, he explained, financed his good works. 'I do not undertake any commercial activities', he said, 'which conflict with the charitable aims and objectives of AGI.' Jamie Dimon's visit to Rwanda alongside Blair to seek investment opportunities was brushed aside as consistent with AGI's programme.

To his good fortune, Blair's reputation was not further damaged by either the banking crash in London or the economic recession of 2008. Rather, Gordon Brown was in the firing line for having encouraged reckless growth, relaxing controls on greedy bankers and failing to build up a surplus during the post-1997 boom. While the former chancellor was held culpable for Britain's soaring debt of over £1 trillion – the second highest in the industrialised world – and soaring welfare benefits, Blair escaped serious criticism. He was detached, appearing to live in voluntary exile.

That impression was underlined during Elisabeth Murdoch's fortieth birthday party at her country estate in Burford in October 2008. Among the hundreds of guests invited by Matthew Freud, her husband, was Martin Armstrong, the headhunter who had first suggested that J. P. Morgan employ Blair. The customary introductory fee from the bank had not materialised, so, in some anger, he approached Blair.

'I'm the guy who placed you with J. P. Morgan,' said Armstrong.

'Good for you,' replied Blair and walked quickly away.

By early 2009, partly thanks to J. P. Morgan and Blair's friendship with Hillary Clinton, newly installed as the US secretary of state, his opportunities for offering advice about 'governance, modernisation and implementation' were growing. Other than Bill Clinton or Henry Kissinger, few others could confide to a network of potential clients that they had access to President Obama and other world leaders.

But trading access to earn millions of pounds, Blair soon discovered, could be a grubby business. Among those who offered money to mitigate their own tainted reputations was UI Energy of South Korea. The company, embroiled in a corruption scandal since 2003, sought an introduction for an oil contract. Blair accepted the fee – and once again persuaded the British Advisory Committee on Business Appointments that 'commercial sensitivity' should prevent disclosure of his contract. The secrecy was fortunate: in 2012, the South Korean regulator compulsorily delisted UI Energy from the local stock exchange.

Under that same veil of secrecy, Blair recruited David Lyon from

Barclays Capital to offer financial advice to his clients. Tony Blair Associates, operating under a licence from the Financial Services Authority, filed sparse accounts through Firerush Ventures No. 3 LP. The obfuscation was intentional.

Among TBA's new clients was Mubadala, an investment fund controlled by Sheikh Mohammed bin Zayed al-Nahyan. After several visits to Abu Dhabi, in each case by private jet, Blair agreed to provide 'global, strategic and political advice' to Mubadala and to monitor the fund's investments in mineral-rich countries. Soon after, Mubadala bought a share of the Zubair oil field in Iraq. In a statement that was repeated frequently to distance himself from any controversy, Blair denied ever giving advice about the purchase.

Denial also covered his relationship with Qatar, a gas-rich state further up the Gulf coast that was a bitter enemy of Abu Dhabi and the other Emirates. The corrupt dictatorship there supported extremist Muslim groups, suppressed freedom of the press (despite owning the Al Jazeera TV network) and was offering bribes to win the right to host FIFA's football World Cup in 2022. The Qataris hired Cherie rather than Tony. Like her husband, she had organised her interests carefully, establishing her commercial activities alongside the Cherie Blair Foundation for Women and the Africa Justice Foundation, two charities financed by rich Americans.

Amid some acrimony, Cherie had resigned from Matrix Chambers, where she had operated as a barrister, and opened Omnia Strategy, a consultancy advising Middle Eastern and African governments. Among those grateful for her help was Sheikha Mozah bint Nasser al-Missned, a wife of a Qatari royal. In 2009, on her behalf, Cherie sent messages to Hillary Clinton, urging her to engage in a woman-to-woman meeting to improve relations between the two countries. After an exchange of nineteen emails, Cherie won the day. 'When I see what a difference you are making,' she flattered Clinton, 'it reminds me why politics is too important to be left to the bad people.'

Few politicians were as 'bad' as Colonel Gaddafi. Tony Blair remained attracted to the dictator, whom he revisited several times after May 2008. Travelling with him were J. P. Morgan bankers seeking a licence to trade in Libya. During a meeting arranged by Blair, Gaddafi agreed to the bank's request. Blair next asked for money that would go towards education programmes for Palestinians. Gaddafi agreed, but delivered – after much lobbying – only $1 million, two years later.

After his visit, Blair wrote a letter of thanks suggesting that Gaddafi should also consider funding projects in Africa, 'since you know I am doing a lot of work there and know of good, worthwhile projects for investment'. In April 2009, he returned to Tripoli from Sierra Leone in a jet provided by the colonel. Waiting for him was Tim Collins, the American billionaire. Collins, an admirer of Ruth Turner and the Faith Foundation, had been encouraged by Blair to meet Gaddafi to discuss the provision of malaria nets for Africans. During the meeting, the colonel urged Collins to invest in a holiday resort on the Libyan coast. To Collins's surprise, Blair encouraged the idea. 'This is a Muslim country which forbids alcohol and Western music,' Collins told Blair. The former prime minister, Collins realised, was trying to earn a commission. 'I don't need Blair for business,' he thought, outraged that he had been brought to Libya under false pretences.

After the meeting, Collins turned to Blair. 'This guy Gaddafi is batshit crazy,' he exclaimed. 'I'd rather go hungry than deal with a guy who's a complete lunatic.'

Collins drove to the airport alone, while Blair remained to negotiate contributions to AGI, broker other business possibilities and discuss a prisoner exchange. The stumbling block was the refusal of the British government to free from a Scottish jail Abdelbaset al-Megrahi, convicted for involvement in the Lockerbie bombing. Gaddafi threatened that, unless the release was agreed, he would cut commercial ties with Britain. Blair assured his host that he would try to broker a deal.

Throughout all these exchanges, he seemed unconcerned about placing himself in such invidious circumstances. Over the following year, he was also seen stepping on and off Kagame's Bombardier jet in

Israel, Zurich and Abu Dhabi. Collins was not alone in reassessing his judgement of Blair. 'Perhaps I've been naive,' he reflected. 'He wants to be a player in the spotlight to save the world.' But he pushed his doubts aside.

Similar mixed sentiments had been aroused in Jerusalem. In early 2008, Blair had presented Ehud Barak with a detailed plan drafted by the Quartet's staff to lift hundreds of Israeli roadblocks across the West Bank to improve the Palestinians' economic and social life. Barak immediately asked General Michael Herzog, a veteran of peace negotiations, to study which blocks might be removed. Working through the night, Herzog's staff produced an amended plan. As some roadblocks disappeared, Palestinians hailed Blair's success and Israelis re-emphasised their faith in an exceptional friend. 'That was the high point,' Herzog later recalled. 'It didn't get any better. Only worse.'

Over the first year and a half of his new life, Blair spent about four days every month in Jerusalem, travelling occasionally between the city and the West Bank to discuss financial investment in the Palestinian territories. Shocked by the realities of life on the West Bank, he realised that economic progress was impossible without a political settlement. This became his albatross. Although he was initially trusted by Abbas, neither the Israeli nor American governments needed Blair as an intermediary in the political peace process, and he was denied any influence. Diplomats and Israeli officials watched his authority 'swiftly drip away', as one observer reflected. His original conviction about his power to shape events withered as the Israelis discovered that Washington had limited his authority. The ex-prime minister found himself excluded from discussions and relegated to caring for minor issues.

Negotiations in Israel were mind-numbingly time-consuming. Israeli officials were intractable, even preventing James Cameron's film *Avatar* from being released on the West Bank (although, after an excessive struggle, they relented). Nevertheless, there were some minor achievements. With considerable effort, Blair negotiated Israel's agreement to the UN spending $500 million on new houses in Gaza and, by shuttling from Jerusalem to meet Abbas in Ramallah, the 'capital' of Palestine on the West Bank, he persuaded the Israeli government to allow Wataniya, a Kuwaiti and Qatari company, to establish a second mobile network across the West Bank, albeit with a more limited spectrum than originally envisaged; and there was also a concession for British Gas to extract gas off the Gaza coast. Both Wataniya and British Gas were advised by J. P. Morgan, and Blair voiced outrage when anyone implied that there was a conflict of interest. He hailed those agreements to Hillary Clinton as part of his 'transformative change agenda'.

The small triumphs did not silence the mounting criticism over his failure to broker an agreement between Israel and the Palestinians. Potential investors told Blair that their money was conditional on a settlement but, even after minuscule progress, he was condemned for failing to tour Gaza. He blamed the discovery by Israeli intelligence of a jihadist threat to murder him; his critics said he was obeying Netanyahu and Bush to isolate Hamas and so prevent any agreement.

To his detractors, his invisibility suggested disengagement. Blair confided to friends his dismay over his exclusion from the Middle East peace negotiations and even from politics in Britain, including the Labour Party. The compensation was the pleasure of eating in the sun at Turkiz and other seaside restaurants in Tel Aviv. Feted as a hero, he had been introduced to the generous hospitality of Israel's multimillionaires, especially Ofra Strauss, an attractive, dark-haired, rich divorcee. His frequent visits to Strauss's home fuelled gossip of an affair, which he, Strauss and Cherie all denied. Through Strauss, he mixed with billionaires who offered him advice. Like scores of others, Arnon Milchan, a film producer, and Avi Tiomkin, a hedge-fund adviser, were electrified by Blair's entry into their homes. Encouraged by their warmth, he slipped into sharing their fears about Islamic extremism, and his sympathy for Israel's position grew.

On 27 December 2008, the Israeli army invaded Gaza in retaliation for rocket attacks launched by Hamas, the Palestinian group who had seized power the previous year. Over three weeks, nearly

1,400 Palestinians died and thousands of buildings were damaged or destroyed. At the beginning of the fighting, Blair was on holiday. Later, he stood on the sidelines, embarrassed by his isolation from Gaza but refusing to criticise Israel for any excess. His silence fed the Palestinians' conviction that he was prejudiced, but at least he had instant entrée to Israel's prime minister, unlike other Europeans. That access did not change after Olmert resigned in disgrace and, in February 2009, Benjamin Netanyahu was elected.

Blair and Netanyahu forged a bond of trust just as Obama, addressing a rally in Cairo in June, proposed new negotiations between Israel and the Palestinians. Blair urged Netanyahu to reciprocate. Although in September the Israeli flew to New York to meet Abbas, Hillary Clinton and George Mitchell, who had been appointed to lead a new round of peace talks, Blair was again excluded from the process. Washington was decidedly uninterested in the Quartet. Robert Danin, dubbed 'the Tranquilliser', was replaced as Blair's chief of staff by Firas Raad, a softly spoken member of the Jordanian royal family. With Washington's declining support and Raad's appointment, the Quartet had become more ineffective and even invisible. Blair was rarely seen in Jerusalem, other than to receive a $1 million award from an Israeli charity for his 'unique, profound contribution to humanity, on a global scale'. The Palestinians were unimpressed, but Blair showed no concern about their disdain.

His priority was to complete his memoirs in anticipation of Labour's defeat in the 2010 election. Finally, there was an opportunity to settle some scores against Brown and the media. He had survived their harassment, he wrote, thanks to him 'trying to wear what was effectively a kind of psychological armour which the arrows simply bounced off, and to achieve a kind of weightlessness that allowed me, somehow, to float above the demonic rabble tearing at my limbs. There was courage in it and I look back at it now with pride. I was cornered, so it was either go down or fight.'

The combination of his lifestyle, the mounting number of fatalities among British soldiers in Afghanistan and his country's wrecked economy had unleashed unexpected vitriol among both Conservative and Labour Party members, and Blair's defiance was no protection from his vulnerability over Iraq. The public were angry and, after the withdrawal of the last British troops, Brown could no longer resist the demand for a comprehensive inquiry. On the advice of Gus O'Donnell, the Cabinet secretary, its chairman could not be a judge: the general perception of Brian Hutton's bias had discredited his profession. Accordingly, Brown, acting on O'Donnell's advice, appointed John Chilcot. As a member of Robin Butler's inquiry, Chilcot was well acquainted with the intelligence background and, O'Donnell reasoned, could master the remaining issues. To help him, O'Donnell selected Margaret Aldred as the committee's secretary. With her Cabinet Office experience of the Iraq and Afghan wars, she was expected to guide the committee's panel to the relevant files, manage the testimony of officials and supervise the writing of the report. The criterion for selecting the four remaining members of the committee was safety. The two respected historians, Martin Gilbert and Lawrence Freedman, had never upset the Establishment; Roderic Lyne, a retired diplomat, was never one to rock the boat; while Baroness Usha Prashar, an untalented quangoist, fulfilled the requirement of diversity. The five appointees were tasked with disentangling events since 1998.

Understanding the web of exchanges between Britain's politicians, civil servants and the military required forensic investigation and astute analysis. The committee would also need to unravel the relationships between the British, American, Iraqi and European governments. Finally, the committee's remit was to probe the secrecy spawned by sofa government. The nature of Blair's exchanges with Bush, Boyce, Dearlove, Powell, Campbell and many others might be indicated in documents (although Blair had deliberately limited the number of written records), but only subtle questioning could discover whether he was culpable of deliberate deception.

To meet those demands, the five panellists would require the skills of jurisprudential examination. None had those gifts. Chilcot and Aldred were uninspired officials; and while Gilbert, Freedman and Lyne were intelligent, none had ever distilled a similarly complex controversy into a pungent conclusion – and Freedman had drafted Blair's Chicago speech. Their limitations would have been concealed if O'Donnell's edict that the hearings be conducted in secret had survived. O'Donnell anticipated that Chilcot would adopt Butler's efficient process and complete a satisfactory report by the end of 2010. That tidy plan was challenged by outraged MPs. Unable to resist their demand that the hearings should be held in public, Chilcot succumbed, and the 'cover-up' began to unravel on 24 November, when the first of 190 witnesses gave evidence.

By the time Blair appeared, on 29 January 2010, the treatment of the preceding eighty-three witnesses had exposed the panel as neither savvy nor well briefed. Chilcot had failed to appoint an experienced lawyer either to interrogate the witnesses or to present the official documents as evidence during their testimony. Without the cut and thrust of cross-examination to elicit explanations for the contradictions between the witnesses, no sensational revelations had emerged. Polite questions had produced bland replies. The tone of the hearings was familiar to those discussing history at a friendly dinner party in Notting Hill Gate.

Tanned and still youthful, Blair arrived to deliver a well-crafted narrative. He denied deceiving the nation for seventeen months after November 2001 over his intention for war, or making any private deal with Bush during 2002. 'Mine was not a covert position but an open position,' he said. During the meeting with Bush in April 2002 and thereafter, Blair told the inquiry, 'It was always clear that there would be regime change.' He insisted that his denial in July 2002 to the Commons Liaison Committee of any plan for war was not a lie. 'We had not decided,' he said, because he 'could not be sure that the UN route would not work'.

Chilcot failed to refer to the discussion in Blair's office on 23 July 2002, after Dearlove returned from Washington, when war was deemed certain. Two years later, Blair had told the Butler inquiry that during 'July and August . . . I was increasingly getting messages saying . . . "are you going to war?" and I was thinking "this is ridiculous"... we've not decided on military action, we've not decided on what we're going to do'. Since giving that testimony, new evidence had emerged to contradict his assertion. Private letters between himself and Bush, recordings of the video conversations between the prime minister and president, and the internal messages between Bush's senior advisers, based on their conversations with Blair's confidants, all showed that Blair was committed to supporting an invasion the following year. Instead of confronting Blair, the panel's questions did not undermine his own interpretation of Dearlove's report, the errors in the dossier or his certainty about WMDs. He was not asked about the contradictions between John Scarlett's private assessment that the intelligence on WMDs was 'sporadic and patchy', his own foreword to the dossier declaring that the JIC had established 'beyond doubt' that Saddam possessed WMDs, and his statement to the Commons that the intelligence was 'extensive, detailed and authoritative'.

Helped by a meek panel, Blair escaped unchallenged after mistakenly asserting that he had 'always' favoured the 'large-scale package' for the military commitment. No one questioned his assertion that 'we didn't [commit troops] for influence'. No one asked about his failure to inform the Cabinet of his plans, or his endangering the military and the region by failing to make robust plans for the post-war occupation of Iraq. Instead, the quintet allowed Blair to set out a scenario based on selective hindsight rather than what he said at the time.

In Blair's revised version, the world was changed by 9/11. Dictators like Saddam, armed with WMDs and advocating the 'dangerous ideology' of Islam, meant that in 'my judgement you don't take any risk on this issue'. The mistaken intelligence, he emphasised, was irrelevant. Cutting short Hans Blix's hunt for WMDs was similarly immaterial. 'Even if Blix had [had] another six months,' said Blair, 'it would have made no difference.' Although Saddam did not possess WMDs in 2003, he had the 'intent' to possess them, possibly by 2010. That 'long-term threat' had to be prevented. The panel did not press Blair to produce evidence for his conjecture and, in a familiar occurrence of not listening to his replies, failed to seize upon his unexpected revelation about deciding to go to war in January 2003 even without UN backing. That contradicted his original agreement with Peter Goldsmith – namely, that Britain could go to war only if the UN passed a second resolution.

The missed opportunities came to a climax with Blair's own omission. At the end of the session, he was asked by Chilcot, 'Is there any final comment, beyond those you've already made, that you wish to add before we close?'

'No,' replied Blair.

Behind him, the packed audience included the families of soldiers killed in Iraq. They had expected him to express regrets for the dead. His silence evoked angry protests. He was unconcerned. 'You get to a position', he told an interviewer, 'where the criticism you get, you just have to live with. It's the way it is. When you are someone like me, you create a lot of controversy one way or another. You just decide to do what you are going to do and let that speak for itself.' He blamed his woes on the British media's malice. Their preoccupation, he complained, was 'how to belittle what I am doing, knock it down, write something bad about it. It's not right. It's not journalism. They don't get me and they've got a score to settle with me. But they're not going to settle it.'

His sense of victimhood was matched by that of Gordon Brown. The prime minister was also lashing out at those who refused to appreciate his talent. He had survived attempted Blairite coups, first by Patricia Hewitt and Geoff Hoon, then later by James Purnell, a junior minister who resigned from the Cabinet and appealed to Brown also to quit 'to give our party a fighting chance of winning [the election]'. At the last moment, Purnell was abandoned by David Miliband, who remained foreign secretary. Blair watched his legacy disintegrate. His refusal to nurture successors had left the party slipping towards the abyss. His one achievement was to help Gloria de Piero, a dark-haired TV presenter and a close friend, become the favoured candidate to succeed Hoon as an MP.

Labour's defeat in the 2010 election left Blair depressed. His judgement about Brown had been confirmed. More painful was his own exclusion from the political debate. He had much to say, but few wanted to hear. His alienation from Britain was confirmed when he was not invited to the wedding of Prince William and Kate Middleton, and by the Queen's unprecedented refusal to award the Order of the Garter to a former prime minister. Her unease over Blair's conduct after Princess Diana's death had turned to general suspicion towards him. But then Blair had made his choice between obeying the Establishment's rules and pursuing his own personal enrichment, and that choice had consequences.

FORTY-NINE

The Tragedy of Power

Frustrated in Britain and Israel, Blair found his strength was his permanent optimism about the future. His opportunities to become rich appeared to be limitless. The downside was that, as the number of people employed by his charities and businesses increased to over 150, he was under pressure to generate yet more income. Among his new clients was Vinod Khosla, an American billionaire associated with Bill Clinton's controversial green-energy investments. As a 'face for hire', Blair made appearances at receptions to promote the 'green' ventures, until the businesses crashed and Khosla lost hundreds of millions of dollars. Next, he accepted a contract from PetroSaudi, a newly formed group led by a colourful group of directors who paid him £41,000 a month and 2 per cent commission on any deals he brokered with Chinese officials. That arrangement was also short-lived, with PetroSaudi being accused of bribing Malaysian politicians. Almost inevitably, Blair accepted Richard Branson's invitations to visit Necker, part of the British Virgin Islands, but eventually discovered that the tycoon refused to reimburse him for advice.

For those prepared to pay, Blair seemed unconcerned by controversy. Spurred on by J. P. Morgan and others interested in Libya's oil money, Blair had visited Colonel Gaddafi six times during the two years since he had left Downing Street. Saif Gaddafi, the dictator's son, facilitated Blair's relationship with his father and was rewarded, after paying £1.5 million to the university, with a place and eventually a PhD at the London School of Economics. That quid pro quo would be condemned by an official inquiry and the LSE's director would resign.

Building on her husband's new relationship with Gaddafi, in April 2010, at a dinner in her Buckinghamshire home, Cherie received a substantial contribution to her Foundation for Women from Oxand, a French consultancy that was pursuing business in Libya. Neither Cherie nor her husband appeared to be troubled by possible conflicts of interest.

In November 2010, Blair arrived at Nnamdi Azikiwe airport in central Nigeria on a private jet with Kate Gross and Catherine Rimmer, his most trusted staff, and his protection officers. He was met by Wiebe Boer, the representative of Tony Elumelu, a local multimillionaire banker who had set up a foundation to promote entrepreneurship. At Blair's suggestion, Elumelu had agreed to co-fund with Bill Gates the employment of two AGI advisers for the Nigerian government and one for Liberia. Elumelu's interest was not entirely philanthropic. He hoped that a close relationship with Blair would open doors for his business interests in Europe and America. Similarly, Blair relied on the banker to ease his ambitions in Nigeria.

Elumelu had arranged for Blair to meet President Goodluck Jonathan. Blair was to offer the services of AGI and the Faith Foundation to reconcile Muslims and Christians, especially in the war-stricken north of the country. After an intelligence briefing at the British embassy, Blair had requested what the president's staff called a 'one-on-one audience'. Jonathan's staff regarded the private meeting as 'Blair satisfying his ego, to feel a sense of importance in the intimacy'. After the meeting, Blair was joined by Jamie Dimon. The American banker was asked by Jonathan to invest in a national power grid. He declined, but he did offer to manage Nigeria's sovereign wealth fund. No other bank was asked to tender for the profitable chore and J. P. Morgan's bid was accepted.

Dimon was not present when Wiebe took Blair for an informal Sunday lunch at the presidential palace. In the garden, surrounded by the president's entourage, Blair explained the potential benefits of their relationship. 'When you become president,' said Blair, 'your experience is the lowest and your approval is the highest. When you finally leave, your approval ratings will be the lowest but your experience will be the highest.' Laughing, Jonathan praised Blair's wisdom, especially his advice about 'time management' – the simple task of scheduling an effective day's work. As the banter continued, Blair said, 'You know, one of the conditions of aid will be that you must give gays their rights in Nigeria.' The foreign minister jabbed his finger at Blair: 'OK, but we will only sell you our oil if you in Britain and America agree to allow polygamy. If you don't allow polygamy, we will black you.' Amid the laughter, Blair stopped arguing his case.

From Nigeria, he flew with Dimon to Sierra Leone and then Monrovia, Liberia. The presidents of both West African countries had small AGI teams advising them. J. P. Morgan invested in a project in Liberia, while Ian Hamman, one of the bank's mineral experts, was mining diamonds in Sierra Leone. The intertwining of Blair's charity and commercial work was irrefutable.

Dotted throughout his travel were further well-paid speeches, including an address in Orlando to the International Sanitary Supply Association, manufacturers of lavatory cleaners. During his speech, Blair confessed that 'What is rather shocking is that I have a so much better understanding of the Israeli/Palestinian issue than I did when I was prime minister. That's just the way it is, I guess.' He did not mention that his visits to Jerusalem had fallen off just as freedom protests erupted in the Arab world. Starting in Tunisia, the demand for democracy had spread to Egypt, Libya, Syria and down the Gulf. Blair shared Hillary Clinton's pleasure when President Hosni Mubarak of Egypt resigned, and believed that, eight years after the toppling of Saddam, the Arabs had finally seized the opportunities provided by his ideology of liberal intervention. His 'better understanding' failed to predict the obvious: that Mubarak would be replaced by an extremist Muslim Brotherhood government that would destabilise Egypt, Libya and the Middle East.

In February 2011, after failing to persuade Gaddafi to cease his brutal suppression of an uprising, Blair asked David Cameron to grant the dictator safe haven. The prime minister refused. Blair then urged Gaddafi to end the violence by leaving the capital. 'If you have a safe place to go, then you should go there because this will not end peacefully unless that happens.' He warned the colonel that he was approaching 'the point of no return'. Having lured Gaddafi to abandon extremism and come in from the outside, he could not deliver any protection, and the Libyan leader was killed by a mob in October 2011. Blair was powerless despite Hillary Clinton's email about his efforts for the Quartet: 'You are truly doing "the Lord's work" but not sure even He could get it done.'

The Israelis had not shared his jubilation about the Arab Spring. On the contrary, American negotiations for a settlement, based on the Palestinians recognising a 'Jewish state' in return for Israel agreeing to the creation of a Palestinian state and a freeze on building more settlements on the West Bank, had foundered amid bitter recriminations between Benjamin Netanyahu and Mahmoud Abbas.

In July 2011, with Hillary Clinton's blessing, Blair began shuttling between Jerusalem and Ramallah to persuade Abbas to recognise a 'Jewish state' in order to form the basis for a peace agreement. In reply, Abbas threatened to appeal to the UN to recognise Palestine as a state. A successful vote at the UN would wreck any chance of an agreement with Israel. Abbas rejected Blair's entreaties, which only increased Netanyahu's belligerence. Abbas urged Blair to protest publicly. Blair refused. Even one of Olmert's advisers advised him to reconsider: 'You've got to call a press conference and complain about Bibi. You're being played by him. He's wrapping you up in his promises and lies, and you don't say a word.' The adviser had one more go – 'You're like the Pope. You have no [military] divisions except media attention' – yet still Blair refused to confront Netanyahu. In Ramallah, his stock fell. 'What's Blair's value?' Abbas asked, and refused to meet him again before flying to the UN in New York. 'Useless, useless, useless,' was his spokesman's verdict on the envoy.

In September, Blair gathered with Hillary Clinton and other players at the Carlyle Hotel in New York. His haunted look reflected his acknowledgement of failure. 'We'd gone from bad to worse,' recalls one of the participants, 'and then the criticism of Blair really started.' His trips away from Jerusalem increased, sometimes lasting for nearly two months.

In his absence, his staff moved from the Colony Hotel to a seven-storey building in an expensive area of east Jerusalem. Since both Washington and Brussels refused to finance the increasing cost of Blair's operation, he had arranged for the Kuwaiti government to secretly provide money. The transfer of the cash, Blair admitted to the State Department, required 'bending some budget rules', which had in turn caused 'internal chaos' in Kuwait. The Kuwaitis were not financing a success: Blair was making no progress in improving the Palestinian economy. A plan to create an industrial zone had been abandoned, while British Gas's intention to explore off the Gaza coast was stymied by the Palestinian refusal to prevent the profits being spent by Hamas.

During his brief visits, Blair socialised with his new friends and regularly met Ehud Barak and Netanyahu. He never revealed to his staff what was discussed. His frequent access to the Israeli prime minister suggested that he wielded remarkable influence, but in reality he underestimated the complexities and concealed his impotence by radiating self-confidence.

To his good fortune, the paralysis in Jerusalem passed unnoticed among his new clients, including Nursultan Nazarbayev, the president of Kazakhstan. Ever since the break-up of the Soviet Union, this one-time satellite state had become a credible target for British investors seeking contracts from a country whose fortunes depended upon a consortium of Western corporations extracting oil from beneath the Caspian Sea. In 2000, Blair had welcomed Nazarbayev to Downing Street, allowing Kazakhstan's first president, elected in 1991 as the only candidate with 91.5 per cent of the votes, to hold baby Leo. Over the following years, Whitehall had supported the dictator's bid to transform his peasant economy, although the new wealth had spawned corruption and violence. To cement relations, Prince Andrew was dispatched to promote British industry. The prince forged financial relationships with controversial Kazakhs, which damaged his credibility, and, in the same vein, Blair encouraged Dick Evans, the former chairman of BAE, to become chairman of Samruk, the Kazakh state holding company for most of the country's industries.

Morality did not appear to be a consideration. The issue of whether to deal with corrupt dictators, all intolerant of minorities and opponents, across Asia, the Arab world and Africa was a familiar one for Western governments. Their justification was that self-denial was expensive and 'opening up' these societies offered an eventual prospect of democracy. Some considered that Blair's special status denied him that defence. His speech in Chicago in 1999 had advocated intervention against dictators, but his acceptance in 2011 of Nazarbayev's lucrative offer of employment indicated that those principles had been forgotten. The embarrassment followed soon after. Kazakh security forces in a regional town shot dead fourteen unarmed protesters and wounded over sixty others. There were also reports of opponents being tortured. 'I don't dismiss the human rights stuff,' Blair said. 'These are points we make. There's a whole new generation of administrators there who are reformers, and we're working with them.' In return for his fee, he also appeared in 'In the Stirrups of Time', an hour-long video extolling Nazarbayev in which Blair, sitting beside the president, repeatedly eulogised his new client. Alastair Campbell and Tim Allen, a former Downing Street spokesman who had set up Portland PR, were also contracted to promote Nazarbayev. In each case, the incentive appeared to be money.

Similar considerations led Blair to Conakry, the capital of Guinea, another impoverished West African dictatorship infected by corruption. He arrived in 2011 to offer advice to Alpha Condé, the president who had wrested power from the military but was intolerant of the opposition parties. Guinea had become the target of rival tycoons eager to develop the country's rich mineral resources. Among those interested were Mubadala of Abu Dhabi and J. P. Morgan's mining specialists in

West Africa. As before, Blair denied any link between his presence and his paymasters. Rather, he explained, he had arrived to outline the benefits of AGI. He was following in the footsteps of billionaire investor George Soros, whose better-funded international advisory team was offering a similar service. To avoid using his own money, Blair obtained funds from the US aid programme.

By then, the value of his advice was being challenged, not least in Kuwait. His expensive report, 'Kuwait Vision 2035', had been greeted with derision by those who read a lengthy repetition of Kuwait's well-known problems and the presentation of impractical solutions. And then Ismail Khudr al-Shatti, the project's prime supporter, abruptly departed from the government, terminating the venture. Blair's personal investment in the project had been so limited that the sixty-five staff involved did not notice him showing much concern about the scorn the report received. To save face, the Kuwaitis buried the bad news.

Blair's frenetic journeys – often in a black Bombardier Global Express business jet dubbed Blair Force One – between West Africa, the Gulf, Kazakhstan, Israel, China, America and occasionally Britain sustained his divorce from reality. Accompanied by his protection officers, he worked from his old Downing Street red box, trusting his team to prevent any information about his activities getting out. Altogether, his constant deal-fixing, which saw him flitting across the globe between various five-star hotels owned by the Four Seasons group, and lucrative speech-making created an unusual backdrop to his bid to become president of the European Council in 2012.

To establish his credentials, Blair set himself apart from his commercial life. 'I'm basically a public-service person,' he explained on BBC television. Two-thirds of his time, he said, was spent doing pro bono work, and the rest was devoted to earning enough to deal with his expanding payroll. To succeed, Blair needed to douse the European federalists' criticism of him being 'Euro-lite' and being burdened by the unforgiving baggage of Iraq. With his familiar self-confidence, he assumed that he could ignore the antipathy towards Britain's refusal to join the euro or the Schengen agreement on common frontiers. Instead of initiating an open campaign for the presidency and spelling out his vision, he denied that he was seeking the job, while quietly expecting that it would simply be offered to him.

To help his cause, he unobtrusively made lightning trips to visit the European leaders, especially Angela Merkel, Nicolas Sarkozy and Silvio Berlusconi. He also asked Hillary Clinton and David Cameron to urge Merkel to give her support. The more overt campaigning was left to Jonathan Powell and Peter Mandelson. According to a senior official in Brussels, both behaved as if Blair was a 'slam dunk to get the job. But he was deluded about the support for him. He was never in with a chance.'

His submerged campaign was interrupted by John Chilcot's request that he return for another public session in January 2011. Since his previous appearance a year earlier, Blair's hair had turned grey and, despite spending an hour most days in the gym, his youthful looks had faded. For his second appearance, the panel was better briefed, not least because they had obtained copies of exchanges between Blair and Bush demonstrating Britain's commitment to the invasion. Criticised for their lackadaisical style in the previous session, they attempted to appear more rigorous.

The panel focused on the allegations of Blair's deception – although the word was never used. Why, he was asked three times by Roderic Lyne, the former diplomat, was the Cabinet Office's 'Options Paper', prepared in March 2002 and describing the government's range of policies towards Iraq, never offered to Cabinet ministers? Blair spoke at length but never directly answered the question. He denied ordering that the paper should not be distributed but was never pushed to explain why it was not circulated.

In a baffled manner, he insisted that, after the Crawford meeting in April 2002, the Cabinet regularly discussed regime change. The facts contradicted him. Two days earlier, Stephen Wall, the senior official responsible for Europe, had told the panel that, while attending nearly every Cabinet meeting during 2002, he 'probably' only became aware, like most ministers in those gatherings, that Blair intended to join the invasion in January 2003. Blair disputed this account. There could be no doubt, he said, that after April 2002 the Cabinet knew that war was an option. Yet, as Lyne indicated, Cabinet minutes showed that Iraq had never been discussed between 11 April and 23 September. All Blair could offer in reply was to dispute the records. The unasked supplementary question left dangling was whether Blair's refusal to allow a discussion about Iraq by the Cabinet was indicative of his purposeful deception regarding his intentions. He would never be challenged with that crucial accusation.

Peter Goldsmith's recollection of events also undermined him. In January 2003, said the lawyer, Blair was told that UN resolution 1441 could not authorise war. Britain needed a second resolution. Blair's comment about Goldsmith's advice on the eve of his visit to meet Bush in Washington was that it was 'not helpful'.

The two questions Chilcot should have posed were: had Blair pressured Goldsmith to change his advice? And why was the Cabinet not shown the complete version of the lawyer's final paper? Neither was asked. Instead, Blair regretted that Goldsmith had not been 'more closely involved', but insisted that their disagreements were mere lawyers' debates. He dismissed Goldsmith's complaint that he had been 'discouraged' by Powell and Sally Morgan from giving formal advice in writing that the first resolution, 1441, did not authorise war. Under no circumstances, Blair said, would he have allowed 'a chink of light' based on a lawyer's advice to 'breach the political line'. That, he said, would have been 'a catastrophe'. On that issue, the panel was required to decide whether to believe Goldsmith or Blair.

Hans Blix's mission would be harder to resolve. Over the previous eight years, Blair had moved a long way from justifying the war because of Iraq's WMDs. By 2011, his claim was that Saddam had posed a permanent threat to mankind. He told the panel that he had never felt real confidence in Blix, and disagreed that the UN inspectors' increasing access to the sites identified by Western intelligence proved that

Saddam was co-operating. On the contrary: first, he explained, Saddam had refused to allow Iraqi scientists to be properly interviewed by the UN inspectors; and, second, Saddam's concessions were all made under 'the pressure of 300,000 soldiers' on his border. 'He was stringing us along, and we needed a change of heart on co-operation.' Saddam's record showed that his aim was to 'outfox the international community'. The real threat, said Blair, presenting his new argument, was not that Saddam actually possessed WMDs but that he would return 'to his old games'. None of the panel retorted that the assessment by Britain's intelligence services about Saddam's 'old game' had been grossly mistaken, and that their incompetence had caused deep anger.

Finally, the panel did not present any discomfiting reports about the fate of Iraq after the war. In his testimony, Blair denied ever contemplating that the situation in post-war Iraq 'should be left to the Americans'. The panel failed to confront Blair with the evidence of Whitehall officials and generals who specifically recalled him referring to his reliance on Washington.

And that led to a most delicate issue. During the four years after the war, the generals had complained to Blair about insufficient money, men and equipment. The climax of one argument was General Walker's threat to resign over lunch at Chequers. Yet Blair told the panel, 'I cannot recall being told we needed resources and I said "no". Money really wasn't the problem. If it was a resource problem, we would have paid the bill. We had troops and resources to manage this. So far as resources, that was not the issue being raised with me. I would always agree to more resources.' The testimony of the leading military figures between 2003 and 2007 again contradicted him.

On his day in the spotlight, Blair's memory repeatedly jarred with the facts. Baroness Prashar asked the questions about post-war Iraq. He told her that Paul Bremer, the American governor of Iraq, 'did a pretty good job. When he was there, Iraq was on an upward path.' It is now generally accepted that Bremer's demobilisation of the Iraqi army and dismissal of Ba'athist civil servants had hastened Iraq's plunge into civil war. Even in his memoirs, Blair recorded that Bremer's operation needed 'a drastic boost'. Prashar did not ask Blair about this contradiction. Equally surprising was the panel's reaction to Blair's robust assertion that 'I did not get the impression he [Bremer] was refusing to discuss it with the British.' John Sawers, Jeremy Greenstock, General Walker and Jack Straw all complained to Blair that Bremer was ignoring his UK allies. But Prashar lacked the ability to challenge Blair.

Overlooking these inaccuracies led the panel into a cul-de-sac. The heart of Blair's argument rested on his interpretation of events in postwar Iraq. He believed that the conquered people were keen to embrace liberal democracy but were thwarted by al-Qaeda, supported by Iran, stepping into the vacuum. Their regime of terror, said Blair, could not have been predicted. Iraq was just one part of the struggle against Islamic extremism. The aftermath of 9/11, he continued, had generated a stream of dangerous bids for power. This 'evil' brand of Islam, he told the panel, one that demanded the destruction of Israel, the imposition of Sharia law and the destruction of everything Western to create a single caliphate, had to be confronted.

His latest interpretation of history was barely challenged. Halfheartedly, Lyne pointed out that Iraqi extremists rather than al-Qaeda and Iranian fundamentalists had instigated the civil war, and their terror started only after Saddam's removal. Blair brushed Lyne's musings aside, without answering the principal complaint: that the increasing horrors across the Arab world had been instigated by the invasion of Iraq. If asked, Blair would have quashed such a notion. Mirroring Israeli opinion, Blair asserted that Saddam was a life-threatening menace whose demise was justified, and that the carnage that followed was unavoidably necessary.

That opinion was not shared by all his friends in London. One of the few upon whom he could still rely was Rupert Murdoch. Throughout his decade in Downing Street, Blair had encouraged visits by Murdoch and his lieutenants. Their relationship had intensified after Rebekah Brooks became editor of the *Sun* in 2003. After his resignation, Blair and Cherie regularly met Murdoch and his Chinese wife Wendi Deng in New York and London. One benefit was Murdoch's £100,000 contribution to the Faith Foundation. In March 2010, he invited Blair to become godfather to his daughters Grace and Chloe and to attend their baptism on the bank of the River Jordan. Dressed in a white suit, Blair requested no photographs.

Maintaining close relations with Murdoch was important to him. The tycoon provided introductions to a network of billionaires. In return, Blair immediately offered support when, on 4 July 2011, the *Guardian* revealed that an agent acting for the *News of the World* had hacked into the voicemail of Milly Dowler, a thirteen-year-old schoolgirl who had disappeared while returning home from school on 21 March 2002. During the police search for Dowler, voice messages had been deleted from her mobile phone, giving her parents hope that she was alive. In reality, she had been murdered, and her body was discovered in woodland six months later. The *Guardian* mistakenly alleged that the newspaper's agent had deliberately deleted the phone messages, which had aggravated the parents' distress. Brooks was editing the newspaper at the time (she had since been promoted to oversee all of Murdoch's British newspapers) and was caught in a storm of public outrage over her alleged conduct.

Later that day, Blair emailed her: 'Let me know if there's anything I can help you with. Thinking of you. I have been through things like this.' Six days later, Murdoch made a publicised visit to London to support Brooks and his newspapers. The following day, 11 July, Blair telephoned Brooks. During a one-hour conversation, Blair offered himself to her and the Murdochs as a secret unofficial adviser. Her crisis, said Blair, would pass, and in the meantime she should 'toughen up', 'keep strong' and not make any rash decisions. News International, he suggested, should hire a robust QC to run an independent inquiry and publish a 'Hutton-style report'. Blair also offered his advice on managing the continuing storm: 'Publish part one of the report at the same time as the police close their inquiry and clear you,' he said, anticipating the result, 'and accept shortcomings and new solutions and [publish] part two when any trials are over.'

Blair misjudged the public's disgust. Four days later, Brooks resigned as chief executive. 'I'm really sorry about it all,' he emailed. 'Call me if you need to. T x.' The next day, in advance of her appearance before a Commons select committee, he texted: 'If you're still going to Parliament, you should call me. I have experience of these things! T x.'

Over the following months, Blair met Murdoch in America and, on separate occasions, teamed up with the tycoon's wife during trips to China, where he offered his services as an adviser to the China Investment Corporation, a sovereign wealth fund. His overtures were rejected, but during the process he became closer to Wendi Deng. Twice during June 2012 he visited the attractive forty-three-year-old at her husband's London flat, and in August was seen alone with her at 5 Hertford Street, a Mayfair club. Deng was clearly smitten and realised the danger. In an email message to herself, she wrote that Catherine Rimmer opposed the relationship: 'Katherine [*sic*] Rimmer does not like me because she does not want Tony gets [*sic*] in trouble with me.'

On 7 October, Blair arrived at Murdoch's 1,000-acre home near Carmel in California. Deng had told her husband that she was staying at the ranch with a girlfriend. Her friend departed before Blair arrived. Some of her staff were also ordered to leave the house, and the Metropolitan protection officers were quartered in a nearby hotel. The staff who remained witnessed events amounting to a close relationship between Blair and Mrs Murdoch. Her husband was unaware of Blair's visit.

Those observing Blair wondered whether he was losing the plot. While his Quartet work had declined, he still jetted around the Middle East to promote the Faith Foundation, give media interviews, make a paid speech or pitch his services for hire. His message had become ordinary. At a conference on Africa in 2012, he told the audience that there was 'something wonderful, vibrant and exciting' about the continent's culture and traditions, and, speaking about the prospects of economic development, warned, 'With electricity, given the technology we now have at our fingertips, everything is possible. Without it, progress will be depressingly slow. Likewise with roads and, often, ports.'

Similar banal musings had seeped into his promotion of the Faith Foundation. To finance his ambitions, he had accepted $500,000 from Victor Pinchuk, a Ukrainian oligarch, and $1 million from Michael Milken (the model for Hollywood's Gordon Gekko and his 'greed is good' mantra), who was convicted in 1990 for fraud. Neither maverick was noted for his particular interest in religion, but both succumbed to Blair's charm.

Pinchuk and Milken would have been puzzled by the attendance of Faith Foundation staff at a conference in Vienna about 'interfaith dialogue' and the promotion of human rights funded by Saudi Arabia, one of the world's most intolerant regimes, renowned for punishing minor infractions of Sharia law with public beheadings. As Martin Bright, an admirer of Blair, would discover after joining the foundation, there were irreconcilable conflicts between Blair's supposed beliefs and his priority of not irritating any paymaster. Bright would leave after complaining that Blair 'doesn't do humility and nor do his organisations. Perhaps that's his tragedy.'

There were no boundaries when it came to sustaining his lifestyle. In September 2012, Jamie Dimon asked Blair to help Ivan Glasenberg, the competitive chief executive of Glencore, the world's biggest commodity trading house, buy Xstrata, a rival. One year earlier, after the company had been launched on the stock exchange, Glasenberg's personal stake in Glencore had been valued at $9 billion. Now, the aggressive South African wanted to use Glencore's shares to buy his competitor and become even bigger. However, Mick Davis, Xstrata's equally bruising boss, did not agree to Glasenberg's price. To win, Glasenberg needed the support of Sheikh Hamad bin Jassim bin Jaber al-Thani, the prime minister of Qatar, which owned nearly 12 per cent of Xstrata's shares.

Glasenberg wanted to hammer out a deal with al-Thani face to face, and sought an introduction. 'Try Tony Blair,' suggested Michael

Klein, a New York banker. 'I know Tony fairly well, and he got to know al-Thani in Downing Street and later through his Quartet work.' Klein suggested that Blair could make the telephone call in anticipation of a meeting already arranged at Claridge's hotel in London. A fee was agreed and Blair was briefed by Glasenberg. Blair's pitch, said Glasenberg, would be that Qatar's image in London had been damaged by the revelations of a murky deal facilitated by Qatari money to bail out Barclays Bank after the 2008 crash. To rescue its reputation and prevent Barclays' stock price from falling, Blair was to tell al-Thani that Qatar should support Glencore.

Blair delivered the script and also agreed to be present when al-Thani arrived at 11 p.m. in the hotel suite. Over the following hour, Blair sat silently in an armchair – 'there for the urging' in support of Glasenberg. At the end, the Qataris agreed to sell their stake. After his victory, Glasenberg could not decide whether Blair had been helpful or whether his huge fee was a waste. For the super-rich, the payment of a few million pounds was superfluous. After all, money could buy few better names than Blair's, as Kazakhstan's President Nazarbayev had discovered.

In July 2012, Nazarbayev asked Blair for advice about a speech he was to make at Cambridge. The problem for the president was how he should address the deaths of the fourteen civilians during the protest in December. Considering that British paratroopers had shot and killed thirteen civilians in Londonderry in 1972, Nazarbayev's record was unexceptional. 'Tragic though they were,' wrote Blair about the Kazakh deaths, 'that should not obscure the enormous progress that Kazakhstan has made.' In his speech, continued Blair, the president should deal with the shootings 'head on' using the phrases and sentiments provided by Blair to express his understanding of the international anger but asking his critics to recognise the progress made by his country and accept that, in the future, 'We are going to have to go step by step.' Nazarbayev followed Blair's advice, and was also grateful that the former prime minister encouraged David Cameron to plan a visit to Kazakhstan in June 2013.

Soon after, Blair chose to deny that he personally 'makes money' in Kazakhstan. His total income, he said, came from J. P. Morgan, Zurich Insurance and from speeches. Few were convinced, but the truth was buried. He did disclose that, in 2012, the income of the Windrush companies had increased from £12 million to £16 million. Of that, £12.5 million went on expenses and the remainder was profit. The deliberate obfuscation was his original description of the Windrush group as providing advisory services for governments, while Firerush worked on behalf of private businesses. His explanations made little sense. The following year, his accounts would show that Windrush's turnover was £14.9 million with £2 million profit, while £13 million remained deposited in the company's bank account. This presentation of his business interests would allow Blair to say in 2015 that he was worth 'only £10 million'. No one could authoritatively challenge the disclosed chain of payments of £57 million over four years on travel, rent and salaries, while the interlinked companies in turn reimbursed sister businesses for management fees, services and administrative expenses. Some speculated that Blair was using the tax and legal systems to channel yet more of his income through a number of new, unknown companies.

That suspicion arose after he consolidated his new relationship with Mubadala in Abu Dhabi. Mubadala was investing in Vietnam, Serbia, Colombia and West Africa, and Blair was contracted to earn commissions of up to 20 per cent by brokering deals between the fund and those countries. His selling point was that he could open the door to national leaders; his handicap was his inexperience in closing big commercial deals. In other words, he lacked the persuasive skill to get the vital signature on a contract, and without a final signed agreement he was not entitled to any commission.

He was on surer terrain selling his expertise to governments. Thus, for instance, operating as Tony Blair Associates, he pitched to Colombia's president Juan Manuel Santos a scheme to prevent the employees and brokers of the country's mining industry stealing a large chunk of its annual £2 billion income. 'Improved delivery', he wrote, mining his own tried and tested rhetoric, 'was one of the great achievements of the Blair administration.' He offered assistance from the 'founders of deliverology, a New Labour model for government reform'. His self-promoting proposal continued, 'Mr Blair, with his extensive on-the-job experience and a politician's instincts, will personally lead this project.' He also offered 'to serve as an adviser in domestic matters or questions of international politics'. President Santos agreed the deal in autumn 2013. Four months later, Mubadala bought a gold mine in Colombia.

Similar pitches to 'deliver the reform programme' succeeded in Serbia, Mongolia and Brazil. Erik Camarano, the chief of the Movimento Brasil Competitivo, a group dedicated to improving the Brazilian economy, had met Blair in Davos in 2011. Two years later, he part-funded a £3.7 million fee to hire Blair to improve government operations in the São Paulo region by 'producing a strategic vision'. Similar New Labour jargon had secured a contract to advise Edi Rama, the leader of Albania's Socialist Party, on winning the national elections and, later, to provide advice on governance. 'With Tony Blair and his team', said Rama, 'we will have on our side a very important partner, with unique experience and all the right advice to build a successful government and to make a reality of our programme for an Albanian Renaissance.' With Blair's help, Albania was also given candidate status in Brussels to join the EU. Blair shared the income with Alastair Campbell, appointed as an adviser to Albania, and Cherie, who arrived in Tirana on a private plane provided by Rezart Taçi, an Albanian oil tycoon.

Nothing profitable and legal seemed to be excluded from Blair's list of possible projects. During that summer, he was hired by an American hedge-fund owner in the south of France to accompany him to billionaires' yachts along the Côte d'Azur in a search for investors. To the surprise of his hosts, Blair would smile, say little and earn a percentage in the event of success.

At that point his track record was associated with success. In 2013, Mubadala had reportedly invested $5 billion to mine bauxite in Guinea. Blair was the country's star. Naturally, he was invited to a conference at the Etihad Towers hotel in Abu Dhabi in November 2013 called 'Guinea Is Back: Guinea's Development Partners and Investor Conference'. No mention was made of any link between him and Mubadala's investment. Instead, referring to AGI's presence in Guinea, he delivered a ten-minute speech that described his team working 'shoulder-to-shoulder with senior leaders in the heart of governments . . . to drive delivery of results on the ground'.

Not everyone was persuaded of the benefits. A senior aide to President Jonathan had cast doubt on the project's merit to Nigeria. Tony Elumelu, he suspected, had wanted to use AGI to place his people in key government positions, but the AGI staff had failed to offer any value. 'They sent their foot soldiers through the government but nothing changed. They hit a brick wall,' the aide recalled. After two years, Tony Elumelu agreed. Supporting AGI in Nigeria, he decided, 'cost too much and I didn't think it was worth it'. He withdrew his funding. Blair was not discouraged. The original introduction had been beneficial. In 2013, Kate Gross called Jonathan's aide on Blair's behalf one weekend. 'Tony,' she said, 'would like to speak to the president about Sikorsky helicopters.' The chief executive of a Canadian company wanted to pitch his aircraft to the head of state to overcome an American embargo. The aide arranged an immediate conversation between the Canadian executive and the president. AGI had proved its value for Blair.

Unperturbed by Elumelu's withdrawal of funding, rather than investing his own money to continue the project Blair obtained $2 million from USAID. He presented the gloss to Lionel Barber, the editor of the *Financial Times*: 'The purpose is not to make money. It is to make a difference.' In reality, the one common factor among his associates was always their wealth. Thus, a new Israeli friend was Moshe Kantor, a rich Russian-born businessman and aggressively Zionist oligarch who recruited Blair to his fledgling European Council on Tolerance and Reconciliation. There could be no reasonable explanation for Blair's commitment other than money.

The incongruity was apparent during his regular visits to Ehud

Barak's apartment, which spanned the entirety of the twenty-eighth floor of Akirov Towers, overlooking the Mediterranean in Tel Aviv. In 2012, Barak resigned as defence minister and resumed life as a consultant for Israeli companies across the world. The two former prime ministers forged a profitable alliance, even as Blair's position as the Quartet's envoy became discredited and Barak, despite his military heroism, was criticised within Israel for using his experience of office to become rich. It appeared no coincidence that Barak would be consulted by Nazarbayev in Kazakhstan and by various West African presidents, and that Blair mentioned Israeli drones to President Buhari of Nigeria.

Blair's new relationships eroded his immunity to criticism from previous allies. Having lost the Palestinians' trust and without access to Mahmoud Abbas, he found his role as a mediator had vanished, and some EU officials, after reading the reports of his commercial deals, demanded his resignation. To placate the critics while protecting Blair, the EU Commission withdrew its £1.5 million annual contribution to Blair's operation, ostensibly because the money was needed for refugees. Hillary Clinton came to the rescue by committing America to pay all of Blair's costs.

Initially, he received the same co-operation from her successor, John Kerry. In mid-2013, Kerry restarted the peace process, setting a fixed timetable of nine months for a comprehensive agreement between Israel and the Palestinians, based on an economic package put together with Tim Collins, the American businessman who had travelled with Blair to Libya and who contributed to the Faith Foundation. Blair joined them on 26 May, at a meeting of the World Economic Forum on the Dead Sea in Jordan. The secretary of state's 'surprise' announcement to an audience of Israelis and Arabs was a $4 billion package for the Palestinian economy that had been put together by Collins and a McKinsey team arranged by Blair. At Blair's behest, Gaza was excluded. Once again, Blair appeared to be at the centre of the peace process and had good reason to assume that Collins would support his role as envoy. 'How hard would it be to reach a peace agreement?' he asked the audience rhetorically. 'The answer is, not very hard at all.' He misjudged the mood in the hall, as did Munib al-Masri, a Palestinian billionaire whose speech outraged the Israelis. The audience's anger caused State Department officials to doubt Blair's 'butterfly judgement'. Kerry questioned whether Blair should be sidelined.

Nevertheless, during those months, Blair privately urged Netanyahu that peace depended upon him taking a risk, both with the Palestinians and with his Israeli voters. Netanyahu would say that he followed Blair's advice by freezing the construction of new settlements and releasing many convicted Palestinian murderers. But, at that moment, Blair's precarious position in Jerusalem was further undermined by events in New York.

On 11 June, Murdoch and Wendi Deng hosted a dinner for a group of friends and visitors from London. Unknown to his guests, and especially to his wife, Murdoch's lawyers were to file for a divorce the following day. Over many months, Murdoch had become weary of his wife's verbal humiliations, her frequent absence at parties and on foreign trips, and by the endless visits to their Manhattan home of her Chinese friends. Her habit of speaking Chinese in his presence was particularly irksome. Their fourteen-year marriage, he decided, had run its course. The excuse to call it a day was presented by the investigation into the *News of the World*'s hacking. In the course of sifting through millions of emails in News Corp.'s computers, emails from Deng were unearthed that suggested a close relationship with a tennis coach in Carmel, another with Eric Schmidt, the founder of Google – and a third with Tony Blair.

The evidence of her conduct was shown to Murdoch by his son. Specifically, there was one memorandum Deng had written to herself: 'Oh shit, oh shit. Whatever why I'm so so missing Tony. Because he is so charming and his clothes are so good. He has such a good body and he had his really, really good legs Butt . . . and he is slim tall and good skin. Pierce blue eyes which I love. Love his eyes. Also I love his power on the stage . . . and what else what else what else . . . '

Other messages suggested that Blair had met Deng in New York, London and Beijing. The Chinese authorities prized a security video recording the two walking together through the lobby of a Beijing hotel. Of outstanding relevance was Deng and Blair's overnight meeting on 27 April 2013 at Murdoch's ranch in Carmel. Blair had met Murdoch the following day in Los Angeles and, while asking for more money for the Faith Foundation, had not mentioned meeting his wife. In his version of events, Murdoch later explained that, after returning from Australia, 'I naturally asked the staff in Carmel and it opened up.' He was told that, during their meals, Blair and Wendi would feed each other, and that Blair was seen joining Deng in her bedroom and closing the door.

Hours after the announcement of the divorce, Blair telephoned Murdoch. He insisted that he was innocent. After a brief conversation, Murdoch refused to take any more of his calls. Blair nevertheless spoke regularly with Deng on the phone. Both his and Cherie's denials that there had been a sexual affair were ridiculed by Murdoch, who was supported by his staff.

Blair was damaged by the global interest in the scandal. For six years, he had enjoyed a strife-free honeymoon as a respected globetrotting statesman earning sufficient money to maintain a millionaire's lifestyle. Now, Tim Collins and others regarded Blair's conduct as beyond the pale. Collins, an observant Christian, was particularly appalled. 'The Wendi Murdoch affair put me off,' he recalled. 'The real man was revealed. He's incapable of self-criticism. I felt so naive.' Collins was equally disenchanted by Blair's stridency against Islamic extremists. 'He was meant to reconcile the faiths, not attack them,' Collins complained, and withdrew his support from the Faith Foundation. 'Even Ruth Turner was disillusioned,' he added. (She would later resign from the Faith Foundation.) Blair's status as the Quartet's envoy was imperilled. But, like a spider darting about on top of water, he would not succumb. 'He hung around the Quartet,' complained Collins, 'using it as a calling card long after he could have an impact. Blair was no longer relevant.'

His reputation dived further after he delivered a eulogy at Ariel Sharon's funeral in January 2014. Wearing a skullcap and seated next to Netanyahu, Blair outraged the many Palestinians who still mourned the death of 20,000 Arabs during Sharon's invasion of the Lebanon in 2002. The kudos Blair earned from the Israelis for his attendance was lost on Kerry. The American team in Jerusalem raged about his prejudice in favour of the Israelis, his conflicts of interest, the annual cost of his operation – in excess of £10 million – and his shifting opinions. Long liberated from Westminster, he had forgotten the limitations imposed upon politicians by those with vested interests. The Americans wanted his dismissal, but held back as they watched his gyrations.

In August 2013, Blair had energetically advocated intervention to remove Syrian president Bashar al-Assad and to encourage the country's reformists to take control. He joined the clamour for an air attack on Syria in revenge for the 'moral obscenity' of Assad's fatal gas attacks on civilians, and urged Britain's MPs to vote for bombing the country because 'we have to understand the consequences of wringing our hands, not putting them to work'. If Assad were not removed, he predicted, the country would become 'mired in carnage' and a 'breeding ground for extremism'. The MPs rejected his advice. Blair's legacy had left Labour MPs distrustful of intelligence reports and sceptical about any plan for Syria after Assad.

A year later, Blair completely reversed his view. In a speech in April 2014, he urged co-operation with Assad. In the 'Titanic struggle' between moderates and extremists promoting 'dangerous and corrosive Islamic ideologies', he told his audience in London, 'We have to take sides.' Defeating 'the biggest threat to global security', he said, depended on the West co-operating with Russia and China, and therefore supporting Assad, despite his murderous conduct.

Some suspected that his somersault reflected an understanding with his paymaster in the Gulf. The United Arab Emirates opposed the Muslim Brotherhood government in Egypt. With their support, a violent uprising in June 2013 deposed the elected administration and restored the army to power under General Abdel Fattah el-Sisi. Among those dispatched to Cairo at the UAE's expense as an 'economic adviser' was Blair. Despite the bloody military revolt, he hailed Sisi's coup as the 'absolutely necessary rescue of a nation'. The hundreds of deaths during the uprising, he said, were justified because 'all the choices facing Egypt are ugly . . . but simply condemning the military will not get us any nearer to a return to democracy'.

Three years after welcoming Mubarak's downfall, Blair's tolerance of dictators reflected his complaint about the impotence of European and American politicians over radical Islam. The West, he said, should assert the supremacy of its values in the Middle East. Such stridency cast Blair as prejudiced.

In July 2014, at the very moment that war erupted again in Gaza and Israeli shells were killing Palestinians, he returned to Britain to host a surprise sixtieth birthday party for Cherie and 150 guests at his Buckinghamshire home. The contrast between photographs of celebrities dancing, his new commercial interests in Israel and pictures of Palestinians suffering underlined his conflicts of interest. Isolated from the Palestinians and scorned by EU officials, he was also adrift from Washington. Blair knew he was on borrowed time.

To save his job, he flew to Cairo to persuade General Sisi to broker a peace deal between Hamas and Israel. His initiative cut across Kerry's efforts. For the secretary of state, that was the final straw. Kerry wanted Blair's resignation but did not want to be held responsible for the deed. He waited until November 2014, when Federica Mogherini, an Italian politician, became responsible for the EU's foreign affairs. Ignoring Blair's charm offensive, Mogherini told him that she wanted control over Europe's policy in the region and that he should resign. Blair agreed, so long as the announcement was delayed until May 2015.

To repair his self-esteem, he welcomed the decision by Justin Forsyth, a former special adviser in Downing Street and an ex-employee of AGI, to use his position as chief executive of the Save the Children charity to present Blair with a prize in recognition of his 'leadership in international development' at a gala in New York. Forsyth's endorsement was supported by Jonathan Powell, a member of the charity's board. Forsyth had forgotten that, six years earlier, his organisation had supported a complaint by twenty-one aid agencies who condemned Blair's mission in Palestine for having 'fundamentally failed'. That contradiction was noted by more than 87,000 people, including members of the charity's staff, who signed a petition of protest. Blair looked embarrassed at the award ceremony because the protest had snowballed after *GQ* magazine, not coincidentally, named him 'philanthropist of the year' at the same time. Both awards appeared to have been prompted by Blair's requests.

With his employment with the Quartet about to end, he established a discreet office in Israel and sought a closer relationship with the UAE. One cloud was the state of Mubadala's faltering finances. As oil prices fell, the Emirates' finances were squeezed. At the insistence of the crown prince, the value of the fund's contracts was questioned. As with other funds in Abu Dhabi, Mubadala's managers had been swindled by fixers and over $1 billion had disappeared. Suspicions of fraud were directed at senior advisers who had sought to cultivate Blair. Ignoring that hiccup, in a lengthy proposal he suggested a new five-year partnership. 'There is virtually nowhere in the world right now', he wrote, 'where we could not work or provide the necessary contacts either politically or commercially should we want to.' He continued: 'As with any country, there are from time to time issues or problems that arise and require fixing. These could be diplomatic or commercial or even relational challenges. We stand ready to offer our help in solving these issues.' Mubadala's managers anticipated that he would ask for £25 million, plus commission.

At Mubadala's request, he flew to Vietnam to offer his advice on restructuring state enterprises and making the country more attractive to foreign investment. Shortly after, David Cameron visited with a large trade delegation. Blair offered the same service to Aleksandar Vučić, the Serbian prime minister who had served in Milošević's government. Blair's fees were paid from Abu Dhabi. On each visit to a foreign country, he would call at the British embassy for briefings, occasionally staying overnight, undeterred by the fact that he was advising a sovereign government in ways that could conflict with British interests. The sentiment among some in London was suppressed irritation, but no one in Whitehall dared challenge the former prime minister. On the contrary, he was encouraged to join Peter Sutherland, the former chairman of BP, on the advisory panel that supervised the construction of a $45 billion oil pipeline from Azerbaijan to the Mediterranean. He was also paid to advise Ilham Aliyev, Azerbaijan's president and an ally of Britain, whenever required. The threads of Blair's relationships led in many directions. BP – once dubbed 'Blair Petroleum' because of the close relations between the then prime minister and the corporation – secured Blair's services not only in Azerbaijan, but also in seeking new concessions for the company in Abu Dhabi. Sheikh Mohammed bin Zayed al-Nahyan, Blair's employer at Mubadala, was also the head of Abu Dhabi's Supreme Petroleum Council. Entwined in that commercial association was Blair's enthusiasm for recycling his role with the Quartet. Soon after a discreet conversation with Zayed al-Nahyan in Jones the Grocer, a coffee house adjacent to Mubadala's headquarters, Blair flew to Qatar to meet Khaled Meshaal, a Hamas leader. Ostensibly, Blair was offering Hamas a prize. In exchange for a permanent ceasefire, he explained, Gaza's border would be opened and billions of dollars invested to help the Palestinians. Although Netanyahu had not approved the plan, Blair sought to prove his credibility by offering Meshaal a meeting with David Cameron in Downing Street in June 2015. Hamas rejected the invitation, but the offer raised a litany of questions about Blair's profitable proximity to government leaders and his many commercial retainers, especially with J. P. Morgan, whose client needed Hamas's acquiescence to develop the gas fields off the coast of Gaza.

By February 2016, Blair's resumé as a broker of influence presented him as being at the heart of a network of commercial contacts in twenty-five nations that operated in parallel with AGI and the Faith Foundation in another twenty countries. His latest accounts disclosed that his annual turnover had increased to £19.4 million, with increased profits of £2.6 million. 'In a series of deep business and government connections around the world', he explained, 'we do business and philanthropy.'

His self-description had surprised the organisers of 'Eat', a conference held in Stockholm on 1 June 2015 to discuss feeding the hungry. Blair was invited to make a twenty-minute speech. He sought a fee of £250,000, plus £80,000 in expenses. He was offered £125,000, which he rejected.

The snap rejection of what by any standards was a large fee reflected a politician guided by an unusual code of integrity. That weakness existed during his premiership but went unseen by not only the public, but also civil servants and Labour MPs. By obscuring his attitude towards spending and making money and his disregard for the traditional culture of government during his decade in Downing Street, Blair persuaded millions of people in Britain and abroad to believe in his and New Labour's exceptional virtues. Subsequently, his conduct in committing the country to war in Iraq and Afghanistan challenged their trust. His broken vows could no longer be concealed by the disseminators of government information. We now realise that the path to the two wars was not an aberration but all of a piece with the way his government behaved across its entire domestic agenda, especially in the areas of health, education, energy and immigration. In a tragic sense, Blair had been consistent.

During his time in power, the three most important public servants in his administration – Robin Butler, Richard Wilson and Andrew Turnbull – had served him competently and loyally. During those years, each had judged that Britain's leader was, at worst, an enigma. They later changed their opinions and, in their different ways, concluded that, as prime minister, Blair had not been a laudable guardian of the public's trust. No other prime minister in recent history has been similarly castigated after leaving office. Richard Wilson's heartfelt verdict echoed their judgement: 'There are events during my period as Cabinet secretary that make me shudder at what I remember because we had high hopes and we were so disappointed. He promised so much, but in the end so little was achieved.'

Acknowledgements

I owe a huge debt to many people who were generous with their time and help. By the end of the two-year project, I had interviewed over 180 people, some several times. I will not name them individually. Most are apparent from their quoted comments in the text; a minority preferred to remain anonymous. I am immensely grateful to them all.

At the outset, I was indebted to Sarah Fletcher for her research at Westminster. I am also grateful to Sarah Mole for her research, while Alistair Morton provided a succinct guide to government statistics.

Above all, I could not have written this book without Claudia Wadsworth's remarkable research. Over many months, Claudia produced original information across the whole range of topics covered herein, which made the writing both a pleasure and a challenge.

Regarding the military aspect, I spoke to all the senior generals, admirals and air marshals who served Blair. That good fortune owed much to the advice offered by General Christopher Elliott, whose recent book, *High Command: British Military Leadership in the Iraq and Afghanistan Wars*, provided an invaluable analysis of the problems faced by Britain's military during the Blair government.

Jonathan Cummings and Matthew Kalman were helpful researchers in Israel.

Others to whom I am grateful are Neil Barnett, Jan and David Blackburn, Adam Boulton, James Brabazon, Phil Clark at SOAS, Phil Collins, David Cornwell, Dominic Cummings, David Easton, Robert Fox, Penny Furniss, Brian Griffith, Mark Hollingsworth, Solomon

Hughes, Trevor Kavanagh, Tim Knox at the Centre of Policy Studies, Brian and Anne Lapping, Richard Norton-Taylor, Alex Perry, Dominic Prince, Patrick Smith, Andrew Weir and Myles Wickstead of *Africa Confidential*, Hew Strachan, Paul Vallely, James de Waal, the late Henry Worsley and the authors of *Blair Inc.*, Francis Beckett, David Hencke and Nick Kochan.

Many other contributors, especially Blairites, prefer to remain anonymous.

I am hugely grateful to Richard Cohen, an accomplished publisher and author, for editing the manuscript. Richard was generous, inspired, meticulous and made an invaluable contribution to the book.

Ian Bahrami was, as always, an outstanding copy-editor. Thanks to Sarah Barlow for her remarkable proofreading. At Faber, I was helped by Angus Cargill, my editor, and Rachel Alexander. For many years, none of my books has been completed without an enormous debt being owed to two stalwart friends: David Hooper, my libel lawyer, and Jonathan Lloyd, my agent at Curtis Brown.

Above all, I owe so much to Veronica. Her loyalty and support are invaluable and irreplaceable.

Bibliography

Abse, Leo, *Tony Blair* (Robson, 2001)

Bailey, Jonathan, Richard Iron and Hew Strachan, *British Generals in Blair's Wars* (Ashgate, 2013)

Barber, Michael, *Instruction to Deliver* (Methuen, 2008)

Beckett, Francis, David Hencke and Nick Kochan, *Blair Inc.* (John Blake, 2015)

Blair, Tony, *A Journey* (Random House, 2010)

Boulton, Adam, *Blair Administration* (Simon & Schuster, 2008)

Bower, Tom, *Branson: Behind the Mask* (Faber and Faber, 2014)

—— *Gordon Brown* (Harper Collins, 2004)

—— *No Angel: The Secret Life of Bernie Ecclestone* (Faber and Faber, 2012)

—— *The Paymaster* (Simon & Schuster, 2001)

Butler, David, and Dennis Kavanagh, *The British Election of 1997* (Macmillan, 1997)

Campbell, Alastair, *The Blair Years: Extracts from the Alastair Campbell Diaries* (Arrow, 2008)

—— *Prelude to Power: The Alastair Campbell Diaries Vol. 1* (Hutchinson, 2010)

—— *Power and the People: The Alastair Campbell Diaries Vol. 2* (Hutchinson, 2011)

—— *Power and Responsibility: The Alastair Campbell Diaries Vol. 3* (Hutchinson, 2011)

—— *The Burden of Power: The Alastair Campbell Diaries Vol. 4* (Hutchinson, 2012)

Cowper-Coles, Sherard, *Cables from Kabul* (HarperPress, 2012)

Crisp, Nigel, *24 Hours to save the NHS* (Oxford, 2011)

Dannatt, Richard, *Leading from the Front* (Corgi, 2011)

Darling, Alistair, *Back from the Brink* (Atlantic, 2012)

Draper, Derek, *Blair's 100 Days* (Faber and Faber, 1997)

Elliott, Christopher, *High Command* (Hurst, 2015)

Finlayson, Alan, *Making Sense of New Labour* (Lawrence & Wishart, 2003)

Goodhart, David, *The British Dream* (Atlantic Books, 2013)

Greene, Toby, *Blair, Labour and Palestine* (Bloomsbury, 2013)

Jackson, Mike, *Soldier* (Corgi, 2008)

Kampfner, John, *Blair's Wars* (Free Press, 2003)

Kavanagh, Dennis, and David Butler, *The British General Election of 2005* (Macmillan, 2005)

King, Anthony, and Ivor Crewe, *The Blunders of Our Government* (Oneworld, 2013)

Levy, Michael, *A Question of Honour* (Simon & Schuster, 2008)

McBride, Damian, *Power Trip* (Biteback, 2013)

Mandelson Peter, *The Third Man* (HarperPress, 2010)

Meyer, Christopher, *DC Confidential* (Weidenfeld & Nicolson, 2005)

Oborne, Peter, and Simon Walters, *Alastair Campbell* (Aurum, 2004)

Owen, David, *In Sickness and in Power* (Short Books, 2005)

—— *The Hubris Syndrome* (Methuen, 2012)

Peston, Robert, *Brown's Britain* (Short Books, 2005)

Pollard, Stephen, *David Blunkett* (Hodder & Stoughton, 2005)

Powell, Jonathan, *The New Machiavelli* (Vintage Books, 2011)

Rawnsley, Andrew, *Servants of the People* (Hamish Hamilton, 2001)

—— *The End of the Party* (Penguin, 2010)

Rentoul, John, *Tony Blair* (TimeWarner, 2002)

Seldon, Anthony, *Blair* (Simon & Schuster, 2004)

—— *Blair Unbound* (Simon & Schuster, 2007)

—— and Dennis Kavanagh, *The Blair Effect* (Cambridge, 2005)

Shaw, Jonathan, *Britain in a Perilous World* (Haus, 2014)

Stothard, Peter, *30 Days* (Harper Collins, 2003)

Straw, Jack, *Last Man Standing* (Panorama, 2013)

Thatcher, Margaret, *The Downing Street Years* (Harper Collins, 1993)

Warner, Norman, *A Suitable Case for Treatment* (Grosvenor House, 2011)

Wilson, Rob, *The Eye of the Storm* (Biteback, 2014)

Wolmar, Christian, *Down the Tube* (Aurum, 2002)

Woodward, Bob, *Plan of Attack* (Simon and Schuster, 2004)

Notes and Sources

Providing sources in books that rely on any off-the-record conversations is always unsatisfactory. Unusually, however, a considerable number of interviewees in this book agreed to go 'on the record'. Their names appear in the text alongside their comments. However, some constraints remain. For various reasons, most did not want their names to reappear regularly in this list of sources. Some are mentioned once, some occasionally, while others go unmentioned. Assiduous readers seeking the source of a quotation may be irritated by those omissions, but using an alternative identification – such as 'private information' – would, I believe, be worse, so I hope the compromise is acceptable.

Unless sourced to a book, newspaper or television programme, most of the quotations in the book are from named civil servants, politicians or military personnel whom I interviewed. Regarding the references from the inquiry chaired by John Chilcot, I have only included dates when a witness gave oral evidence twice, or when his or her evidence also included a written submission. In some instances, the reference only mentions a page in the transcript.

INTRODUCTION

xvi *Soldiers and corporate chief executives* . . . *New York Times*, 4 December 2014

CHAPTER 1

1 *Butler's protests were the death* . . . Campbell, *Power and the People*, pp. 47, 50
4 *'He didn't even ask me* . . .' Butler, interview with author
5 *'He didn't really get* . . .' Campbell, *Power and the People*, p. 104
5 *Simon Jenkins, another shrewd* . . . *The Times*, 2 May 1997
6 *'an old-school* . . .' Powell, *The New Machiavelli*, p. 18
6 *The first sign of* . . . Mandelson, interview with author
10 *'I've decided to make* . . .' Butler, interview with author; Seldon, *Blair*, p. 280
10 *'It was my idea* . . .' Blair, *A Journey*, p. 114
10 *'My core staff* . . .' ibid., p. 19
11 *That, he mistakenly* . . . Chilcot, Wilson, 25 January 2011
12 *'You can keep it, Clare'* Campbell, *Power and the People*, p. 21
13 *'communication is fifty per cent* . . .' Blair, p. 27
13 *The most important ally* . . . Seldon, *Blair*, p. 196

CHAPTER 2

16 *Beyond that, he was oblivious* . . . McTernan, interview with author

16 *We had come to power with . . .'* Blair, pp. 204–5
16 *He was supported by . . .* House of Commons, 20 November 1995 and 11 December 1995
16 *Tim Walker and other . . .* Walker and Flesher, interviews with author
17 *Many of his constituents . . .* McTernan, interview with author
18 *Blair agreed with Straw . . .* Clarke, interview with author
18 *'Because I represent Blackburn . . .'* Walker, interview with author
18 *'Straw's also not interested . . .'* O'Brien, interview with author
18 *'Blair', observed Butler . . .* Butler, interview with author
18 *It was clear that Straw's . . .* Wilson, interview with author
19 *'Increase the countries on . . .'* Walker, interview with author
19 *Among those to be granted . . .* Flesher, interview with author
20 *'Law and order . . .'* Blair, p. 630
20 *In reality, Downing Street's . . .* Clarke, interview with author; *The Times*, 22 May 1997; Campbell, *Power and the People*, pp. 31, 55
20 *'placatory signals'* Blair, pp. 204–5

CHAPTER 3

21 *Four days after the election . . .* Langlands, interview with author
22 *A plan introduced in 1988 . . .* Rivett, *National Health Service History*, 'Labour's Decade 1998–2007', p. 213: www.nhshistory.net/cvrivett.htm
24 *'had not got a clue . . .'* Hill, email to author
24 *'The state was still . . .'* Blair, p. 214
25 *Although he instinctively accepted . . .* Butler, interview with author
25 *'Save the NHS' was . . .* Smith, interview with author
25 *Over the following weeks . . .* Edwards and Fall, *The Executive Years of the NHS 1985–2003* (Radcliffe, 2005), pp. 154 and 161, and interviews with author
27 *Hart resisted explaining . . .* Hart, interview with author; Seldon and Kavanagh, *The Blair Effect*, p. 284; Rivett, p. 170; Dowling, *GPs and Purchasing in the NHS: The Internal Market and Beyond* (Ashgate, 2000)
28 *'He doesn't have the faintest . . .'* Hart, interview with author
28 *He would rely on . . .* Campbell, *Power and the People*, pp. 47, 50, 105–6
29 *'The chancellor would like . . .'* Hart, interview with author
30 *'Go and see Gordon . . .'* Langlands, interview with author
30 *'I can't give these . . .'* ibid.; Edwards and Fall, p. 164
30 *Millions were spent . . .* Edwards and Fall, p. 158
30 *'We had prepared . . .'* Powell, p. 177
31 *'Very odd-looking . . .'* Campbell, *Power and the People*, p. 108; *The Blair Years*, p. 263

CHAPTER 4

34 *Since 1995, the education budget . . .* In 1997, the education budget was 4.6 per cent of GDP, about £50 billion. Lupton and Obolenskaya, 'Labour's Record on Education: Policy, Spending and Outcomes 1997–2010', Centre for Analysis of Social Exclusion (CASE), LSE, 'Social Policy in a Cold Climate', Working Paper 3, July 2013, pp. 16, 20
37 *The 1988 Act imposed . . .* Thatcher, *The Downing Street Years*, p. 593
38 *'We have a crap teaching . . .'* House of Commons Select Committee on Education, 8 March 2010; Barber, *Instruction to Deliver*, p. 28
38 *Both Left and Right . . .* Gillard, *Education in England: A Brief History* (2011), p. 5: www.educationengland.org.uk/articles/25academies.html

41 *By 2002, they were ordered . . .'* Ofsted, 'National Literacy and Numeracy Strategy 1998–2002', p. 3; Walford, *Blair's Educational Legacy?* (Routledge, 2010); Cassen, 'Tackling Low Educational Achievement', Rowntree Foundation, 2007; Cassen, *Making a Difference in Education: What the Evidence Says*, chapter 6 (Routledge, 2015); 'Social Policy in a Cold Climate', a series of papers edited by John Hill

41 *To enforce the changes . . .* Barber, p. 32

41 *They were to be reopened . . .* The legislation was the School Standard and Framework Act, 2 June 1998

41 *Nearly every teacher . . .* Clarke, interview with author

41 *'Why are the schools . . .'* Woodhead, interview with author

42 *'Ofsted should be used . . .* ibid.

42 *'Yes, yes, yes . . .'* Woodhead, interview with author

43 *That autumn, Blunkett . . .* Brown, 'The Key Role of Educational Research in the Development and Evaluation of the National Numeracy Strategy', *British Educational Research Journal*, p. 10

43 *The Tories had told teachers . . .* Lupton and Obolenskaya, p. 14

43 *The best and the worst . . .* Brown, 'Magic Bullets or Chimeras? Searching for Factors Characterising Effective Teachers and Effective Teaching in Numeracy', paper given at the British Educational Research Association Conference, University of Leeds, 2001; Brown, 'The Key Role of . .', p. 7

43 *Student teachers, warned Brown . . .* Brown, interview with author

44 *Giddens's way with language . . .* Seldon, *Blair*, p. 380

CHAPTER 5

45 *'It's a sad day . . .'* Bower, *The Paymaster*, pp. 135, 138

46 *'Peter has let his ego . . .'* Campbell, *Power and the People*, pp. 105, 117, 120

46 *Blair walked into . . .* Bender, interview with author

46 *'No. 10's bright new . . .'* ibid.; Campbell, *Power and the People*, p. 121

47 *An outstanding performer . . .* Finlayson, *Making Sense of New Labour*, p. 16

47 *'Tony Blair has this week . . .'* The Times, 6 September 1997

48 *'change and modernise'* ibid., 8 September 1997

48 *'Modernisation' was the theme . . .* Campbell, *Blair Years*, pp. 247–8; *Power and the People*, pp. 146, 162

49 *To avoid further embarrassment . . .* Campbell, *Power and the People*, p. 86

50 *'In so far as . . .'* Levy, *A Question of Honour*, p. 133; Campbell, *Power and the People*, pp. 171, 176–8, 198

51 *'Peter Mandelson seems to . . .'* The Times, 9 August 1997

51 *On Brown's behalf . . .* The Times, 18 October 1997; Campbell, *Power and the People*, p. 179; *Blair Years*, p. 253

52 *'well aware what . . .'* The Times, 27 October 1997

52 *'Theirs is not a relationship . . .'* Turnbull and Tebbit, interviews with author

52 *'we're dead . . .'* Campbell, *Power and the People*, pp. 185–6

52 *'We do not propose . . .'* ibid., pp. 191–2

53 *'The consequences were . . .'* Blair, pp. 126–7

53 *Events were moving . . .* Campbell, *Power and Responsibility*, p. 405; Levy, p. 137

53 *The £1 million . . .* Campbell, *Blair Years*, pp. 257–8; *Power and the People*, p. 206

54 *'Our sin in this case . . .'* Powell, p. 213

54 *'To be fair . . .'* Blair, p. 129

55 *Back in Ecclestone's . . .* Ward, interview with author; Bower, *No Angel: The Secret Life of Bernie Ecclestone*, p. 200

56 *'The whole of Whitehall . . .'* Mosley, interview with author

57 *'To my knowledge . . .'* Levy, p. 137

58 *On the same day . . .* Rawnsley, *The End of the Party*, pp. 95–6; Campbell, *Power and the People*, pp. 221, 225; *Blair Years*, p. 261

58 *'We must not let . . .'* Campbell, *Power and the People*, pp. 43, 449

58 *'was taking a real . . .'* Campbell, *Blair Years*, p. 261; Powell, p. 214

59 *Straw then promptly . . . Evening Standard*, 13 November 1997

59 *'I think that most . . .' The Times*, 16 November 1997

59 *'I've been hung out . . .'* Ecclestone, interview with author

59 *To avoid chaos . . .* Campbell, *Blair Years*, p. 262

60 *'I have been evasive . . .'* Campbell, *Power and the People*, pp. 208–10

60 *'would return to . . .'* Bender, interview with author

61 *'Call the dogs off'* Powell, p. 110

61 *'The attention-seeking . . .'* Campbell, *Power and the People*, pp. 64, 94, 102–4, 108; *Blair Years*, p. 222

CHAPTER 6

62 *'I know we have . . .'* Burridge, interview with author

64 *'Clare's sound on . . .'* Guthrie, interview with author

64 *Blair halted his 'pompous . . .'* Campbell, *Power and the People*, p. 53

65 *'It's been written . . .'* Tebbit and Essenhigh, interviews with author

67 *'He doesn't have a clue . . .'* Guthrie, interview with author

67 *'Now there's a real politician'* Gibson, interview with author

67 *Well prepared for the meeting . . . The Times*, 18 June 1997

68 *'Believes that he was . . .'* Campbell, *Blair Years*, p. 211; *Power and the People*, pp. 58–60

68 *'the most reviled presidential . . .' The Times*, 28 May 1997; Campbell, *Blair Years*, p. 208; *Power and the People*, p. 43; Blair, p. 231

68 *'no longer ignore . . .'* Powell, pp. 263–5

69 *'The world needs our leadership'* Blair, p. xviii

69 *The opinion polls . . . The Times*, 27 June 1997

69 *'I have to tell you . . .'* Campbell, *Power and the People*, p. 231

69 *Robinson had been unapologetic . . .* Bower, *Paymaster*, p. 150

70 *'He's a sad, sad . . .'* Campbell, *Power and the People*, p. 255

71 *'I'm surrounded by . . .'* ibid., p. 261

71 *'an intriguing guide . . .' The Times*, 14 January 1998

71 *A ponderous leader . . .* ibid., 20 January 1998

71 *'complained interminably . . .'* Powell, p. 184

71 *'Tony was not a natural . . .'* ibid., p. 63

72 *'put the boot into . . .'* Bower, *Gordon Brown*, p. 267

73 *'helped by a bottle of sherry'* Essenhigh, interview with author

74 *To try to help . . .* Campbell, *Power and the People*, p. 419

CHAPTER 7

77 *Those few experts . . .* Keay, interview with author

78 *'Irresponsible . . .'* House of Commons, 18 April 1998

79 *'They just don't get it'* Rickett, interview with author

82 *In New Labour's lexicon* . . . McNulty, interview with author

CHAPTER 8

83 *'Immigration won't be an issue . . .'* O'Brien, interview with author

84 *'No,' replied Straw.* Walker, interview with author

84 *'I want to make . . .'* Eland, interview with author

84 *'We must not let . . .'* Flesher, interview with author

84 *Straw was deaf to* . . . ibid.

85 *'the relief of Mafeking . . .'* O'Brien, interview with author

86 *O'Brien also stated* . . . Portes, 'Migration: An Economic and Social Analysis', October 2000, para 6.8

86 *'Gordon has agreed to pay . . .'* O'Brien, interview with author

86 *Although Straw rejected* . . . Flesher, interview with author

87 *'a failure of policy . . .'* Omand, interview with author

87 *'a soft touch'* Walker, interview with author

87 *Blair's lack of interest* . . . Flesher and O'Brien, interviews with author

89 *The number of immigrants* . . . Straw, *Last Man Standing*, p. 295

90 *'What more do you want . . .'* Boys-Smith, interview with author

90 *'what mattered to me . . .'* Blair, p. 631

90 *'We were quickly dubbed . . .'* ibid., pp. 204–5

91 *The government's policies* . . . Boys-Smith, interview with author

92 *'I was shocked by . . .'* ibid.

92 *The civil service* . . . Blair, pp. 204–5

CHAPTER 9

93 *'found himself banging . . .'* Powell, pp. 71–3

93 *'Why Britain Needs . . .'* The Times, 15 January 1998

94 *She continued talking* . . . Blair, p. 217; Powell, p. 184

94 *'driving Tony absolutely crazy'* Powell, p. 184

95 *'Well, what you shouldn't . . .'* Rawnsley, *End of the Party*, p. 289

95 *'drain government of its role . . .'* Wilson, interview with author

95 *'The problem with the traditional . . .'* Blair, pp. 18–19

95 *To allay Blair's fears* . . . Powell, p. 81

96 *Having risen to the top* . . . The Times, 8 June 1998

96 *The direction of the NHS* . . . Wilson, interview with author

96 *'Hospitals are too much like . . .'* McKeon, interview with author

97 *Later, on three separate occasions* . . . The Times, 29 September 1998; *Observer*, 11 June 2000

97 *Over the thirty years* . . . Independent, 27 June 2012, quoting the National Audit Office

97 *Blair confessed he was* . . . Blair, speech to Labour Party conference, 1999

98 *In the jargon he used* . . . Campbell, *Power and the People*, p. 647

98 *On reflection, Blair realised* . . . Bower, *Paymaster*, pp. 174–7

99 *Blair left for his summer holiday* . . . ibid., pp. 136ff

99 *In July 1998, he faced* . . . Mandelson, *The Third Man*, p. 253

99 *The government's policies were* . . . Langlands, 'NHS Leadership', King's Fund, 24 March 2011

100 *'They're well meaning . . .'* Mandelson, interview with author

100 *'Why did you appoint...'* Mandelson, p. 215
100 *'Blair's real delinquency...'* Clarke, interview with author
100 *'Dobson spent a lot of time...'* Langlands, 'NHS Leadership'
101 *But that did not explain why...* report by Sir Brian Jarman of Imperial College
101 *'Well, he didn't raise it...'* McCrea, interview with author
102 *He could not foresee...* Civitas, 'After Francis', studies by Dr Zack Cooper and others, 2010, p. 22
102 *'Tony didn't complain...'* Dobson, interview with author
104 *In November, Blair again ignored...* Bower, *Paymaster*, p. 193
104 *'the coming of age...'* *The Times*, 28 October and 6/7 November 1998
105 *'Scandal is an absolute...'* Blair, pp. 130, 220
105 *'The PM...'* Bower, *Paymaster*, p. 204
105 *And he blamed Campbell...* Campbell, *Blair Years*, p. 349–53; *Power and the People*, p. 608; Mandelson, p. 204
106 *'this sweet, sticky web...'* *The Times*, 29 December 1998
106 *'Thereafter,' wrote Mandelson...* Mandelson, p. 25
106 *'I have no doubt...'* ibid., p. 276
106 *'This must be the year...'* Wilson, interview with author
107 *'They had no idea...'* Campbell, *Blair Years*, p. 408
107 *'very offensive...'* *The Times*, 2 February 1999
108 *'information-age government'* Bender, interview with author
108 *'We will be forward-looking...'* 'Modernising Government', White Paper, p. 15
108 *'We were left talking...'* 'The Spin Doctors', *Panorama*, BBC TV, 13 March 2000
109 *'Blair, Brown and Dobson...'* Annual conference, Healthcare Financial Management Association, 1999
110 *Already under fire...* King's Fund, 'Independent Audit of the NHS under Labour 1997–2004', p. 24
110 *'A new prime minister...'* Powell, p. 29
110 *Blair dismissed their...* Campbell, *Power and Responsibility*, pp. xv, 125, 141; www. ncbi.nlm.nih.gov/pmc/articles/PMC1127646
111 *Only later would Blair...* Blair, p. 5
111 *'He seemed unaware that...'* Campbell, *Power and Responsibility*, pp. 92–4, 99

CHAPTER 10
112 *Success, he said...* Blair, pp. xxxiii, 99
113 *'Should we do more...'* *The Times*, 2 December 2005
113 *'They assumed...'* Woodhead, interview with author
114 *'Tony wanted speedy results...'* Blunkett, interview with author
115 *Despite financial support...* Gillard, *Education in England*, p. 8, and reports by NAO and IPPR
115 *Both wanted a manifesto commitment...* Eisenstadt, 'Providing a Sure Start: How Government Discovered Early Childhood', 2011, p. 130
116 *'The honeymoon is over'* Eisenstadt, interview with author
116 *Brown had seized upon...* Lupton and Obolenskaya, p. 7
117 *He failed to mention...* Brown, 'The Key Role of..', p. 10
117 *His data ignored...* Lupton and Obolenskaya, p. 29
119 *Treasury officials warning him...* *The Times*, 2 April 2007
119 *'damaging impression...'* Blair, p. 116

CHAPTER 11

121 *'We can't let it . . .'* Campbell, *Power and the People*, p. 415
121 *'convinced that he could resolve . . .'* Powell, p. 55; Campbell, *Power and the People*, p. 524
121 *Ignoring the Foreign Office's . . .* Campbell, *Power and the People*, pp. 416, 418
121 *International diplomacy was more . . .* Powell, p. 262
121 *Clinton, however, would consider . . .* Campbell, *Power and the People*, pp. 516–9, 538
122 *'It really is pretty scary . . .'* Seldon, *Blair*, p. 387
122 *At their joint press conference . . .* Seldon and Kavanagh, p. 396; Campbell, *Power and the People*, p. 287
122 *Blair had read . . .* Blair, pp. 209, 224
123 *'devoured' Jenkins's life of Gladstone . . .* Powell, p. 32
124 *Modern European history had little . . .* Blair, p. 224
124 *Robin Cook, who would push . . .* Campbell, *Power and the People*, p. 301
124 *Blair now waited for Clinton . . .* Campbell, *Blair Years*, p. 278; *Power and the People*, p. 560
125 *the president would drop . . .* Campbell, *Blair Years*, p. 334; *Power and the People*, pp. 590–2
125 *'improving the possibility . . .'* *The Times*, 17 November 1998
125 *'paper tiger . . .'* ibid., 18 November 1998
125 *The Cabinet agreed to the bombing.* Campbell, *Blair Years*, p. 332
125 *'I sensed . . .'* Campbell, *Power and the People*, p. 596
126 *The RAF, he told MPs . . .* Guthrie, interview with author
127 *Owen noted that Blair . . .* Owen, *In Sickness and in Power*, p. 254
127 *Blair retorted that . . .* Campbell, *Power and the People*, pp. 512, 516, 520
127 *'I saw it essentially as . . .'* Blair, pp. 227–9
128 *'Jonathan Powell,' noticed Guthrie . . .* Guthrie, interview with author
128 *'show who was boss'* Campbell, *Blair Years*, p. 368
128 *The Americans, he added . . .* Guthrie, interview with author; Campbell, *Blair Years*, p. 262
129 *'I thought he was going to hit me'* Campbell, *Blair Years*, pp. 370–1
129 *'No amount of NATO bombing . . .'* *The Times*, 24 and 27 March 1999
130 *Blair was uncertain about . . .* Blair, p. 237
131 *'This is not moral . . .'* *The Times*, 22 April 1999
131 *'This could be the end . . .'* Seldon, *Blair*, p. 395
131 *'I'm not interested in your . . .'* Campbell, *Blair Years*, p. 376
132 *'We are going for broke'* Campbell, *Power and the People*, pp. 718, 725; *Blair Years*, p. 382
132 *he used Cook's unexpected dash . . .* Guthrie, interview with author
132 *'If we don't win this . . .'* Campbell, *Blair Years*, p. 380; *Power and the People*, pp. 732–3
133 *revised meaning of 'force for good'* Blair, p. 248
133 *For the British diplomats . . .* Myer, interview with author
133 *Alarmed by the rise of . . .* Rawnsley, *End of the Party*, p. 44
135 *'This is a battle for . . .'* Powell, p. 267; Campbell, *Blair Years*, pp. 385–6
135 *Cook was a snake . . .* Seldon and Kavanagh, p. 15
136 *Other ministers offered . . .* Campbell, *Blair Years*, pp. 394–5
137 *The bombing, wrote Simon Jenkins . . .* *The Times*, 4 June 1999
137 *'It was a gamble . . .'* ibid., 5 June 1999
138 *'The Kosovo conflict . . .'* Blair, p. 227

CHAPTER 12

139 'TB seemed lost . . .' Campbell, *Power and Responsibility*, p. 107
142 'I love aspiration . . .' Blair, p. 115
142 'Coming here reminds me . . .' *The Times*, 28 January 2005
142 'We live in a new age . . .' Blair, p. 570
143 *Blair was modernising . . .* Campbell, *Power and Responsibility*, p. 119
143 'turning point . . .' *The Times*, 18 November 1999
144 'cynicism was dreadful . . .' Blair, p. 254; Seldon and Kavanagh, p. 17; Campbell, *Power and Responsibility*, pp. 112, 116, 278
145 'sinecure cynics who . . .' Blair, p. 301

CHAPTER 13

146 *In hindsight, he blamed . . .* Blair, p. 263
147 'It wasn't significant for Blair . . .' Dobson, interview with author
147 'I returned to find a burning . . .' Milburn, interview with author
148 'since 1997 the service had recruited . . .' Bower, *Gordon Brown*, p. 334
148 *Pushing one button . . .* Anderson, interview with author
148 *Labour's partisan opposition . . .* Blair, 'Antagonism of Choice', speech to Labour Party conference, September 2003
149 'Don't ever speak to me . . .' Campbell, *Power and Responsibility*, p. 237
149 *Among the victims was . . .* ibid., pp. 118, 122, 164, 168, 189–91
150 *He also accused Blair . . .* *New Statesman*, 14 January 2000
151 'It was the most important battle . . .' Powell, p. 111
151 'always more money' Campbell, *Power and Responsibility*, p. 211
152 'overenthusiastic briefing' *The Times*, 22 January 2000
152 'We're putting money in . . .' Le Grand and Milburn, interviews with author
153 'We didn't have the same . . .' Powell, p. 186
153 *He explained his failure . . .* Milburn, interview with author
154 *More money . . .* Campbell, *Power and Responsibility*, pp. 243–4; Bower, *Branson: Behind the Mask*, p. 214
155 *the Treasury's Red Book . . .* Powell, p. 111
155 'all part of an effort . . .' Campbell, *Power and Responsibility*, pp. 274–5
157 'he wasn't believed . . .' *The Times*, 17 July 2000
157 'Yes, Labour's love affair . . .' ibid., 15 June 2000
157 *Later, in a memorandum to . . .* ibid., 17 July 2000
158 'were too late . . .' ibid., 19 July 2000
158 'the headlines were dominated . . .' webarchive.nationalarchives.gov.uk/20050302192710/number10.gov.uk/page1523
159 'redesign the NHS . . .' Milburn, interview with author

CHAPTER 14

161 *The market was assumed . . .* 'Energy: The Changing Climate', p. 20: www.theiet.org/factfiles/energy/uk-energy-policy-page.cfm
163 *Speaking before a huge audience . . .* ibid., p. 23
164 *Blair was persuaded . . .* Ward, interview with author
165 *edicts from departments . . .* Powell, p. 180

CHAPTER 15

170 *'You didn't manage them . . .'* Wilson, interview with author

170 *'Unleashed by Number 10 . . .'* Straw, p. 320

171 *Blair was also frustrated . . .* Blair, pp. 204–5

171 *Immigration was still not a priority . . .* Roche, interview with author

171 *Thanks to a threatened rebellion . . . The Times,* 10 June 1999

171 *She wanted to see black faces . . .* Boys-Smith, interview with author

172 *'The old approach . . .'* Spencer, interview with author; Spencer, 'Immigration', in Seldon, *Blair's Britain 1997–2007* (Cambridge University Press, 2007), pp. 347–9

172 *Labour's progressives, who embraced . . .* Goodhart, *The British Dream,* pp. 216, 285, 310

173 *During her two visits . . .* Roche, interview with author

173 *'30,000 failed applicants' The Times,* 19 July 2000

174 *with other 'progressives'* Goodhart, p. 217

174 *'I was saying the kind . . .'* Balch, 'Labour and Epistemic Communities', p. 11

174 *In his report, Portes emphasised . . .* Portes, para 6.47

174 *'It would be counter-productive . . .'* ibid., para 3.13

174 *Without fear of contradiction . . .* ibid., para 6.8

174 *510,000 immigrants who arrived . . .* ibid., para 6.15

174 *With Spencer's support . . .* ibid., paras 6.40, 6.43

175 *'greater diversity into UK schools'* ibid., paras 6.58, 6.42

175 *'There is little evidence . . .'* ibid., 6.29

175 *'Migrants will have no effect . . .'* ibid., 6.30

175 *Nine years later . . . Daily Mail,* 5 March 2014

175 *His solution to reducing isolation . . .* Portes, para 5.33

175 *'There was no policy for . . .'* Spencer, interview with author

175 *the British would unquestioningly accept . . .* contra Goodhart, p. 219

175 *Portes's assurance that . . .* Portes, para 2.3

176 *'modernise the work permit system'* Spencer, interview with author

176 *By then, the number of such permits . . .* Balch, p. 10

176 *Roche avoided the phrase 'asylum-seekers'* Boys-Smith, interview with author

176 *'I remember coming away . . .'* Goodhart, p. 218

176 *Straw was keeping his head down . . .* Straw, interview with author

177 *'liberal' judges and . . .* Blair, p. 206

177 *'Don't mention immigration . . .'* Powell, p. 114

177 *Blair endorsed the chancellor's . . .* Balch, p. 7

177 *'Well done, Barbara'* Roche, interview with author

177 *Blair had embraced . . .* Balch, p. 8

178 *'It was a policy . . .'* Roche, interview with author

178 *encouraged some Muslims . . .* Goodhart pp. 229, 239

178 *'I've had a roasting from . . .'* Boys-Smith, interview with author

179 *Although there was no historic . . .* Goodhart, p. 227

179 *'It's the civil servants'* Campbell, *Power and Responsibility,* p. 231

179 *The previous September, Gould . . . The Times,* 25 September 1999

180 *Nevertheless, at his Boxing Day party . . .* Campbell, *Blair Years,* pp. 448, 518; *Power and Responsibility,* pp. 286, 572

180 *To build new centres for 40,000 . . . The Times,* 19 May 2001

180 *'RC had definitely . . .'* Campbell, *Power and Responsibility,* pp. 580, 582, 617

180 *'would fuel rather than . . .'* Mandelson, p. 331

181 *Unlimited immigration was acceptable* . . . Campbell, *Blair Years*, pp. 518–9; *Power and Responsibility*, pp. 572, 575

CHAPTER 16
182 *'big leap' The Times*, 8 December 1999
182 *England's eleven-year-olds* . . . Barber, pp. 39, 44, 185
182 *'In just over two years* . . .'ibid., pp. 34–5; Ofsted, 'National Literacy and Numeracy Strategy 1998–2002', p. 6
183 *The figure in 2001 would be* . . . Lupton and Obolenskaya, p. 16
183 *Since the number of schoolchildren* . . . ibid., pp. 18, 29
183 *in 2001 Labour spent less* . . . Seldon and Kavanagh, p. 274
183 *Two years after the 424 condemned* . . . Leo et al., *Academies and Educational Reform* (Multilingual Matters, 2010), p. 33; Morris, *The Times*, 20 May 2000
183 *They were to be recategorised* . . . *New Statesman*, 20 March 2000
183 *His worst moment* . . . *Daily Telegraph*, 1 March 2001
184 *'Inspections* . . .' *The Times*, 12 April 2001
184 *He demanded 'results'.* . . Blunkett, interview with author
184 *'You can't run the system* . . .'Bichard, interview with author
185 *'valued by very many parents* . . .' *Guardian*, 30 March 2001
185 *The Church of England* . . . Barber, p. 39
185 *They would separate themselves* . . . Gillard, *Education in England*, p. 149
185 *The first two Muslim schools* . . . *The Times*, 10 January 1998
186 *His spokesman went public* . . . ibid., 13 February 2001
186 *Prime ministers were allowed* . . . Blair, pp. 287–8
186 *He believed that his new delivery unit* . . . democms.them.co.uk/client_files/www. reform.co.uk/files/key_lessons_of_the_blair_years.pdf

CHAPTER 17
187 *Cook embellished his* . . . *The Times*, 28 July 1998, quoting the Legg report
189 *The new review empowered* . . . Tebbit, interview with author
189 *In a government driven* . . . Strachan, Tebbit and Fry, interviews with author
190 *Neither man, in Boyce's judgement* . . . Boyce, interview with author
190 *Officials began compiling* . . . Johns, interview with author
191 *Blair asked no questions* . . . Chilcot, Blair; Boyce, interview with author
191 *'You are not focusing* . . .'Seldon, *Blair*, p. 135

CHAPTER 18
192 *he would decide on his staff* . . . Campbell, *Power and Responsibility*, pp. 527–8, 549
192 *I have a real sense of* . . .'Mandelson, p. 306
194 *To enquiring journalists* . . . *The Times*, 24 January 2001
194 *He had indeed telephoned* . . . Campbell, *Power and Responsibility*, p. 503
194 *Mandelson was outraged* . . . Mandelson, pp. 309ff
195 *'wearing our blue badges'* . . . *Financial Times*, 20 July 2001
196 *'a sleazeball was allowed* . . .'Price, interview with author
196 *'I like Blair* . . .'*Voyager*, BMI's in-flight magazine, summer 2001
196 *'No, I don't'* *Newsnight*, BBC TV, 16 May 2002
196 *The new partnership* . . . *Mail on Sunday*, 12 May 2002
197 *'systematic attempt* . . .'*Daily Mail*, 14 May 2002

197 'At Last a US President . . .' *The Times*, 15 December 2000
198 *Matthew Parris in 1998* . . . ibid., 6 March 1998
199 'You may be looking . . .' Shaw, interview with author
199 *The public's confidence* . . . Anderson report, 'Foot and Mouth Disease 2001: Lessons to Be Learned', p. xiv
200 *The government was spending £8 billion* . . . Bender, interview with author
200 *In a video conference* . . . Shaw, *Britain in a Perilous World*, p. 37
200 'Life is a living hell' . . . Powell, pp. 124, 140
200 'a sufficiently compelling vision . . .' Mandelson, p. 324
201 'like something on a shoe' Campbell, *Power and Responsibility*, pp. 583, 584
201 *Despite warnings by MI5* . . . *The Times*, 10 March 2001
201 'I love his deviousness . . .' Campbell, *Blair Years*, p. 594
202 *Campbell attacked the tabloid* . . . *The Times*, 7 June 2001
203 *He felt misunderstood* . . . Blair, pp. 335–6
203 'I did lack courage' ibid., pp. 124, 332, 335–6; Mandelson, p. 340
203 *Millar sent a 'vile' email* . . . *Mail on Sunday*, 14 June 2003
204 *Blair lacked the imagination* . . . Blair, p. 340

CHAPTER 19

207 'My inheritance from Jack . . .' Blunkett, interview with author
207 *Immigration from the Indian subcontinent* . . . *The Times*, 25 August 2001
208 *As usual, the rising number* . . . Goodhart, p. 217, citing Matt Cavanagh
209 *Blair 'shared a conviction* . . .' Cavanagh, 'Immigration under Labour', p. 30 (IPPR, 2010)
209 *Blunkett failed to get to grips* . . . Pollard, *David Blunkett*, pp. 253–8; Blunkett, Walker, Boys-Smith, interviews with author

CHAPTER 20

211 'a real doubt whether . . .' Crisp, *24 Hours to Save the NHS*, p. 9
211 'I was always interested in NHS staff . . .' Crisp, interview with author
212 'a betrayal of public service ethos . . .' Blair, p. 284
212 'Why did the army succeed?' Seldon and Kavanagh, p. 13; Barber, p. 204
213 *the trend as monitored by* . . . King's Fund, 'Independent Audit of NHS under Labour 1997–2005', p. 18
213 *had risen by less than 1 per cent* . . . *The Times*, 28 March 2002
213 *Aggressive incentives were one solution* . . . Rivett, p. 98
215 *he obviously remained undecided* . . . Milburn speech, *The Times*, 7 November 2003
215 'how little I understood' Blair, p. 262
216 *Sixteen months earlier, he had made* . . . *The Times*, 1 March 2000
216 *the NHS's chief executive opposed* . . . Campbell, *Power and Responsibility*, p. 669
217 'It's going to be hell . . .' Barber, p. 67
217 'a rebirthing experience' *The Times*, 22 June 2007
218 'I'm not going to be pushed out' Mandelson, p. 341
218 'They basically lied to me about it' Campbell, *Blair Years*, p. 557
219 *His message was 'deliverology'* . . . Barber, p. 102
219 'officials lacked confidence in the government' ibid., pp. 105–6
219 'coherence at the centre of government' ibid., p. 113

CHAPTER 21

220 *Sir Herman Ouseley would identify . . . Guardian* 1 April 2004
221 *Blair's ideas encouraged . . . The Times*, 3 September 2001
221 *'I feel my persuasiveness . . .'* Mandelson, p. 337
221 *he was barely consoled . . .* Campbell, *Power and Responsibility*, pp. 658–9
221 *'It's intimidation in order to dislodge me . . .'* Mandelson, p. 338
221 *Mulgan was asked to produce . . .* Mulgan, 'Life After Politics: New Thinking for a New Century', p. x, quoting Finlayson, p.124
222 *'Flaky'* Campbell, *Power and Responsibility*, pp. 660–80
222 *Brown continued to create problems.* Mandelson, p. 348
222 *Although Naomi Eisenstadt . . .* Eisenstadt, p. 53; Ball, 'National Evaluation: Getting Sure Start Started', DFES, July 2002, p. 58 (www.ness.bbk.ac.uk/implementation/documents/159.pdf)
222 *Instead, middleclass mothers . . .* Eisenstadt, p. 49
222 *By then, at least £100 million . . .* Bower, *Gordon Brown*, p. 365
223 *Labour could not trust the civil servants . . .* King and Crewe, *The Blunders of Our Government*, p. 337
223 *His tangled message . . . The Times*, 6 September 2001
223 *'They could not understand why . . .'* Blair, p. 623
223 *His polished revision rebuked . . .* Seldon, *Blair*, pp. 223–6
224 *'It was not America alone . . .'* Blair, p. 345
224 *'The only course . . .'* ibid., p. 349
226 *'at the forefront of my mind'* ibid., pp. 385–6
226 *Blair took in Dearlove's conviction . . .* Chilcot, Dearlove letter, 3 December 2001
226 *the president's speech to Congress . . . The Times*, 22 September 2001

CHAPTER 22

227 *'our values versus theirs'* Blair, pp. 343–8, 357
228 *Even the White House noted . . . The Times*, 3 October 2001
228 *'Mission creep and . . .'* ibid., 26 September 2001
228 *'I misunderstood the depth . . .'* Blair, pp. 365–7
229 *with 81 per cent telling . . . The Times*, 26 October 2001
229 *'I think we need a strategy . . .'* Chilcot, Wilson
230 *'close relationship with . . .'* Chilcot, Dearlove transcript, pp. 9, 24
231 *'We didn't see it as our job . . .'* Chilcot, Scarlett transcript, p. 28
233 *'succeeded in destroying . . .'* Lord Butler, 'Review of Intelligence on Weapons of Mass Destruction', paras 171, 181, 200
233 *a 'worst-case scenario'* ibid., para 209
233 *restarting a nuclear programme.* ibid., paras 225–6, 235
234 *'Phase Two of the war on terror'* Chilcot, Ricketts
234 *If not, then a rogue dictator . . .* Chilcot, Blair, 21 January 2011
235 *'Is Boyce looking for a reason to quit?'* Campbell, *Burden of Power*, pp. 111, 114
236 *Bush had received a memo . . .* US National Archive EBB No. 326, citing John Prados, 'The Iraq War – Part 2: Was There Ever a Decision?'
237 *'This is something . . .' The Times*, 25 February 2002, 1 March 2002, 4 March 2002 and 8 March 2002
237 *a 'break-out' to develop WMDs.* Butler report, paras 255, 261
237 *'very little intelligence'* ibid., paras 276–8, 281

238 'We have to re-order...' Chilcot, Blair, 21 January 2011, p. 44
238 'I would still have thought it right...' Fern Britton interview, BBC TV, 13 December 2009
238 'more neocon than the Americans...' Rawnsley, *End of the Party*, pp. 89–90
239 'Can we have some papers on Iraq?' Darling, interview with author; Chilcot, Wilson, 25 January 2011
239 'a mismatch' Chilcot, Turnbull, 25 January 2011
240 'Not exactly division...' Campbell, *Burden of Power*, p. 183; Blair, p. 401
241 'I didn't know what...' Chilcot, Wilson, 25 January 2011
241 who 'despised him' Campbell, *Blair Years*, p. 608
241 'It's keeping our hands...' Chilcot, Dearlove transcript, pp. 26, 29
241 'I resolved to be part...' Blair, p. 402
241 'I knew that regime change...' ibid., p. 400
242 'never asked in London...' Campbell, *Blair Years*, p. 612; *Burden of Power*, p. 197
242 'Their choice made no...' Chilcot, Manning, document 5
242 'Fuck Saddam...' Seldon, *Blair*, p. 573
242 'I made up my mind that...' *New York Times*, 6 April 2002
243 'How many prime ministers...' Campbell, *Burden of Power*, pp. 200, 632
243 'I am one of the Western leaders...' Owen, *In Sickness*, p. 265
244 The message from Manning was... Chilcot, Manning, p. 130
244 'I have no war plans on my desk' Woodward, *Plan of Attack*, p. 129; Boulton, *Blair Administration*, p. 118
244 so long as Bush... Chilcot, Boyce
244 'Leaving Iraq to develop...' *The Times*, 6 April 2002
244 'he had decided to join Bush...' Owen, *In Sickness*, p. 275; Chilcot, 'Conditions for Military Action', 21 July 2002
244 had pledged 'in blood' Blair, p. 400
245 'The shutters are firmly down' Tebbit, interview with author; Chilcot, Wilson, 4 December 2009, pp. 8–9
246 'I knew Bush had not decided' Blair, p. 405
246 'You know, George...' Rawnsley, *End of the Party*, p. 99
246 'the intelligence and facts...' Dannat, *Sunday Times*, 1 May 2005
246 'It's worse than you think...' ibid.; *New York Review of Books*, 9 June 2005
246 'Hussein is still trying...' House of Commons, 18 March 2003
247 'Even the Commons Defence Committee...' ibid., HC 93-1, 15 May 2003
248 'I was taken aback...' Chilcot, Wilson, 25 January 2011

CHAPTER 23
249 'We're going to be tougher' Boys-Smith, interview with author
249 'become more integrated...' *Independent*, 9 December 2001
249 The headlines dismayed Blair. Boys-Smith, interview with author
250 'Tony ignores the fact that...' Seldon, *Blair*, p. 635
250 'You could be reducing...' *The Times*, 2 April 2002
250 '80,000. With cash benefits...' ibid., 25 August 2001
250 'swamping' schools and... Pollard, p. 278
251 The message to Spencer... Spencer, interview with author; *The Times*, 16 September 2002; Campbell, *Blair Years* p. 638; Seldon, *Blair*, p. 635
251 In 2000, an additional... Portes, p. 22

251 *'I want people to come here freely . . .'* Pollard, p. 281

251 *and was attacked as racist.* The Times, 16 September 2002

251 *Since 1997, at least 67,000 . . .* Pollard, p. 274; Blunkett, House of Commons, 2
December 2002

252 *'I'm all for good immigration.'* Turnbull, interview with author

252 *Blunkett did not reveal . . .* Barber, p. 135

252 *In London, Andrew Turnbull agreed.* Turnbull, interview with author

252 *'Is this handleable? . . .'* Blunkett, interview with author

CHAPTER 24

254 *'same old gossip . . .'* The Times, 19 January 2001

254 *'Tony Blair is the best friend . . .'* ibid., 22 November 2001

255 *'This is bollocks'* Bower, *Brown,* p. 380; Campbell, *Burden of Power,* p. 97

255 *Wanless was outraged . . .* Bower, *Brown,* p. 378ff

255 *'It did sometimes feel . . .'* Campbell, *Burden of Power,* pp. 156–9

256 *'The mood in the media . . .'* Campbell, *Blair Years,* p. 602

256 *David Blunkett and John Reid . . .* Campbell, *Burden of Power,* p. 140

257 *'He hasn't changed . . .'* ibid., pp. 154–6

258 *The spokesman could also . . .* The Times, 12 February 2002

258 *Moore denied that . . .* Guardian, 14 February 2002

259 *'slowly the whole foundation . . .'* The Times, 22 May 1998

259 *Among the list of government-inspired . . .* Powell, pp. 206–7; Campbell, *Burden of
Power,* pp. 58, 154–6, 162–5, 183

259 *'unlike 1998 . . .'* Barber, p. 57

259 *their senior managers . . .* Rivett, p. 67

261 *Blair praised Richard Grainger . . .* King and Crewe, p. 196

261 *'culture of the community'* Blair, p. 576

262 *he redefined his 'golden rule' . . .* Seldon and Kavanagh, pp. 172–4, 418

262 *'new discipline established . . .'* Barber, p. 57

263 *'barrister's ability to soak up . . .'* Powell, p. 42

263 *'a sense of drift . . .'* Crisp, pp. 14–15, 202

263 *'the difference between . . .'* Crisp, interview with author

264 *'I had a simple . . .'* Crisp, p. 157, and interview with author

264 *'still very wedded'* Crisp, pp. 75–6

264 *In frustration, he appealed . . .* The Times, 7 August 2002

264 *He rejected the evidence . . .* Le Grand, *Financial Times,* 25 May 2011

265 *'a big bad moment'* Campbell, *Blair Years,* pp. 624–5

266 *Campbell issued a . . .* Campbell, *Burden of Power,* p. 324

CHAPTER 25

267 *That one day's results . . .* Guardian, 14 June 2011; Brown, interview with author

267 *He heaped the blame on . . .* Barber, p. 186

268 *'The results will improve . . .'* Blunkett, interview with author

268 *The standards among . . .* Brown, 'Are We Getting Better at Educating?' KCL lecture,
June 2010, slide 4; Brown, 'Magic Bullets or Chimeras?' pp. 4, 8; Ofsted, 'National
Literacy and Numeracy Strategy 1998–2002', p. 11; Civitas, 'Blair's School Legacy Is
a Sham', 2007; Civitas, 'Straight As? A-Level Teachers' Views on Today's A-Levels',
2009; Civitas, 'The Ins and Outs of Selective Secondary Schools', 2015

268 *Innumeracy among children* . . . Brown, 'The Key Role of . . .', p. 27; Robert Peal, 'Progressively Worse', Leverhulme Trust paper, 2014; Sutton Trust, 'Blair's Education – An International Perspective'; House of Commons Children, Schools and Families Committee, 'From Baker to Balls: The Foundations of the Education System', April 2010

269 *'In some cases, research . . .'* Brown, 'The Key Role of . . .', p. 29

269 *His target had been* . . . Ofsted, 'National Literacy and Numeracy Strategy 1998–2002', p. 3

269 *'Too often . . .'* Barber, p. 145

270 *Morris was focused on* . . . Brown, 'Strategy or Straitjacket', study commissioned by the Association of Teachers and Lecturers, 2002, p. 5

270 *'standards not structures'* Barber, p. 23

270 *He ignored her advice* . . . Lupton and Obolenskaya, p. 27

272 *'grade manipulation'* Seldon and Kavanagh, p. 261, citing Tomlinson

272 *a 'misleading' assurance* . . . www.civitas.org.uk/pdf/resultsgeneration.pdf

272 *'Are we in trouble . . .'* *Daily Telegraph*, 27 October 2002

273 *'makes me weep'* Education Committee, House of Commons, 8 March 2010

274 *The country would need* . . . *The Times*, 28 November 2002

274 *'Will you push through university top-up fees?'* Clarke, interview with author; Blair, p. 487

275 *'People have been licensed . . .'* Mandelson, p. 378

275 *declared his support for* . . . Seldon, *Blair*, p. 634

275 *He even advocated a debate* . . . ibid.

CHAPTER 26

277 *'I don't want to look at myself . . .'* Meyer, interview with author; 'Conditions for Military Action', Cabinet Office, Defence and Overseas Secretariat briefing paper, 21 July 2002; Owen, *In Sickness*, p. 275

277 *'That's all history, Mike . . .'* Rawnsley, *End of the Party*, pp. 184–5

277 *He predicted Saddam's overthrow* . . . Owen, *In Sickness*, p. 274; Danner, 'The Secret Way to War', *New York Review of Books*, 2006

278 *he spoke with certainty* . . . Owen, *In Sickness*, pp. 270, 275

278 *'sort of Rolls-Royce . . .'* Chilcot, Powell letter, 19 July 2002

279 *'Mr Blair has no clue . . .'* *The Times*, 31 July 2002

279 *'I really think we . . .'* Chilcot, Short, 2 February 2010

279 *'very little intelligence'* Butler report, para 293

280 *'If the government insists* . . . Essenhigh, interview with author

280 *'profoundly unsatisfactory'* Dannatt, *Leading from the Front*, p. 283

280 *The military's fate depended* . . . Essenhigh, interview with author; Tebbit, interview with author

281 *The Treasury, he knew* . . . Chilcot, Boyce and Manning

281 *'If we get disarmament . . .'* Chilcot, Manning

281 *However, his sympathy was crushed* . . . Blair, p. 407

282 *the JIC applied 'greater firmness'* Butler report, paras 303–4

282 *'a substantial rewrite . . .'* Campbell, *Burden of Power*, p. 293

282 *For others, the confusion* . . . Chilcot, Scarlett, p. 43

283 *'a fellow depressive'* Campbell, *Blair Years*, p. 569

283 *'a ring of secrecy'* Chilcot, Manning

284 *Blair had fragmented Whitehall* . . . Turnbull, interview with author
284 *Dearlove accepted his* . . . Chilcot, Scarlett, p. 30
285 *Jones was not an 'authoritative' expert* . . . Butler, interview with author; Chilcot, Scarlett, pp. 27, 47
286 *They even disseminated* . . . Butler report, para 486
286 *'unduly influenced'* ibid., para 450
286 *'last call for any items* . . .' Butler report, paras 338, 507; ISC report, Cm 5972, para 10, p. 52; Chilcot, Scarlett, p. 7
287 *'More weight was put* . . .' Butler report, para 338
287 *'reading like the* Sunday Times *at its worst'* Hutton inquiry, 20 August 2003
288 *'a pretty rare event* . . .' Butler report, paras 573–6; Chilcot, Dearlove, second session, 30 July 2010, pp. 28–9, 34
288 *'Blair loved his close relationship* . . .' Turnbull, interview with author
288 *'fragile and dangerous'* Chilcot, Dearlove, p. 64
288 *Blair had the impression* . . . Chilcot, Blair, 29 January 2010; Butler report, paras 573–8
288 *On the basis of Dearlove's briefing* . . . ISC report, Cm 5972, para 79
288 *'did famously influence* . . .' Chilcot, Scarlett, p. 20
288 *'felt it was pretty compelling stuff'* Campbell, *Blair Years*, p. 637
288 *'We must make clear* . . .' Seldon, *Blair*, p. 582
290 *no subsequent inquiry* . . . ISC report, paras 76–8; Butler report, para 464; Butler, interview with author
291 *Manning and Powell, who were* . . . Turnbull, interview with author
291 *the overwhelming majority of ministers* . . . Chilcot, Wall, p. 88
291 *'grim meeting'* Cook, *Point of Departure* (Simon and Schuster, 2003), p. 212
293 *'The infamous 45-minute claim* . . .' Blair, p. 406
293 *'extremely uncomfortable'* Chilcot, Dearlove, first session, 16 June 2010, p. 60
293 *He would also discover* . . . Chilcot, Dearlove, second session, 30 July 2010, p. 30
294 *'I counted, was a big player* . . .' Blair, p. 410
294 *'This is what we have to do* . . .' Dannatt, p. 283

CHAPTER 27
299 *The government, Hartley* . . . 'The Energy Review: A Performance and Innovation Unit Report', February 2002, p. 7 (www.gci.org.uk/Documents/TheEnergyReview. pdf)
300 *Blair accepted Hartley's* . . . Ian Rutledge, 'New Labour, Energy Policies and Competitive Markets', pp. 907, 918, April 2002
300 *'Blair Set to Put* . . .' *The Times*, 2 September 2002
300 *'He's behaving outrageously* . . .' Mandelson, p. 354
301 *Two years later* . . . Seldon and Kavanagh, pp. 195, 205, citing NAO report
302 *since 1997 a million jobs* . . . ibid., pp. 197, 201–3
302 *John Prescott had begun* . . . *The Times*, 24 September 1997
303 *Blair supported his chancellor's* . . . King and Crewe, pp. 204ff; Seldon and Kavanagh, pp. 216ff
303 *Instead, Downing Street employed* . . . King and Crewe, p. 316
304 *Blair was against nuclear power* . . . *The Times*, 24 February 2003; Wilson, interview with author
304 *'undermined the drive* . . .' BBC News, 24 February 2003

304 *he asked John Birt to draw up*... Turnbull, interview with author
304 *'I was as isolated...'* Blair, p. 412
305 *Blair went to her London home*... Levy, p. 213
307 *'I'm going to sack him'* Powell, p. 127

CHAPTER 28

308 *'The military...'* James de Waal, 'Depending on the Right People: British Political–Military Relations 2001–10', Chatham House, 2013, p. 6
309 *JIC assessment, based on Curveball*... Butler report, para 349
310 *after an embarrassed silence*... Fry, interview with author; West, interview with author; Hoon, interview with author
310 *Later, he would credit Boyce*... Blair, p. 411
310 *Walker resisted issuing*... Walker, interview with author; Elliott, interview with author
311 *Hoon, too, appealed to Blair.* Hoon, interview with author
311 *'because we are trying to avoid war'* Turnbull, interview with author
312 *By excluding the MoD*... Tebbit, interview with author
312 *'I was rebuffed...'* ibid.
312 *'This is what I want...'* Hoon, interview with author
313 *'You cannot send the armed forces...'* Essenhigh, interview with author
313 *'I was disappointed that Blair...'* ibid.
313 *'That was playing politics...'* Walker, interview with author
314 *Often, during over*... Butler report, paras 609–10
314 *'I'm sure we received...'* Straw, interview with author
315 *The region, as he later wrote*... Blair, pp. 387–8
315 *He looked blank.* Boulton, interview with author
315 *'We invaded Iraq...'* ABC TV, 27 February 2003
316 *Dearlove blamed the inspectors' luck*... Chilcot, Scarlett, p 36
316 *'I see that as a policy issue'* Chilcot, Scarlett, p. 41
317 *'SIS [MI6] had over-promised...'* Omand, interview with author; Chilcot, Scarlett, p. 36; Chilcot, Dearlove, first session, 16 June 2010, p. 90

CHAPTER 29

318 *Blair telephoned Michael Barber.* Barber, p. 170
318 *'Why can't we just sort this out?'* Campbell, *Burden of Power*, pp. 419, 423, 427
319 *But the fall was for*... Balch, p. 10
319 *Despite his fluent jargon*... Mandelson, interview with author
320 *'It's best if I sophisticate this...'* Blunkett, interview with author
320 *'The facts show...'* Pollard, p. 277
320 *'TB was looking more worried...'* Campbell, *Blair Years*, p. 665

CHAPTER 30

321 *Their relationship, the MI6 chief thought*... Chilcot, Dearlove, first session, 16 June 2010, pp. 76, 89
321 *unofficially classified Curveball*... Tyler Drumheller, 'On the Brink', Public Affairs, 2008; Owen, *In Sickness*, p. 304
321 *Hoon knew that the chiefs*... Hoon, interview with author
323 *General John Reith, responsible for*... Chilcot, Reith

323 *Boyce again told Blair* . . . Chilcot, Boyce

324 *Hoon's statement did provoke* . . . Chilcot, Wall, pp. 88–9

325 *'George, shouldn't we do something . . .'* Sands, *Lawless World* (Viking Penguin, 2006), citing Rycroft's memo about the Blair–Bush conversation

326 *'a provocation'* Butler, interview with author

326 *'Can we pull out of the invasion? . . .'* Tebbit, interview with author; Hoon, interview with author

327 *'The plan was we did not need a plan . . .'* Cross, *Sunday Times*, 21 October 2007

327 *To head off an anti-war march* . . . ISC report, para 130

328 *'It was a bad own goal . . .'* Campbell, *Blair Years*, p. 664

328 *Manning even deluded himself* . . . Chilcot, Manning, p. 136

329 *'Blair never listened to Chirac . . .'* Chilcot, Wall, pp. 54–5

329 *Blair swept his warnings aside* . . . Seldon, *Blair*, p. 594

330 *'Are you sure Saddam has WMDs? . . .'* Hoon, interview with author

331 *Without that document* . . . Chilcot, Boyce

331 *'I understand'* Hoon, interview with author

332 *'You don't have to do it . . .'* Rawnsley, *End of the Party*, p. 160

332 *'I was wrong on every count'* Chilcot, Manning, p. 81

332 *Before Goldsmith returned* . . . Blair, p. 422

332 *'assumed wrongly'* ibid., p. 436

333 *regarded as his exclusive 'client'* Chilcot, Goldsmith

334 *'I couldn't work out . . .'* Chilcot, Walker

335 *An ICM opinion poll found that* . . . *The Times*, 31 March 2003

335 *'It does really get to you . . .'* Stothard, *30 Days*, p. 189

336 *At the end of the day, he flew* . . . Campbell, *Burden of Power*, pp. 535–8

336 *After his retirement, Boyce* . . . House of Lords, 6 November 2009

337 *With exquisite symmetry, Fiona Millar* . . . Campbell, *Burden of Power*, pp. 541–3

CHAPTER 31

338 *a third group would describe Brown* . . . Seldon and Kavanagh, p. 165; Rawnsley, *End of the Party*, p. 194; Peston, *Brown's Britain*, p. 217

338 *Blair usually anticipated* . . . Chilcot, Wilson, 25 January 2011

338 *he encouraged Jeremy Heywood* . . . Rawnsley, *End of the Party*, pp. 195–6; Campbell, *Burden of Power*, pp. 529–30

339 *In the tit-for-tat* . . . Powell, pp. 114, 209

339 *Compared to securing Brown's* . . . Campbell, *Burden of Power*, pp. 541–3

340 *Brown had assumed that* . . . Office of Budget Responsibility, working paper no. 7

340 *Despite the rising bedlam* . . . Bower, *Gordon Brown*, p. 370

341 *'hardship and distress'* King and Crewe, p. 147

341 *'They basically lied to me . . .'* ibid., p. 144

341 *Only half that number* . . . 'Households Below Average Income Report', *The Times*, 14 March 2003; Seldon and Kavanagh, pp. 173–4, 316, 319–20, 327

341 *'Call me Cherie . . .'* Campbell, *Power and the People*, p. 506

342 *'There's finally progress'* Barber, p. 131

342 *Bureaucrats were 'gaming . . .'* Gubb, Civitas, 'The NHS: Is the Extra Money Working?' p. 18, citing Audit Commission

342 *'Hit the target and miss the point'* Anthony Harrison, 'Reducing Waiting Times', *Journal of Health Service Research Policy*, vol. 14, no. 3, July 2009

343 *'They're tinkering at the edges . . .'* Anderson, interview with author
345 *In his distrust of politicians . . .* Crisp, email to author, 30 March 2015
345 *'We must shift from "NHS delivery" . . .'* Warner, interview with author
347 *'We made a mistake'* Hutton, interview with author; Rivett, p. 162
347 *Andrew Foster, responsible for . . .* Foster, interview with author; *Health Service Journal*, 25 March 2010
347 *'unproductive interference . . .'* Blair speech, 24 February 2004
348 *'We created overcapacity . . .'* Crisp, interview with author
348 *They omitted to disclose . . . Financial Times*, 1 October 2014
349 *'The NHS got a huge jolt . . .'* Hutton, interview with author
349 *Blair was the party leader despite . . .* Rawnsley, *End of the Party*, p. 229
350 *'Tony felt cornered'* Mandelson, p. 365
350 *In Blair's interpretation, Brown . . .* Blair, p. 485
351 *After telephoning some . . .* Powell, pp. 121, 156; Campbell, *Burden of Power*, p. 565
352 *'I had told Blair in 2001 . . .'* Milburn, interview with author; Mandelson, p. 364
352 *Chris Smith emerged from . . . The Times*, 19 May 2003
352 *Blair was again torn . . .* Powell, p. 296
353 *'I really never looked back'* Blair, pp. 56, 60, 68
353 *'I was just a front man . . .'* ibid., p. 73
353 *'His way of managing Gordon . . .'* Powell, p. 108
354 *Blair's weakness was . . .* Blair, pp. 493–9
356 *'I realise that physicians . . .'* Foster, interview with author
356 *Dirty staff were causing . . .* Rivett, p. 224
357 *Within a year, British doctors . . .* King's Fund, 'Where's the Money Going?' February 2006
357 *After taking account of . . .* ibid.
357 *The estimated cost of . . . The Times*, 31 October 2004
357 *'We changed the doctors' contracts . . .'* Powell, p. 181; 'Explaining NHS Deficits', Dept of Health report, pp. 63–4, 2007
357 *'Foundation hospitals . . .' The Times*, 8 May 2003
358 *Blair's misfortune was . . .* Gubb, Civitas, 'The NHS', p. 50
358 *'supreme fulfillment of my mission . . .'* Blair, pp. 496–7
359 *Britain's survival rates* Office for National Statistics, p. 43, 2006; King's Fund, 'Health and Ten Years of Labour Government', p. 10, 2007
359 *Much of the extra money . . .* Gubb, Civitas, 'The NHS' p. 21
360 *'We had too much . . .'* Crisp, pp. 91–2, 135
360 *'Reid didn't care . . .'* Alberti, interview with author
361 *NHS hospitals would be . . .* Warner, *A Suitable Case for Treatment*, p. 61
362 *Gaming by managers . . .* Turnbull, interview with author
362 *'too many targets . . .'* Crisp, p. 65
362 *No one in Downing Street . . .* Warner, pp. 99, 157, 164, 288

CHAPTER 32
364 *Any mention of 'ability' . . . Oxford Review of Education*, April 2009, p. 271
364 *That embarrassment was hidden . . .* Cassen, interview with author
364 *By 2006, 10.4 per cent of the young . . .* Lupton and Obolenskaya, p. 9
364 *Exhaustive research by . . .* Cassen, *Making a Difference in Education*
364 *He would resurrect . . .* Powell, p. 181; Campbell, *Burden of Power*, p. 563

365 *£50 million on a*... Gillard, *Axes to Grind: The First Five Years of Blair's Academies*, 2007, p. 21: www.educationengland.org.uk/articles/25academies.html (and see Gillard, *Education in England*)

365 *The latter, a fifteen-year programme*... Lupton and Obolenskaya, pp. 12–13

366 *'Won't all this*...' eprints.lse.ac.uk/32289/1/Lewis_Sure_start_childrens_centres_2011.pdf

366 *'wrong... We were short on*...' Eisenstadt, p. 100

367 *The old inequalities*... ibid., p. 161

367 *Research by academics*... *Guardian*, 14 December 2010, 12 July 2012

367 *'have not yet borne fruit'*   Eisenstadt, p. 157

367 *'Blair will stay to fight*...' *The Times*, 15 July 2004

368 *Ofsted's results, she argued*... Brown, 'The Key Role of...', p. 26; Brown, 'Magic Bullets or Chimeras?' p. 23

368 *The inspectorate's inadequate figures*... Brown, 'Is the National Numeracy Strategy Research-Based (1999/2000)?' n.d., p. 13

368 *'Deliverology' was corrupting education*. www.civitas.org.uk/pdf/FastTracktoSlowProgress.pdf

368 *walking barefoot across*... Barber, p. 203

CHAPTER 33

370 *'a drag on our system'* Chilcot, Walker and Boyce

370 *British soldiers were seen sunbathing*... Chilcot, Boyce

371 *Short encouraged her officials*... ibid.

371 *'It was a breakdown*...' ibid.

372 *'Bits and pieces'* Chilcot, Dearlove, second session, 30 July 2010, p. 10

372 *Although Kevin Tebbit*... Tebbit, interview with author

372 *Under the headline*... *The Times*, 1 May 2003

372 *'It is startlingly apparent*...' Chilcot, Jackson, 28 July 2010

373 *accused of being 'General Hypocrite'*... *Sunday Times*, 10 December 2006

374 *The 5,000 battle-ready commandos*... Owen, *In Sickness*, p. 298: Chilcot, Sawers memo, 11 May 2003

374 *'There's only so much*...' Walker, interview with author

375 *'I didn't think they were*...' ibid.

375 *'complete misunderstanding about*...' Chilcot, Walker

375 *'no thoughts that*...' ibid.

375 *He cautioned that*... Chilcot, Fry, p. 87

376 *'unlikely to be aggressive'* Chilcot, 21 January 2011, citing JIC paper, 19 February 2003

376 *Blair's mask did not reveal*... Tebbit, interview with author

376 *The Tories had won impressively*... Powell, p. 296

377 *After sixteen months' proximity*... Blair, p. 463

377 *Or at least that was the argument*... ITV interview with Blair, December 2009; Chilcot, Boyce

377 *Giving Hans Blix more time*... Blair, p. 427

378 *Blair was repeating Curveball's invention*... *The Times*, 31 May 2003

379 *'It's another attack*...' Campbell, *Blair Years*, p. 699

379 *Campbell for his part took comfort*... Campbell, *Burden of Power*, pp. 597, 643

380 *'The best way would be to get*...' ibid., p. 602

381 *The public, Blair understood* . . . Blair, pp. 454–5

382 *'open a flank on the BBC'* Campbell, *Burden of Power*, pp. 635, 668, 683

382 *'a decisive meeting'* Tebbit, interview with author; *The Times*, 14 October 2003

382 *'to fuck Gilligan'* Boulton, p. 211; Campbell, *Burden of Power*, p. 618

383 *'handled' by Tebbit* . . . *The Times*, 8 January 2004

383 *Hoon directed spokesmen* . . . Hoon, interview with author; Smith, Hutton inquiry, 20 August 2003

383 *'provide as much information* . . .' Blair, p. 456

384 *provoking Tory MPs* . . . *The Times*, 17 July 2003

384 *'There was no inevitability* . . .' Blair, p. 479

385 *'The truth is that* . . .' ibid., pp. 380, 449, 465

385 *'The problem was that this* . . .' ibid., pp. 457–8

385 *'It was truly a ghastly moment'* ibid., p. 459

386 *'utterly transparent'* ibid.

387 *'rampage through the media* . . .' ibid., p. 589

388 *'lied and bullied his way* . . .' *Newsnight*, BBC TV, 11 May 2007

CHAPTER 34

390 *Blair would not mention that* . . . *The Times*, 25 February 2004

390 *His next step was to allow* . . . Pollard, pp. 279, 283

390 *'wave through' applications* . . . ibid., p. 279

391 *'There is no obvious upper limit* . . .' *Newsnight*, BBC TV, 12 November 2003

391 *'I made a mistake* . . .' Blunkett, interview with author

391 *'started playing footsie* . . .' Milburn, interview with author

392 *'ambiguous and on condition'* Prescott, *Prezza: My Story, Pulling No Punches* (Headline Review, 2008), p. 310

392 *'that a deal had actually* . . .' Mandelson, p. 372

392 *'a thousand people kicking* . . .' *The Times*, 12 January 2004

393 *'There will be absolutely no retreat* . . .' *Guardian*, 3 December 2003

393 *'This is where [Clinton's] resilience* . . .' Blair, p. 233

393 *On the morning of the vote* . . . Rawnsley, *End of the Party*, p. 235

393 *'relations between the Chancellor* . . .' *The Times*, 28 January 2004

394 *'There was no dishonourable* . . .' Blair, p. 460

395 *'simply playing to the gallery* . . .' *The Times*, 14 May 2004

395 *'Too good to be true'* Seldon and Kavanagh, pp. 104–5; Rawnsley, *End of the Party*, p. 239

397 *'I really didn't want that'* Blair, p. 463

397 *'unwise because it was never* . . .' ibid., pp. 495–6

398 *'Why are you still sitting here?'* Rawnsley, *End of the Party*, p. 270

398 *He told Brown* . . . Blair, pp. 506–9

399 *'At the beginning* . . .' Blunkett, interview with author; Pollard p. 280

400 *Unusually, the Tories were* . . . *The Times*, 3 April 2004

400 *With the polls showing that* . . . ibid., 6 April 2004

400 *To restore himself alongside* . . . Seldon, *Blair*, p. 635

400 *'real abuses of* . . .' *The Times*, 7 and 28 April 2004; Blair article in *The Times*, 16 September 2004

400 *And, to ingratiate himself* . . . ibid., 26 October 2004

CHAPTER 35

401 *'I thought it was dishonest'* 4 *Corners*, Australian TV, 15 February 2005
402 *'convincing intelligence'* ISC report, para 66
402 *Blair, her report concluded . . .* ibid., p. 57
402 *'Why did he [Saddam] . . .'* Blair, p. 374
402 *The Anglo-American bombing . . .* ibid., p. 382
402 *Possibly, Saddam was misled . . .* The Times, 18 March 2004
402 *The following year, Blair . . .* Blair, p. 376
402 *'assumed an active chemical . . .'* ibid., p. 381
402 *'At stake . . .'* ibid., p. 389
404 *'The overall situation . . .'* Walker, interview with author
405 *Despite Jack Straw's later denials . . .* Richard Norton-Taylor, *Guardian*, 23 January 2015
406 *So many countries . . .* Greene, *Blair, Labour and Palestine*, p. 98
406 *'Without a political objective . . .'* Jackson, interview with author
406 *'conditions' and 'solutions'* Bowen, interview with author
407 *the army's fate languished . . .* Fry, interview with author
407 *Then Gordon Brown demanded . . .* Chilcot, Walker
408 *'I've drawn a line . . .'* Walker, interview with author; Powell, p. 115
409 *'bring down the government . . .'* Powell, p. 126
409 *'I wasn't sure that Tony . . .'* Mandelson, p. 296
410 *'I think Tony Blair uses . . .'* The Times, 22 March 2002
410 *'I am not seeing Tony . . .'* Mandelson, p. 386
410 *At her behest . . .* Levy, p. 217
411 *'He's in a fight . . .'* Pollard, p. 292
411 *But, at the end of May . . .* ibid., p. 296
411 *'There never was a moment . . .'* The Times, 17 September 2004
413 *'They had taken six months . . .'* Chilcot, Walker
413 *The extra soldiers . . .* The Times, 9 July 2004
414 *'do better in Afghanistan . . .'* Fry, interview with author
415 *'finish the job'* Elliott, *High Command*, p. 113
415 *'If you're not happy . . .'* Walker, interview with author
415 *'I want to go to Afghanistan . . .'* Fry, interview with author
415 *'The chiefs say . . .'* Hoon, interview with author

CHAPTER 36

416 *About 30 per cent of children . . .* The Times, 27 April 2004
417 *'Links between expenditure . . .'* ibid., 7 January 2005
417 *Blaming bad teachers . . .* ibid., 23 February 2005
417 *Although 21,700 more teachers . . .* Seldon and Kavanagh, p. 276
417 *'ten-year-old pupils were ranked . . .'* Blair, p. 523
418 *Immigrants, maintained Blair . . .* ibid., pp. 523–4
419 *'Let's move on . . .'* Clarke, interview with author
419 *'Are you serious, Trevor?'* Kavanagh, interview with author; Powell, p. 137
419 *'Changing a country . . .'* Blair, p. 28
420 *'How are we planning . . .'* O'Brien, interview with author

CHAPTER 37

423 *Dearlove had told Taylor's . . .* ISC report, para 51

423 *the agency was admitting*... Butler report, para 413

423 *a corrupted processing system*... ibid., para 422

423 *'The dossier*...' ibid., paras 454, 458, 466

424 *an instrument of persuasion*... ibid., para 462

424 *the dossier was not remotely connected*... ibid., para 319

424 *Dearlove was taken to task*... ibid., paras 67, 331, 464

424 *'high regard*...' ibid., para 469

425 *'Perhaps we were too polite*...' Butler, interview with author

425 *'We conclude that it would*...' Butler report, para 392

426 *Tony Blair, he told*... New Statesman, 30 September 2004

426 *He would later accuse Blair*... Question Time, BBC TV, 28 April 2005

426 *'In the final analysis*...' Blair, p. 424

427 *The two generals agreed*... Dannatt, interview with author

428 *'I didn't realise*...' Jackson, interview with author

428 *'We're not doing any good*...' Fry, interview with author

428 *Paralysis hung over Northwood.* ibid.

CHAPTER 38

429 *with the polls showing*... The Times, 29 April 2004

430 *'what you did*...' Blair, pp. 581–2

431 *'Tony had gone*...' Levy, p. 226

431 *'TB really was*...' ibid., p. 232

432 *'pretty corrupt*...' The Times, 25 August 2004

432 *'previously saved £3 million*...' ibid., 16 May 2005

432 *twenty-five of the 292 peers*... ibid., 14 November 2005

433 *'Mad, bad and dangerous'* Mandelson, pp. 405–6

433 *'You can't talk about*...' Powell, p. 125

434 *'Tony's overriding concern*...' Mandelson, p. 201

435 *the debt had risen from*... Seldon and Kavanagh, p. 181

436 *'the mood trumps*...' Blair, p. 513

437 *'fantasy island*...' The Times, 7 February 2005, 17 June 2005

437 *570,000 illegal immigrants*... ibid., 1 July 2005

437 *The Tories' best*... Blair, pp. 523–5

438 *'I believe in you*...' The Times, 14 February 2005

438 *This line of attack*... Blair, p. 511

439 *'We've lost'* Rawnsley, End of the Party, p. 313

439 *This was not his sentiment*... Blair, p. 511

439 *Labour was predicted to win*... Only 61 per cent of the electorate voted, with Labour securing 35.2 per cent of the vote. In 2005, the party won 9.6 million votes; in 2001, it won 10.7 million votes; and, in 1997, it won 13.5 million votes

439 *Blair half doubted*... Mandelson, p. 409

439 *'ungenerous' and 'grim'*... Blair, p. 529

439 *'Gordon will make*...' The Times, 29 April 2005

440 *She had just submitted*... ibid., 21 April 2006

CHAPTER 39

444 *The publication of these proposals*... Warner, p. 91

446 *Naturally, he would not admit*... Blair, p. 211

447　*There were no new ideas . . .* McKeon, interview with author

447　*The problem is always . . .* Crisp, email to author, 30 March 2015

447　*being strangled by . . .* The Times, 31 August 2004

449　*Just after the election . . .* Warner, p. 157

450　*Besides more doctors . . .* Gubb, Civitas, 'The NHS', p. 10

450　*staff productivity had risen . . .* ibid., p. 32, citing King's Fund report

450　*unit costs in hospitals . . .* King's Fund, 'Our Future Health Secured? A Review of NHS Funding and Performance', 2007, p. 30: www.kingsfund.org.uk/sites/files/kf/field/field_publication_file/our-future-health-secured-review-nhs-funding-performance-full-version-sir-derek-wanless-john-appleby-tony-harrison-darshan-patel-11-september-2007.pdf

450　*The Healthcare Commission reported . . .* King's Fund, 'Spending on Healthcare. How Much Is Enough?' 2006

450　*Pressed on why . . .* Warner, p. 293; Crisp, p. 140; report, Parliamentary Select Health Committee, December 2005

451　*Half of the annual increase . . .* Department of Health, 'Explaining the Deficit', 2007, pp. 64–5

451　*Within three years, GPs' . . .* Gubb, Civitas, 'The NHS', p. 33

451　*John Reid paid out . . .* Chisholm, interview with author

451　*Weak hospital managers . . .* King's Fund, 'Health and Ten Years . . .' p. 7; House of Commons Committee of Public Accounts 2006–7, HC 506

451　*The resulting higher pay . . .* King's Fund, 'Our Future Health Secured?', p. 10; Alberti, interview with author

451　*In sum, by 2005 . . .* King's Fund, 'Health and Ten Years . . .', pp. 7, 40; Ham, *Health Service Journal*, 24 March 2010, p. 14; Gubb, Civitas, 'The NHS', p. 4, citing Office for National Statistics and OECD

452　*Britain's premature death rates . . .* Gubb, Civitas, 'The NHS', p. 15

452　*Warner had sent Crisp and Hewitt . . .* Warner, p. 157

453　*Over half were serial . . .* ibid., p. 78

453　*Amid coughs and pauses . . .* Calum Paton, House of Commons Select Committee on Health, written evidence, May 2006

454　*Only £475 million would . . .* King's Fund, 'Where's the Money Going?' February 2006

454　*Contrary to Richard Douglas's . . .* Nuffield, 'Pay Reform – Facts, Achievements and Lessons Learnt', 2014

454　*He ignored a report . . .* Crisp, p. 93; Warner, p. 51; *Financial Times*, 6 February 2008

454　*We lost clear direction* Crisp, p. 51

454　*Under Crisp, the funding . . .* Hansard, House of Commons, 15 November 2005; Department of Health, 'Explaining NHS Deficits', February 2007

454　*Similar mismanagement had . . .* Gubb, Civitas, 'The NHS', p. 34

455　*the 350 PCTs would increase . . .* Paton, House of Commons Select Committee on Health, written evidence, May 2006

455　*Probably I only found . . .* Blair, pp. 216, 223

455　*All the mantras . . .* ibid., p. 212

456　*I had lost power . . .* Crisp, p. 164

CHAPTER 40

458　*There was a chasm between . . .* Goodhart, p. 223

458　*What does Tony think . . .* McNulty, interview with author

459 *Rather than 13,000* . . . Goodhart, p. 215; *BBC News*, 30 June 2005; Spencer, 'Immigration', p. 355

459 *Justin Russell, his special adviser* . . . Goodhart, pp. 270, 283

460 *But the revival of his interest* . . . McNulty, interview with author

460 *'I really did feel* . . .' Blair, p. 584

460 *'You completely shafted me* . . .' Powell, p. 126

460 *In retaliation, Brown* . . . McBride, p. 175

461 *Blair retaliated by* . . . Powell, p. 126

461 *'We began to lose control* . . .' ibid., p. 298

462 *He insisted on a Fundamental* . . . Blair, pp. 587, 682

462 *'You asked for a fucking* . . .' Powell, p. 113

462 *Belatedly, Blair recognised* . . . Blair, p. 586

CHAPTER 41

464 *'settle Iraq and* . . .' Blair, p. 530

464 *'put[ting] some backbone* . . .' Tebbit, interview with author

466 *the prime minister agreed* . . . Walker, interview with author; Fry, interview with author

471 *'We can do Iraq and Afghanistan'* Walker, interview with author

472 *'we did not have any clear* . . .' ibid.

472 *Knowing that Blair was* . . . Elliott, p. 172

473 *The number he had chosen* . . . Cavanagh, 'Ministerial Decision-Making in the Run-Up to the Helmand Deployment', *RUSI Journal*, p. 51; Elliott, p. 155

473 *'If that's your view* . . .' Walker, interview with author; Elliott, p. 132

474 *'As John made very* . . .' Blair, pp. 610–11

474 *'although Tony and Reid* . . .' Powell, p. 269

474 *'We would be perfectly happy* . . .' House of Commons Defence Committee, 8 February 2011

CHAPTER 42

476 *as David Normington was forced* . . . House of Commons Education Committee, 12 October 2005

476 *The improvements in the test results* . . . National Foundation for Educational Research Standards at KS3, November 2005; House of Commons Public Accounts Committee, January 2006

477 *'National tests* . . .' Primary National Survey, 2004

477 *well-trained American teachers* . . . Cassen, *Making a Difference in Education*, chapter 6, pp. 2–3; 'Every Child a Reader and Every Child Counts', White Paper, 2005

477 *Some £885 million* . . . House of Commons Public Accounts Committee, January 2006

477 *one major project to improve* . . . National Foundation for Educational Research Standards at KS3, November 2005

477 *even sympathetic politicians* . . . House of Commons Education Committee, 12 October 2005 (www.publications.parliament.uk/pa/cm200607/cmselect/cmpu-bacc/261/261.pdf)

477 *Just nine out of 21,000* . . . *The Times*, 16 March 2005

477 *The government was committed* . . . ibid., 17 March 2005

478 *His argument about education* . . . Blair, pp. 580–1

478 *the country had fallen from* . . . *The Times*, 14 September 2005
478 *Those 71,000 non-graduates* . . . ibid., 22 September 2005
479 *Ghettoisation in faith schools* . . . *Guardian*, 18 January 2005
479 *Bell was supported* . . . ibid., 15 October 2005
479 *Kelly encouraging primary schools* . . . *The Times*, 22 December 2005
479 *'politically correct interference* . . .' Blair, p. 577
480 *'extraordinarily poorly written'* House of Commons Select Education Committee, 12 October 2005
480 *'The trouble is* . . .' Powell, p. 68
480 *The number of schools deemed* . . . Lupton and Obolenskaya, p. 32; *The Times*, 12 January 2006, citing NAO report
481 *'There was a significant* . . .' *Public Finance*, 23 September 2005
481 *'English ten-year-olds* . . .' Specialist Schools and Academies Trust Annual Conference, 30 November 2006
481 *That, reported the academics* . . . Lupton and Obolenskaya, p. 35; Toynbee, *Guardian*, 2 July 2013
481 *Studies conducted at* . . . Civitas, 'Blair's School Legacy Is a Sham'; 'Straight As? A-Level Teachers' Views on Today's A-Levels'; 'The Ins and Outs of Selective Secondary Schools'; Lupton and Obolenskaya, p. 33, citing Durham University's Curriculum, Evaluation and Management Centre (CEM)
482 *The reading skills of ten-year-olds* . . . Brown, 'Going Back or Going Forward? Tensions in the Formulation of a New National Curriculum in Mathematics', n.d., p. 4, noting that most schools refused to co-operate with PISA in 2003. The PISA results in 2006 showed declining standards over the previous five years in the international rankings of British children in maths – seventh to seventeenth – and reading – eighth to twenty-fourth. The government blamed parents. Brown commented that, in truth, there was no change in standards between 2006 and 2009. In contradiction, a TIMSS study showed a sharp improvement in maths and science between 2003 and 2007
482 *Setting targets had failed* . . . Brown, King's College London lecture, slide 24
483 *'He would rather sacrifice* . . .' Powell, p. 35
483 *On the night* . . . *The Times*, 15 March 2006
483 *Enquiries revealed that* . . . ibid., 23 March 2006
483 *A paper by Robert Cassen* . . . Cassen, Rowntree report, 2007
483 *the attainment of disadvantaged pupils* . . . Lupton and Obolenskaya, pp. 27–8
483 *Despite the huge expenditure* . . . 'Social Mobility Strategy', LSE, 2011
483 *The number of state-school pupils* . . . Lupton and Obolenskaya, p. 45
484 *'primary schools in the poorest* . . .' Toynbee, *Guardian*, 2 July 2013
484 *The only children* . . . Sutton report, June 2007
484 *The exam results* . . . NAO report, 2007
484 *he would use inaccurate* . . . Blair, p. 523
484 *he upped his target* . . . ibid., p. 577
484 *educating less than 3 per cent* . . . Lupton and Obolenskaya, p. 29
484 *She advocated that pupils* . . . Gillard, *Axes to Grind*, p. 29

CHAPTER 43
485 *The civil servants' excuse* . . . McNulty, interview with author
486 *'I was cornered* . . .' Blair, pp. 573–4

486 *'What is to be gained . . .'* Rawnsley, *End of the Party*, p. 362
487 *To save her political . . .* Powell, p. 220
487 *Stevenson had decided that . . .* Levy, pp. 252, 259–60
487 *'There were very good . . .'* Blair, p. 607
487 *He criticised the media . . .* ibid., p. 589
487 *Ninety minutes later . . .* ibid., p. 608; Hutton, interview with author
488 *'Gordon is going to . . .'* Rawnsley, *End of the Party*, p. 363
488 *'mafia-style politics'* Powell, p. 226

CHAPTER 44

490 *Traditional NHS administrators . . .* Mays and Tan, *Journal of Health Service Research Policy*, vol. 17, supplement 1, January 2012, p. 135
490 *Economists in the Department of Health . . .* Smee, *Speaking Truth to Power: Two Decades of Analysis in the Department of Health* (CRC Press, 2005), p. 26
491 *Researchers, he wrote . . .* Ham, 'Reforming the NHS from Within', King's Fund, 2014, p. 12
491 *'vast network of . . .'* Blair, p. xxiii
491 *'Attendances at A&E . . .'* Warner, pp. 122, 125
492 *the cost of the IT project . . .* King and Crewe, p. 196
492 *'short-term imperatives . . .'* King's Fund, 'Audit of the NHS under Labour 1997–2005', 2007, pp. 20, 44
492 *'We succeeded in strategy . . .'* Powell, p. 187
492 *'a real and imminent . . .'* The Times, 27 June 2006
492 *'Tony's fascination with technology'* Powell, p. 175
492 *To her alarm . . .* Reform, 'NHS Reform: The Empire Strikes Back', January 2007
493 *'We'll put doctors . . .'* Lancet, vol. 369, issue 9,574, May 2007, p. 1,679
494 *'We consciously decided . . .'* Powell, p. 300
496 *she would be officially . . .* King and Crewe, p. 174
496 *'We were mired by . . .'* Blair, p. 594
497 *'Eighteen months of . . .'* ibid., p. 608
497 *'frivolous . . . Unfortunately for . . .'* Powell, pp. 230–1
497 *she had criticised Maria Hutchings . . .* The Times, 9 January 2007
499 *Worse, it was clear . . .* Flesher, interview with author
499 *'Those dinosaurs . . .'* The Times, 8 May 2006

CHAPTER 45

501 *'I've always accepted . . .'* The Times, 21 November 2005
501 *To douse the uncertainty . . .* Keay, 'Can the Market Deliver Security and Environmental Protection in Electricity Generation?' Chapter 10 in Rutledge and Wright (Eds), *UK Energy Policy and the End of Market Fundamentalism* (Oxford University Press, 2011)
501 *Despite spending £2.5 billion . . .* The Times, 26 September 2005
502 *The result of Blair's latest . . .* Rutledge, 'New Labour, Energy Policy and "Competitive Markets"', *Cambridge Journal of Economics*, 2007, vol. 31, issue 6, pp. 901–25
502 *So far, only 2.4 per cent . . .* The Times, 11 February 2005
503 *a 'fantasy-land' . . .* ibid., 17 May 2006; www.oxfordenergy.org/wpcms/wp-content/uploads/2011/01/July2006-UKEnergyReview-MalcolmKeay.pdf
504 *'the (very small) risk . . .'* 'Meeting the Energy Challenge', DTI White Paper, 2007, p. 132

504 *The number of those suffering* . . . www.theiet.org/factfiles/energy/uk-energy-policy-page.cfm, pp. 26–7

506 '*hopelessly, absurdly* . . .' Blair, p. 533

507 *Euro scepticism, he jibed* . . . *The Times*, 25 June 2007

508 '*around three times higher*' Rickett, 'Paper on Renewables' Target', 2007, p. 2

508 '*Overnight* . . . *our drafts* . . .' Rickett, interview with author. During that period, the proportion of electricity generated from renewables grew from 2 per cent to 3 per cent. By 2015, it was 7 per cent. www.theiet.org/factfiles/energy/uk-energy-policy-page.cfm, p. 22

CHAPTER 46

511 *as part of NATO* . . . House of Commons Defence Committee Report, 8 February 2011

512 '*I returned to Afghanistan* . . .' Butler, 'Setting Ourselves Up for a Fall in Afghanistan', *RUSI Journal*, March 2015

512 *Others, including General Peter Wall* . . . House of Commons Defence Committee report, para 48, 8 February 2011

513 *No one asked* . . . House of Commons Defence Committee debate, 29 March 2011; Browne, interview with author

513 *Even Blair would say* . . . House of Commons Defence Committee report, para 55

514 '*had no grip on Butler*' ibid., paras 49–50

514 *Britain was slipping into* . . . *The Times*, 1 July 2006

517 '*We're going to a baseball match*' Bower, *Branson: Behind the Mask*, p. 39

517 '*I managed circumstances* . . .' House of Commons Defence Committee debate, 29 March 2011; Browne, interview with author

519 *Success would require* . . . www.iraqinquiry.org.uk/media/47317/lessons-identi-fied-basraprt-06-07.pdf

521 '*We need to be shedding* . . .' Dannatt, interview with author; Elliott, interview with author

521 '*Stirrup's not prone* . . .' Elliott, p. 207

521 *He found no mention* . . . Dannatt, p. 291

522 '*War is not clean*' Flesher, interview with author

522 '*It was always about Dannatt*' Browne, interview with author; Dannatt, p. 263

523 '*haemorrhaging*' Powell, p. 301

524 '*We need to get people* . . .' Wegg-Prosser, *Guardian*, 20 September 2013

525 '*a disgraceful attempt* . . .' *The Times*, 7 September 2006

526 '*Very well done* . . .' Wegg-Prosser, *Guardian*, 20 September 2013

527 '*feeling utterly sick*' McBride, *Power Trip*, p. 228

528 *Their deaths were blamed* . . . Haddon-Cave inquiry, 2009

528 '*You sit down* . . .' Richards, interview with author

528 '*sometime soon* . . .' *Daily Mail*, 12 October 2006

528 '*I wasn't best pleased*' Blair, p. 470

529 *Both the chiefs and politicians* . . . Fry, interview with author

530 *That explanation was* . . . *The Times*, 18 November 2006, citing interview with author on al-Jazeera TV

530 '*We spent most* . . .' Powell, pp. 270, 276

530 '*lost sight of strategy*' Cavanagh, 'Ministerial Decision-Making . . .', pp. 53–4; Elliott, p. 80; see Cavanagh, 'Inside the Anglo-Saxon War Machine', *Prospect*, October 2010

531 *Shirreff duly wrote* . . . Shirreff, interview with author; www.iraqinquiry.org.uk/media/ 47317/lessons-identified-basraprt-06-07.pdf

532 *'I dunno* . . .' Boulton, p. 112

532 *But Blair was waiting* . . . Chilcot, Fry, pp. 105–8

532 *'We're loyal supporters* . . .' Shaw, interview with author

532 *'the progress in Iraq is remarkable'* *The Times*, 22 February 2007

532 *'You're not security-cleared* . . .' Elliott, p. 124

532 *'was just beginning* . . .' Blair, p. 652

532 *'I was left with* . . .' ibid., p. 571

CHAPTER 47

533 *'I want to get on* . . .' *BBC News*, 29 January 2007

533 *'on top form* . . .' Blair, pp. 593, 600

534 *'to lie for him'* *The Times*, 13 March 2007

535 *'I have taken absolutely* . . .' ibid., 28 February 2007

535 *'Mr Blair has made* . . .' ibid., 9 September 2006

536 *David Bell, the permanent secretary* . . . ibid., 15 March 2007

537 *'In schools, standards up* . . .' Blair, p. 637. A TIMSS survey in 2011 placed England tenth out of forty-two countries

537 *Alan Smithers reported that* . . . Sutton Trust, February 2013

537 *'the longest period of* . . .' Blair, p. 637

538 *'right decision to make* . . .' *The Times*, 2 April 2007

538 *'mishandling' of the succession* . . . Rawnsley, *End of the Party*, p. 442

539 *'New Labour', he said* . . . *The Times*, 2 January 2007

540 *'a new kind of politics* . . .' Blair, p. 58

541 *energetically denied that* . . . *The Times*, 1 June 2007

541 *'To an extent immigration* . . .' Blair, p. 630

541 *the retired chiefs turned* . . . House of Lords, 15 November 2007

541 *'I am right* . . .' Norton-Taylor, interview with author

543 *'Mr Blair may be widely* . . .' *The Times*, 2 May 2007

543 *'New Labour rather than the Tories* . . .' ibid., 26 June 2007

CHAPTER 48

552 *'wall of noise'* *New York Times*, 4 December 2014

557 *'We don't tell* . . .' Beckett, Hencke and Kochan, *Blair Inc.*, p. 213

558 *While the former chancellor* . . . Office for National Statistics, 2014

559 *'When I see what a difference* . . .' *Guardian*, 2 July 2015

560 *Blair assured his host* . . . Beckett, Hencke and Kochan, p. 128

563 *'trying to wear* . . .' Blair, p. 573

565 *'July and August* . . .' Butler report, paras 289, 313

567 *'You get to a position* . . .' *Sunday Times*, 20 November 2009

567 *'how to belittle* . . .' ibid.

CHAPTER 49

569 *PetroSaudi being accused* . . . *Sunday Times*, 9 November 2014

572 *'If you have a safe place* . . .' Hillary Clinton emails, US State Department

572 *'What's Blair's value?'* Kalman, *Guardian*, 18 December 2012

575 *'I'm basically a* . . .' *Politics Show*, BBC TV, 27 June 2011

576 *he denied that he was* . . . *Financial Times*, 29 June 2012; *Guardian*, 2 July 2015
576 *Two days earlier, Stephen Wall* . . . Chilcot, Wall, pp. 88–9
581 *he offered his services* . . . *Sunday Times*, 29 April 2012
582 *he had accepted $500,000* . . . Beckett, Hencke and Kochan, p. 254
584 *personally 'makes money'* . . . *The Economist*, 20 December 2014
584 *payments of £57 million* . . . *Sunday Telegraph*, 11 January 2015
585 *'With Tony Blair and his team* . . .' ibid., 19 May 2013
585 *Mubadala had reportedly invested* . . . Beckett, Hencke and Kochan, p. 208
586 *'shoulder-to-shoulder* . . .' ibid., p. 194
586 *'The purpose is not to* . . .' *Financial Times*, 29 June 2012
587 *the EU Commission withdrew* . . . The EU paid €7.8 million between 2008 and 2012
587 *'How hard would it be* . . .' Alex Perry, *Newsweek*, April 2015
590 *'we have to understand* . . .' *The Times*, 27 August 2013
590 *Some suspected that* . . . Bloomberg speech, London, 23 April 2014
591 *'all the choices facing* . . .' *The Times*, 27 August 2013
592 *condemned Blair's mission* . . . Kalman, *Guardian*, 8 September 2008
592 *Blair looked embarrassed* . . . *The Times*, 26 November 2014
593 *'whose client needed* . . .' Hearst, *Middle East Eye*, 1 September 2015

Index